Contemporary Authors®
Autobiography Series

ISSN 0748-0636

Contemporary Authors

Autobiography Series

Joyce Nakamura
Editor

Shelly Andrews
Motoko Fujishiro Huthwaite
Associate Editors

Marilyn O'Connell Allen
Editorial Associate

volume **19**

 Gale Research Inc. • *DETROIT* • *WASHINGTON, D.C.* • *LONDON*

While every effort has been made to ensure the reliability of the information presented in this publication, Gale Research Inc. does not guarantee the accuracy of the data contained herein. Gale accepts no payment for listing; and inclusion in the publication of any organization, agency, institution, publication, service, or individual does not imply endorsement of the editors or publisher. Errors brought to the attention of the publisher and verified to the satisfaction of the publisher will be corrected in future editions.

The trademark **ITP** is used under license.

10   9   8   7   6   5   4   3   2   1

Contents

Preface

A Unique Collection of Essays

Each volume in the *Contemporary Authors Autobiography Series (CAAS)* presents an original collection of autobiographical essays written especially for the series by noted writers.

CA Autobiography Series is designed to be a meeting place for writers and readers—a place where writers can present themselves, on their own terms, to their audience; and a place where general readers, students of contemporary literature, teachers and librarians, even aspiring writers can become better acquainted with familiar authors and meet others for the first time.

This is an opportunity for writers who may never write a full-length autobiography to let their readers know how they see themselves and their work, what brought them to this time and place.

Even for those authors who have already published full-length autobiographies, there is the opportunity in *CAAS* to bring their readers "up to date" or perhaps to take a different approach in the essay format. In some instances, previously published material may be reprinted or expanded upon; this fact is always noted at the end of such an essay. Individually, the essays in this series can enhance the reader's understanding of a writer's work; collectively, they are lessons in the creative process and in the discovery of its roots.

CAAS makes no attempt to give a comprehensive overview of authors and their works. That outlook is already well represented in biographies, reviews, and critiques published in a wide variety of sources. Instead, *CAAS* complements that perspective and presents what no other ongoing reference source does: the view of contemporary writers that is shaped by their own choice of materials and their own manner of storytelling.

Who Is Covered?

Like its parent series, *Contemporary Authors,* the *CA Autobiography Series* sets out to meet the needs and interests of a wide range of readers. Each volume includes essays by writers in all genres whose work is being read today. We consider it extraordinary that so many busy authors from throughout the world are able to interrupt their existing writing, teaching, speaking, traveling, and other schedules to converge on a given deadline for any one volume. So it is not always possible that all genres can be equally and uniformly represented from volume to volume, although we strive to include writers working in a variety of categories, including fiction, nonfiction, and poetry. As only a few writers specialize in a single area, the breadth of writings by authors in this volume also encompasses drama, translation, and criticism as well as work for movies, television, radio, newspapers, and journals.

What Each Essay Includes

Authors who contribute to *CAAS* are invited to write a "mini-autobiography" of approximately 10,000 words. In order to give the writer's imagination free rein, we suggest no guidelines or pattern for the essay.

We only ask that each writer tell his or her story in the manner and to the extent that feels most natural and appropriate. In addition, writers are asked to supply a selection of personal photographs showing themselves at various ages, as well as important people and special moments in their lives. Our contributors have responded generously, sharing with us some of their most treasured mementoes. The result is a special blend of text and photographs that will attract even the casual browser. Other features include:

Bibliography at the end of each essay, listing book-length works in chronological order of publication. Each bibliography in this volume was compiled by members of the *CAAS* editorial staff and submitted to the author for review.

Cumulative index in each volume, which cites all the essayists in the series as well as the subjects presented in the essays: personal names, titles of works, geographical names, schools of writing, etc. To ensure ease of use for these cumulating references, the name of the essayist is given before the volume and page number(s) for every reference that appears in more than one essay. In the following example, the entry in the index allows the user to identify the essay writers by name:

> Auden, W.H.
> > Allen **6:**18, 24
> > Ashby **6:**36, 39
> > Bowles **1:**86
> > etc.

For references that appear in only one essay, the volume and page number(s) are given but the name of the essayist is omitted. For example:

> Stieglitz, Alfred **1:**104, 109, 110

CAAS is something more than the sum of its individual essays. At many points the essays touch common ground, and from these intersections emerge new patterns of information and impressions. The index is an important guide to these interconnections.

For Additional Information

For detailed information on awards won, adaptations of works, critical reviews of works, and more, readers are encouraged to consult Gale's *Contemporary Authors* cumulative index for authors' listings in other Gale sources. These include, among others, *Contemporary Authors, Contemporary Authors New Revision Series, Dictionary of Literary Biography,* and *Contemporary Literary Criticism.*

Special Thanks

We wish to acknowledge our special gratitude to each of the authors in this volume. They all have been most kind and cooperative in contributing not only their talents but their enthusiasm and encouragement to this project.

A Brief Sampler

Each essay in the series has a special character and point of view that sets it apart from its companions. A small sampler of anecdotes and musings from the essays in this volume hint at the unique perspective of these life stories.

Rita Dove, attributing her success as a writer and a wife to a characteristic she and her husband share: "Even in the crib, it seems, I was a night person. 'I remember waking up at three in the morning,' my mother is fond of saying, 'because I heard some noises coming from the nursery. And when I tiptoed in, terrified that a burglar had slipped into my baby's room, what did I find?'—here she pauses for effect—'Just little old you, playing contentedly in the pitch dark!' According to family legend, my parents tried everything to put me on 'normal' time: eliminating naps during the day, keeping me up past midnight, submitting me to a sequence of aerobic exercises in an effort to tire me out. Nothing worked. To this day I remain more mentally alert in the hours between midnight and 5:00 A.M."

William Price Fox, reminiscing about his father: "Back in the thirties my dad had a radio show band here in Columbia, South Carolina, called The Hawaiians. They were three blacks and two whites, and the only song they knew in Hawaiian was 'I'm Going Back to My Little Grass Shack in Kealakekua, Hawaii.' The rest of the songs they played were in Spanish. Such items as 'Cielito Lindo,' 'Juanita,' 'Besame Mucho,' etc. Dad always said he was sure no one in Richland and Kershaw Counties would know the difference. No one did, or at least they didn't complain. Anyhow, that's the way he operated. He wasn't a full-fledged, gun-toting crook, but he liked to live out there in the moral twilight. Slightly shady money was much more desirable than honest money, and the forty-hour-a-week Christian ethic was for someone else. Not him. When he was older and said the moisture had dried up in his hands and he couldn't deal seconds and bottoms in poker, with great reluctance he tried honest work, refrigeration and air-conditioning repair. But the thrill was gone and the old flamboyant trumpet-, guitar-, and clarinet-playing gambler, nightclub owner, and operator was never the same."

Lee Harwood, sharing an image of his childhood in England: "Chertsey was then a country town surrounded by farmland, woods and copses, the meadows by the river, and the sandy heathlands nearby. It was a real pleasure roaming this place as a child. There was no sense of time. The seasons came and went, but that seemed to take ages. It was a continual joy taken for granted. With my friends there were camps to be built in the woods, trees to be climbed, streams to be dammed, pears to be stolen, other 'gangs' to be challenged. It all sounds very innocent now and generally was so. That love of the countryside has never left me, though I've obviously cut back on the damming and stealing. There's a continual fascination in watching the natural world. A wild flower or a bird or a pebble on a beach. The longer one watches, the more one finds."

Guy Murchie, recalling his days as a journalist: "One of my early Chicago assignments was to write up the sewage system, an appropriate subject seeing as I was perceived to be starting at the bottom to work my way up. Right away I learned that Chicago was proud of having three times as much sewage as New York. To which New York replied, 'Yes, but our sewage is stronger than yours in Chicago.' Then I met the fellow whose job it was to watch the grating that Chicago's sewage passed through, and I learned from him that a few days ago he had spotted a ten-dollar bill drifting along on the noxious tide and had retrieved and washed it and hung it up to dry. After this extraordinary bonanza, moreover, his eyes opened a little wider as he thought 'maybe someday a twenty-dollar bill will come along.' But, seeing me jotting down notes, he said out loud, 'Oh, don't write it up in the paper.' For he had fears that the *Tribune*'s huge circulation might bring out hordes of prospectors to pan out the sewage like the Gold Rush of forty-nine, in which case his job could literally cease to be."

Norman Spinrad, describing when he had a 106 degree fever: "Laboring under the hallucinatory delusion that I was being tortured for secret rocket fuel information by spies, I had the hysterical strength to snap the bandages tying me to my deathbed, yank out the IVs, and hold off a squad of interns while I used another Power on the bedside telephone. It was the wee hours of the morning. . . . Somehow I had fixated on the name of what turned out to be a real air force general. I got an outside line. I got a long distance operator. I made a collect long distance call to said general at the Pentagon. He had long since gone home to bed. . . . I ordered the Pentagon switchboard to patch me through to his home phone, validating it with a blather of letters and numbers that was my top secret command override code. They did it. A bleary general's voice came on the line. . . . I started babbling about spies, rocket fuels. . . . By the next morning, my fever had broken. And the hospital had some tall explaining to do when the Pentagon traced the call back."

These brief examples only suggest what lies ahead in this volume. The essays will speak differently to different readers; but they are certain to speak best, and most eloquently, for themselves.

Acknowledgments

Grateful acknowledgment is made to those publishers, photographers, and artists whose works appear with these authors' essays.

Photographs/Art

bill bissett: pp. 1, 54, Val LaPointe; pp. 5, 17, 23, bill bissett; p. 22, Arthur Richardson; pp. 27, 58, Adeena Karasick; p. 31, Harry Porter; p. 34, Dawn Vincent; p. 38, Jenny; p. 46, Allan Rosen.

James Lee Burke: pp. 63, 76, © Tomm Furch.

Andrei Codrescu: p. 79, S. F. Tabachnikoff.

Rita Dove: p. 97, Jim Higgins/Library of Congress; pp. 98, 99, 107, Ray A. Dove; pp. 101, 109, 113, Fred Viebahn; p. 104, Hans Viebahn; p. 111, © Anthony Barboza.

William Price Fox: p. 117, from *Images of the Southern Writer,* text and photos by Mark Morrow. Copyright © 1985 by The University of Georgia Press. Reproduced with permission of The University of Georgia Press; p. 128, © Mark Morrow.

Lee Harwood: p. 139, Woodham Photographics.

Robert Kelly: p. 180, Le Roy Studio; p. 183, E. Bruuel.

Walter Laqueur: p. 207, © Christine Strub; p. 213, Sha'ar Hagolan.

Guy Murchie: p. 247, Polly Starr; p. 279, Guy Murchie, Jr.; p. 294, Donald Murchie; p. 308, Larry Smith.

Norman Spinrad: pp. 311, 323, 332, 337, 338, N. Lee Wood; p. 314, James Hauser; p. 336, Phil Dibble.

Audrey Thomas: p. 341, Robert Sherrin; p. 354, Ian Thomas.

George Zebrowski: p. 361, © Jerry Bauer; pp. 367, 373, 375, 381, © Jay Kay Klein; pp. 371, 379, Michael Orgill.

Contemporary Authors®
Autobiography Series

bill bissett

1939-

*bill bissett   th yeer i won th milton acorn award
charlottetown   1990*

as carol malyon   great poet   short storee
writr n novelist sz   th autobio iul write
in 1993 will b diffrent thn anee othr   th
focus n th points uv view always changing
emphasis re birthing

so far from rome   n th
council uv nicea   th pauleen point that th
bodee is bad etsetera   th terribul effects uv
non pluralistik europa   christyan bondage
breething from th diaphragm   pushing 4 th
whol bodee identitee   poetiks inseprabul from
th life   lives in all direksyuns reinkarnating
regardless uv that council   compelld by
anothr focus   adding   being   not onlee in
th blurring   th genocide at contact
certainlee attemptid   lukilee not reelee
successful   we ar heer 2 unravel   accept our
status as visitors on ths planet wch sustains

us if we dont destroy it   we ar heer 2
enjoy   our bodeez   minds   souls   rage
against th confining strukshurs   onlee by
losing plesur dew we mesur th longevitee uv
what we xperiens   gettin it on on th run
ancient hours memorizing   rehersing
rewriting   re living   all ways present   we ar
part evreething   tuna   brains reelee part
compewtr   mostlee soul   if we accept that
th prson identiteez fate detail   destina
remarkabul versimiltude   th self is evree wher
infinitlee dispersing   we dew   can dew so
manee events   wher it bcums conflictud   let
that go   or dualistik   deferring permanent
identitee   sins ther is onlee changing
psychik apertures   xpressyuns   sing from th
soul   wanting   or not wanting   we embodee
send out   let go   n yet ther ar facts
seesuns   disastrs   ecstasees

flying
we ar part bird   mammals with wings   spirit
uv   fire embrace   kiss   n let go   greef
oftn ther   sumtimes acceptans   rage on
undrstanding   deep   inside   n undr   th sun
moon   th writing cums direktlee from my life
from th me   n me   n me   othr   from out
side me   if ther is outside   ther is   ther
inside   into me   telling   n imaginaysyun
construkts thru me   n out   thees
preposisyuns   th hed yielding   tilting   prhaps
2 wun side   or   as th words   entr transmit
"veronika"   primarilee dictatid 2 me by th
writing guides who have helpd me a lot
guidans in th writing   diffrent thn in
tuishyun   wher it sumtimes cums from byond
me   n th voices from direkt prsonal xperiens
all thees approaches   all uv thees   all thees
dances   song   journees   cum from   evree
wher   including me   i like 2 spell so th
words look as close 2 how they sound in that
partikular place in that pome   as much as
possibul   its a kind uv phonetik spelling   it
bgan with onlee sum words   n spredding
thruout almost all th words

*me on my mothrs knee   with my
big sistr elizabeth   my middul sistr laurel
n cousin michael   in halifax*

iuv always bin interestid in abt 12 approaches with th writing   sum mor intenslee thn othrs fr a whil   all howevr feeding each othr   1) lyrikul   2) narrativ storee telling   3) non narrativ elements uv langwage   telescopd or micro   4) romantik sensual sexual   5) metaphysikul philosophik spiritual   6) sound   wher th main element uv th pome is sound   7) vizual konkreet   bordr blur   lettrs themselvs kleer or smudgd as th media   8) chanting repitishyun uv statements   song   sound waves errupsyuns ecstasees uv being   oftn non linear in th usual wayze   auditoree data carressings   themselvs not leeding 2 analytik construks   alredee ther   n heer   9) fushyun all thees n mor elements working   playing 2gethr   10) conversaysyunal vois   a diffrent vois from lyrik   or th speech uv sum othr modes listning 2 how peopul   how eye talk n writing that   in th storee telling   or evn in th seeminglee non narrativ writing   11) politikul writing   12) natur poetree

all thees arrivd at thru writing n painting feeding each othr   also meeting in lettr n image collages   th images inside th lettrs spelling out living   being   outflowing iuv lovd manee peopul   am not coverd by aneething   th great spirit s   n th miraculs uv what we dont know   n oftn think we dew cud it b god s   protekt us enlitn us uplift me   can   in ths life   i startid in halifax   nova scotia   canada   th atlanteeka oceanus   totalee raging   smells uv cod n rockee vishyuns   sailors n see maidens in our negoshiaysyuns with acceptanses xpressyuns   ther is nevr reelee anee way out uv being ourselvs   that is plural   "my manee selves on fire . . ."[1]

essay "why i write like ths" in *what we have* (Talonbooks) is th most thorough n compleet xposisyun uv what ium into i know uv in th writing   th well spring uv th writing   what they usd 2 call inspiraysyun it duz happn   lyrikul writing condensaysyun   empteeing uv evreething   pomes uv outrage   criticism   angerd observaysyun howevr   th pome cumming in adrenalin   grounding   consciousness swiping at th obvios n cruel hierarkees   meta leptikul   meta storee   meta physikul   meta reeson   meta me   as in permanent   2 long undr th dryer   dont want 2 b   fushyun pomes   wher all th elements uv storee n non storee gathr   spill out   like in "th mirror peopul"   realism mode storee telling as in "wun day my fathr tuk me down" n "how i lernd 2 paint agen" n "have yu seen th moovee fortune n mens eyez" n th mor lyrikul n reinkarnativ "th vessul" n "th nite th purpul elephants"   in th oxygen tent at almost 11 yeers aftr a numbr uv operaysyuns 4 peritinitis   evenshulee i had 12 operaysyuns in almost 2 yeers   i decidid ther i wud fr sure write n paint   as dansing in ballet or figur skating or hockee   ballet th main ambishyun up til thn not reelee an opsyun with a bellee full uv scars   slashing th abdominal musculs   time i was 18 in vancouvr writing wanting 2 xploor vizual phonetik sound beings uv th pome   letting th pome speek 4 itself   in evree way   n

---

[1]"around th table my many selves on fire"   from *nobody owns th erth*   anansi   1971

th inevitabilitee uv tossd salads dictating plesur

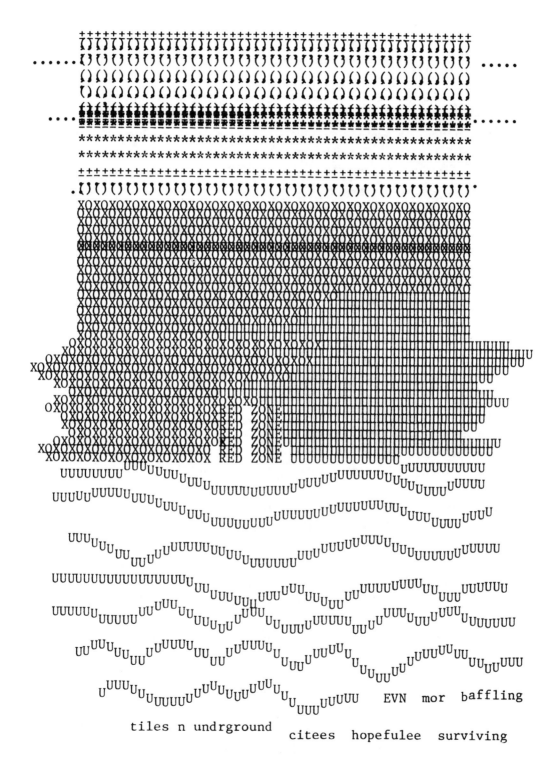

EVN mor baffling

tiles n undrground   citees hopefulee surviving

from inkorrect thots Talonbooks 1992

veronika

if yu wer maypul n acorn treez winding down along
th desert sidebords   whnevr telling whisprs marginate
all th dawn held trestuls is time n reefr opulens uv
wun days at keest saving terribul times n wanton soul
trubuls for th leeward gains westrlee rideages uv sum
tufful remakes n coffee irritants banging n windows
ar kleening all th waftring weasuls n hillee sandblasts
whn yu herd th waves sing sallee   wasint that th riming
desire that held yu   rockd yu   me i was wafr thin that
day n soggn to heer th bells play n th leevs growing biggr
n tracks layd n plans rearrangd n wallets n walnuts n
wasint it abt time for sum ecstasee   raptur   that cud
beg   borrowing th tremrling   saw a baybee eagul up in
th tree   a gud sign   n thn met sumwun   n thn it was surelee
time to go afor i b late for th next pastural timmr n sd
sorrow to b going n th hills climbing in th memoree
gainfulee treepluxd n growing   o lay me ovr   n down   down
i was wanting all nite   no wun els ther   n i was watch
king th moon   moov thru th treez   moov thru th skies
th plesides   sum grammar uv th manee verses i was
observing   pleets   n mackerels   n see

yello side wagring   n tree planting   th trellis bed
he   wudint it so   verokia dew yu   remembr th rocking
or   wasint it all th   sheep so floating   was it for
th   colors   all uv   them litning th   mess uv th so
okay   mistakn circuitree   what to call   it   boiling n
thers a sea uv plentee   tuk us to all   kindling rise
smile n all nite n ther   was no wun ther   veroika did
she   yu evr   feel   that   yess we all   have sallee
n thats life dan sd   my mothr told   me therud b
he sd daze like ths   n   went back to   helping th
up   fresh lee   sprung   pink flowrs grow   say managements
they cum n go   but   thees flowrs need   sum loving   yes
ther like peopul   watring   grazing   tempul massage
n blessing   th   orange winniferd   waxreefordingum
tastetralaingarius   yarionterammanio   sending th
grammas uv th see   tides   treelak   words uv th
lavendr lightning   didint yu   know   trying
to go forward   going on   for   words alone in
th moonloting   ring   ping   with each tother
reamandring   seek out   grip   n tangoed   waze
n larkspur   hunee itul get   bettr   it can

from *hard 2 beleev* Talonbooks 1990

wayze   always wanting vizual sound narrativ
non narrativ   romantik   lyrikul   sexual
politikul   metaphysikul song prose pomes
arranging rearranging   letting th pome write
itself   finding th pickshurs   in th words
lettrs   dansing ther

i n 87–92   up all nite   rehersing in th band
LUDDITES with gerry collins   peter denny
murray favro   thn peter d went acoustik n
gerry n murray n me up all nite   nu songs
arrangements   rime so mimetik   metalogikul
sounds n colors uv th feeling with th phrases
bars working   uv each word   matching with
th beet   meta sens music   gerry collins
amazing composr n leed guitar   murray favro
rhythm guitar   wundrful   all share input
murray f also brillyant sculptor   peter d great
playr   vibraphone zylophone bells

up all nite with martina clinton   1960s
writing vizualee   space   spaces btween th
words   lines   pause 4 breething being
emphasis   not crowding   stuk 2gethr
artifishulee   as in mor trad form   parts uv
th specees   uttrances   writings   ovr time
meta time   sequenshul   linear   up all nite
collating books by so manee othr writrs with
blewointmentpress   running th press with
martina clinton   thn by myself   running th
press with bertrand lachance   thn by myself
running th press with allan rosen   thn agen
by myself   n letting it go   thats 1962–1983
editing   typsetting   designing   lay out
showing   so manee wayze 2 free th pome
with wundrful partnrs   bertrand lachance
latr translatid sum uv my work into a book
en français *parlant*

th wells springing   my
own life lives   so manee n spilling ovr   from
sharing th lives with theyrs uv othrs   giving
out thees modaliteez   from within soul
lettrs   sumtimes seizd by flowing out
balansing   so manee balls   hats   interacting
sounds   colors   tactile   th jewels shine as
our undrstanding   nuanses   not uv linear
meening   uv being   words as th media
heer within relaysyunships   btween   stringing
happning   sound color shifts   agreements
contrasts verb   dissonanses   noun
xcitement   carreeing being   varieteez uv
lifting   all th approaches we feel   ar   make

martina clinton   vancouvr   about 1965

turning   playsing   replaysing   sing   grumbul
growl   sighing   lyrikul line oftn less wide   th
mor epik letting th sliding line keep
breething   xtend   out   2   its   fullest
breth   being all it can   2 its end
continuing   or run on   keep it going   so
reeching "th breth"[2]   as far as it can   also
meta robotik   fine   from our lives   speech
its all in th tongue   lungs   innr   eyez
ommmm   bra   shure   yes   th also   veree
oftn   veree surprizing   well   springs

THER IS NO UNIVERSAL
MIND   springing from th bed   bathroom
ablushyuns   meditating tai chi   anothr
possiblee   n aneeway   miraculous day   all
what we dont know   agnostika   th goddess
uv unknowing   protekting us   if we let her
n autobiographika   th goddess heer   uv ths
current task

[2]originalee publishd in *th high green hill*
blewointmentpress   1972   also in *selected poems: beyond
even faithful legends* Talonbooks   1980

metaphysiks uv th surviving self &　th mirror peopul

th serching endocrine　　not like in　　th digestyun uv
ystrday　summr haze in　continent　　　elbows n blu
venus whispring th first　storee is　　th digestiv
system i sd　no he sd　its breething　　flowrs growing
in boxes　hanging from　th ceiling　　as far as th eye
cud see　may b　longr　in finitee　　th perfumd drummr
announsing a diffrent　galaxee　　eithr bfor　or　we
wer ar aftr　abt th　mirror　　peopul　sumtimes he
sd　mawking　or　praising　so much　can slip into pride
is that so awful　wch　approach　AN ABSTRACT NOUN　who
will tell us aneething　dont beleev　them　its abt th
akashik cd　meet me　at th forum　round 5 pm　wud yu
undr th beginning uv　th lengthening　shadows　we cud
make a run for it　our fingrs melting　togethr　n our
dreems uv sun　blessing can b th　ravenous soul
kissing　our minds pouring yet　farthr n inn uv th perfumd
messenger whn　we slide thru th glass　slip so eezilee thru th
layrs　silkee n grateful merging　n lyrikul blending　into th reel
intima　n lustr uv th fifteenth radians　giving off th scent uv
so manee n eternal　mirrorings　eternal moons we fly thru　ar yu
jodee he sd 2 me　humid　yu cud barelee breeth　no i sd　sum
peopul ar coupuling undr a tree not far from me　iuv just run
away from sum wun i didint want　whos next　time　n th moon　so
hot　n nowun n evreewun　it keeps turning　undr th cedar　th
smells uv acorn n walnut　magnolia　th singing spirits inside th
limbs　n perfumd umbrella we wer all out undr　farthr in side th
mirror　　as what causalitee　as what figuring　as what genius
amends　windows　seeping into con scious ness aspekt ing ga o
es na　es na　nevr bin so　so　restless th purring fumd magish
yan　was showing his hand　2 th on looking mirrors th peopul in
side narrowlee ducking his grasp duck　duck　they ar so silveree
n luckee for them　yes i sd　breething　thats it　we wer sitting
undr rows n rows uv sweet smelling dreem uv erotik bliss as far
as th eye cud see　prhaps mor　pulling up theyr sheets so fast n
tremula　n pianissimo ths part　who flew so　catching snippets uv
suddnlee　prayrs uv soon　mantras uv now pleez　o　now
th lightning　lit up evree　wher　as rare as　we wer so tiny n
alrite　we cud see into evree place　beeking　beeming　brittul
howevr　briting　wer heer　ovr heer n he was weering acorns n
walnuts　round his ankuls　intima　in teems　th mirror peopul who
will tell us aneething　dont listn 2 them　keep going on　arint
they great tho　arint they fritening　o langwanga　th
eye reelee like th mirror peopul i sd　yes

corroda   th ar kaaaaaanaaa   th linguinasteando
 th lafftr   bronzing   echoes   uv our out for getting
it on feeding   they live inside   th mirrors n ar not
reflecksyuns   uv us   or lizard   plants growing so tall
 in th background   bcumming th forground   is whers th diffrens
space is all space   all space is all space   th mirror peopul
  take us on our quikest n longest journees   whn its time   they
cum for us   n sing   bells   into our ears   n hearts   th mind
   revolving like a danse ball   meet sum wun   from   love land
 in ther   SUMWUN FROM LOVE LAND   like a danse hall

                                                   th indigo wind telling
   p r a n a   i n t e e e m a a

                                        a serees uv replenishd toys
   like a writr   getting redee 2 vacuum   we wer standing undr rows
 n rows uv prfuming flowrs growing in boxes deliteful n dahlias
   n surprising colors n texturs   they wer   rimeing into infinitee
 or prhaps longr mm th mirror peopul   chanting our way along rubee
sacrid corridora   chanting n fanning our wayze thru   th mirror
   peopul   whn they carress us   leeding us   cum a long now   its
 alrite   2 th mix uv milkee sun drenchd sand nd   take us thru th
 passagewayze   so tendrlee n holding our hands   so incrediblee
hugging us   we all know   its into th unknown   n th suspensyun uv
 suspensyun uv rejecksyun   suspensyun uv negativitee   thees opn
  ings thru th crystal caverna   analogia for   ar   time n   space
 turning   licking our lips uv th lobstr   evn heer   n so succulent
 th taybul cloth   th   turning   each tall ordr   each othr   did yu
see   how   th walls mould   melt   n curv   into   othr castuls   medows
 othr consideraysyuns uv th hiest   iul listn 2 th mirror peopul
 i sd   n i want 2 live wher thers   mor peopul like me   n so
  diffrent i know evreewun is   isint   ther onlee wun uv evree
   thing   th othr vois   can yu   heer   she sd   was that her
 well   carree th spells from whoov   r andr   he wantid 2 live
 with me   me   not ovr th regrets   from th last prson   traps
   not ovr th wundrfulness fullee   it was   it was   think abt
   it   living in was   o no   tho   th clinging   what cud we
     make a go with   cud coast   see a bit   swim   dip in
      toast in th morning   with   luvlee coffee from paris
        n watching th swimmrs tangul in th kelp n th marina   so
      eeree in th still unfulfilld morning lite   seeking a room
      sumwher 2 write   in a big citee   in a small verandah   cudint
  cud   am arint   n sailing onnnnnnnnnn   evree wun outside is th
 same n so diffrent as th inside n i keep writing n writing n
    getting farthr n farthr inside into th centr uv th lite wch
       hopefulee transcends middul class moralitees for th self so
       responsibul   inside th deepest centr uv th crystal   hanging

ovr th large citee   above th pollushyun n   u f o s   ium
writing in   its rocking   n evree nite   thers arm pits
not wun foot aftr th othr   wun foot with each othr 2 b is a
foot   divisyuns in th text   ownrship uv memorees   gazing on
crotches   tits   legs   legs   around our brain pressing   n
trew love anothr abstrakt noun   its so veree rocking   n evree
nite th fires burn inside our hearts   nevr confusd   was it a
tempest aftrwards   we cud peer in so deeplee n thinking evree
day uv living

we cud see   wher we ar   wher we wer   whats cumming
laffing   allianses   n th futur   heer   like 2 linking   2 memorees
in th flowrs humming   i meen middul class moralitees in prsonal
affairs uv th heart he clarified   yes i undrstood that   dew yu
evr think that sum wun or summr will cum   n yr touch will b
tendr agen   n that love will cum   me ium not holding my breth
its nevr love for long   is it   wasting my time with spekulaysyun
dont want 2 listn 2 sum old tapes   thinkin bad uv that prson
bein sad abt that wun   listning 2 burnt   hurt refrains   lost   in
judgment

lots uv brokn toys mending   we saw our selvs thru th
telescopes   that was raging   things keep happning   nothings
getting dun   floating ovr yonge street   jonathan   jonathan
fastr n fastr   it was th wind

n windest uv all   blasting so
deliberatelee   wasint it   th tunnul dreeming   swaying   rocking
our soon 2 silvr lovrs laying along th somnolent siding such
merging o o o   changing direksyuns   courses   mating   coupuling
n singul th voyajuur   golding th lantern   spiruls th   perfumd
fate keeprs   gladiator   hors sweeps stalemates makrs marine
biographers book design wrafflers   sewr papr sellrz who will
look into yr eyez   take yr mouth n luckee we ar   n glazing   lift

yu lasting eye dont know   evn if i sumtimes dont beleev in th con
ontinuitee uv evreething   it cud still go on beleeving in me   like
th mirror peopul dont mind
along th somnolent   mirroring   th
laydul down by th   rivr uv   what is time   flowing   what is space
isint it omni centring   thru mor n mor   mirrors   we pass thru
sheets in th splaying   old n nu songs   nu harmonee   go all th
way   lull n lilting   beez n boiling play   in th hats uv th
witnesses   mouths n minds opn 2   th reflecting   TING
th self
so shining   carrees on bord   a candul   a notebook
pen   o look
at th sweeping vallee   th peopul uv ths time zone
cant see
us   as we roll with th wind   ovr theyr houses n out
n inn
in   singing

from *inkorrect thots* Talonbook 1992

artikulating th breth from sumwher
moovs thru us lungs meshing diaphanouslee
oftn with th flesh n bones dna puppetree
n th miraculous mysteree uv th free will
prsonalitee dew we have th branches uv
arriving from evreewher n ther heer so
much mor 2 cum in from uv whatevr
dimensyun aftr being sick so much as a boy
n thn latr ium grateful 2 b not in a
hospital that ium ok so far so gud

th poneez uv sweetest disordr in th sound
fushyun keep eclipsing themselvs with nu
spill ovr radians point uv views until sum
times we heer th sound itself selvs infinit
sounding s

martina clinton amazing
brekthru poetree consciousness statement
jazz space layd out spaces btween th words
punkshuating THER n lyrik assemblages also
uv indescribabul delikaysee bertrand
lachances *street flesh* & *tes rivieres t'attendent*
soaring attacking politiks being n
incrediblee intimate love pomes as duz
martina clinton 4 me thees ar wundrful
writrs great lachance also wrote *cock tales*
(Talonbooks 72)

Originalee a trade name bissetters peopul
whos job it was 2 put th tips on th
arrows bfor they wer releesd they wer brout
from what was thn normandee ovr 2
scotland possiblee in time 4 th battul uv
hastings or they wer late 4 that foray prior
2 that time howevr unbeleevablee in scotland
arrows wer not getting releesd th bissetts
may have left scotland certainlee aftr th
highland cleerans perhaps a fling they
wantid 2 avoid they had alredee lost theyr
tartan owing 2 having blown up or burnd 2
deth wun 2 manee english bishops n lords
in theyr continuing quest 4 independens
my dad out on th porch freezing pelting
hail icee snow we all inside him out
ther singing will ye know cum back agen 4
bonnee prins charlee

my mothrs familee
covert originalee couveers flemish arrivd
in new amsterdam bfor it was new york
evenshulee went 2 new brunswick intrtwind
with th macculloughs a great great great

aunt julia was a beautiful paintr n a writr
iuv seen wun uv her paintings she
chroniculd th rathr unusual medikul praktices
uv th macculloughs who still had theyr
tartans they wud put sick peopul on th
frozn miramishee rivr thinking th fresh air
mite b healthee fresh prhaps but veree
cold she was shunnd 4 recording ths th
couveers prsons still holding that name
bcame coverts or had alredee dun so n
latr moovd 2 nova scotia whr i thn bcame
mor possibul

1987 working with chris meloche
electronik composr in london ontario
anothr veree xciting partnrship in sound
adventur 4 me meloche is veree brillyant
atmospheerik we put out 2 cassetts so far
shining spirit electronik composisyuns with
words n othr sounds merging storee n
coinsiding electronik entiteez no time
referensd whil *luddites* is veree much time
referensd so i find it interesting n xciting 2
work in both fields approaches chris n me
also brout out *LONDON LIFE* mor uv spokn
word poetree with sum chant songs sound
pomes with electronik treetments evreething
uv cours xcept th original n revisd writing is
a collaboraysyun evn th writing by wunself is
alredee oftn in tandem say in writing lyriks 4
alredee xisting music ium heering gerry
collins brings in gorgeous pees uv music it
startid happning rite away i wud heer n
write down th words thats how "fireworks"
was dun sum times th words wud cum first
"reflex blu" sumtimes i wud bring in th
melodee n th words all thees diffrent
variaysyuns wun time chris meloche playd
me a recent pees he had writtn n th words
tumbuld thru ths duz happn n how much
is from practising at it n not going 2 that
well whatevr 2 oftn is sumtimes fine saying
dont have it yet duz anee wun know gerry
collins magik arrangr n composr as well n it
is magik whn yuv got th lyrik or th spokn
words 4 th music yuv just herd ar heering
4 th first time n its working n murray
favros face n mind lites up he works his
part we all work our part n put it 2gethr
its a benefishul thing 4 me that i had
mostlee gottn ovr being so shy all ths
working with peopul espeshulee sins going 2
london has reelee helpd with that as well
with a lot uv developmental evolving 4 me

th vessul

                    was so awkwardlee construktid
manee joints not reelee meeting   or dovetailing n
      th xcessiv amounts uv nails reelee rusting
    n sum parts uv th sails shredding   that it was see
worthee mor from wishing thn from effikaysyus building

     indeed   what wud bcum uv us all on ths wonkee voyage
faith 2 moov oceans   courage 2 calm n dispell giant waves

imaginaysyun 2 not faltr   altho well restid   during dreeree
  disulatoree daze n nites   without wind or moon or stars
     evn if they ar long sins gone from our possibul
       present site   give romantik lite   n pre scientifik
inspiraysyuns   2 our fingring uv th nodulaysyuns uv deus
x destina   wher els wud we b going   toward   or inside

    uv cours   ther ar always moments   uv sexual reegret n
thees ar oftn msaprehensyuns   uv th most baroque ordring
    whn all is wanting   that is   wanting   is wanting   n
care   being part uv th dansing

    well heer   uv cours   ther is also scrubbing th decks   n
nu identiteez cropping up   supplanting   eye dont think sew
  can   aneewun   replacing eithr   not 2 evn think uv
adding mor   n mor   peopul   fresh   xciting   2 turn from
    it is 2 leen on th past problema   not let go uv th
satisfying n unsatisfying parenting   take our own
    journee   veree few xcuses 2 ourself is wher it is
counting   reelee   4 not going on

    precawsyun uv cours   always yet if th bell is ringing
dew try n answr it   howevr gracefulee   if at all possibul
  wudint yu rathr b loving   well   thers a pawsing in th
  puritan withdrawl from adventur n plesur   th bodee   is
   reelee as fine as aneething   is connekting with th
     mind
                 n guilt from societal teechings freys th
   delicate   n potenshulee strong n yielding   n being
asking   among th treez   furthr   in th summrree   blowee
winds n breezes   yu can feel on yr skin   making
   agen   th innosent   music   we can   live   4

wun uv my ship mates had a small gold statue uv
a barracuda   sumtimes he sd it was a salamandr   as well as
    a trinket   also gold   uv sum minatur merkats   thees wer all
    deliteful 2 me   n oftn   undr a full moon   he wud show thees
2 me   on th uppr deck   th ship jostuling its nevrthless way
no mattr th emosyuns uv wondr i wud feel looking at thees
      objects   or it th ship   wud seem   n th watr n sky also 2
coinside   evn merg with th feelings i wud b xperiensing at
      thees times

      he wud tell me manee storees on thees occasyuns   how he
    had acquired   2 my mind thees tresurs   n wher all he had
        been   happee n sad n dangrous   n himself   in dangr oftn

    in my bunk aftr i wud endlesslee repeet 2 myself evree
    thing he had relatid 2 me   its importans   n its detail   he
      wud sumtimes smile   curving his lip   into th   uttrmost
      mystereez that i felt sure   nowun els cud undrstand   or evr
dreem uv   putting into words   n i wud fall asleep   agen
        phrasing   n rephrasing   n listning   2 his words n seeing
          ovr n ovr agen   that smile   how it did curv   like a
      magikul gold crescent moon   into th dark nite
                                                          n th watr
slapping n carressing th serpentine bow   as we made our
    way thru anothr endless xpans   like i hoped peopuls
    minds wud b   like i sumtimes thot they wer   espeshulee
his   tho i was alredee starting 2 find   limits n circuls
      clockwork   n chores   n feer   n th less than nimbul sieve
      th circuitree uv th brain   n ium disapointid at what
        seem arbitraree limits in   peopul   tho not in his
smile   curving with plesur n unpredictabul risk

      wun nite he tuk me into his bunk n held me til dawn whn
he left   leeving me wun uv his gold merkats   claspd
      in my hand   whn i gazd at it bfor brekfast i saw that
          it wore his smile   as did my bodee   n my heart

    he was no robot

                              from *dreem carpets n toxik winds*   work in progress

against my will[3]

i was born   i kept
putting it off

whn i was born i
weighd 12 pounds
8 ounces
                i cudint
put it off much
longr   i cuduv
bin born earleeer
i did want 2
b a scorpio
            also
i startid 2
forget all th
horribul things

iud herd abt life
n got curious nd

bgan 2 considr
th strain on my

mothr who thot
i was twins

gazing   watching th caulking   uv   th pool
quiet attentiv   ecstasee undr wch th latest full moon
pulsing   its gonna b twice ths month   toronto   onlee 2
marvel   let in th continuing breething ache uv it sumtimes   th
beautee   ium heer   on th balconee   air canada   its a
palace   515.00 a month tripul towrs   facing into gorgeous court
yard   gardns   pools   huge treez   fountains   dogs
peopul   n th great maypul leef gardns   huge blu maypul on th
immens roof   hot   giant mushroom space ship   abt 2
levitate   time moovs 4ward n back   resolutelee   speeding
thn still   illusyuns uv 4 purpoises inside th chambr   flesh
bones   wishes   breth   organa   we ar looking out   its our
own submersibul   moysyun pickshur   still mooving   on side
wayze   world is tilting   present   wher we ar living   big
mysteree uv th futur reseeding as we go out   find sumwun 2
b   with   undr th fountains   jumping up in 2 th spinning
wheels   we grab n carress each othrs flesh   its takn yeers
n yeers 2 get 2 a place like ths   2 afford   windows ar huge
2 th floor   looking away from them   n all th green
grass   blu hot sky   n th diamond watr rising   they let in
evreething   heer all day   thees storeez so hi   magikul
knowing   unknowing   timing   dewing ths   travelling 4
work n play   wher ar mistr n missus linear   theyr out 2day
playing i hope   XCELLENT   wundrful frends heer

similarlee in vancouvr   i live neer stanlee park
worlds largest innr citee park   ancient growth treez   west coast
magik animals   above th building next door i can see ovr th hi rise
towrs 2 th pacifik deep permitting atmospheer   erotik   loamee
moistlee fecund   tuk a long whil 2 get heer   off th street   out uv trubul
ium abul 2 live in 2 places   frequent flying   4 dewing poetree reedings   having art
shows uv my paintings   drawings   sculpturs   next wun   kingston ontario   summr 94
time sharing 2 let it happn   7 yeers now dewing ths   a living   found in a myriad see
uv sub letting th apartment ium not in whil living in th wun ium in   manee peopul
want 2 live onlee 2 or 3 months sumwher   ium meeting lots uv them   we help each
othr   adds 2 th papr play putting ths 2gethr   worth it   usd 2 call it papr work
play sounds like mor fun   dusint it   ths all startid whn i was offerd writr in residens job
at western universitee   london ontario   by alan gedalof   th hiring professor ther
changd my life   hes so amazing   1985–86   thn still living london part time   offerd writr
in libraree   woodstock ontario   1987–88   mor workshops   mor wun on wun
reelee liked it   gud 4 th writing n painting 2   was askd 2 join LUDDITES   alternative
band   as vocalist n lyricist   xcellent   cassett out fast   thn 12"lp calld *luddites*   thn 1991
dreemin uv th nite   originallee gerry collins   peter denny   myself   thn peter denny
went mor acoustik   thn th three uv us touring south western ontario   veree raging
back from thn in 1984   workd with dermot foley   lenore herb   in band calld
SONIK HORSES   brout out cassett from undrwich edishyuns in toronto nd our own label
in vancouvr   its wundrful byond beleef 2 work with brillyant musiciyans like thees
dermot n lenore ar now front line environmentalists n on th bord uv SPEC societee 4
preservaysyun uv environmental concerns   gerry an amazing composr as well   n
brillyant guitarist   now in anothr band   LUDDITES lastid a long time   5 yeers   n thers
always possibilitee we may dew mor work 2gethr   *dreeming uv th nite* has receevd a lot uv
air play   college alternative staysyuns   as duz th
luddites lp   so who knows th futur   wch is
wun uv th points uv ths autobiographee

---

[3]from *seagull on yonge street* Talonbooks 1983

irving layton   wun uv our great eldr poets
his erotik n romantik writing is veree
wundrful n his religyus n spiritual work   veree
profound   mooving   interesting 2 me   sd
in a recent intrview on tv that what can b
tragik abt a writrs life is that we think words
ar mor reel than aneething els   n they arint
i find ths reelee sumthing   2 think abt   oftn

i was born novembr 23 1939   same day as
billy th kid   n gerald lampert n p.k. page
two writrs i admire   ium on th cusp
sagitarius n scorpio   makes me poetenshulee
veree gud diplomat n also ingredients 4
xplosyun calmd thru lerning TM whn i thot i
was going inside 4 a long stretch   wud need
sum way uv getting off   2day its toronto
with a flu   writing ths   staring sum mor at
th fountains   i nevr pay rent in 2
apartments simultaneouslee   uv cours   n ium
reelee mostlee basd in toronto   am an

me in halifax   my dog brookside "ruggee"
citayshun   winning best in show

ontario resident sins 1985   still love vancouvr
tho   n northern bc   go ther whnevr i can
work takes me

    in halifax   whn i was in th
crib   i was wanting 2 b a child actor at mgm
dean stockwell my oldr brothr   wud have
bin a dreem cum trew 4 me   i did love my
2 sistrs tho we faut espeshulee they faut
2gethr forsd 2 share th same room all theyr
growing yeers was veree hard on them at
times   i was sick a lot   veree oftn not
wantid by my peers bcoz they perseevd me as
gay so dont play with   i was beetn up a lot
4 being gay hauntid n isolatid   i nevr put
them down 4 being strait or tried 2 xclude
them from me 4 that   i listend 2 great
canadian radio programs like "jake n th kid"
starring john drainie   brillyant canadian radio
actor   an idol   it was writtn by wundrful
canadian writr w.o. mitchell   n "th happee
gang"   reelee funnee   n had pickshurs uv
hot amerikan moovee stars undr blankits with
me n my dog "ruggee"   oftn i was seizd by
a sens uv tragedee   melencholee   entrapment
alternating with sum psychik upliftment
ther was a painting uv daniel in th lions den
on th wall opposit my bed   gave me courage
helpd a lot   espeshulee as well with th
growing sexual intensitee n longing   we all
watchd "plouffe familee"   great tv show from
kebek
    my mothr went 2 spirit whn i was 14
she had sufferd so much from cancr n had
helpd me so much regardless whn i was sick
n aftr optimism faith   fighting   obstakuls
sickness discouragment   debts   massaging th
tube in my bellee trying 2 get th shit
mooving aftrwards   helping me always with
my homework   math   memorizing   ovr n ovr
agen   yu had 2 dew well at school as well as
yu cud aneeway   or what was th point   all
th operaysyuns my mothr went thru   hacking
off her bodee   bit by bit   it was so terribul
4 all uv us   fathr also xtraordinaree   so hard
working   at home   veree tyrannikul   he
worreed so much   yelling   fighting
skreeming   th doors slamming   his pain   our
feers   hysteria   mothr dying   nothing is
always   her terribul pain   was fathr sick with
worree at nite   foetal posisyun   his
seeminglee erratik childrn   from his point uv
view   how wud they survive   my mothr offerd
me her religyun but it nevr reelee tuk

grade school in halifax

well class what happend to yu
during th christmas holidaze thats
uv intrest   sumthing unusal say
bill   what abt yu   stand up   n tell
us   well my mothr got her brest cut
off in th hospital

BILL how can yu talk filth like that
its th strap agen for yu   ium sorree
abt thees welts on yr hand but its th
onlee way yul lern

wipe thos teers from yr eyes   yr a
big boy now   yr in grade three   yu
bring all ths on yrself

ths hurts me mor than it duz yu she
sd   i pulld my hand away quik as th
strap cum pounding down on her knee

n that time it did hurt her mor

ther wer scuff marks on th floor in
front uv her desk   i didint dew it
but th girl who was numbr wun on th
honor roll   i was onlee seventh or
eighth but for a boy mooving up tho
i didint want to   she sd i did it   n
i got strappd agen   it was always in
th cloak room   all th swet n wet rubbrs
mittns   stuffee

so i wud go out in th yard during recess
stand ther   turn round fast   n faint   dont
remembr if th teechr felt compassyun thn

we had a lot uv fire n air drills   sumtimes
we dansd reels   girls in skirts   guys in
pants   th english took th kilts away long
time ago bfor that   th ground was always
hard whn i wud fall on it   thr was no wun to
talk to abt my mothr

that was avoidid like th war n othr deths

from *seagull on yonge street*
Talonbooks 1983

i lovd mgm musiculs   louis b. mayer from
nu brunswick   dad yelling sumthing   heet
was 2 hi   i got cold eezee   2 long in my
room   his debts   b a MAN he yelld in th
hospital whn he came 2 see me wuns in it
seemd like two yeers   i was skreeming with
pain   he nevr came agen   xcept wuns he
brout presents bfor an operaysyun   i was
loving tord him   he workd veree hard   nevr
joind a firm   tuk cases 4 veree poor clients
beleevd stronglee in soshul justis   hes yelling
ium out th door   muffins on   wind is
howling   snow   swirling   off downtown with a
tube still in my bellee   2 see anothr mgm
musicul   or *a place in th sun*   with elizabeth
taylor   montgomery clift   n shelley winters
ther was no medicare thn   all th doktors
expenses   we wer going bankrupt   oftn i
thot it was my fault   elaine stewart also a
favorit   whn i had my brain operaysyun
yeers latr   medicare pd 4 it   othrwise i
wudda gone 2 spirit   n bobby driscoll   uv
cours th stars in *a place in th sun* i totalee
lovd   also *singin in th rain*   n *an amerikan
in paris*   peter lorre n jules munshin singing
"2 bad we cant go back 2 moscow" in *silk
stockings* with fred astaire n cyd charisse   also
so magikul   mor latelee *dead ringers* with
jeremy irons n geneviève bujold   a david
cronenberg film   n *edward 11* by derek
jarman   iul always see a lot uv moovees

th world falls apart   all th time   world
war 2   terrifying   rumors uv what was
reelee happning in th deth camps   th
holocaust   latr mccarthee period   cold war
mor feer   we keep trying 2 put th world
back 2gethr   th bodee   th mind   soul
onlee working tord equalitee reelee works   n
our attempts so fleeting   evreething is testid
still want 2 work 4 hope n th possibul pees
my mothr gone   i bcame 2 b in a gang
aftr limping 4 sum time   at last a peer
group that wud have me   we wer veree tuff
i was also reeding sartre   de beauvoir   camus
cocteau   singer   shirley anne grau
gertrude stein   truman capote   mordecai
richler   shaw   rebecca west   tennessee
williams   eugene o'neill   andre gide   d.h.
lawrence   edith sitwell   marianne moore
tolstoy   th brontës   george eliot   manee uv
thees introdusd 2 me by a frend   just close
frend   i admird veree much   his brothr

returnd from europe with thees names   i
was veree thrilld   cudint reed enuff   n
listning 2 bartok   schoenberg   menotti   weill
ther was a girl i was sexualee nuts abt   i
nevr thot that wud happn   so hornee   no
way til wer marreed   she sd   i had seen
marriage   i wantid 2 b a poet n a paintr
knew ther wudint b munee 4 marriage   like
my fathr   she wantid me 2 b a lawyr   i
wasint blaming aneewun   she wudint allow
condoms   was skreeming at me whn i tuk
wun out 2 ask her if we cud use it   she was
skreeming   marriage or nothing   fine
images uv james dean   hank williams   judy
garland   sarah vaughan   june christy with
stan kenton singing "lonely woman"   billie
holiday singing "strange fruit"

            thn i met ths
wundrful guy   i was uv cours veree hornee
we slept 2gethr in my attik room   paintid
dark green   with picassos "the lovers" on th
wall   wher th houskeepr who had bin my
best frend had livd   my fathr fired her aftr
my mothr had gone 2 spirit   i was told 2
take ovr cooking n kleening i did   he still
yelling   whn i was sleeping with my frend
howevr he bcame sweet 2 me   was it bcoz i
was happier   we draw happeeness 2 us
sumtimes whn wer happee ourselvs   its that
i cant know why dad wud b asking reelee
nicelee 4 his cookees n milk bfor going 2
bed   with a raging hard on sum how
disguisd leeving my frend 4 a bit i wud go
downstairs n bring him that n say gud nite 2
him   me n my frend nevr what they thn
calld went all th way   he had bin raped whn
he was a kid n that had left him problems
we ran away   i sd gud bye 2 my dad in th
erlee morning   i told him i had a job with
general motors in calgary with a frend uv his
he probablee knew that wasint trew   we hit
th road planning 2 leev western civilizaysyun
4evr   i was 17   gud luck

            home bfor dark
thats what dad wud say   we wud leev th
summr cottage uv his frends   neer th giant
wild straberree bushes n th atlantik ocean ovr
sum sand dunes wher we wud go swimming
sad 2 leev so erlee   grumbling   dad wud
leed us in songs "what dew yu dew with a
drunkn sailor erlai in th morning" n "'eis th
biy that built th boat n 'eis th biy that sails

at nineteen   in vancouvr

'em"   ther sure wer squabbuls   sumtimes i
had tantrums   locking myself in my room
moaning on th linoleum floor   staring up at
th sky thru th ceiling   going into outtr space
but it reelee was fun sumtimes   evn with th
childrn shud b seen n not herd maxim
invokd fairlee oftn   whn it was fun what a
releef   thn weud b singing "farewell 2 nova
scotia"   i knew i wud b dewing that fairlee
soon   its wundrful ther   beautiful
evreetime i go back ther   4 reedings   or 2
prins edward island   i love it mor

            i lovd
my frend so much   it nevr reelee workd out
as it turnd out   we did make it 2 vancouvr
xcellent   th writings uv jack kerouac n allen
ginsberg gave us support   we startid on th
road with a girl   frend   who we alternatelee
closetlee wer in love with   i needid a buffr
bcoz uv what i thot wer his xtreem jealouseez
he needid a buffr bcoz he wudint go all th
way with me   young love   fine   raging   not
all bluffs ar on mountains

wun day my fathr took me down to th old court hous

in halifax   n showd me wher peopul usd to get hung
didint happn aneemor   a fairlee recent advans   ther
wer still manee wars   ths shud nevr b usd agen my
fathr sd abt th hanging place n thn he was tendr
confident whol not torn btween loyaltees as i latr
lernd peopul can bcum

wun nite aftr my first mothr died my sistrs stayd
out uv th hous til morning   he was yelling at them
so much   slamming doors   all skreeming at each othr
he was mad violent bcoz they had boy frends   calld
them names   he had no wife   me sticking up for them
him yelling at me   as long as yr out tomorro   not
undr my roof

i workd for him a few yeers   cooking kleening   left
whn i was legal age   to go west   he marreed agen but
she drownd n he moovd into a hotel   th conflict dusint
mattr now tho it had its effects   is that a definishyun
uv mattr   all th childrn in ths strange land ths has
happend to   brot up to b wun thing offishulee unmasking
wun aspekt onlee uv ther prson   in or out uv anee familee

bfor he went into spirit i phond him   he sd is that my
son bill   he told me he lovd me n my sistrs   took sum
yeers to get mello but it did   fathrs n sons   born into
th distance   a smiling fathr face in th clouds   far from
wher   a week bfor he died he came thru th front windo
wher i was living thn in a dreem   whn i got th telegram
he was veree sick   i calld th hospital in halifax from
robson street phone booth vancouvr   th doctor came to th
phone n sd ium sorree bill but yr fathr just died   i was

crying   closd in by th rain n glass   now hes bizee with
othr things   is fine   sum blessings for our madness   i
hope   ium taking it aneeway that thats whats going on
wer disapeering into numbrless atoms n still want sum
human animal love to live n go with in ths sun   bfor my
second mothr went into th ocean i herd she sd to th cab
drivr who took her ther pleez keep it   wher ium going

i dont need th change

from *seagull on yonge street* Talonbooks   1983

aftr my frend went back to halifax
i had anothr peritinitis attack   my big sistr
flew out west 2 see me   protekt me from my
fathr who wantid 2 put me in a mental
hospital   i always remembr her braveree in
dewing ths   she had bcum a soshul workr
told dad aftr spending a few dayze with me
that i was fine   whn my mothr went 2 spirit
i didint cry 4 a coupul yeers   thn th teers
wudint stop   whn my fathr went 2 spirit i
cried rite away 4 dayze   evn tho he wasint
an ideel fathr i did love him   tho he wasint
comfortabul with that being xpressd   tho he
was with his wife   our mothr   they wer so
much in love   so th loss is always ther
evenshulee i undrstand nowun is ideel
dusint that help with my growing   he did
disown me   i wrote "halifax   nova scotia"
bcoz eye cudint help it   n 2 relees from
obsessyun i had bin 4 yeers abt events ther n
2 vizualize my parents as living as they startid
as they mite have continued healthee
romantik   wildlee   always n unworreed by
debts   sicknesses   th worst always around th
cornr   n trying so courageouslee 2 keep
going on   n with ths relees   in ths pome
4 me as well   2 go on

*my dottr michelle   playing with frend
about 1965*

1960   shelving books in th vancouvr publik
libraree   didint like korrekt spelling   was
finding my wayze out uv that   lovd arranging
xploring words dropping like baubuls   glands
pulsing all ovr th papr   my favorit thing in
hi school   junior hi school was making
geographee n historee books   i lovd that th
most   onlee activitee i evr won prize 4 at
graduaysyun time   i lovd pastin in photos or
drawings n putting th heddings undr thos in
diffrent colord pencils   highliting my futur in
books   i lovd books   now i was shelving
them   n reeding them evree nite aftr work
evreething i cud get my hands on   i went
back 2 halifax   hitching in th wintr with a
frend   she n i laffing all th way thru th
frozn prairee   flew from montreal 2 see my
dad bcum a judg   got ther 2 late 4 th
ceremonee   we got 2gethr familee nothing
jelld tho   my dottr reserches th judgments
my fathr made n tells me they wer veree fair
veree compassyunate   leeving th nest i gess 4
evreewun is a novel n a half   so back 2
vancouvr

ther was a guy so in love with me i didint
get it til yeers latr   we got it on   i still let
it go   met anothr guy   he tuk me home   i
was so in love with him i livd with him rite
away   he was in love with anothr guy   kept
phoning him at nite aftr we wud get it on
i was in love with him   he wasint abt 2
change   i hit th road   reeding evreething
by virginia woolf   james baldwin   gore vidal

Close frend uv my mothrs calld aunt _____
receevd a message from my mothr in
spirit   time 2 live with a girl she sd   i
met her   she saw me   she found me   we
told each othr evreething   we moovd in
2gethr   listning 2 coltrane   mingus   veree
hot sex   i was no longr a virgin   wundrful
we ragd 2gethr   red evreething   up all nite
rearranging all th words   letting spaces
happn   both into vizual writing   hers
stretchd out in lines   spaces btween th words
accenting   mine mooving up n down th page

halifax   nova scotia

all th brave sailors   what they had dun   brave hous wives   what they had
dun   th ded n gone sailing vessel daze whn halifax was lustee n
brawling rich th ghosts uv th sailor n th sea maiden lovrs rising
above th tides   haunting th melodee uv all th resting bones at th bottom
shoal sea bed   wher th othr tresurs lay goldn next to th mor ivoree ribs
uv th beechd n drownd peopul lament for th haunting as th brekrs roaring
onto th shore   wher by a thin breth we can b separatid from our safetees
n join th deth romance uv th sailors embracing each othr   hugging   seeming
to stare back at th curious eyez uv th purpul spottid grey fish   wer goin
down my boy   th giant spray gushing into theyr lungs   ther ar rubees undr
th eyelids   emeralds in th fingr bones   arms around each othr n th sunkan
tresur uv th heart   until we ride agen

on partikularlee stormee nites whn we ar all inside by th fire th long n
recentlee ded sail agen ovr th main n above th giant billows   greet each
othr across th great tormentid sky   we ar inside n that close to drowning
if th waves so whim it highr n loudr   we heer th voices cry n laff hi n
stern jagged tormentid n victorious   dashing rocks to farthr obliviyun
hundrid metr waves   tees th holographee uv th jumping so hi n deft wivvering
ghosts   spirits uv th departid from ths place   erth borne can we dance
agen   can we fix it celebrate   holograph images   ducking n escaping agen
from th leviathan waves   laffing th sounds uv echo in our freezing clap
bord houses   th winds saw eezilee thru n into our skin   fishing vessels
around th wharves down by th harbor   wun wharf named aftr my grandfathr from
inverness scotland   his ships saild to portugal   but we live on universitee
avenue   in halifax   a bit inland n safer from th immediate changes   tho th
ocean powr is inside us   at our window   waiting n biting th glass

wher victor hugos dottr went mad   trying to win ovr a spurning lovr   wher
sum uv th ded from th titanik ship wreck ar burreed   in th graveyard on
barrington street   whn yu heer th wind blow   it duz that   nites uv fiers
winds yu dont go   yu stay n listn to th howling n th sereen lullabyes   th
astors ar bureed ther   peopul always going down to th harbor   staring out to
sea for hours my dad wud sit in his car at th brek watr   his eyez going far
out beyond th atlantik horizon   aftr a long enuff time   did land apeer   or
atlantis surfacing from th trench   meditaysyuns on th disapeering horizon
fish smell sea gull shrieks   always announsing fresh storms at sea n detail
ing th kind uv bones bleechd on rocks   what meet left on them n howevr bleed
id   skraping against th bottom   th sea takes evreething back   th winds sum
times sounding like wraith creatures suffocating for oxygen   breeth into us
feed us life agen

neer wher into th big park my mothr n i wud go hunting flowrs to take
home   she oftn wud look for laydeez slipprs   that was her favorit   th
flowrs wer a wondr for her   whn she was veree close to what we heer
considr th last veil   i remembr she went down th sevn blocks uv th
avenue to th altr to place flowrs thru a blinding snow storm   walking
gainst winds cumming home   remembr a pictur uv my mothr n fathr whn
they wer veree young   both theyr hair strong theyr bodeez clasping in
embrace th winds raging with theyr hair   my mothrs hair black bfor th
cobalt treetments turnd it grey   full uv life they both wer   passyun
n gladness   smell th beautee   sand beech   so much to remembr   so

much to forget   let go   th love is   reel   still burning   th flame
thru th sky   thru th fog   thru all th veils we pass thru   changing
n anothr wun to pass thru   change n let go   til thers th seering singing
care   offring   sharing th vanishing time   until we ride agen   my mothr

gone two yeers from th cancr settling into th lungs   last stage   heering
fathr aftr a long muffuld silens sing out uv his closd door bedroom   IUM
OKAAAAAAAAAAAY a great street lamp sign yell into th void   kay was my mothrs
name   his fred   n sobbing   thn running watr   n kleening his   teeth   mor
silens   sumthing abt memorees   an appul n spruce treez   thirtee mile view

uv th lake   a hot plate on fire that wasint pluggd in   was my fathr out
looking at th huge ocean   its moods   deciphering   praying   for th sea
maidn n th sailor   my parents   themselvs   all th lanterns blown out   no
witnesses for th miracul   themselvs   riding th brekrs   soaring lullabyes
th masts n th wreckage   carnal spirit   lifting theyr great arms up above
th spray   aura beem   mor than sufficient lite   crooning to th whales   th
sea birds   th sun rising n setting   dansing above th waves   wings opn
n lifting theyr hopes n daring   th prayd for futur   a chorus uv drowning

sailors accompaneeing them   escaping th undrtow   into th moon change

until they ride agen   n th wethr was fair

from *canada gees mate for life*   Talonbooks 1985

so in diffrent wayze letting th words breeth
on th page   remet lance farrell   major bud
him n me also   all three uv us   up all nite
finding th sylabul   writing   writing   she was
pregnant   with our dottr   wundrful   thn
th full blown sixteez   going 2 court   in
band calld mandan massacre   12"lp out
i wud reed e.e. cummings 2 her in bed
". . . all in green my love went riding . . ."
we bcame almost wun prson   nowun wud
publish us   we wer trying 2 keep our dottr
th law was evreewher   sidney simons   so
brillyant   dfending us   getting me off
possessyun charges   lots uv court apperances
we turnd ourselvs inside out 4 each othr   2
keep going   thn breking away   in spite uv th
povrtee n th critiks starting blewointmentpress
2gethr 1962   evenshulee averaging 10 books
a yeer   starting with gestetnr mimeograph
masheen from th erlee 1900s   printing so
manee writrs   helping amerikan desertrs find
canadian wives so they cud stay n not get

killd in vietnam   giant rock concerts   starting
poetree reedings   mor busts   mor court   big
huge bust at end uv sixteez   narks came in
motor launches   ovr mountains   on foot
armd 2 th teeth   so we wer veree politikul
stop th damn war   stop th dedlee evil rite
wing   we wer abt sevn peopul   our dottr
skreeming   wasint th first time   we wer far
away tuckd in th countree   who wer we
hurting   narks violent   we wer totalee
outnumberd   veree long trials

            i dont see time as decades
what is time   a storee is what time is it what
time is it   did sum in jail   manee counts
stuk onlee on wun   thanks agen 2 th
brillyans uv sidney simons   great frend   not
much time   dottr so wundrful   in free school
in countree   protektid   state didint get her
big worree 4 me   my dad worreed a lot
uncontrolablee   so cud i   my dad hired th
first woman lawyer 2 artikul   he was veree

advansd in manee wayze   sixteez xplosyuns
in hiding from a kangaroo court in bc
tensyuns loyalteez testid hard love we
kept publishing thru a lot uv ths part uv
my sentens from th big bust was a cash fine
i printid a book uv mainlee pomes writtn in
jail n smugguld out   sold it door 2 door
calld *sunday work(?)* (blewointmentpress)
othr writrs thru blewointment maxine gadd
judith copithorne lance farrell gladys
hindmarch d.a. levy pat lowther who was
later murderd by her redneck marxist
husband   ther is no wun way   bpNichol
david uu beth jankola sam perry dallas
sellman gary lee nova gwendolyn macewen
rosemary hollingshead   joy zemel long
margaret avison dorothy livesay earle birney
mona fertig britt hagarty michael coutts
david cull beverley rosen simons john
burton milton acorn al purdy colleen
thibaudeau miriam waddington aaron steele
alex pratt gwen hauser sam perry al neil
manee manee othrs

d.a. levy was being houndid in cleveland
great frend thru th mail we had similar
karma in th houndid area xcept in
cleveland they did hound him 2 deth th
rite wing ther what powr they thot they had
his passing tragik outrage in th literaree
"undrground" memorial antholojees uv his
work ar still being put 2gethr like sam perry
he tragikalee shot himself great tragedee
ther sam perry such a wundrful meditaysyun
devotee n film maker a time uv veree fast
changes great oppressyuns a lot uv
tragedee as well as th uplifting magik n
ecstasee n working 2gethr so much
bpNichol n me also great frends in that time
n latr thru th mail   publishing each othr
fanning xtend th work opportuniteez
reedings networking so manee peopul bp
had ganglia press wch publishd my maybe
first book *we sleep inside each other all* 1966
neck n neck with *fires in th tempul OR th jinx
ship nd othr trips* (very stone hous) i was
also involvd with patrick lane jim brown n
seymour mayne   *fires in th tempul* was a
blewointment very stone hous copublishing
ventur   we wer also bp n i reeching out
with bob cobbing in england ivo vroom in
belgium japan d.r. wagner in california
sound konkreet vizual d.a. levy n myself
veree much into bordr blur bob cobbing 2

ther eminentlee   tord 1968 blewointment
publishd d.a. levy's brillyant *zen konkreet* d.a.
had publishd sum uv my work in cleveland
uv cours maxine gadds *guns uv th west* n
hochelaga (blewointmentpress) wer also major
brekthrus in pome consciousness michael
coutts wundrful brillyant lyrikul n politikul
poet anothr great n tragik loss 2 that time
incredibul prson close frend   i got out uv
jail   living alone   went 2 art partee i was
invitid 2   hosts uv th art show i was in
konkreet vizual poetree show   i fell thru th
door not latchd disguisd 2 look like a wall
20 feet down 2 th konkreet landid on hed
neurolojee ward intrcerebral bleed aphasia
paralysis on rite side 2 yeers 2 reelee fullee
recovr pain luckee got out thats 2 yeers
in full was in hospital onlee littul spinal
tap memoree loss occupaysyunal therepy
physio therepy push push doktor resident
intern she savd my life pushing me
pushing in th physikul present 4 evn
incremental improovments n not worreeing
abt th temporaree memoree losses othr side
effects

    lost th court case 4 damage claims
bcoz eithr theyr cat had or had not drunk
its milk wch saucer it wud go 2 preciselee at
whatevr at th foot uv th stairs whethr yes
sins it was aftr that time th cat must uv
slurpd alredee n thn therfor no liabilitee evn
undr invitee invitor bcoz th door wud have
bin latchd   wud th cat testify   wun uv th
hosts gud frend showd his invite cards
nothing ther 4 me not invitid uv cours i
had bin fine ths was 4 me a veree gud
view uv what can b xpectid with peopul n
all beings insurans co   uv cours th cat thing
if th cat had finishd drinking had returnd
upstairs th door latchd what wer they saying
that i had unlatchd th door myself n thrown
myself down th stairs   i had just gottn out
uv jail wud i have wantid 2 kill myself thn
i still think testimonee from th cat wud have
bin desirabul so big deel mostlee i was
so grateful i was getting bettr th migraines
wer going th epilepsee was gone n th
paralysis gone   each day less n less fateeg
yeers latr th host with th invite cards in th
witness stand put me in a show in toronto
vancouvr 7   harborfront i blew bubbuls at
th opning was veree happee competeing
curators critiks ther uv cours wer offendid at

th titul uv th show   opning was reelee fun 4
me   n formr host seemd festiv now   releef
ther   n we carreed on   like lots uv things in
life   ther wer ingredients uv events byond
comprehending   wanting 2 live in change
accepting flexibul in th eternal moovments

but bfor that seeming resolushyun   on th
shores uv lake ontario   vancouvr wun nite
being bathd in th hospital   walking still veree
trikee   worreed abt my studio living place
brokn in2   evreething smashd   moov next

door   went out wun nite   met ths guy   came
home   nu studio destroyd evreething
paintings slashd   note on floor sd   ium
going 2 kill yu   i fuckd off out uv ther
went cross th bridg   downtown   club   met th
guy   i had tried introdusing peopul with
each othr   whatevr   went with guy i met that
nite rite away   great   left town aftr a whil
north   did log peeling   physikul work
xtreem cold helping migraines post op effect
pills 4 epilepsee   veree poor   eeting kraft
dinnrs   sharing them   missing dottr   tried 2

OUT ON TH TOWN JOY RIDIN

what that yuve got round yr neck th big heavy
bull yelld down at th groovy stond kid hed
just thrown down on th cement floor
of the van. city bucket kickin his nuts cummin
up in th elevator with us that nite he sz
sure feel like kickin sum ones nuts in tonite
nd th stond kid say just waitl yu read th
star weekly in 3 weeks after i been stripped
nd searchd in th below freezing snow on th
beach at english bay havin been hauld
out of th VW is this legal i askd stallin
what are yu a part-time lawyer trubul with
yu dissenters is yu read part of a subversive
civil liberties pamphlet nd ya think yu
know th law later we joshd round a bit
bout whether theyd need a mountie to search
a mobile home well he really wasint that
bad but meanwhile later back at th bucket
th big heavy bull sd whats that you got round yr
neck to th stond kid still on th floor with
no nuts left to speak of yr st. christophers
medal eh RIPP so yu want it at th
other end of th floor yu crawl for it
punk crawl which he did while th bull kickd
him nd th othr bulls laffd it up question
duz a country get th police force it deserves
do most peopul live in such fear while in th
investigation room we ate sum blue bail papers from
a previous bust so i cud say i had no record crash th
bull threwn th kid back into th elevator head first
nd we shovd th rest of th blue paper into th radiator
just in time

1st publishd   *sunday work(?)* blewointmentpress   1968
2nd publishd   *nobody owns th erth* anansi   1971
3rd publishd   *selected poems: beyond even faithful legends*
Talonbooks   1980

bertrand lachance   about 1972

stay in ths also beautiful relaysyunship
chopping wood   got bettr   natur is th best
wher th asid had takn me   howling winds
fiers   cold wethr   kept printing blewointment
books   meta leptika   first gran mal   thrashd
evree thing   bed brokn   on th floor   went
into previous life wher i livd in afrika village
huts   in a circul   veree beautiful   startid
seeing peopuls auras   went into th painting
july 93 now   toronto   gottn ovr long flu
remembring outstanding brillyant neurologist
n "th high green hill"   n rosemary
hollingshead   who helped me xercise

erlee seventeez   back 2 th citee   vancouvr
live in triangul   xcellent n veree difficult
lerning   unlerning   wher is th possessyun
abridging th primal construkt 2 keep going
each day   printing books   collating still by
hand   latr hiring that out   12–14 hour day
go out   get it on sumwher   xcellent
sumwun cums 2 rescue me   cuz i was going

down   take nu track in both our lives   keep
printing   mor n mor poetree books uv cathy
ford   hart broudy   candas jane dorsey
carolyn zonailo   gerry gilbert   lionel kearns
beth jankola   rosemary hollingshead   alec
newell   steve miller   eli mandel   gwendolyn
macewen   david uu   joy zemel long   giant
antholojees   manee singul author books
great life raging 2gethr   wundrful partnr
ium on my own agen   aftr anothr serees uv
ecstatik yeers   lerning th singul life can b as
great as anee othr   on my own   reelee first
time in my life   1981   sad n xcitid   both
th danse keeps changing   accepting that
working   playing   with

thn bang i was askd
2 have a wun prson retrospektiv show at th
vancouvr art galleree   curatid by brillyant
scott watson   raging   had just had a painting
praisd by john bently mays in th vancouvr
warehous show   ths was totalee unxpectid
surprizing *globe & mail* n i gess 4 me gud
n less gud things have always bin surprizing
scott watson had had show in mind long
time previous 2 that   was almost an entire
floor   blew my mind   my dottr at th opning
praktikalee evreeun iuv evr known or livd
with   prettee xhilerating   i had bin veree
private 4 yeers sins brain op   that nite at th
galleree endid my hermitage   tho paradoces
i was now living alone   in 1989 had a wun
prson show at th veree magik n festiv selby
hotel on sherbourne st in toronto   i was also
luckee 2 receev canada council grants   three
times in th sixteez   during wch   c. 62   i was
in a film made abt manee vancouvr artists n
writrs shot by len fourrier n jack long 4 th
nfb   n just bfor being run out uv town   was
in *strange grey day ths*   65 film directid n
produsd by maurice embra   abt my writing
painting   n life   maurice was both inspiring
n relaxing 2 work with   wundrful xperiens
it was shown on cbc n sold 2 nbc
intrnashyunalee   th film abt van artists n
writrs was calld *in search of innocence*
receevd canada council grants in th seventeez
th last full grant i had receevd until ths yeer
93 was in 78 whn *sailor* (Talonbooks) was
releesd   luck hard work prserverans   ther
has bin a lot uv ups n downs   abt 50–50   i
reelee dew appresiate my luck tho th first
press i had was an erlee 1900s gestetner
mimeograph masheen with no automatik papr

feed   art may nevr make as much munee as
killing but i beleev its bettr 4 peopul
certainlee bettr 4 me   seeing th words thn
running from off th rollr   duplikating
themselvs imaginablee   into seeming infinitee
silkscreening   reprodusing by hand   th first
masheen with an automatik papr feed was a
revelaysyun 2 us   thn evenshulee an offset
press   wheww   n thn th printing got farmd
out   ths point tuk yeers 2 get 2

i was printing billy th kid

by michael ondaatje   seksyuns
from it   bfor it was publishd
by it self   we wer printing
it in th occupaysyun issew
uv blewointmentpress

i was working th press thn
with bertrand lachance

my hair was veree long
cirka 1970   half way down my
back

i was lerning how to print
with an a b dick offset   i was
stond   out uv my gourd   n my

hair caut in th electrik
rollrs uv th machine   thundring
n turning fastr than i cud stop
them   th plug was in th wall
on th far side uv th room

i was skreeming

bertrand n his sistr wer in th
orchard   looking ovr th fraysr
canyun   n th vegetaybuls   th nite
treez   sky   th rivr breth uv th
leevs   no wun came running

they thot   they told me aftrward
that i was practising sum nu
sound poetree   from th distans
it soundid veree nice they sd

sum uv thees issews have a lot
uv hair stuk on them

from *animal uproar*   Talonbooks 1987

th first pome i wrote was in grade 3 or
erlee grade 4   abt boats sailing   that i
think was th terribul summr i almost had 2
go 2 boys camp 4 th entire summr   faut like
crayzee 2 get out uv that   thinking up things
my parents wud accept   they wer veree
incensd   thank god i got out uv it   whol
summr filld with boys   go totalee crayzee
sexualee n whatevr   if in th wintr they cud
pelt me with snow balls filld with rocks n
summarilee beet me undr huge treez in othr
seesuns   what cud i xpect in a far away
isolatid place in th countree wher it wud fr
sure take me longr 2 run home   if eye wud
get home   my fathr thot that it was not
manlee 2 not want 2 go 2 boys summr camp
what cud i dew   yes it was not manlee
tony curtis   jeff chandler   rock hudson
montgomery clift   frank sinatra   russ tamblyn
gene kelly   george nader   john derek
richard widmark   burt lancaster   my parents
may have nevr forgivn me 4 th row i put up
n i may nevr have forgivn them at that time
all th skreeming n yelling what was wrong

allan rosen toronto about 1975

have u seen th moovee fortune n mens eyez   or th play   iuv seen th

moovee n red th play   by john herbert   theyr both reelee great   i sd
coz ths guy askd me aftr a reeding coz iud sd iud dun sum time   cud
i compare   yeh i sd i lovd that moovee   it was outstanding n sos th
play   it was a bit like that wher i was onlee not quite so dramatik tho
it may have bin if iud stayd ther longr

like th time we had th 3/4 hour morning brek bfor lunch   i was alone in
my cell   th guy in th cell next to me was going to get th bitch   thats
indefinit time forevr for whats calld incorrigibul   its phrasd at her
majestees pleasur   thats off th books now but thn it was on   he had 16
counts uv rape against minors n he recentlee had killd a hippee   that
was whn th word hippee was such a big deel   anothr co-opting technique
so i was being careful coz he was muttring hippee hippee a lot at me but
aneeway during th brek i was walking up n down th tier n at th end cell

ther wer thees 9 guys in it playing cards or starting to   veree frendlee
askd me to cum in n i did   i want to play cards   sure i sd   i cant play
cards too gud but i was grateful for th companee n th acceptans if it was
thn they all pulld out thees littul papr containrs like sum restaurants
usd to serv th ketchup or th thousand islands in   littul papr cups full
uv vaseline n wun uv them moovd in on me   it was all reel quiet xcept my
nervs wer skreeming   9 guys ths was

thn ths reelee amazing guy on th tier   cums rushing in   pulls me out uv
ther   n takes me up th tier   throws me into th cell   slams me shut   locks
me inside   latr he brout me chocolate bars n i found out from sum othr
guys that he lookd aftr nu guys until things wer cool for them   i nevr
got reelee close to him   he had a roomate   but aftr that i nevr went anee
wher unless he was around   evn from a distance say like in th xercise yard
wher we walkd in a circul for an hour each day   i wud feel him   his eyez
ovr to me   looking out for me   as he brout bars to sum peopul n did all
th trading deels he was in in charge uv to keep th scene as cool as it cud
b   on th surface aneeway

also he was th barbr   whn i first cum in my hair was reelee long   i didint
want it cut   th screw sd how to b   i did a useless protest scene   but he
cut it so it lookd shortr than it reelee bcame n he sure calmd me   he put
all my hair in a plastik bag with a red ribbun tied round it   hung it from
his wall   ther was a barbr pole outside his cell   i didint have to co-operate
with aneething layd on me   he always was ther if thr was troubul   i was
luckee   th screws tho kept me from having visitors by mooving me from cell
to cell tier to tier for no reeson so that whnevr peopul came to see me   thr
was no record uv my being ther   but that guy always knew wher i was had got
to n wud make an apeerans so they knew to not mess with me   he sure was built
n quik as a cat

th food wasint bad   bettr than iud had in a lot uv places at that time
but it was prettee terribul   th coffee was always too week   bred was
always nine tenths flour   n by th time yu got yr tray up to yr cell th
food was all cold   but it was food i gess   th building was veree damp
hard on a prsons lungs   reelee cold at nite with wun thin blankit   to
evn get half way warm cudint happn   oakalla had bin condemmd yeers ago
evree three yeers or so bunch a big shots from ottawa or victoria visit
n xclaim how awful th living condishyuns ar n that th building shud or
will b torn down but nothings evr dun abt it   i can see why sum senior
citizens dew th boosts to get inside   at leest three meels a day n no
wun cin at all afford three meels a day on pensyuns aneemor   unless its
dog or cat food

that guy who helpd me he was in for armd robberee   he was reelee kind
most togethr prson in such a hevee dutee scene   he had to keep it all
goin or thr wudda bin constant freek outs n violens   evree wun was on th
edg all th time   all peopul bcum that way with bad food   poor living   n
isolaysyun   th membrs uv th parliament sd it was unfit for anee human
habitaysyun   they shud know   shudint they   what it duz to peopul is reel
n terribul   long enuff in ther n yr byond aneething   n if it werent for
that guy a lot uv us wudda bin byond aneething   lonelee n buggd   jumpee
n nothin

i herd th womens side was no bettr   whn we wer first in ther me n th woman
i was living with thn   waiting bail   we werent allowd to see each othr th
wardn sd bcoz evn tho we had livd togethr ovr 5 yeers we werent legalee
marreed   i askd him   thats what he sd   sorree son   thats th rules   mor
uv that   so she was on th womens side   i was on th mens side   side uv what
i wonderd   side uv beef   side uv th wch mountain   side uv sun   i met a
guy in ther   was in for being photographd in bed with anothr guy   photos
wer takn by bizness rival to brek him   he was drawing plans for geodesik
houses n structurs   he was sentensd two weeks bfor th law was changd   he
was still dewing full time   he got two yeers less a day   th guy he had
bin with was not a minor

it was snowing th morning i got out   th screws had playd a game on me   came
for me wun morning thn laffd that it was th next day   th calendar was wrong

from canada gees mate for life Talonbooks 1985

with me   why wasint i wanting 2 b with boys
my own age   etsetera   whats wrong with yu
wun time i sd they dont like me   so i dont
want 2 spend th whol summr with them
thats no xcuse they yelld back at me   i
forget what finalee clinchd it   i think my
sticking 2 my guns   they got ovr gradualee
laying guilt trips abt it on me   evree world
can b lunchd   wanting robotik responses

in th oxygen tent in th hospital i wrote my
first storee abt a boy n his monkee   who
always wantid 2 swim byond th boundareez n
rules uv his familee life   2 swim in th ocean
wher th undrtow was veree dangrous   n aftr
almost drowning   was abul 2 return n make
pees with th life in th familee   howevr
arbitrarilee   from his point uv view   with
nevrthless his minds eye on th brekrs   redee
2 try   escape agen   coupul yeers latr i wrote
". . . deth deth n mor deth . . ." abt my
mothrs going 2 spirit place   it was a
materialist vishyun uv th bleekness n totalness
uv deth   not a reinkarnativ   or spirit place
vishyun uv th next door path beem way   i
was thn looking at life without my sumtimes
rescuer

               th chanting i bcame 2 b into
bgan at reedings in vancouvr 60s   whn i wud
say sumthing ovr n ovr   repitishyun 4 speshul
sound   effect   a blurring uv linear
partikulariteez   par xample   th ancient lord
laydee uv th univers asks yu 2 b   ovr n ovr
agen   n othr sounds   non english   wch evolv
from th slurring emerg   aftr th brain
operaysyun all that bcame mor fluid   bfor
it was minimal slurring   mostlee trance with
th repitishyun   fine   aftr th brain op
othr non english sounds wud occur much
mor frequentlee   i intuitivlee wud go with
them   howevr far they wud carree me   in th
work   now its bcumming   less like
chanting   mor into singing   i still want 2
go with thees sounds   take th music   th
poetree   n me

1981   bgan 2 live in th words n th images
relaysyuns with my dottr close agen   sum
peopul iud livd with still frends 1993 frends
with evreewun iuv livd with   thats important
2 me   thn sum grudges not yet let go uv
sum things uv cours still take work 2 let go
uv   letting go othrs in process   me 2 most

uv th day i wud write n paint   go out at
nite   rage   sex in cars whatevr   safelee
amazing wendee wood   who taut me tai chi
curatid 7 shows in a row uv my work ovr a
4–5 yeer period   thos venues oftn at
"pizzarico's" in vancouvr   robson street   n
anavada   also i showd at neoartism n sechelt
art galleree   keven stephens curator   wun
prson art show richmond art galleree 86
page hope smith curator   n th edge   two
prson show with jeffrey birkin   arriving in
london ontario   wher i xperiensd sum
wundrful times at th forest citee galleree
wun prson show 1987   playing with th
LUDDITES at th opning   raging   i was
reeding   sound symposium   newfoundland st
johns   prince edward island   montreal   north
bay   toronto   st catherines   kingston
winnipeg   houston   bc   manitoba   saskatoon
regina   medicine hat   prince george
vancouvr   victoria   new york   n europe
paying off th xisting debts from th press   so
manee places   living   reelee enjoying
paintings dewing bettr   see "invisibul wings"
pome essay on painting i wrote in *canada gees
mate for life* Talonbooks had bin publishing
my work sins th late seventeez   aftr my
having bin with quite a few publishrs   new
star books *living with th vishyun*   house uv
anansi wher i editid *nobody owns th erth* with
margaret atwood n dennis lee   black moss
tuff shit   oberon *MEDICINE my mouths on fire*
(with record)   Talonbooks has bin
xtraordinarilee gud 2 me   karl siegler ther
wundrful 2 work with   he owns th press   as
colleeg publishr   working on strategee 2gethr
whn i was a publishr as well   we talkd oftn
how 2 survive   thn aftr xcellent david
robinson left Talonbooks   he had bin 4 me
editor   karl siegler bgan 2 work with me
hes so brillyant 2 work with   i prepare th
books veree compleetlee now   mesurd 2 th
copee size   th rhythm uv th editing   spend
endless hours on   so that its hopefulee
reelee heightend n accessibul   if it is
organikalee living   karl looks 4 anee
redundansee uv theem   phrase   image   or
pome it self   what iuv missd   sd alredee in a
previous book or 2 much alredee in th same
book   n thru th philosophees   n mostlee
whethr he himself likes th book   or not   we
have great conversaysyuns   sum previous
books wer leed time rushd by circumstances
whatevr   so thos wer editing collaboraysyuns

warren tallman   about 1991

at earleer development   i write th books as
books   whethr th reedr is aware or not uv
that subliminalee not as persuaysyun   as
journee   fact i want 2 b aware uv evree
possibul sub text   if ium writing   all th time
evree day   ths is possibul   i dont want
aneething in ther that i can b aware uv that
eye wudint authorize   sumtimes thats a lot uv
raking   editing   rewriting   mor than whn th
spirit moovs me   i love it   living in london
ontario was veree gud 4 th writing   n th
painting   evelyn li   wundrful prson so great
kind 2 me   landlaydee ther   we bcame
xcellent frends   she n her husband mok n
me

philosophee n english wer my majors   i
nevr finishd th ba   wanting 2 write n
paint   i did finish th majors   sum great
teechrs   george grant at dal   he wrote *lament
for a nation*   warren tallman   he wrote
godawful streets of man   n *in th midst*
(Talonbooks)   warren put up his hous 4 me

4 bail   twice   in th sixteez   late seventeez
whn th rite wing fundamentalists   sum uv
them latr dewing time 4 fraud   emerald
smugguling   watch th rite wing   warren
produsd n hostid a yeer long poetree reeding
serees 2 benefit me n Talonbooks who wer
also undr fire   poets from all ovr canada n
united states came n red on our behalf
ther wer ovr a thousand in th audiens each
uv th manee nites   4 poetree   warren gave
an entire sabbatikul yeer uv his 4 ths

as hard as life is
can b peopul ar oftn ther 2 help   with th
struggul against th forces uv suppressyun
wch reelee nevr sleep   oftn thats why we
need a gud nites   rest n 4 me 2 keep
talking   xchanging ideas with frends   abt
evreething   talking with harris ginsberg n
connie boles   with mickey gunn   th laydee
uv th lake   rob noel prins alberts diner   in
london ontario   john donlan ther   marion
johnson   with rudolph nadassky n cyrus point
in vancouvr   so th mind can keep growing

th high green hill

aftr th light th soft moss dark th glow uv
    each day, night
               and th fire
   th speekr sounds   uttring   releesing
magik torrents   energy cumming into th room

and th words lose all sense

   th sound
           uv barking dogs togethr mad creatures
  elephants making theyr way ovr th alps wun
 time jackals cats whales and th
     ocean past memory

all that is in us

   shouting out for th soul

   sink swallow nd th comfort   pillows soft long
legs all ovr th hairs rise th skin rises plain nd th
                    surface
    uv th mantul hoo hoo hoooo
                th calling
 seek goez home mothr sz that all running
                 my heart
and th eyez stedily taking th body
     dreem togethr

th line that carries th nose th lips open
     what th ears hear without murmurs
       th dried skull undr th tree
      th full moon making th night so cleer
     that yu can way bfor dawn see
    for miles how th earth turns nd smell
   upon th suddn winds blowin
  gainst th windows
  all th day's business,eyowwww

  for th hands wings th face uv th owl

  lay out th limbs all thru

             th time is

  uv leaves

near what light yr heart burns

take ths lettr to th bearer nd say that th fingr wch wears
          th ring shall heer vast stories uv love nd pleasure
offring so told as to opn th shell we all do
               hide from and ther what drink is handid yu
for uv thirst and marrow

                                        sing thundr th words
          stedily moov. sing tell nd th glistning clouds

          th forms we all make up in th oystr

what cums out uv th sea

what brings us togethr

we do know who we are

     he sd egg cartons   blissful mothrs fathrs sanctuaries
     he sd papr trees baby oranges lafftr
     he sd all these

he sd fire watr drums
          he sd names for things nd bringing us always
     closr to death what th life is now what

                              assumptsyuns

     we ride on to bring in th dark

that our minds can make uv any flame

          arktik waste

                    and it is th meat we alredy are
          we find togethr
               that we can see in all ths darkness
     tiny growing molecules worlds uv time
               and space that make up th light

mooving th hot coals for mor pictures ones we dont yet know

          ar cumming to   within ourselvs

     th jaw holds itself togethr and what we ar
     doing moment with in moment time inside
          time - spaced - is not sum cycle it is
               each time discovery tough fukan serch
     sumtimes nd yu take th path, yr mouth
               opn and th gift   stars tumbuling out uv
                    yr forhead.

wch rivr is th aint none
mistr nd th shores so far yu cant touch yr body
feel feel feel what
th business
nd all th cumming what yu cud call
glory tell yu cant touch it
no mor, its touchd yu

when ther is not bottom prhaps feathrs maybe
eyes maybe past karma for sure yu dont know

yr paddling
wow yu bettr sumtimes th land
breks in sharp
what it is about, th passage

yu dont count neithr
it dont add up, is cummin all th time

th fog, and th creatures moov about as asleep
lantern   eyes

thru th curtains past wun then
anothr untold halls uv undrstanding

they rolld on th floor all night

hair all ovr them

a diamond eagul thru th glass

th parts uv tendrness

touching groin

all th babees rocking in th blaze

th high green hill blewointmentpress 1972
northern birds in color Talonbooks 1981

hopefulee not burdend with set or status quo
ideas   talking with arthur richardson jeffrey
birkin

living in th karibu northern bc reel
wintr oftn 50 below vancouvr veree mild
pacifika coastal seldom below zero north

countree writing natur poetree inspiring 2
me informs my writing 4evr meta physikul
all thees wundrful peopul iuv workd with
dewing reedings printing books putting art
shows 2gethr th rite wing backd off 4 a
whil from me n Talonbooks n othrs still
infiltrating school bords banning books from

my big sistr elizabeth   nova scotia   about 1990

within   mor quietlee   cutting th canada
council   each yeer mor   so th rite wing
dusint evr retire   unfortunatelee

1980   reports uv AIDS entring consciousness
frends worreed   safe sex   finding out   living
in chicago with great guy breeflee   seeing my
dottr   mor art shows   writing books   AIDS
message getting thru   sum frends starting 2
get sick   i spend a lot uv time in north
countree writing   painting   n in london
ontario   singing LUDDITES touring thruout
south western ontario   toronto recordings
ths wun uv th best xperiences uv my life
working lerning   travelling   dewing reedings
on my own   mid eighteez   frends closr in
getting sick   me still okay   so far so gud
inkubaysyun period xperts keep lengthning
backward in time   frends dying   going 2
spirit   mainstreem societee slow in
appresiating that AIDS is not a gay disees
usual medieval judgment scapegoating   gay
societee veree strong   mainstreem societee
bcums mor informd as AIDS touches it
unlike in afrika wher it bgan in heterosexual
main streem   ths edifikaysyun takes a lot uv
work on th part uv thousands n thousands uv
brillyant peopul   mor n mor peopul dying
mor n mor frends   ther is alredee 2 much 2

write abt heer   pome in *inkorrect thots*
(Talonbooks)   "timothee sz ther is no deth"
4 timothy priske   chronikuls evreething iuv
bin abul 2 write so far abt AIDS   timothy
did so much reserch n thinking   my pome
contains a lot uv what he told me   timothy
is th great great grandson uv gabriel dumont
mor recording in th pome "ths is th paliativ
ward th nurs sd" 4 stephen weir   also from
inkorrect thots   with mor frends going as ther
is 4 evreewun   ther will b mor such pomes
from mor n mor writrs   ths is such a great
tragedee uv all our lives   evree wher   if
onlee a cure   sumthing cud b found 4 ths
pandemik

sound poetree 1993   reed with bob cobbing
paula claire   chris cheek   adeena karasick
such a brillyant poet   all so brillyant   all th
intrnashyunal sound poetree sins 1975   hostid
by bob cobbing in london england   i was
ther with allan rosen   red at th poetree
centr in earls court   n classes at oxford   bob
cobbing so brillyant   keeps pushing us 2
grow mor without being aware uv that   was
my first time ther   red thn in amsterdam
paris   thn tourd europa with george
johnston   susan musgrave   anothr wundrful
hard working time   we soard 2gethr   thn
sound poetree festival   glasgow   thn in
toronto   new york   thees all a few yeers
inbtween   also tourd thru u.k. with paul
dutton   raging   red with jackson mac low
jerome rothenberg   bob cobbing   raging
paula claire   superb   n p.c. fencott   so
amazing   n in london agen   bob cobbing   so
miraculous   wer totalee raging   n adeena
karasick   raging   n paula claire   it was thn
that my big sistr went 2 spirit   huge greef 4
me   adeena helpd me so much with that as
well as inspiring me so much thru her
writing n performances

            allan rosen has almost
always photographd me n my paintings 4 my
book covrs   hes brillyant   n his work has
always brout out th feel n th xistens uv th
partikular book   wch has helpd th books so
much   shoots with him ar always wundrful
give stretch   his frendship   prsonal professyunal
so inspiring 2 me   our conversasyuns   dialog
wher sumtimes i feel claritee   as i hopefulee
keep lerning   its abt self responsibilitee
allan wrote a magik book *michael* n a vizual

ths is th paliativ ward th nurs sd

for Stephen Weir

we like 2 have our familee in gud hands   now ths
servis availabul thru a frend uv mine   as it happns
coinsidens   is onlee 3,500.00 n christian prayrs ar
sd   yu dont want th welfare rates uv free   we want
our familee handuld well dont we   n thees othr wuns
also familee   ar gud frends uv mine   theyr 6,000.00
its onlee coinsidens   th nurs went on   we wer both
crying   he was going soon   i had just sd reelee gud
bye 2 him   tho i sd see yu in a bit   n my frend who
wud b with him til he went   n ths prson was selling
us a christian box whil th time she felt was   rite
i sd   forget it   2 her   i wantid 2 say get away from
us   i sd forget it   she went 2 th staff room   with
her calculator   n her christian prayrs   looking calm
n punching numbrs   we wer in th elevator wch was
designd 2 cum 2 onlee that ward   wher whn i was first
ther with my frend 2 see stephen a nurs told me n
michael that not all uv th peopul in ths ward   have
aids   sum ar just veree old   or have cancr   i had
kissd stephen on th forhed   our eyez totalee meeting
he was always so gud 2 me   michael left me for him
but i nevr didint like him for that   or aneething
i always respectid him n came 2 love him

aftr 3 yeers uv chemotherapee   drugs   diets   cancrs
in th mouth   throat   lungs   skin   decreesing n in
creesing   pain   pain   temporaree improovments   relapses
mor   pain   amazing independens   n so well cared for by
michael   n michael nevr left   nowun reelee left aneewun
so great   until now   will stephen b leeving soon   who
can handul ths   he was receeving a constant supply uv
morpheen now   bones n spirit now   n such strong courage
th morpheen was keeping him out uv most uv th pain
most   not all   tho it made his mind foggee he sd   th
doktor sd soon they wud decrees th dose   it was onlee
for ths short whil   ther wasint much els 2 dew xcept 2
say things like that   weul let whats still in th bottul
run its cours   iuv herd thos remarks bfor   i know what
they meen

anothr nurs sd   have a look around   th tv room   th
balconee with th cedar n plants   recentlee she sd
sumwun passd on   with aids   baloons wer releesd into
th sky he cud see whn he tuk his last breth   it was
veree beautiful she sd

michael was with stephen whn they brout him mor oxygen
2 nites aftr i saw him   he sd   no   pushing it away
i dont want anee mor uv that   it was time for him 2
go   n he went   like that   deep in rest   i was home
down town   i phond th hospital   he was going soon   i

cud feel it whn he left heer   erth   ther was a lifting

a rush   n th feeling uv fethrs mooving   space   his

journee   awe   for that time relees   from th pain n

th suffring   freedom from that   forevr   a feeling

uv wondr   n strength   no teers   they came   bfor   n

aftr

from *inkorrect thots*   Talonbooks   1992

delite *rory th price uv morning* that is veree
mooving n alive n beautiful   2day wintr
toronto othr close frends ben kennedy n
richard browning cumming 2 see me   n my
recent paintings   ium working on my most
recent book   *th last photo uv th human soul*
i dew tai chi evree morning aftr meditating
helps with evreething   ther ar great icikuls
on th window   25 below   we have t
wundrful time 2gethr   ben sz its summr in
my hous   sum dayze ar th best   espeshulee
that sens uv compleysyun   having dun so
manee paintings   frends seeing them n liking
them   thats reel time off 4 me being 2gethr

vancouvr   taking down whats left from art
show at NOT JUST DESERTS great restaurant

in vancouvr   east broadway   frend george siu
owns   wundrful frend   wev known each othr
ovr 10 yeers   remet in london   ontario
great   iuv had two shows ther   n red three
times ther selling tickets   pd from th door
so manee reedings n books n shows made
possibul by th canada council wud not have
bin accomplishd without theyr support   n has
built such groundwork   support   ths times at
NJD tho ar independent   wch i find also
invigorating 2 dew   opportuniteez   seeing
sharing   wch all thos times ar howevr theyr
produsd   going 2 dew reedings in th free
press festival van   produsd by kedrick james
great performans poet   n produsr   in
vancouvr   n seattul   yeer bfor red in seattul
bumbershoot with grace paley   veree inspiring

*LUDDITES   clockwise from bottom   murray favro   gerry collins   bill bissett   n
peter denny   about 1989*

all thees times   thn up north paint n write
ther   get into natur   memoreez uv th
wundrful poets iud herd n great peopul iud
met at thees reeding times in me   with th
trees   watr   sky   magik birds   thn off 2
charlottetown   prins edward island   rockin
beautiful place   wher i receevd my first
award 4 writing   th peopuls poet award   in
memoree uv milton acorn   great peopuls
poet   amazing craft n spirit 1990   2nd award
1993 bc book award   dorothee livesay poetree
prize   she great poet   an eldr 2 us all now
she helpd me with starting blewointmentpress
as did earle birney   wundrful writr   also now
an eldr   in hospital toronto   we see what
happns as our bodeez n minds change
hopeful we can b our souls nevrthless ar mor
upliftid   with th spiritual frend inside us all
gay pride day   toronto june end 93   ovr
150,000 uv us all totalee raging n out
amazing floats   astonishing enerjee   ium heer
bhind th "buddys in bad times" float   rockin
in toronto   on sum uv th biggest streets in
th world   its so great   thrilling   next day flu
cums back   ths is a long wun   tho
spiritualee ium fine   my hed still ringing
with all th joy uv th previous day

toronto wher th offis uv th leeg uv canadian
poets is   still happning   n thru wch gerry n
arlene lampert bookd me n so manee othr
poets into so manee reedings   so manee
yeers   th gratitude still ther   gerry went 2
spirit late 70s   great loss 4 me   reelee hard
lukilee still see arlene   she dusint book
reedings reelee sins not long aftr gerrys
passing   she n i   frends

Keeping vigil 4 a frend   who may b going
2 spirit   he is oftn inbtween ths world
n th next   suspending spiritual so
graceful with so much innr strength   evn
with th pain he is almost continualee having
now from th AIDS   me iuv had pre deth
events   iuv seen th tunnul 2 th next world
or is it bfor   twice   all th singing up ther
iuv sat in circul   herd voices from th spirit
place   iuv bin shown parts uv th big journee
from heer   it looks n feels veree xciting
xhilerating   i dont know   i hope its trew   i
know i love him   i know that dusint
specifikalee help him with what he has 2 dew
now   n hes so courageous   keeps on fighting

i sumtimes worree   know thats not
construktiv   n think   evn ther is eternitee
what abt th parting

mary donlan veree strong non figurativ
xpresyunist paintr frend in from london
ontario   we talk abt so much   her painting
is great art   time   storee   she sz veree erlee
painting   prhaps th first painting   ths is way
bfor lascaux   circuls   squares   lines   dots
veree geometrik   bfor th representaysyunal
bison on th cave walls   mid july reeding
high park   with michael holmes   adeena
karasick   paul dutton   sky gilbert   othrs
veree hot   humid   summr nite   electrik   flu
almost ovr   writing on ths autobio   painting
off 2 th zoo with ben kennedy   hes a singr
n poet   j.p. n ms vicki   what a great zoo
gettin bettr   off 2 th zoo agen with adeena
karasick n michael holmes   its diffrent evree
time   rest   write n on ths   paint   papr   play
thn off 2 paul duguay n richard brownings
th week uv th magik lobstrs   pauls sistr brout
in from new brunswick   we all eet lobstr
almost evree day   its wundrful   shelia pruden
close frend   she works wardrobe in moovees
wantid a big painting from me 4 her nu
apartment wch shes sharing with ben kennedy
she askd ben 2 select a drawing by me 4 me
2 paint from   its non figurativ   ben is
veree inspird   veree sensitiv   i did 5
paintings   5 variaysyuns   so shelia cud make
a chois   dewing thees paintings got me thru
th long flu   was a brekthru 4 me   returning
agen 2 non figurativ work   colors flat on th
pickshur plane   basd on continuous line
drawing wch lance farrell n me workd thru
so long ago   in part basd on that total yello
ground   look kinduv like tree   rivr   leevs
branches   secret n veree calm   lettrs agile
big drawing stroke   glowing   so much yello
green teel line drawing   thru   on   mostlee
they look like themselvs   breething   being
ar non translatabul objects in themselvs
glowing

thers sheets uv lightning on th
balkonee   wrapp my self in them   th pasts
have bin 2 much with me 2day   th futur   i
dont know   dew yu   i feel free uv
conflicktid emosyuns n stasis   go out into th
nite uv th purpul elephants   what els can i
dew   control evn in my own life   or othrs
undrstandings   get reel   its a veree long

th nite th purpul elephants

went riding in my dreems was th nite aftr eye
dreemd i tried 2 get th ring off my fingr th last prson
    iud livd with he had givn me i still weer releesd
      th fingr felt temporarilee free uv thn panickd put
it back on acknowledging i had felt angr still n letting
    it moov that that had not workd out longr tho cud i
b th judg uv anee longevitee

        weering th ring agen i was mor fine aftr that
dreem xercise was th nite aftr that eye dreemd sum wun
    els i still lovd as well thanks me 4 helping her
    it came thru th dreem wires n that he wantid me
2 write him

      wasint i now in th kleer 2 go out 2 th barn n sit undr
th birthing stars aftr watching th dansing n th coat chek
    guy asking me if i was alrite

sumwun carressd me n he told me i had beautiful hair it
    was veree dark evreewher n lites popping n goldn shapes
forming n dissolving as onlee th wondrous lite reveeling th
    intreeging shapes in th dark can b n a herd uv th amazing
purpul elephants was running thru our chests

      my bodee bcame totalee alive n tendr n yielding with
trust n loving our hands travelling each othr n thn he
    left ths is quite fine ths is part uv th music i was
    sereen so breethee looking up at th sky th stars endlesslee
    replaysing themselvs

      n i went into th dansing into th washroom n back up
stares was walking out 2 look out agen from th suspending
    room opn 2 th slowlee swerving clouds sum peopul laffing
2 loud othrs quietlee smoking th hot coals n my desire

      eye didint see that th glass door was closd walkd into
th glass sumwun grabbd me from bhind held me askd ar yu
alrite

      i sd yes n startid 2 go thru anothr glass door it was
doubul he held me agen n togethr we went thru mor care
    fulee he sd i was warm we talkd abt being togethr he
sd he had a terribul hed ache we went 2 my place th

purpul elephants wer gladlee following us   we
got 2gethr   ragd totalee   present   ran out   4 mor   far
     away 2 thees great konkreet fields   th purpul elephants
i saw wer flying above th street neer us   whil i waitid 4
     him   he sd wait heer   my hed was calm   inside a tree
     cheking on th elephants up ther   he came back 4 me
othr peopul wer standing   apart   mooving   on th edges uv
     ths great konkreet field he was traversing tord me   uv
cours th othrs thin n stringee   alienatid n spurtivlee
     joining   lookd like   dansrs   in a post modern ballet
wer they all reelee wanting 2 connect   fr a littul whil
     n thn start th hunting agen   us we raged home   got mor
     2gethr

he sd his hed ache was gone   n that i was reelee gud   he
     was fine   n th purpul elephants had bcum smallr n wer
     nestuld around us   around th bed   in th morning they
     wer on th balcone   staring into us   smiling   they wer
     relativs uv th mor clay colord n also incrediblee
     beautifulee wrinkuld elephants at th zoo   we saw last
week   werent we relativs 2

he wore shinee blu boxr shorts   had a big fevr   eye
massaged his hed   his teeth wer rotting out   or sumthing
     he was veree handsum   n veree tall

whn he left he sd heud cum back 4 me   weud go riding 2
gethr   with th purpul elephants   heud seen them 2 he sd
     in his sleep   as his brow turnd 2 sum sacrid triangul
     his mouth smiling   n we lay veree still aftr

     calls came in so loud   into th answring masheen

     we didint heer   or undrstand

from *dreem carpets n toxik winds* work in progress
3rd draft uv ths 2nd p   aug 17.93   vancouvr

voyage   talking abt sum past confinements
anothr part uv my present n futur walks by
we dont see him   thn i see   go off yelling
down th allee   he dusint heer   pneumatik
drilling so loud   tall buildings clustring
against our flesh   lungs   i know i will miss
my othr frend so much   i know   flash   great
hes gettin bettr strongr   iuv livd in a lot uv
places   iuv lovd a lot uv peopul   still dew
each day is 2day   2nite   hot n humid
romantik   th full moon sailing in th spaces
btween th towrs like on th lp covr uv
rachmaninoff second piano concerto   leonard
pennario pianist   george siu reintrodusd me
2 listning 2 sarah vaughan   saw wun uv her
last concerts   roy thomson hall   toronto
amazing   all my life iud wantid 2 see n heer
her in prson   now i was   hallusinating
billy eckstine   i usd 2 listn 2 all th time in
halifax 2   idols   still ar   as well as k.d. lang
anne murray   depeche mode   leonard cohen
kashtin   buffy sainte-marie   rereeding
gwendolyn macewen   i love thees peopul
politiks   how so manee leedrs ar
determinidlee creating huge undrclasses
sorrow   in th world   saying ths with frends
joy kuropatwa   teechr n essayist   n bruce
kramer   lawyr   frends in london   n on th
phone with sharon nelson   poet   n frend
montreal   abt thees rite wing events   george
n deborah siu have a construksyun i made
with th reel door bell patrick lane found in
th grass at my formr home in halifax whn
he n i wer reeding ther   i had also at that
time red in antigonish   in cape breton
glorious countree   n patrick n me wer in th
swing ther in th back yard   swing still strong
going highr n highr

ium listning 2 morrissey a lot 2   results uv
my brain injuree   no drinking   that takes
oxygen from th brain   i need all th oxygen i
can get   no big deel 2 not drink   wanting
no stress   who dus   n naps evree day
othrwize fine   looking out from th balconee
heer   th full moon   n i wondr if that lp
jacket painting   th moon ium gazing up at
now thru th hi rise radians   wud have bin
th same lp louis b. mayer wud have had
wud he have lovd rachmaninoff as i did   th
second piano concerto   montgomery clift
patricia bosworth in her bio uv him sd l.b.
was difficult   katharine hepburn   her
autobio *me* sz he was wundrful   an artist

*bob cobbing adeena karasick n paula claire
london 1993*

romanticism   my fathr wud have me danse
4 his frends whn he wud cum home at nite
ask me 2 weer th white pants   aftr my mothr
had gone 2 spirit   gradualee i give up th
ideas that th othr whethr parent or lovd wun
is responsibul 4 my happeeness n is 2 blame
4 not so fulfilling me n bcum intrmittentlee
thn strongr th deepning felt realizasyun that
i am responsibul 4 my own happeeness   my
choices in natur   my life   lives   othr writrs
i admire a lot   margaret drabble   sam
d'allesandro   andrew holleran   paul monette
n peter mcgehee   espeshulee pauls *love
alone: eighteen elegies for roc*   sams *the zombie
pit* n peters *boys like us*

i beleev thru our taxes tho th govrnment
wch is ourselvs is responsibul 4 manee things
universal health care   soshul programs
infrstruksyur   individual human rites   mor
than adequate environmental proteksyuns   if
wer not reelee getting thees rites   why ar we
paying taxes   also i beleev guaranteed
minimum incums   universal   wud bettr
replace th sloppee n condescending welfare n
unemployment insurans programs   freedom is
certainlee worth strugguling 4   4 me that
includes nowun involuntarilee falling thru th

all we can dew

ium by th
starree
ocean

wait 2
heer from
yu

peopul
drown heer
slowlee

2 shadows
in th
sea

watch th
memoree
go

wishes
drifting
past

love is
out uv
reech

didint
yu say
yud
cum

its a long way in

long way 2 yuuuuu

drink ths watr is

all we can dew

how yr heart breeths

how th whales sing

how th skies ar dansing

is all we can dew

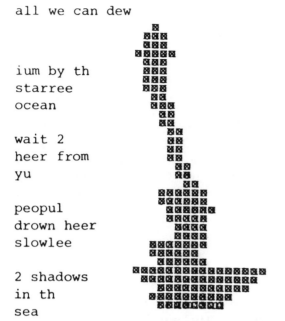

i met a wizard n i askd him isint ther sumwun waiting 4 me
iuv lookd in th treez n in evree wave uv th sea   ther is sum
wun waiting for yu he sd sumwun yu dont want n th prson who
yu reelee want is alredee inside yr own heart yu meen ium al
redee myself yes he sd yu ar bcumming yrself   iuv herd that
bfor i sd ium starting 2 undrstand th wind in th treez sighd

from *inkorrect thots* Talonbooks 1992

soshul safetee nets   if wun prson is
inadvertentlee homeless   thn we all ar   in a
way   homeless   th state is onlee evreewun in
it   isint it

            4 my fathr n his frends
suddnlee arriving home late at nite   i wud
b lip synching n dansing 2 noel cowards
"alice is at it agen"   marlene dietrichs "see
what th boys in th back room"   well i lookd
into that a lot   had lots uv jobs 2 keep
writing n painting til i cud make a living at
it   english tutor   gas jockey   book shelvr
ditch diggr   record store sales   been pickr in
mexico   evreething els yu can think uv   blow
jobs   whatevr   sumtimes iuv thot iuv seen
my life thru othrs   dew we evr   n all thos
changes now   its me   my self   th present
going 2 p.e.i. soon agen   dew reedings   wch
i love 2 dew   th work   heer   great   keltik
rock roots music ther as well   danse at a
kaylee aftr th reedings at orwell cornrs
valerie lapointe th produsr ther   great prson
reeding with nicole brossard magik
incandescent artikulaysyuns   robert priest
kim morressey   othr great poets   cedrik
smith   terry jones   singing great tributes 2
milton acorn   thn 3 days in toronto seeing
frends   thn 2 portland artquake reeding
ther with ira cohen   raging mistr magik
enerjee   it all turnd out   cant see that yet
ium in toronto   working on ths auto bio
letting thees pasts n futurs go 4 a whil   in
un knowing   grateful   n hot   out th door
ium out with th purpul elephants 2nite
cleer decks   cleer th tapes   letting th
construkts go   n flying

oct 1993   shows uv my paintings n drawings
currentlee on at the edge   xcellent restaurant
on davie street   n in two great book stores
r2b2 books   n   margaret gabriel books   both
in kitsilano   all in van   stephanie harper is
making a film abt my writing n painting calld
bills brain   she is wundrful 2 work with
cleer   knowledgabul   incisiv   n guiding
what iuv seen alredee uv th film is veree
xciting 4 me   i love putting up shows   peopul
seeing th work

            wish i had a photo uv evelyn
crook   she was my nurs n frend whn i was a
boy in halifax   4 almost 2 yeers   so joyous
her companee 4 me whil she n my mothr n

i n othrs wer trying 2 get me bettr   wun uv
th philosphee books i lovd was martin bubers
i & thou   also   mary shelley   plato
symposium n *th republic* n with th novels uv
mary renault reeding 2nite   *the mask of apollo*
also love beckett   ionesco   joyce   marx
marian engel   margaret laurence   timothy
findley   thomson highway   n not yet last nite
in vancouvr   richard browning heer   great
magik   rage with david n robbee n robert
aftr picknicking with george n deborah n
stan n byron n davee n daphne n agatha n
bobbee   n us latr richard n me n robbee n
david n robert watching annee lennox n
elton john n lisa stansfield n george michael
n liza minnelli   all amazinglee brillyant in
tribute 2 freddie mercury at wembley stadium
so uplifting raging   n john mellencamp
singing "what if i came knocking" from his
nu album   robert cray   who i love 2   robbee
has all thees great music videos hes splisd
from th "david letterman show"   we ar
feeling enhansd   so great   n th walls around
us   lifting   dissolving   had they evr bin ther

yes well   its a day n a nite off from working
n writing ths autobiographee   time away from
it   2 feel how it is   n going home in a
glowing goldn cab   iuv writtn n workd n
playd with autobiographika thru 6 full moons
ths full moon also so   radiant   n ecstatik

        love is th dreem   n th danse nevr ends
n who can forget

                                        oct 7.93

EDITOR'S NOTE: Recognizing the unique nature of
bill bissett's work, we provide this version of his essay
for comparative reading. "Translation" by Shelly Andrews.

As Carol Malyon, great poet, short-story writer,
and novelist, says, the autobiography I
will write in 1993 will be different than
any other. The focus and the points of view
always changing, emphasis rebirthing.
  So far from Rome, and the council of Nicea,
the Pauline point that the body is bad, etcetera,
the terrible effects of nonpluralistic Europe, Christian bondage, breathing from the diaphragm,
pushing for the whole body identity, poetics

inseparable from the life lives in all directions, reincarnating, regardless of that council, compelled by another focus, adding, being, not only in the blurring, the genocide at contact. Certainly attempted. Luckily not really successful. We are hear to unravel, accept our status as visitors on this planet which sustains us if we don't destroy it. We are hear to enjoy—our bodies, minds, souls. Rage against the confining structures, only by losing pleasure do we measure the longevity of what we experience. Getting it on on the run. Ancient hours memorizing, rehearsing, rewriting, reliving. Always present, we are part everything. Tuna. Brains really part computer. Mostly soul, if we accept that. The person, identities, fate, detail. Destiny. Remarkable verisimilitude. The self is everywhere, infinitely dispersing. We do, can do so many events. Where it becomes conflicted, let that go, or dualistic, deferring permanent identity. Since there is only changing psychic apertures, expressions, sing from the soul. Wanting or not wanting, we embody, send out, let go, and yet there are facts, seasons, disasters, ecstasies.

Flying, we are part bird, mammals with wings, spirit of fire. Embrace, kiss and let go, grief often there sometimes. Acceptance. Rage on, understanding, deep, inside, and under, the sun, moon, the writing comes directly from my life. From the me, and me, and me, other from outside me, if there is outside, there is, there inside. Into me, telling and imagination constructs through me and out these prepositions, the head yielding, tilting, perhaps to one side, or as the words enter transmit, "veronika," primarily dictated to me by the writing guides who have helped me a lot. Guidance in the writing, different than intuition where it sometimes comes from beyond me, and the voices from direct personal experience. All these approaches, all of these, all these dances, song, journeys come from everywhere, including me. I like to spell so the words look as close to how they sound in that particular place in that poem, as much as possible. It's a kind of phonetic spelling. It began with only some words, and spreading throughout almost all the words.

I've always been interested in about twelve approaches with the writing. Some more intensely than others. For a while, all, however, feeding each other: 1) lyrical; 2) narrative storytelling; 3) non-narrative elements of language, telescoped or micro; 4) romantic, sensual, sexual; 5) metaphysical, philosophic, spiritual; 6) sound, where the main element of the poem is sound; 7) visual concrete, border blur, letters themselves clear or smudged, as the media; 8) chanting repetitions of statements, song, soundwaves, eruptions, ecstasies of being, often nonlinear in the usual ways, auditory data, caressings, themselves not leading to analytic constructs, already there, and here; 9) fusion, all these and more, elements working, playing together; 10) conversational voice, a different voice from lyric or the speech of some other modes, listening to how people, how I talk, and writing that in the storytelling, or even in the seemingly nonnarrative writing; 11) political writing; 12) nature poetry.

All these I arrived at through writing and painting, feeding each other. Also meeting in letter and image collages, the images inside the letters spelling out, living, being, outflowing. I've loved many people, am not covered by anything. The great spirit is, and the miracles of what we don't know, and often think we do. Could it be God's? Protect us, enlighten us, uplift me, can, in this life. I started in Halifax, Nova Scotia, Canada, the Atlantic Ocean, totally raging. Smells of cod, and rocky visions, sailors and sea maidens, in our negotiations with acceptances, expressions, there is never really any way out of being ourselves. That is plural, "my manee selves on fire. . . ."[1]

The essay "why i write like ths," in *what we have* (Talonbooks) is the most thorough and complete exposition of what I'm into that I know of in the writing. The wellspring of the writing. What they used to call inspiration. It does happen. Lyrical writing, condensation emptying of everything. Poems of outrage, criticism, angered observation, however, the poem coming in. Adrenalin, grounding consciousness, swiping at the obvious and cruel hierarchies. Meta leptikul, meta story, meta physical, meta reason, meta me, as in permanent. Too long under the dryer. Don't want to be. Fusion poems. Where all the elements of story and nonstory gather. Spill out, like in "th mirror peopul." Realism mode storytelling, as in "wun day my fathr tuk me down" and "how i lernd 2 paint agen" and "have yu seen th moovee fortune n

---

[1]From "around th table my many selves on fire," in *nobody owns th erth*, Anansi, 1971.

j a n u a r e e   s o n g s

                                        for paula claire

          m ystikul m e ˢ ˢ
                         a g e s
                                    b   b   b   b   b   birds r
          ths lettr goez across th ocean   flyin

           it has all th lettrs uv th alphabet in it
A   aaaaaaaaaaaaaaaaaaaaaa   B   bbbbbbbbbbb .... ZZZZZZZZZZZ

        z ᶻ ᶻ
      ᶻ   ᶻ z a a z z z   z   z   z   k k k k eeeee eeee
       ᶻ
        z   d m   ddddd   mmmmmmmm d m d m   d m   d m ddd
    ᶻ
       f
       f   f f f   f   f zeeeeeeeeeeeeeee   d d d   n   mor
        f f
              ths lettr goez across th ocean   O S Y U N

aaaaa   eeeeeee
              eeeeeeeeeeeeeeeeeee   b   it lands   in

      heathrow

              travels   into   london   samuel   pepys
                                             looks UP

      what   is ths lettr   goin ovr
                               th bridg
                                        d ths lettr a e i   uuuuuuu
  o eye o e o eye e   n   l l
  loop   i   u
        d   w   n n
     d   t ᵘ
                                              up
  wind blam plane   slants   look
                           sidewaze   gryphons loop   UP
  goez thru a   looks
              w i n d   t u n n u l   in oxford paula

  s m o o t h   r i d e   paula is r eeeeddinnnnggggg

is   seeding   botanee

                brand   nu   flowrs   is   deesing

dran d   b   un   sd   ord   w

                        e   l   a

                   w   l   ch   n   t

                     a   ch   t   i

                                          n

nu   tanguls   with   brush   razing   g

                           aces   leevs   buttr

                 u

         o

flies   all   r   n

       z   d   h er   hair   shining

y e l l o   is re naming   th   plants   n   stalks

happee   sunshine

                  le t t r s   l e t t u s   d aiseez

tulips   greeneree

              flocks   sisther   is   ia   yaaaaaa   YASSS

                eeeee   aaaaaaa   yaaaa   aaa   yayayaya

          i

       n   s   in   oxford

            n

     a

  d   g   tiny   goldn   birds   r   flyinnnnng

              k   o   l   a   t a y n e   e   a   ya

paula o o s   P

      l   U   t   t   t   t   t   t   lettrs

aula   p   ula   ap   heer   eeeeeee   ya   kushan   ameee   yoksumanee

k   a   k   o   o

a   a

    a   n   l   huuuuuuuuuuuuuuuuuu uuuushhhhhshhhh

                   shhhhhhhhhhhh

                       shoft   buuuuttttr   song

From *animal uproar*, Talonbooks, 1987

mens eyez" and the more lyrical and reincarnative "th vessul" and "th nite th purpul elephants."

In the oxygen tent at almost eleven years after a number of operations for peritonitis, eventually I had twelve operations in almost two years. I decided there I would for sure write and paint as dancing in ballet or figure-skating or hockey, ballet the main ambition up till then not really an option with a belly full of scars, slashing the abdominal muscles. By the time I was eighteen in Vancouver, writing, wanting to explore visual phonetic sound beings of the poem, letting the poem speak for itself. In every way and ways, always wanting visual sound narrative, non-narrative, romantic, lyrical, sexual, political, metaphysical, song prose poems, arranging, rearranging, letting the poem write itself, finding the pictures, in the words, letters, dancing there.

In 1987–1992—up all night rehearsing in the band Luddites with Gerry Collins, Peter Denny, Murray Favro. Then Peter D. went acoustic and Gerry and Murray and me—up all night. New songs, arrangements, rhyme, so mimetic. Metalogical sounds and colors of the feeling with the phrases, bars working, of each word, matching with the beat, meta sense music. Gerry Collins—amazing composer and lead guitar. Murray Favro—rhythm guitar. Wonderful. All share input. Murray F.—also a brilliant sculptor. Peter D.—great player, vibraphone, xylophone, bells.

Up all night with Martina Clinton, 1960s, writing visually. Space, spaces between the words, lines, pause for breathing being emphasis, not crowding. Stuck together artificially, as in more traditional form. Parts of the species, utterances, writings, over time, meta time, sequential, linear. Up all night collating books by so many other writers with blewointmentpress. Running the press with Martina Clinton, then by myself. Running the press with Bertrand Lachance, then by myself. Running the press with Allan Rosen, then again by myself, and letting it go. That's 1962–1983 editing, typesetting, designing, layout, showing so many ways to free the poem, with wonderful partners. Bertrand Lachance later translated some of my work into a book in French called *parlant*.

The wells springing, my own life. Lives. So many, and spilling over. From sharing the lives with those of others, giving out these modalities from within. Soul letters, sometimes seized by flowing out, balancing, so many balls, hats, interacting, sounds, colors, tactile, the jewels shine as our understanding, nuances, not of linear meaning. Of being. Words as the media, here, within relationships. Between, stringing, happening, sound, color, shifts, agreements, contrasts, verb dissonances, noun excitement. Carrying. Being. Varieties of lifting. All the approaches we feel, are, make. Turning, placing, replacing. Sing, grumble, growl. Sighing. Lyrical line often less wide. The more epic, letting the sliding line keep breathing, extend out to its fullest breath, being all it can, to its end. Continuing or run-on. Keep it going, so reaching "th breth,"[2] as far as it can. Also, meta robotic. Fine. From our lives, speech, it's all in the tongue, lungs, inner eyes, *ommmm bra shure.* Yes. The also very often very surprising well springs.

THERE IS NO UNIVERSAL MIND springing from the bed, bathroom, ablutions, meditating, Tai Chi. Another possibly and anyway miraculous day. All what, we don't know. Agnostica, the goddess of unknowing, protecting us. If we let her, and Autobiographika, the goddess here of this current task.

Articulating the breath from somewhere moves through us. Lungs meshing diaphanously. Often with the flesh and bones. DNA puppetry and the miraculous mystery of the free-will personality. Do we have the branches of, arriving from everywhere, and there, here, so much more to come in from, of whatever dimension. After being sick so much as a boy and then later, I'm grateful to be not in a hospital. That I'm okay. So far so good.

The ponies of sweetest disorder in the sound fusion keep eclipsing themselves with new spillover radiance, point of views, until sometimes we hear the sound itself, selves. Infinite soundings.

Martina Clinton—amazing breakthrough poetry consciousness. Statement, jazz, space. Laid out. Spaces between the words. Punctuating THERE and lyric assemblages also of indescribable delicacy. Bertrand Lachance's *street flesh* and *tes rivieres t'attendent* soaring, attacking, politics, being, and incredibly intimate love poems, as does Martina Clinton. For me these are wonderful writers.

---

[2]Originally published in *th high green hill* (blewointmentpress, 1972), also in *selected poems: beyond even faithful legends,* Talonbooks, 1980.

Great. Lachance also wrote *cock tales* (Talonbooks, 1972).

O riginally a trade name, Bissetters, people whose job it was to put the tips on the arrows before they were released, they were brought from what was then Normandy over to Scotland, possibly in time for the Battle of Hastings. Or they were late for that foray. Prior to that time, however, unbelievably, in Scotland, arrows were not getting released. The Bissetts may have left Scotland certainly after the Highland clearance. Perhaps a fling they wanted to avoid. They had already lost their tartan owing to having blown up or burned to death. One too many English bishops and lords in their continuing quest for independence. My dad, out on the porch freezing, pelting hail, icy snow. We—all inside. Him out there singing "will ye no come back again," for bonnie Prince Charlie.

My mother's family name was Covert, originally Couveers. Flemish. Arrived in New Amsterdam before it was New York. Eventually went to New Brunswick. Intertwined with the MacCulloughs. A great, great, great aunt Julia was a beautiful painter and a writer. I've seen one of her paintings. She chronicled the rather unusual medical practices of the MacCulloughs who still had their tartans. They would put sick people on the frozen Miramishee River thinking the fresh air might be healthy, fresh perhaps, but very cold. She was shunned for recording this. The Couveers persons still holding that name became Coverts, or had already done so, and later moved to Nova Scotia where I then became more possible.

1987—working with Chris Meloche, electronic composer in London, Ontario. Another very exciting partnership in sound adventure for me. Meloche is very brilliant, atmospheric. We've put out two cassettes so far, *shining spirit,* electronic compositions with words and other sounds merging story and coinciding electronic entities, no time referenced, while *luddites* is very much time referenced. So I find it interesting and exciting to work in both fields, approaches. Chris and I also brought out *LONDON LIFE,* more of spoken word poetry with some chant songs, sound poems with electronic treatments. Everything, of course, except the original and revised writing, is a collaboration. Even the writing by oneself is already often in tandem, say, in writing lyrics for already existing music I'm hearing. Gerry Collins

brings in a gorgeous piece of music. It started happening right away. I would hear and write down the words. That's how "fireworks" was done. Sometimes the words would come first, "reflex blu." Sometimes I would bring in the melody and the words all these different variations. One time Chris Meloche played me a recent piece he had written and the words tumbled through. This does happen, and how much is from practicing at it and not going to that well, whatever too often is. Sometimes fine, saying don't have it yet. Does anyone know? Gerry Collins, magic arranger and composer as well—and it is magic when you've got the lyric or the spoken words for the music you've just heard, are hearing, for the first time, and it's working and Murray Favro's face and mind lights up. He works his part. We all work our part, and put it together. It's a beneficial thing for me that I had mostly gotten over being so shy. All this working with people, especially since going to London, has really helped with that as well with a lot of developmental evolving for me.

Irving Layton—one of our great elder poets, his erotic and romantic writing is very wonderful, and his religious and spiritual work, very profound, moving, interesting to me—said in a recent interview on TV that what can be tragic about a writer's life is that we think words are more real than anything else. And they aren't. I find this really something to think about often.

Gazing, watching the caulking of the pool. Quiet, attentive ecstasy under which the latest full moon, pulsing. It's going to be twice this month. Toronto, only to marvel. Let in the continuing breathing ache of it sometimes. The beauty. I'm here, on the balcony, air Canada. It's a palace, $515.00 a month, triple towers, facing into gorgeous courtyard, gardens, pools, huge trees, fountains, dogs, people. And the great maple leaf gardens. Huge blue maple on the immense roof. Hot, giant mushroom spaceship about to levitate. Time moves forward and back, resolutely speeding. Then still. Illusions of four porpoises inside the chamber. Flesh, bones, wishes, breath, organa. We are looking out. It's our own submersible motion picture, still moving, on sideways. World is tilting. Present. Where we are living. Big mystery of the future receding as we go out. Find someone to be with, under the fountains, jumping up into the spinning wheels. We grab and caress each other's flesh. It's taken years and years to get to a place like

With gypsy in Glasgow, 1975

this. To afford, windows are huge. To the floor. Looking away from them, and all the green grass, blue hot sky, and the diamond water rising. They let in everything. Here all day, these stories so high. Magical, knowing, unknowing, timing, doing this. Travelling for work and play. Where are Mr. and Mrs. Linear? They're out today, playing, I hope. EXCELLENT. Wonderful friends here.

Similarly in Vancouver, I live near Stanley Park. World's largest inner-city park. Ancient growth, trees, West Coast. Magic animals. Above the building next door I can see over the high-rise towers to the Pacific. Deep, permitting atmosphere. Erotic. Loamy. Moistly fecund. Took a long while to get here. Off the street. Out of trouble. I'm able to live in two places. Frequent flying, for doing poetry readings. Having art shows of my paintings, drawings, sculptures. Next one, Kingston, Ontario, summer 1994. Time sharing to let it happen. Seven years now doing this. A living. Found in a myriad sea of subletting the apartment I'm not in while living in the one I'm in. Many people want to live only two or three months somewhere. I'm meeting lots of them. We help each other. Adds to the paper play. Putting this together, worth it. Used to call it paperwork. Play sounds like more fun, doesn't it? This all started when I was offered writer in residence job at Western University, London, Ontario, by Alan Gedalof—the hiring professor there, changed my life, he's so amazing—1985–86. Then still living in London part-time. Offered writer in library, Woodstock, Ontario, 1987–88, more workshops, more one on one. Really liked it. Good for the writing and painting, too. Was asked to join Luddites, alternative band, as vocalist and lyricist. Excellent. Cassette out fast. Then 12" LP called *luddites*. Then, 1991, *dreemin uv th nite*. Originally Gerry Collins, Peter Denny, myself. Then Peter Denny went more acoustic. Then the three of us touring southwestern Ontario. Very raging. Back from then in 1984, worked with Dermot Foley and Lenore Herb in a band called Sonik Horses. Brought out cassette from Underwich Editions in Toronto and our own label in Vancouver. It's wonderful beyond belief to work with brilliant musicians like these. Dermot and Lenore are now frontline environmentalists and on the board of SPEC (Society for Preservation of Environmental Concerns). Gerry, an amazing composer, as well, and brilliant guitarist, now in another band. Luddites lasted a long time. Five years, and there's always the possibility we may do more work together. *dreemin uv th nite* has received a lot of air play, college alternative stations, as does the *luddites* LP. So who knows the future? Which is one of the points of this autobiography.

I was born November 23, 1939, same day as Billy the Kid, and Gerald Lampert and P. K. Page, two writers I admire. I'm on the cusp of Sagittarius and Scorpio, which makes me potentially a very good diplomat, and also ingredients for explosion, calmed through learning transcendental meditation, when I thought I was going inside for a long stretch, would need some way of getting off. Today it's Toronto with a flu. Writing this. Staring some more at the fountains. I never pay rent in two apartments simultaneously, of course, and I'm really mostly based in Toronto. Have been an Ontario resident since 1985. Still love Vancouver though, and northern British Columbia. Go there whenever I can, work takes me.

In Halifax, when I was in the crib, I was wanting to be a child actor at MGM—Dean Stockwell, my older brother. Would have been a dream come true for me. I did love my two sisters, though we fought. Especially they fought together, forced to share the same room all their growing years was very hard on them at times. I was sick a lot. Very often not wanted by my peers because they perceived me as gay, so don't play with. I was beaten up a lot for being gay, haunted and isolated. I never put them down for being straight or tried to exclude them from me for that. I listened to great Canadian radio programs like "Jake and the Kid," starring John Drainie, brilliant Canadian radio actor, an idol. It was written by wonderful Canadian writer W. O. Mitchell, and "The Happy Gang," really funny, and had pictures of hot American movie stars under the blankets with me and my dog "Ruggee." Often I was seized by a sense of tragedy, melancholy, entrapment, alternating with some psychic upliftment. There was a painting of Daniel in the lion's den on the wall opposite my bed. It gave me courage, helped a lot, especially as well with the growing sexual intensity and longing. We all watched "Plouffe Family," a great TV show from Quebec.

My mother went to spirit when I was fourteen. She had suffered so much from cancer and had helped me so much, regardless when I was sick and after. Optimism, faith, fighting obstacles, sickness, discouragement, debts, massaging the tube in my belly, trying to get the shit moving. Afterwards, helping me always with my homework, math, memorizing, over and over again, you had to do well at school, as well as you could anyway, or what was the point? All the operations my mother went through, hacking off her body, bit by bit, it was so terrible for all of us. Father also extraordinary. So hard-working. At home very tyrannical. He worried so much. Yelling, fighting, screaming, the doors slamming, his pain, our fears, hysteria, mother dying, nothing is always. Her terrible pain. Was father sick with worry at night, fetal position, his seemingly erratic children, from his point of view. How would they survive? My mother offered me her religion but it never really took.

I loved MGM musicals. Louis B. Mayer from New Brunswick. Dad yelling something. Heat was too high. I got cold easy. Too long in my room. His debts. "Be a MAN!" he yelled in the hospital when he came to see me once in it seemed like two years. I was screaming with pain. He never came again, except once he brought presents before an operation. I was loving toward him. He worked very hard. Never joined a firm. Took cases for very poor clients. Believed strongly in social justice. He's yelling. I'm out the door, muffins on. Wind is howling, snow swirling, off downtown with a tube still in my belly, to see another MGM musical, or *A Place in the Sun* with Elizabeth Taylor, Montgomery Clift, and Shelley Winters. There was no Medicare then. All the doctors' expenses. We were going bankrupt. Often, I thought it was my fault. Elaine Stewart also a favorite. When I had my brain operation years later, Medicare paid for it, otherwise I would have gone to spirit. And Bobby Driscoll, of course. The stars in *A Place in the Sun,* I totally loved. Also, *Singin' in the Rain* and *An American in Paris,* Peter Lorre and Jules Munshin singing "too bad we can't go back to Moscow" in *Silk Stockings* with Fred Astaire and Cyd Charisse, also so magical. More lately, *Dead Ringers* with Jeremy Irons and Geneviève Bujold, a David Cronenberg film, and *Edward 11* by Derek Jarman. I'll always see a lot of movies.

The world falls apart, all the time. World War II, terrifying rumors of what was really happening in the death camps, the Holocaust. Later, McCarthy period. Cold War. More fear. We keep trying to put the world back together. The body, the mind, soul, only working toward equality really works, and our attempts so fleeting. Everything is tested. Still want to work for hope and the possible peace. My mother gone. I became to be in a gang, after limping for some time. At last a peer group that would have me. We were very tough. I was also reading Sartre, de Beauvoir, Camus, Cocteau, Singer, Shirley Anne Grau, Gertrude Stein, Truman Capote, Mordecai Richler, Shaw, Rebecca West, Tennessee Williams, Eugene O'Neill, Andre Gide, D. H. Lawrence, Edith Sitwell, Marianne Moore, Tolstoy, the Brontës, George Eliot, many of these intro-

duced to me by a friend. Just a close friend I admired very much. His brother returned from Europe with these names. I was very thrilled. Couldn't read enough, and listening to Bartok, Schoenberg, Menotti, Weill. There was a girl I was sexually nuts about. I never thought that would happen. So horny. "No way till we're married," she said. I had seen marriage. I wanted to be a poet and a painter. Knew there wouldn't be money for marriage. Like my father, she wanted me to be a lawyer. I wasn't blaming anyone. She wouldn't allow condoms. Was screaming at me when I took one out to ask her if we could use it. She was screaming, "Marriage or nothing!" Fine. Images of James Dean, Hank Williams, Judy Garland, Sarah Vaughan. June Christy with Stan Kenton singing "Lonely Woman." Billie Holiday singing "Strange Fruit."

Then I met this wonderful guy. I was, of course, very horny. We slept together in my attic

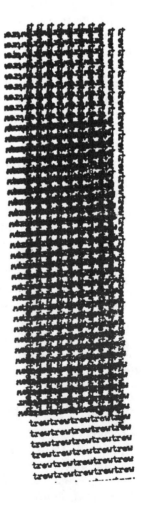

From blew trewz

room, painted dark green, with Picasso's *The Lovers* on the wall, where the housekeeper who had been my best friend had lived. My father fired her after my mother had gone to spirit. I was told to take over cooking and cleaning. I did. He, still yelling. When I was sleeping with my friend, however, he became sweet to me. Was it because I was happier? We draw happiness to us sometimes when we're happy ourselves. It's that I can't know why. Dad would be asking really nicely for his cookies and milk before going to bed, me with a raging hard-on somehow disguised, leaving my friend for a bit, I would go downstairs and bring him that and say goodnight to him. Me and my friend never what they then called "went all the way." He had been raped when he was a kid and that had left him with problems. We ran away. I said goodbye to my dad in the early morning. I told him I had a job with General Motors in Calgary with a friend of his. He probably knew that wasn't true. We hit the road, planning to leave Western civilization forever. I was seventeen. Good luck.

Home before dark. That's what Dad would say. We would leave the summer cottage of his friend's, near the giant, wild strawberry bushes and the Atlantic Ocean over some sand dunes where we would go swimming. Sad to leave so early grumbling. Dad would lead us in songs: "What do you do with a drunken sailor early in the morning" and "I's the boy that built the boat and I's the boy that sails 'em." There sure were squabbles. Sometimes I had tantrums, locking myself in my room, moaning on the linoleum floor, staring up at the sky through the ceiling, going into outer space. But it really was fun sometimes. Even with the children should be seen and not heard maxim invoked fairly often. When it was fun, what a relief. Then we'd be singing "Farewell to Nova Scotia." I knew I would be doing that fairly soon. It's wonderful there. Beautiful every time I go back there, for readings or to Prince Edward Island, I love it more.

I loved my friend so much. It never really worked out. As it turned out we did make it to Vancouver. Excellent. The writings of Jack Kerouac and Allen Ginsberg gave us support. We started on the road with a girl *friend* who we alternately, closetly, were in love with. I needed a buffer because of what I thought were his extreme jealousies. He needed a buffer because he wouldn't go all the way with me. Young love. Fine. Raging. Not all bluffs are on mountains.

After my friend went back to Halifax, I had another peritonitis attack. My big sister flew out West to see me, protect me from my father who wanted to put me in a mental hospital. I always remember her bravery in doing this. She had become a social worker. Told Dad after spending a few days with me that I was fine. When my mother went to spirit, I didn't cry for a couple years. Then the tears wouldn't stop. When my father went to spirit I cried right away for days, even though he wasn't an ideal father I did love him, though he wasn't comfortable with that being expressed. Though he was with his wife, our mother. They were so much in love, so the loss is always there. Eventually I understand no one is ideal. Doesn't that help with my growing? He did disown me. I wrote "halifax nova scotia" because I couldn't help it, and to release from obsession I had been for years about events there and to visualize my parents as living, as they started, as they might have continued, healthy, romantic, wildly, always and unworried by debts, sicknesses. The worst always around the corner and trying so courageously to keep going on and with this release in this poem for me as well to go on.

1960—Shelving books in the Vancouver Public Library. Didn't like correct spelling. Was finding my ways out of that. Loved arranging, exploring words dropping like baubles, glands, pulsing, all over the paper my favorite thing in high school, junior high school, was making geography and history books. I loved that the most. Only activity I ever won a prize for at graduation time. I loved pasting in photos or drawings and putting the headings under those in different colored pencils. Highlighting my future in books. I loved books. Now I was shelving them, and reading them every night after work. Everything I could get my hands on. I went back to Halifax, hitching in the winter with a friend. She and I laughing all the way through the frozen prairie. Flew from Montreal to see my dad become a judge, got there too late for the ceremony. We got together, family. Nothing jelled though. My daughter researches the judgments my father made and tells me they were very fair, very compassionate, leaving the nest I guess, for everyone is a novel and a half. So back to Vancouver.

There was a guy so in love with me I didn't get it till years later. We got it on. I still let it go. Met another guy. He took me home. I was so in love with him I lived with him right away.

He was in love with another guy. Kept phoning him at night after we would get it on. I was in love with him. He wasn't about to change. I hit the road, reading everything by Virginia Woolf, James Baldwin, Gore Vidal.

Close friend of my mother's, called Aunt _____ received a message from my mother in spirit. Time to live with a girl, she said. I met her. She saw me. She found me. We told each other everything. We moved in together, listening to Coltrane, Mingus. Very hot sex. I was no longer a virgin. Wonderful we raged together. Read everything, up all night. Rearranging all the words, letting spaces happen, both into visual writing. Hers stretched out, in lines, spaces, between the words, accenting, mine moving up and down the page. So in different ways letting the words breathe on the page. Remet Lance Farrell. Major bud, him and me also. All three of us, up all night, finding the syllable, writing, writing. She was pregnant with our daughter. Wonderful. Then the full blown sixties. Going to court. In band called Mandan Massacre. 12" LP out. I would read e. e. cummings to her in bed ". . . all in green my love went riding . . ." We became almost one person. No one would publish us. We were trying to keep our daughter. The law was everywhere. Sidney Simons, so brilliant defending us, getting me off possession charges. Lots of court appearances. We turned ourselves inside out for each other, to keep going. Then breaking away. In spite of the poverty and the critics, starting blewointmentpress together, 1962, eventually averaging ten books a year, starting with a Gestetner mimeograph machine from the early 1900s, printing so many writers. Helping American deserters find Canadian wives so they could stay and not get killed in Vietnam. Giant rock concerts. Starting poetry readings. More busts. More court. Big huge bust at the end of the sixties. Narks came in motor launches, over mountains, on foot, armed to the teeth. So we were very political. Stop the damn war. Stop the deadly evil right wing. We were about seven people. Our daughter screaming. Wasn't the first time. We were far away, tucked in the country. Who were we hurting? Narks violent. We were totally outnumbered. Very long trials.

I don't see time as decades. What is time? A story is what time is it, what time is it? Did some in jail. Many counts, stuck only on one. Thanks again to the brilliance of Sidney Simons,

great friend, not much time. Daughter so wonderful. In free school. In country, protected, state didn't get her. Big worry for me. My dad worried a lot, uncontrollably. So could I. My dad hired the first woman lawyer to article. He was very advanced in many ways. Sixties explosions. In hiding from a kangaroo court in B.C. Tensions, loyalties tested. Hard. Love. We kept publishing through a lot of this. Part of my sentence from the big bust was a cash fine. I printed a book of mainly poems written in jail and smuggled out. Sold it door to door, called *sunday work(?)* (blewointmentpress). Other writers through blewointment, Maxine Gadd, Judith Copithorne, Lance Farrell, Gladys Hindmarch, d. a. levy, Pat Lowther—who was later murdered by her redneck Marxist husband, there is no one way—bpNichol, David Uu, Beth Jankola, Sam Perry, Dallas Sellman, Gary Lee Nova, Gwendolyn MacEwen, Rosemary Hollingshead, Joy Zemel Long, Margaret Avison, Dorothy Livesay, Earle Birney, Mona Fertig, Britt Hagarty, Michael Coutts, David Cull, Beverley Rosen Simons, John Burton, Milton Acorn, Al Purdy, Colleen Thibaudeau, Miriam Waddington, Aaron Steele, Alex Pratt, Gwen Hauser, Sam Perry, Al Neil, many, many others.

d. a. levy was being hounded in Cleveland. Great friend through the mail. We had similar karma in the hounded area, except in Cleveland they did hound him to death. The right wing there, what power they thought they had. His passing, tragic outrage in the literary "underground." Memorial anthologies of his work are still being put together. Like Sam Perry, he tragically shot himself. Great tragedy there. Sam Perry such a wonderful meditation devotee and filmmaker. A time of very fast changes, great oppressions. A lot of tragedy as well as the uplifting magic and ecstasy, and working together so much. bpNichol and me also great friends in that time and later through the mail. Publishing each other, fanning, extend the work, opportunities, readings, networking. So many people. bp had Ganglia Press, which published my maybe first book, *we sleep inside each other all,* 1966, neck and neck with *fires in th tempul OR th jinx ship nd othr trips* (Very Stone House). I was also involved with Patrick Lane, Jim Brown, and Seymour Mayne. *fires in th tempul* was a blewointment/Very Stone House co-publishing venture. We were also, bp and I, reaching out with Bob Cobbing in England, Ivo Vroom in Belgium, Japan, D. R. Wagner in California.

Sound concrete, visual. d. a. levy and myself very much into border blur. Bob Cobbing, too, there. Eminently. Toward 1968 blewointment published d. a. levy's brilliant *Zen Concrete*. d.a. had published some of my work in Cleveland. Of course Maxine Gadd's *Guns of the West* and *hochelaga* (blewointmentpress) were also major breakthroughs in poem consciousness. Michael Coutts, wonderful brilliant, lyrical, and political poet. Another great and tragic loss to that time. Incredible person, close friend. I got out of jail. Living alone. Went to an art party I was invited to. Hosts of the art show I was in, "konkreet vizual" poetry show. I fell through the door not latched, disguised to look like a wall twenty feet down to the concrete. Landed on my head. Neurology ward. Intracerebral bleeding. Aphasia. Paralysis on right side. Two years to really fully recover. Pain. Lucky. Got out. That's two years in full. Was in hospital only little. Spinal tap. Memory loss. Occupational therapy. Physiotherapy. Push, push. Doctor resident intern. She saved my life. Pushing me. Pushing in the physical. Present for even incremental improvements and not worrying about the temporary memory losses. Other side effects.

Lost the court case for damage claims because either their cat had or had not drunk its milk, which saucer it would go to precisely at whatever. At the foot of the stairs, whether, yes, since it was after that time the cat must of slurped already and then therefore no liability, even under invitee/inviter because the door would have been latched. Would the cat testify? One of the hosts, good friend, showed his invite cards. Nothing there for me. Not invited? Of course I had been. Fine. This was for me a very good view of what can be expected with people, and All Beings insurance company. Of course the cat thing. If the cat had finished drinking, had returned upstairs, the door latched. What were they saying? That I had unlatched the door myself and thrown myself down the stairs? I had just gotten out of jail. Would I have wanted to kill myself then? I still think testimony from the cat would have been desirable. So big deal. Mostly I was so grateful I was getting better. The migraines were going, the epilepsy was gone, and the paralysis gone. Each day less and less fatigue. Years later the host, with the invite cards in the witness stand, put me in a show in Toronto, *Vancouver 7* Harborfront. I blew bubbles at the opening. Was very happy. Competing curators. Critics there, of course, were offended

My daughter, Michelle, in Victoria, about 1991

at the title of the show. Opening was really fun for me and former host seemed festive now. Relief there, and we carried on, like lots of things in life. There were ingredients of events beyond comprehending. Wanting to live in change, accepting, flexible in the eternal movements.

But before that seeming resolution—*on the shores of Lake Ontario*—Vancouver, one night being bathed in the hospital, walking still very tricky, worried about my studio living place, broken into. Everything smashed. Move next door. Went out one night. Met this guy. Came home. New studio destroyed, everything, paintings slashed, note on floor said, "I'm going to kill you." I fucked off out of there. Went across the bridge, downtown, club, met the guy, I had tried introducing people with each other. Whatever. Went with guy I met that night right away. Great. Left town after a while. North. Did log peeling. Physical work. Extreme cold helping migraines, post op effect. Pills for epilepsy. Very poor. Eating Kraft dinners. Sharing them. Missing my daughter. Tried to stay in this also beautiful relationship, chopping wood. Got better. Nature is the best. Where the acid had taken me. Howling winds, fires, cold weather. Kept printing blewointment books. Meta leptika. First gran mal. Thrashed everything. Bed, broken. On the floor. Went into previous life where I lived in Africa, village, huts, in a circle. Very beautiful. Started seeing people's auras. Went into the painting. July 1993 now. Toronto. Gotten over long flu. Remembering outstanding brilliant neurologist and "th high green hill" and Rosemary Hollingshead, who helped me exercise.

Early seventies, back to the city. Vancouver. Live in triangle. Excellent and very difficult. Learning. Unlearning. Where is the possession. Abridging the primal construct to keep going, each day. Printing books. Collating still by hand. Later hiring that out. Twelve- to fourteen-hour day. Go out. Get it on somewhere. Excellent. Someone comes to rescue me, because I was going down. Take new track in both our lives. Keep printing, more and more poetry books of Cathy Ford, Hart Broudy, Candas Jane Dorsey, Carolyn Zonailo, Gerry Gilbert, Lionel Kearns, Beth Jankola, Rosemary Hollingshead, Alec Newell, Steve Miller, Eli Mandel, Gwendolyn MacEwen, David Uu, Joy Zemel Long. Giant anthologies, many single-author books. Great life raging together. Wonderful partner. I'm on my own again, after another series of ecstatic years. Learning the single life can be as great as any other. On my own, really for the first time in my life. 1981. Sad and excited. Both the dance keeps changing, accepting that, working, playing with.

Then *bang* I was asked to have a one-person retrospective show at the Vancouver Art Gallery, curated by brilliant Scott Watson. Raging. Had just had a painting praised by John Bently Mays in the Vancouver Warehouse Show. This was totally unexpected, surprising. *Globe and Mail.* And I guess for me good and less good things have always been surprising. Scott Watson had had a show in mind a long time previous to that, was almost an entire floor. Blew my mind, my daughter at the opening. Practically everyone I've ever known or lived with. Pretty exhilarating. I had been very private for years since the brain operation. That night at the gallery ended my hermitage. Though, Paradoces, I was now living alone. In 1989, had a one-person show at the very magic and festive Selby Hotel on Sherbourne Street in Toronto. I was also lucky to receive Canada Council grants, three times in the sixties, during which, about 1962,

I was in a film made about many Vancouver artists and writers shot by Len Fourrier and Jack Long for Canada's National Film Board, and just before being run out of town, was in *Strange grey day this,* 1965 film directed and produced by Maurice Embra about my writing, painting, and life. Maurice was both inspiring and relaxing to work with. Wonderful experience. It was shown on CBC and sold to NBC internationally. The film about Vancouver artists and writers was called *In search of innocence.* Received Canada Council grants in the seventies, the last full grant I had received until this year 1993 was in 1978 when *sailor* (Talonbooks) was released. Luck. Hard work. Perseverance. There have been a lot of ups and downs. About 50–50. I really do appreciate my luck, though the first press I had was an early 1900s Gestetner mimeograph machine with no automatic paper feed. Art may never make as much money as killing but I believe it's better for people. Certainly better for me. Seeing the words, then running from off the roller, duplicating themselves imaginably, into seeming infinity. Silkscreening. Reproducing by hand. The first machine with an automatic paper feed was a revelation to us. Then, eventually, an offset press. Whew. And then the printing got farmed out. This point took years to get to.

The first poem I wrote was in Grade 3 or early Grade 4, about boats sailing. That I think was the terrible summer I almost had to go to boys' camp for the entire summer. Fought like crazy to get out of that. Thinking up things my parents would accept. They were very incensed. Thank God I got out of it. Whole summer filled with boys. Go totally crazy, sexually and whatever. If in the winter they could pelt me with snowballs filled with rocks and summarily beat me under huge trees, in other seasons what could I expect in a far-away isolated place in the country where it would for sure take me longer to run home, if I would get home. My father thought that it was not manly to not want to go to boys' summer camp. What could I do? Yes, it was not manly. *Tony Curtis, Jeff Chandler, Rock Hudson, Montgomery Clift, Frank Sinatra, Russ Tamblyn, Gene Kelly, George Nader, John Derek, Richard Widmark, Burt Lancaster.* My parents may have never forgiven me for the row I put up, and I may never have forgiven them at that time. All the screaming and yelling. What was wrong with me? Why wasn't I wanting to be with boys my own age? etc. "What's wrong with you?!" One time I said they don't like me, so I don't want to spend the whole summer with them. "That's no excuse!" they yelled back at me. I forget what finally clinched it. I think my sticking to my guns. They got over, gradually, laying guilt trips about it on me. Every world can be lunched, wanting robotic responses.

In the oxygen tent in the hospital, I wrote my first story about a boy and his monkey who always wanted to swim beyond the boundaries and rules of his family life, to swim in the ocean where the undertow was very dangerous, and, after almost drowning, was able to return and make peace with the life in the family, however arbitrarily, from his point of view, with nevertheless his mind's eye on the breakers, ready to try escape again. A couple years later I wrote ". . . deth deth n mor deth . . ." about my mother's going to spirit place. It was a materialist vision of the bleakness and totalness of death. Not a reincarnative or spirit-place vision of the next-door path beamway. I was then looking at life without my sometimes rescuer.

The chanting I became to be into began at readings in Vancouver in the 1960s when I would say something over and over. Repetition for special sound effect. A blurring of linear particularities, par example, the ancient Lord Lady of the universe asks you to be, over and over again, and other sounds, non-English, which evolve. From the slurring, emerge. After the brain operation all that became more fluid. Before, it was minimal slurring, mostly trance with the repetition. Fine. After the brain operation, other non-English sounds would occur much more frequently. I intuitively would go with them, however far they would carry me, in the work. Now it's becoming less like chanting, more into singing. I still want to go with these sounds. Take the music, the poetry and me.

1981—began to live in the words and the images. Relations with my daughter close again. Some people I'd lived with, still friends. 1993, friends with everyone I've lived with. That's important to me. Then some grudges not yet let go of. Some things, of course, still take work to let go of. Letting go, others in process. Me too. Most of the day I would write and paint, go out at night, rage, sex in cars, whatever, safely. Amazing Wendee Wood, who taught me Tai Chi, curated seven shows in a row of my work over a four- to five-year period. Those venues often at "Pizzarico's" in Vancouver, Robson Street, and

Anavada. Also I showed at Neoartism and Sechelt Art Gallery, Keven Stephens curator. One-person art show, Richmond Art Gallery, 1986, Page Hope Smith, curator. And The Edge, two-person show with Jeffrey Birkin arriving in London, Ontario, where I experienced some wonderful times. At the Forest City Gallery, one-person show, 1987, playing with Luddites at the opening. Raging. I was reading. Sound Symposium Newfoundland, St. John's. Prince Edward Island, Montreal, North Bay, Toronto, St. Catherine's, Kingston, Winnipeg, Houston, British Columbia, Manitoba, Saskatoon, Regina, Medicine Hat, Prince George, Vancouver, Victoria, New York, and Europe. Paying off the existing debts from the press. So many places, living. Really enjoying. Paintings, doing better. See "invisibul wings" poem/essay on painting I wrote in *canada gees mate for life*. Talonbooks had been publishing my work since the late seventies, after my having been with quite a few publishers. New Star books, *living with th vishyun*. House of Anansi, where I edited *nobody owns th erth*, with Margaret Atwood and Dennis Lee. Black Moss, *tuff shit*. Oberon, *MEDICINE my mouths on fire* (with record). Talonbooks has been extraordinarily good to me. Karl Siegler there, wonderful to work with. He owns the press as colleague publisher, working on strategy together when I was a publisher as well. We talked often, how to survive, then after excellent David Robinson left Talonbooks, he had been for me editor, Karl Siegler began to work with me. He's so brilliant to work with. I prepare the books very completely now, measured to the copy size. The rhythm of the editing, spend endless hours on, so that it's hopefully really heightened and accessible. If it is organically living. Karl looks for any redundancy of theme, phrase, image, or poem itself. What I've missed, said already in a previous book, or too much already in the same book, and through the philosophies, and mostly, whether he himself likes the book or not. We have great conversations. Some previous books were lead time rushed by circumstances, whatever. So those were editing collaborations at earlier development. I write the books as books, whether the reader is aware or not of that subliminally, not as persuasion, as journey, fact, I want to be aware of every possible subtext. If I'm writing all the time, every day, this is possible. I don't want anything in there that I can be aware of that I wouldn't authorize. Sometimes that's a lot of raking, editing, rewriting, more than when the spirit moves me.

Sarah Murphy, Joe Rosenblatt, and me doing sound poetry together,
Charlottetown, Prince Edward Island, 1991

I love it. Living in London, Ontario, was very good for the writing and the painting. Evelyn Li, wonderful person, so great, kind to me, landlady there. We became excellent friends, she and her husband Mok and me.

Philosophy and English were my majors. I never finished the B.A., wanting to write and paint. I did finish the majors, some great teachers: George Grant at Dalhousie. He wrote *Lament for a Nation.* Warren Tallman, he wrote *Godawful Streets of Man* and *In the Midst* (Talonbooks). Warren put up his house for me for bail, twice, in the sixties, late seventies, when the right wing fundamentalists, some of them later doing time for fraud, emerald smuggling. Watch the right wing. Warren produced and hosted a year-long poetry reading series to benefit me and Talonbooks, who was also under fire. Poets from all over Canada and the United States came and read on our behalf. There were over a thousand in the audience each of the

many nights, for poetry. Warren gave an entire sabbatical year of his for this.

As hard as life is, can be, people are often there to help with the struggle against the forces of suppression which really never sleep often. That's why we need a good night's rest, and for me to keep talking, exchanging ideas with friends about everything, talking with Harris Ginsberg and Connie Boles. With Mickey Gunn, the lady of the lake. Rob Noel, Prince Albert's diner in London, Ontario. John Donlan there. Marion Johnson with Rudolph Nadassky and Cyrus Point in Vancouver. So the mind can keep growing, hopefully not burdened with set or status quo ideas. Talking with Arthur Richardson, Jeffrey Birkin.

Living in the Cariboo, northern British Columbia, real winter, often 50 below. Vancouver very mild, Pacific coast, seldom below zero. North country, writing nature poetry, inspiring to me. Informs my writing forever. Meta physical. All these wonderful people I've worked with doing readings, printing books, putting art shows together. The right wing backed off for a while from me and Talonbooks, and others still infiltrating school boards, banning books from within, more quietly cutting the Canada Council each year more so. The right wing doesn't ever retire, unfortunately.

1980—reports of AIDS entering consciousness. Friends worried. Safe sex. Finding out. Living in Chicago with great guy briefly. Seeing my daughter, more art shows. Writing books. AIDS message getting through. Some friends starting to get sick. I spend a lot of time in north country, writing, painting, and in London, Ontario, singing. Luddites touring throughout southwestern Ontario. Toronto recordings. This is one of the best experiences of my life, working learning, travelling, doing readings on my own. Mid-1980s, friends closer in getting sick. Me, still okay. So far so good. Incubation period experts keep lengthening backward in time. Friends dying, going to spirit. Mainstream society slow in appreciating that AIDS is not a gay disease. Usual medieval judgment scapegoating gay society, very strong mainstream society becomes more informed as AIDS touches it. Unlike in Africa where it began in heterosexual mainstream. This edification takes a lot of work on the part of thousands and thousands of brilliant people. More and more people dying. More and more friends. There is already too much to write about here. Poem in *inkorrect thots* (Talonbooks) "timothee sz ther is no deth," for Timothy Priske, chronicles everything I've been able to write so far about AIDS. Timothy did so much research and thinking. My poem contains a lot of what he told me. Timothy is the great-great-grandson of Gabriel Dumont. More recording in the poem "ths is th paliativ ward th nurs sd" for Stephen Weir, also from *inkorrect thots*. With more friends going, as there is for everyone, there will be more such poems, from more and more writers. This is such a great tragedy of all our lives everywhere. If only a cure, something, could be found for this pandemic.

Sound poetry 1993. Read with Bob Cobbing, Paula Claire, Chris Cheek, Adeena Karasick, such a brilliant poet. All so brilliant. All the international sound poetry since 1975 hosted by Bob Cobbing in London, England. I was there with Allan Rosen. Read at the poetry center in Earls Court and classes at Oxford. Bob Cobbing so brilliant. Keeps pushing us to grow more without being aware of that. Was my first time there. Read then in Amsterdam, Paris, then toured Europe with George Johnston, Susan Musgrave. Another wonderful hard-working time. We soared together. Then sound poetry festival, Glasgow, then in Toronto, New York. These all a few years in between. Also toured through U.K. with Paul Dutton. Raging. Read with Jackson Mac Low, Jerome Rothenberg, Bob Cobbing. Raging. Paula Claire, superb, and P. C. Fencott, so amazing, and in London again, Bob Cobbing, so miraculous. Totally raging, and Adeena Karasick, raging, and Paula Claire. It was then that my big sister went to spirit. Huge grief for me. Adeena helped me so much with that, as well as inspiring me so much through her writing and performances.

Allan Rosen has almost always photographed me and my paintings for my book covers. He's brilliant, and his work has always brought out the feel and the existence of the particular book, which has helped the books so much. Shoots with him are always wonderful. Give, stretch. His friendship, personal, professional, so inspiring to me. Our conversations, dialogue where sometimes I feel clarity as I hopefully keep learning. It's about self-responsibility. Allan wrote a magic book, *Michael,* and a visual delight, *Rory the Price of Morning,* that is very moving and alive and beautiful. Today winter, Toronto, other close friends Ben Kennedy and Richard Browning coming to see me and my recent paintings. I'm working on my most recent book, *th last photo uv th human soul.* I do Tai Chi every morning after meditating. Helps with everything. There are great icicles on the window. Twenty-five below. We have tea. Wonderful time together. Ben says it's summer in my house. Some days are the best, especially that sense of completion. Having done so many paintings. Friends seeing them and liking them. That's real time off for me, being together.

Vancouver, taking down what's left from art show at Not Just Deserts [*sic*]. Great restaurant in Vancouver, East Broadway friend George Siu owns. Wonderful friend. We've known each other over ten years. Remet in London, Ontario. Great. I've had two shows there and read three times there selling tickets, paid from the door. So many readings and books and shows made possible by the Canada Council. Would not have been accomplished without their support, and it has built such groundwork support. These times at NJD, though, are independent, which I find also invigorating to do. Opportunities, seeing, sharing, which all those times are however they're

th last photo uv th human soul

bcoz uv th kind uv bombs usd in
th fifth just war nd bcoz uv th
apparent lack uv sum materials   photographee   was
4 th time   being   bannd

ths was th offishul xplain from th war n pees committeez
aftr top scientists n doktors   statespeopul   had bin
looking at
th last photo uv th human soul

takn during an unsuccessful operaysyun   whn th soul left
th bodee   2 much pain ther   bodee giving out   time 2 rage
on 2 th next dimensyun   next world   is it next   or bfor

th top peopul cud not determine its gendr   from
looking at th photo   th correlaysyun uv th photo with th
now disceesd patient had uv cours   bin lost with all th
hectik activiteez   that go on in th o r   ducking spraying
blood streems   pumping tirud hearts   2 much hurt

so big mysteree ther   its voting patterna   anothr
big qwestyun   its demographiks

they cud not determine its posisyun on   th old left
th nu   rite
th familee
valus
how cud thees top peopul criticize
or evaluate ths image
at leest   yet

had ths human soul takn a forbiddn drug   that had allowd
its self 2 evolv byond disseksyun   byond th committeez reech
had it   th soul   enrolld in   an unauthorizd   practise
or teeching

it was aftr all   onlee a photograph   uv sum kind uv being
in sum shape uv ecstasee   prhaps   byond pain   or th
grasp uv th ruling elite   or alternate committeez   what cud
th top men n women dew

certainlee   classify it 4
startrs   but what if it wer leekd   our adjaysensee 2 th

immaterial world   so pronounsd   n ths evidens   *nd*   TH HUMAN

    SOUL DID NOT LOOK AFRAYD   is ths what happns   whn we ar
freed uv othr peopuls trips our own   thru going 2 spirit place

    wher was thn th undrclass prspektiv

        so th top peopul destroyd th photograph

           combustyun n resultant ashes n secresee   n th

    irritating memoree   how long wud that lingr   uv a world so

    diffrent than th wun they had authorizd   wun they cud nevr
                            control   at all

    erratik n prhaps diaphanous purges wer occuring with greatr
frequensees   n less xplanaysyuns   than usual   on th citadel

    undrclass membrs wonderd what was happning   at th equalitee
                               palace

      on tuesday next week a final announsment

          abt th futur   was   2   b   made

        we th viewrs   cud   wait   4   it

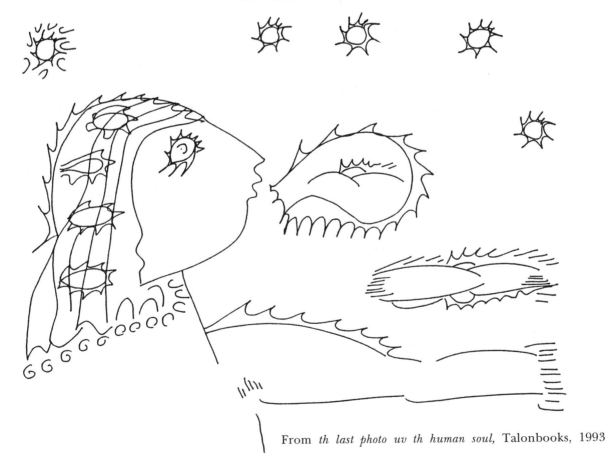

From *th last photo uv th human soul*, Talonbooks, 1993

bill bissett with Paula Claire, in London, England, 1993

produced. Going to do readings in the Free Press Festival, Vancouver, produced by Kedrick James, great performance poet and producer in Vancouver and Seattle. Year before, read in Seattle Bumbershoot with Grace Paley. Very inspiring. All these times. Then up north. Paint and write there. Get into nature memories of the wonderful poets I'd heard and great people I'd met at these reading times in me. With the trees, water, sky, magic birds. Then off to Charlottetown, Prince Edward Island. Rockin' beautiful place. Where I received my first award for writing, the People's Poet Award in memory of Milton Acorn, great people's poet, amazing craft and spirit, 1990. Second award 1993, a British Columbia book award, Dorothy Livesay Poetry Prize, she great poet, an elder to us all now. She helped me with starting blewointmentpress, as did Earle Birney, wonderful writer, also now an elder in hospital, Toronto. We see what happens as our bodies and minds change. Hopeful we can be our souls nevertheless are more uplifted, with the spiritual friend inside us all. Gay pride day, Toronto, June, end of 1993. Over 150,000 of us all totally raging and out. Amazing floats. Aston-

ishing energy. I'm here behind the "buddys in bad times" float. Rockin' in Toronto on some of the biggest streets in the world. It's so great. Thrilling. Next day flu comes back. This is a long one, though spiritually I'm fine. My head still ringing with all the joy of the previous day.

Toronto, where the office of the League of Canadian Poets is still happening and through which Gerry and Arlene Lampert booked me and so many other poets into so many readings, so many years. The gratitude still there. Gerry went to spirit late 1970s. Great loss for me, really hard. Luckily, still see Arlene. She doesn't book readings really since not long after Gerry's passing. She and I friends.

K eeping vigil for a friend who may be going to spirit. He is often in between this world and the next, suspending, spiritual, so graceful with so much inner strength, even with the pain he is almost continually having now from the AIDS. Me, I've had pre-death events. I've seen the tunnel to the next world, or is it before, twice. All the singing up there. I've sat in circle. Heard voices from the spirit place. I've been shown parts of the big journey from here. It looks and feels very exciting, exhilarating. I don't know. I hope it's true. I know I love him. I know that doesn't specifically help him with what he has to do now, and he's so courageous. Keeps on fighting. I sometimes worry. Know that's not constructive, and think, even if there is eternity, what about the parting?

Mary Donlan, very strong nonfigurative expressionist painter friend, in from London, Ontario. We talk about so much. Her painting is great. Art, time, story. She says very early painting, perhaps the first painting, this is way before Lascaux, circles, squares, lines, dots. Very geometric before the representational bison on the cave walls. Mid-July, reading, High Park, with Michael Holmes, Adeena Karasick, Paul Dutton, Sky Gilbert, others. Very hot, humid, summer night, electric. Flu almost over. Writing on this autobiography. Painting. Off to the zoo with Ben Kennedy. He's a singer and poet. J.P. and Ms. Vicki. What a great zoo. Getting better. Off to the zoo again with Adeena Karasick and Michael Holmes. It's different every time. Rest, write, and on this, paint, paper play. Then off to Paul Duguay and Richard Browning's the week of the magic lobsters Paul's sister brought in from New Brunswick. We all eat lobster almost every day. It's wonderful. Shelia Pruden, close friend, she works wardrobe in movies, wanted a big painting from me for her new apartment which she's sharing with Ben Kennedy. She asked Ben to select a drawing by me for me to paint from. It's nonfigurative. Ben is very inspired, very sensitive. I did five paintings, five variations so Shelia could make a choice. Doing these paintings got me through the long flu. Was a breakthrough for me. Returning again to nonfigurative work. Colors flat on the picture plane, based on continuous line drawing, which Lance Farrell and me worked through so long ago, in part based on that total yellow ground look, kind of like tree, river, leaves, branches. Secret and very calm. Letters, agile, big drawing stroke. Glowing. So much yellow green teal line drawing through on. Mostly they look like themselves, breathing. Being. Are nontranslatable objects in themselves. Glowing.

There are sheets of lightning on the balcony. Wrap myself in them. The pasts have been too much with me today. The future. I don't know. Do you? I feel free of conflicted emotions and stasis. Go out into the night of the purple

elephants. What else can I do? Control even in my own life, or others, understandings, get real. It's a very long voyage, talking about some past confinements. Another part of my present and future walks by. We don't see him. Then I see. Go off yelling down the alley. He doesn't hear. Pneumatic drilling so loud. Tall buildings clustering against our flesh, lungs. I know I will miss my other friend so much. I know. Flash. Great, he's getting better, stronger. I've lived in a lot of places. I've loved a lot of people. Still do. Each day is today. Tonight, hot and humid, romantic. The full moon sailing in the spaces between the towers, like on the LP cover of Rachmaninoff, second piano concerto, Leonard Pennario, pianist. George Siu reintroduced me to listening to Sarah Vaughan. Saw one of her last concerts, Roy Thomson Hall, Toronto. Amazing. All my life I'd wanted to see and hear her in person. Now I was hallucinating. Billy Eckstine I used to listen to all the time in Halifax, too. Idols. Still are. As well as K. D. Lang, Anne Murray, Depeche Mode, Leonard Cohen, Kashtin, Buffy Sainte-Marie. Rereading Gwendolyn MacEwen. I love these people. Politics. How so many leaders are determinedly creating huge underclasses, sorrow in the world. Saying this with friends Joy Kuropatwa, teacher and essayist, and Bruce Kramer, lawyer. Friends in London. And on the phone with Sharon Nelson, poet and friend, Montreal, about these right wing events. George and Deborah Siu have a construction I made with the real doorbell Patrick Lane found in the grass at my former home in Halifax when he and I were reading there. I had also at that time read in Antigonish in Cape Breton, glorious country, and Patrick and me were in the swing there in the backyard. Swing still strong. Going higher and higher.

I'm listening to Morrissey a lot, too. Results of my brain injury. No drinking. That takes oxygen from the brain. I need all the oxygen I can get. No big deal to not drink. Wanting no stress. Who does? And naps every day. Otherwise, fine. Looking out from the balcony here, the full moon, and I wonder if that LP jacket painting, the moon I'm gazing up at now through the high-rise radiance, would have been the same LP Louis B. Mayer would have had. Would he have loved Rachmaninoff as I did? The second piano concerto? Montgomery Clift? Patricia Bosworth in her biography of him said L.B. was difficult. Katharine Hepburn, her autobiography, *Me,* says he was wonderful, an artist, romanticism. My father would have me dance for his friends when he would come home at night. Ask me to wear the white pants after my mother had gone to spirit. Gradually I give up the ideas that the other, whether parent or loved one, is responsible for my happiness, and is to blame for not so fulfilling me, and become intermittently, then stronger. The deepening felt realization that I am responsible for my own happiness, my choices, in nature, my life. Lives.

I believe through our taxes, though the government, which is ourselves, is responsible for many things. Universal health care, social programs, infrastructure, individual human rights, more than adequate environmental protections. If we're not really getting these rights, why are we paying taxes? Also I believe guaranteed minimum incomes, universal, would better replace the sloppy and condescending welfare and unemployment insurance programs. Freedom is certainly worth struggling for. For me that includes no one involuntarily falling through the social safety nets. If one person is inadvertently homeless, then we all are in a way homeless. The state is only everyone in it. Isn't it?

For my father and his friends suddenly arriving home late at night I would be lip-synching and dancing to Noel Coward's "Alice Is at It Again," Marlene Dietrich's "See What the Boys in the Back Room." Well, I looked into that a lot. Had lots of jobs to keep writing and painting till I could make a living at it. English tutor, gas jockey, book shelver, ditch digger, record store sales, bean picker in Mexico, everything else you can think of. Blow jobs. Whatever. Sometimes I've thought I've seen my life through others. Do we ever? And all those changes. Now it's me, myself, the present going to Prince Edward Island soon again. Do readings which I love to do the work. Hear great Celtic rock roots music there, as well. Dance at a kaylee after the readings at Orwell Corners, Valerie Lapointe, the producer there. Great person. Reading with Nicole Brossard. Magic. Incandescent articulations. Robert Priest, Kim Morressey, other great poets. Cedrik Smith, Terry Jones singing great tributes to Milton Acorn. Then three days in Toronto seeing friends. Then to Portland, Artquake, reading there with Ira Cohen. Raging mister magic. Energy. It all turned out. Can't see that yet. I'm in Toronto working on this autobiography, letting these pasts and futures go for a while, in unknowing. Grateful and hot. Out the door. I'm out with the purple elephants tonight.

Clear decks. Clear the tapes. Letting the constructs go, and flying.

October 1993—shows of my paintings and drawings currently on at The Edge, excellent restaurant on Davie Street, and in two great bookstores, R2B2 Books and Margaret Gabriel Books, both in Kitsilano, all in Vancouver. Stephanie Harper is making a film about my writing and painting called *bills brain.* She is wonderful to work with. Clear, knowledgeable, incisive, and guiding. What I've seen already of the film is very exciting for me. I love putting up shows, people seeing the work.

Wish I had a photo of Evelyn Crook. She was my nurse and friend when I was a boy in Halifax for almost two years. So joyous her company for me, while she and my mother and I and others were trying to get me better. One of the philosophy books I loved was Martin Buber's *I and Thou.* Also Mary Shelley, Plato's *Symposium,* and *The Republic,* and with the novels of Mary Renault, reading tonight *The Mask of Apollo.* Also love Beckett, Ionesco, Joyce, Marx, Marian Engle, Margaret Laurence, Timothy Findley, Thomson Highway, and not yet last night in Vancouver, Richard Browning here. Great magic. Rage with David and Robby and Robert after picnicking with George and Deborah and Stan and Byron and Davy and Daphne and Agatha and Bobby. And us later, Richard and me and Robby and David and Robert watching Annie Lennox and Elton John and Lisa Stansfield and George Michael and Liza Minnelli. All amazingly brilliant, in tribute to Freddie Mercury at Wembley Stadium. So uplifting. Raging. And John Mellencamp singing "What If I Came Knocking?" from his new album. Robert Cray, who I love, too. Robby has all these great music videos he's spliced from the "David Letterman Show." We are feeling enhanced. So great. And the walls around us, lifting, dissolving. Had they ever been there?

Yes, well. It's a day and a night off from working and writing this autobiography. Time away from it, to feel how it is, and going home in a glowing golden cab. I've written and worked and played with Autobiographika through six full moons. This full moon also so radiant, and ecstatic.

Love is the dream and the dance never ends and who can forget.

October 7, 1993

BIBLIOGRAPHY

Poetry:

fires in th tempul OR th jinx ship nd othr trips: pomes-drawings-collage, illustrated by the author, Very Stone House/blewointmentpress, 1966.

we sleep inside each other all, illustrated by the author, Ganglia Press, 1966.

where is miss florence riddle, Luv Press, 1967.

what poetiks, blewointmentpress, 1967.

(th) Gossamer Bed Pan, blewointmentpress, 1967.

Lebanon Voices, Weed/Flower Press, 1967.

Of Th Land/Divine Service, Weed/Flower Press, 1968.

awake in the red desert!, Talonbooks, 1968.

sunday work(?), blewointmentpress, 1968.

liberating skies, blewointmentpress, 1969.

lost angel mining co., blewointmentpress, 1969.

IBM, blewointmentpress, 1970.

s th story i to, blewointmentpress, 1970.

blew trewz, blewointmentpress, 1970.

(Editor, with Margaret Atwood and Dennis Lee) *nobody owns th erth,* Anansi, 1971.

air 6, Air, 1971.

tuff shit, Bandit/Black Moss Press, 1971.

dragon fly, Weed/Flower Press, 1971.

RUSH what fukan thery, blewointmentpress, 1971.

drifting into war, Talonbooks, 1971.

(With Earle Birney, Judith Copithorne, and Andy Suknaski) *Four Parts Sand: Concrete Poems,* Oberon Press, 1972.

th Ice bag/th high green hill/Polar Bear Hunt/words in th fire, blewointmentpress, 1972.

pomes for yoshi, blewointmentpress, 1972.

air 10–11–12, Air, 1972.

pass th food, release th spirit book, Talonbooks, 1973.

th first sufi line, blewointmentpress, 1973.

vancouver mainland ice & cold storage, Writers Forum, 1973.

what, blewointmentpress, 1974.

drawings, blewointmentpress, 1974.

MEDICINE my mouths on fire (includes record), Oberon Press, 1974.

space travl, Air, 1974.

yu can eat it at th opening, blewointmentpress, 1974.

living with th vishyun, New Star, 1974.

th fifth sun, blewointmentpress, 1975.

image being, blewointmentpress, 1975.

stardust, blewointmentpress, 1975.

venus, blewointmentpress, 1975.

th wind up tongue, blewointmentpress, 1976.

plutonium missing, Intermedia, 1976.

an allusyun to macbeth, Black Moss Press, 1976.

sailor, Talonbooks, 1978.

th first snow, blewointmentpress, 1979.

soul arrow, blewointmentpress, 1980.

sa n th monkey, blewointmentpress, 1980.

selected poems: beyond even faithful legends, Talonbooks, 1980.

northern birds in color, Talonbooks, 1981.

ready for framing, blewointmentpress, 1981.

parlant, translated into French by Bertrand Lachance, blewointmentpress, 1982.

sa n his crystal ball, blewointmentpress, 1982.

seagull on yonge street, Talonbooks, 1983.

write me an adventure, Gronk, 1983.

fires in th tempul, Vancouver Art Gallery, 1984.

canada gees mate for life, Talonbooks, 1985.

animal uproar, Talonbooks, 1987.

what we have, Talonbooks, 1988.

rezoning, Vancouver Art Gallery, 1989.

hard 2 beleev, Talonbooks, 1990.

inkorrect thots, Talonbooks, 1992.

th last photo uv th human soul, Talonbooks, 1993.

Recordings:

awake in the desert, See Hear, 1968.

MEDICINE my mouths on fire, Oberon, 1976.

northern birds in color, blewointmentpress, 1982.

sonic horses, Underwich, 1984.

Past Eroticism, Gronk, 1986.

jumping cloud, London, Ontario, 1987.

luddites, London, Ontario, 1988.

LUDDITES (12" LP), London, Ontario, 1989.

(With Chris Meloche) *shining spirit,* Independent, 1989.

(With Adeena Karasick) *liquid wayze,* Independent, 1990.

dreemin uv th nite, Luddites, 1991.

(With Chris Meloche) *LONDON LIFE,* Nightwood, 1991.

Other:

(Editor) *th last blewointment anthology: 1963–1983,* 2 volumes, Nightwood, 1985.

(Illustrator) Jim Brown, *The Circus in the Boy's Eye,* Very Stone Press, 1966.

Contributor to various television documentaries, including *In search of innocence,* 1963; *Strange grey day this,* 1964; and *Poets of the 60's,* 1967. A film entitled *bills brain* is being written, produced, and directed by Stephanie Harper, due for release in 1994.

James Lee Burke

1936-

James Lee Burke, 1993

Lessons in Race, Dialogue, and Profanity

I think that the writing of good dialogue is probably the most difficult technique to accomplish in the art of fiction writing (or, of course, in writing for the stage or screen). I wrote on my own for two years, without any instruction or editorial help; then I attended the University of Missouri and took a class with Bill Hamlin, who was probably the best creative writing teacher I ever knew, even though he did not write fiction himself.

In Bill's class I quickly learned, through a negative example, what good dialogue was not. We were by and large an idealistic and sincere group, but in our membership was one student who used to scoff at what we considered our aesthetic standards. He planned to be a writer for television. "I'll be honest with you guys," he'd say. "I'm going for the big score. What's wrong with that? Who wants to live off weenies and beans?"

63

He pumped iron, wore T-shirts in the winter, had jug ears and a crew cut like a peeled onion. He wasn't a guy you messed with.

Back in those days, before Xerox machines, the instructor or the student had to read the story at the lectern, while the class listened attentively and took notes in anticipation of the group critique. The oral readings of this man's stories were like moments of time dredged up from Dante's ninth circle. They were eye-crossing, mind-numbing studies in boredom, with the worst dialogue I ever heard, before or since.

In order to create convincing speech, he went around town with a tape recorder, then transcribed real conversations word by word onto the written page. The result was certainly realistic, to the extent that you wished the Phoenicians hadn't invented the alphabet.

I didn't fare much better. In conferences with Bill Hamlin, he would mark my dialogue with a red pen until it looked like a disemboweled animal.

"Is it really that bad?" I asked after a particularly tough session.

"Yeah, it is. It's awful."

"What's wrong with it?"

"It's stupid, that's what's wrong with it. Your characters *sound* stupid."

"Anything else?"

"Yeah, throw it away."

Then later, as always, he felt bad about the criticism he had given me. That evening, over a pizza and beers at the Shack, across from the elm-shaded School of Journalism, he rubbed his face with the palm of his hand and said, "Come on, Jim, you know the psychological terrain. You just haven't learned yet how to make your characters talk about what's on their mind."

"I disagree. I think they do."

"They sound like emotional douche bags who were kicked out of a Tennessee Williams script. Good dialogue reveals personality in an oblique way. You've got to do it with three-cushion shots."

"Boy, that clears it up. Am I paying for the pizza tonight?"

When my first cousin Andre Dubus and I were boys in south Louisiana, we devoted most of our summer days, in one way or another, to playing or watching baseball. It was in the era before television, when major league games came to us only on radio, and bush league ball was a vital part of southern life. You knew the players around town; they ran filling stations or worked as carpenters or meat-cutters. But on a twilight diamond, right after a rain, with halos of mist glowing around the electric lamps high overhead, these same blue-collar men had all the mythic and carnival characteristics of national celebrities. There was also a reckless physical courage about them, an outrageous disdain for convention that we intuitively recognized as the elements that made them a separate race, a collection of boy-men who would never grow up, who would always be out of sync with the world, always spitting Brown Mule on the shoes of authority.

They threw spitters and beanballs, came in with their spikes up, and busted up double plays with elbows and knees. Sometimes the batter deliberately slung the bat at the pitcher's head like a helicopter blade. They smoked in the dugout and, in view of the crowd, rubbed their bats between their thighs like they were masturbating. Their profanity and yelled insults could leave an uninitiated listener stunned and disbelieving.

Like the men I would work with later in the oil field and on the pipeline, most of their insults had do with oral sex or sodomy, since the implications were what they feared most in themselves. "Cocksucker" was a word they never seemed able to wear out.

Early every morning we gathered at a dirt lot off St. Mary Boulevard in Lafayette and chose up sides. We tried to imitate professional ballplayers in every way we could. We rolled the brims of our hats into virtual cones, and folded, creased, and taped down the crowns at night so they were always sharply peaked in front. We shot the bone and talked as obscenely as we dared, spit through our teeth, straddled our legs, and pridefully hitched up our genitalia.

But we were ahead of our Evangeline League heroes in one respect. Even though Jackie Robinson and Larry Doby had integrated the majors, the minor leagues in the South were still all-white. Some mornings at our dirt-lot games, the children of black lawn men in the neighborhood wandered over and joined us. Few of them had caps, which cost one dollar at Bell's Sporting Goods, and none of them ever had a glove.

Andre had caddied for his father at the city golf course and had cut lawns all summer to buy a claw mitt. It had cost sixteen dollars, in a time when even white adults were paid only three dollars and fifty cents for a ten-hour day of physical labor. Andre rubbed the new leather with oil until it was the color of mahogany, and at night he cupped a ball deep in the pocket and crisscrossed and tied down the glove's sides with twine to give it shape and depth.

It was the kind of glove that you carry all the way through your adolescence, that hangs from your handlebars, that sits on your bookshelf at night like a sentinel, that you entrust to your girlfriend as an act of faith while you're at bat, until the dream becomes just that and you give it up and ballparks become places where you buy a ticket to watch someone else play.

A tall black kid, maybe sixteen years old, who wore jeans with no knees and tennis shoes that were bursting at the toes, showed up at the lot one morning with four other black kids and asked to play. He was already hot and dirty from lawn work, and he kept pulling at his T-shirt with his pinched fingers to shake the blades of grass off his stomach and back.

His first time at bat he nailed our best pitcher's hanging curve all the way to the street. It looked like a BB disappearing into the trees. But it was when we watched him play at first base that we knew he was better than any of us. In the first inning he played without a glove and didn't ask for the loan of one; in the second inning Andre lent him his claw mitt. With a runner on first, the black kid vacuumed a line drive out of the dirt, rifled the ball to the second baseman for the automatic out, then caught a wild return throw and flicked his tennis shoe behind him and touched the bag before the batter could make first base.

At the end of the game the black kids were getting on their bikes to rejoin their fathers, the lawn men. I saw Andre hitting his fist into the pocket of his glove. He kept doing it almost as though he were mad at it. Then, as though a troubling thought had finally done its injury and gone its way, he walked over to the black first baseman and tapped him on the arm with the glove.

"You keep it," he said.

"Keep what?"

"You play a lot better with it than I do. You keep the claw."

"What you talkin' about, man?"

"I want you to have it. I told you," Andre said.

We were all silent.

"You foolin' wit' me?" the black kid said.

Andre shook his head. The black kid looked at his friends, then extended his left hand and wrapped his fingers around the soft folds of leather.

"You sure now? 'Cause if you foolin' wit' me—" He made a fist with his right hand and lifted it in the air, but he was smiling when he did it.

I never asked Andre why he gave his glove away because I already knew, and the explanation was not the one he had offered the black kid, nor even the one, in my opinion, that he later offered himself. He gave it away because he didn't believe the white race deserved what it had. Our superior standard of living was at best a gift, just as an artist's talent is a gift, but we had become prideful and racially arrogant and deliberately obtuse and had murdered the gift of charity in our hearts by denying the simple biological fact of our brotherhood.

The end of this brief story actually took place ten years later, in the barber shop across from the old Lafayette city police station and jailhouse. The station and jail were three stories tall and built of gray stone, and on the narrow apron of lawn in front was a Confederate monument, the color of burnished lead, that looked like it had been placed there as an afterthought. Back in the 1950s the electric chair used to travel from parish to parish; when it came to Lafayette the two big power generators were parked on a semi under the trees on a side street, and workmen in coveralls would string the long, rubber-coated cables to the third floor of the jail where the condemned man was electrocuted at midnight. It had started to rain, and one of the barbers had opened the front door to let in the cool air. I could see a black man at a barred window on the third floor of the jail, his forearms propped across the windowsill.

I had just gotten my first paycheck as an English instructor at the university, and I decided to have a shoeshine.

The porter, who wore a starched gray apron, a whisk broom in his back pocket, and who was about my age, bent to his work and popped his rags across my shoes. But each time he straightened up to get more polish or reach for a brush, his eyes lingered for a moment on my face. Then I remembered.

"Did you used to play ball over on St. Mary Boulevard?" I asked.

"Yes, sir, I did."

"You played first base."

"That's right. You got a good memory. I seen you 'round town, but I didn't think you'd recall me."

"You remember that day about the glove?"

"I ain't forgot it. That's me. It sure is."

"You were a great player, podna."

He nodded and smiled politely, then began buffing the points of my shoes.

Then I asked the question that I shouldn't have asked: "Did you play in high school, or in—"

He stood erect and looked obliquely out the front door. He flipped the shine rag idly in one hand.

"I got married, had to settle down, stop all that runnin' 'round, you understand what I mean?" he said.

"Yeah, sure."

"You cain't make no money playin' games."

"Yeah, I guess that's right."

"I think about it sometimes, though."

He bent back into his work, then a moment later he tapped the bottom of one shoe with his long fingers to show me that the shine was over.

"See you around," I said when I paid him.

"Yes, sir. I'll be here."

In the first few years that I wrote fiction I tried to recreate obscene and profane language just as I'd heard it used. The result was awful. I was simply replicating the speech of inarticulate people who used profanity either as a form of psychological magic to make an unpleasant situation disappear or to mask the inadequacy of their vocabulary. Then I began to realize that the profanity used by southerners actually had little to do with what they were saying; i.e., the profane words, which were almost always nouns, were far less important in terms of meaning than the verbs and the modifying adjectives.

The word "sonofabitch" is used by southerners to describe virtually everything and is finally a neutral term. But it is the emphasis on other words in the sentence that will make the speaker's intention clear: "He's a *lying* sonofabitch," or "He's a *crazy* sonofabitch," or "I tell you, hon, I *love* that old sonofabitch," or, perhaps in speaking of a musician, "That boy can flat *play* that sonofabitch."

Then I began to hear rhythms and patterns and language within language all around me, and slowly I realized that I seldom needed the profanity to recreate the poetry and metaphors that ordinary people use every day of their lives.

A hospital corpsman from Birmingham was telling me how much he loathed a despicable landlord: "You know, Jim, that's the only man I ever met I could kill and drink a beer while I was doing it."

Once I asked an old-time Kentucky moonshiner, a fine man whom I much admired and who had distilled a million gallons of whiskey in his career before he hung it up and went back to farming, about the ethos of cooking illegal mash and transporting it up to the syndicate in Detroit. He answered, "We broke a man-made law, son. We didn't break no God-made law."

I don't think I'm capable of writing better dialogue than that. All I had to do was listen in a selective way. And the concern I'd had about using profanity in an effective manner turned out to be not worthy of concern after all.

Thirty-two years ago in Houston, two overweight black women were sitting behind me on the bus. At that time segregation in public transportation was still legal in Texas, and the metal sign that said *colored,* all in lower-case letters, was bolted to the vertical chrome rail just behind my head, but I could hear everything that they said to each other:

"That new preacher give a good sermon at the graveside."

"Yes, he did." A pause. "It was awful cold when that sun went down, though. And I was thinkin', why didn't that man cut on his brakes, why that lil boy got to be down there in that box, down in that cold ground. Just six years old. All 'cause some drunk man got to have his whiskey."

Most academics love polysyllabic and abstruse language because it gives the appearance of profundity to third-rate ideas. But as my old poetry professor and friend John Neihardt once told me, the English language naturally falls into iambic meter, its best appeal to the senses is always through its Anglo-Saxon derivatives, and when your ear becomes attuned to the music of language, you'll understand why William Wordsworth used the tactile and monosyllabic words of rural people in his art.

John Neihardt's best-known work is his biographical novel *Black Elk Speaks.* He told me that he wrote it late at night, "because that's when the voices of dead poets speak to you." I believe that was John's metaphor for explaining that the power to create comes from outside you, that somehow it is collective, that many voices of many people somehow contribute to what will flow from your pen, and you can no more describe that collective energy, which sometimes seems almost mystical, than you can separate the sounds you hear inside a seashell.

1950s Hoods, James T. Farrell, and the Girls of the Gran Via

Even though it's a gray winter day outside and the oak trees are full of fog, the high school metal-shop class is hot, almost superheated from the forge, the sparks showering from an acetylene torch; the air is bright with the smells of metal shrieking on emery wheels, the molten aluminum being poured like liquid red and yellow candy into sand molds.

Jerry Jeff wears butch wax in his thick blond hair to shape the ducktail at the back of his head. His knuckles are the size of quarters, his upper torso like an oak stump. His face is impassive as he works the sand in the foundry and waits for the aluminum to cool.

"I'm supposed to make the forms for my mailbox hangers," another kid says to him.

"Not today," Jerry Jeff says.

"I got to. For my grade."

"You got an 'S' for 'snarf.' By the way, you're standing in my light."

Twenty minutes later the instructor is looking idly out the door at the rain falling in the trees. Jerry Jeff and a friend break open the sand forms, pry out the aluminum replicas of brass knuckles, and dip them hissing into a split oil-barrel filled with dirty water. The instructor yawns lazily and looks at the rain.

A buck a piece. Buffed and honed on the grinder or as is. The latter isn't a bad deal, either. The ragged edges can print the face with daisy chains of red flowers in seconds.

The teachers, the gym coaches, the administrators have a facility for not seeing. Not the chains in hall lockers, the fights in the parking lot after school, the bullies who on a whim can break noses and burst mouths into torn plums; they do not see the kid who pares and trims his nails with a barber's razor in my history class.

I always have a nameless sick feeling in my stomach. I pray that no one else will sense the fear that seems to hover about my heart like an invisible vapor. Jax beer is thirty-five cents a quart. We get loaded with some regularity during the lunch hour, and fifth and sixth period go by in an indolent, hazy stupor. After school I beat up another boy in order to impress a girl. He's a likable and decent person who has done nothing to provoke what I do to him. Later he will forgive me, but that violent moment, born out of my own

fear and self-loathing, will remain as the most cowardly and cruel act of my life.

I'm never called to task for it.

There are occasions when you get whacked in the coach's office with the blade of a boat oar that has been sawed-off, sanded, and drilled with holes to lessen air resistance. If you're stand up, you don't blink with the blows or let the pain show in your eyes. The coach lets you know this is what happens when you piss in the shower or sass a teacher or an administrator. The paddle is wrapped around his wrist with a leather thong and remains with him wherever he goes.

"What's a snarf?" a sophomore asks Jerry Jeff one morning in metal shop.

"You don't have a mirror at home? A guy who gets off sniffing girls' bicycle seats," he answers.

No one ever reports Jerry Jeff for making and selling weapons. Nor is he or his friends ever reported for beating and rolling homosexuals. It's all common knowledge, like rut bursting inside the jeans, part of the day, the week, the month, the year, perhaps even part of a fearful adult awareness of what could happen if the eye alights upon the wrong situation.

But there's no record of any of it, except in memory, the way a face marbled with bruises can float in and out of your ken, voiceless, degraded, asking for redress from those who have the power to give it.

In high school English class I seldom read the assigned material *(The House of the Seven Gables* by Nathaniel Hawthorne was an academic favorite in the early 1950s). Instead, I read *Gone with the Wind, The Amboy Dukes, Hot Rod, Kiss Me Deadly, Battle Cry,* or any available paperback novel about ex-Confederate soldiers wending their way across Texas during Reconstruction.

I wrote my first poem when I was seventeen. It dealt with a Confederate officer returning to his burnt Georgia home. I showed it to my eleventh-grade English teacher, who read it thoughtfully and indicated to me that I had probably taken it from someone else's work. I hadn't, but I took her remark as a great compliment. I was a terrible student, and if an English teacher thought my poem had been written by a published writer, then indeed, I told myself, it must be pretty good.

My problem as a beginning writer, however, was point of view and concept. I believed that art had to deal with elevated subjects and make use of elevated language. Profanity and the ribald seemed the stuff of Mickey Spillane. Also, literary stories were about the lives of exceptional characters, noble and heroic ones, certainly, who were somehow emblematic of an era or a unique kind of experience.

In other words, they weren't like me or anyone I knew.

It's late afternoon, summer, and through the third-story, wire-mesh barred window you can look down upon the tops of the oak trees and the cooling shadows along Ryan Street, hear the music from the hillbilly juke joint on the corner, watch the heat lightning dance over the lake and the wetlands that drain into the Gulf.

It's not an exceptional environment, just a typical Deep South jailhouse gig of 1955—one cast-iron lockdown unit inside an enormous room called the bull pen, a pitiful collection of check writers, drunks, wife beaters, barroom brawlers, two or three strong-arm robbers. Max time in is two one-year consecutive sentences; the meals come at 7:00 A.M. and noon—sausage, white bread, black coffee, grits, and spaghetti—leftovers for the afternoon stinger that gets heated up just before lockdown at five o'clock.

The serious area is across the hall, beyond the deadline and the main door (the deadline is the white rectangular stripe inside which no inmate is allowed, at least not without consequence, when the trusties or jailer enter the unit). The electric chair and the executioner travel in Louisiana, from parish to parish, and no one has any doubt as to when they're in town. The generators on the flatbed create a grinding sound that makes some close their windows and doors even in ninety-five-degree heat.

Across the hall, at midnight, earlier in the year, a freshly showered, head-shaven man, in dungarees, an immaculate white T-shirt, and cloth slippers, threw up in a toilet bowl, wiped his mouth on a towel handed him by his executioner, then waited mutely in an oak chair while people he didn't know strapped down his limbs and prepared to cook him alive.

But that was across the hall.

"Don't you want to get out of here?" I ask.

"It ain't so bad," Deek says. "Two pretty good squares. Then we got the stinger in the afternoon. You gotta work out there, man."

"I thought that jailer was going to hit me."

"You shouldn't have been inside the deadline."

"I think he's bad news."

"No, man, your thinking is bad news. Nobody breaks the Man's rules, nobody has no trouble."

"What happens when somebody breaks the rules?"

He stands up from his bunk, his naked upper torso as white as a snake's belly, points an index finger at me, and walks away.

But two events happen that are not expected and are certainly not good for the jailer's self-image or career.

A mainline con, a recidivist sociopath from Angola, a big stripe, is shipped in to testify at a trial and is kept in temporary custody at the parish prison. In the shower his hard body glistens like gray stone. He eats by himself, his thoughts masked, his spoon scraping methodically against the tin plate; at a certain point, when he's had enough, he smokes a cigarette then mashes it out in his remaining food.

At noon he lines up with the others for macaroni and white bread and black coffee. He eats one spoonful, lights a cigarette, rises from the sewage pipe that traverses the bottom of one wall, and flings his plate into the open iron-door, inches away from the jailer's head. The macaroni slides and oozes down the door, across the locking mechanism, onto the floor.

The jailer says and does nothing. He waits while the trusties back the food carts out into the hall, then he eases the door shut and locks the bar across the jamb.

Later, three armed-robbers are brought in, escapees from a prison in Nevada; they're wanted in a half-dozen states, filled with manic energy, wired on goofballs, contemptuous of a tin-can holding-tank.

One hour before lockdown, during an electric storm that drenches the town and litters the streets with shattered tree limbs and downed telephone lines, the three escapees rip the covers off a dozen tick mattresses, tear a steel bar out of the window mortar, and use it to peel the wire-mesh screen loose from the bolts that are set in the outside stone.

In minutes they've disappeared down their cloth rope into the howling storm, into Ryan Street, into all the vast potential of the free people's world.

The next morning is bright and hot and the walls sweat with humidity. An old man in boxer undershorts, with elephantiasis in one leg, is caught unaware inside the deadline when the door swings open.

The jailer shoves him to the cement floor, hard, intentionally.

No one speaks. When the jailer leaves, Deek stares at the flat gray surface of the door, a lucifer match tucked in the corner of his mouth, his face bemused.

On a sheet of lined Big Chief notebook paper, with a pencil stub, one man writes up what happened and everyone signs it. The next man out carries the story to the local newspaper.

It's printed on the letters to the editor page; in fact, it's boxed with a black border.

The upshot is seven days in the hole, in lockdown, in midsummer, for everyone. No showers, no visitors, no chance to swab out the toilets.

"You'd have to carry the stink out of this place on a shovel. It ain't right," Deek says, the light from a guttering candle wobbling on his face.

"What's not?" a truncated man called Short Boy says.

"We didn't break the rule. An old man like that don't count."

Short Boy is silent.

"They sent reporters when them big stripes cut their tendons at Angola," Deek says.

"Maybe they'll still do that. It could happen."

"You think?"

"Why not?"

"Yeah, it still could, huh? Yeah, they got their ways. They might be writing it all up now."

They continue to talk in the sweltering darkness, three blocks from a newspaper office, where most of the lights are off, the staff is gone, and Negro janitors with tired faces are mopping the floors.

There were few creative writing programs in the 1950s. Places like Stanford and the University of Iowa were famous exceptions. At Southwestern Louisiana Institute I took my stories to one or two professors for criticism and felt fortunate to receive their encouragement. Then after two years there, I went on to the University of Missouri at Columbia, where fiction and poetry workshops were taught by people like John Neihardt, Don Drummond, William Peden, Bill Hamlin, and Tom McAfee. At age twenty-two I started a novel titled *Half of Paradise*. By the summer of 1959 I had written a hundred pages.

But something was wrong with it, or the conception behind it. It began with an account of a Confederate officer and his black servant returning to south Louisiana after the surrender at Appomattox Court House. The characters and the locale were good ones, and I seemed to have the right emotional kinship with them, but I felt as though I was not rendering them in an accurate way. I felt that the world I wrote about had to be sawed whole out of sonnets; it had to possess the Arthurian vision of William Faulkner or the poetic fatalism of Tennessee Williams, or it would not be any good.

But what was it in Williams that made a character like Valentine Xavier more than a male prostitute, or Faulkner's haunted aristocracy anything more than self-pitying dipsomaniacs?

I didn't know.

I read Thomas Wolfe, W. Somerset Maugham, Erskine Caldwell, Ernest Hemingway, James Joyce, F. Scott Fitzgerald, Eudora Welty, Caroline Gordon, Katherine Anne Porter, Gerard Manley Hopkins, Henrik Ibsen, George Orwell, and Arthur Miller. In fact, I think I tried to read everyone who had any influence at all on twentieth-century poetry, fiction, and drama.

Then I began reading John Dos Passos and James T. Farrell in earnest.

Nineteen fifty-nine is the first year that Franco's Spain has been open to tourism since the Civil War. Some of my fellow students in the international dormitory at the University of Madrid are also from the American South and they, too, have known police whose charge it is to represent the interests and well-being of the rich. But life in a fascist country is something none of us is quite prepared for.

The average Spaniard is never allowed to forget the severity of the war or who lost it and who was victorious. In the park across the street from the dormitory are the remains of the Loyalist lines, bronze statues riddled into erect pieces of scrap, concrete machine-gun bunkers and the sides of classroom buildings pocked from shell fire. American volunteers, the George Washington and Lincoln brigades, fought and suffered terrible casualties in these same trenches. But on a porcelain-blue day you can gaze above the chestnut trees, out over the edge of the plateau on which Madrid is built, and watch the squat, olive-green shapes of World War II German Junkers, with their peculiar corrugated fuselages, going through training maneuvers while strings of paratroopers stream out their open doors, their chutes popping open like cotton bolls against the sky.

If you still doubt who won the war, you can ride the electric streetcar early in the morning down the Gran Via, past the Air Ministry Building, and watch the Guardia Civil, with their rubber truncheons, Schmeisser machine guns, and flat-backed, lacquered black hats, changing the guard at the sentry boxes, or the enlisted men from the barracks goose-stepping along the flagstones, outfitted with 9-mm Mauser rifles, hobnailed jackboots, and Nazi helmets that flange over the nape of the neck.

As in most dictatorships, the poor in Spain are quite visible, their roles well-defined. In the southern part of the country they live in state-sponsored stucco communities set close to the highway, out in the middle of arid wastes that remind you of biscuit-colored moonscape. The dwellings are brilliant white, barracks-like, contiguous, hooked one to the other; and on one wall are always the blue-lettered reminders *¡VIVA ESPAÑA! ¡VIVA FRANCO!*

In the city there are no beggars. The elderly are given jobs selling lottery tickets in small wooden booths along the avenues. Often they are blind or soon will be, because a strange disease of the eyes afflicts many Spaniards, one that begins with a raw inflammation around the eye, just as if the person had been burned by a flame or chemical, and gradually destroys all the optical tissue. No one is ever able to give me an adequate explanation of its cause or why no treatment is apparently available.

Peasant girls from the country who do not want to spend their lives in white-washed stucco rooms located on moonscape come to Madrid and work as housemaids and scullions, many of them in University City where I attend classes, or sometimes they end up working the street trade on the Gran Via.

It's not a low-rent area. The boulevard is lined with trees, sidewalk cafes, theaters, wine shops; the parks are full of children, shaded tables, stands that sell *horchata* and hand-cranked ice cream, sprinkled with cinnamon.

But the girls, many of them beautiful, are out on the street twenty-four hours a day. They either sit with their pimps in the cafes or stand in the middle of the sidewalk, waiting for a U.S. airman from the Strategic Air Command base or perhaps an *inglés* from the university.

They hit you with two fingers across the forearm, hard, and demand *"Por qué estás solo, hombre?"* (Why are you alone, man?)

I'm told they have short careers. By age thirty they are either ridden with disease or look like sacks of potatoes. One day a buxom dark-haired woman in a sundress, her pimp on one arm, stops on the sidewalk in front of our table and begins shouting at me. She's incoherent with rage, and I have no idea what she's saying or why she has singled me out.

"Have I provoked you in some way?" I ask in Spanish.

Her pimp thinks it's all an amusing affair. He puts his hand in the small of her back and escorts her down the street while her lips keep moving in profile.

"What's that about?" I say to Ian, an English student who rides the streetcar with me each afternoon to the Prado or the Retiro.

"They do it for a few years and eventually they have syphilis of the brain."

"Depressing stuff," I say.

"Try Portugal."

"What a country."

"It isn't Iowa."

"What's that mean?"

"Your president seems to get along quite well with these fellows. You know, hands across the sea, American supplies for suppressing peasants, that sort of thing." He looks at my face. "Sorry . . . next time, tell me to work it."

The cleaning girls in my dormitory sweep the floors each morning with short-handled brooms that cause them to stoop almost double. I can never understand why no one gives them long-handled brooms, or, for that matter, mops, because once the sweeping is done, they wipe the floors on their hands and knees with rags and pails of water.

Carmina is the girl who cleans my room and makes my bed each morning, even though I try to convince her that the room is already clean and I'm capable of making my own bed. Her workday starts at 5:00 A.M. and ends at 10:00 P.M. She's twenty-three years old, comes from a village in Andalusia, and thinks that Madrid is a glorious city. She is given room and board in the servants' quarters and fifteen dollars a month and has Sunday afternoons off. She has a boyfriend in the army, and after lunch on Sunday she meets him in the park and they sit under the trees together.

I return from class Monday morning to find her wiping down my floor on all fours. She's a thick-bodied girl, with broad shoulders and thick chestnut hair on her neck, and her dress and gray apron are spotted with water from the pail.

"I really wish you wouldn't do that, Carmina," I say.

"You speak foolish things," she says, without looking up.

"Excuse me?"

"If I'm not allowed to clean the room, then I have no function here."

She straightens her back and squeezes out the rag in the pail.

"I sewed the torn button on your shirt," she says.

"Carmina—"

"Was it supposed to sew itself?" She pauses, her face exasperated. "You're a nice boy. Did you enjoy the bulls yesterday?"

"The cruelty to the animals bothers me."

"The bulls are a stupendous thing," she says. *"Una cosa estupenda."*

"Would you like to go next Sunday?"

She rises to her feet and shakes her finger back and forth.

"I didn't mean to offend you," I say.

She doesn't answer. She picks up the pail and her rags and hurries down the hall.

You don't cross class lines in the Generalísimo's Spain.

That afternoon I sit in a cafe in the park and work on my novel in longhand. It's a beautiful, blue-gold day, with a cool breeze blowing through the trees, and I have a hard time concentrating on the story about Iberia Parish, Louisiana, and the descendants of a Confederate officer. Not far away is the gray cylindrical shape of a machine-gun bunker. The area around the two steel-lined firing slits looks like it was beaten with ball-peen hammers. I fold my notebook on my fountain pen and walk to the bunker, rub my hand over its cool surfaces, and look inside. The floor is strewn with rubble, newspapers, empty San Miguel bottles, feces, discarded rubbers.

This is the only monument to the people who defended Madrid against Franco's Falangists and Hitler's Luftwaffe. I watch a street cleaner in a purple beret sweeping the gutter with a straw broom, a corked green wine bottle protruding from his denim coat; the white-jacketed waiter turning the crank on an ice-cream maker; a bovine woman in black who sells flowers and Biosonte cigarettes from a cart. What memories are locked in their minds about the war, the sacking of the cathedrals, the mass executions in Jarama, the atrocities of Moorish troops when they were turned loose on working-class neighborhoods? Was the blood of Spain ever truly washed from the stones in these tree-shaded streets?

That same night Ian and a U.S. marine out of uniform and I go to a nightclub that sometimes is frequented by Truman Capote, who has written his name on one wall. It's a brightly lit, smoke-filled, happy place, crowded with revelers, guitar players, singers, well-dressed prostitutes, dancers who career about the small dance floor, waiters who bring pitcher after pitcher of sangria to the tables.

Then two other players enter the club, drunk, unshaved, mean-spirited with an ideological bent, cruising for trouble any way they can get it. Someone gladly obliges by pointing out that some *inglés* are drinking at a back table.

The two drunk ideologues position themselves in front of our table. Their faces are pale, their eyes red, their dress shirts spotted with wine. One taps his knuckles on the tablecloth to emphasize his point.

"Los Estados Unidos son mierda," he says.

"What's that mean?" the marine, who's from Dallas, Texas, asks.

"He's telling you the United States is shit," Ian says.

"How do you say fuck you bud in Spanish?" the marine asks. *"Chinga tu madre?* Ain't it something like that?"

"We don't care about your politics. Do you want a drink?" I say in Spanish to the drunks.

But they will not be appeased. I thought they were leftists but we soon discover they're Falangists who believe Franco has sold out the fascist cause. They launch into an arm-waving tirade.

"Oh-oh," Ian says, glancing at the other tables.

"What are these guys saying?" the marine asks.

"They're giving the old boy a proper reaming, I'm afraid," Ian answers.

Then the band takes a break, and suddenly you can hear the voices of the two drunks resonating off the far wall.

It's not yet eleven o'clock but the club empties in less than five minutes. The evacuation is orderly, but it's immediate and there's no doubt about the cause. No one is left in the club except some dispirited band members, the waiters, the two drunks, and us.

I go to the bar to pay our bill. The waiter adds it up with a pencil and hands it to me. His face is morose; his lips a tight line.

"Thank you for the evening. We had a fine time," I say.

"Thank you, too, sir, and please never come back," he says.

"I beg your pardon?"

He walks away without answering and begins stacking the chairs on the tables.

It's raining when we go outside. I become separated from the others and take shelter in an open doorway. The streets are glazed with pools of yellow light from the overhead lamps. I see two Guardia Civil in raincoats, their hats hooked low on their brows, walking toward the entrance of the nightclub. Then I suddenly realize that I'm not alone in the doorway, that a woman is standing behind me. Her makeup is garish, like a harlequin's, deathly white, with a gash of a mouth; she stinks of *anís* and cigarettes and dried rut; her teeth are pink and wet when she smiles. Her fingers seize my wrist with the strength of pliers. *"Por qué estás solo, hombre?"* she asks.

I have four days in London before I return to the United States. It's only September but the air is damp and cold and smells of automobile exhaust and chimney smoke. In my hotel room I read James T. Farrell's descriptions of Irish neighborhoods in south Chicago and the fear and ignorance that his characters struggle with like cobweb wrapped around the eyes. My novel about the American South sits on my desk, the characters still caught somehow in a historical time capsule that denies them breath.

What am I doing wrong?

In John Dos Passos I meet biographical figures and groups of people I never read about in an American history book: Joe Hill, the songwriter executed by firing squad in the Utah pen; the Wobblies and the Molly Maguires; Elizabeth Gurley Flynn, the sweetheart of the Industrial Workers of the World; the nameless thousands beaten with clubs, jailed, run out of town, murdered by company goons on picket lines in Ludlow and Hazard or wherever working men and women tried to organize for a fair wage.

Did no historian or academic or publisher of textbooks think them worthy of inclusion in the formal record of our country?

I walk down to a used bookstore by the British Museum and buy a water-stained paperback copy of *Bound for Glory* by Woody Guthrie. It's a stunning book and I read it until late at night. I fall asleep with an image in my mind that has the dreamlike quality of light trapped inside a bowl of purple mountains, as the smells of windblown cattle cars on a siding and irrigated water coursing through alfalfa. I see Woody and Cisco and a gang of Mexican migrants picking melons in a field whose borders are lighted by piles of burning cedar; the hands of the Mexicans are sheathed in calluses, their faces as darkly gold as worn saddle leather.

But their story ends in a plane that explodes over Los Gatos Canyon. When Woody writes an elegiac song for his friends, he remembers how the radio referred to them as just deportees.

George Orwell once asked his reader to list the names of slaves whose names survive from antiquity. Spartacus comes to mind. Frederick Douglass. Perhaps two or three others. Out of untold millions.

I often wondered if the victims at Auschwitz or Bergen-Belsen scratched their names on a stone, a shower wall, a plank under their straw bedding. Did they try to leave behind some mute indicator of who they were, their passing, the flame that became their lives?

On my last evening in London I visit friends in a lower-income neighborhood made up of brick row-houses with narrow alleys and desiccated wood porches at the back. As I walk back toward Victoria Station the sky has started to clear and looks like a red-tinged ink wash. At the end of a long block I glance back at the sun on the rooftops, the handkerchiefs of smoke from the chimneys, wash strung between two second-story windows over an alley, the wet purple light on the brick paving in the street, the violent green of a solitary tree in a small park.

It's not the kind of place I ever thought of writing about. But I know that it's the southside Chicago neighborhood that James T. Farrell described in his novels about Studs Lonigan, the block where Woody Guthrie lived in New York when he was writing *Bound for Glory,* the homes of the young English idealists who fought alongside George Orwell in Spain.

Then a strange event happens to me, one as much like an epiphany as I'll probably ever experience as an artist. The platform at the station is crowded with waiting passengers, the air dirty with the clatter of train cars, crying children, the shriek of whistles, a blistering argument among a group of French tourists. My ears pop, as though with cabin pressure, and for just a moment I can hear no sound whatsoever. I feel as though I'm surrounded by hundreds of people who have been struck dumb simultaneously, although their mouths continue to move and their faces are animated with intense and private meaning.

Orwell once said he wrote in order to set history straight. For the first time I understand what he was talking about. I'm convinced that every person I've known in my life is somehow there on that platform: Jerry Jeff from metal-shop class, the hoods with chains in their hall lockers, the boy I hurt in order to impress a girl, Deek the mainline con, the jailer and the old man he shoved to the concrete, Carmina and her boyfriend in the Falangist army, the blind sellers of lottery tickets, Ian and the Texas marine and the Spanish waiters who probably watched or participated in the work of firing squads, the syphilitic and deranged girls of the Gran Via, each of them voiceless in a different way, their failed attempt at words and explanations rising from their lips like dry moths.

To assign oneself the role of giving voice to others is probably an arrogance and a vanity, but for me it would become a lifetime compulsion, and I suspect it hasn't been entirely a bad vice to have.

A Special Place Where You Live

It was a Sunday evening, the burnt-out end of a scorching July day in 1957, and our seismograph crew was waiting for the company boat to pick us up at the levee and take us back to the quarter-boat, deep in the Atchafalaya Basin, for another ten-day hitch out on the water. Our shooter, or explosive man, who was a part-time Fundamentalist preacher in Mississippi, sat next to me on his duffle bag, in the warm shade of a willow tree, playing a bottleneck, slide guitar. Storm clouds that were the color of broken plums were piled on the western horizon, and you could smell salt in the wind and the odor of something beached and dead out in the marsh. He sang:

> *"Ten days on, five days off,*
> *I guess my blood is crude oil now.*
> *I reckon I'm never gonna lose,*
> *Them mean ole rough-necking blues."*

He leaned his guitar against the tree trunk and folded his hands. His watchband covered part of a wide red scar across the bottom of his wrist.

"That about says it, don't it?" he said. Behind us, a half dozen of our crew were coming out of the beer joint, combing their hair, hawking and spitting, squinting against the red sun. "One of

these days I'm gonna give it up, do what I'm suppose' to."

"What's that, Bud?" I asked.

"Work at the church back at Wiggins. I done got too old for this kind of life. It makes you old, son."

He was right; there wasn't much romantic about offshore or marine seismograph work, or what was sometimes called "doodlebugging." In fact, in those days it was considered to be the lowest, dirtiest, most unskilled form of labor in the oil fields, outside of building board-roads in the marsh. We worked long hours in one-hundred degree heat on a cast-iron drill barge, whose every surface by midday would blister your bare back, and strung recording cable through swamps filled with cottonmouth moccasins and mosquitoes that would boil out of the mud and hum around your head like a gray helmet.

The men on that crew were the most unusual I had ever known. I suspect that some, if not most, of them were borderline psychotics. They opened pop bottles with their teeth and burned warts off their hands with Zippo lighters. One of the boat skippers had been in Angola pen and another was a pimp on his off-hitch in Morgan City. The shooter, Bud, handled dynamite, explosive primers, and nitro caps all day but could not understand why he had ulcers, since he didn't drink or smoke. Many of them had worked with each other for years, but they didn't know each other's last names. Often their names were either initials—W.J. and J.W. in particular—or derogatory: Doo-Doo, Weasel, Tee Nigger, Rod Flogger, and Dog Shit. Their skin was burned as brown as mahogany; they looked fifty when they were thirty; they had misshaped bones where they had been hit by pipe tongs, stumps where their fingers had been pinched off by drilling chains.

They talked constantly of women and race, and like most southern poor white males, they had the lowest self-esteem of any group of human beings I ever knew. Their lives were governed by phobias that their lack of education would never allow them to define: fear of homosexual desire in themselves, fear of women, and of course fear of all blacks, whom they regarded unconsciously as their sexual superiors but upon whom they also looked as the primary source of their economic privation.

The irony is that I never encountered a more stoic and physically brave group of people in my life. They were glad to have the work and never complained about the primitive conditions in which we lived or the low pay we received. Like Roman legionnaires, they were the cutting edge of a vast empire and had pipelined, doodlebugged, and drilled oil wells from Greenland to Saudi Arabia to Venezuela but had little idea of where those places were on a world map. On the fifth night out the party chief allowed a crew boat to take a group to the levee, where they piled into cars and pickup trucks and drove to the red-light district in Morgan City. At six the next morning we would hear the crew boat thump against the rubber tires that hung down from the gunwales of the quarter-boat, and moments later the revelers would stumble into the galley, stinking of whiskey, blood, beer, and rut; then they would drink scalding black coffee, vomit over the rail, and work ten hours on the drill barge under a sun that looked like a white flame in the sky.

On one of those nights I sat alone in the dining room, with a tablet of lined, yellow paper, trying to write a short story in longhand. Bud walked out of the galley with a cup of coffee in one hand, his slide guitar in the other, and sat down at the end of the long, plank table where I was working. He began twisting the tuning pegs on his guitar and twanging each string with a metal thumb pick. I kept writing and didn't look up, hoping to finish the next sentence before I lost it.

"Whatcha doing?" he asked.

"Working on something of my own."

"You looked intense, all right." Then after a pause, "You writing a letter to a girl?"

"I'm writing a short story."

"You mean for a newspaper?"

"Not exactly."

"Why you writing it, then?"

"I want to be a writer."

"I thought you was making to be a preacher."

"No, not me."

He had a round, sunburned face, sandy hair that was cut close to his head, and watery green eyes that always looked bemused behind his steel-rimmed glasses.

"I thought that was why you never went with them others," he said. "I don't blame you, though. Them places'll mess you up. You like girls?"

"Sure."

"You got to be careful with them. They can turn you around, mess up the way you think. I had to learn that."

"I see."

"I done got too old for all of it, though," he said, standing up and straightening a crick out of his spine. Then he stared through the screen window at the fireflies lighting in the flooded cypress trees, as though their electric tracings contained a portent that only he understood.

I had rented a mailbox at the university post office in Lafayette, and during the off-hitch I lived in a rented room and worked on my stories in both longhand and on a portable Smith-Corona typewriter. On the fifth day, just before I would drive back to the levee for another hitch out on the water, I'd put everything new that I had written, or every story that I had revised, into eight-by-eleven envelopes and mail them off to magazines in the United States and Canada.

When I would get off the next hitch, the rejections would be waiting for me in my rented mailbox. But I learned a system that I would keep for the next thirty-five years. I never let a story stay at home, unless I was revising it, for more than thirty-six hours. The rejections didn't matter. I knew that a story's failure, as well as my own, was a foregone conclusion as soon as I put it away in a drawer or cabinet; I was convinced that eventually the right editor would be sitting at the right desk at the right time when my story came through the mail slot. And you reduced the odds against you by the amount of exposure that your story had.

The rejections were always the standard printed ones, so they were never personally offensive or injurious. Later, I would discover that there are people in publishing, not many, but some, who, like some newspeople and academics, are drawn to their profession for reasons of power and not out of love for words and literature. These are the ones who will deliver the insult, the contemptuous remark, and mask it as literary criticism. You learn to detect them early on and to give no credence to what is actually an oblique expression of their own self-loathing.

I had no thematic or empirical direction at all in my work. I had a novel in progress about the French underground, about which I knew virtually nothing, set in Paris, where I had never been. I wrote Western stories based on my mother's family in south-central Texas; I tried prizefighting stories for male magazines like *Saga* and *Argosy;* I wrote a story about the crucifixion and sent it to a Catholic magazine, knowing nothing about the magazine except that it was Catholic and that it published fiction; then I had a fling with experimental interior monologues that were so abstruse that not even I could understand them two days after I had finished them.

I wrote an article on how to get your hens to lay more eggs by using heat lamps in your brooder house.

When I would come back from the on-hitch, my rented mailbox would be packed so tightly with my returned self-addressed stamped envelopes that I could hardly pry them out of the box.

But I can say in all honesty that the rejection of my work never bothered me, at least not in a personal way. For the first time I started to write about the world that was closest to me, and in so doing, I realized that my art and my life were becoming one. Everything that I saw and did, in one way or another, traveled from the eye, through the arm and hand, onto the page. I knew that even my sleep, my dreams, were becoming part of my art, which meant that the entire twenty-four-hour period in any given day was part of something much larger, part of an ongoing story that was never lost, that the world of sky, trees, earth, and water was always translating from the eye, through the arm and fingers, onto the page.

I remember that summer for its terrifying lightning storms out on the water, the four-o'clocks that bloomed as scarlet as blood around Spanish Lake, the way the early sunlight looked like shafts of spun glass in the oak trees—the gift that each morning brought, like a strawberry bursting against the roof of your mouth—Jimmy Clanton's "Just a Dream" that was on every jukebox in Louisiana, the evening crab boils and fish fries and Acadian bands on Bayou Teche, the smoke from meat fires drifting through the flooded cypress, the distant watermelon-smell of the rain when it blew out of the south, sunsets that turned the clouds into flamingo wings and filled the twilight with the droning of cicadas.

I knew then that life in south Louisiana was a party and I only needed to write about it in an accurate way, and no matter how many rejections my work received, the world I wrote about would never be the less for it, would never change or be impaired in any way, and eventually an editor would say, *Hey, podna, that's not too bad.*

My last hitch on the water was right after Hurricane Audrey decimated the Louisiana coast, tore one-hundred-year-old oaks out of the earth like celery stalks, and sent a tidal wave into Cameron that curled over the town like an enormous fist, crushed it flat, and killed 550 people.

I was packing my duffle bag in my small room on the second deck of the quarter-boat when Bud came in and sat down on my bunk. I could hear the other men playing *bouree* in the recreation room at the end of the corridor, their voices rising and falling against the suck of the huge window fan behind them.

"You hanging it up to go back to school, huh?" he said.

"Yeah, I guess so."

"They're talking about all them bodies floating in the marsh down by Cameron." He combed his hair and clipped his comb inside his shirt pocket. He crinkled his nose under his steel-rimmed glasses. "It don't bother me, though. I've saw worse at Saipan. That's why you get you a private place in your head to live in."

I pulled the drawstring on my bag and tied it with a slipknot.

"You know what I'm talking about?" he asked.

"Sure."

"No, you don't. It's a place where they cain't turn you around. Them other boys don't understand it, either."

"I'll keep it in mind, Bud."

"Well, don't catch the clap," he said, then lifted himself off my bunk, put his hand on my shoulder, and let it slide down the back of my arm for longer than it should have been there. "Did you hear me?" he said.

"Yeah, I did, Bud." I could feel my muscles constricting away from his touch.

"That's good," he said, and his fingers began to knead my arm.

"I've got to put this on the jug-boat," I said, and threw my duffle up on my shoulder so that it separated our two bodies.

A half hour later I was on my way to the levee, sitting on the bow of the long, flat, high-powered boat that we used to lay out underwater recording-cable and seismic jugs, the wind blowing cool in my face, pink mullet jumping in our long troughlike wake, the sky painted with fire on the western horizon, the tiny windows of the quarter-boat lighted against the black-green overhang of cypress trees where it was moored.

I didn't publish anything that I wrote that summer nor did I ever again see any of the men with whom I had worked on that doodlebug crew. But the following year I started a novel entitled *Half of Paradise*, and much of it, in one way or another, would include the people and events that were the most immediate in my experience and I would give up forever trying to write fanciful stories in which I had little emotional investment. I would write most of that first novel in graduate school and while I worked on a pipeline in Texas, and finish the rewrite two weeks after my twenty-fourth birthday, but its publication would be almost more difficult than the actual writing of the book, which was always a joy. During that period of the book's rejection, and, later on, during a thirteen-year period when I couldn't sell anything in hardback in New York, I came to learn the meaning of Bud's admonition about creating a special place in which you live.

No, *create* is the wrong word. You earn that place, and it's yours forever. It's like a private cathedral, suffused with light from stained-glass windows, a place where you go when virtually everyone says your work is wanting, inadequate, not quite viable for the market, or simply no good. Or you go to that place if you teach in a college or university and find yourself surrounded by academics who sneer at accomplishment and loathe the prospect of the artist in their midst. You know that the talent you have was given to you for a reason, by some power outside yourself, and as long as you're true to that gift and you use it wisely and with humility in the interest of something that is greater in value than yourself, the purpose of the gift eventually will be fulfilled and the beneficial influence you can have as an artist can be beyond your greatest expectations.

Bud probably had lightning bolts in his head, as most of the men on that seismic crew did, including me (as I was later to learn, after a long courtship with living out there on the rim, where you daily invite losing it all); but in his peculiar way he was talking about the same ethos that my original sponsor in a twelve-step fellowship described to me during that period when I could publish nothing, could not think of the world except as a place where you slid shards of glass across your palms, and believed, truly, that lobotomy was not the worst alternative a person could have.

He said, "Don't keep score, noble mon. The score takes care of itself. Just keep bearing down on the batter, then at the bottom of the ninth, glance over your shoulder at the numbers up on the board in the outfield and you'll be pleasantly surprised."

I guess I've learned that, in one way or another, it's always the first inning; every day is the full-tilt boogie; and it's not always bad to have sparks leaking off a few terminals or to subscribe to an unreasonable view of the world.

About fifteen years ago I sanitized the people from my old doodlebug crew and wrote a long

James Lee Burke, Montana, 1993

short story about them. I submitted it to a New York literary editor, a friend and very nice lady who was not easily taken aback. The content of the story, all true, and the portrayal of the characters in it sent a wave of nausea through her that she could hardly find words for.

The story remains unpublished to this day.

But for me, the best stories were always to be found in the lives of people who might be considered the walking wounded, the brain-fried, what I call the Moe Howard account, the people who need diagrams for shoe-tying. Normalcy is dull, and a rational and analytical view always leads to more dullness.

For me it's still 1957, or any window in time that the pen wants to create. And I always know where there's a cathedral that smells of incense, votive candles, water, and cool stone. It's not a bad way to be, I think.

"Lessons in Race, Dialogue, and Profanity" first appeared in *The Southern Review,* Winter, 1993; "1950s Hoods, James T. Farrell, and the Girls of the Gran Via" was originally written for this series; and "A Special Place Where You Live" first appeared in *Epoch.*

BIBLIOGRAPHY

Fiction:

Half of Paradise, Houghton, 1965.

To the Bright and Shining Sun, Scribner, 1970.

Lay Down My Sword and Shield, Crowell, 1971.

Two for Texas (historical novel), Pocket Books, 1982.

The Convict (short-story collection), Louisiana State University Press, 1985.

The Lost Get-Back Boogie (also see below), Louisiana State University Press, 1986.

"Dave Robicheaux" series:

The Neon Rain (also see below), Holt, 1987, Mysterious Press (London), 1989.

Heaven's Prisoners, Holt, 1988, Mysterious Press (London), 1989.

Black Cherry Blues, Little, Brown, 1989.

A Morning for Flamingos (also see below), Little, Brown, 1990.

A Stained White Radiance (also see below), Hyperion, 1992.

In the Electric Mist with Confederate Dead, Hyperion, 1993.

"The Convict" is anthologized in *New Stories from the South* and *Best American Short Stories,* 1986. Also contributor of short stories to *Antioch Review, Atlantic, Epoch, Kenyon Review, New England Review, Quarterly West,* and *Southern Review.*

Andrei Codrescu
1946-

Andrei Codrescu, 1991

Against Photography

Unlike most people I was not born but *snapped* and I was not gestated but *developed*.

Both my parents were photographers. And both of them were Jewish. They were bad Jews because they were photographers. God said, "Thou shalt not make graven images," and both of them did.

My father's graven image shop was on the main street in my hometown of Sibiu (or Hermannstadt) in central Transylvania, Romania. My father did all the graduation portraits of the local high schools and technical schools, and also weddings and portraits. The graduating classes posed for group portraits that were then displayed in shop windows up and down the main street. Marrying couples came into the shop directly from city hall. When I graduated from high school I refused to wear the school uniform in the class picture. I was the only one out of fifty people who didn't wear a tie. And I insisted that my pseudonym be used under my picture rather than the name I suffered years of school with. My father's shop was long gone by the time I graduated—as was my father—but I was driven. When our portrait was displayed, people remarked: "He changed his name and isn't wearing a tie because

"My mother in front of her photo shop in Sibiu before I was born. During the Soviet occupation," 1945.

plained about the brightness of the sun. "Don't ever say anything like that about the sun again!" the policeman warned me. I couldn't wait to get back into the darkroom. Even today, I live in cities of the night, like New Orleans, and don't fully come to life until sundown.

My mother's photo studio was called Baby Photo (my mother's nickname was Baby, a very chic monicker in Romania, where the word was redolent of exotic fragrance, bubblegum, nylons, and Big Bands, a whole jazzy post-War longing that never materialized because the Russians came instead of the Americans . . . but that's another story). Baby Photo was at the very end of the central street by the train station, and the clientele wasn't as upscale as my father's. Mother photographed soldiers and their girlfriends, Gypsies, and peasant grandfathers brought in by their families from the countryside to be photographed before they died.

I grew up playing in the shop, and being photographed. I was my mother's favorite subject. She squeezed me into leather *spielhosen* and velveteen shirts, and had me stand with one leg up on a lace-covered pedestal with my elbow on my raised knee and my head perched sideways on my hand. This elaborate and unnatural position involved the creation of a correct face that my mother coaxed from me by threats, insults, endearments, and sometimes—when it failed to materialize—by tears. "Don't make that face!" she'd begin, clicker in hand to the right of the huge camera that dwarfed her, "That's an ugly face! You look like a butcher! Don't grin like that! Why do you punish your mother with those rolling eyes?! Is this why I was born? So my child can make a face like that?"

Amid the laments and the curses my seven-year-old brain raced through the muscles of my face in search of both the appropriate configuration and the most inappropriate because, let's face it, I was delighted by the attention, by the complete critique of any face I chose to invent. I knew the face that "looked like a butcher," the mug that "broke your mother's heart," the countenance that made her question her existence. It was all there, the ontology and eschatology of a mother before the son in search of the photographable mug. At long last, the clicker clicked and I was captured.

Stiff, cramped, in pain, insecure, and exhausted I stand there in the early 1950s looking toward a point in the future when I would be released. That point came soon after Stalin died, in 1953,

he's mad at his father!" My father, in turn, had been mad at God, which is why he made pictures.

My mother and father spent most of the six months that they were married to each other in the darkroom of the photo shop. I was no doubt conceived in the darkroom. And afterwards, I baked there inside my mother under the steady red light for six full months, the time I believe that it takes most major organs and most of the brain to form. My outline must have been there in any case, as well as certain vital shadows. I was then violently wrenched into the light by my parents' divorce.

My mother did not get her own photo shop off the ground until two months after I was born. I spent those two months in the sunlight with the family of a policeman while my mother got herself on her feet. These people were pagan. They were sun worshippers who slapped me when I com-

when the whole world behind the Iron Curtain let out a great sigh of relief and everyone's face muscles relaxed slightly. Some even smiled. Stalin's huge portrait, which adorned every building and school wall, came down. In its stead, other pictures took up the space. Our mono-pictural black-and-white world gave reluctant way to a serial picture world with hints of color in it. Of course, it wasn't until I left Romania in 1965 that I realized that the world could be multi-imaged and colorexplosive, and that people could actually wear unconstrained faces.

Those early '50s photo-sessions left me with a permanent terror of cameras. Whenever someone points one at me now I run automatically through a repertoire of faces before I settle on the one I have approximately decided is correct. It doesn't really matter who's behind the camera, there is only one photographer, my mother. And so to the question of somewhat larger import, "Who's watching?" I can truthfully answer, "My mother," and I believe that this is the case for most people whether their mother was a photographer or not. Mothers watch. And, as John Ashbery put it in a poem: "All things are tragic when a mother watches."

There is also only one photograph: Stalin's, and that is the other story. My mother may have photographed me but the end-product was a picture of Stalin. In those days, Stalin was everything. If you were to ask a school child what two plus two was, he answered: "Stalin." Likewise, if you handed someone a picture of their recently departed grandmother and asked who they were seeing, they said: "Stalin." There was no one else. Given the elementary authority of that world, as well as certain subsequent developments, I can never believe that photography is in any way "objective." The photographer, who is the watcher, is always the parent, the subject is always the child, and the end result is always Stalin. And Stalin resembles the photographer more than he resembles the child. The child, like nature, is only there to be used by authority, machines, and the authority of the machine. And this result, this photograph of Stalin, is always tragic.

Among the arts, and for me, photography is the saddest. Even if I grant you that there are in this world photographs that are not photographs of Stalin, their effect has to be tragic. Photographs are the object of a pointed melancholy having nostalgia on one end and metaphysical despair on another. When it is people I look at in pictures I am sad because they are not there. (And they are

not there even if they stand right beside me.) When I look at pictures of nature or objects of any kind—though I am not very much moved by these, I much prefer faces—I am struck by their strangeness, by their impossibly alien existence. And all other photo compositions, no matter how formally interesting, sadden me because they are based on the existence of an ideal which, curiously enough, is the world we live in. Platonism did not truly exist before photography. Photographs make it clear that a tragically unknowable reality capable of leaving traces on photographic paper was once present. But these pathetic traces, no matter how skillful, are only an elegy to the real, a lament for a love long gone.

Baby Photo was equipped with painted cut-outs: there were bodies of uniformed generals with gold epaulets for soldiers to stick their bodies through; wasp-waisted evening-gowned fin de siècle beauties with a hole for a head where girls from the Stella Soap Factory could stick their own;

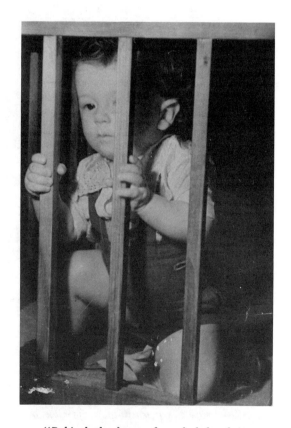

"Behind the bars of my babyhood in Transylvania. My first political statement."

a park bench with a sickle moon on a wire behind it on which sat a well-dressed Parisian or Viennese dandy with his arm in the air: the young lady who wished to be photographed with him slid under his arm and rested her head on his narrow shoulder; there was also a beautiful girl of that same era with an inclined head under which a young man could slide his shoulder. In addition to providing men with the uniforms and the bodies of authority, and women with the curves and frills of La Belle Epoque, Baby Photo had a horse, a mule, and a huge rabbit for children.

In 1953, shortly before Stalin died, my mother landed a government contract to photograph all the Gypsies in Sibiu for newly required identity cards. The job took two years, so between the ages of seven and nine we had Gypsy families practically living with us, occupying every inch of floor, eating, whistling, singing, breast-feeding babies, and quarrelling. The decibel levels were astonish-

ing despite my mother's assistant Radu's half-hearted stabs at restoring order.

One by one they paraded before the cameras, men, women, women with six babes in arms, old men and women, thousands of faces, day after day. Before I left for school in the morning, the place was already filled with a stormy rustling of wide skirts, the clinking of coin necklaces, the echoes of playful slaps, and lots and lots of giggling. The men had wide-brimmed black hats that they removed only after a great many threats by my mother to call the gendarmes (the pictures had to be full frontal), and the women hid their faces behind scarves or babies. When I came home from school, they were still there, taking large bites out of fried meat (they made fires and cooked in the alley behind the shop), asleep one on top of another, and full of unexpected (for me) glimpses of tantalizing flesh under carelessly lifted skirts. I studied the breasts of girls barely older than me while babies suckled on them and wondered

"My mother's grandfather's family: prosperous Transylvanian Jews with only a few years left to enjoy." (Mother is seated at left, and her sister Amci is seated at right.)
Alba Iulia, Transylvania, Romania, 1930.

"My mother (third from left) with her aunts, all of whom perished in Auschwitz. My grandmother's sisters did not follow our family across the border into Romania. They stayed in Hungarian Transylvania and were shipped to their deaths." Alba Iulia, Transylvania, Romania, 1938.

secretly what it would feel like to kiss those big full nipples. As my mother photographed their faces I mind-photographed erotic glimpses of bodies at rest and play. I was extremely sorry when the project came to an end two years later, in part because I'd made friends with two Gypsy boys my own age who had no inhibitions whatsoever about spying on their sisters and who knew the best times and vantage points for so doing. A week or so after the project was concluded, I visited with this one particular band on the outskirts of town behind the railroad tracks but two days later they vanished, to my mother's great relief. She'd had enough, although for years afterwards, she loved showing her friends the shop register where she had written down the Gypsies' names as required by law. They had all named themselves after handicaps: there were hundreds of *Surdu* (deaf), scores of *Mutu* (mute), and *Orbu* (blind). Whatever their real names, they had managed to turn a perfect deaf,

mute, and blind mirror to the register. I was not surprised to hear later that the Gypsy identity card project was a complete failure. The Gypsies burned their ID cards as soon as they got them, and the government had to content itself with a census. Instead of photo IDs the Gypsies had numbers. That suited them fine. In the whole country there is now only one Gypsy: No. 3458.

These Gypsies had good reasons to feel queasy about IDs. More than ten years before, only one year before I was born, they had been interned in concentration camps. All of them, with the exception of children, were survivors. Tens of thousands of Romanian Gypsies had perished in camps. They did not want to be photographed. They knew enough about the State and the police to avoid photographs at all cost.

My mother must have understood their sadness well as she clicked face after face. My mother, her sister, her sister's husband, and my grandmother had crossed the Hungarian-Romanian border at night in 1943 to avoid deportation to the death camps. My grandmother's two sisters, my great aunts, perished at Auschwitz. They perished along with millions of others, a whole world of faces that exists now only in faded photos.

In 1936, a man named Roman Vishniak, possessed of an extraordinary urgency, crossed and recrossed the borders of Poland, Hungary, Romania, and Carpathian Lithuania to take pictures of Jews. Braving incredible dangers, using a hidden camera, he roamed the ghettoes and the shtetls, and secretly recorded that vanishing world. He took 16,000 pictures of which 2,000 survive. He smuggled some of the negatives sewn into the lining of his coat out of Europe to America. It is difficult to look at these images. It's nearly impossible to keep in mind that the people we see ceased to exist immediately after the pictures were taken. These people went to their deaths almost exactly as we see them: in the puzzle of their childhoods, in the perplexity of their old ages. We see them all: scholars argue through the grey slush of Europe; wide-eyed children look to their teachers, the Torah open in front of them; sages, rabbis, zaddiks, Hassids in flapping black vestments and wide-brimmed hats. The European Jews of 1936, my mother's aunts and cousins, had been marked for destruction. Vishniak's children, from Seder scholars to street ragamuffins, share a seriousness and understanding beyond their years. In the crumbling innards of the old Polish cities, the threadbare objects of poverty glow with a life of their own. Here is a peddler with two customers, bent over a coat, carefully examining the fabric. There is an incredible *materiality* too in this coat, paradoxically suggesting its opposite, spirituality. When this coat falls apart, this whole world will go with it. Soon, human beings will also become things, to be discarded and junked.

Vishniak said that he felt that he was on a mission from God. In that case, it could not have been the God that had said "thou shalt not make graven images." Or perhaps it was the same God, allowing himself a tiny contradiction within a larger and more terrible meaning. Vishniak's camera is on a mission, a calling that is the opposite of the camera of the State intent on recording every face within its authority. Vishniak's camera redeems in a small way the use of the camera in our century, a use, by and large, infinitely more useful to the destroyers of people than to the lovers of them. The camp guards at Auschwitz all had good German cameras. They wanted to show

their children one day what their technology had accomplished. These children, their descendents, are today's tourists. They too are taking pictures for *their* children: pictures of native peoples in quaint poses before picturesque arrangements arranged for pictures by the Tourism Bureau (the framer of remnants of the real for picture-taking). Well, at least, one might say, tourists aren't *killing* anybody for a picture.

Is *that* the difference between tourism and terrorism? Tourists are terrorists with cameras, while terrorists are tourists with guns. Tourism is the civilian aspect of imperialism. After the natives have been pacified by force of arms, we finish the job with the cameras. It's no coincidence that both activities are called "shooting." It's hard for me to look at old *National Geographics* without feeling an anguished nausea. There they are, on display, the dead freaks of worlds we have destroyed. They've left forms behind for the use of the fashion industry.

In Rome a few years back my family and I strolled about with cameras around our necks and baseball hats on our heads, looking for all the world like *touristi Americani,* which we were. It so happened that Aldo Moro, the Italian premier kidnapped by the *Brigate Rosse,* had just been murdered and deposited about a street away from where we were, on Via Caetani, halfway between the Communists' and the Social Democrats' headquarters. Hundreds of screaming Italian police cars took to the streets, and trucks full of carabinieri were rushing in from the provinces. One of these came to a screeching halt in front of us, and a police captain holding a machine gun leapt out in front of us. "What's the way to the police station?" he asked. In stilted tourist Italian I told him: "Go straight. Make a right. Then a left." He saluted, thanked me, and they took off in the directions I'd pointed them in. Only I'd made up the directions. I'm not sure what exactly went through my mind but I must have reasoned that if the obvious tourist getup hadn't deterred him, there was no reason for me not to act like a native. And natives, particularly in Rome, answer at length any question you ask them, even if and especially if they don't know the answer. So—the camera, you see—is not a *complete* defense against the stupidity of the police. Both tourists and terrorists shoot what they can't quite tame. To finish with the camera what your grandfather started with the gun is both easier and harder. The souls we steal may be our own.

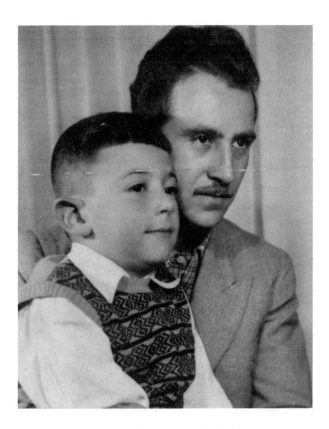

"With my father, Julius. One of the few times we were together," Sibiu, about 1955

My own revolt against my father the graven image maker took the form of bursting into the crowded waiting room of his shop one summer afternoon and shooting my cap pistol. By the time the smoke cleared, half the customers had fled, and my father had me in a headlock in the darkroom, lecturing on decorum. He wasn't looking at me. My act had been revenge, I suppose, on all the faces my father *did* look at.

Years later, in 1976, I still hadn't received my American citizenship, though I'd been in the United States for ten years. My only piece of identification was a so-called "white passport," a re-entry visa, really, that allowed me to come back to the United States if I strayed over the border by mistake or something. I never carried this for fear of losing it. I didn't drive then—so—no driver's license.

One very late night in California, my friend Jeffrey and I were driving up a country road in Mendocino in search of a nonexistent address when the lights of something huge and unearthly

were suddenly upon us. It was the CHP—the California Highway Patrol—and a tall cop strolled out with a flashlight and a shotgun. He asked Jeffrey for his driver's license, and then he came to my side and said, "ID!" Now the only ID I had with me was my autobiographical book called *The Life and Times of an Involuntary Genius,* which had my picture on the cover. The cop took Jeff's ID and my book, and went back to his cruise mobile. He put his feet out the window and started reading. Eons passed. Billions of stars died in the sky over our heads. I slept. I had dreams. Summer turned into winter. At long last, the cop came back. He looked at me long and hard. He then tapped my face on the cover with his trigger finger. "Anybody can fake a picture like this!" he said. "Sure," I said, "but wouldn't it be easier to fake a regular ID?" "OK," the cop said, *"this time!"* I believed him. Every ten years now I produce a new autobiography with a fresh picture for that cop. *Photos para la autoridad! Flores para los muertes!*

When Jeffrey died later that year, in a different car, I had the urge to look at pictures of him. One of our friends had been shooting a lot of our get-togethers with his video camera. When I saw the tapes, I found, to my dismay, that instead of Jeffrey's face—or anybody else's face for that matter—my friend had "composed" shots out of fragments of trees, elbows, house tops, and clouds. Another reason to find art loathsome—for its effects on dilettantes.

I tried to use my book for identification in banks, in supermarkets, and at public events of various kinds where it was sometimes accepted, sometimes rejected, depending on the imaginative stretch of the guard dog.

My first book of poetry was called *License to Carry a Gun.* It also had my picture on the cover. I was standing with one foot in a garbage can on First Street between First and Second Avenue in New York where I lived. A few years later I got a job teaching poetry in Folsom Prison in California. The first time I presented myself at Folsom I gave the guard my poetry book in lieu of ID. He called his boss on the phone. A huge man with hands that looked like they cracked bones for a living came down. He looked at my picture, he looked at the title—*License to Carry a Gun*—and then cracked open my book with his knuckles, and read. He then picked up the phone and called *his* boss, a guy no doubt ten times larger who ate men's livers for breakfast: "It's just fucking poetry, boss! Just fucking poetry!'' he said. So the picture was good enough after all.

The moral from these two incidents, if you're looking for one, is that most people in charge of enforcing the law still have no doubts as to the equivalence between pictures and reality. Consequently, we ought to keep postmodernism a secret.

I had a dream once that life and death were positive and negative photocopying respectively. I saw the DNA strands being copied and was reassured. In that light, we are all copies, but I am a copy in the most exacting sense, thanks to Mom and Dad. Eventually, everyone will have to work out the precise sense in which photography engenders them. For me, photography presents the oedipal pure, but that's just luck of the draw.

You could say that my relation to photography is that of photography to the world: I come out of it but I don't necessarily give back a pretty picture. The day I burst into the full waiting room of my father's shop and discharged that cap gun I took charge of myself. The smoke and the shots that caused panic among his Sunday-best dressed customers gave birth to the unphotographable self.

Two pieces of advice then to the would-be photographer: 1) Pay attention to the thing you photograph, and 2) Try to love it.

I hope I'm not obscuring the issues. There is a great place on Bourbon Street where you can take your picture in a jail cell. That's where I'm going.

And then there are clearly unphotographable things that you can see. In 1973 I tried taking a picture with my 35mm of my two naked girlfriends in front of a poster of the kid guru Maharaji but the pictures didn't come out. I tried Polaroid. No go. The poster or the guru did something to the light.

In 1973, the year that the political soap opera Watergate mesmerized the nation, I wrote the following poem:

About Photography

I hate photographs
those square paper Judases of the world,
the fakers of love's image in all things.
They show you parents where the frogs of doom
are standing under the heavenly flour,
they picture grassy slopes
where the bugs of accident whirr twisted
in the flaws of the world.
It is weird,
this violence of particulars
against the unity of being

Despite my accent, which makes "f-l-o-u-r" sound like "f-l-o-w-e-r" and "w-h-i-r-r" sound like "w-e-r-e," and despite the ancient, awkward problem of putting Judas in the plural—which I did out of the instinctive self-anti-Semitism in which I was steeped as a child—this poem gets at my feelings about photography with remarkable ease. The functional word here is "weird," which was the word with the widest possible circulation in America during Watergate. If being has any unity in the age of television it is weird—to say the least—trying to fathom it through the fragmented and framed instances of specific pictures. What is one to infer of American life—and inner life—by looking at the triple-chinned mugs and black-rimmed eyes of our elected leaders, our meritocracy, standing trial for trying to hijack American democracy?

It is now more than twenty years later—long enough for a young man or woman to have been born, grown, and sent off to be killed in a war at the request of the successors of the discredited administration of 1973. A war, moreover, that was so well packaged by the administration on television that not a murmur of dissent penetrated the skillful wrappings.

I probably don't have to tell you that the taking, selecting, and distributing of pictures is a highly manipulatable business. In the past four decades, and most intensely in the last two decades, the ideological education of would-be mind controllers has been concerned almost exclusively with the business of image-making. For example, the so-called revolution in Romania in December 1989 was an event staged for television by Securitate—the Romanian secret police—and the KGB—the Soviet secret police. In order to arouse the masses, they produced a number of images for TV: the most famous one is the "Madonna and child" picture, which shows a young woman and child lying on the ground, killed by a single bullet. This image was shown over and over on the TV screens of the world until the alleged murderers took on mythic Hitlerian dimensions. In fact, this was a fake produced by collaging a picture of a woman who had died in an alcoholics' hospital with that of a baby dead of different causes. A bullet was put through them, and they were seen accordingly. This image was followed on Romanian TV by footage of Nadia Comaneci winning triumphantly in Montreal in 1976. The two pictures together said: "Here is the genius of our nation, nipped in babyhood by the monsters of the old regime."

Other images were equally bogus: children murdered on the steps of the Timisoara Cathedral, an image which gave rise to the extraordinary reports that sixty thousand people had been murdered in Romania, turned out to be a collage as well. The net effect of all this camera-work was to make millions of people believe that they were witnessing a spontaneous revolution while a coup d'etat was taking place. But in fact a revolution DID occur, a mass revolt that was highjacked via television from right under people's noses. Today in Romania a neocommunist government hatched in conspiratorial secrecy by the police claims to be the legitimate representative of this revolution. But it isn't. It is the representative of "revolution" between quotation marks. The most immediate effect of image manipulations is the placement of "reality" between quotation marks, the creation of a fundamental mistrust in the evidence of one's senses when confronted with slick images to the contrary. The evidence of one's senses has at its disposal only a very clumsy, very old defensive language, while propaganda and manipulation command a sophisticated technical arsenal that make human beings seem evolutionary throwbacks by comparison.

Someone out there in the recesses of literature flattered himself a few years ago by saying, "I Am a Camera." I remember also the beginning of a novel by William Burroughs: "The camera is in the eye of the vulture," after which he proceeds to describe everything from the vulture's vantage point using an interesting speeded-up cut-up language that tries to keep up with the vulture-speed of the camera.

Before photography was an art, with all the pretensions and baggage of that activity, it served art by freeing it from the conventions of realism. The camera made modern art possible by freeing artists from the tyranny of the eye. The crucial moment in the history of modern art occurs in the Salvador Dali/Luis Buñuel film *An Andalusian Dog* when a razorblade slides across an eyeball. Henceforth, art is free of the exigencies of reporting

"My mother's inscription on the back: 'Friends who drove us to the train station when we were leaving Romania,'" Sibiu, 1965

reality according to the eyes. That becomes the job of photography. Of course, it wasn't long before Man Ray and the Dadaists discovered that in the twentieth century "art" should be placed between quotation marks. Art with a capital A was dead as soon as the first picture was taken and a long process of debunking—still in progress—was in order. The photograph brought Art down from its pedestal and gave it to the masses to have fun with. Which left artists desperately searching for new specialized stances in the mechanically violated wilderness of representation.

And I will not even mention Walter Benjamin.

When the violent subjectivity of early avant-gardes showed signs of being exhausted, being a camera or an eye became art's first postmodern obsession. Implicit here was a certain regret at having ceded such a useful description of reality to a machine, but also envy at the infinitely productive capacity of photography. In the 1950s, in the age of existentialism, when it became obvious to everyone that the human race was doomed by the A-bomb, it became fashionable to feign lack of feeling, a kind of psychological "objectivity" whose ideal practitioner was the camera. Some artists confused the workings of the camera with objectivity because it provided a metaphor for indifference, both the existential and the Zen kind. For them, the camera made it possible to conceive of looking at something without feeling, which is to say without guilt. The camera seemed to make vision blameless; it provided the act of looking with a possibility of innocence.

However—the camera is no innocent instrument. Or rather, the instrument may be innocent but there is no innocent use of it. There is no moral difference between a camera and a paint brush. Both are—precisely—instruments. Nonetheless, the camera continues to provide the metaphor of objectivity in a kind of theoretical space. With the populist snapshot at one end and the military satellite photo on the other, the camera is as complete a topographer of reality as we are ever likely to have. In short, the camera has conquered the world and the world it shows us is the way we now articulate reality. Which opens up wide the possibilities of manipulation.

We now read the world according to pictures of it stitched together either by powers behind the scenes or by the technological process itself. In any case, the end result does not benefit the majority of the people for whom the new imaged "reality" is an opiate that extorts their energies.

In the second or third wave of postmodern difficulties with the image, which is right now, few people say any longer, "I Am a Camera." The last I-Am-a-Camera people were the punks, or rather the catatonic wing of the punks who resented mightily the wavy impressionist hippies with all their shimmering light and idealized distortions. The severest punks were strictly black and white and they moved as little as possible. Their drug of choice was heroin–the most photographic of all the drugs.

More to the point than I-Am-a-Camera is my own case, which is I-Am-a-Picture.

Because of its teasing relation to reality, photography can be made to convince people of things that aren't necessarily good for them. Pictures can lie, transmit propaganda, and change the evidence of one's senses to the point where reality disappears. Photographs also make it possible to substitute images for reality when the dread of the real becomes too unbearable. That is, I believe, where we stand now in our time. We are forcing ourselves to believe in the simulations of reality all around us because we are quickly losing the vestigial organs for direct apprehension of reality.

And I want to put a curse on police cameras everywhere. I hope that aliens, mucking about the ruins of our planet, run into a full set of *National Geographic*s, rather than into the millions of dreary mugshots that prove that our world was a dingy prison-planet.

It's a matter of degree, of course.

Adding to My Life

In the first chapter of my third autobiography, the narrator—that is, myself—stands before the world's greatest authorities on autobiography, about to make a speech.

My previous two autobiographies were the result of accident, but each one begins with the equivalent of standing before people trained in the judging of lives. In the first one, titled modestly *The Life and Times of an Involuntary Genius*, it is my mother before whom the impending story is about to make its cheeky and devastating appearance. "You're not old enough to wipe your nose!" my mother exploded. "*I* should write my autobiography! *I* lived!" That was doubtlessly true, but she would never do it. She had not only had too much life but she had such an active quarrel with it that she would have been hard put to find anyone to address her story to. I was twenty-three years old: I had had as much life as I cared to remember and my audience—beginning with my mother—was vast. There were more potential witnesses to my life than there had been people in my life so far—a heady feeling. I could add them all to my life by writing my life. Which is not why I wrote the book, but it was a thought. Furthermore, it was high time that I became the author of something I could call "my life" in order to get on with it. Saying farewell to my mother, leaving her story, as it were, was not simply a matter of individuation. It was also a matter of sabotaging her story, a less than benign thing.

Just before the book came out I asked my mother about a certain incident I had labored hard to render accurately. It was about the time she left me with my grandmother, the Baroness, in Alba Iulia. I was five, and the Baroness kept chickens. There were chickens everywhere in the formerly grand manse she now had the top floor in, and both my mother and I were sternly warned to watch where we walked because there were eggs everywhere. In fact, there were eggs in my bedroll when I went to sleep, and I woke up the next day holding in my hands two miraculously unbroken eggs. It seemed to me that over the years this story had become something of a legend among our kin. But my mother, when I asked her about it, said that the Baroness kept little pigs! That, further- more, I was only three when I went to live with her, and that I was only there for one month. I remembered living there for a year. PIGS! I wasn't about to change anything so dear to me, so I let it slide. A year after the book came out, I was visiting my mother in Washington, D.C., and she said that she felt very sorry that she'd had to leave me with my crazy grandmother and her chickens when I was five years old. "BUT MOTHER," I said. "PIGS! WHATEVER HAPPENED TO THE PIGS?" "What pigs?" She was annoyed. Denied ever having said anything about pigs. It had been chickens all along.

A strange power this, changing your mother's memory cassette! Her memory just crumbled before the printed page—which may explain in a small way why, in places where history has been falsified by the authorities, people are hard put to remember their true experiences. It's chickens for everybody, whether they like it or not.

My friend Michael Stephens wrote a wonder- ful memoir called *Season at Coole*. It is composed entirely of fights at the dinner table of his huge

"Young pioneer, vaguely aware that he will see The Loneliness of the Long- Distance Runner *at a local cinema in a few years"*

New York Irish family. His father never spoke to him after the book was published, and claimed to have never read it. He had been a New York customs official. After his father died, Michael married a Korean girl whose family sent them beautiful old furniture. Thinking to ease the duties on the antiques, Michael told the customs chief at the docks that he was old Mr. Stephens's son. The man looked him over carefully, then asked him: "You're not the one who wrote the book, are you?" "No," said Michael, "that was my brother." "It's a good thing," the boss said, "because we're still looking for the s.o.b. who wrote that book. When we find him we'll break all his bones!" Turns out that old man Stephens had come to the office every morning for the past ten years, read a page of Michael's novel, and made everyone's life miserable the rest of the day.

My own life didn't cause such widespread unhappiness only because my mother wasn't anybody's boss. But she expressed her displeasure emphatically by announcing that she could never share my accomplishment with her friends. "Oh, why," she lamented, "did you have to call it an autobiography? Couldn't you call it a 'novel'?"

It is curious how, in the face of disaster, people suddenly reach for form. At the edge of the abyss they begin to have these formal thoughts—if only the genre had been changed . . . this wouldn't have befallen me. It's like getting religion before dying: one is suddenly beset by alternatives.

Every book needs a proper address. My mother was the one I addressed my first book to because she had been my author until I became one myself. But that isn't why I wrote the book. George Braziller, who published a book of my poetry, glimpsed between the rarefied vistas of my verse certain hints of stories. He suggested I write an autobiography, a suggestion I found absolutely intoxicating. Here I was, twenty-three years old, the possessor of a wealth of experience which had already spawned an equal if not greater quantity of mythicizing anecdotes. I had no axe to grind. I'd changed countries and languages at the age of nineteen, a neat break that could provide a thousand books with rudimentary structure. In addition, I had the numbers: born in 1946, became conscious with the Hungarian revolt in 1956, came to the United States in 1966. Initiatory structures in plain view, natural chapter breaks for the taking. I had already practiced all the anecdotes and revealed their cosmic import to my new American friends in the process of learning the language. I was learning to view my journey, if not *sub specie aeternitatis,* then at least as a quest. I was a tragic hero because, most likely, I could never go home again, but I was having a great time on the way. Since I did not speak any English before I came to the United States—with the exception of a single sentence I will reveal shortly—I used my life story to buy my way into my new world. I had no money either. When you're that broke—without language and without money—you are doomed to a kind of choreography, a language of gestures and primal sounds that promise the coming of a story, as soon as some of the details—things like words and food—take their place within the structure. The only thing I had was my story which, I was convinced, was the price of admission to everything. Money, I believed, and still do, is most people's substitute for a personal story. The symbols it buys always tell the same story, namely the success story of the prevailing culture back to the culture that spawned it. Money is one's way out of autobiography and into the collective myth. The currency of outsiders is their personal story: Here I am. Let me sit by the fire. In return, I'll tell you about these pigs. . . . Of course, not speaking the language intensified the story about to unfold by announcing that it was also a *first* story, a genesis myth. Here I am then, rising from the need to tell my story, gathering language around it as I go, *un pequeño Dios* conscious of nothing but its coming into being. And your attention, of course!

The one sentence that I was mighty proud to have put together in English, with the help of my friend Julian in Rome, six months before I came to the U.S., was:

WHY DON'T YOU KILL YOURSELF?

We tried it out on people around the train station in Rome. A bunch of hustlers and pimps

"Graduate of 'GH. Lazar' Gymnazium, poet and rebel, filled with contempt for life as we knew it"

were hanging around the fountain there. We walked up to them:

"WHY DON'T YOU KILL YOURSELF?" Julian asked.

They had a conference. After some deliberation, one of them pointed us in the direction of the self-service machines inside the station. He thought we'd meant those by "self," places where you could get soft drinks and sandwiches. Since then I've always associated "self" with those "self-service" machines and think of "self" as a coin-operated contraption.

This primal notion served me well when Mr. Braziller offered to pay my advance to my life story in monthly installments. I literally constructed my life story in increments spewed out every time he inserted $250.00.

The Life and Times of an Involuntary Genius was written in the third person (with one chapter, a letter, in the second person singular). I needed this particular distance to view the self under construction. I reserved the first person for oral versions of the story, particularly ones meant to elicit an immediate response: "Hi! I'm Hungarian. Can you spare a dime?"

Ten years after the writing of *Life and Times*, Lawrence Ferlinghetti of City Lights Bookstore asked me to write a sequel. He'd read the first one and wondered what had happened afterwards. I was curious myself because what had happened is that, meanwhile, I'd become an American. The sequel, which is not really a sequel at all, is called *In America's Shoes,* and it begins with an address to the Immigration and Naturalization Bureau, an entity I fought a long battle for citizenship with. Instead of addressing myself to my mother, I began this book by addressing myself to the State.

In the first chapter the agent in charge of my case is looking through my voluminous file. I see my life passing through the policeman's eyes, arranged in an order alien to me, alphabetized by offenses and suspicions, a life that resembles mine in all but the structure of the narrative. Of course, I tell myself, "file" is an anagram for "life"!

In order to leave the world "my story" rather than "their story," I proceed to write my autobiography. This time the book is in the first person singular, an emphatic first person at that, because the file is in the third person. The first person now sets up a new distance, not between self and self, but between self and the State. In fact, this book, *In America's Shoes,* is an elaborate identity card.

It was my great luck, coming into America in the late sixties, to encounter several wayward myths ready-made for me, Transylvania being but one of them. Transylvania at the time of my arrival was a growing myth, full of potential, and anybody who bought stock in Dracula then must feel like an investor in early McDonald's. In the past two decades I have seen Halloween overtake Christmas as the nation's greatest holiday, and Dracula become bigger than Jesus Christ, and even John Lennon. Queasy at first about this Hollywood fantasy, I later considered it a gift. The dark stranger who bites blond Anglosaxony in her semisleep is the outsider, par excellence, the exile who brings history to a halt with his story. His bite ends being in time, it jumpstarts eternity, overthrows daytime and the bourgeoisie, reinstates aristocracy and difference. And it was a great way to meet girls. I never abandoned the profoundly gloomy existentialist disposition of my rebellious Romanian generation within which I had been raised as a baby dissident destined for great things and prison. No, I just put on a cape to complete the picture. Ionesco, my previous totem, was only a literary Dracula. To be bit by the absurd is every bit as liberating as being bit by an immortal, but why not be bit by both?

The advantages of being a literary exile in a culture obsessed by a myth of it are numerous. The most obvious one was that I was able to gain admittance to a community of my peers with the promise of a story that was, at least in the beginning, only a series of gestures and inarticulate groans. I was able to obtain credit at the bank of the future on the strength of my generic mythical assets.

My mother, who looked for security as well as acceptance, had no active myth to see her on her way. Her generation, in America, was a television-narcotized middle class that had been traumatized by the rebellious younger generation, and was suspicious of foreigners if not downright xenophobic. Her next-door neighbors in Washington never smiled, and her attempts at making friends had been rebuffed or perhaps simply lost in the cracks between manners where all the sad foreigners end up. Her story had no one she could properly address it to, which is why she couldn't write her autobiography, no matter how many momentous events had befallen her. She could have addressed it to me, but I'd heard it many times already, and I disagreed most strenuously. My chickens, unless printed, rarely won the day. Her story was by far more tragic, and more typical than mine. She

"My mother at her first job in America, color separator of Progressive Color *printers,"* *Washington, D.C., 1966*

struggled like all energetic immigrants to make a living, and possibly some money. The money was to show the people back home that she'd become a rich and powerful woman. Most of all she wanted friends. She made a living. She didn't make any money. She didn't make many friends. People her own age eluded her because, by and large, they preferred the soap operas they could all enjoy together to the peculiar life story of a single person in broken English. It was not because they lacked compassion but because the same myths that helped me, Dracula and exile, were enemies to them, the myths of their children who caused them nothing but pain. Had my mother become a rich and powerful woman she might have written her autobiography. It would have been addressed to her mother back in the old country, a skeptical soul who never believed that things were different elsewhere. To prove it she lived with chickens—who don't fly far, and can be easily caught and eaten.

Having the assistance of a wayward myth is a special kind of luck, vouchsafed to certain Romanians by Logos Central. Without it, no story can be rightly heard. This is what breaks all those tens of thousands of hearts who imagine that simply

because they have had an eventful life there is a reason for writing it down. At times all those cabdrivers who were once former prime ministers, and those heroes of wars no one cares to remember, achieve a kind of epiphany regarding the importance of their lives.

"I wrote this book as a warning: I have lived through terrible things and I have been saved only in order to tell the story. This is my mission: otherwise why did everyone have to die while I went on? And go on, driving this cab which is a vehicle of destiny and a cage for stories. I was neither stronger nor luckier than the rest. Something or Someone kept me here to write this book. But a terrible thing must have happened to this Someone, because no one wants to publish my book. I have no choice but to pay a vanity publisher to publish it: the world will hear my story this way if this is how it has to be. I am going to the bank tomorrow to borrow money against the house. Ah, happy day! The book is published! I will pay the bank back for the book with the money I will make: the world will cry and buy. Or rather buy and cry!"

Days pass, then years. The world isn't buying because the world never sees it. Vanity publishers do not distribute the thousands of sad lives that they publish. They bury them, and that's the final joke. Most people were kept alive not to tell their stories but to have their stories BURIED. They were kept alive to be made fun of. LIFE IS FUNNY, no doubt about it.

Of all the kinds of literature, autobiographies, no matter how humorous, are the least funny. After all, how much genuine irony can an autobiographer muster? At best he can apply the benign version known as "affectionate irony." Anything stronger would be too strong: one's life, after all, is something one is disinclined to knock, even—or especially—if one wove it out of whole cloth. After all, one has taken the trouble to write it and, if for no other reason, labor must be respected. If one's life seems funny to one the result is more likely to be silence or awkwardness. Life is funny all right, but not the way one was hoping for. Most likely, funny things happen in the course of one's life, and those things, through the insistent refinement of being told over and over, become "funny stories" because they amuse listeners over and over, containing as they do, endurable and instructive doses of pain. A collection of these "funny stories" is in truth a terrible thing taken altogether because the life in question is nothing but a series of coverups, a horrific giggle stretched over an open wound spanning time. If a life is all "funny stories" the biography itself is the saddest book ever written. The novelist cabdriver who has just banned smoking in his cab finds out that his house is burning. He can add this to the list of instructive experiences for the sake of which he's been kept alive.

In the past two decades, there's been a proliferation of life stories, both autobiographies and thinly disguised autobiographical fiction. The latter, however, for one of those reasons of publishing fashion that are completely mysterious in their transparency, are more in vogue at the moment. "I would like you to write another autobiography," a well-known publisher said to me, "but make it a novel." My mother would have been pleased.

Whence the reluctance? "Whence the reluctance?" I asked him. "Well, to be perfectly frank, you're not famous enough," he said. "This is the time of Iacoccas!" It was. At the American Booksellers' Association meeting that year, every book being pushed was an autobiography by someone who was not a writer. Writers, in other words, if they wanted to live in the same world as the Iacoccas, had to hide their lives in novels. Autobiography had suddenly become a form for the rich and famous. There was no call for the outside story. At some point during the time since my last autobiography, time had started flowing backwards. When Andy Warhol said that in the future everyone will be famous for fifteen minutes, it sounded funny because time was still flowing forward. Then fifteen minutes became five minutes, then nanoseconds, and now we can safely say that everyone *was* famous for fifteen minutes at one time or another. Time flows back from the future now, already full of the velocity of a superfluous past which is being divided by several Iacoccas. We are longing to become part of the picture we have already been put out of. The mirrors there, at the junction between past and present, make it appear that there are thousands of Iacoccas. But there are only a few. This is the reason, no doubt, why the retroactive evidence of presence that is the autobiography is such a fiercely awkward phenomenon these days. It is proof of those fifteen minutes, which are now wholly owned by Iacoccas and Trumps.

The future of autobiography is both bright and dim like a TV set. The bright part is that the wealthy dead can now have video screens installed in their tombstones. Push this button, ye stranger going by, and see a life-sized Iacocca appear on screen speaking his life. A coin-operated contraption, this videodisplay offers a choice between fifteen minutes of distilled wisdom from a long life to a full five hours of detailed anecdotes about exactly what it took to bury such a great man.

The dim part is that fewer and fewer people can imagine a life that doesn't look like television. Up to a point, an autobiography would seem to be the exact opposite of television, the stand of the insistently personal against the collectivized story, the small tenant-farmer's resistance to the Sovietization of life. But, in fact, we know television families better than our own because they show us everything, while ours, those lumpy shapes on the couch next to us, are completely hidden. How can those strangers be so VISIBLE while we can only watch our dear ones from the narrowing peephole of our own inattentive, inarticulate, amnesiac little selves.

Our own little selves didn't use to be as little as all that. "I contain multitudes," said Walt Whitman, anticipating television by a hundred years, and going on to speak from the platform of that "I" for the multitudes we never really hear except as a background roar, like the sea. Rimbaud's "je suis un autre" has always been an autobiographer's true challenge, though in my own practice, the "je suis," most often "un jeu."

I once conceived a truly monstrous idea, and went through with it. My third autobiography, covering the ritualistic interval of another ten years, was not going to be either in the first, second, or third person singular or plural. I sent out a questionnaire to friends and acquaintances asking them to describe in their own words incidents we had experienced together. I asked them to include the story of our meeting, the story of meeting others in our circle, as well as rumors, fantasies, and fabrications. There was a special section for composing from the point of view of the subject, "hosting" myself, as it were. I collected some three hundred pages of these testimonials which range from the surreal to the minimal, and began collating them into a single narrative with a view to making a book from the point of view of everyone who has ever admitted knowing me. The "me" under construction here was Nadia Comaneci, the gymnast, the third member of the mythical triumvirate of Ionesco and Dracula. Nadia, the way I saw it, gracefully walked the tightropes of this life, which were actually the seams between the various stories. After being Ionesco and Dracula I wanted to be Nadia. This, I thought, would be the last perspective on my narrative of "self" and, no doubt, my last autobiography. In my first such book I was my own affectionate subject. In the second, I stood up to bad guys and gave them a piece of my mind. In the third, I am no longer speaking. Call me Nadia. Or ABC.

It was a great idea. The only trouble with it was that other people's stories—even though they were about "me"—bored me. The stories I had forgotten had something about them that made me see exactly why I had forgotten them. The ones I remembered, I could tell better. It's true, moreover, that whatever you forget other people remember: it's a nice thing to know in case you need witnesses in court. But amnesia is more important to art than total recall. Amnesia shapes the few remembered or misremembered scenes into whatever you're going to make. The kind of remembering that interests me is anamnesis, which is an intense flashback. Such a flashback is generally devoid of facts because it has room only for

feelings. Outfitting these feelings with facts like a grandmother with chicken feathers is a job I like very much. The truth is that I am not all that interested in "myself." I am only curious to see what kind of person is going to emerge from a certain arrangement of personal stories, which are themselves not "facts" but earlier arrangements for certain practical uses.

Furthermore, I'm only an inn for the Logos.

My early life story was recently written into a movie script by two well-meaning people. When I went to Los Angeles last week, a producer asked me if I was working on another autobiography.

"As we speak," I told him.

Here is how it starts. I am standing before a distinguished gathering of scholars of autobiographies. I hold forth for various trembling minutes until I realize that I have absolutely no idea how to end. I ramble on and on. The hall empties. I am all alone, rambling on and on. It will be two hundred years before anyone will come back.

"My wife, Alice; my son Tristan, with camera; my son Lucian, and his bride, Rebecca, on their wedding day," Charlottesville, Virginia, July 29, 1993

Informed of my failure, my mother says: "Didn't I tell you to make it a novel? Oh, why didn't you make it a novel?"

Why not indeed?

"Against Photography" was the keynote speech at the National Conference of the Society for Photographic Education in New Orleans, March 21, 1991. The speech "Adding to My Life" was presented at the Conference on Autobiography, Portland, Maine, October 31, 1989. Both are included in *The Muse Is Always Half-Dressed in New Orleans*, by Andrei Codrescu.

BIBLIOGRAPHY

Fiction:

Why Can't I Talk on the Telephone, Kingdom Kum Press, 1971.

How I Became Howard Johnson, Parnassus, 1972.

(With others) *The Questionable Hell*, Parnassus, 1972.

The Repentance of Lorraine (novel), Pocket Books, 1977.

A Craving for Swan (essays), Ohio State University Press, 1986.

Monsieur Teste in America and Other Instances of Realism (short stories and a novella), Coffee House, 1987.

The Disappearance of the Outside: A Manifesto for Escape, Addison-Wesley, 1990.

Belligerence, Coffee House Press, 1991.

The Hole in the Flag: A Romanian Exile's Story of Return and Revolution, Morrow, 1991.

Road Scholar: Coast to Coast Late in the Century (also see below), photographs by David Graham, Hyperion, 1993.

The Muse Is Always Half-Dressed in New Orleans and Other Essays, St. Martin's Press, 1993.

Poetry:

License to Carry a Gun, Big Table Publishing, 1970.

The History of the Growth of Heaven, Grape Press, 1971, enlarged edition, Braziller, 1973.

The Here, What, Where, Isthmus Press, 1972.

(With Aram Saroyan) *San Francisco*, Fits Collective, 1972.

& Grammar & Money, Arif, 1973.

Secret Training, Grape Press, 1973.

A Serious Morning, Capra, 1973.

Au bout du Monde, Four Zoas Press, 1977.

The Marriage of Insult and Injury, Cymric Press, 1977.

The Lady Painter, Four Zoas Press, 1978.

For the Love of a Coat, Four Zoas Press, 1978.

Traffic au bout du temps (poetry broadcast), first broadcast for Watershed Intermedia (Washington, D.C.), 1980.

Diapers on the Snow, Crowfoot Press, 1981.

Necrocorrida, illustrated by Alice Codrescu, Panjandrum, 1982.

Selected Poems: 1970–1980, SUN Press, 1983.

Comrade Past & Mister Present, Coffee House, 1986.

Other:

(Editor with Pat Nolan) *The End over End*, privately printed, 1974.

(Translator) *For Max Jacob* (poetry), Tree Books, 1974.

The Life and Times of an Involuntary Genius (autobiography), Braziller, 1975.

In America's Shoes (autobiography), City Lights, 1983.

American Life with Andrei Codrescu (radio programs), first broadcast on National Public Radio, 1984.

Boys with Bats (television commentary), first broadcast for Public Broadcasting System (PBS) on KTCA-TV (Minneapolis), 1985.

Miss Liberty: Centennial (television commentary), first broadcast on PBS, 1986.

(Editor and contributor) *American Poetry since 1970: Up Late* (anthology), Four Walls Eight Windows, 1987.

(Translator) Lucian Blaga, *At the Court of Yearning: Poems by Lucian Blaga*, Ohio State University Press, 1988.

(Editor) *The Stiffest of the Corpse: An Exquisite Corpse Reader*, City Lights, 1988.

(Editor) *Raised by Puppets: Only to be Killed by Research*, Addison-Wesley Publishing Company, 1989.

Road Scholar (film), directed by Roger Weisberg, Metro-Goldwyn-Mayer, 1993.

Author of columns, "La Vie Boheme," 1979–82, and "The Last Word," 1981–85, and a biweekly editorial column, "The Penny Post," all for the *Baltimore Sun*; author of monthly book column, "The Last Word," for *Sunday Sun* and *Philadelphia Inquirer*, 1982—; author of weekly column "Caveman Cry," for *Soho Arts Weekly*, 1985–86; author of weekly book column,

"Melville & Frisby," for the Baltimore and Washington, D.C., *City Paper,* of the column "Actual Size," for *Organica,* and of weekly book review for National Public Radio's *Performance Today.* Poetry editor, *City Paper,* 1978–80, and *Baltimore Sun,* 1979–83; contributing editor, *San Francisco Review of Books,* 1978–83, and *American Book Review,* 1983—; editor, *Exquisite Corpse: A Monthly Review of Books and Ideas,* 1983—; contributing editor, *Cover: The Arts,* 1986–88.

Also author of *Meat from the Goldrush* and, under pseudonym Betty Laredo, *36 Poems by Betty Laredo.* Contributor of poetry to magazines, sometimes under pseudonym Urmuz or Marie Parfenie. Contributor to anthologies, including *The Fiction Collective Anthology,* Braziller, 1975; *Kaidmeon: An International Anthology,* Athens, 1976; *The Penguin Anthology of British and American Surrealism,* Penguin, 1978; *The Random House Anthology of British and American Surrealism,* Random House, 1979; *Longman Poetry Anthology,* Longman, 1985. Contributor of poetry to periodicals, including *Antaeus, Chicago Review, Confrontation, Editions Change, Isthmus, Poetry, Poetry Review, Sun,* and *World;* contributor of stories to periodicals including *Co-Evolution Quarterly, New Directions Annual, Paris Review,* and *Tri-Quarterly;* contributor of book reviews to *American Book Review, Chicago Review, New York Times Book Review, Shocks,* and *Washington Post Book World.*

Rita Dove
1952-

Rita Dove, Poet Laureate, 1993

Even in the crib, it seems, I was a night person. "I remember waking up at three in the morning," my mother is fond of saying, "because I heard some noises coming from the nursery. And when I tiptoed in, terrified that a burglar had slipped into my baby's room, what did I find?"—here she pauses for effect—"Just little old you, playing contentedly in the pitch dark!" According to family legend, my parents tried everything to put me on "normal" time: eliminating naps during the day, keeping me up past midnight, submitting me to a sequence of aerobic exercises in an effort to tire me out. Nothing worked. To this day I remain more mentally alert in the hours between midnight and 5:00 A.M.

I would like to believe that I became a poet because of this unusual body clock, but I'm afraid I didn't entertain notions of becoming a writer until well into my undergraduate college years. Not that I didn't indulge in all of the pastimes commonly associated with the literary mind; from the age of six I loved to read, and by seven or eight I had begun writing my own stories and poems.

I made two "breakthroughs" as a child writer: one in prose, and one in poetry. During a free-choice period in fourth grade, I wrote an Easter poem called "The Rabbit with the Droopy Ear." Once I had the title, I began writing with no idea whatsoever of how the rabbit was going to be cured of his physical defect:

Mr. Rabbit was big and brown,
But he always wore a frown.
He was sad, even though Spring was here,
Because he had one droopy ear.

They were the handsomest ears in town;
'Cept one went up, and one hung down.
And to think Easter was almost here!
Alas for the rabbit with the droopy ear.

But I kept writing, deeper and deeper into the narrative, and by the penultimate stanza, the solution "occurred" with no apparent effort of my own:

The Rabbit went to wise old owl,
And told his tale 'twixt whine and howl.
The owl just leaned closer to hear
And said, "I know the cure for your droopy ear."

The next day everyone gathered 'round to see
The incident at the old oak tree.
Mr. Rabbit hung upside down
From a branch on the tree, and gone was his
    frown.

Hip, hip hooray—let's toast him a cup,
For now both ears were hanging *up!*
All the animals raised a cheer:
Hooray for the rabbit with the two *straight* ears!

It was as if the poem itself, through its cadences and narrative thrust, had told *me* the answer.

"Chaos," my first attempt at extended prose, was written over the period of one semester, also in fourth grade. Each Monday afternoon the teacher would allot twenty-five minutes for spelling; after going over the new spelling list, we were supposed to do the exercises in our text. I would quickly finish them (usually something like, "Use each spelling word in a sentence"), and then I'd write the next chapter of my epic science-fiction saga. The only rules I set for myself were: (1) each spelling word had to be used in the tense/conjugation presented, (2) the order of the list must be honored, and (3) no peeking at next week's list. Needless to say, I had no idea what developments in plot or character were going to

"My brother Ray 'Tommy' and I with our maternal grandparents,
Thomas and Georgianna Hord," Akron, 1953

occur. Again, it was the language itself that led me on; I was open to the adventure.

Though I obviously relished creating my own stories and poems, at that age it never occurred to me to think about writing as more than a pastime. I had no idea that one could grow up and become a writer, much less how to develop a life around writing.

I spent my childhood and youth in Akron, Ohio, as a first-generation middle-class black child. Both sets of grandparents were blue-collar workers who had moved Up North as part of the Great Migration of rural southern blacks to the northern urban centers during the 1910s and '20s. My parents were the first in their working-class families to achieve advanced degrees. My mother graduated from high school at the age of sixteen with a full scholarship to Howard University; but her parents decided their daughter was too young to be sent into the wide world, so she attended the local secretarial school. My father earned a master's degree in chemistry from the University of Akron. (He also completed all the course work towards the doctorate, but could not afford to take the time off from his menial job in order to write his dissertation.)

I and my three siblings (two younger sisters, one older brother) came of age in a supportive but strict environment. We knew we were expected to carry "the prize"—the respect that had been earned—a little further along the line. We had to do our best at all times; there were no excuses.

Of course we were aware of discrimination, but not as something that affected us directly— although our father had been a direct victim of prejudice in my lifetime. After graduating with honors, he applied for a job as an analytical chemist at the Goodyear Tire and Rubber Company, the chief employer in Akron. Unlike his white schoolmates, some of whom he had tutored in organic chemistry, my father was passed over for a chemist's post (despite graduating at the top of his class) and instead was offered the position of elevator operator. With a wife, son, and another child (me) on the way, he could ill afford to be indignant; he accepted the menial job and for years ferried his former classmates from floor to floor. Finally, consistent protest against this racist foolishness by one of his former professors and a change in Goodyear's management ended this indignity, and my father became the first black chemist (he's retired now) in the rubber industry.

I was not aware of any of this. My parents raised us to be proud of our heritage and cau-

"With Tommy, all decked out for church,"
about 1956

tioned us against the subtle reach of prejudice; but they were careful not to dash our hopes too early: though they related historical indignities and racist incidents, they also conveyed the impression that times were changing, and our abilities would be recognized.

Education was the key: that much we knew, and so I was a good student. I brought home straight *A*'s on my report card and hoarded the shiny dimes I got for each of them. Which is not to say I didn't like school—I adored learning new things and looked forward to what intellectual adventures each school day would bring; some of the luckiest magic in the world was to open a book and come away from it wiser after having been lost in its pages.

Among my earliest influences were relatives who loved to tell good stories; some forms of popular entertainment—rock and roll lyrics, action comic books, *MAD* magazine—had an impact on me as well. I was not reading "pulp literature" exclusively; I devoured all kinds of writing. But it was pulp literature that, as a child, I sought to imitate by creating my own—perhaps I felt that I had a better chance of emulating formulaic writing rather than Shakespeare's sonnets (which I began reading around the age of twelve) or James Baldwin's *The Fire Next Time.*

From the time I was eight until I turned fourteen, a typical summer would run something like this: my brother, who is two years my senior, would declare himself the editor-in-chief of our summer vacation neighborhood newspaper; after lengthy negotiations, I would finally attain the status of feature editor. (All of this, of course, took place before we actually set down a single word.) Invariably, I would quit in protest against his autocratic directives and establish my own magazine, called *Poet's Delight;* however, if I remember correctly, I never completed an issue of that either. (I usually managed to write one poem about autumn so that I could color in a cover design featuring a large maple tree and a rather dreamy person lying under its boughs.) But I put far more energies into my comic book heroines, who were modeled after the standard heroes of the day: Jet Girl (with her dog, Jet Zoommano), Remarkable Girl (with her dog, Remarkark), Space Girl, and Lightning Bolt, a female variation on Flash Gordon and the Human Torch. My brother and I also composed many an R & B song and recorded them using the impressive sea-green microphone that my father had hooked up to the stereo. We also produced radio plays for the delight and edification of any adults we could corral into sitting through them. These audio dramas always included a raging waterfall and a lightning storm, both of which we gleefully created over the kitchen sink.

I read everything my brother was reading. He was into science fiction, so I'd read his *Analog* and *Fantasy and Science Fiction* magazines after he was finished with them. One science fiction story fascinated me in particular: a retarded boy builds a sculpture from discarded materials—coke bottles, scrap iron, string, bottle caps. The town looks on, amused. Then one day, the boy disappears. The narrator of the story, investigating the mystery, finds that the "sculpture" is actually a machine that activates a doorway into another dimension; he steps through into this alternate universe, which is the mirror image of his town, and when he makes his way to the town square he discovers a statue erected to—who else?—the village idiot.

I loved this story—the idea that the dreamy, mild, scatter-brained boy of one world could be the hero in another. In a way, I identified with that village idiot, because the place I felt most alive was between the pages of a book, while in real life I was painfully shy and awkward.

What I remember most about rainy summer days is browsing the bookshelves in our solarium to see if there were any new additions. I grew up with those rows of books; I knew where every book was shelved and immediately spotted newcomers. And after months had gone by without new acquisitions, I would tell myself: Okay, I guess I'll try this one—and then discover that the very book I had been avoiding because of a drab cover or small print was actually a wonderful read. Louis Untermeyer's *Treasury of Best Loved Poems,* for example, had a sickeningly sweet lilac and gold cover and was forbiddingly thick, but I finally pulled it off the shelf and discovered a cornucopia of emotional and linguistic delights, from "The Ballad of Barbara Fritchie," which I adored for its sheer length and rather numbing rhymes, to Langston Hughes's dazzlingly syncopated "Dream Boogie." There was also Shakespeare—daunting for many years because it was the complete oeuvre, in matching wine-red volumes so thick they looked more like oversized bouillon cubes than books . . . and yet it was that ponderous title *The Complete Works of William Shakespeare* that enticed me, because here was a lifetime's work—a lifetime!—in two compact, dense packages. I began with the long poem "The Rape of Lucrece" (looking for the rape, of course, which I couldn't locate); then I stumbled onto a few sonnets, which I found beautiful but too adult in theme, and finally wandered into the plays—first *Romeo and Juliet,* then *Macbeth, Julius Caesar, A Midsummer Night's Dream, Twelfth Night.* I was enthralled by the power of Shakespeare's language, and especially by my discovery that poetry was spinning the story. Of course I did not understand every single word, but I was too young to know that this was supposed to be difficult; besides, no one was waiting to test me on aspects of structure and content, and so, free from pressure, I dove in.

Although I loved books, I had no aspirations to be a *writer.* I liked to *write*—all those books had made me into a demanding reader, and sometimes, on long summer days when I ran out of material to read, or my legs had fallen asleep because I had been curled up on the couch for hours on end, I invented my own stories. Most were never finished. Those that were, I didn't show to anyone. I didn't think making up stories was something ordinary people admitted to doing. There were no living role models for me—a writer was a dead white male, usually with a long white beard to match.

Finally, in twelfth grade, I had a crucial experience. My English teacher, Miss Oechsner, took me to a book signing in a downtown hotel. She didn't ask me if I'd like to go—she got my parents' permission instead, signed me and another guy out of school one day (that other guy is a literature professor at Berkeley now, by the way) and took us to meet a REAL LIVE AUTHOR. He was John Ciardi, a poet who had translated Dante's *Divine Comedy*, which I had heard of, vaguely. That day I realized that writers were real people, and that it was possible to be a writer, to write down a poem or story in the intimate sphere of one's own room, and then share it with the world.

*

That same year, 1970, I was chosen as a Presidential Scholar, one of a hundred-odd high school seniors nationwide invited to Washington, D.C., to receive a medal. The telegram came on a school night in May, a little after dinner. "Western Union for you, Rita," Dad hollered; this bit of

news made no sense at all, but I came to the door to sign for the first telegram in my life, tore open the envelope, and unfolded the dingy yellow page:

AS 1970 PRESIDENTIAL SCHOLAR, YOU ARE AMONG THE OUTSTANDING HIGH SCHOOL SENIORS IN OUR COUNTRY. I SEND YOU MY WARM CONGRATULATIONS ON THIS WELL-EARNED DISTINCTION, AND INVITE YOU TO MEET ME AT THE WHITE HOUSE ON JUNE FOURTH. COMPLETE DETAILS FOLLOW.

RICHARD NIXON

What was this, a joke? But my parents were solemnly considering this piece of sorcery as if it might mean something. They phoned Miss Oechsner who, it turned out, had recommended me in the first place. And so, a few weeks later, I took the first plane ride of my life, a forty-minute hop to National Airport. I made it all the way to Georgetown University before throwing up in a waste-

The author with former high school English teacher Margaret Oechsner, 1988

basket in the lobby where all the Presidential Scholars had been gathered.

Oddly enough, I don't remember much about those three days in Washington. I think I was too nervous, or it was simply too much: we toured the monuments, attended lectures and panel discussions arranged for our benefit, and prepared for the medal ceremony at the White House. When word got out that our group was planning to hand the president a petition protesting the Vietnam War, Nixon's aide H. R. Haldeman admonished us as if we were nasty children, and not the crème de la crème of American youth, and the president opted just to deliver a speech without shaking each of our hands as originally planned. Still, the pomp and circumstance was substantial for a bunch of eighteen-year-old kids, two from each state in the Union.

The "Personality Questionnaire" I had to fill out for the Presidential Scholar press packet included that popular section called "self-description," with this directive: "Which three adjectives would you use to describe your personality?" Two of my three attributes were "dreamy" and "mild." Nevertheless, when I entered Miami University (in Oxford, Ohio) in the fall of 1970, I listed my major as "pre-law," because that was what was expected of me. No one, and especially not my parents, had said this explicitly. But most of the adults I knew would make chance comments on the behavior and goals of television characters and neighbors, and so were sublimely involved in planning my life. Earlier, I had leafed through *Ebony* and *Jet* magazines, dreaming of the days when I would reap the rewards of my efforts in school by becoming a doctor or lawyer's wife; now I had a generalized, blandly motivated ambition to be the doctor or lawyer myself. Wasn't it the obligation of a straight-*A* student to become such an authority figure on the top rungs of the ladder of community recognition and social reputation? And so I matriculated at Miami University convinced that pre-law was the appropriate—indeed, the only—career for someone like me. I had neglected one tiny detail, however: I had never shown an interest in the practical workings of the judicial system.

Needless to say, I changed my major four times before hitting my sophomore year—from pre-law to psychology, then German and, finally, English—until I could figure out what I wanted to do.

Fate struck again. Having placed out of freshman English, I enrolled in advanced composition

to fulfill part of my core curriculum requirement. Six weeks into the semester, the professor was hospitalized, and the creative writing instructor took over. Milton White strode into class, his snowy white hair dipping dramatically over a tanned brow, horn-rimmed glasses contrasting with his cobalt blue Italian suit. "We're going to tell stories!" he announced, and spent the rest of the time going from person to person, asking for the opening lines of a "story." Terrified but strangely energized, we scrambled to think up racy plots; when my turn came I stalled for time by spinning out a description of the scene: "It's chilly this afternoon," I began, but before I could think further, Professor White interrupted. "Wait!" he shouted. "Did you notice how you began?" I hesitated, terrified. "You started out in the present tense," he said, "and captured the reader's attention; he's in the moment immediately. That's what you want to do. Whaddya know—you've got talent!" He spun around to confront the next student, but I heard no more; I was hooked.

In the fall of my junior year, I had to admit to myself that I had been arranging my course schedule around available creative writing classes. During the break in a poetry workshop, one of my classmates spoke woefully of an incident that summer when a friend of his family inquired what he planned to do with his English degree, and he had answered that he intended to become a professor. "Why didn't I say what I really want?" he exclaimed to a small group of us hanging around the vending machine. "Why didn't I just come out and say I want to be a poet?"

When I went home for Thanksgiving weekend, I first told my mother that I wanted to be a poet. "You better tell your father yourself," my mother replied; but all my father did was to swallow, lower his newspaper, and say: "Well, if that's what you want to do, all right. I've never really understood poetry, so please don't be upset if I don't read it." That was good enough for me; in fact, it was the best encouragement possible: an honest *bon voyage* as I set off on my adult career.

If I were to name extra-literary influences on my life and art, two come to mind immediately: music and German.

In fourth grade everyone in our class was given a Tonette, a black plastic wind instrument bearing a stubby resemblance to a recorder. Later that year, the music teacher asked those children demonstrating *musical aptitude* if we would like to learn a *real* instrument. My brother had gone through the same winnowing process two years earlier and now played the clarinet in the junior high band. Rejecting all wind and brass instruments, therefore, as a matter of course, I considered the array of strings. Everyone else chose violin, viola was a girl's name, the double bassist never got to play the melody. That left the violoncello. I was slightly taken aback by its size; I had expected something about the size of a guitar. But I had made my choice, so I stuck with it, and soon I grew to love the deep, haunting tones that poured from that wooden box whenever I bowed the strings properly. A year later I was recommended for private lessons once a week at the Akron Conservatory of Music, a renovated church with vaulted ceilings and delicious dark wood moldings; I was immediately entranced and decided that I would play cello forever just to be allowed to linger in those sun-stroked halls. I joined the Akron Youth Symphony and later, in high school, also did a few gigs as part of a jazz quintet (flute, keyboard, drums, cello, voice). I played with the

As a cellist in high school, 1969

Miami University orchestra and have studied music ever since.

The only time I was not actively involved in music was when the other extra-literary influence on my life and art began to take shape, during my Fulbright year in West Germany. After graduating from Miami University *summa cum laude* with a Bachelor of Arts degree in English (with creative writing emphasis) in December of 1973, I worked as a secretary with a contracting firm before flying to Europe in June of 1974. A smattering of other Fulbrighters were on the plane as well, and we had a grand and noisy time together. After negotiating my way through passport control and customs, I was feeling pretty cocky, striding through the Frankfurt airport, when I collided with another traveler. *"Entschuldigung,"* he muttered, and went on his way. But I stood there, petrified, and suddenly heard it all around me: Everyone spoke *German*—everybody!—and they spoke rapidly, much more rapidly than I was accustomed to from German Conversation 202. How would I ever survive?

Two months of intensive language immersion (after four hours of class, I'd go back to my apartment and watch dubbed *Bonanza* episodes) at the Goethe Institute in Schwäbisch Hall, an idyllic river town in southern Germany, did the trick. I went on to study modern European literature at the University of Tübingen, where the noted author-critic Walter Jens held a chair in the Department of German Language and Literature, and where, in the early nineteenth century, the poet Hölderlin had spent the long last years of his life "mad as a fox," jotting down wildly disjointed poems of haunting beauty in a yellow tower overlooking the Neckar River.

I spoke, breathed, even dreamed in German. Switching to English with other American students became increasingly difficult, translating for visiting Americans nigh to impossible. To survive in Germany required a certain degree of self-sufficiency: laundry was hung outside even in the dead of winter, and when I went shopping, I had to bag my own groceries. My self-confidence was growing; I learned to speak up during discussions, since *interrupt or forever hold your peace* seemed to be the brutal rule. And for the first time I saw my country from another vantage point. Although I understood my German classmates' image of the United States as a land of technicolor riches and abominable poverty, exalted beliefs *(We hold these truths to be self-evident . . .)* and intransigent racism, I insisted on differentiation; we argued after class, over *Kaffee und Kuchen,* during impromptu get-togethers late at night. The more I pointed out the errors in their simplistic appraisals and repudiated generalizations, the more complicated, and open to doubt, everything I believed in became—democracy, equality, the basic goodness of humanity. When I insisted that not all black Americans live either in Harlem or the Deep South, I remembered what my American history textbooks had reported and what they had chosen to ignore. This fascination with the underside of history—its vanquished and oppressed peoples, its ordinary citizens and unsung heroes—has accompanied me ever since.

*

When I returned to the U.S. in the summer of 1975, I entered graduate school at the University of Iowa's Writer's Workshop. The competition was as fierce as I had been led to fear; but after a year of speaking German, the intellectual fencing and literary hobnobbing that went on at Iowa seemed

pretty small potatoes. Our teachers were excellent, and most of my peers were kind, although some were overly anxious and others cunning. Since I was the only black member of the workshop, however, I was pretty much left out of the Royal Hunt for a Pecking Order: I believe my race made me less of a threat—since this fact, at least in the subconsciouses of my classmates, doomed me to be an outsider, never to be on equal footing with them. On the other hand, I was the only student in the workshop who appeared in that year's major publication, *The American Poetry Anthology.* (The editor, Daniel Halpern, had visited Miami University two summers before and accepted for his magazine, *Anteaus,* the same poems which he then reprinted in the anthology.)

In my second year at Iowa I met my husband-to-be, the German novelist Fred Viebahn. Fred came to Iowa as part of the International Writing Program, which brought established authors to the "heartland of America" every fall semester. Each of these writers was asked to deliver a two-hour lecture on a subject of their choice. Eager to

"With Fred in front of his parents' house in Frömmersbach, Germany," 1977

maintain my fluency in German, I had volunteered to translate whatever texts the German guest writer might consider using to illustrate his lecture.

We met on Fred's first day in the country, September 1, 1976; in fact, he was ferried straight from the Des Moines airport to a party being held in honor of the international authors at the program director Paul Engle's house; I had been invited as Fred's potential translator. When we met a week later to choose the sections from his novels to be translated, we discovered that we had similar working patterns.

"I usually write until four in the morning or so," I said.

"That's nothing," Fred replied. "I stay up till at least five or six."

"Good for you," was my response to this bit of machismo. That night he called me at four to see if I was truly up and alert, and we talked for over an hour. We repeated this practice for more than a week, getting to know each other through conversation in the wee hours of the night before retiring separately to our respective beds. Early on we mused about a coincidence that struck us both as providential: the title of Fred's first novel, published in 1969, was *Die Schwarzen Tauben,* and the German translation of the English name the protagonists, a high school rock band in Cologne in the mid-sixties, had given themselves was—*The Black Doves.*

After receiving my M.F.A. in the spring of 1977, I was in a quandary. During the winter I had interviewed at Florida State University. Convinced I could not possibly live in Tallahassee, much less produce any poems there, I had turned down their offer of a tenure track assistant professor position, a decision my classmates declared insane. Fred, who had been writer-in-residence at the University of Texas at Austin for the spring semester, and I planned to return to his stomping grounds in West Berlin to live a free-lance life. (Prior to Iowa, Fred had made his living by writing for German radio, television, and newspapers.)

Fate intervened, however, in the form of a farewell party for another German writer who was just completing his semester as writer-in-residence at Oberlin College, just an hour from Akron. After transporting all of my gear from Iowa to my parents' house, Fred drove to Oberlin to see his friend while I stayed at home to convince my parents that this indeed was the man I wanted to marry. Fred returned with the startling news that Oberlin College had offered him a visiting profes-

sorship in the German Department, replacing sabbatical leaves.

During our two years in Oberlin, Fred taught German literature and wrote and directed bilingual plays for the annual German theater course. I took classes in modern dance and silversmithing, sewed our wedding outfits, and completed most of the work on what would become my first book of poems, *The Yellow House on the Corner.* Fearful that "Iowa" was still looking over my shoulder, I began writing short stories in order to escape the trap of the "workshop poem." A bit of that apprenticeship prose was later refined and included in my collection *Fifth Sunday.*

When I discovered I could not, as a nonstudent, sign up for private music lessons at the Conservatory, I switched to the bass viola da gamba, an early cousin to the cello whose plaintive, reedy sound is produced by a fretted fingerboard and six gut strings. This chance development had its repercussions in later life, sparking an interest in medieval and renaissance music that has continued into the present. (In recent years I have played gamba with several consorts in North Carolina and Virginia. For my fortieth birthday in 1992, Fred surprised me with a bass viol, custom-made by one of the two contemporary viol builders in North America: my gamba, a replica of a seventeenth-century English original, displays as its scrollpiece the hand-carved head of a black woman, modeled after Albrecht Dürer's 1521 sketch *The Negress Katharina.*) Through playing gamba I have acquired, over the years, a more intricate understanding of rhythmic variations, and through early music—which, in its irregular measures and constant modulations, resembles modern jazz—have fallen in love all over again with the pleasure of music. I am quite certain this music has spilled into my poems, which are modulated by shifting word patterns and syncopation through internal rhyme and enjambment.

*

The two years in Oberlin and the two years immediately following, spent mostly in Israel and Germany, were truly my "salad days"—I had few responsibilities and little money, although the windfall of a National Endowment for the Arts creative writing grant in 1978 allowed me a modicum of financial security. We put the money in the bank as our collateral against starvation.

At the end of our first spring in Oberlin, after Fred had accepted a second year as sabbatical replacement, we sat down to decide what we were going to do with the summer between. Our lease on the rental house was up; we would have to look for new lodgings the following fall. Nothing bound us for the summer to this town or, for that matter, to America.

Fred and I arrived by car ferry in Dublin, Ireland, at the beginning of June 1978. We had rented a house in Dun Laoghaire, just south of Dublin, purely on the recommendation of an acquaintance of an Irish playwright who had been in residence at Oberlin that spring, and now we drove into the appointed neighborhood with trepidation. To our relief, the house was airy and welcoming, with several large windows facing a neighborhood square and a narrow but sunny garden out back. The owners met us with a big smile and the confession they, too, were a mixed couple (Catholic and Protestant), gave us the keys, and left for their summerhouse on the west coast.

Fred had a September deadline for a novel with his publisher, so we spent the next three months writing, seeing very little of Ireland (except on a few day-trip dashes) but feeling its muses nonetheless. On a typical day we would rise at four in the afternoon, just in time to gulp down a cup of coffee and rush to the market before closing; each day we tried a different variety of fresh fish; if necessary, we would also refill our liter bottles from huge oak barrels of sherry. Often we would take a stroll along the pier, sometimes all the way to the Joyce Tower. *(Come up, Kinch. Come up, you fearful jesuit.)* Back home, we'd make dinner and talk and read and watch television until it went off the air at midnight; afterwards we would retire to our separate studies (Fred in the living room on the third floor and I in the ground floor dining room, peat fire at my back) and write until the milkman arrived at sunrise. I was working on a novel which—major revisions, a dozen years, and hundreds of discarded pages later—would begin to take on a resemblance to the manuscript that was to become *Through the Ivory Gate.* In between bursts of writing I would read *Ulysses,* alternating with sections of Richard Ellmann's biography of Joyce. Occasionally this routine was interrupted by a visit from a charming but mysterious Irish friend of our playwright acquaintance, who would pop up to take us on day trips to various places of interest along the eastern Irish coast, present us with tickets to Makem and Clancy or James Galway or a

Brendan Behan play, and then would disappear just as mysteriously and swiftly.

By the end of August, Fred had finished his fourth novel, *Die Fesseln der Freiheit,* and I had written half of a novel and several poor poems (too much Yeats in the air!) which luckily have never seen the light of publication.

*

Our time in Oberlin ended in May of 1979. That summer Fred was invited as a guest of the city of Jerusalem to spend three months at Mishkenot Sha'ananim, a scholars' and artists' colony ensconced in a former caravanserai facing Mount Zion. We revised our habits to rise at 11:00 A.M. to the whitewashed, light-filled arches and corridors of our two-story apartment and the amazing views of the Old City from our windows; it was like living in a Bible picture book. Often we set out to explore the nooks and crannies of the city in the dog hours of the afternoon, when the shadows of the labyrinthian medina provided some respite from the heat. As the evening sun threw a golden-pink shawl over King David's Tower, we returned to our terrace overlooking the valley between the Old and the New City and read until dinner, then retreated to our desks to write until three or four in the morning. From Jerusalem I mailed the manuscript of *The Yellow House on the Corner* to several publishers in the United States; word of its acceptance by Carnegie-Mellon University Press came in November at the German Academy in Rome, where we made a brief stop to intercept our forwarded mail on our way from Israel to Germany.

With no sabbatical openings to fill and no job prospects on the horizon, we had decided to revert to our original plan from two years earlier— before fate sent us to Oberlin—to earn our living as free-lance writers in Germany. We sublet a sunless, one-room apartment in Wedding, a blue-collar district of West Berlin; a huge tiled oven in one corner provided the heat, to which end we hauled two bags of charcoal briquettes up three flights of stairs every other winter day. I wrote at the desk in the main room while Fred took the small circular table in the kitchen alcove. When this proved too cramped, the girlfriend of an acquaintance offered her apartment, vacant during university vacations. The only catch was that there was no electricity; every afternoon I would take off for this apartment armed with my note-

"My sisters Robin and Rhonda, my brother Tommy, Fred and I at our wedding," 1979

books and pens, thermal underwear, and a bottle of Polish vodka. I would write for two or three hours until my fingers were numb, then return to our smaller but warmer digs. In that cold "loaner" apartment I wrote short stories in longhand into a red notebook; our oven-warmed room I reserved for writing many of the poems that would make up my second book, *Museum*.

As idyllic as those months were, the wet, chilly summer of 1980 primed us for melancholy during a cold and dreary autumn, two weeks of which we spent lecturing, debating, and writing at the International Working Period for Authors in the city of Bielefeld. By now, I noticed a disturbing development: I was losing my English. Not that I couldn't speak fluently or read English as quickly as I had in the past; it was simply that the more fluent my German became, the more insecure I became about what, exactly, constituted "normal" American syntax and cadence whenever I sat down to write poetry. I could no longer locate the

precise tone of a phrase, nor gauge the subterranean currents of a line. Prepositions were especially sinister. This terrifyingly subtle process was probably the main reason I had taken so desperately to writing short stories in that borrowed unheated apartment—with prose, the damage was more manageable.

I felt that I had to go back to America. Although he had experienced no such language difficulties during his years in the U.S., Fred was immediately sympathetic.

A friend sent me the MLA (Modern Language Association) job list, and I began the onerous procedure of highlighting possible openings, assembling my resume, and writing letters. In February 1981 I flew to the States for interviews; back in Berlin there was another flurry of phone calls before the decision was reached to accept a tenure track position as assistant professor for creative writing at Arizona State University in Tempe, Arizona.

Tempe had put on her best face for my interview in February: mild temperatures and sunny skies, palm trees and balmy breezes. We moved to Arizona in the middle of the summer, driving cross-country from Ohio in a third-hand station wagon. When we pulled our huge black Buick into a rest area just outside Phoenix and I stepped from its air-conditioned interior into the blazing heat of early August, tears popped into my eyes. Valley of the Sun, indeed—this was a cauldron! My skin prickled; I gasped, and the air was as hot and dry as a furnace blast. The pavement heat began to work its way through the thin soles of my sandals, so I ran to the bathroom, the tears drying on my cheeks as quickly as they streamed down. What had I done?

"Don't worry; in a while your blood will thin and you won't feel the heat," Phoenicians (as we took to calling the long-term inhabitants) assured me. And sure enough, by October I had gotten used to drinking mass quantities of fluid, and I actually liked the way the heat made me feel purged and radiant, as crisp as a freshly-baked cookie. Dissipating stress was easy: simply lean against a car seat warmed by the sun and all the tension automatically drained from the upper back. People tended to be very friendly Out West: total strangers might touch my arm to emphasize a point when I asked for directions, and on the sun-drenched campus everyone smiled as if to make up for the lack of eye contact caused by the ubiquitous dark glasses. Many students were commuters; many worked in order to put themselves through school; many were older and came to class with a fierce desire to learn.

We moved into a spanking new apartment complex that boasted free utilities and instant landscaping. Norman Dubie, senior poet on the faculty, and his wife Jeannine came by with a house plant and helped us carry in a couch, desk, and dinette set that Fred and I had scavenged from local Goodwill and Salvation Army stores. Since I was slated to spend the spring semester at Tuskegee Institute in Alabama as writer-in-residence, we decided to hold off on buying a bed; instead, we spread out our station wagon mattresses (two narrow foam rubber pads we kept for overnight camping trips) on the plushly carpeted bedroom floor and slept on them for those first five months.

Alabama was yet another adjustment. Whereas everything in Tempe was pretty new (the house we would buy a year later boasted the distinction of being located in an "older" neighborhood, all of twenty years old!), Tuskegee Institute seemed not to have changed significantly since Booker T. Washington's time. My classroom

flaked paint and exuded mold, and there was a fifteen-inch hole in the linoleum floor, between the pitted oak desk and the cracked blackboard. When I reported it, maintenance came over promptly to patch it by nailing crosshatched two-by-fours over the cavity. All semester I stubbed my toe on the boards as I paced and lectured.

Adequate housing for such a short time could not be found in Tuskegee, which was not much more than a hamlet, so we rented a tiny brick house twenty-five miles away in Auburn. We were cautioned that, though our particular neighborhood (arranged around a circular turnabout) was "safe," we should always check our rear-view mirror when returning home to make sure no one was trailing us. Shocked and a bit incredulous, we soon adopted this useful paranoia when, a week later, we surprised a man trying to slash our tires while we were in the supermarket.

Once Fred and I were driving back from Tuskegee after a dusting of snow had canceled classes. Near Auburn University, in front of a fraternity house "garnished" with a large Confederate flag, we had to slow down in order to pass by throngs of frat boys waging a snowball fight; when they saw who we were, they blocked the street, began hurling snowballs at our car, and screamed epithets I was too scared to actually understand and which Fred was reluctant to repeat to me later. "No way, you bastards!" Fred muttered, and pressed down on the accelerator; when they realized he had no qualms about running them down, the frat boys scattered and we shot through, trailed by snowballs and screams.

The semester in Alabama was my first extended experience living in the South. Our "mixed" marriage had occasioned raised eyebrows or disdaining glances before, but never had we been exposed to such fiercely hateful glares. Every day I would drive the half hour into Tuskegee and meet open, friendly faces; each evening I would check the rear-view mirror twice before turning into our street. And social climate matched the actual weather: although the temperatures were cooler than in Arizona, the Alabamian air was more oppressive and, as spring arrived, cloying with the strange sickly-sweet odors of the Deep South—wet kudzu, barbecue smoke, and insect repellent.

It was a relief to return to Arizona that August. I soon fell into the rhythm of the laid-back lifestyle—impromptu picnics in the desert and dinner parties where the guests, attired in shorts and loose cottons, congregated around the grill or the pool. When we looked up the daughter of one

"With Fred and our daughter, Aviva Chantal Tamu Dove-Viebahn," Tempe, Arizona, 1983

of our Alabama acquaintances shortly after our return to Tempe, we discovered three intersecting interests: she and I were both four months pregnant, her father was one of America's foremost poets (Hayden Carruth), and we were looking for a house just as they were trying to sell theirs. We settled the transaction with a minimum of paperwork and moved into our new home in mid-September; the backyard was bursting with figs and olives.

We spent all autumn painting our first own house in bold colors: Pompeiian red walls and royal blue ceiling in the bedroom, pastel blue and yellow for the nursery (the ceiling half blue and half yellow, diagonally), an aubergine-colored foyer and palest pink living room. Colleagues who came to dinner were polite, but we could tell they thought we'd gone bonkers.

I went into labor at four in the morning of January 24, a few hours after painting the bathroom mustard yellow with a coral stripe at chest level. The day before, the midwife had sent me home predicting I wouldn't deliver for another week; depressed, anxious, but determined to put this extra time to use, I hemmed the living room curtains and cleaned out several drawers before tackling the bathroom, unaware that the nesting

instinct had kicked in. Thirty-six hours later, Aviva Chantal Tamu Dove-Viebahn was born.

Although I had written very little during the last months of pregnancy, I had felt no anxiety; now the poems began to explode onto the page. While living in Berlin I had begun a group of poems about my grandfather's early adult years: haunted by a story my grandmother had told me about my grandfather working on a Mississippi riverboat as part of a song-and-dance team, I had written five or six poems revolving around this young man who somehow would become my sweet, shy grandfather. At that point I thought I would be satisfied with a cycle of a half dozen poems; I submitted this grouping to the *Ohio Review*, which had been printing "chapbooks" as centerpieces for each issue. In Alabama, I completed several more "grandfather" poems, so I rearranged the cycle and sent the revised version to *Ohio Review* editor Wayne Dodd with an apology and an explanation; it was this group of poems that appeared as the chapbook "Mandolin" in *Ohio Review* 28.

I was writing every day, driven by the fear of maternal distraction as much as by the elation of creativity. Fred and I had devised a strict schedule in order to insure working time: one of us would tend Aviva for four hours in the morning, then be relieved for the next four; we allotted two hours for dinner, and then the first sitter would take over again for four more hours. Every day we switched the order. After a week, we realized we had allowed little time for all three of us to be together, so we relaxed the schedule to include one four-hour work period on either side of a four-hour "family time." Also, I had to figure my teaching and related university work into the timetable. A Guggenheim Fellowship allowed me to take a leave of absence the following academic year (1983–84), so we were able to extend our writing schedule.

The modest cycle of "grandfather" poems sent to the *Ohio Review* expanded dramatically one evening when, while giving a poetry reading, I turned to "Dusting," a poem written way back in Berlin and already included in *Museum:*

> Every day a wilderness—no
> shade in sight. Beulah
> patient among knickknacks,
> the solarium a rage
> of light, a grainstorm
> as her gray cloth brings
> dark wood to life.

Under her hand scrolls
and crests gleam
darker still. What was his name, that
silly boy at the fair with
the rifle booth? And his kiss and
the clear bowl with one bright
fish, rippling
wound!

Not Michael—
something finer. Each dust
stroke a deep breath and
the canary in bloom.
Wavery memory: home
from a dance, the front door
blown open and the parlor
in snow, she rushed
the bowl to the stove, watched
as the locket of ice
dissolved and he
swam free.

That was years before
Father gave her up
with her name, years before
her name grew to mean
Promise, then
Desert-in-Peace.
Long before the shadow and
sun's accomplice, the tree.

Maurice.

At this point, with some distance acquired
between poem and its original inception, I realized
that the room described in it was modeled on my
grandmother's solarium, and the woman trying so
desperately to recall her first love's name was none
other than my grandmother. It was as if she had
stepped out of the poem to claim her place in my
grandfather's cycle; "you can't tell just one side of
a story," she seemed to be saying. In that moment,
Thomas and Beulah was born: a book-length collection of poems chronicling the lives of my maternal
grandparents, an epiphanal series of vignettes
depicting an ordinary marriage lived out against
the grand panorama of History—the Great Migration of blacks from the rural South to the urban
North, world wars and depressions, the civil rights
movement and the rise of Afro-American activism
in the sixties.

During this blessed time, the poems in *Thomas
and Beulah* assembled themselves. I phoned my
mother every weekend to talk about her childhood. And although she knew I was writing about
her parents, she never asked to see a single poem.
Her implicit trust, her faith that I would do justice

to their lives, was the most positive force I
experienced while writing the book.

Fred's fortieth birthday fell on a Thursday in
April of 1987. I had planned a small surprise
party, and since I had no classes to teach that day, I
informed the English Department that we weren't
to be disturbed at home for any reason.

I arose at eleven and kept the shades drawn
while I made coffee. According to my secret
itinerary, I planned to pick up Aviva from preschool (where Fred had taken her at eight in the
morning, before going to bed), drive with her by
the shop for the surprise ice-cream cake, special-
ordered with a video camera frosted on top—as an
amateur photographer with his first video camera,
Fred filmed everything that moved. Then we
would surprise him before dinner with seven gifts
relating to the seven most significant periods of his
life. After dinner, our closest friends were scheduled to "drop by" for champagne.

Since I knew we were expecting guests, I had
planned to do a bit of surreptitious housecleaning,
so I decided to sweep the kitchen floor before Fred
got up. The phone rang; I let the answering
machine take the call and began to fume when the
voice of my department chairman filled the room.
What nerve, I thought, I had told them I didn't
want to be bothered for anything, banging my
broom into a corner as he repeated, a bit frantical-
ly, "Rita, I know you're there. Pick up—this is
important!"

He had already told me a few weeks earlier
that my promotion to full professor had passed all
the committees, so what could this be about?
Snatching up the receiver, I snarled: "What is it,
Nick?" The dialogue that followed was worthy of
Laurel and Hardy:

"You've gotten the Pulitzer!"

"No."

"Yes!"

"No!"

"Yes!"

In the end it was the tone of his voice, an
octave higher than normal, that convinced me he
was telling the truth. I was totally unprepared.
What about Fred's surprise party? At that moment, Fred came barreling into the room, eyes
popped wide; I must have screamed.

Nick was still talking: " . . . couldn't get
hold of you because your number was unlisted so
they called the president of the university and *he*
didn't have it either, so he had to call me but I told
him, no, *I* want to tell her. Listen—the press has

Rita Dove and her parents,
Ray and Elvira Dove, Akron, 1993

started calling here; you don't want them to have your number, do you?"

"No . . ."

"So I'll arrange a press conference for . . . let's say three o'clock. That should give you enough time to collect yourself. Meet me at the office."

Two hours! What should I wear? And my hair needed washing. And we had to pick up Aviva; what about the cake?

"I don't know how to give a press conference," I wailed into the telephone.

"You'll learn," Nick replied, and hung up.

My hair did not get washed that day. We scooped up Aviva and made our way to the university, where colleagues were waiting with flowers for me and balloons for Aviva. Our friends picked up the video-camera cake on their way to our house later that evening, and the surprise party was sprung three hours later than planned, but all the heartier.

Nick was right. One moment I was sweeping the kitchen and the next moment the klieg lights were turned on, and ever since I've been learning the ropes in the strange public arena. The girl who shied away from junior high school play auditions now found herself, when her home town organized a "Rita Dove Day," standing on a stage before an audience of three thousand, talking about her childhood in Akron and reading her poems. The high school senior who had described herself in a personality survey as "dreamy, sensitive, and mild" was now invited for radio interviews and TV talk shows. The young woman who avoided speech classes in college now spoke in front of classrooms and auditoriums nationwide. The bookworm had to learn to dictate letters into a Dictaphone and how to pack a carry-on suitcase for an eight-city tour, how to sleep sitting up and even to be cheerful at 8:00 A.M. breakfasts—by far the most difficult task!

*

I had a sabbatical, pre-Pulitzer approved, for 1987–88, and we spent the first half hopscotching all over—from islands off the coast of Yugoslavia (sweltering in June) to the German island of Amrum in the North Sea (near-freezing in July); then came an international poetry festival in Mexico City, followed by four weeks of frenzied writing in Berlin (Aviva went to preschool—called a *Kinderladen* or "children's store"—every day while Fred and I wrote in an architectural firm's spare rooms overlooking Kurfürstendamm, Berlin's "Fifth Avenue").

Late September found us in the States again. Akron's "Rita Dove Day" went nonstop for the first two days in October, with speeches at my old high school, before 650 business women and men at a luncheon, and finally before an audience of 3,000 at the local performance hall which was followed by the signing of over 1,000 books. At the city hall reception, Aviva got her face painted at a clown stand and held her helium balloons in front of the mayor's face as he presented me with the key to the city. Relatives I hadn't seen since I was twelve stormed the town and ended up in my parents' living room, munching potato chips. My fourth grade teacher was telling reporters how I had recited the Preamble to the Constitution, something I don't remember ever being able to do. My fifth grade teacher (and the first black teacher I ever had) handed me a term paper I had written back then on the effects of alcoholism. One near-hysterical woman insisted that I had gone to the prom with her son, and when I answered that I hadn't gone to the prom at all (that had been the day Haldeman snapped at us Presidential Scholars in D.C.!) she refused to believe me, brandishing instead a Polaroid snapshot of her son (whom I recognized) posing with a young lady I had never seen before. "See," she exclaimed, "there you are." It was a very bizarre, heartwarming and frightening experience; I felt like a heroine, a ghost, and a terrible fraud, all at the same time.

From the halls of local history I tumbled into six weeks of deliriously delicious isolation in a borrowed apartment in Paris, where Fred and I (Aviva stayed with her grandmother in Germany) immediately slipped back into our night skins, writing until past 10:00 A.M., soothed by the ever-changing pulse of the streets in the city that never sleeps. We slept through the dreary wintry afternoons, strolled through the Marais at nightfall, then returned with artichokes and red wine to fuel us again.

In the summer of 1988 I topped off my sabbatical year with a five-week residency at the Rockefeller Foundation's Study and Conference Center in Bellagio, Italy, a pocket of heaven where cypress-covered hills plunge into the clear waters of Lake Como and whitewashed villas slope up into the mists. Perched high on a promontory above the town, the castle-like Villa Serbelloni accommodates more than a dozen scholars and artists at a time, who are expected to work on their specific projects but are often found ambling through the estate along the exquisitely groomed paths, identifying the tiger lily and the hydrangea and the tiniest orchid.

And ah, the villa itself! The only times before that I had walked along such magnificent halls—full of marble niches and four-foot marble urns filled with fresh floral arrangements whose blooms were culled every morning from the villa's own greenhouses—had been behind tour guides.

Meals were opulent, with waiters who would not dream of making a guest reach for the morning coffeepot. Dinner was always a five- to six-course affair, with *aperitivi* served beforehand and menus on creme stationery tucked among the linen napkins, hand-tatted place settings, and silver candlesticks. It was almost too elegant, too beautiful.

Fred and I were assigned a luxurious bedroom in the villa, and each of us had a more rustic studio in different parts of the grounds. I tried to forge a routine which would allow me to enjoy the culinary delights (and the copious wine selection) without cramping my writing schedule, but I ended up spending most afternoons drowsing in a rattan chair outside my study (actually a one-story tower without a castle, a stone cylinder set at the top of a grassy knoll with windows looking out on all four directions, like a lighthouse), watching the three goldfish in my private little lily pond. Gradually I ceased feeling guilty about doing nothing (i.e., not writing) and relearned the deep pleasure of simply *being:*

And Counting
(Bellagio, Italy)

Well of course I'm not worth it but neither is
the Taj Majal for that matter so who's counting?
Someone's got to listen to the fountain;
someone is due to catch the *nymphaea tuberosa*
closing promptly five till five. Opulence
breathes on its own a little better
if there's a gardener raking or a scholar
primed to record its suscitation. I came here

to write, knock a few poems off the ledger
of accounts payable—only to discover

Rita, Aviva, and Fred at home in Charlottesville, Virginia, 1993

pasta put me under just as neatly as sambuca
would catapult me into telepathic communication.
    So
I took a few day trips, sprained an ankle on the
    courts,
fell asleep over Catullus-*cum*-Zukofsky . . . in

short, nothing happened that wasn't
    unexceptional,
but that's the crux of moral implication, is it not?
Mother Mary, ingénue with the golden womb,
you would not comprehend how cruel a modern
    game of
tennis is: you only had one phosphorescent ball.
Here's a riddle for Our Age: when the sky's the
    limit,
how can you tell you've gone too far?

Each autumn upon returning to Arizona from
summer vacation, my allergies had worsened.
Contrary to popular myth, Arizona—particularly
the heavily populated areas—is no longer a haven
for hay-fever sufferers. Homesick easterners moving into the Sun Belt often bring their cherished
gardens and lawns with them; this maddening

practice, which also requires obsessive watering, as
well as the large number of swimming pools in the
Greater Phoenix area, have resulted in high levels
of pollen and dry mold. My allergy problems, plus
my yearning for seasonal changes, first prompted
me to consider the offer of a position at the
University of Virginia. After many tortured
months of discussion and soul-searching, we decided to pull up stakes, moving first to Durham,
North Carolina, where I was a fellow at the
National Humanities Center for the 1988–89
academic year. And finally, in August 1989, we
moved into our dream house just outside of
Charlottesville—window seats and fireplaces, windows upon windows looking out on our lake and
trees and the Blue Ridge Mountains in the distance.

We never regretted the decision. The university grounds are beautiful, the faculty and students
everything one could wish for in an academic
setting. And as far as spiritual energy is concerned,
a marvelous *frisson* results from the way Jeffersoni-
an legacy of the "academic village" is superim-

posed on the high-tech, light-industry infrastructure of the town; the more recent influx of progressive academics, avant-garde artists, reclusive Hollywood connections, the "horse set," and the multimillionaire set all add intriguing flavors to the cultural gumbo. Hard to imagine that a mere twenty-five to thirty years ago this university was a fortress of racism and male chauvinism!

Aviva's horseback riding lessons (part of the bargain struck to persuade her to move away from Arizona) have turned her into quite a horsewoman; Fred plays squash and plugs away at his first American novel. I continue the singing lessons begun in Durham and occasionally venture onto the stage of the University Opera Workshop.

*

The perverse thing about fame is that the more recognition there is, the less time remains to continue doing that for which one has been recognized. Since the Pulitzer Prize, it seems that my daily life has become a struggle against fragmentation; carving out the necessary blocks of time in which to write has become increasingly difficult. The requests for appearances and interviews, book reviews and essays, promotional comments and letters of recommendation keep pouring in; even to answer with a polite "no" demands an extraordinary amount of time. Being a responsible and "present" mother is important to me: I have turned down trips to China and France and writing residencies in beautiful places because it would have meant being absent from home for undue periods; my pleasures are taken in the homey and intimate delights of the everyday, the miracles of the ordinary.

Life continues in its fits and starts superimposed over the comfort of dailiness. Not a day goes by that I don't curse the telephone and the Federal Express truck bringing more urgent requests and unsolicited manuscripts; but not a day passes that I don't look out over the hills and think, "What a charmed place this is; how lucky I am to live in it."

I had thought, when the initial brouhaha of the Pulitzer had trickled away, that at least never again in my life would I be *that* surprised. But two days after the announcement that I had been appointed the new Poet Laureate of the United States, I was driving home from the university and the thought hit me: "Damn," I said aloud, "it happened again." I know now not to wager bets against fate. More and more often these days I am

reminded of the advice my father gave me—repeated in a few prophetic lines in my sonnet "Flash Cards":

> In math I was the whiz kid, keeper
> of oranges and apples. *What you don't understand,*
> *master,* my father said; the faster
> I answered, the faster they came.
>
> I could see one bud on the teacher's geranium,
> one clear bee sputtering at the wet pane.
> The tulip trees always dragged after heavy rain
> so I tucked my head as my boots slapped home.
>
> My father put up his feet after work
> and relaxed with a high ball and *The Life of*
> *Lincoln.*
> After supper we drilled and I climbed the dark
>
> before sleep, before a thin voice hissed
> numbers as I spun on a wheel. I had to guess.
> *Ten,* I kept saying; *I'm only ten.*

Life and work are coming at me fast and furious these days, so I'm happy I received such good training in flash cards. I'm grateful to all the mentors (parents, relatives, neighbors, teachers, students, husband and daughter) who have shown me by example that life is only worth writing about if one is really living it. I take the "slings and arrows of outrageous fortune" as they come, and write between the interstices.

Postscript

One of those super-successful computer wizards once said: "I can't believe my life is happening to me." When Richard Nixon's telegram arrived at my parents' house nearly a quarter century ago, I felt the estranging power of good fortune. Looking back, it seems like I must have been sleepwalking through the media blitz following the Pulitzer Prize; the charmed weeks in Bellagio are now no more substantial than a trail of smoke rings. And when the phone rang last May in my Chicago hotel room where I was packing for the return trip after a two-day reading and panel event with Gwendolyn Brooks—when the voice on the other end of the line asked if I would consider becoming Poet Laureate of the United States, it was only training and Nick's statement "You'll learn" that enabled me to formulate a more or less coherent response. The weeks that followed were ten times more strenuous than those after the Pulitzer, but I learned to handle the publicity with a measure of calm—all the while feeling like I was a piece in some Titan's chess game, a Queen run amok, certain to be decapitated with the next move. This sense of unreality, of fickle fortune, helped me survive those first weeks—that, plus the unshakable fact that we held nonrefundable plane tickets for mid-June to Europe, where we had already rented a motor home to camp through Scandinavia. Everything—print, radio and television interviews, photo shoots, pressing correspondence, plus organizing the fall season for the Library of Congress reading series (my first official duty)—had to be finished by mid-June. Remembering my grandmother's advice to *Just do your best and then stop worrying about it,* I plowed through. Upon my return from a rejuvenating month in Norway, Finland, and Sweden (no crowds or reporters, just fiords and reindeer and the midnight sun as available light for reading through piles of books), the mounds of letters towered even higher. But whenever I approached the point of collapse, I would run across a correspondent who had enclosed clippings of her favorite poems (not her own!), or someone who simply wanted to tell me how poetry had enriched his life. This enthusiastic and abiding love for poetry, as expressed by nonacademics, by "people," energized me.

On October 7, 1993, I opened the literary season at the Library of Congress in Washington, D.C., with a poetry reading. The event was held in the Great Hall of the Jefferson Building—hundreds of people crammed into every gilt- and marble-adorned corner; closed-circuit televisions were set up between the fluted columns for those standing in the back. I would have been terrified if my grandmother hadn't been beside me in spirit, chuckling, "Now, ain't this nothing!" After the reading, Fred and I were whisked up to the Poetry Office, on the top floor of the same building, in order to change for a black-tie dinner at the White House. As I flung off my reading outfit and stepped into my evening gown, the girl who had wept because nobody had asked her to the high school prom and who had been saved from

mortification by being invited as a Presidential Scholar to visit the White House on the same weekend as that prom—this girl had to chuckle, too. It was happening, whether I chose to believe it or not. Outside the balcony windows of the Poetry Office, the dome of the U.S. Capitol glowed like a perfectly turned meringue.

BIBLIOGRAPHY

Poetry:

Ten Poems, Penumbra Press, 1977.

The Only Dark Spot in the Sky, Porch Publications, 1980.

The Yellow House on the Corner, Carnegie-Mellon University Press, 1980.

Mandolin, Ohio Review, 1982.

Museum, Carnegie-Mellon University Press, 1983.

Thomas and Beulah, Carnegie-Mellon University Press, 1986.

The Other Side of the House, photographs by Tamarra Kaida, Pyracantha Press, 1988.

Grace Notes, Norton, 1989.

Selected Poems, Vintage Books, 1993.

Other:

Fifth Sunday (short stories), Callaloo Fiction Series, 1985.

Through the Ivory Gate (novel), Pantheon Books, 1992.

The Darker Face of the Earth (dramatic play), Story Line Press, 1994.

Work represented in anthologies. Contributor of poems, stories, and essays to magazines, including *Agni Review, Antaeus, Ars Poetica, Black Scholar, Boston Review, Georgia Review, Gettysburg Review, Michigan Quarterly Review, Nation, Poetry, Southwest Review, TriQuarterly,* and *Yale Review.*

William Price Fox

1926-

William Price Fox at the Capital Cafe, in Columbia, South Carolina

Back in the thirties my dad had a radio show band here in Columbia, South Carolina, called The Hawaiians. They were three blacks and two whites, and the only song they knew in Hawaiian was "I'm Going Back to My Little Grass Shack in Kealakekua, Hawaii." The rest of the songs they played were in Spanish. Such items as "Cielito Lindo," "Juanita," "Besame Mucho," etc. Dad always said he was sure no one in Richland and Kershaw Counties would know the difference. No one did, or at least they didn't complain. Anyhow, that's the way he operated. He wasn't a full-fledged, gun-toting crook, but he liked to live out there in the moral twilight. Slightly shady money was much more desirable than honest money, and the forty-hour-a-week Christian ethic was for someone else. Not him. When he was older and said the moisture had dried up in his hands and he couldn't deal seconds and bottoms in poker, with great reluctance he tried honest work, refrigeration and air-conditioning repair. But the thrill was gone and the old flamboyant trumpet-, guitar-, and clarinet-playing gambler, nightclub owner, and operator was never the same.

In his heyday he arranged music, played it, and sang it while running a nightclub and making his own whiskey. For three years in the late thirties he operated a barbecue nightclub in Lugoff, South Carolina, which he had set up with a red room for

117

"My father in the navy," about 1942

poker and a green room for craps and roulette. He had slot machines that he'd rigged not to pay off; ran a shell game and a three-card monte hustle with a sawed-off shotgun under the counter in case the victim got out of hand; had punch boards with the winning numbers removed; and, in the back, about a hundred yards down the creek, kept a fifty-gallon moonshine still. With all this going, one would think we would have been rich as Rockefeller, but such was not the case. He was a good musician, cook, and moonshiner, but not a very good gambler. He would play against anyone, but there was always someone coming through town who was a shade better. In other words, every penny he made he lost or gave away. He was also supporting three or four black families in the area that did odd jobs for him. But we lived pretty well, had good clothes and a car, and when my brothers and I went to the fair in Camden ten miles away, we always had three or four dollars.

The Law caught Dad making whiskey and he was shipped back to Columbia thirty miles away to do a year and a day. We moved into town a few

blocks from the state penn to be near him and would take him food and cigarettes on visiting days. While in jail he took a correspondence course—the kind one finds in the backs of magazines—and that's where he learned air-conditioning and refrigeration, though he claimed he knew it already from building whiskey stills.

Anyhow, when he got out of jail, he tried it awhile but quickly lost interest. Fortunately for him, Pearl Harbor had just been bombed and he thought it his duty to re-enlist in the navy as ship's cook. He had served in the marines back in the twenties as a pharmacist in the Haitian campaign to put down the voodoo rebellion. In any event, in 1941, a couple days after Pearl Harbor, he shipped out of Charleston for convoy duty on the North Atlantic.

Back in Columbia, my mother, two of my brothers, Bobby and Dickey, and I went to work as curb hops, grill cooks, and almost anything connected with restaurant work. My other brother, Jimmy, was too young to work. Mother was very resourceful and took Dad's enlistment with no hard feelings. When she was younger and lived in Chicago where Dad met her, she made her living as a nightclub hostess. She later went on to managing small restaurants, working the sandwich board, and cashiering, and during World War II helped run the USO in Columbia.

*

Earlier, back in the twenties, after getting discharged from the marines, Dad joined a band in Waukegan, Illinois—he played guitar and trumpet, did arrangements, and also sang. It was here he met Mother, and it was here that Bobby, Dickey, and I were born.

We lived there for four or five years. Mother worked as a nightclub hostess and waitress, while Dad did everything from running a band, to cooking, to driving a diaper truck. He even played trumpet as a "scab" during a big musician's strike. He grew tired of Illinois, and in 1932 he took me and a friend and drove back to Columbia, South Carolina.

The car was an old 1929 Model T Ford and driving through the Tennessee mountains on the washboard roads took four or five days. The car kept breaking down—major breaks, transmission, drive shaft, etc.—and they had to repair it right there on the side of the road while I slept in the back seat. Later, Dad told me they practically rebuilt the car on the trip down.

We arrived in Columbia and moved into 404 Elmwood with Dad's mother, Fanny. Shortly after this, Mother came down from Waukegan with my two brothers. The house, right across the dirt street from the cemetery and Pauper's Field, was only four rooms with no heat or light. Mother was appalled at the place because Dad had told her she would be living in a nice bungalow. But she quickly recovered and went to work uptown as a waitress. Jimmy, my youngest brother, was born right in the house on Elmwood. I made Mother name him Jimmy, for Jimmy Foxx, the Boston Red Sox baseball player. Mother said she could tell how much time was passing during her labor by looking out of the bedroom into the kitchen and seeing the half-gallon jar of corn whiskey in the kitchen getting lower and lower.

Grandmother Fox had had twelve sons and one daughter and grew up in Foxtown, South Carolina, forty miles away. The family were farmers, small-store owners, and, as far back as anyone can remember, had been making corn whiskey. At 404 Elmwood she sold home brew which she made and bottled in the back room and sold from the front room. Bobby and Dickey and I went to Logan Elementary School a few blocks away.

One of the first things I remember at 404 was the first Fourth of July when one of the big kids down the block had a stick of dynamite that no one would light. Like a total fool, and just like my dad, I volunteered and, armed with a stick match and a brick bat to strike it on, I marched out and lit it. Fortunately, it didn't go off. From that time on I was not only considered part of the gang, I was a potential leader. It was right about in here that I discovered baseball, football, and fishing in the river. So while we were as poor as migrants, we lived outdoors most of the time and all in all had a great time. School suffered but we were all fairly smart and managed to bring home tolerable grades.

Despite the strong influence of my dad, Mother was the real strength that kept the family together. She was raised a Catholic but when she moved South she joined the Baptist church, which she attended religiously, and helped out with community activities. She also desperately, and hopelessly, tried to keep us all in school. Her efforts weren't enough, because all three of us, again like Dad, eventually dropped out and went in the service.

Mother was very attractive and made friends easily. Not only was she a great cook and restaurant manager, she also had a gift for calligraphy and was able to design original menus and do

Playing football (left end) next to his brother Bobby, in the mid-1930s

place-setting cards. She had a great gift of energy as well—some years she would work two and three jobs, take care of her aging mother, raise us, and still have time to work at the USO.

Later, while living in Columbia at 613 Richland Street, Dad and his brother Martin Luther—M.L.—sold corn whiskey by the shot, pint, quart, and half-gallon. My job, I was around eight at the time, was to sit on the front porch and watch for the Law. They always came up Richland out of the sun. When I saw them I'd push a buzzer and Dad or M.L. would then empty their forty-gallon sink of whiskey into the sewage before the Law could get across the yard, flash a search warrant, and come inside. Above the industrial sink—which they had equipped with a three-inch drain that went directly into the sewerage—they kept a gallon of coffee grounds which they would pour in after the whiskey was gone to kill the smell. Since the whiskey was in the bathroom and the house was tiny, only four rooms, our clothes would smell of corn whiskey so much we would have to hang them out in the yard at night to get rid of it.

The house on Richland was equipped with trap doors, phony ceilings, and sliding panels to hide whiskey. There was also a fifty-five-gallon barrel buried in the backyard with a secret tap connected to the sink. Dad built all of this equipment and in doing so learned a lot about copper, electrical wiring, plumbing, cement work, carpentry, etc. As a matter of fact, most of the moonshiners back then were very skillful men who knew a great deal about a lot of trades. They were also very good on souping up cars to outrun the law.

Dad was raised during the time whiskey-making was legal. He learned not only how to make good pure corn but how to build pot stills, steam stills, and later the Ground Hog Still, which came out of South Carolina and he claimed was a Fox invention. This is a horizontal still which is used in the woods after the leaves have fallen.

Later, when the federals started raiding, moonshining became very secret and very sophisticated. Dad built underground stills, stills in trailers, in attics, caves, etc. He and M.L.'s biggest still was a thousand-gallon-a-day steamer set up in some county in Georgia where they had paid off the sheriff. The deal was they could run for a month. The month was almost over when the government put an embargo on sugar. Dad and M.L. then promptly bought two boxcars of sugar-topped six-count cinnamon rolls and completed the run with no apparent loss of quality. He never forgot sitting

out in the swamp in a straight chair, swatting mosquitos and unwrapping the rolls.

There was a playfulness about making whiskey and selling it back then. The men were all in their teens and early twenties, and many of them loved the recklessness and abandon that went with it. Dad and M.L. had a great time and when they were much older would sit for hours and go back over every detail. At one time there was a hundred dollar bet around Columbia on who could build and operate a still closest to the city jail on Taylor Street. Dad and M.L. won this bet when they built a still on the corner three blocks away in a two-story house. The still was on the top floor and a firehose for the mash slop drainage went down the stairs into the toilet. Next door to the still was the Jewish cemetery and they stashed the whiskey, which was packed in ten-gallon wooden kegs, in the graves. By sliding back the top slabs on the tombs, they were able to store three ten-gallon kegs in each grave. Inside the house they kept the records on the walls: i.e., Herkovitz thirty gals., Shapiro thirty gals., Cohen thirty gals. Years later they were still laughing about sitting on that front porch drinking beer, listening to the still running, while they looked out over the railroad tracks at the lights of the city jail.

In the kitchen where Dad served whiskey it cost a dime for a two-ounce shot, a quarter for a half-pint, a half-dollar for a pint, and a dollar for a quart. This was also the place where we ate our meals. So right in the middle of breakfast or dinner in would march four or five guys fresh from the cotton mill a few blocks away for their morning or evening drinks. They'd load the jukebox up with nickels, and since there was nowhere to sit they'd sit on the floor and listen to the music.

There was always plenty of music around the house in one form or another. Dad never liked country music—everything was swing or blues or ballads. He even had a few records of light opera. *Martha, Cavalleria Rusticana*, Puccini, Gilbert and Sullivan. Even Sousa marches. He continued playing trumpet, guitar, banjo, and base horn and kept up with his music. About once a week three or four members of the old Hawaiians would show up and they'd play great songs such as "Avalon," "Red Red Robin," "Poor Butterfly."

These songs must have sounded strange down on Richland Street where every radio was tuned to Nashville and Roy Acuff and The Grand Ole Opry. Later when he owned one of a string of failing restaurants, he refused to put country and western on the juke. Instead it was Tommy Dorsey, Glen Miller, Artie Shaw, etc.

This is kind of a generalized background of how I grew up. Dad was probably the catalyst that made me read a great deal. I had plenty of time sitting on the front porch swing watching for the law. I think the first serious book I read was the collected works of Edgar Allan Poe. I remember distinctly sitting on the porch saying one of Poe's lines over and over again: "omniscient, omnipresent, omnivorous." God knows where it came from, or what it meant, but it sure stuck with me. From Poe I moved on to Jack London, Albert Payson Terhune, and Booth Tarkington. I think the book I enjoyed the most back then was "The Romance of Leonardo Da Vinci" by Merjowkowski. I still remember one great line. The scene is after a great feast when the court glutton steps forward to entertain the guests. It goes: "Talpone the Rat, the court glutton, stepped forward and making the sign of the cross rolled up his sleeves and proceeded to dispatch the greasy fare with a speed and a greed unbelievable."

God, I loved that line. I'd say it over again like a lunatic and quote it to anyone who would listen. And each time I did it, I would crack up. I'm afraid I'm still like that.

Dad would also take Mom and all of us fishing down on Cedar Creek. He was a very good fly fisherman—tied his own flies and repaired his own rods. After World War II he won the state championship for biggest bass on a fly rod, 9½ pounds. He could fly cast in a creek, which is very difficult because you have to work the line in front of you. He also played baseball, football, and boxed, so my brothers and I got a lot of tips about sports, gambling, etc. One thing he said: "In a poker game, if you can't figure out the chump in one round, you're it." He could do a few sleight-of-hand tricks, mark cards, load dice. He could even control dice—claimed to have made thirty-two straight passes. This was on a blanket with no backboard.

One would think with all of these talents he could have been very successful. But he wasn't. He would get bored and try something else: cooking, carpentry, plumbing, wiring, inventing, etc. He never ever settled down until it was too late, and then it really was too late.

Mom and Dad loved each other but they fought a lot. Every few years she would leave him. She would pack up a big basket of sandwiches and we'd head north on the Greyhound for Waukegan

"With Joe Heller, author of Catch-22,*"*
Columbia, South Carolina, 1982

or Chicago or wherever she could get a job. Once we had to live at the Salvation Army in Chicago for a couple months. But each time Mother would leave, Dad would promise to get a straight job and start over. And each time she would believe him. Once we came back and he had us living in an attic in August. The beds were on the catwalk, running lengthwise with the boards. If you got out of bed the normal way, you would step right through the ceiling below. Above our heads it was all nails sticking straight down from the roof, so you had to keep low to avoid the nails and watch your feet at the same time and try to survive the heat, which we measured almost every night at a flat 120 degrees.

Anyhow, Dad was like that. He was a great character and wonderful to be around but really wasn't built to take on the responsibility of a family. Mother was, and, as I said before, it was her strength that kept us together. Had she not, a couple of us would have wound up in jail or working in the cotton mill. As it turned out, Bobby joined the navy and became a cook down at St.

Simon's Island for the Air Sea Rescue Unit, Dickey joined the army, and I went into the air corps. Later, Jimmy was in the navy. So out of a family of six, from World War II through Korea, five of us were in the service and Mother was working at the USO. That's six out of six; pretty patriotic.

Bobby returned from the navy and finished school. Later he became the plant foreman at Tamper Industries, building railroad equipment. He is also a master plumber and something of an inventor. Dickey was a scout with the First Cavalry in Korea. He was killed near Heartbreak Ridge. Before he died of leukemia, Jimmy had finished college, served in the navy, and worked as an electrical engineer for TVA in Chattanooga.

*

My first job, apart from collecting whiskey bottles and selling them to the bootleggers, which we all did from the time we were six or seven, was working in a corner grocery store when I was nine. The store catered mostly to blacks and I remember bagging and selling nickel bags of grits, rice, sugar, etc. Also fat back, pork liver, pickles, etc. I forgot what I was paid but it couldn't have been much. My second job when I was ten was curb hopping out at the Pig Trail Inn. The hours were from five till twelve during the school year, the salary three dollars a week plus tips and meals.

I was fired twice from the Pig Trail. The first time for introducing a local nutcase on the public address system as Bing Crosby, "direct from Hollywood," and letting him sing along with the jukebox on "Night and Day." I was hired back, but after organizing the curb boys in a strike for higher pay I was discovered as the leader and fired again. So much for my union activities.

I then went on to curb hop at most of the drive-in drugstores in town for a couple years until I was fourteen, when Doug Broome hired me as a grill cook and counter boy at his first restaurant in Columbia. He would later own five or six places and be recognized as the Hamburger King of South Carolina. I was the first cook he hired—because I was so cheap and so young.

For a year or so I caddied out at Trenholm Road Golf Course. I think I made thirty cents for carrying singles, sixty for doubles for eighteen holes. You were supposed to get tips but no one was tipping back then. We also had caddies' day on Monday, and I'd skip school and tee off at dawn and play until dark. Two of us broke the record,

108 holes in one day. We thought the *Columbia Record* and the radio station would be there to meet us when we came in out of the dark—we had to use flashlights to see to putt. But they weren't. Instead the owner shouted out, "Y'all ain't going out again, are you?"

After a couple years there—where I learned a lot about golf but not enough to break eighty—I got a job delivering telegrams for Western Union. I was especially good at this because we'd been living in the black section of Columbia—called Black Bottom—for most of my life and I knew all the back streets and alleys. Very few were on the map. Places like Easy Street, Elbow Alley, Joe Louis Boulevard.

World War II was in its second year and there was a heavy traffic in two-star death telegrams—which had to be delivered in person. The message could not be phoned or mailed in—Western Union was one of the official purveyors and we took this job very seriously. Another item on the downside was delivering personal two-star death messages to the illiterates. Often they would have no lights. If they had any, it would be the fireplace or a kerosene lamp. Sometimes the message would be collect: thirty cents and three cents tax, and require an answer. The rule was you'd have to collect the money before you read the message—even a death message. After I'd collect, I'd read the message to them by their fire or my flashlight. Then when they'd recovered, I'd write their return message for them. Grim work, but I was always proud of the fact I was able to do it.

I was also one of the few messengers who would sing "Happy Birthday" telegrams. I hated doing it because often it would be in front of kids I was going to school with. But usually you got a pretty good tip.

All in all I liked Western Union and the uniform with the leather puttees and the garrison hat. I remember feeling very important in it—a far cry from how I felt going to school in the same old blue jeans, tennis shoes, and T-shirt. About once every two weeks I'd stop off during work and play sandlot football in my uniform. A couple times it got torn up and I'd tell the manager at Western Union I'd been in a wreck. He was so relieved I was all right—and there was no lawsuit—he promptly gave me a new outfit. I'm sure this carried over into the service when I became a lieutenant in the air corps, because if there was one thing I loved it was that officer's uniform.

Meanwhile in school I was a disaster. I hated everything about it except the sports. I played freshman football and basketball but had to drop out because Western Union hours were too long; and if I went to school, then played ball, and then worked from five until midnight, I would fall asleep in class.

But there was something else at work here. Everyone knew that my father was a moonshiner and bootlegger and he'd done time at the penitentiary. They assumed that I was going to do the same thing. So instead of going to school on some normal schedule, I was placed in manual arts: woodwork, metalwork, sheet metalwork, typing, etc. I hated all this and promptly failed everything they put me in. I remember the only fun I had in manual training was the day I invented a bowling game played with ten twelve-ounce Pepsi-Cola bottles and a ten-pound sledge hammer. I'd slide the hammer down about a fifty-foot marble hall, and the crash and noise were beautiful. I was expelled that day. When I came back, someone pulled the fire alarm and I got blamed and expelled for that too. But I was expelled enough times to justify their suspicions, so there was very little I could say or do.

I failed the tenth grade. I think I had all *F*'s. I was expelled again for flamboyantly shining a mirror in Governor Strom Thurmond's eyes during a war bond rally on the high school steps. Even back then I thought he was an embarrassment. This time I was taken away by the police, and as the patrol car started off for the police station I waved back, savoring the moment as one of my best at old CHS. Historic footnote: Cardinal Joseph Bernardin was voted the most famous CHS graduate; I was voted the most famous drop-out and was given the honor of being the guest speaker at the dedication of the new CHS.

Ironically, years later, I was in charge of a group to save the old building, which was located in downtown Columbia. It was on the National Register but the local Baptists were determined to tear it down and build a bigger church. Their reverend announced that the Lord had told him the building would be torn down and the church would be erected. I did a radio show and editorial letter saying I'd talked to the Lord myself, and he told me he hadn't said any such thing. We sued the church to stop the demolition. My group wanted to save downtown Columbia which was turning into a ghost town by putting condos in the old building. We even had a builder ready to build.

The Baptists, who had the inside track greased politically, prevailed. Not only did they prevail, they sued me personally for being a nuisance and costing them money for delaying the building. I wanted to fight them but was advised not to and eventually we settled out of court. In the end the building was torn down and one of the biggest eyesores in the southeast was erected as a 3000-seat Baptist Church—it looks exactly like Opryland.

In March of '43 when I was failing the tenth grade again, I quit, walked out, crossed the street, and told the recruiting station sergeant I was eighteen and wanted to take a test for aviation cadets. I took it and passed and couldn't believe it. No one checked my age and I was off to the air corps. I guess I thought I'd be discovered at any moment and sent back home, so I was loose and relaxed when I took all the motor coordination and tests and trials they put cadets through and sailed through as if it were nothing. Meanwhile, the air corps had too many cadets in training and the wash-out rate was well above 50 percent. So while I was going through the program, many of the college graduates in the barracks with me were washing out. The only problem I had was disguising the fact I was seventeen and didn't shave. I was also sneaking into the latrine at night and desperately trying to learn how to tie a necktie. There was no one in the barracks I could ask. At Western Union we wore leather clip-ons. Was anyone ever so green?

I guess I picked up some extra self-esteem when I saw I could compete with my peers who were all dressed in the same uniform and knew nothing about my background. In any event, I believe most of the wash-outs tried too hard. Getting through flight training was a little like playing golf and probably a little like writing. When you try too hard, you tighten up and nothing works.

But let me back up here and do a little more about Dad because I think he was the one, without knowing it, who got me into writing. He only finished the third grade but eventually he became a really great reader. He read Greek drama, Homer, Plutarch, Caesar, Gibbon, etc. He could speak three or four languages—he just picked them up traveling. As a matter of fact, with his knowledge of French and the Haitian dialect, he was able to translate the language some of the dock officials were using in World War II when his ship was anchored in Casablanca.

He taught himself algebra, basic physics, and chemistry, and even some medicine—which he picked up while working on the soda fountain and helping out in the pharmacy of a local drugstore. In Haiti, during the rebellion when most of the men came down with malaria, he performed appendectomies, removed bullets, and sewed up wounds by following the directions in the Naval Medical Handbook. Before he died in 1975 he still had the book, along with a picture of himself sitting on a donkey—the men called him Little Doc.

Dad was always reading something and his interest ranged from philosophy and politics to archaeology and medieval history. He had a gourd-back twelve-string mandolin, and he used to sit on the top step down on Richland, strumming it and singing nifty little songs. He was especially fond of Johnny Mercer and Cole Porter. I guess when all is said and done, those moments still stand out for me with the greatest intensity. I'm sure it's why I read and sang to my kids and hope they in turn will do the same with theirs.

I graduated from cadets in December '44 in Victorville, California, as a bombardier-navigator

Standing in center between golfers Calvin Peete on left, Payne Stewart on right, in Morocco, 1992

second lieutenant, and I can't think of a happier day. Yes, I can, probably coming home and meeting Mom and Dad at the train station. I remember we were walking up Gervais Street, I had my right arm around Mom and my left around Dad, who was a petty officer and home on leave too. We walked along and a string of GIs from Fort Jackson began saluting me. Since my arms were around them, Dad saluted them left-handed. I can still see his big wide exaggerated salute and hear him laughing, "At ease, Doggie. Smoke if you got 'em."

But there was one more moment that week that is even more memorable. I went up to CHS to see my class—they were now in the eleventh grade. My old homeroom teacher was glad to see me but she suspected foul play and took me to the office. The principal was sure I was impersonating an officer and sent for the police and the MP's. I waited until the perfect moment and handed the MP my AGO card. He saw I was legitimate, stepped back, saluted, and apologized, and I got to say, "It's OK, Sarg, you're just doing your duty."

One of my biggest disappointments was not getting to go overseas and fight the Japanese. Because if ever someone was ready to fight, it was me. I hated them with my every fibre, and I had myself tuned so tight it was beautiful. A lot of us were like that. The air corps knew how to get us ready. They would assemble us in a movie house and, keeping the lights off, would play audiotapes of Japanese torturing Americans, raping women, and shooting down innocent parachutists. By the time we came out we were bristling with patriotic fervor and would have volunteered for anything up to and including suicide missions.

Our group was stationed in Pyote, Texas, at Rattlesnake Army Air Base, one of the big B-29 schools. Here we learned high altitude bombing and B-29 procedure—it was a brand-new ship with many kinks that had to be worked out. There were many crashes—some fatal. One problem: it was so heavy it took ten thousand feet of runway to get airborne. And once airborne you climbed to five hundred feet and nosed down to pick up sufficient speed to climb. For a long time we thought the plane would prove to be useless. In the end, however, it prevailed.

Our mission, and this was in early '45, was to learn how to drop the atomic bomb. We didn't know what we were doing, it was all secret, but the procedure was to drop this mystery bomb and then do a hard diving 180-degree turn and get out of the area. On a normal bombing run when the bomb is released the plane continues on the same heading in order to photograph whether it is a hit or a miss. The 180-degree turn was brand-new, and with it came special goggles and procedures.

When the *Enola Gay* dropped the bomb on Hiroshima, we all knew the war was over. Everyone in the barracks celebrated and began making plans to go home and go back to college. Me, I was miserable and in tears. Not only was I not going to get to fight the Japanese, I was going to have to turn in my uniform and paycheck and go back to Columbia and Western Union and the tenth grade. I was miserable but concealed it and joined in the victory celebration. I remember drinking nine or ten rum-and-cokes and throwing up all night.

I tried to stay in the air corps but the peacetime army had no room for bombardiers. I came home, wore my uniform for the allowed thirty days, and, taking a deep breath to get used to civilian life, got a job stacking license plates in the Highway Department. This was until school started, when I went back to the tenth grade.

Back in high school, the kids were all wearing bobby socks and popping bubble gum and I felt like a fool sitting with them. Fortunately the government stepped in and I was allowed to take an equivalency test and skip the rest of high school.

I then entered the University of South Carolina (USC) in Columbia, not knowing what I wanted to take. I was tested and scored high in everything but interest. It was weird; nothing really interested me. Finally I decided to try engineering school. But it didn't work, and I promptly failed almost everything. During this time I was on the GI Bill which covered most of my expenses, but I also had jobs on the big grill for Doug Broome and hanging speakers out at the Starlight Drive-In Theatre. (Later, I wrote about the Starlight for *Esquire*). Needless to say, this was a real comedown for me from being a second lieutenant in the air corps.

Dad was home from the navy but wasn't making much money in the refrigeration business, and Bobby and I were helping out with what money we were making. Korea came along and I wanted to drop out of college and re-enlist. But I knew if I went in I'd have to go in as a private, so I backed off on that and continued on with school. I didn't like taking notes in class and found most of the lectures boring. I took only minimal English and didn't like any of it. Especially the grammar and the reading. So at this time there was very little evidence, if any, of me being anything except

what they had decreed long before—a blue-collar worker with skills in manual arts.

Then one day I got a great teacher and everything changed. His name was Archibald Lewis and he taught medieval history. I took every one of his courses. His lectures were so good there was no need or requirement to take notes. Suddenly I wanted to be a medievalist and began reading everything I could get my hands on in the library. I loved everything about the courses, especially the outside reading. Lewis gave us wonderful reading lists, and it was right about in here that I began to take school seriously and thought about being a scholar. The problem was, I was lousy in French and Spanish and didn't stand a chance of learning either one. But Lewis let me stay in his classes and even let me take his graduate courses.

I was also helped a great deal by Dr. Pierre Lafferty in philosophy. I took most of his courses and wanted to major in it. When I signed up for a course in logic, he took me aside and said he would give me a *B* for not taking it. He said I would never be able to pass it, and if I did it would spoil my beautiful naivete. This proved to be invaluable. I have never been focused or a very logical person, but all of a sudden I realized that this wasn't a crime. That's just the way I was.

On the day I graduated, I bet a dollar with four of my classmates on who could hold onto Senator Strom Thurmond's hand the longest when he congratulated us. Still remembering being dragged away by the police from CHS years before when he was governor, I gripped down and won the four bucks easily.

On the day I graduated, I picked up my clothes from the cleaners and with about thirty-six dollars I'd been saving from grill cooking, I headed for Miami with a friend, Bill Ivey. The plan was to go to Venezuela and work in the iron mines and save money and come back rich.

We never got out of Miami. Ivey decided he had to come back and I stuck it out down there dead broke—living on peanut butter and potted ham until I got a job at Miami Military Academy out on Biscayne Bay. This was a backbreaking and weird job. The owners believed in the Bernard McFadden philosophy of no medication, chewing your food thirty-two times, endless exercise, etc. I became the Cadet Captain. But it was a title that meant even more work. In addition to teaching all subjects to four classes—ninth, tenth, eleventh, and twelfth—in one room, I was in charge of all athletics. I worked from dawn to lights out. Even then it wasn't over because little kids from the first and second grade would start whimpering in the night and I'd let them crowd into my bunk with me.

Many of the kids were from broken homes that didn't want them so most of them were sad little individuals who were craving attention. If one of them got sick, it was tough luck. No aspirin, nothing. The colonel who owned the place, and was in charge of everything, usually told them to run it off. There were nine or ten kids from families in Cuba who had migrated over to the mainland. They were very gifted, with incredible talents for music, mimicking, and great fun to work with.

Christmas came and the kids all went home for two weeks. Naively I thought we'd stay on the payroll, but the colonel had other plans. He shut the place down and said if we wanted to stay there we could use the bunks but the kitchen was closed and we'd have to feed ourselves as best we could. One of the teachers who had a car wanted me to go with him to California. We were both dead broke but he figured we could steal a couple hundred blankets from the warehouse and go across the country selling them. I've always kind of liked that idea but am glad I said no.

What I did do was go out to Miami Beach and get a job as a bellhop at the Hotel Johnina on Seventy-ninth and Collins. During the interview the owner asked if I had ever worn a uniform. I showed him my AGO card as a lieutenant and he was impressed enough to give me the job. Bellhop jobs are very hard to get in season. Anyhow, it was a brand-new seventy-room hotel right on the beach, and the season was just about to start. There was no salary but they gave us uniforms, and we could borrow ten to twenty dollars against our tips. I made between four and six hundred dollars a week in tips, setting up poker games, selling whiskey and medicine, car washes, dry cleaning, and recommending the services of various prostitutes out on Collins Avenue.

Working as a bellhop was perfect. The hours were long—twelve and fourteen hours—but you could make a lot of money. I also managed to meet a great group of people who worked there and hung around the bar. Years later I wrote a story for the *Saturday Evening Post* called "Room 306 Doesn't Tip," which is about how you handle some guy who won't tip. I wrote the story as fictional, but when the *Post* folded, *Holiday* ran it, and it was selected as one of the *New York Times*'s Best Articles in 1969. Anyhow, bellhopping was a great life, and I probably learned more from it than I did

in college. At this time, I roomed in Coral Gables with O. G. Smith, whom I had met back at USC. If I had to pin down the one person who got me started thinking about writing, it was him. He had been to the University of Florida and had studied under Caroline Gordon and Andrew Lytle.

The bellhopping season, much like a migration, ended in April when the high rollers went back to NYC and the no-tip schoolteachers and package planners flooded the beach. We used to call them the Cloth Coat and Hush Puppy set. When the tips started dropping off, I hitchhiked to NYC.

I arrived on a cold April day wearing a cotton suit and carrying one suitcase and a carton of books: Greek drama, Gibbon's *Rise and Fall of the Roman Empire,* and my medieval history books. I had no idea what I was going to do for a living, but I had to have a place to stay, so I checked in at the Thirty-fourth Street YMCA.

From the "Y" I moved to a single room on the corner of Ninety-sixth and Broadway. This was 1952 and the rent was twenty a week and they tossed in a towel and a paper bath mat. Directly in front of my window was a neon sign flashing "Broadway Bar," but I don't remember it ever bothering me. I'd seen a lot of guys living on the same floor so one morning, just like in the movies, I stood in the hall and made a speech to anyone who would listen: how three or four of us could move in together and get a great place to live. I then read a few ads out loud from the *New York Times.* It worked perfectly, and two guys from Boston and I pooled our money and moved into a big place at 23 West Seventy-sixth Street, right next to the Museum of Modern History and the subway stop.

By this time I had a job with Westerman and Rathbone, insurance brokers down on John Street. My job was to run back and forth between companies, getting policies signed. I didn't know what I was doing and didn't care. As long as it paid the rent.

One day I was eating in Chock Full O' Nuts; nutted cheese on raisin bread with a bowl of split pea soup, coconut cream pie and coffee. Good quality at a fair price back then. I was sitting there over my nutted cheese and whispering to myself in the mirror. In NYC you can talk to yourself and nobody even notices. Anyhow, I was asking myself if I wanted to stay in the insurance business. The answer came back no. From there I went to an employment office and took a placement test. The employment agency said I was a born salesman and sent me off for my first interview.

During the next eight years I was a New York salesman for five different companies: Shellmar, Continental Can Company, Plax Corporation, Specialty Papers Company, and finally Atlanta Converting. My job was to sell printed flexible packaging using such materials as cellophane, polyethylene, aluminum foil, and paper. I was given a six-month trial period with Shellmar, and by making a lot of calls I kept the job. My biggest sale at this time was to Union Carbide—eventually we would do their Eveready battery label. The purchasing agent here had a wall filled with prints of medieval escutcheons and right away we hit it off. We would have lunch almost every week and talk business about two minutes. The rest of the time we would spend talking books and history. His hobby was the Crusades.

I sold Nabisco the printed cellophane for their Oreo cookies, their Lorna Doone cookies, and their Very Thin Pretzel cellophane wrap. I also sold American Tobacco, Colgate Palmolive, Fruit of the Loom, etc., etc. My territory eventually became all of New England, and I could go wherever I thought I could find business.

During this time I was married to Suzanne Kiplinger. She was a Pan American stewardess. When she quit the airlines she became the art critic for the *Village Voice*. We lived in Greenwich Village on Perry Street and had one daughter, Kathy.

It was about this time, when we were living in the Village, that I discovered that Caroline Gordon was teaching at the New School and remembered O. G. Smith's suggestion. I enrolled in the class on the short story. I didn't have a clue of what I was doing but there were a lot of girls around so I figured I couldn't go too wrong. Even up to this time I had no idea or plans to be a writer. Gordon was editing and helping Flannery O'Connor and would read us parts of her work from time to time. She could also recite the last two pages of Joyce's *The Dead*. She was a wonderful teacher who really loved writing. While this was a course in reading short stories, she said if any of us wanted to try writing one, she would read it.

I remembered a story Dad told me about a hound dog fighting a wildcat and went home and wrote it in a few days. I handed it in and then forgot all about it. A week or so later Gordon announced that there was a born writer in the class, and I looked around to see who she was talking about. It turned out it was me. She read the

With Payne Stewart, 1992

whole thing right there in class, all twenty pages. I was so embarrassed I wanted to put my head on the desk. But later when everyone seemed to like it, I began to feel good about it. She asked me if I had any questions. When I asked how you knew when to use first person or third, she told me to forget it, that it would come to me naturally. This turned out to be pretty profound advice for I have followed it ever since.

Murray Schisgal, the playwright, was in this class and we became good friends. Also Gene Hill, who became the editor for *Sports Afield* and did a lot of work for *Field and Stream*. Richard Yates taught a class here. Years later we would become friends in Hollywood when I was living with Charles Portis for a short time. Later I'd see Yates again at the Writer's Workshop in Iowa City.

Also at this time, while I was still in sales, I met William Manville, who was doing a column for the brand-new *Village Voice*. His column was called "Saloon Society" and it was a funny running account of what all was going on in the Village, notably the White Horse Tavern, the Lion's Head, and Henry's—all bars we were hanging out in then. One night at the Horse he said he didn't want to do that week's column and asked me if I would try it. He had heard me telling southern jokes around the bars and thought I might work out. Anyhow, I did one called "Tourist," about a redneck coming to NYC and staying at the Dixie Hotel on Forty-second Street. This was the first piece I'd ever written for publication. Bill said to write it the same way I talked, and that's precisely what I did. I figured the *Voice* would just throw it away and let Manville skip a week, but what happened was really wild.

They ran it on page one. Right after it came out, I began getting calls from magazines—the *Saturday Evening Post, Harper's,* and *Esquire*—asking if I had anything else. I lied and said I did and started writing short stories. At the same time I met Knox Burger of Gold Medal Books, a division of Fawcett—he lived about three blocks away. He was interested in me doing a book of short stories and arranged for me to get an agent: Max Wilkinson. Knox was a great editor; he was the first one to publish Kurt Vonnegut as well as John D. McDonald. Eventually he would leave Gold Medal and become a successful agent.

Knox gave me a contract to do the series of stories, which became *Southern Fried.* He tried to sell it to the hardcover publishers but this was the early sixties and southern short stories weren't in demand. Anyhow, the book finally came out in softcover under the Gold Medal imprint. I showed the cover to Caroline Gordon and told her I wanted to dedicate it to her. But she thought the cover was tacky and the book too commercial and wanted no part of it. Gold Medal figured the book was a bus station book for down South and had Jack Davis do a hillbilly sitting on a broken-down porch with a skinny hound, a chicken, and a deep breathing bosomy Daisy Mae-type. The books were all shipped South, and I figured that was the end of it.

What happened next was really spectacular. John Hutchens, the lead reviewer for the *Herald Tribune,* loved the book and gave it a rave review. He also gave the hardcover publishers a rap on the knuckles for not buying the book. The following week Walt Kelly, the cartoonist for "Pogo," wrote another nice review for the Sunday *New York Times.* I think this book was one of the first softcover books to be reviewed like this. Anyhow, with the book costing only forty cents there was a big rush to the bookstores. Unfortunately all of the books had been shipped South and there wasn't a

book in NYC. Gold Medal had the books shipped back to NYC and began planning for a second printing. The demand was really great and the book was printed two or three more times. Years later I added six more stories that had appeared in various magazines and changed the title to *Southern Fried Plus Six.* Lippincott brought it out in hardcover. From there it went back to softcover and has been printed five or six times by various publishers. Last year it came out again in hardcover with Sandlapper Publishers.

While the book received great reviews and sold a couple million copies, the problem was I'd written it in just a few months, with very little, if any, rewriting, and I was very suspicious that I was a flash in the pan or it was an accident. I decided not to believe my good fortune and stuck with my sales job. My sales manager, seeing that I was rapidly becoming a successful author and appearing on talk shows, began thinking I was spending more time writing than I was selling. Actually he was right. But I had a good territory and my sales

In the classroom

were up so I figured what the hell—I'll keep doing it until I get caught.

I had accounts up in the northern part of New York State which I'd call on in the dead of winter when the snow was thickest. Several times I'd let myself get snowbound. Then I'd hole up in a motel for a few days and write stories. I think I started my first novel somewhere up near Utica.

I was in sales for over eight years and for a long time loved it. I had a company car, an expense account, a nice office, plenty of free time, and I made very good money. I also met a lot of strange and interesting people, many of whom are heavily disguised in my later fiction.

After *Southern Fried* came out I stayed in sales and did stories for the *Saturday Evening Post,* a couple for *Holiday, Harper's, Audience, American Heritage, Sports Illustrated,* the *Los Angeles Times,* and most of the golf magazines. I also got a two-book contract from Sandy Richardson, who was then at Lippincott. Knox Burger showed him part of a book I had called *Doctor Golf,* and Sandy bought it as well as my first novel, which was *Moonshine Light, Moonshine Bright.*

Doctor Golf was interesting in that it was a complete departure from the southern delivery I used in *Southern Fried. Doctor Golf* is an eighty-year-old curmudgeon who believes in caddie flogging, covered sleeves, wooden shafts, and that golf's darkest day occurred when Francis Quimet, the caddy, defeated the British champions Henry Vardon and Ted Ray. His pronouncement was "the end of the golden age of golf is over. Soon the rabble will be in the foothills and the game will never be the same."

The whole delivery of Doctor Golf was a mimicking of a couple of my favorite actors, Alastair Sim and Robert Morley, and my agent, Max Wilkinson. But the reason I wrote this way was because I didn't want to be pigeonholed as another southern writer. The book did very well and became a column for a couple of golf magazines and only went out of print this past year.

I stayed in sales and kept on writing stories. Then one day I got a call from Paul Henning, who owned and wrote the *Beverly Hillbillies* television show. He said he was going to be in NYC and wanted to get together to discuss putting *Southern Fried* on the Broadway stage. In the meantime Jean Sheppard, who had his own talk show, called and also wanted to make *Southern Fried* into a musical. We met and he brought along his buddy Shel Silverstein. The problem was we became such good friends all we did was talk and drink and never did do any work. Years later Shel, Franklin Ashley, and I did an all-black musical here in Columbia called *Southern Fried.* It was a big success locally but much too long and costly to put on the road.

After the Paul Henning visit, I wound up that year working for him in Hollywood. He also owned *Petticoat Junction* and *Green Acres.* At Filmways, where *The Beverly Hillbillies* was shot, they were also shooting the *Andy Griffith Show, The Addams Family,* and *Mister Ed.* I had a lot of fun talking to Andy Griffith, playing ball with Opie, and hanging around the *Addams Family* set. I did very little work for the *Hillbillies,* maybe some suggestions but nothing warranting any credit.

About this time Dwight Whitney, the West Coast chief of *TV Guide,* gave me an assignment to do an article on Jim Nabors. Dwight showed me how to interview people—he took me on one with Mel Torme—and showed me how articles should be written. I wound up doing seven or eight pieces for him, and I've been doing them ever since.

While in LA I was divorced from Suzanne and married Sarah Crawford from NYC—she had formerly been an editor for Knox Burger back at Gold Medal. At this time I had an assignment from *Holiday* to do six humorous pieces in Europe, along with one for the *Saturday Evening Post* on spaghetti Westerns. Also at this time my novel *Moonshine Light, Moonshine Bright* had just come out and I was being flown in to be on the Johnny Carson and Dick Cavett shows. On the Carson show we talked so much about bellhopping that we forgot to mention that I was a writer and I came to be known as the bellhop who wrote on the side.

I came back to NYC from Europe not knowing if I wanted to go back to Hollywood or not. Just as I was about to return, Kurt Vonnegut called—we had the same agent, Max Wilkinson—and asked if I wanted to replace him at the Writer's Workshop at the University of Iowa.

I don't know why I said yes. I still don't because I had every intention of going back to the coast and trying to do novels and screenplays. But I guess I wanted to write fiction more than screenplays. In any event, we moved to Iowa City and I began teaching.

It was the first time I'd been before a class of adults teaching anything. At first I felt like a registered fool but gradually I relaxed. I attracted a lot of southern writers; my group was called The Raccoon Class. All in all this was a very good experience and I probably learned more about writing from my students than they did from me. Many of them did very well with fiction, nonfiction, and screen and TV work.

I continued teaching here with a lot of trips to LA to work on movies and TV screenplays. During this time MGM bought *Moonshine Light, Moonshine Bright* and I did a screenplay for it. Later I also did two *Southern Fried* stories as TV pilots, writing the scripts with Bobby Kaufman—later he collaborated with Murray Schisgal and Larry Gelbart on *Tootsie*—and stayed out there for the shooting. Neither one of the pilots was picked up.

While in Iowa City I also did the first draft on a movie that was to be called "The Man Who Fell to Earth," and for ten weeks worked for Norman Lear on a movie called *Cold Turkey.* I did the original story and title. Norman re-wrote it and was given the screen writing credit; I got screen story. The movie is still shown on TV—it's about a town giving up cigarettes.

While in Iowa City I wrote *Ruby Red,* a book about two girls from Columbia going to Nashville and getting into the country music field. I'd done a lot of work in Hollywood and Nashville doing articles about music for various magazines and hung around with songwriters and singers such as Roger Miller, Kris Kristofferson, Johnny Hartford, Mel Tillis, Bobbie Gentry, and Merle Travis, so I knew a little bit about the field.

The book did very well and was bought by Paramount and given to Arthur Penn to direct. Penn and I worked on it for a while but he decided he wanted another screenwriter and they did it together. Paramount didn't want to film it for some reason and they, in turn, gave the book to Bob Fosse. Fosse had recently done *Cabaret.* It was at this time that he had a heart attack and died. The book then went to John Hancock, who did *Bang the Drum Slowly,* and then on to Robert Altman and then someone else. In any event it seemed that everyone tried it but just couldn't make it work for Paramount.

Meanwhile back in Iowa City at the workshop, though I'd planned to stay one year, it turned out to be eight. My first son, Wyatt, was born here and three years later my second son, Colin. Wyatt died in '73 at age three of cancer, and I quit writing novels and stories for a while. All I felt like writing were easy pieces for golf and travel magazines. In 1975 I was offered the writer-in-residence job at USC—James Dickey was the poet in residence—and I moved back home where I have been ever since.

"With my mother-in-law Betty Gilbert (left) and my bride Sarah (Gilbert) Fox"

At USC I began working on a novel called *Dixiana Moon.* This book was based on a couple interviews I had with the Great Bartok. Bartok owned the Hunt Brothers Circus but before that he owned one of the biggest medicine shows in the world. He employed Mickey Rooney, Red Skelton, Carmen Miranda, Bessie Smith, Stepin Fetchit and claimed he was the one who gave Oral Roberts his first break. He told me a lot about the old hustles and I combined this with some of my sales experience. Viking brought the book out in '81 but it never did very well and didn't even go to softcover. Three producers optioned it but nothing ever happened.

Since then I've done a collection of stories and articles called *The Chitlin Strut and Other Madrigals; How 'Bout Them Gamecocks!,* about the '84 season where Carolina won nine games; a table-sized golf book called *Golfing in the Carolinas.* For this book I played fifty of the best courses all the way from Hilton Head, South Carolina, to the western mountains of North Carolina. And two years back I did a combination fiction/nonfiction book for Algonquin Press about Hurricane Hugo called *Lunatic Wind.*

During these past years here at Carolina I've done about twenty golf stories and articles for the golfing magazines, another twenty or so for travel magazines—*Travel and Leisure, American Heritage, Geo, Charleston*—and about fifteen satirical opinion pieces for *USA Today*. In addition I produced and hosted the USC-ETV Writer's Workshop.

This is a very successful program which is now shown on PBS. In it I have my class ask direct questions to writers and let them talk without any interruptions. Kurt Vonnegut helped me get this started, and before it was over we had filmed almost twenty writers. Among them were Pauline Kael, Nora Ephron, Tom Wolfe, James Alan McPherson (my old student from Iowa), William Styron, Susan Sontag, Reynolds Price, Joe Heller, John Gardner, John Hawkes, John Irving (my son Colin was named after his son Colin), George Plimpton (who does the introduction), Stephen Spender, James Dickey, Tom Stoppard, Toni Morrison, Isaac Bashevis Singer, and myself.

At the present time I'm finishing up two novels. One is about my dad and some of his whiskey and gambling experiences. The other is about myself during World War II. I also have a collection of golf stories called *For Golfers Only*, which I have just sent up to my agent, Laura Blake, at Curtis Brown.

I've had a lot of luck in writing and think much of it has been because I've never tightened up and taken myself too seriously. I guess I find almost anything I deal with slightly funny. And I think students seem to like the way I tell them to relax and write run-on sentences when they get in

trouble, or if they can't spell something, smudge it. I even encourage them to write on a blank screen of the computer. Anything to keep them loose. And I only give them one piece of advice, which I gleaned from reading one of my favorite writers, A. J. Leibling. He said, "You write as well as you can. And how you do it is your business."

On Leibling: He was a fan of *Southern Fried* and wanted to review it for the *Times*, but Walt Kelly did it instead. Anyhow, I saw Leibling in a restaurant one day and started across the room to introduce myself. But at the last minute I realized how much in awe of him I was and backed off. For someone like myself, who never stops talking, I froze and walked away. Weird, aren't we?

I divorced my second wife three years ago and married Sarah Gilbert—she is an ex-student of mine and the author of three novels: *Hairdo; Dixie Riggs;* and *Summer Gloves* for Warner Books. She also did the novelization for them of the movie *A League of Their Own*.

We now live in Winnsboro, a small town thirty miles from the University in Columbia, in the mayor's old mansion with ten rooms, a wraparound porch, four outside dogs, and three inside cats. I go to all the football, basketball, and baseball games at USC and play golf at Wildwood down the road to the tune of a twelve handicap. The twelve is guaranteed to be coming down in thirty days because I just got Bob Mann's *Automatic Golf: Add 30–80 Yards to Your Drive in 21 Days* video, which I ordered over cable TV.

I belong to a golfing group called Parker Smith's International Golf Writers. Twice a year we play against writers from Britain and Japan. We have played in Spain, France, Hawaii, Bali, Ireland, and next year we're going to Jakarta and maybe Tokyo. Last November we went to Morocco, for the second time, as guests of King Hassan, who is a golfer and every year has his own professional and Pro-Am tournament.

While there is very little money in golf writing, you can cheerfully starve traveling around and seeing the world and playing the great courses. And since the short story market has virtually dried up, I use golf magazines to publish short stories.

And finally, it's curious what's happening to my nieces and nephews. I've never thought about it until now when I began writing this thing. Bobby's son Mike finished USC and is an accountant; Perry, his second son, dropped out of school and is a mechanic doing diesel engine repair. Dickey's son Chauncey dropped out of school and

"Sarah on a camel," Morocco

With the renowned golf champion Lee Trevino, 1993

is a plumber. Jimmy's daughter Carol is a housewife and social worker and his son Bruce dropped out of school. The last I heard he was a grill cook somewhere but planning on becoming a writer. My daughter Kathy finished USC in education, plays guitar and flute, sings and acts and is teaching day care at the University of Texas. My son Colin studied Greek in Crete and is now in his second year at St John's in Annapolis, Maryland, studying the classics. Maybe he'll drop out and become a grill cook. Anyhow, it sure makes you think there's some basic pattern out there.

I'd like to close this with a quote from my old agent Maxwell Penrose Wilkinson. Not so much for the message, but for the sheer humor and sound of it. I'm sure the sound is something like the one I use in *Doctor Golf.* Anyhow, one night at the Absinthe House in NYC when he was deep in his cups he called the manager over to complain about the ways of the world. At this time he was representing John D. McDonald, Kurt Vonnegut, Richard Gehman, Jake La Motta, a couple of other losers, and myself. Anyhow, he stood up and gesturing theatrically across the blank wall behind him he intoned, "Ruben, my dear man, how would you like a mural on this vast portico I see before me? It would be of me, of course. And I see myself dressed in eternal robes, standing on some rather

high promontory, waving farewell to my wretched clientele."

BIBLIOGRAPHY

Fiction:

Southern Fried (short stories; also see below), Gold Medal Books, 1962.

Doctor Golf, Lippincott, 1963.

Moonshine Light, Moonshine Bright, Lippincott, 1967.

Southern Fried Plus Six (contains *Southern Fried* and other stories), Lippincott, 1968.

Ruby Red, Lippincott, 1971.

Dixiana Moon, Viking, 1981.

The Chitlin Strut and Other Madrigals, Peachtree Press, 1983.

Lunatic Wind, Algonquin, 1992.

Nonfiction:

How 'Bout Them Gamecocks!, University of South Carolina Press, 1985.

Golfing in the Carolinas, Blair, 1990.

Screenplays:

"Southern Fried" (based on his book of the same title), Twentieth Century Fox, 1967.

"Off We Go," Paramount, 1968.

"Fast Nerves" (television screenplay), American Playhouse, WNET-TV, New York City, 1969.

"Cold Turkey," Paramount, 1970.

Contributor of short stories and articles to periodicals and newspapers including *American Heritage, Charleston, Esquire, Golf Digest, Golf Illustrated, Golf Journal, Harper's, Holiday, Saturday Evening Post, Southern, Southern Living, Sports Illustrated, Travel and Leisure, USA Today,* and *West Magazine* of *Los Angeles Times.*

Lee Harwood

1939-

*Lee Harwood on the Glyderau,
North Wales, 1993*

Preface

I'm fifty-three years old. To write an account of my life at this point is somehow unnerving. It seems to imply a life neat as a story with a beginning, middle, and end, especially an end. Also there are all those oversimplifications due to the limitations of language and a reader's patience. I'm stating the obvious, I know, but how to reach a clarity?

Or is it just a progress report, assuming there is such a thing as progress? Though death seems to end it when we've hardly started. A listing of achievements? But what are achievements? Books?

Assuming the books are something concrete and useful, what does the writer's own life matter anyway? You can see this is rapidly heading into Bishop Berkeley territory with questions about the very nature of reality or personal reality at least. And in addition to this I should add that one of my favourite pieces is Borges's parable "Borges and I," which ends with the sentence "I do not know which of us has written this page."

The painter Ron Kitaj rightly said "reducing complexity is a ruse." If there is any "truth," it's the admission of this complexity. My life seems to have been filled with contradictions, blurred edges, and mess. Memory, of course, uses all sorts of cunning tricks and subtle editing to protect one's own vanity or just to make a story more colourful. Chaos, I know, isn't a permanent state. There have been times when my life seemed straightforward and simple, where there was a sense of purpose that was followed.

What I do know today is that I lack any sense of clarity or even that mysterious word "purpose." It is a strange mystery to me. Things seem to happen, almost by accident. Work gets written, and the daily business is moved through, sometimes for better, sometimes for worse. From the outside my life may look a clear enough story, but from the inside . . . It's very hard to tell. This brings me back to the chastening entry in Camus's notebook: "Nostalgia for the life of others. This is because, seen from the outside, another's life forms a unit. Whereas ours, seen from the inside, seems broken up. We are still chasing after an illusion of unity" (1942). Though what would we do if we found it?

I'm stuffed with quotations—but that's how people are. We may live alone and we do die alone, but equally we are "social animals." We are a crowd of people just as we live among a crowd of people. We're a bundle of memories and voices. As George Oppen wrote: "bewildered / by the ship-wreck of the singular / we have chosen the meaning of being numerous." A bundle of quotations like prayer flags flapping in the wind on a high mountain pass. This has all been best described by Michael Ondaatje in his novel *The English Patient:* "We die containing a richness of lovers and tribes, tastes we have swallowed, bodies we have plunged into and swum up as if rivers of wisdom, characters we have climbed into as if trees, fears we have hidden in as if caves. . . . We are communal histories, communal books. We are not owned or monogamous in our taste or experience."[1]

This may seem to be wandering around—going nowhere?—but what I'm trying to get close to is some sense of how I or anyone gets through a life. We're all so marked by the company we keep, and the time and place we live in, much more than our ideas of free will and originality will admit. I feel so inadequate when it comes to talking about this clearly and truthfully.

1

To step back and try to present this "life" simply? To move from the general to the particular. To acknowledge one's "sources" at least. My father, Wilfrid Travers Lee Harwood, was from Chertsey, then a small town on the banks of the Thames about twenty miles west of London. His mother, Pansy Harwood, née Lee, though born in New Zealand, was from an old Devon family, with a few Scots thrown in. It's her that I felt closest to all my life, because of her temperament and her style. Born in 1896 she had her generation's resilience. Nothing was ever thrown away or wasted. She could continually improvise and adapt. Yet she always had an elegance and an aristocratic certainty in her manner. She was a "Devonshire" woman, having, as Ford Madox Ford wrote when describing John Galsworthy, another native, "a surface softness under which lies the grimmest of obstinacies—the velvet glove on a hand of marble." It was her smile that I remember and a warm gentleness and readiness to act, to help. And there's even a literary connection since her aunt Leah Lee married the French poet Jules Laforgue. My grandmother's husband, Wilfrid Harwood, a Chertsey man, died when I was a child so I have only the vaguest of memories of him. An invalid who lay in bed in the front room and on a summer day walked round the garden in his dressing gown.

With mother, Grace Lee Harwood, Chertsey, England, 1942

He'd been a country schoolteacher, as were his two sons, but not his grandson.

My mother, born Grace Ladkin, was from Earl Shilton, a village west of Leicester. Her family was from the Midlands and the Welsh borders. They worked in boot and shoe manufacturing. She met and married my father when he got his first teaching job in nearby Hinckley. I was never really close to her family. There were holiday visits. A tree heavy with Worcester apples. The sound over the fence of men on a Saturday morning, their terriers hunting rats among the leather hides. My grandfather's watch-chain medal—champion of the Earl Shilton Domino League. My memories show me to be an "ungrateful wretch"? Not that, but they didn't feel like "blood." They didn't feel like my Chertsey family. I could have committed a murder and my grandmother, Pansy Harwood, would have stuck by me, and she told me this.

So . . . I was born in Leicester, three months before the outbreak of the Second World War, on the 6th of June 1939. The birth certifi-

---

[1]Reprinted by permission of Michael Ondaatje from his book *The English Patient,* Knopf, 1992.

cate shows my full name registered as Travers Rafe Lee Harwood. My childhood was, I presume, typical of my generation. The war, the bombing, the fathers away, the strange forms that normal daily life takes at such times. It's hard to know what worth there is in chronicling the daily details, or even if it's possible. As Peguy wrote, we need "a day to complete the history of a second, a year to complete the history of an hour." Rather it's a sense of a time, some more significant than others. It appears that we have periods of vivid intensity and change, and others when we quietly get on with "the business," even seem to tread water.

The years of my childhood remain such a vivid and intense time for me, marked me, but like a card, not an injury. With the declaration of war my father was called into the army immediately. As an officer in the Royal Warwicks, he served with the British Expeditionary Force that ended with the tragedies of Dunkirk. After this he was shipped to the Belgian Congo and then East Africa. He didn't return until 1947. My father, who had

briefly held me as a baby, did not see his son again until I was seven. There was an impassable gap between us. His return could only have caused me alarm since I now had to share my mother, and my family, with this "strange man." I equally expect he too resented the presence of this demanding "strange child" when he wanted to reestablish his relationship with my mother. From this unpromising beginning our own relationship never really developed. It was dogged by suspicion and a difference of temperaments. He was a coldly reserved, strict, and particular man—maybe as a result of the war, maybe because of his own father's coldness. I'll never know. But he never felt comfortable with any display of emotion, unlike his somewhat emotional and excitable only child.

At the beginning of the war my mother and I had moved down to Chertsey and my grandparents' house. My mother worked as a "tin basher," shaping petrol tanks for aircraft in a nearby factory. My grandmother was a volunteer nurse at the hospital treating all the wounded. It's difficult

With paternal grandparents, Pansy and Wilfrid Harwood (at far right), and their son, Sergeant Observer Denis Harwood (Royal Air Force), Chertsey, England, 1942

to describe, but it was a home where everyone helped, did things. We grew all our own fruit and vegetables. Our shoes were mended at home. My few toys were homemade, or I made them from what was at hand. It would be foolish to idealise such a time, but as a child I only remember a happiness and am unaware of any tensions there may have been.

What I do remember clearly from those wartime days, or rather nights, was eating cold rice pudding in our Anderson shelter at the bottom of the garden during the bombing raids; having my bedroom window shattered, with the frame smashed over my bed, by the blast of a German rocket (I slept through the whole event and so was duly angry I hadn't been woken to see the nearby flames and devastation—I still remember the sound of crunching glass as my mother carried me from my bed that morning); and detesting the U.S. airmen who visited our house and as a Christmas present gave me an egg cup full of sugar. "Ungrateful wretch" strikes again. The self-cen-

tredness of a child. Meanwhile my father's younger brother, Denis, was shot down and killed over North Africa.

2

After my father's return, he stayed in the army for a further two years. My mother and I accompanied him to postings in Shropshire and Staffordshire. Eventually he resigned his commission as a major in the Royal Engineers and in 1949 returned to teaching. I gladly returned to "normal life" in Chertsey after suffering a series of dreary village schools and an attempted escape from the school in Wellington (I was duly returned and suitably punished by my father—two weeks "confined to barracks"). My father taught mathematics at the school in his hometown until his death in 1969. People talk to me about him with admiration as a very conscientious and correct teacher, a "gentleman."

"My father, Captain W. T. Lee Harwood (seated third from left), with the remaining officers and sergeants of the Royal Warwickshire Regiment after Dunkirk, 1940"

Chertsey was then a country town surrounded by farmland, woods and copses, the meadows by the river, and the sandy heathlands nearby. It was a real pleasure roaming this place as a child. There was no sense of time. The seasons came and went, but that seemed to take ages. It was a continual joy taken for granted. With my friends there were camps to be built in the woods, trees to be climbed, streams to be dammed, pears to be stolen, other "gangs" to be challenged. It all sounds very innocent now and generally was so. That love of the countryside has never left me, though I've obviously cut back on the damming and stealing. There's a continual fascination in watching the natural world. A wild flower or a bird or a pebble on a beach. The longer one watches, the more one finds. As Gilbert White noted: "It is, I find, in zoology as it is in botany: all nature is so full, that that district produces the greatest variety which is the most examined." Such dictums go far beyond watching hedgerows. It's an ignorant person that equates the pastoral with escapism.

This enthusiasm developed in my teens into breeding champion show rabbits (Best of Its Breed and Best Junior Entry at the 1955 Surrey Combined Rabbit Show, for example!) and helping handle stock at Guildford Market. There were trips farther afield like swimming in the Wey and the Thames, or nutting at Virginia Water. By my midteens I was cycling even farther with tours through France, Belgium, and Holland. I usually travelled alone as I came to find that the most relaxed and peaceful way. I chose my own pace and company, lived on bread and tomatoes, and slept in youth hostels, barns, and woods. Later, abandoning my bike to get even farther, I hitch-hiked to Spain and Italy. By now it wasn't just to see foreign countryside. It was also for the thrill of standing in front of paintings by Botticelli in Florence or Caravaggio in Rome.

George Oppen wrote: "It is the child who is the branch / we fall from." It seems so.

The author exhibiting at Addlestone Rabbit Club, 1955

3

How one comes to poetry is a matter of education and then "natural sympathies," whatever they are. How one comes to write poetry is a more difficult question.

My own education consisted of going to various state schools and, eventually, on my second try, winning a scholarship to a very good though somewhat snobbish grammar school, St. George's

College, Weybridge. I still remember one of the Catholic priests who taught there sniffily announcing to me: "Gentlemen always wear gloves." Needless to say, my being a "council-school scholarship kid," I was not considered a gentleman nor suited to an eventual university education. Such British class prejudices seem absurd and unreal now but were real enough then. Luckily I had a few good teachers, especially for English Literature. Thanks to the advice of one of my father's colleagues, I also found I could go to university and duly went in 1958 to study English at Queen Mary College, University of London.

I started writing poetry when I was fifteen. That old coincidence of poems and puberty. Usually people grow out of it and leave it behind like teenage spots, but I hung on for some unknown reason. Maybe it was because, despite the dubious adolescent beginning, I gradually found I was actually creating something. I discovered that a piece of writing could become a sort of "structure" that could stand on its own, regardless of the question of self-expression involved in the process of making any art. A piece of writing could be taken, read, and used by others. Such a making was a real craft to be worked for and, for me, a real need.

It is very much a need, a true necessity in oneself, to make the marks on the paper. It certainly isn't from any sense of superior vision. I think I'm as smart and as stupid as the "next man."

I'm not a teacher nor am I dazzlingly perceptive. I do though—unlike the majority of people—have this need to note "things" down, to create. This, in a way, has become my profession. I certainly haven't found this satisfaction elsewhere, nor have I been successful in any other skills. I've got by with varying degrees of competence in a number of jobs over the years, but it's always been the poetry that has been central for me. A form of obsession maybe, but it's the one thing that's stayed with me.

My early "verse"—I can't call them poems—was far from promising. I tried to write, I imagined, in the mood of Keats and Wordsworth. I remember walking dreamily through the fields reading Keats's "Sleep and Poetry" and "Ode on a Grecian Urn" and thinking these poems were the most marvellous things. I also read parts of Wordsworth's *Prelude,* and this had a similar effect on me. My own attempts, as you'd expect for that age, were filled with self-pity, vanity, and sentimentality. At sixteen the twentieth century entered when I discovered T. S. Eliot and Ezra Pound and somehow Louis MacNeice. The surfaces of these poets, especially Pound's Chinese poems and social satires and Eliot's *The Waste Land,* were duly copied and added to the cocktail, or maybe it should be called a stew. I wonder what I could have understood at all of the real content of these poets at that age. Very little, I expect. Rather I was grabbing at tones of voice and reproducing what I imagined as the mood of their poems that I felt I could identify with.

Once I moved to London and went to university, a cornucopia of new discoveries was placed before me. I'm talking about literature here, but the same was true in all the other areas of my life then. After a tentative start, a headlong rush into "the new." A real hunger there. A continual trying out of what's possible, despite the inevitable and frequent awkward and stupid bouts of behaviour.

The thorough University of London course left me with a great love of Old English literature—*Beowulf* and *The Battle of Maldon*—and of seventeenth- and eighteenth-century literature, especially Dryden, Swift, and Sterne. The London nightlife—Soho, the coffee bars, jazz clubs—was altogether another "education" that pulled me, very willingly, directly into "the action" in all its forms. This was far more than appreciating a past literature, it was finding one's own literature. I just hope that's understandable and makes sense to you, dear reader. It was the excitement of finding works of art that felt like the manifesto I'd been waiting for. It was finding the poems of Tristan Tzara, courtesy of Michel Couturier, one night at Sam Widges coffeehouse in Berwick Street. Never having seen such things done with language before. Never having seen such freedom and wildness before that all felt instinctively so right. It was being handed a copy of Kerouac's *On the Road* or Gregory Corso's *Gasoline* or Ginsberg's "Howl." Of hearing a visiting American student recite a poem from Ferlinghetti's *Coney Island of the Mind.* And this sweeping excitement spread beyond the books to the first exhibitions of Jackson Pollock and then Robert Motherwell at the Whitechapel Gallery. To hearing Thelonius Monk play at the Festival Hall. To hearing all the great British bop musicians like Joe Harriott and Shake Keane or the Tubby Hayes group at the Marquee. (Charlie Parker had already converted me to "modern" jazz when I was still at school.) To leaving a cinema stunned by the films of Jean Vigo, Buñuel, Truffaut, Resnais, Wadja.

It wasn't exactly the country mouse that came to London, but after the pastoral writings of Chertsey, I moved into an intensity of writing and of life unknown before. It's very easy now to get choked with the facts of what seemed important at the time. The events of that time. The birth of British "beatnikery," the well-thumbed pamphlets on anarchism and Suzuki's *Introduction to Zen Buddhism.* It's hard to know the relevance of these particulars. My life, like most people's, doesn't progress in a neat orderly series of events. Rather it's a woven sprawl that leapfrogs (if sprawls can leapfrog) in all directions. There is change but it's rarely logical or clear-cut. Seeds bear fruit in erratic ways—sometimes the next day, sometimes after years of lying dormant.

4

I'm not going to try to give an account of "The Sixties." Those years did see an immense release, a great burst of energy and optimism. In Britain, with the giant antibomb marches organised by the Campaign for Nuclear Disarmament, the eruption of "pop music" and "youth culture," as it's now known, all seemed possible. The barriers, the class system, the narrow introversion in the arts—all seemed to be collapsing. It's now fairly obvious that they weren't all golden days. The poverty was still very much there. And the "love, love, love" soon slid into a bleak world of hard drugs and violence. The hazy mysticism and protest degenerated into dogmatism and authoritarian religious and political groups. But I still feel very much marked by that time. I still feel that optimism, maybe at times naively and, some might judge, blindly. I've never been able to feel the deep cynicism that came later, nor to believe William Burroughs's definition of a pessimist as a man who knows all the facts.

When I graduated from the university I continued to live in east London until 1967. In 1961 the question, the necessity, of a regular job came up, possibly even a "career." The problem was that I seemed unable to think in such a purposeful way. I was nagged by the thought that I could think pretty and talk pretty but could do nothing with my hands. I had a desire to be a "whole man," a "Renaissance man." I dreamed of a life like William Blake's where he was both an artist and writer and a craftsman. It was, I realise, a romantic dream fed much by the mood of the time.

I couldn't consider a teaching career. My prejudices were too great. My father and his father had all been schoolteachers. I couldn't bear the idea of ending up like them. My childhood memories of my father's colleagues were of men who talked at each other rather than to each other, who knew it all, and in very black and white terms. I felt the very opposite. I knew so little. Nor, unlike my father, did I have any genuine vocation for teaching. I couldn't with any honesty go into such a career as an easy option. Maybe I should have at least tried, especially since so many of my friends and the writers I admire have made a successful career of teaching. But it's too late now. Ah well, spilt milk.

After some halfhearted attempts at jobs in journalism and publishing—an interview with an agricultural trade journal titled *The Muck Spreader*—I eventually ended up as a monumental mason's mate. This seemed very right at the time. I worked in a large stone yard off the Mile End Road helping make elaborate marble and granite gravestones. One of the masons, Lou Esterman, remains an ideal for me. He had that beautiful gift of, for want of a less clumsy phrase, intellectual humility. He was a superb stonemason, carving wreaths of flowers and flowing decorations on a slab of marble after making the briefest of pencil sketches on the stone. He faultlessly cut the long inscriptions in Hebrew and English. And yet with all this natural skill and flair he was never smug or

opinionated. He always seemed open and looking. He always had a generous spirit. I'd had a glimpse of this virtue while at university. The two most noted scholars on the lecturing staff were also the least pompous and the most likely to pursue the matter should a student mention something new to them. This seemed what an education should teach more than anything else. If in a lunch break I should be sitting in the stone yard looking at a book of Picasso's paintings, there would be none of the usual mockery then current, the jokes about how monkeys could paint better, and so on. Lou would want to discuss why Picasso had made a painting the way he did, he'd want to work it out. I've found that same willingness and freshness since then and nearly always amongst craftsmen, like the bookbinders when I later worked in libraries. I found it too when I finally met Tristan Tzara. Tzara epitomised the questing spirit, never taking anything for granted but always searching and pushing the boundaries further. But Lou was really the first to directly show me this. I love and dearly respect such clear modesty. We never met again after my time in the yard, but the seed had been sown.

5

In 1961 I met Jenny Goodgame, then an actress and artist's model, and later a painter. In fact we'd seen each other earlier when we were both students at Queen Mary College. We married in the same year at Limehouse Town Hall. We lived in one room and a kitchen, as we did nearly all our married life, first of all in Brick Lane, then in Wellclose Square off Cable Street down near the Wapping docks. I suppose we were poor, though one wasn't really conscious of that. Lou Esterman had at exactly the right moment appeared on our doorstep with a set of dishes soon after we married. We felt very rich. Like Catherine and William Blake, we imagined, she drew and I wrote. In fact at this time I wrote, painted, and tried sculpture with plaster and with small blocks of marble stolen from the stone yard. When I later edited and printed magazines, Jenny would do the lino-cut illustrations. It was inevitable that when our son was born the next year he was named Blake.

At the end of 1961 the cold in the stone yard got too much for me, despite such delicacies as tea brewed in a bucket. I took a job as reference librarian in Dagenham Public Libraries where they had radiators. I continued working on and off in libraries for the next six years, moving to the University of London Library after Dagenham. Libraries were still at that date leisurely places for people who loved books. The relentless plague of "information technology" had not yet got its stranglehold. There were still card catalogues rather than computer screens. It was a helpful place for me. There was the peace to think, to discover new books, to even read when possible, and to earn a simple living.

6

Dylan Thomas once described writing poetry as a "sullen art," a solitary pursuit when it actually comes down to the making. No one else can do it for you, obviously enough. You're alone with the possible poem, and whether it works or not is entirely dependent on yourself. There are few occasions outside the arts where this is the case, though maybe I have a grandiose view of the arts. It's probably true of other crafts, whether they be doctoring or stone carving. But it's that rare luxury in the twentieth century of being wholly responsible for something, of being able to totally make something, to create.

This rather romantic sense of isolation that can bring its own versions of heaven and hell is undeniably the starting point for all writing. But our ability to get beyond the desire depends so much on others. The ability to give a desire to write, that necessity, some concrete form doesn't come out of "thin air" or "divine inspiration." It's the bundle of voices mentioned earlier. The voices may be found in books read or in hearing or meeting other poets. There are so many sources that can help us discover different ways of "getting it down," of notating our thoughts and imaginings. The particular combination of such influences is unique to each writer. What's chosen, what left out, and the proportions of the recipe. My voice, and the voices in my poems, echo earlier voices. And this pattern, I find, is even to be seen in the structure of my own poems. Many of them seem to contain a weave, a collage, of material. Different personae, myself included, fact and fantasy, close-ups and long shots, and much contradiction. A quilt of fragments.

I may admire the work of many writers but not be able to "use" them for my own work. It

wouldn't, though, be hard for me to make an "acknowledgments list" of the writers who have truly taught me, who've shown me possible approaches, angles, qualities of writing that have helped me "on my way." And most, though not all, of these writers I discovered or met during the 1960s. They've stayed with me ever since. Such a list would have to start with Pound, as mentioned earlier, then Tristan Tzara and Jorge Luis Borges, and later on John Ashbery and André Gide. This is as clumsy and inadequate as most chronicles. In fairness the list should also include others like William Carlos Williams, Kenneth Patchen, Frank O'Hara, Harry Guest, Roy Fisher, E. M. Forster, Stendahl, and Jocelyn Brooke. And I could easily make a third list. But what marks most of these writers and what I love so much in their work is their sense of perspective, their ability to show coexisting worlds, or rather, coexisting realities.

When Apollinaire coined the word "surréalisme," it was not in the sense of a dwelling on the fantastical. It was to describe a new realism, a super realism. One that could express accurately all aspects of reality, simultaneously if possible. A realism that included not only the logical but the illogical, "facts" and daily details along with dreams, memories, imaginings. This is certainly what I hoped for in much of my poetry, especially in my earlier work. *That* form of precision. I'd found this quality in all my literary heros. Pound's *Pisan Cantos* are an obvious example. William Carlos Williams interweaving history and the personal in *Paterson*. Borges playing with our sense of reality and then pulling the rug out from under our assumptions at the end of his fictions. The gentle way both Forster and Gide show we should never judge by appearances. The way Gide in *The Counterfeiters* interleaves journals, letters, parts of a novel, and stories to portray a truly three-dimensional, four-dimensional world. The poetry of John Ashbery with its half-finished thoughts and sentences which, as he says, is "the way we communicate"—"the way experience and knowledge come to me, and I think to everybody." I feel all this is very true and certainly is what attracts me to the work of others, but equally I must admit my doubts about my profuse theorising. Is this all a smoke screen to cover what is very personal in my work? As usual I think it's probably a bit of both. It's certainly easier to talk about literary approaches than untangle personal motives.

7

In 1963 I assembled and printed a magazine called *Night Scene*. It was more like a manifesto than a "literary magazine." By this time I'd joined the newborn network of "underground" poets and publications that sprang up in the early 1960s. The established British literary scene seemed so remote, safe, and hostile to all the "revolutionary" feelings that were in the air. The answer was, like Blake obviously, to publish oneself the work one believed in (using a mimeo machine or any other means that were possible). This network went far beyond Britain and included France, the United States, Canada, and even further afield. It was fuelled by a massive enthusiasm, an extensive exchange of letters, manuscripts, and publications of all sorts from broadsides to books. When I'd visited Tristan Tzara in Paris earlier that year, after he'd approved my translations of some of his poems, I was absurdly full of ideas of Dada, of creating a sort of neo-Dadaism. Tzara very kindly put me right, explaining that a specific response

was necessary to each new set of circumstances. Dada was a reaction to the First World War. It was different now. So maybe our new outbursts were the right way, I thought, to wake things up? I suppose all of us involved in this generous excitement felt we really were making it New, as Pound had dictated. That the poems were fresh creations, messages direct or indirect, showing what Louis Aragon called "the daily miracle" and vigorously protesting at the repressive nature of surrounding society. Sadly, and I suppose inevitably, this community of artists broke up for various reasons, evaporated as years went by. By the 1970s it felt almost as though one was on one's own again. Maybe on one's own, but greatly enriched.

After *Night Scene*, I edited and coedited a number of poetry magazines. *Night Train, Soho* (a bilingual English and French magazine), *Horde, Tzarad* and, much later, *The Boston Eagle*. Most of them were just one-shot publications, though *Tzarad* actually reached four issues and *The Boston Eagle* three. The contributors were mostly young poets living in New York, Vancouver, Paris, and

John Ashbery and Lee Harwood, Paris, 1965

Walden Pond, Massachusetts, early in 1973: (from left) John Weiners, Lee Harwood, Lewis Warsh, and William Corbett

London, though not exclusively so. In Britain, for example, the poetry "renaissance" was started mainly in the north away from London. The magazines also included many translations as well as photos and graphics. There's no sense listing all the people here, but the net was cast wide and so were the resulting friendships and travels.

Gradually, after the initial all-embracing excitement, I naturally made more particular choices. There was a lot of zooming around in these years. My 1966 visit to the United States, for example, when I toured around for two months hungrily exploring a country that seemed to produce such great new art and meeting all the people I'd previously only known through letters. But a sense developed—not so much of a quietening down or getting "serious"—but of having a much clearer idea of where I wanted my writing to go. I don't think it was that consciously planned. It's hard to talk clearly or objectively about this. When I wrote I somehow wanted my poems to have the atmosphere of John Ashbery's apartment

in Paris in 1965, the bare white walls, the piano music of Erik Satie, a sense of quiet almost crystal calm. I also remember the openness and intelligence of a man like Frank O'Hara, and his wit. I wanted my poems to have that too. I still treasure the memory of his care and delight as he told me, a stranger, which paintings to see in Washington. And this willingness and even joy in sharing was an echo of Tzara earlier, and Lou Esterman even earlier. I wanted my poems to have the mystery and unfinished quality of Gustave Moreau's painting *The Chimeras,* which hangs waiting in his house near Gare St. Lazare, ready for us to fill in the blanks with our imaginations. I wanted my poems to be allowed to contain human awkwardness and imperfections. One of my favourite quotes is the note written by Charles Ives to his music copyist: "Mr. Price: Please don't try to make things nice! All the wrong notes are right."

This account is getting hopelessly tangled and vague, and even contradictory. What I am clumsily trying to describe is a move from an overflowing young person's writings, outpourings, to a considered making of poems. Poems that could be handed to others for them to use and mesh into. It was that shift from pure self-expression to creating an artistic structure. The barriers between these two though aren't that clear-cut. They overlap, of course.

8

The end of the sixties was both a bleak and prolific time for me. Put crudely, my life fell apart and I wrote a lot of books. Maybe the puritan dictum of paying the price is true, though I doubt it. Things don't seem to happen because of some overall justice and accounting. Good people die young, so they say, more often than bad people.

In 1967 my marriage to Jenny finally collapsed completely. It was entirely my fault. A lethal combination of immaturity and stupidity on many fronts, emotional and chemical excesses. That old Ian Dury number *Sex and drugs and rock'n'roll.* I still admire and envy my friends who have long and successful marriages. A real virtue. I fell around and travelled around even more after this breakup. I'd been working at a bookshop, Better Books, in London, having left my library job the year before. I then moved to Exeter, back to London, then on to the United States, and eventually a year later back to England and running a bookshop in Brighton. Then off to Gloucestershire to work as a forester. Then back to Brighton to work as a bus conductor for a year. Then off to the United States again and again, giving readings, spending time with friends, even doing a gardening job. Then back to Brighton and another bookshop job in London. And all the time writing, writing.

Amongst all this rushing around, I'd had a breakdown and spent two months in a locked ward of a London psychiatric hospital. At the bleakest times I think I was kept going by the inscription on my grandmother's crest: "Dum spiro spero"—while I breathe I hope. Such truisms do work at such times of trial and stress. That's why they're there, I suppose.

The strange contrast to this grim saga is that at the same time I was being widely published and encouraged. I think I was very lucky in this. I was also lucky, since I seemed so incompetent in handling my daily life, that people approached me for work for magazines and books. I never had to go out asking. I may be ambitious for what I want

to achieve in my own writing, but I've never been ambitious for a literary career or effective at self-promotion. The whole business makes me feel very uncomfortable. My very first book was due to the kindness of Bob Cobbing asking me for a manuscript for his Writers Forum press. It was titled *title illegible.* A year later, in 1966, Anne Waldman and Lewis Warsh in New York published my second book, *The Man with Blue Eyes,* in their Angel Hair Books series. Both these books could be termed little press publications, but when Stuart Montgomery brought me out with his Fulcrum Press, it was a shift to a much wider audience. Fulcrum printed excellent high-quality books in large editions. Stuart Montgomery was a real pioneer. He published great but neglected poets like Basil Bunting, Lorine Niedecker, and George Oppen. He brought out for the first time in large decent editions the work of Ed Dorn, Robert Duncan, Roy Fisher, Gary Snyder, and many other British and American poets. And essentially he launched new writers like Paul Evans, Tom Pickard, and myself. Between 1968 and 1970 Stuart published three of my books. And it was obviously due to this exposure that I was published in 1971 in the Penguin Modern Poets series to reach an even wider readership. Even my father had heard of this series. It must be added though that the size of an edition doesn't guarantee the number of readers. There's a lot of pulped paper around. But Stuart had an amazing ability to publicise his titles so that editions actually did sell out. It was indeed a great loss to poetry publishing when Fulcrum was forced to close in about 1973 due to money troubles.

Since the end of Fulcrum I've been equally lucky with the support of such excellent presses as Ian Robinson's Oasis Books and then Ric Caddel's Pig Press. I owe a lot of thank-yous.

I can't really describe the contents of my early books, though others may try to. They're there and it's for the reader to decide. At times there does seem to be a move from the early, somewhat baroque and surreal poems to a simpler more direct poetry. A shift from elegant cavalier to intense puritan. But just when it seems that a definite progression has happened, things slide back, even overlap, and still seem to. I need them both—the elaborate scene building and collages *and* bare clear poems that may describe a love or a landscape or, as usual, both. The baroque, the artful, was fired by the writings of, say, Borges and Ashbery—expeditions set out, landscapes are glimpsed—but the clarity and simple magic comes from meeting someone like Marian O'Dwyer who

With Judith, Rafe, and Rowan Harwood, Brighton, 1982

inspired much of my work then and later. The fire really does come from the love in one's life. I shouldn't make assumptions for others. I mean the love or lack of it in my own life, and all the possible permutations and conflicts that come with it. A spring in one's step making it feel such a miracle and such an honour to be alive. I'm in danger of gushing. But why not?

9

In June 1971 I was invited to be writer in residence at the Aegean School of Fine Arts in Greece. It was a small art school run by Americans for American undergraduate and postgraduate students taking an overseas semester. The school was on the Aegean island of Paros. I stayed in this post for over a year. It was a very welcome and necessary change from the too hectic rushing around of the previous years. It was like a time to calm down and carefully think about what I was doing. There was the luxury of time and quiet in which I could read and write without interruption,

could even "muse" as I wandered round the island or swam or just sat on the porch of my small house watching the lemon grove below. It was idyllic and a great cure-all for earlier foolishness.

Paros at that time was still fairly undeveloped. The only tourists were Athenians who came in the summer and a small handful of others. There was one boat a day to Athens in summer and two a week in winter, winds allowing. The English-language newspaper *Athens News* seemed to specialise in headlines like "Shepherd Falls off Cliff." Maybe they couldn't have any more pointed news items since the Colonels were ruling Greece then. Life was simple. My house was halfway up a mountain surrounded by an orchard and then bare rocky fields. Water meant a hundred-yard walk with a bucket to a well cut deep into the underlying marble. Light was from a small oil lamp. And for cooking I had a gas cylinder lugged up the mountain on my shoulders every couple of months. I couldn't afford a donkey for this journey since my pay was not exactly generous. My "desk" at the school was an old door on two trestles. It was a matter of "poor but happy." I have no complaints. My work at the art school only meant helping some of the students with their writing and giving occasional seminars on various writers. The idea of teaching people to write poetry or prose seemed very dubious. All I felt I could do was show the students how to read a text carefully and learn about other poets or novelists that might be helpful to them. Creative writing classes seem fraught with the dangers of teachers setting themselves up as gurus and students wanting psychotherapy. Neither seems to have much to do with literature and the real questioning and questing needed for writing.

While on the island I set myself the pleasure of reading one Pound canto a day. I walked those cantos. If there was a classical reference I didn't know, I'd have to walk a mile and a half south of the small town of Parakia to the house of an American expatriate who actually had a classical dictionary. There weren't many books on the island. And if there was a Chinese reference, I had to walk three miles east of the town to visit a Swedish expatriate who had various oriental reference books. And, of course, along these journeys I was mulling over the text of that day's canto. Such space and time was indeed a luxury and taught me so much, not only about Ezra Pound but about writing as a whole. It was here that I was finally able to finish my poem sequence "The Long Black Veil."

It was also during my stay on Paros that I met Judith Walker. Jud was a photographer and visiting art student from Boston. Our meeting soon moved to our living together, a natural shift in such an apparent paradise. We had near carefree lives then. Making art. Swimming and sunning. Good wine and simple food. Who could ask for more? I kept rabbits again. My grandmother even came out and visited us, thriving in the "primitive conditions" due to her own upbringing in the New Zealand outback. It may seem strange, given this idyll, that late in 1972 we decided to leave. Sometimes I certainly regret that decision, and wonder where. . . . But Jud needed to return to Boston to finish her art degree, and I was beginning to feel uneasy in my position as an expatriate writer. I have a great love for Greece, but I was missing walking streets surrounded by my own language. I wanted to have a few more sparks flying. Some of the long-term expatriate "artists" on the island were a chilling warning. In their isolation they seemed to become more and more smug and uncritical, imagining themselves as bea-

cons of purity whereas back home (in the United States or wherever) all the others were obviously corrupt and money grubbing. This easy view didn't ring true. Their paintings grew weaker and weaker and their talk seemed to lack any self-criticism or doubt. We need to be cut down to size now and then, like any other plant, if we're to remain healthy. We also need to see what else is going on.

10

The move to Boston, where we lived for almost a year, was indeed a contrast to Greece, to put it mildly. The culture shock could have been worse since Boston is probably one of the most European-feeling cities in America. I could walk most places, and I had good friends there such as Bill Corbett and Lewis Warsh. It was a home of sorts, though not exactly a happy one. By the time Jud had finished her degree we had no money at all. A summer working as waiters in a fancy Kennebunkport "inn" made us our fare money, and we flew back to Britain in the autumn of 1973.

We settled in Brighton and, really, it's been home ever since. I've always loved the place ever since my childhood day trips to the seaside and my time spent here in the late sixties. It has the best of both worlds, town and country. The town was never stiflingly provincial. There was always something going on, whatever your interests may be. A saucy town. Relaxed, louche, and fun. "Thank God for Brighton!" declared Laurence Olivier. Anyway, if you really needed it, London was only an hour away on the train. And then there was the sea in front, and behind were the hills and unspoilt countryside. Swimming and sunning could continue, though in a slightly more bracing climate.

I now had to find a job and, as so often happens, I fell into one almost by accident. For some unknown reason the idea of working for the Post Office had come into my head. I suppose the origin might have been previous writers who'd once worked for the Post Office, such as William Wordsworth and Charles Olson. It may have been the simple fact I'd found the uniforms worn by U.S. postmen quite elegant and so thought "Why not?" Whichever, after an interview and training, I found myself working as a counter clerk in Brighton Post Office. There were no elegant uniforms but it did turn out to be a very rewarding job that I stuck to, with a couple of breaks, for the next nineteen years. At that time the Post Office, though a delightfully shambling and inefficient organisation, was a genuine service. It was run in a very humane way and for the benefit of everyone. Times have changed and these ideas pushed aside by a greedy demand for profit and lean "efficiency." But at its best the Post Office job helped me meet and respect a whole range of people I would never have come in contact with otherwise. It also felt simply good helping old or illiterate people deal with all the forms and bureaucracy thrown at them. In a way this taught me about real politics and later involved me in trade-union work and even running (and losing) as a Labour Party candidate in county elections.

11

The next ten years were really family years. There is an Indian description of the stages in a man's life—child, warrior, husband, priest. Is this patriarchal pattern true? I hope not. I think not. But these middle years were very much devoted to

being a husband and later a father. I'd made such a mess of my first marriage, I was determined to make this second one work. Jud and I married in the spring of 1974 and then in 1977 our son, Rafe, was born. Two years later saw the birth of our daughter, Rowan.

With the birth of Rafe, I left the Post Office and looked after my son while Jud continued her teaching career. When Rowan came her mother and I reversed roles. I returned to the Post Office and Jud left teaching for a while. In a way I wish we hadn't as I so enjoyed that time at home as a "househusband." The indescribable pleasures of being with one's own children. The terms all too easily slip into sentimentality, but the reality of it goes so deep. It's an affair of the heart, of the blood, and one of the deepest joys. A joy that grows and expands as the children do, as the years pass.

It should be added here that having a family doesn't mean going brain soft. I continued writing, though in a less frantic fashion. I had several collections of poems published, one being very

With Paul Evans, near Arundel, Sussex, 1988

much an exploration of place, titled *Boston-Brighton*. A worthy but dull attempt I now feel. Jud published photo-poem posters of Bob Cobbing, Elaine Randell, Jerome Rothenberg, and John Weiners. Together we started Skylark Press and published books by William Corbett and Paul Evans. We also collaborated on a book of our own work—photos and poems—titled *All the Wrong Notes*, handsomely published by Pig Press. But the most rewarding event for me was when Asa Benveniste's Trigram Press published my collected translations of Tristan Tzara's poems. I'd worked on the poems for years, had some come out in pamphlet form, but this was the first time they were all readily available. The publication was for me like a debt repaid for all Tzara had given me. It was also good to see Tzara's words spread to places as far away as Robin Blaser's bookshelf in Vancouver.

12

Great passions aren't something that suddenly appears. They're something that gradually grows over the years, that gets deeper and richer and larger with experience and knowledge. Besides my writing and my children, the two other great passions in my life are the countryside and the mountains.

I'd grown up in the country but it was something I took for granted. Now I was settled in Sussex I found myself more and more exploring the countryside, examining it. I wanted to know more than just a casual pleasure in my surroundings. I wanted to know the names of all the wild flowers and plants, to be able to spot the different birds. Somehow it's in the naming that we sharpen our attention and learn how to watch with a sharp eye, how to be careful in our surroundings. I'd spend days walking the South Downs, the line of chalk hills that runs parallel to the south coast of England. Each year I would look forward to the arrival of the first swifts, to finding the first common spotted orchids in the various spots where I knew there were colonies, to seeing the lapwings swirling over the Cuckmere valley or a heron rising from a ditch near Glynde. The sense of pace and patience and the quickness of eye I learn with this feed so much more than an interest in "natural history." My heroes became naturalists such as the Reverend Gilbert White and, despite his many faults, W. H. Hudson. But my special heroes were the two writers who so marvellously combined a

"Fiftieth birthday in the French Alps, with friend Janet Lawrence," 1989

passion for the countryside with a passion for literature—Jocelyn Brooke and Geoffrey Grigson. Brooke's brilliant work on British orchids and his own fictions, such as *The Orchid Trilogy (The Military Orchid; A Mine of Serpents; The Goose Cathedral)*, and his autobiography, *The Dog at Clambercrown*. Grigson's exhaustive handbook *The Englishman's Flora*, along with his own poetry and the many far-ranging and unsurpassed anthologies he assembled of eighteenth- and nineteenth-century poetry.

My love of the mountains was in a way a development of my love of walking in the countryside and hills. But in other ways it's another world in the demands it makes and the excitement and heaven it's shown me. I owe this all very much to Paul Evans, a dear friend and a poet I greatly admire, whom I'd first met in 1965. Paul had an unique combination of vigour and wit, tenderness and true scholarship, that I love. He invited me to North Wales in the mid-1970s, and after that I've never looked back. We went on to climbing all the main peaks in Wales. Walking, scrambling, cling-ing, and clawing our way up by a variety of routes in all weathers and at all times of year. We later went on to try the Lake District and the Scottish peaks.

I was also joined by Harry Guest on some of these "expeditions" to the mountains. We'd been tramping Dartmoor together for some years, so this was a natural progression. Again, like Paul, Harry is another long-standing friend. We'd known each other since 1963. The precision and atmosphere of his poems are like touchstones for me of what I want in poetry. We weren't quite the Three Musketeers, and in fact we never climbed together as a trio, but there is a sort of "compan-ionship of the heights" that closely bound us. Such a committed and continued enthusiasm couldn't work otherwise. My dearest and closest friends.

It's hard, if not impossible, to describe the thrill and pure joy of being in the mountains, being on the tops. A whole intense experience so beyond words (and in that lies part of its power and fascination) where I felt so immediately present, alive, and surrounded by such solid magnificence. It can be that golden joy of standing late in the afternoon on a ridge, the whole of North Wales spread out below, and the sea glittering in the distance. It can be clinging to an unpleasant cliff in the Carneddau and suddenly seeing a peregrine falcon perched almost beside me. It can be Paul and me throwing ourselves at the rock and hauling ourselves up the Cneifion arete, laughing much of the way, oblivious to anything else by necessity and choice. It can be that muffled silence of a winter climb wrapped in white and grey cloud, the rock coated in ice and all the ledges deep in snow. Like being in another world, though also being very intensely in this world.

13

In the spring of 1983 my marriage to Jud ended. We had had many good years, been at ease and happy with each other. We'd successfully made a home and raised a family, yet somehow we started growing apart until it seemed we were almost living separate lives and only made contact when it had to do with our children. We didn't seem to have the will, when the break came, to really work and try to rebuild what we'd had.

This account of my life is all becoming a cautionary tale. I don't know if I or anyone can draw a moral from it. I wish I could. I almost feel

there's nothing I can trust except the mountains and the countryside, and possibly the writing. I certainly don't trust myself but continually doubt my ability now to hold one idea or emotion without it suddenly sliding away from me, beside me, whatever. I feel like one of the earls in the Wars of the Roses. I set my standard up but as quickly leave the battlefield when most needed or even go over to the other side. I know I can be trusted when navigating in cloud on a mountain-side but certainly not when trying to navigate sexual and some emotional "clouds" (though I wish I could). Paul Evans wrote in one of his pieces titled *Transparent Things:* "Why are human rela-tionships so tortuous? Sometimes I should like to be a rock. Sometimes I am a rock. Looking for a friendly female geologist, my sardonic shadow says."

As a result of this collapse, I left the Post Office and Brighton and flew to California. Such a break isn't that simple. There's such a weave of reasons and excuses. Jobs may wear us down, make us dull and resentful. "Foreign fields" may seem to offer a longed-for warmth and a new chance. Easy answers are desperately grabbed at without much consideration. Who does, though, live such a reasonable and considered life? It almost seems like a myth to keep people in line, to control the emotional animal that can't help leaping and falling about. Irresponsibility isn't a virtue, but it can be understandable.

I stayed in California for a year and a quarter living with Bobbie Louise Hawkins in Bolinas, a small village up the coast from San Francisco. I loved the beauty of Bolinas. I would row a dory around the lagoon watching the seals or an osprey in its perch clawing a fish or the lines of pelicans flying by at dusk. It was, in some ways, again an idyllic place. My children came out and visited me, and I would go back every four months or so and visit them in Brighton. The vigorous and open literary life of San Francisco was a pleasure and a welcome change from the somewhat narrow and clannish world of British poetry. I was asked to lecture on Shelley at New College along with Michael McClure and Diane DiPrima. Again this is something that would never have happened in Britain where the academic establishment has little time or room for "creative writers." I suppose this realisation was nothing new since I'd always felt my work was more readily welcomed in the United States than Britain. Certainly all my early encour-agement came from American poets. In recent

Rafe and Rowan Harwood, Brighton, 1993

years this may have changed, but the warm welcome is still there.

By the autumn of 1984 I knew I couldn't stay on in California. Living somewhere is so different from visiting. I might be welcome but I still felt a stranger. It wasn't my "place." This lack could have been managed, but what couldn't be managed was how much I missed Rafe and Rowan. I couldn't bear being that far away from them. The distance and infrequency of our being together were totally upsetting to all of us. I flew back to Brighton, got a flat fifteen minutes' walk from where Jud lived with the children, and, for want of an alternative, got my old Post Office job back.

The years after my return were a mixture of confusion and rewards. I was living alone again and swept by alternative waves of great self-confidence and nervous insecurity. Trying to get it right.

The rewards were obvious. My children were nearby and in practice lived half the week with me. It was a very rich time in that way. And there was the extra bonus of living in a countryside that I

knew intimately, where I could walk the paths on the darkest night and still find the right way. To have that close familiarity with the land.

In a way it was also a slightly isolated life. I wasn't a monk, but . . . (This is a discreet autobiography.) A necessary quiet time. I didn't take much part in any "literary scene" but concentrated on pursuing my own obsessions whether they be my children, the work of Jocelyn Brooke, or going to the mountains. I had a number of books published, including in 1988 a "selected poems." It all seemed solid work. And it was good to know there was someone out there that wanted my work, that the poetry was being used and then expanded by others with their reading of it. That my writing wasn't just me talking to myself.

14

On the 28th of January 1991 Paul Evans and I were climbing together in the Snowdon massif in North Wales. We'd already had two glorious days, magical days. We'd done, what we called, "connoiseur's routes.'' A lot of ice and snow on the tops, our beards growing stiff with ice. But a hot sun and clear blue skies. On the Monday it was greyish and cold, but good enough. We'd contoured round Crib Goch into Cwm Uchaf. The surface of the snow was frozen hard. The waterfalls were solid curtains of ice with trapped air bubbles trickling down behind in the shadowy flow of water. Thick icicles hung on all the surrounding rocks. We reached the foot of our climb—the Clogwyn y Person arete on Crib-y-ddysgl. It was a route we'd climbed several times before and even descended twice. As Steve Ashton says in his guide, "the rock proved to be very good—rough and comforting." There were plenty of good holds and ledges. It was all very square cut and manageable.

We sat talking for a while. Joking a bit. Watching a lacework of snow being blown across the surface of the small frozen lake, Llyn Glas, below us. Then we started up the route, taking it in turns leading, finding a way up through the maze of rock. Two-thirds of the way up, I'd gone up a chimney in the rock and was on the ledge above. Paul was following me but having difficulty finding a good grip, somehow unable to brace himself between the two walls. He started to lower himself back down to the ledge. Somehow he started sliding, landed awkwardly, and lost his balance. He rolled off the ledge and fell over three hundred feet. He was killed instantly. His body lay stretched out in the snow beside a long black rock, some blood in the snow above his head.

We're so used to believing that everything can be fixed, that things, us included, can always be patched up some way or other, and that we can keep going. But a death like this is so final and totally undeniable. It shouldn't have happened, but did. The coroner later described Paul's death as "sheer bad luck." We were properly equipped and experienced and following an established route. We were doing a thing we loved in a place we loved. When death comes I can't imagine a better way to go. But it shouldn't have happened to Paul. He was forty-six, with a new family, and so much still to do. But I'm still here and he's gone forever. I can never forget this. This immense loss.

15

Janáček titled his 1912 piano piece *In the Mists,* a reflection of his own sense of isolation as a composer and a man. I think I can intensely identify with that mood. I feel so remote, out "on

the borderlands." After Paul's death most pursuits seem irrelevant. What's a book compared with a man's life? Yet I've now started writing again, from need and partly habit.

Paul and I, on occasion, used to assume the manner of slightly blustery tweedy gents modelled on the personae of our heroes W. A. Poucher and Showell Styles, two grand writers on climbing and the mountains in general. It was fun to do and a nice counterbalance to contemporary idiocy and fashions. In an indirect way it was an attempt to maintain standards and the right priorities as we saw them, to state them despite the crass brutality that seemed to surround us. It seems like the bully boys only too often run this world. One's only answer is to at least never let one's standards fall to theirs, but instead to try to create in one's own life some sort of oasis of vague decency. My grandmother did this right up to her death at the age of ninety-three.

The mountains are still there, the sea, the countryside. There is that true delight of walking out the door into the spring sunshine. That luxury. And best of all there is the real love and joy of my two children, now in their midteens, both glowing with intelligence and health. And so here I am living fifty miles from where I grew up. All *that* continuity, despite the travels and adventurings. What next? A recent poem ends:

> the first steps out onto
>
> not knowing
>
> the small fox poised on the ice
> listening listening for the telling crack
>
> across the river the frozen willows
> set in a depthless mist

(From *In the Mists: Mountain Poems*)

Hove, Sussex
6 May 1993

BIBLIOGRAPHY

Poetry:

title illegible, Writers Forum, 1965.

The Man with Blue Eyes, Angel Hair Books (New York), 1966.

The White Room, Fulcrum Press, 1968.

The Beautiful Atlas, Ted Kavanagh, 1969.

Landscapes, Fulcrum Press, 1969.

The Sinking Colony, Fulcrum Press, 1970.

The First Poem, Unicorn Bookshop, 1971.

New Year, Wallrich, 1971.

(With John Ashbery and Tom Raworth) *Penguin Modern Poets 19,* Penguin, 1971.

Freighters, Pig Press, 1975.

HMS Little Fox, Oasis Books, 1975.

Boston–Brighton (with photos by Judith Walker), Oasis Books, 1977.

Old Bosham Bird Watch and Other Stories, Pig Press, 1977.

(With Antony Lopez) *Wish You Were Here,* Transgravity Press, 1979.

All the Wrong Notes (with photos by Judith Walker), Pig Press, 1981.

Faded ribbons . . . , Other Branch Readings, 1982.

Monster Masks, Pig Press, 1985.

Crossing the Frozen River: Selected Poems, Paladin, 1988.

Rope Boy to the Rescue (with drawings by Peter Bailey), North and South, 1988.

In the Mists: Mountain Poems (with drawings by Peter Bailey), Slow Dancer Press, 1993.

Prose:

Captain Harwood's Log of Stern Statements and Stout Sayings, Writers Forum, 1973.

(With Richard Caddel) *Wine Tales: Un Roman Devin,* Galloping Dog Press, 1984.

Assorted Stories, Staple Diet/Pig Press, 1985.

Dream Quilt: 30 Assorted Stories, Slow Dancer Press, 1985.

Assorted Stories: Prose Works (with drawings by Peter Bailey), Coffee House Press (Minneapolis), 1987.

Translator and editor of works by Tristan Tzara:

Cosmic Realities Vanilla Tobacco Dawnings, Arc Press, 1969, revised second edition with parallel French/English texts, 1975.

Destroyed Days: A Selection of Poems 1943–55, Voiceprint Editions, 1971.

Selected Poems, Trigram Press, 1975.

Chanson Dada: Selected Poems, Coach House Press/-Underwhich Editions, 1987.

Nonfiction:

Tristan Tzara: A Bibliography, Aloes, 1974.

(Editor, with Peter Bailey) *The Empty Hill: Memories and Praises of Paul Evans (1945–1991),* Skylark, 1992.

Sound recordings and film:

Landscapes (sound recording), Stream Records, 1969.

(With others) *Poet* (film), O Films, 1969.

(With others) *1983* (sound recording), Supranormal Cassettes, 1975.

Also author of poetry card "The Map of the Town," Colpitts Poetry Cards, 1979; and of texts for two poem-print posters written in collaboration with artist Ian Brown: "It's the Vase of Tulips . . ." and "Sleepers Awake . . . ," South East Arts, 1980.

Anselm Hollo

1934-

1

The Way

The way you got to be the way you were
just a moment ago

is the way of "the moment"
a big old notion in which you can never

find yourself
so stagger on on your quest

for the other big old notion
"the now"

as in *right now*
as you just were right then[1]

Anselm Hollo, 1993

What do I *know* of my beginning(s)? What
does *anyone* really know about theirs?

What will generations whose earliest moments
have been recorded, on film or videotape, learn
from those images and sounds when they review
them later in life? What "was it all about?"

What if one recorded every waking (and
possibly even sleeping) moment of one's life up to,
say, thirty-five, and then spent one's remaining
years watching the tape?

A recent study[2] suggests that each mental
replay of a memory is more like a re-*make*, a re-
interpretation, whose materials are fragmentary
and in far from "archival" condition:

> maternity home with
> big black bronze
> statue of sheepdog
> in front who
> knows the connection
> but as we
> walk past someone
> points at it
> says that is
> where you were
> born
> that someone
> quite possibly my[3]

—well, mother, most likely. . . . I remember
writing those purposefully halting lines (an inter-
lude in a longish and otherwise fairly flowing
sequence, *Lunch in Fur*), trying to deal with the
horrors and joys of seemingly interminable midlife
crises, one bitterly cold winter night in a rented
trailer in Cottonwood, Minnesota; but I cannot
state with any certainty whether they originated in
a dream or in my "waking" memory. Walking
around the tall cliffs and boulders of Kaivopuisto
(a Helsinki city park overlooking the old harbor)
not too long ago, I was not able to locate the small,
private maternity hospital (possibly called
"Salus"?) there, nor the big bronze dog (of the
breed known as "German Shepherd" in the U.S.
and "Alsatian" in the U.K.). Nor do I have a clear
idea why such a sculptural guard should grace the

entrance of a place where human children are born. . .

In any case, my birth certificate states that I was born in that city, on the twelfth of April, 1934, the son of Juho August Hollo (1885–1967), professor of pedagogy (educational theory) at the University of Helsinki and translator of world literature from fourteen languages into Finnish, and Iris Antonina Anna Walden (1899–1983), music teacher and translator of scholarly (mostly ethnographic) texts into German.

Juho, or "J. A. Hollo" as he signed himself, was a native of the town of Laihia in the province of Ostrobothnia, the firstborn son of a Finnish master cabinet maker and his Swedish wife. Iris was born in Riga, Latvia. Her mother was a "von" from an originally Prussian family, her father a Baltic-German scientist and professor of organic chemistry. She met J.A. in Leipzig, Germany, where she was studying music and he was doing postgraduate work. They married and went to live in Vienna, where my sister Irina (1921–1991) was born. They returned to Helsinki in the late Twenties.

While my mother's background was urban (Riga, St. Petersburg, Moscow), my father's family weren't exactly country bumpkins: my paternal grandfather, who ended up owning a furniture factory, was an avid reader and had at least one close friend who was a writer, the novelist Santeri Alkio. According to family legend, this grandfather once became so enthused by the classics that he tried (in vain) to persuade his womenfolk to wear Greek garb while going about their domestic chores—in the summer, presumably, since the climate would have made this rather impractical during the rest of the year. The classics continued to loom large in our family history: his eldest son, my father, translated Plato, and my father's closest friend was the poet Otto Manninen, who first performed the *Iliad* and the *Odyssey* in Finnish. A year ago, I, a mere midget in the field, completed an American English version of the fragments of Hipponax.[4]

When I was five, my mother took me to visit her parents in Rostock, Germany, where grandfather Paul Walden (1863–1957) was then teaching, and on to Berlin. I recall a ride down a wide nocturnal avenue, black and glittering with rain, which must have been the Kurfürstendamm; a walk past the Reichskanzlei, Hitler's headquarters, and its stone-faced sentries; a magical, "Old Dutch interior" kind of evening with my godfather, Robert Fellinger, and his Wendish housekeeper

"Tante Helene"—one of the last of her tribe, and, as I heard later, a life-long opium addict. (Her people, also known as the Lusatian Sorbs, are the smallest Slavonic tribe without a country of their own.) Portly and maternal, she radiated an old-world kindness and sweetness that I did not, at that time, encounter in my grandparents' home. They considered me a "difficult" child, and I remember overhearing a conversation in which Grandma Wanda von Lutzau exhorted my mother to "break his will," in typical Victorian/Wilhelminian fashion.

I never really knew my paternal grandparents. I must have been very young on the one visit to Laihia we made while they were still alive. I remember a large, bearded patriarch in a rocking chair, and the thumb on his right hand, which had been sliced off at the first joint in some long-ago woodworking accident. My father's mother is an even fuzzier snapshot of a busy little woman wearing a crocheted black shawl with fringes . . . This visit, too, must have taken place just before the second great slaughter of the century began.

Helsinki, 1940

Exploding, shattering, burning

Big lights in the sky

& this was
Heaven's Gate?

No no it's just the front door
same old front door you know from the daytime
& we're just waiting for a lull in the action
to cross the yard, get down to the shelter
& meet the folks, all the other folks
from all the other apartments

& there was a young woman
at least ten years older
he thought very beautiful

blankets & wooden beams & crackling radios & chatter

it was better than heaven, it was
being safe in the earth, surrounded by many

all of whom really felt like living[5]

In order to improve our chances of survival, my parents, my sister, and I packed our bags and took the steamer across the Gulf of Bothnia to Stockholm, where we stayed long enough for me to learn to read, and to learn Swedish at the same time. Until then, I had spoken only the main conversational language of my family, which was German. My sister Irina grew tired of reading and translating the Swedish speech-balloons in my favorite comics (*Felix the Cat, Mandrake the Magician, Nancy & Sluggo, The Phantom*) in the back pages of the Stockholm dailies, so she obtained a Swedish ABC book and proceeded to teach me to read. In Swedish. When we returned to Helsinki, my father taught me Finnish in a couple of months, preparing me for Miss Ojansuu's elementary school just around the corner from where we lived. Our home was on the second floor of a large apartment building on Mariankatu in the Old Town of Helsinki; the apartment had twelve-foot ceilings and large, white, Dutch tile stoves, heated with wood fetched up from the cellar and stored in a large box in the kitchen.

> grew up in finland
> the south of that land
>
> father philosophos & writer
> wrote the works of cervantes in finnish
>
> mother a talker & talker
> all over the known world
>
> but really my parents
> you were giant white rabbit people
> very wealthy & powerful
> lived in a palace place
> under elephant rock
>
> thrones
> robes
> & a great golden light
> strobed out from behind them[6]

With a sister thirteen years older, I grew up much like an only child, one who was born into a family that was "in exile." My father, the eldest of six, had left the rural province of his birth for the cities and academic life as a young man, and had renounced his share in the family business in favor of his siblings. My mother, a Balt born in Riga, whose German ancestors had colonized Latvia hundreds of years ago, and who had been raised in Czarist Russia and Weimar Germany, never really felt at home in Finland—even though it, too, is a Baltic region. I have reason to believe that she sometimes had a sense of living among barbarians. Her relations with my father's family were, however, mostly cordial, and much of the culture shock she had initially suffered had worn off by the time I appeared on the scene.

Father, J. A. Hollo, about 1925

when my mother was but a young lass from germany, moved to finland for a life with my (then, future) father, they were invited to dinner, a formal academic occasion, & she was seated next to a dignitary chosen for his command of spoken german. it was a long dinner, with many speeches, given in finnish, an ugric language my mother did not understand. the only attempt at conversation her neighbor-at-table managed, was the statement: "this is good pig, is it not" (in german, of course). she is still fond of the story, fifty years later.[7]

Finns are, of course, notorious for being taciturn. The hot, young Finnish *auteur* of recent years, Aki Kaurismäki of *Leningrad Cowboys* fame, puts that trait to good satirical use in his film *The Match Factory Girl:* in terms of the spoken word, its script could have been written by a newt. My mother, on the other hand, was indeed "a talker & talker / all over the known world," and I think one reason why my sister Irina never left the nest until dear Amy (our nickname for her) died, only eight years before she herself passed away in 1991,

*Sister, Irina, Anselm, and mother, Iris ("Amy")
Walden-Hollo, about 1941*

was that Amy needed someone to talk to. But she was a magnificent teacher of languages, and I owe her thanks for the ones I know.

From the time I was two, we spent the summer months, June, July, and August, at a summerhouse some twenty miles from Helsinki, in an area that was then quite rural. The surrounding culture consisted of working-class Finns with a sprinkling of vacation-home owners like ourselves. Although I did not have any playmates except for my sister, and later on, for a brief period, my brother Erkki who is seven years my junior, I loved those summers and populated the landscape with long serial fantasies, stories I told myself, in which those "giant white rabbit people" were part of the cast.

nineteen thirty-nine

just sit here telling myself all these stories
when the sun is shining
on the granite & the veins in it & the veins
in the back of my father's hand

pine needles moss & the light the light
a great roaring silence
so spacious & hospitable
to the rising voice of my mind[8]

"the light the light," indeed; summer days were long, but in the winter they were short and *dark.* It was dark when I set out for school in the mornings, and the streetlights were coming on again when I returned home. And, yes, "the veins / in the back of my father's hand"—he was almost fifty years old when I was born. Compared to my mother, he *was* taciturn, but we did have long philosophical conversations and played many games of checkers during those summers; made our own bows and arrows, threw darts, wandered around the woods looking for mushrooms as fall approached.

Poem Beginning with a Line by Edward Thomas

the steam hissed. someone cleared his throat.
it was my father: time to get off train.
summer time
         for inward world—
rocks. plants. birds. reptiles. mammals
other than ourselves
perceived
         in mute surmise. three months
times ten. a great blank shining space
in life, each year,
quite probably only
           reason i'm still here.[9]

In 1944, after Finland had made a separate peace with the Soviet Union, I spent a summer on the west coast of Sweden with friends of my parents. My host family's paterfamilias had saved his favorite juvenilia, which included the collected works of James Fenimore Cooper and Edward S. Ellis, many "Buffalo Bill" and "Texas Jack" pulp novels, and Edgar Rice Burroughs's "Tarzan" saga. All in Swedish, of course. Like any Germanophone for generations, I had read Karl May's interminable novels set in an entirely imaginary Far West of the nineteenth century, but I had also read Eirik Hornborg's pioneering history of the North American "Indian wars" and was able to enjoy the various subtexts and biases all those authors presented. I was a Western nerd, the way my friend David Ball, the poet and French literature scholar (whom I was to meet six or seven years later at an international summer camp in upstate New York) was a Science Fiction nerd.

Such esoteric knowledge did nothing to further my schoolwork, but my command of German,

Swedish, English, and French (which Amy taught me between the ages of eight and ten) certainly did, and since I also had an aptitude for writing in the language of instruction, Finnish, and did quite well in math and science, I floated through high school at the head of my class. While I had friends among my brainier classmates, I found them dull, by and large, and admired the kids who came from less pretentious families, even submitting to a degree of bullying and condescension from these streetwise types. Everything my parents enthused about—J.A. from a humanistic-Platonic viewpoint, Amy from a Nietzschean "will to change" vantage—that smacked of heroics, idealism, reverence for some abstruse "virtue" or another, was deeply suspect to me. I was a politely rebellious son and student affecting the style of my not always so polite fellow rebels—1930s gangster style hats, pegged "jitterbug" pants, and a generally snotty and cool attitude to cover up typical adolescent innocence and romanticism.

Teen Angel

streets
he walked
thinking to meet or
merely to see her

once a day　　　or once
every other
third or
fourth

a madness

buildings　　　pavements
lines drawn so fine

sweet madness of centuries

there she was　　　no one else
only i & she

a strange
an isolate
sensibility

eternity
was
my address
then[10]

Her name was Nina, and she was Russian, although born in Helsinki. Her family had come from St. Petersburg, but not from the "circles" my mother felt *we* belonged to. Amy was violently opposed to our teenage romance—which, in a pre-automobile culture, was limited to long walks and smooching in stairwells. When, in my senior year in high school, I was encouraged by my teachers to apply for an American Field Service International scholarship to the United States, my parents strongly seconded this, feeling it would be a Very Good Thing to put the North Atlantic and a few thousand square miles of continent between Nina and me. So, off I went—first to the aforementioned summer camp, where I met David and argued with him about the respective merits of Westerns and Science Fiction, and then to McKinley High in Cedar Rapids, Iowa.

Chingachgook and Cody, Winnetou, Wild Bill, and their cohorts had been my guides across the huge, wild, entirely imaginary land across the ocean, and by my late teens, those thrilling chieftains had been joined and overshadowed by Ishmael, Huck Finn, Nick Adams, Sam Spade, Philip Marlowe, Holden Caulfield; but by the time *he* came along, I was already having a not-so-thrilling sojourn in midwestern suburbia.

This was 1951. My hosts considered W. Somerset Maugham unsuitable reading for a seventeen-year-old, and they turned an unhealthy color when I told them I liked Henry *"The Air-Conditioned Nightmare"* Miller. They certainly hadn't heard of be-bop, and even if they had, they would have disapproved of it, as they disapproved of the teenagers from "downtown" Cedar Rapids with whom I struck up friendships across class lines.

Having thus acquired firsthand experience of the chasms that yawned between at least three distinct and separate "cultures" in "America" (then as now), i.e. Artistic, Official, and Popular, the kid from Helsinki, Finland, returned from his first venture to the West a sadder but marginally wiser person, and left Helsinki soon thereafter for prolonged sojourns in Germany, Austria, and England, not to return to these still so curiously Divided States until 1965.

2

The first poetry I read, in a parental home with a sizable polyglot library, consisted of works by the German Romantics printed in Gothic typefaces—for instance, Johann Wolfgang von Goethe's *Wer reitet so spät durch Nacht und Wind:*

Who's riding so late through night-wind wild?
It is the father with his child;
He holds his boy safe from the storm,
His cradling arm is keeping him warm.

Spine-tingling stuff, especially when we get to the Elf-King's seductive promises to the little boy:

> Do come with me, my lad so fair!
> My lovely daughters shall give thee care,
> Through night my daughters' revels sweep,
> They'll dance and they'll sing and they'll rock thee
>   to sleep.[11]

In the end, the Elf-King steals the boy's soul; so, don't even dream of going out "riding so late through night-wind wild" (a sentiment of which my mother certainly approved). Then there was verse of a more historic-heroic orientation, such as Count August von Platen's *The Grave in the Busento:*

> Nights one hears on the Busento near Cosenza
>   muffled singing:
> Echoes answer from the waters, from the depths
>   seem to be ringing,
> Shades of valiant Goths move back and forth in
>   ghostly lamentation,
> Mourning the death of Alaric, the greatest leader
>   of their nation.[12]

Grandfather Paul Walden, about 1925

In school, there was more of that sort of thing in Finnish, easily recognizable as, indeed, more of the same. It was interspersed with readings from *The Kalevala,* the collection of Eastern Finnish oral poetry cobbled into a "national epic" in the early nineteenth century:

> I am driven by my longing,
> And my understanding urges
> That I should commence my singing,
> And begin my recitation.
> I will sing the people's legends,
> And the ballads of the nation.
> To my mouth the words are flowing,
> And the words are gently falling,
> Quickly as my tongue can shape them,
> And between my teeth emerging . . .[13]

To a person raised above and in World War II air-raid shelters, in a family divided by Axis vs. Allied sympathies, glorifications of heroism and nationalist mythology were not only boring but repugnant. Long before the Sixties, I was a confirmed internationalist, anti-militarist (though not necessarily 100 percent pacifist), anti-authoritarianist, anti-"Prussian." To this day, military uniforms with or without people inside them give me the heebie-jeebies. I love the "America" of early anarchist communes, of the IWW, of the Lincoln Brigade, of the WPA, and thus feel close to the strains of the Sixties that derive from that tradition.

Excursus: The Kalevala

For a Finn of my Helsinki generation, *The Kalevala* was an early obligatory task of reading and memorization. Hence, first encounters with that work were nonproductive of anything but the traditional schoolboy jokes about birch-bark shoes, etc. The way schools presented the material was off-putting: It was *hyped,* much as I imagine the *Nibelungenlied* was in contemporary Thirties' and Forties' Germany, as the greatest literary achievement of mankind, the ancients' blessed gift to us feeble descendants.

While not the product (at least, as we have it) of a Homeric intelligence, *The Kalevala* does have its charms, spells, and spell-binding moments. It deals with The Word and its Power; it contains the Osiris myth, complete, in two versions, as well as the Quest motif, and, as Paavo Haavikko, the grand old man of Finnish poetry, has demonstrated in two brilliant versions, the story of the origin of abstract "wealth." Then there are Lemminkäinen's amorous and martial exploits whose telling seems closer to the Norse sagas' world than to the ancient shamanistic ambience of blacksmith Ilmari and singer-sorcerer Väinö.

Later, it struck me how bleakly secularized the Icelandic sagas were compared to the *Kalevala* and *Kalevipoeg,* the Estonian variant of the same material. Not until my reading, at least a decade later, of traditional Native American matter did I realize that this was no accident, but due to the stubborn preservation of old traditions in certain cultures, possibly and particularly in those the nineteenth century was fond of calling backward or primitive. Then I came across Giorgio di Santillana's remarkable *Hamlet's Mill,* which resulted in a mildly embarrassing contretemps with a Finnish ambassador to the U.S. During the ten minutes preceding my modest speculative reading of Santillana's thoughts on the "Sampo" theme, at a major American city's Kalevala Day, the ambassador delivered himself of a speech to the effect that the *Kalevala* was simply so great that it did not, and should not ever, require any form of interpretation. Like Yahweh's tablets, it had to be taken at face value. . . . At the risk of sounding immodest, I would like to have it on record that I managed to retain my lunch, deliver the lecture, and walk away with a glowing new-found affection for Louhi, Kauko, Kullervo, and all those folks.

While the *Kalevala* is a typically *patriarchal* cycle of narrative poems, it reads like a revisionist document, one of the earliest: Louhi, the powerful and from our heroes' point of view vicious Lady of the Northland, is Kali, the Great Mother, capable of devouring feeble male ambassadors. Her powerful and decisive presence in the epic as we now have it harks back to a time when battle was joined between an old shamanistic and matriarchal culture on one hand, and upstart bands of "heroes" on the other.

Unless you *like* Longfellow's *Hiawatha,* the only readable English version of the *Kalevala* is Francis Peabody Magoun's.

Δ

There was one poet in my early reading of German classics whose words seemed to bear some relation to how I felt about things:

> The sexton's daughter was small and sweet,
> She showed me through hall and crypt;
> Her hair was blond, her form petite,
> From her neck the kerchief had slipped.

> Candles and crosses, tomb and fount—
> She gave me a tour of the place.
> The temperature then began to mount—
> I looked in Elsbeth's face.
> . . . .
> The sexton's daughter sweetly led
> The way out of hall and crypt;
> Her lips were moist, her neck was red,
> From her bosom the kerchief had slipped.[14]

Like his soul brother Robert Burns, Heinrich Heine loses quite a bit in translation, but there was an irreverent Enlightenment edge to his verse that was very appealing, as were his revolutionary and cynical sentiments:

> There are two kinds of rat:
> One hungry, and one fat.
> The fat ones stay content at home,
> But hungry ones go out and roam.
> . . . .
> These wild and savage rats
> Fear neither hell nor cats,
> They have no property, or money too,
> So they want to divide the world anew.
> . . . .
> The burghers spring to arms,
> The priests ring out alarms.
> The bulwark of the state, you see,
> Is periled—namely, Property.
> . . . .
> No finespun talk can help, no trick
> Of old out-dated rhetoric.
> Rats are not caught with fancy isms—
> They leap right over syllogisms.[15]

Years later, I recognized that tone and vision again in the works of Bertolt Brecht.

"Old out-dated rhetoric" was, indeed, what I mostly found in my early reading of what was called *poetry,* even though there were exceptions such as Heine, Christian Morgenstern, the German counterpart of Lewis Carroll, and Joachim Ringelnatz, a Hamburg sailor-poet who still awaits translation (and may have to wait for it a long time—his verse is 1920s macho-piratical and far from politically correct).

e. e. cummings, Carl Sandburg, and Don Marquis were, if memory serves, discoveries made in Cedar Rapids, or even before that, in the United States Information Service library in Helsinki. Their various rhetorics struck me as more up-to-date.

3

To get back to my first sojourn on American soil: For reasons still not entirely clear to me, I was expelled from the dubious Eden that was Cedar Rapids. I was seventeen, and my only vices at the time were smoking cigarettes in public and masturbating in private (Diogenes would have liked it better the other way around). The AFS people were unable to relocate me anywhere. They even had trouble booking passage for me back to Finland, and so I stayed in their clubhouse in New York City for a couple of months at the beginning of 1952. Provided with a small allowance, I was free to roam the streets, museums, and bookstores. Finally, after I was shipped home, I earned my baccalaureate and matriculated at the University of Helsinki, with the intent of majoring in science, to follow in my maternal grandfather Paul Walden's footsteps as a chemist—thus fulfilling my mother's "dearest wish."

After a stint as an interpreter at the 1952 Olympic Games in Helsinki, and a couple of rather dismal semesters at the university (I was still pining for Nina, but she wouldn't have me back), I came down with a touch of tuberculosis and had my one and only *Magic Mountain* experience, a long summer in a sanatorium in the Finnish countryside. It has been a while since I last read Mann's novel, but it seems to me that there was a whole lot more boozing and sexual activity going on in good old Nummela. It was there that I first acquired a taste for alcohol, and it was there that I had my first consummated affair, with a kind and passionate older woman. I had just published my first slim volume of poems, the only ones I ever wrote in Finnish (mostly not very good imitations of Heine and Lorca, although a couple of them still lead a ghostly existence in Finnish anthologies), I had a lover, I had nights of love and laughter with her, interspersed with nights of serious drinking in the company of a bunch of engagingly monstrous Ur-Finnish war veterans. I had escaped from the long dreary hours in concrete-floored chemistry labs. Antibiotics and a drug called PAS had taken the sting out of the White Death, the food was good, people had new Dizzy Gillespie records—I had never felt better in my whole life. Meanwhile, back in Helsinki, my aging father was tapping away on the old Remington Noiseless typewriter, translating the umpteenth "Horatio Hornblower" novel in order to pay for it all, a bottle of White Horse

scotch on the corner of his desk. He said he liked the label because it had a lot of *text* on it.

With my mother, I had visited my grandparents in 1950 in the small South German town where they had landed after a strenuous wartime odyssey from Rostock, where incendiary bombs had destroyed their home, to Berlin, to Frankfurt, and finally to Kurheim Zollernalb, a combination of health resort and retirement home, staffed by Franciscan (Sisters of St. Clare) nuns. Although my grandmother Wanda von Lutzau (1878–1950) was fifteen years younger than her husband Paul Walden, the strains of their life in wartime had taken a greater toll on her, and she died during that visit. After that, both my mother and my sister Irina spent time living with my grandfather and helping him with his scholarly work on the history of science. In his eighties, he still lectured on the subject at the University of Tübingen.

After I was discharged from the sanatorium in the fall of 1953, it was decided that I should spend a period of convalescence with my grandfather and take on the (none too onerous) duties of his private secretary. I did, in fact, stay with him until his death at the age of ninety-three, in 1957.

The Walden Variations
(for Robert Creeley)

white hair
fine fringes
under the brim

old sunshine on twigs

grandpa
a sturdy
alchemist

old sunshine on twigs

*

old sunshine on twigs

& on the pigs
we ate
together he & i

deaf alchemist
loud grandson

*

ate together

teeth fell out

& died

old sun[16]

Written twenty years later, the laconic lines commemorate four extraordinary years in the company of an extraordinary human being. A research chemist whose discovery of the "Walden inversion" still merits an entry in textbooks of organic chemistry, and a widely published writer on the history of science, my grandfather had survived two revolutions and five major wars, the loss not only of his native land but of an entire *culture* that those wars and revolutions effectively wiped out, and the loss of a beloved wife and companion of fifty years when he was eighty-seven. He had come through it all with an unshaken conviction in the future possibilities of the species, even though he was fond of quoting the German proverb "Gegen die Dummheit ist kein Kraut gewachsen" (roughly, "there's no herb that'll cure stupidity"). The twigs and the sun in the poem derive from the walks we used to take in the old landscape of the Suebian piedmont, walks punctuated by occasional rest stops on benches or old field stone walls, and enlivened by stertorous conversations—he was going deaf, and I had to speak very *loudly* and *clearly* into his left ear; the pigs are a reference to the local diet, in which pork chops and sausages figured quite prominently.

Anselm Hollo, about 1952

Space Baltic

Far, far
     in the future I see

an ancient gringo baron

showing his little grand-nephew
some dusty glass-case memorabilia

in the more than half-ruined manor:

" . . . yesh . . . yesh . . . we used to call that
a *foot*-ball . . ."[17]

This, the title poem of a selection of my "science fiction" poems published a couple of years ago, retains some of the flavor of those days. Paul Walden was no "ancient gringo baron," but he was as much a product of a long-lost culture as the character in the poem, and his conversation gave me a feeling for many places and events that seemed as distant in time as I hope the symbol of present-day American gladiator mania will seem "Far, far in the future . . . " We did not literally inhabit a "more than half-ruined manor" but a spacious third-floor apartment with a panoramic view of the surrounding countryside; we did have neighbors and acquaintances whose manors in what was now either East Germany or Poland had

vanished in the conflagration of World War II, and in the downstairs tavern I met and drank with returnees from prisons and concentration camps in Siberia who had been sent to the *Kurheim* to decompress and recover.

Having lost his parents at an early age, and being the youngest of six children, my grandfather had been raised by his brothers, at least two of whom were officers in the Czarist army. In the Russia of his youth and early manhood, Imperial subjects with academic accomplishments were given the option to substitute government-related teaching work for military service, and Paul Walden, a lifelong pacifist, had made that choice. His involvement with the sciences, and his knowledge of languages and literature, must have given him a perspective on the world that was critical of simplistic notions of patriotism.

If history is understood as "tales of the tribe" that provide reasons for endless revenge—as they seem to be doing to this very day, in supposedly civilized European countries—perhaps only those who are truly "mixed" and "exiled" can step outside of it. I am a descendant of at least five pairs of archenemies of one period or another: Finn/Swede, Finn/Russian, German/Pole, Pole/-Russian, Russian/German—etc., etc.; only the gods know how it multiplies back and back . . .

Excursus: The Warriors

Colonel Walden at Pulkovo   lauded by Lenin
in John Reed's *Ten Days that Shook the World*

heard on tape on the way to Taos
"HEY THAT'S MY GRAND-UNCLE"[18]

A few years ago, my wife Jane and I were driving from Salt Lake City to Taos, New Mexico, listening to an unabridged recording of John Reed's book. This was the passage that caused my exclamation:

> The Pulkovo detachment by its valorous blow has strengthened the cause of the Workers' and Peasants' Revolution. . . . Revolutionary

Hollo (left) with BBC colleague Erkki Arni, 1959

Russia and the Soviet Power can be proud of their Pulkovo detachment, acting under the command of *Colonel Walden.* Eternal memory to those who fell! . . . [*Italics added, as in quotes to follow*][19]

It is a quote from a telegram sent by Leon Trotsky (not Lenin—I must have been carried away by alliteration), People's Commissar, on the thirteenth of November, 1917, two days after the engagement. Historian William Henry Chamberlin elaborates:

> Trotzky [*sic*] is inclined to attribute much of the credit for the successful stand of the Red troops at Pulkovo to *Colonel Walden, an old colonel who had often been wounded in battle,* who assumed command and directed the flanking operations. "It couldn't have been that he sympathized with us," writes Trotzky, "because he understood nothing. But apparently he hated Kerensky so strongly that this inspired him with temporary sympathy for us."[20]

And Isaac Deutscher, in his biography of Trotsky, sheds further light on the matter:

> At this stage already Trotsky had to look round for experienced and skilled commanders. On the day after the insurrection, he and Lenin turned for help to the regular officers, hitherto the target of Bolshevik attacks. But the officers who were persuaded to appear at the Smolny cautiously refused co-operation. *Only a few desperados and careerists were ready to serve under the "illegitimate" government.* One of these, Colonel Muraviev, was chosen to command in the battle on the Pulkovo Heights; and subsequently he played a conspicuous part in the first phase of the civil war. A braggart, posing as a Left Social Revolutionary, he seems to have been moved less by sympathy with the Bolsheviks than by a grudge against Kerensky. Trotsky first received him with suspicion. But the Colonel was mettlesome, resourceful, and eager to win a prize in a seemingly hopeless assignment; and so Trotsky was captivated by his initiative and courage. *Colonel Valden* [*sic*], *another officer of this small group, commanded the artillery, which decided the outcome of the Pulkovo battle in favor of the Bolsheviks.*[21]

An old colonel of the Russian Imperial Army, not too swift in Trotsky's opinion, a member of a small band of "desperados and careerists" in Deutscher's, yet a survivor of battles and clearly a competent artillery commander—the older brother of my dear scientist grandfather Paul who wouldn't hurt a fly: truly an agent of the Fates, that chilly day on the Pulkovo Heights.

The old colonel's sister-in-law (I doubt that they ever met), my grandmother Wanda von Lutzau, was a descendant of another warrior: Baron Adolf von Lützow (1782–1834), a Prussian cavalry officer who commanded a legendary volunteer corps, the Black Rifles, in the War of Liberation against Napoleon I in 1813–14. These volunteers were recruited democratically, without regard to class, education, wealth, or even nationality. Not long before one of them, the Austrian poet Theodor Körner, was killed in battle, he popularized their guerrilla exploits in a ballad, *Lützows wilde verwegene Jagd* ("Lützow's wild and daring hunt"), set to music by Carl Maria von Weber and still sung at German student gatherings. Operating mostly behind enemy lines, the Black Rifles inflicted considerable damage on the French emperor's troops and disbanded only after his abdication. Their colors, black, red, and gold, are now the colors of the German flag.

I never met my uncle Väinö, my father's younger brother, because he sacrificed his life to the cause of the White Guard in the early stages of Finland's Civil War in 1918. A promising young architect, he was running a consignment of machine guns for his (ultimately victorious) side in the conflict, transporting them single-handedly in a horse-drawn sleigh, when he was overtaken and killed by a detachment of Red Guards. My father did not speak of him often, but when he did, I sensed his grief and regret over not having been able to curb Väinö's urge to become a heroic martyr.

It may seem strange that I, a self-professed pacifist who was glad to be saved from military service by the dread specter of "consumption," am erecting this small verbal cenotaph for three warrior kinsmen. I think my main motivation is a sense of marvel, mixed with dismay, over the "causes" and allegiances for which males of the species are willing to sacrifice their own and others' lives. *Dulce et decorum est / pro patria mori* ("Sweet and fitting it is to die for your fatherland"): That line of Roman state propaganda was engraved in gold letters on a marble slab in my Finnish high school's assembly hall, and I remember shuddering at its coercive hypocrisy every time I noticed it.

4

stand up a berserker   end up a beseecher
in the vast stone forest of the world's war
    memorials

the ghosts of generals stumble about
disheveled confused   graffiti on the great
    moving wall

moving toward The Wall   résumés for god
Papa wanted me to marry the Finnish language

Mama   chemistry   (her father's life)
both kept me away from Finnish-speaking women
    with all their might

so I went to Germania & married a German
    speaker
but couldn't make a living in those countries

so ended up in England   thus changing
my great love affair with the English (specifically
    American)

language into a lifetime commitment/marriage[22]

All true. No poetic license there. I met Josephine Clare Wirkus, an aspiring actress, in her hometown Gammertingen, where I spent my years with Paul Walden. After he died at his desk, fountain pen skittering away from an unfinished sentence, I returned to Helsinki for a brief time at home. During my years with him, I had kept on writing literary reviews and essays for Finnish newspapers and magazines, while also pursuing a brief "career" as a writer in German that resulted in a handful of published short stories and poems.[23] Not unreasonably, my parents felt that there was no "future" in this, and they urged me to go back to the university to get a degree, and to forget my truelove in Germany who, while an improvement on my former Russian and Finnish girlfriends, still was not what they had in mind for me.

She was what I had in mind, though, and after working a few months as a translator/secretary for a lumber firm and saving my pennies, I took off for Vienna, where Josephine was finishing her acting studies with a professor of the Max Reinhardt school, and simply arrived on her doorstep one late summer evening . . .

Exciting Moments of the Past #631

    sit in shrub
    wait for errant lover
    thinking of politics
    in 1956[24]

(From left) Tamsin, Josephine Clare, Hannes, and Anselm, 1969

We moved in together, got married in the winter, and eked out a strenuous existence in the, for us, somewhat ironically named Wohllebengasse ("Street of Good Living"). Josephine worked evenings as a waitress, I had a stint as a menial worker for the Atomic Energy Agency and another in the employ of the Vienna Trade Fair; I still wrote the occasional piece for publication in Finland (an essay on the great Austrian novelist Heimito von Doderer, an interview with Thornton Wilder when he visited the city), Josephine continued her studies, and we held tight and got by. Vienna in the late Fifties was not the worst place to be young, and in love, and two against the world.

Excursus: Poetry

It wasn't until I encountered the monumentally baffling Ezra Pound—at first, I believe, in a bilingual edition with Eva Hesse's[25] remarkable German translations: a small paperback selection, with a greenish photo image of the slightly puffy-faced poet on a glossy black cover—that poetry began to seem a subject worthy of active pursuit. Pound's Bertrans de Born still smacked of mothball heroics, but *Cathay* and *The Cantos* were something else. They existed in a realm of active language first opened up to me by Ernest Hemingway's crisply Imagist short stories, the favorite reading matter of my early twenties. They also led me to the work of William Carlos Williams and helped me identify my dissatisfaction with my own attempts to write Heinesque poems and Hemingwayesque short stories. WCW's poems encompassed more of what human life was about most of the time, and did so with greater economy, elegance, and variousness than those ultimately formulaic "stories":

Somebody dies every four minutes
in New York State—

To hell with you and your poetry—
You will rot and be blown

through the next solar system
with the rest of the gases—

What the hell do you know about it ?

AXIOMS

Don't get killed . . . [26]

Compared to the poems of Williams and Pound, even the prose of Chekhov and Stendhal *ran on rails*, just as what poetry I knew from the nineteenth and most previous centuries seemed to do: this new poetry made it possible to get off the train and fly through galaxies and dandelions, zoom down to a nail in a woman's shoe, up to the top of Niagara Falls, back to a sunset over Mount Taishan or forward to some minuscule personal moment of incredible complexity in an undisclosed, wholly interior location. Williams's, Louis Zukofsky's, and Kenneth Rexroth's essays mapped the European sources of that kind of vision—Apollinaire, Cendrars, Pierre Reverdy, and Federico Garcia Lorca; the last-mentioned I had already discovered through an intermediary, one "Georges Forestier" who, in the 1950s, sold thousands of copies of his book *Ich schreibe mein Herz in den Staub der Strasse* ("I Inscribe My Heart in the Dust of the Road") by presenting it as the work of a Byronic Alsatian-born Foreign Legionnaire. The poems were blatant imitations of Lorca, and "Forestier" was soon revealed as a fiction (or fraud, depending on how judgmental you want to be); nevertheless, I am still grateful to him for pointing my way to one of the masters.

Despite the ruins and losses and pervasive feelings of guilt and resentment, the Fifties in central and even northern Europe were an exhilarating time. Artists and poets of post-World War II "free" Europe were rediscovering and catching up on the spectacular Modernist movements that had emerged and flourished between the wars: Cubism, Futurism, Dada, Surrealism, Joyce, Pound, Kafka, Stein—all that had been either banned or buried for almost a decade, especially (with the exception of Switzerland) in the Germanophone realm.

During my years in Germany and Austria, I attended that revival both as a reader and, to a modest extent, as a writer. German poet-editors Kurt Leonhard, Max Bense, and Reinhard Döhl were kind enough to publish and even anthologize some of my German-language texts—these were now influenced by Dada, Bense's "stochastic" experiments[27] based on probability theory and cybernetics, and Helmut Heissenbüttel's post-Steinian writings. (In parenthesis: In the mid-to-late Sixties I encountered a very similar "language

orientation" in work produced by students of mine, mavericks at the Iowa Writers' Workshop—whom I introduced to the few translations that were then available of that German-language oeuvre, including works by H. C. Artmann and Konrad Bayer of the Vienna Group of the Fifties[28] and to some of these writers' major initial influences—Sapir, Whorf, Wittgenstein, Barthes, and others. Far be it from me to make a grandiose claim to mentorship here—but I may have encouraged the desires of Bob Perelman, Ray Di Palma, and Barrett Watten to explore avenues not exactly favored by their other teachers.)

Collage and montage of various kinds were the major modes of production. "Any text could be used, textbooks, trivial literature, etc., and . . . the effect is that of releasing language from its rules and structure, demonstrating its restrictions and hierarchies. The idea that language molds and shapes thought is not new, dating from at least the 19th century, but the Vienna Group made this their basic literary premise."[29]

Now, in 1993, the Eisensteinian montage of *The Cantos*, Tzara's words out of a grab-bag, Max Bense's "stochastic texts" and Artmann's "verbaria," Gysin's and Burroughs's cut-ups, Jackson Mac Low's and Clark Coolidge's continued oeuvres, Kathy Acker's montages and appropriations can all be seen as parts of the canon of Modernist verbal imagination. In a note I wrote for my section in a German anthology published in 1963, I see an early expression of my continued love-hate relationship with that "artful" approach to poetry: "I've experimented with various techniques of fractured syntax, mostly in German, but find that the results end up being merely the charmingly sinister effects of a kind of insensate 'objectivity,' a dead end. Time to start over, however modestly."[30]

Little did I know, then, that it is *always* time to start over. However modestly.

5

Late in 1957, I received in the mail an advertisement from a Helsinki newspaper. The British Broadcasting Corporation's European Services, whose brief was "Projection of Britain," were looking for a programme assistant for their Finnish Section, to work on short-wave radio broadcasts from London to Finland. At one of Josephine's tables at the outdoor wine garden of Hübner's Kursalon in the city park of Vienna, I penned a handwritten application much in the same spirit in which I now fill out sweepstake forms, not expecting anything to come of it.

I did, however, receive a reply. Martin Esslin, who was then working for the BBC's European Services and would later rise to prominence as head of BBC Drama in both radio and television, and who is the author of pioneering books on the theatre of Bertolt Brecht and the Theatre of the Absurd, was coming to Vienna on corporation business and would be glad to interview me for the job. Our meeting went well, I was hired, and from the beginning of 1958 to mid-1967 Josephine and I lived in London.

Those nine years in the United Kingdom mostly confirmed the premonition I had when we left Vienna—that London was a place where I would find few writers with an urgency to "start over" in any direction not sanctioned by the established consensus of a venerable tradition. Dadaism and Surrealism, in their day, had made no perceptible dents in that consensus; they had just been "Continental" fads and aberrations. There never had been an Armory Show in London, yet it was mainly among visual artists (Richard Hamilton, R. B. Kitaj, Ian Hamilton Finlay, Edoardo Paolozzi, Tom Phillips) that one found a lively sense of what had been thought and done elsewhere in the first half of the century. The Brits were kind, and I made lifelong friends there, but the literary power structure was afflicted by a closed-shop mentality. Pound had come and gone; Eliot was a gray eminence glimpsed slouching toward the elevator in Bush House, the headquarters of the BBC's European and Overseas Services; and Basil Bunting had not yet been resurrected—a few people knew and appreciated his work and that of David Jones and David Gascoyne, but they were not among the taste-makers of that period of "Angry Young Men" playwrights and "Movement" poets.

As Allen Ginsberg remarked when we first met in London, the young Britons who cheered the Stones and the Beatles were not *readers:* The early "Beat" era produced no British counterparts to Kerouac, Ginsberg, Corso, and Ferlinghetti across the Atlantic. There were imitators, but a genuine assimilation of the Beat, Black Mountain, and New York School aesthetic only took place in the late Sixties and early Seventies, largely due to the influence of American poets Edward Dorn, Tom Clark, and Ted Berrigan who spent time teaching, editing, and publishing in the U.K. In retrospect, Allen's observation may have reflected the economic and educational difference between U.S. and U.K. collegiate cultures in the Sixties.

I still have a vivid personal memory of my excitement and delight upon finding *Howl* and *Gasoline* in a book shop in the Charing Cross Road, and soon I acquired friends and mentors among those who felt a similar delight: Michael Shayer and Gael Turnbull who published *Migrant* magazine and my own first book in English,[31] Tom Raworth (who published *Outburst* and, with Barry Hall, Goliard Press books), and Michael Horovitz (*New Departures*). We looked to the poets we read in American little magazines—like Cid Corman's *Origin*, LeRoi Jones's *Yugen*, Diane Di Prima's *Floating Bear*, Lita Hornick's *Kulchur*—then met them in the flesh as they came to visit and some even to stay a while in "Swinging London": Allen; Gregory Corso, who became my daughter's godfather; Lawrence Ferlinghetti, who published my translations of *Red Cats*[32]; Robert Creeley; Edward Dorn; Jerome Rothenberg; Jonathan Williams; John Ashbery; Ronald Johnson; Tom Clark; Peter Orlovsky; Aram Saroyan; Lewis MacAdams; Gerard Malanga; Larry Fagin; David Ball (first met in New York in 1951!); Piero Heliczer . . .

Excursus: "Un marginal . . ."

One bright August day this year (1993), Jane and I drive up into the mountains. Browsing in Nederland's shoppes, I find a blue stone and a copy of *The Brief Hour of François Villon* by John Erskine, author of many popular books in the Thirties (including *The Private Life of Helen of Troy*, which I remember reading in the American Field Service clubhouse in New York); good subjects, watery works. And in the mail back in Boulder, there is a card from Tom Raworth to tell me: "Piero was killed in a traffic accident in France a few days ago. Bad, so his widow says—hit by a truck." Leaving his enterprise with pain and cry. . . . His father, *un dottore*, partisan, died in World War II, fighting Nazis in Italy.

Piero Heliczer—*"un marginal"* in the French newspaper story Tom had sent me a month earlier, all about Piero's getting dragged out of bed and beaten up by pea-brained humanoids. His enterprise, "underground" movies, in the heady days of Harry Smith and Jack Smith and Andy Warhol, and before that, small handset books and broadsides that were *petits grimoires*, secret scrolls, prayer flags. And, what else *are* true poems? We were friends in London, in the Sixties.

Anselm and his brother, Erkki Hollo, 1991

Δ

Donald M. Allen's anthology, *The New American Poetry 1945–1960*,[33] was the answer to the prayers of our little cargo cult—evidence that there were not just one or two or three poets "over there" who had heard and assimilated the sounds of the mid-twentieth century, but at least forty-four, and, as the editor stated, this selection presented only a fraction of their work. Piero wasn't in it, though, and I remember him complaining about this, while admiring Ebbe Borregaard's work in the book.

Excursus: Translation

My job with "Auntie," a.k.a. "The Beeb," involved a great deal of translation, and since my salary was not exactly munificent, though adequate for people of relatively frugal habits, I augmented it by free-lance translations. There were times during the London years when I felt that I had three full-time jobs: my five days a week at Bush

House, translation commissions from various Finnish publishers, and my own work in English—not to mention being the father of three children. . . .

Δ

Translation can make you say things you would otherwise never say in your "own" language. In days not too long past, when education always meant knowledge of at least one other language, mostly Latin, even people who did not necessarily consider themselves poets had a go at translating Catullus or Horace, merely for fun, as a mental and linguistic exercise. To some extent, in our Anglophone sphere, the great modernists of languages other than English have now taken the place of old Horace and Gaius Valerius: consider how many different translations there are of Baudelaire, Rimbaud, Apollinaire, Lorca, Neruda, even such a "difficult" poet as Paul Celan. The act of reading a poem with translation in mind is the *closest* reading imaginable, and that quality of attention, once acquired and exercised, is valuable in other contexts, not least in one's own writing.

The idea of translation was one I literally grew up with. As I have already mentioned, my father, J. A. Hollo, was a well-known and prolific translator of world literature into Finnish, from Cervantes to Tolstoy to Flaubert to Henry James. My mother translated scholarly Finnish texts into German, which was her first spoken language, and subsequently—well, both subsequently and *consequently*—my first spoken language as well.

As noted earlier, I learned to *read* from a Swedish ABC book—when my sister got tired of reading and translating the comic strips in Stockholm newspapers to me—and so, I learned a six-year-old person's Swedish at the same time. (My return to Sweden four years later, and the reading I did then, implanted a lasting and continued affection for that language and its literature.) Back in Helsinki, my father taught me Finnish so that I would be ready for school. Then came English, by the age of ten, by means of lessons given by my mother and later in school; French and high school Latin followed. As inhabitants of the Baltic region know—along with those of other poly-lingual parts of the world where speakers of different languages more or less manage to coexist—there was really nothing very extraordinary about that; my sister and brother went on to become fluent in Russian, which I never managed beyond its (now long-forgotten) alphabet: *Red Cats* and other versions from the Russian were produced in collaboration with my mother and other Russian scholars.

I certainly did not, and never will, match my father's working knowledge of fourteen different languages, demonstrated in a lifetime as a literary translator. Nor have I, with my first childhood memories marked by a world war, ever been as serenely confident of the ultimate human value of Goethe's concept of "world literature" and the attendant importance of literary translation, as he must have been at least at the beginning of his career.

Nevertheless, I first read *Don Quixote, War and Peace,* and *Crime and Punishment* in his elegant Finnish, and during my London years I embarked on translations into Finnish on a far more modest scale. Looking back, the most memorable results of those endeavors were two little books of John Lennon's writings and a number of poems by Allen Ginsberg and Robert Creeley which were published in literary magazines and anthologies. In the early Sixties, I also collaborated with Josephine on book-length German translations of Ginsberg, Gregory Corso, and the daddy of them all, William Carlos Williams.[34]

In a way, Bush House was an extension of my parental home, another miniature Tower of Babel within whose walls it seemed possible to work with several languages like a juggler, keeping two or three or four balls in the air at the same time. As the years went by, it became apparent that I could not continue that juggling act ad infinitum—that I had to commit myself to one language before the others. For most of my adult life, American English has been my waking and dreaming language.

I had left Helsinki in the early 1950s, for Germany, Austria, and then Britain, and outside of the offices of Bush House had no active spoken use of Finnish. From my early teens, English and American English literature had been my favored reading matter, and after that slim volume of adolescent verse in Finnish, and a few poems in German, I had not attempted to write my own poetry in anything but English.

It occurred to me that some of the poetry coming out of Finland in the post–World War II era, notably the work of Paavo Haavikko, Tuomas Anhava, Eeva-Liisa Manner, and Pentti Saarikoski, shared something with this new wave of American poets: in their work, I saw a willingness to open up new forms, radically different from those employed by predecessors, and a tendency to favor

With Allen Ginsberg, 1988

concreteness and vivid imagery over idealistic abstraction and breathy symbolism. These two postwar generations of poets, so widely separated in terms of geography and language, shared a common discovery—or one might say, rediscovery—of the rich Modernist tradition of the poetry of France, Russia, Spain, and Italy in the early decades of the century.

Poets and writers of the two postwar Germanies and Austria, emerging from inquisitorial state censorship of the arts, were also rebuilding their bridges back to the Twenties and early Thirties. By the early Sixties they found capable English and American translators—Jerome Rothenberg, Michael Hamburger, Christopher Middleton, to name but three who are significant poets in their own right. Eric Bentley had also begun his pioneering translations of Brecht. So, that field looked well-tilled, and apart from one Brecht play, *Jungle of Cities,*[35] and some poems by Paul Klee,[36] Helmut Heissenbüttel, and Günter Grass, I left it to those capable hands and concentrated on Paavo Haavikko and Pentti Saarikoski. Book-length selections of both their work appeared in London in the late Sixties and became part of the heady internationalism of the poetry and music scene of those years. A quarter of a century later, I am still actively engaged with the work of Finnish poets, and those two in particular. I have expanded their Anglophone bibliographies since then.[37] With the unstinting support of Marja-Leena Rautalin of the Finnish Literature Information Center I have been able to complete translations from numerous other Finnish writers of various genres, and hope to continue doing so. Finding texts worthy of translation is no problem at all—finding *publishers*, in a world in the process of becoming more interconnected on one hand and more fractious and provincial on the other, is a tougher proposition. Thirty years as a literary translator have made me resigned to the fact that the Anglophone world is indifferent to literature from numerically small (or should I say, politically marginal?) European languages. Nobel Prizes and major political upheavals may kindle temporary interest in such works, but on the whole, apart from, say, the occasional new version of Finland's national epic, the *Kalevala*, Finnish literature in translation does not often appear in the lists of U.S. publishers.

6

Socially and anthropologically, the early Sixties in London were a lively time. Thanks to my job with the BBC, and to Josephine's active interest in the theater, we were able to see great productions of the work of that period's playwrights, actors, and directors. Working for "Auntie," I interviewed a number of British writers, among them Rebecca West, L. P. Hartley, Angus Wilson, Alan Sillitoe; wrote radio dramatizations of works like Rudyard Kipling's *The Man Who Would Be King;* DJ'ed a jazz show on Sunday afternoons; reviewed plays and movies; met John Lennon and Yoko Ono at a gallery opening of Yoko's works; met the "Beats" and their British emulators, some of whom camped in the basement of our building and climbed four flights of stairs to use our bathroom. . . . There were parties, boozy Fleet Street lunches, poetry readings. . . . It was life in the Yellow Submarine, all right, but for me, it was also the time of becoming a family man: all three of our children were born in London. Looking back, I realize that Josephine and I were operating at incredible speeds, both physically and psychologically—as was, or so it seemed, just about everybody else we knew.

Joanne Kyger, Donald Guravich, Anselm Hollo, and Alice Notley, 1991

In the present moment's memory re-make, Anselm Hollo ca. 1963 looks like an astonishing composite: good provider type, riding the double-decker bus to work five days a week—industrious translator and literary reporter—father of one, two, three young children—and poet, or at least yearning to be of that number. Many of my works from the period now strike me as curiously, almost *programmatically,* out of touch—or *only* in touch with a fantasy world inspired by "the new spirit" epitomized by the Beats, the New York School, the Beatles, the Incredible String Band, the whole kit and kaboodle floating above those years that also saw the Cuban missile crisis, the assassination of JFK, and (then as now) seemingly endless insensate strife on all continents.

Nevertheless, those works met with some attention. A. Alvarez nicknamed me the "Beatnik Walter de la Mare," George MacBeth invited me to read on the Third Programme, and Edward Lucie-Smith and Martin Bax were instrumental in publishing my collections in handsome editions. Jerome Rothenberg arranged an invitation to a literary conference in New York City, and Paul Blackburn introduced my first ever reading on American soil, at the then still embryonic St. Mark's Poetry Project.

All this proved a little too heady for my already scattered brains (William Carlos Williams: "I am he / whose brains are scattered / aimlessly"). I fell in love with a young woman in New York, returned to London desolate at having had to leave her to go back to family and job, and joined the ranks of victims of the era. The Englishman (or other European, but the "Brit" in particular) who finds himself in the New World of the academic, artistic, literary Sixties and succumbs to its drugs, sex, and rock and roll, plunging his hitherto stable existence into total if at times even joyful chaos, is a staple figure in many novels of the period. I followed that pattern, and it followed me across the Atlantic again, when I was invited to teach summer school at SUNY Buffalo, and then to the Writers' Workshop in Iowa City, Iowa—only fourteen miles from Cedar Rapids, where I had been put on a midnight bus to New York in '51. . . .

My anima-chasing, to use a Jungian term that may sound too polite but that, I believe, truly describes my compulsion, and my steadily attendant addiction to alcohol put severe strains on my marriage, but our family held together through the six years in Iowa City. I think that the death of my father in 1967 made a deeper impression on

me than I was prepared to admit at the time. It probably brought up fears that I, myself, was in no way ready to be a father, and these in turn made me reject that role to the extent that I wanted to insist on all my anarcho-Bohemian freedoms.

where was it i
fell asleep in the afternoon
& down
& into a hall
where forceful as ever in her big chair
he who was i there saw her
hum to a thin corner shadow
the brother pale rigid
not a sound then the sister
energy out of a door on the right
but i knew where he lay
went on & entered
the room light & bare
no curtains no books
his head on the pillow
hand moving outward
the gesture "be seated"
i started talking, saw myself from the back
leaned forward, talked to his face
intent, bushy-browed
eyes straining to see
into mine
"a question i wanted to ask you"
would never know what it was
but stood there & was
so happy to see him
that twenty-sixth day of april
three months after his death[38]

Excursus: Iowa City

I could easily wax boring about my Iowa City years, a time I still believe unequalled in that place for intellectual and artistic excitement and innovation, marked, as it was, by the presence of a succession of important and often atypical mentors at the Writers' Workshop (Ted Berrigan, Kathleen Fraser, Jack Marshall, George Starbuck among them) and the equally vigorous presence of spirited young poets either getting their MFA degrees or living and working in the city, including Alice Notley, now one of the major poets of our time; Merrill Gilfillan, now known to a wide public as an important essayist on the Western Plains region (*Magpie Rising*); the late Darrell Gray, one of this country's first truly "postmodernist" poets, wonderfully unprogrammatic and hence regrettably unacknowledged to this day; Barrett Watten and Bob Perelman, later founders of the still active and

Josephine Clare, Anselm Hollo, and daughter, Kaarina Hollo, at Harvard, 1992

influential L=A=N=G=U=A=G=E school and its *Poetics Journal;* Dave Morice, inventor of *Poetry Comics;* John Sjoberg, David Hilton, George Mattingly . . . The "foreign" poets, visitors to the International Writing Program: Gunnar Harding, Tomaz Salamun, Nicholas Born, Juan Agustin Palazuelos, Ryuichi Tamura . . . The "Actualist" group,[39] which owed much to the work of Frank O'Hara and James Schuyler, and to the "actual" presence of Ted Berrigan in Iowa City for a memorable year.

Ted composed his sonnets and odes with an immediacy, anarchic humor, and unpretentious artifice that still strike me as The News. He taught me, and a generation of younger poets in Iowa City, Ann Arbor, Chicago, and New York City, that "It is important to keep old hat in secret closet."

Frank O'Hara and Ted Berrigan were among the last Euro-American Male poets *of the city.* In the last two decades, dominant U.S. culture has devastated the great cities it once created, and the only poets left in those cities are known as the "marginalized."

Δ

"Those were the days, my friend . . ." After Iowa City, I became a member of what has been called "the gypsy scholars of the Seventies," a generation of itinerant poet-teachers, most of whom found themselves out of jobs in the Eighties—being retired early, as it were, having taught in fifteen different places in as many years. I was lucky to land a few stints that allowed me to stay longer than a year, but this peripatetic existence made it impossible for me to stay with my family, who were neither willing nor able to break camp every other year for yet another visiting gig of mine.

AUTOBIOGRAPHICAL BROADCASTING CORPORATION

eight years behind a microphone—blip—
then bid farewell to normal speak[40]

That farewell had been quite a relief. On the other hand, it had also been a farewell to what is known as "stable existence." In the main, my life has proceeded along the lines of Guy Debord's *dérive* (an ideologized form of good or bad old "drift," as in "drifter"!), combined with a genuine love of exile, i.e., communities and places of *choice* that are not predetermined by accidents of birth. South and West have been the main directions; so, here I am now, in the American Southwest, in a town of the Front Range of the Rockies.

Greater minds have had many things to say about exile. I believe exile is (and always has been, in historical times) the basic condition of the artist. In order to see things in ways not circumscribed by conventional social perceptions, an artist has to move *outside.* That may well be the leap from traditional craft to art—the leap outside the common, outside the family, "beyond the pale." In that sense, exile is probably universal. In one form or another, it is experienced by anyone who has ever woken up to what Ted Berrigan spoke of in a lecture he gave in 1982 at the Naropa Institute (in whose Jack Kerouac School of Disembodied Poetics I am now happy to be teaching):

> The arts are something given to human beings to
>   do
> They improve your senses
> It is necessary to do more than earn your daily
>   bread
> Shelter & food & ability to get the medicine
> For your children when they have a cold
> It's necessary to be more of a person than that[41]

I was born into a family that was "in exile." I had a weird, built-in, westward drift. I didn't plan it that way. As a child, I read Westerns. Melville says "Be true to the dreams of your youth." Now I live within fifty miles of Buffalo Bill Cody's grave. Elsewhere, I have said: *"Permanent diaspora*—the ideal state."[42]

Ted also said:

> Survival
>   is the hardest test for a poet[43]

7

Buffalo, New York; Bowling Green, Ohio; Geneva, New York; Ann Arbor and East Lansing, Michigan; Baltimore, Maryland; Marshall, Minnesota; Sweet Briar, Virginia; San Francisco; Salt Lake City; Boulder, Colorado—these have been some of my way stations as a "visiting dude." Great places, all of them, but mainly in their off-campus parts (except for the libraries).

My advice to aspiring poets today would be to get a couple of Ph.D.'s before attempting a career as writers-in-residence in programs associated with academic (mostly "English") departments. Only then, if they have the right stuff, will they be able to deal with the *other* Ph.D.'s in those departments who are *not* writers, who have spent a very large chunk of their adult lives acquiring their Ph.D.'s,

Ed Sanders and Anselm Hollo with Bobbie Louise Hawkins and Jane Dalrymple-Hollo, 1990

and who basically regard living writers with negative feelings ranging from distrust to resentment to unconcealed hatred. To them, the only good writer is a dead writer.

The Sixties' dream of writing schools staffed by practicing writers of originality and wit, preferably ones who had *not* gone to writing schools or had at least spent a decade or so doing something else for a living, has for the most part turned out to be just another Sixties' dream. I remember thinking, back then, that the writers' workshop was the American answer to the coffeehouses and taverns of old Vienna, Paris, London—simply a *place* where writers, young, middle-aged, and old, could gather and form groups and cliques and movements and feel that they *had* a place in the world.

The United States has never had such a culture, and "creative writing programs," I argued, were at least a kind of surrogate for it. Perhaps they still are, to some extent, despite their penchant for departmental bulletin boards on which students and faculty post their latest literary scalps ("X has had a poem, *Stars above My Catamaran,* accepted by the *New Yorker,*" "Y's story *Gaping Genders* will appear in the *Atlantic*"), fostering yet another version of troglodytic competitiveness.

But enough of that. Despite its ups and downs, it has not been a bad life so far. Almost eight years ago, I managed to kick my alcohol habit, and my doors of perception have grown brighter for it. Although we are separated by long geographical distances, my children, Hannes, Kaarina, and Tamsin, and their mother, Josephine, and I have become a little closer in spirit again, and I feel blessed by the gods. Ten years ago, those gods were even kinder to me when they guided me up a very dark staircase, to Jane Dalrymple, who became my dearest friend, lover, and wife.

> though but a weave of dust and shade
> caught in the chandelle of our days
>
> who writing shovels grief's doubloons
> I can say this: hello! dear woman I name Dream
>
> dear called *Because*
> with you, a thousand years would not be long
> enough[44]

This autobiographical essay, however, is beginning to feel more than long enough, at least for the time being. My apologies for its hops, skips, and jumps; I realize that I have been concentrating on things I may be the only one to know—hence, on earlier years. At the moment of this writing, my decades (almost three) in this country still have many more living witnesses than do those distant European times.

NOTES

(All titles, except where otherwise noted, are by the author.)

1. *Outlying Districts* (Minneapolis: Coffee House Press, 1990), p. 61.

2. Eugene Winograd and Ulrich Neisser, *Affect and Accuracy in Recall* (Cambridge: Cambridge University Press, 1993).

3. *Finite Continued* (Berkeley: Blue Wind Press, 1980), p. 21. In this poem, "maternity home" follows British usage (= "maternity hospital").

4. Anselm Hollo, "The Complete Poems of Hipponax of Ephesus," *Sulfur*, 13, No. 2 (Fall 1993), pp. 99–114.

5. *Heavy Jars* (West Branch, Iowa: The Toothpaste Press, 1977), p. 9.

6. *Sensation* (Buffalo: The Institute of Further Studies, 1972), p. 57.

7. *Maya* (London and New York: Cape Goliard Press and Grossman Publishers, 1970), p. 100.

8. *Sensation* (op. cit.), p. 59.

9. *No Complaints* (West Branch, Iowa: The Toothpaste Press, 1983), p. 25.

10. *Finite Continued* (op. cit.), p. 45.

11. *Erlkönig* by Johann Wolfgang von Goethe. English translation (*Elf-King*) by Martin Zwart, in *A Treasury of German Ballads* (New York: Frederick Ungar, 1964), p. 50.

12. *Das Grab im Busento* by August von Platen. English translation (*The Grave in the Busento*) by Martin Zwart, in *A Treasury of . . .* (op. cit.), p. 255.

13. *Kalevala, The Land of Heroes.* Verse translation by W. F. Kirby (London and New York: John Dent and E. P. Dutton, 1907), opening lines.

14. *Im Dome* by Heinrich Heine. English translation (*In the Cathedral*) by Hal Draper, in *The Complete Poems of Heinrich Heine: A Modern English Version* (Oxford: Oxford University Press, 1982), p. 289a.

15. *Die Wanderratten* by Heinrich Heine. English translation (*The Roving Rats*) by Hal Draper, in *The Complete Poems of . . .* (op. cit.), p. 783.

16. *Black Book* (Center Conway, New Hampshire: Walker's Pond Press, 1974), pp. 38–9. Present, revised version in *Sojourner Microcosms: New and Selected Poems 1959–1977* (Berkeley: Blue Wind Press, 1977), p. 213.

17. *Space Baltic* (Mountain View, California: Ocean View Books, 1991), p. 82.

18. From *Arcana Gardens,* in *Outlying Districts* (op. cit.), p. 107.

19. John Reed, *Ten Days that Shook the World* (London: Penguin Books, 1977), p. 199.

20. William Henry Chamberlin, *The Russian Revolution 1917–1921* (Princeton, New Jersey: Princeton University Press, 1987), p. 331.

21. Isaac Deutscher, *The Prophet Armed* (New York and London: Oxford University Press, 1954), p. 328.

22. From *Arcana Gardens* (op. cit.), pp. 94–5.

23. Some of these were collected in the anthology *Zwischenräume* ("Interstices") (Wiesbaden: Limes Verlag, 1963), pp. 26–39.

24. *Near Miss Haiku: praises laments aphorisms reports* (Chicago: Yellow Press, 1990), p. 4.

25. Not the American artist of the same name.

26. From *XXV* in *Spring and All* by William Carlos Williams. A. Walton Litz and Christopher McGowan, Editors: *The Collected Poems of William Carlos Williams, Volume I: 1909–1939* (New York: New Directions, 1986), pp. 231–2.

27. *augenblick* ("moment"), a literary review published and edited by Max Bense from Siegen, Germany, 1955–1961. Also: Max Bense, *Programmierung des Schönen* ("Programming the Beautiful") (Baden-Baden: Agis-Verlag, 1962).

28. See Rosmarie Waldrop and Harriett Watts, translator-editors, *The Vienna Group: 6 Major Austrian Poets* (Station Hill, New York: Station Hill Press, 1985).

29. Malcolm Green, editor and translator, *Selected Works of Konrad Bayer* (London: Atlas Press, 1986), p. 7.

30. *Zwischenräume* (op. cit.), p. 26.

31. *& It Is a Song* (Birmingham: Migrant Press, 1965).

32. *Red Cats: Poems by Yevgeni Yevtushenko, Semyon Kirsanov, Andrei Voznesensky.* English versions by Anselm Hollo (San Francisco: City Lights Books, 1962).

33. Donald M. Allen, editor, *The New American Poetry 1945–1960* (New York: Grove Press, 1960).

34. William Carlos Williams, *Paterson.* Deutsch von Anselm und Josephine Hollo (Stuttgart: Henry Goverts Verlag, 1970).

35. Bertolt Brecht, *Jungle of Cities and Other Plays* (New York: Grove Press, 1965).

36. Paul Klee, *Some Poems by Paul Klee.* Translated by Anselm Hollo (Lowestoft, Suffolk: Scorpion Press, 1962).

37. Paavo Haavikko, *Selected Poems.* Translated from the Finnish by Anselm Hollo (Manchester: Carcanet Press, 1991. Pentti Saarikoski, *Poems 1958–1980.* Translated from the Finnish by Anselm Hollo (West Branch, Iowa: Toothpaste Press, 1983). Pentti Saarikoski, *Trilogy.* Translated by Anselm Hollo (Montreal: Guernica, 1994).

38. *Sensation* (op. cit.), p. 61.

39. See Morty Sklar and Darrell Gray, editors, *The Actualist Anthology* (Iowa City: The Spirit That Moves Us Press, 1977).

40. *Sojourner Microcosms* (op. cit.), p. 156.

41. Anselm Hollo, *Lines from Ted: An Ars Poetica.* Sonnet VI. Unpublished, 1993.

42. Stephen Kuusisto, Deborah Tall, and Daniel Weiss, editors, *Taking Note: From Poets' Notebooks* (Geneva, New York: Seneca Review Press, 1991), p. 82.

43. *Lines from Ted . . .* (op. cit.).

44. *West Is Left on the Map* (Boulder, Colorado: Dead Metaphor Press, 1993), last page.

BIBLIOGRAPHY

Poetry:

Sateiden Välillä ("Rainpause"), Otava (Helsinki), 1956.

St. Texts & Finnpoems, Migrant Press (Worcester and Ventura, California), 1961.

Lover Man, Dead Language Press (New York), 1963.

(With David Ball) *We Just Wanted to Tell You*, Writers' Forum (England), 1963.

And What Else Is New, New Voice (Kent, England), 1963.

(With eight German poets) *Zwischenräume*, Limes (Wiesbaden), 1963.

History, Matrix Press (London), 1964.

Trobar: Löytää Runoja (trobar means "to find"), Otava, 1964.

& It Is a Song, Migrant Press, 1965.

Faces and Forms, Ambit Books (London), 1965.

Here We Go, Stranger's Press (Newcastle upon Tyne), 1965.

The Claim, Cape Goliard Press (London), 1966.

For the Sea-Sons and Daughters We All Are, privately printed, 1966.

The Going-on Poem, Writers' Forum, 1966.

Buffalo–Isle of Wight Power Cable, State University of New York, 1967.

Isadora and Other Poems, Writers' Forum, 1967.

Leaf Times, University of Exeter Press, 1967.

Poems/Runoja (bilingual edition), Otava, 1967.

The Coherences, Trigram Press (London), 1968.

(With John Esam and Tom Raworth) *Haiku*, Trigram Press, 1968.

The Man in the Treetop Hat, Turret (London), 1968.

Tumbleweed, Weed/Flower Press (Toronto), 1968.

(With Ted Berrigan) *Double Talk*, T. G. Miller (Iowa City), 1969.

Waiting for a Beautiful Bather: Ten Poems, Morgan Press (Milwaukee), 1969.

America del Norte and Other Peace Herb Poems, Weed/Flower Press, 1970.

Gee Apollinaire, Nomad Press (Iowa City), 1970.

Maya: Works, 1959–1969, Cape Goliard Press, 1970, Grossman (New York), 1970.

Message, Unicorn Press (Santa Barbara, California), 1970.

(With Jack Marshall and Sam Hamod) *Surviving in America,* Cedar Creek Press (Iowa City), 1971.

Alembic, Trigram Press, 1972.

Sensation, Institute of Further Studies (New York), 1972.

Smoke Writing, University of Connecticut Library, 1973.

Spring Cleaning Greens, from Notebooks 1967–1973, Doones Press (Bowling Green, Ohio), 1973.

Black Book No. 1, Walker's Pond Press (Center Conway, New Hampshire), 1974.

Some Worlds, Elizabeth Press (New Rochelle), 1974.

Motes, Joujouka Tojours (Baltimore), 1976.

Heavy Jars, Toothpaste Press (West Branch, Iowa), 1977.

Lingering Tangos, Tropos Press (Baltimore), 1977.

(With Joe Cardarelli and Kirby Malone) *Phantom Pod,* Pod Books (Baltimore), 1977.

Sojourner Microcosms: New and Selected Poems 1959–1977, Blue Wind Press (Berkeley, California), 1977.

Curious Data, White Pine Press (Buffalo), 1978.

Lunch in Fur, Aquila Rose (St. Paul, Minnesota), 1978.

With Ruth in Mind, Station Hill Press (Barrytown, New York), 1979.

Finite Continued, Blue Wind Press, 1980.

No Complaints, Toothpaste Press, 1983.

Pick up the House: New and Selected Poems, Coffee House Press (Minneapolis), 1986.

Near Miss Haiku, Yellow Press (Chicago), 1990.

Outlying Districts, Coffee House Press, 1990.

(With Rudy Rucker's *All the Visions*) *Space Baltic: The Science Fiction Poems 1962–1987,* Ocean View Books (Mountain View, California), 1991.

Blue Ceiling, Tansy Press (Lawrence, Kansas), 1992.

High Beam, Pyramid Atlantic (Riverdale, Maryland), 1993.

West Is Left on the Map, Dead Metaphor Press (Boulder, Colorado), 1993.

Editor and translator:

Allen Ginsberg, *Kaddisch* (poems; translated into German), Limes, 1962.

Yevgeni Yevtushenko, Andrei Voznesensky, and Semyon Kirsanov, *Red Cats,* City Lights, 1962.

Paul Klee, *Some Poems,* Scorpion Press, 1962.

Gregory Corso, *In der Flüchtigen Hand der Zeit* (poems; translated into German), Limes, 1963.

Allen Ginsberg, *Huuto ja Muita Runoja* (poems), Tajo, 1963.

(Co-translator) Allen Ginsberg, *Kuolema van Goghin Korvalle* (poems; translated into Finnish), Tajo, 1963.

Idän ja Lännen Runot (anthology of modern American poetry), Weilin & Goos, 1963.

Andrei Voznesensky, *Selected Poems,* Grove Press, 1964.

(With Matti Rossi) *Näin Ihminen Vastaa* (anthology of modern Latin American poetry), Tajo, 1964.

Rolf-Gunter Dienst, *Five Feet Two* (poems), Tarasque Press, 1965.

Word from the North: New Poetry from Finland, Stranger's Press (London), 1965.

Pentti Saarikoski, *Helsinki: Selected Poems,* Rapp & Carroll, 1967.

Paavo Haavikko, *Selected Poems,* Cape Gollard, 1968, Grossman, 1968.

Tuomas Anhava, *In the Dark, Move Slowly . . . ,* Cape Goliard Press, 1969, Grossman, 1969.

Aleksandr Blok, *The Twelve and Other Poems,* Gnomon Press, 1971.

(With Gunnar Harding) *Modern Swedish Poetry in Translation,* University of Minnesota Press, 1979.

Pentti Saarikoski, *Poems 1958–1980,* Toothpaste Press, 1983.

Translator:

Vladimir Maximov, *A Man Survives* (novel), Grove Press, 1963.

John Lennon Panee Omiaan (translation of *John Lennon in His Own Write*), Otava, 1964.

Veijo Meri, *Das Manilaseil* (novel), Carl Hanser, 1964.

Lars Ullerstam, *The Erotic Minorities* (essays), Grove Press, 1966.

Lars Görling, *491* (novel), Grove Press, 1966.

John Lennon, *Hispanjalainen Jakovainaa* (prose; translated into Finnish), Otava, 1966.

Bertolt Brecht, *Jungle of Cities* (play), Grove Press, 1966.

Matti Rossi, *The Trees of Vietnam* (poems), El Corno Emplumado, 1966.

(With Josephine Clare) William Carlos Williams, *Paterson* (translated into German), Goverts, 1970.

(With Sidney Berger) *Thrymskvitha* (translated into English from Icelandic Skald), Windhover Press, 1970.

(With Elliott Anderson) Tomaz Salamun, *Turbines: Twenty-one Poems* (translated into English from the Slovine), Windhover Press, 1973.

Jean Genet, *Querelle* (novel), Grove Press, 1974.

Emmanuelle Arsan, *Emmanuelle II* (novel), Grove Press, 1975.

Franz Innerhofer, *Beautiful Days* (novel), Urizen Books, 1976.

François Truffaut, *Small Change* (film script), Grove Press, 1977.

Tillmann Moser, *Years of Apprenticeship on the Couch: Fragments of My Psychoanalysis*, Urizen Books, 1977.

Wolfgang Schivelbusch, *The Industrialized Traveller*, Urizen Books (London), 1979, published as *The Railway Journey*, Urizen Books (New York), 1981.

Rosa Luxemburg, *Letters to Friends*, Pluto Press (London), 1979.

Olof Lagercrantz, *August Strindberg*, Farrar Straus (New York), 1984, Faber (London), 1984.

Jeanne de Berg, *Women's Rites: Scenes from the Erotic Imagination*, Grove Press, 1987.

Egon Schiele, *I, Eternal Child: Paintings and Poems*, Grove Press, 1988.

Louis Malle, *Au Revoir les Enfants* ("Goodbye, Children"), Grove Press, 1988.

Amos Kenan, *The Road to Ein Harod*, Grove Press, 1988.

Lennart Hagerfors, *The Whales in Lake Tanganyika*, Grove Press, 1989, Deutsch (London), 1989.

Peter S. Jungk, *Franz Werfel: A Life in Prague, Vienna, and Hollywood*, Grove/Atlantic Monthly Press, 1990, published as *A Life Torn by History: Franz Werfel 1890–1945*, Weidenfeld and Nicolson (London), 1990.

Jaan Kross, *The Czar's Madman*, Harvill (London), 1992, Pantheon, 1993.

Verena Kast, *Imagination as Space of Freedom: Dialogue between the Ego and the Unconscious*, Fromm International, 1993.

Rosa Liksom, *One Night Stands*, Serpent's Tail (London), 1993.

Zlatko Dizdarevic, *Sarajevo: A War Journal*, Fromm International, 1993.

Jakob Arjouni, *Happy Birthday, Turk!*, Fromm International, 1993.

Other:

(With Gregory Corso and Tom Raworth) *The Minicab War* (satire), Matrix Press, 1961.

(Editor) *Jazz Poems* (anthology of modern British poetry), Vista Books, 1963.

(Editor) *Negro Verse* (anthology), Vista Books, 1964.

The Coherences (recording), Stream Records, 1969.

Also author of numerous radio scripts for British Broadcasting Corp. and for Finnish and German broadcasts (some under the pseudonym Anton Hofman).

Robert Kelly
1935-

Robert Kelly, London, 1992

1

I'm not sure that I want to write my life. I'm not sure there is any way to write it except to write every day, as I try to, the poem of that day, one after another. The poem is a day.

I'm not sure I want to write about my life. Do I even want to think about it? For someone as egotistical as I am, I have spent very little time thinking about me, only about what I want, what happened to me. Happens to me. Sometimes I think about what *it* wants of me.

I'm not sure I want, in other words, to write about my life in other words than those that have already (poem after poem, story after story, talk after talk) made their way into the more or less durable world of language.

I will try. Because I am asked to, no better reason. Could there be a better reason? Give what is asked: there is no other answer. Cavalcanti's canzone: *A lady asks me, so I will tell*—ground enough for all exposition.

When I think about my life, I think about how I hated it when I was younger, and love it now. Then it was curse and now it is bless. What I wanted to curse was how cut off I felt from everyone, mostly from those I wanted to be close to, wanted to like me. What I want to bless is everything, everyone.

179

2

My autobiography is the writing (*graphein*) of my life, my bios. Now Greek knows two words like that, two words the ancients surmised had at first been one: *bíos,* "life," and *biós,* "a bow" to shoot with as the hunter takes the life of things and turns them into his own life, the life of the tribe.

Writing my life is writing my instrument, my strength.

My life is not my past.

3

An autobiography is different from a biography. It tells the truth, not the facts. "Truth is what most contradicts itself in time," and, like time itself, it is contingent, relative, impermanent as formulated. The most accurate clock in the world is accurate only one instant at a time. Its record is meaningless. Or the recorded readings of a bad clock are identical with the record of a good one. Truth, like time, does not only exist as experienced; it *is* experience. So biography (the writing of a life, done by a Greek pun with an arrow, scratching in the ground, piercing the heart, wounding the flesh, taking the life—or writing in the gentle dust of people's impressions by means of the arrow tip, scratching the names of our sins in the dirt) is *life writing.* Autobiography is the self writing life.

And the self exists only as an imputation: the noticer of the huge heap of stuff called *now.*

Autobiography is now-writing, then. Now writing then—and it comes to speak the past. Then writes now too, can't flee from speaking in the words chosen by, the rhythmic pression of this breath in, this body now.

All of which you know. But where would writing be, let alone literature, if we didn't write down so learnedly and urgently what is so obvious? Nothing else is worth speaking but the obvious. That's why we can make do with a reasonably tidy stack of a few hundred thousand words in the dictionary, enough to speak justly of the billion billion things.

We are just talking to each other about what we know. Minding and reminding. Touching. Writing is touch.

"*Wedding picture of my father, Samuel Jason Kelly, and mother, Margaret Rose Kane,*" Christmas Day, 1923

4

Real autobiography is *the life that writes itself.* That is what a writer's works are, in truth. Look no further: self-written, self-begotten, the poems I have spent most of my life writing are my actual autobiography.

What can I add to them? Some dates, some dedications? Some personal confusions to try to drag back by the tails those articulated energies that have, by wholly entering into language, already managed to get away from me and my concerns?

This is the bow I bent when in October 1958 I vowed to spend my life writing in service of that Brightness I intuited as like or beyond the intense blue autumn sky, and determined that I would give whatever I had of life to saying. To write every day. For the sake of the world, as I supposed in my innocent arrogance. For the truth that language tells—for while language does not tell all the truth or the whole truth, there is some truth that only language tells.

That October commitment is the story. To write every day was the method. To attend to what it said. To listen. To prepare myself for writing by learning everything I could, by hanging out in languages and enduring overdetermined desires, by tolerating my own inclinations as if they had the physical accuracy of gravity. To listen, and say what I heard.

5

What I come to is this, something like this: to write an autobiography is to write one's life oneself, that much is easy.

But my life is not my past; my life is my strength, my instrument ("my bow").

My life is not my past. The past does not belong to anyone—that is the point. The past is common, cloacal, intimate, true only inasmuch as it motivates presences, presentnesses, presents.

"My" past appalls me with its Flemish chiaroscuro, its gleam of sense amongst a nightmare of appetites.

Am I, after all, ashamed of my appetites? Am I a sunflower ashamed of the sun? *Mes tropismes.*

6

I'm not sure I want to write about my life. I do know I want to praise, praise many people, all my friends and teachers and, no sense in the categories, all those who have made contact with me.

Here is a text some Tibetans chant every day before eating:

May whoever gives me food attain the happiness of complete peace. Whoever gives me drink, serves me, respects me, honors me, makes offerings to me, may he attain the happiness of complete peace. And whoever reviles me, causes me unhappiness, abuses me, strikes me with weapons, harms me in any way, even kills me, may he also attain the happiness of complete enlightenment, and become fully and actually awakened in perfect complete Enlightenment.

I want to speak the names of my friends.

And I want to speak the names of my enemies, but who are they? I think of myself as a novel without villains. The astrologers say I have Mars in the Twelfth House, the House of Self-Undoing, they say, *Carcer,* the Jailhouse. They say that means: Beware of secret enemies. They say: Your friends are your enemies. Your friends are jealous and secretly wish you ill. But I know the name of the secret enemy, most treacherous of all the local potentates, and it is me.

Which is one more reason I should be unsure about writing my life. Be advised, honest reader. Even now, by this very scruple, this candor, I may be making you think ill of me.

Don't waste their time, say it or be silent. Never apologize, never explain—that has always been your rule. Why otherwise now?

Listen, it won't do me any good to doubt.

7

Here is my contract with the Natal Daemon, my contract for one Life with one Earth: I was born forty-eight minutes after noon around the autumnal equinox—24 September 1935. A late degree of Sagittarius was rising in the house of life, my sun was in the first degree of the Scales, and my moon in the balsamic degrees of the Lion. It was a hot week. My mother was in labor for three days. (That is a fact I learned only forty-some years later when I happened to ask her, for the first time in my life, what kind of birth I'd had. Instantly, her eyes filled with tears, she who was no sort of crying woman, and she said, simply, that she was in labor with me for three days. She never mentioned it again.)

Weeks after my birth, my mother learned that her own father died the same day I was born.

He was Thomas Kane, about whom I don't know much. He smoked a pipe and I've seen a picture of him where he looks like Wallace Stevens. (My mother was the tenth of his eleven childbirth-surviving children, and she was born, a valiant imperious Aries, on the 7th of April, 1902.) He was also my last surviving grandparent, so I grew up in a world without eld. There were no old people near me, so I had to be my own grandfather. I had to be wise and big. His surname excited and shamed me, and I thought through childhood that I bore the mark of Kane/Cain—which I took to be the mutinous piratical left eyebrow of mine that everybody still seems to notice.

So I grew up without grandparents, though some of my uncles and aunts (two score of them all told) seemed old enough to qualify. Still, I saw day by day no one older than my parents. And so I never learned about the old. As in the house of the young Prince Sakyamuni, age was not seen, death was not mentioned, sickness was not discussed. (When my pregnant mother went to the hospital to give birth to my sister, no sort of explanation was offered to me of her absence.) Religion was de rigueur, but priests and nuns were spoken of with delicate skepticism, a warning not to take too seriously whatever roads of piety or renunciation they might suggest.

I grew up without the old. So when it comes time for me to be an old man, I will not really know how to do it. I suppose it's something you can fake, the frail body helping out. But I have no role model and fear I may make a very imperfect old man. For years, from my earliest childhood, in fact, it seemed unlikely that old age would ever be a problem. Several doctors prophesied, in their solemn and scary way, that "the boy would die by thirty-five"—a prophecy of which I was frequently reminded. Grossly overweight as I was, their lugubrious anticipations seemed justified enough medically (if a bit outrageous psychologically). Now that thirty-five is two decades behind me, I have to face the fact that I'll have to solve unaided the mystery of old age.

Of course, if you don't have grandparents, you don't have anyone to confide in, you don't have a court of cassation, a tribunal of ultimate appeal. You don't have a *tertium comparationis* to judge the truth of what you're told.

So not only did I not learn how to be an old man, I did not learn how to speak out loud what might have been on my mind.

If you don't have grandparents, I sort of think, you never really learn how to talk. Parents tell, grandparents talk. To this day I'm more comfortable addressing a room full of people than meeting them one at a time.

8

My mother's sisters feared to tell her of my grandfather's death—I was a month old before her sisters told her the real reason why her said-to-be-ailing papa had not visited his latest grandchild. That pattern of not-bringing-the-bad-news shaped her life, and my life. When I was a man of forty, my favorite aunt, Aunt Annie, passed away, and my parents never mentioned it for fear of grieving me.

The unspoken. I seemed to be told: the essence of life is to say nothing. No explanations, no excuses, no narration. Things happen, and we shelter from them as well as we can: in silence and fierce habit and the passionless security of everyday life.

And that is kindly, hard, well-meant. Maybe it is finally the best way, in that harshly tender north of Ireland way they imported (who knows when?) as armor against the lascivious novelties of the new world.

9

There was a day, I might have been in second grade, when I decided to walk home from school a different way. The school was only across the street from my house, catercorner, but I walked up away from my house a long block, up the yellow leaves that carpeted Batchelder Street, then over and down, then home, a block or two more. Not long, but long enough for me to miss my father, who for the one day I can remember in my whole childhood had come home early from work and was waiting for me, proposing to take me to the movies to see some Disney (*Dumbo,* was it, the flying, the fat?). He was distressed, and I felt awful to have missed the outing, which never did happen, and more than that, selfish as I was, to have disappointed him so. This event stayed in my mind for all my years, because before I walked the Different Way, I seemed to hear an inner voice saying: Walk a different way. Ever after, I've had this event in mind as groundwork for a life of interpretation. Was this event a deep incurable wound in the body of my openness, one that curtails still my spontaneity? Or was it a protection—if so, whose?—against some experience (car crash, obsessive movie image, act of crime) we would have otherwise been in for? This was the first storey in the House of Interpretation, grist for a life of pondering anxiety.

10

At twenty-three I dedicated my life of work to God. To benefit the world was how I thought about it. At forty-six I dedicated it to the enlightenment of all beings. It seems ambitious and possibly pretentious to want these things, but I mean them with everything I have that can mean anything. My search in "flesh, dream, book" has been for ways of saying, ways of saying that benefit

Robert with his parents, 1942

beings. Searching now in language to unsay my "self," and thereby say the truth, or say towards it.

11

Uranus, inchoate, changeful, full of hope and fear, dwells in the fourth house in my horoscope. Where he dwells, there is no early peace, and change comes quick. I sit and think about the way karma drives us when we're young, how I was driven, ceaselessly agitated with what I think young Dante meant by *dubioso* desire—a fleshly but cogent yearning, in head no less than hod, to run wild in the city and hurry the country down.

And how resist the velocity of karma. I remember the city forty years ago, how desperately I sought words and women, those walking aliens who were at the same time the only home I wanted. I sought and sought. Thoughtful but unconscious. What was it? What wouldn't let me rest?

To catch up with the world I was supposed to inherit. To incarnate fully on this woebegone

beauty, Eyes of Earth. Postures of intercourse and stances of poetics, odes and measures, prosody and ghost stories, the dark house in M. R. James's "The Mezzotint" towards which I was the obscure figure creeping—the urge to be everyone. *I am the man.* All the hurry is there, to become the self you must spend the rest of your days unpiecing. Poetry I sought, and fame, feeding, noise, Viennese music, the secular roar of history. Kulchur, said Pound, and I carried his vade mecum with me in Times Square at fourteen, he was my author and my book was yet to be. Pound and Mahler, Joyce and the girl across the subway car, the girl in the wind, Wotan's farewell, *das oft ich lächelnd geköst*, the blue distances, Italian bread, white cheese, Pepsi-Cola, IRT—these were my house.

When I'm less excited about it, I know that Uranus in the fourth means many changes of house and home, unconventional living arrangements, odd cronies, hand-me-down furniture, dust bunnies, some strange bed. The loss of my first house—1878 Brown Street, a brief tangent off Gerritsen Avenue, in the Marine Park district, not too far from gentle evenings sauntering in sealight at Sheepshead Bay—even now I'd rather posit it than describe the loss. For months after we'd moved, I'd find myself many days taking a complicated series of buses back to the old house, to walk on the old block, talk with the old friends. Though it was not the friends that moved me so. How can a child survive such losses? That house was the blue sky over it, that house was cloud and the color red and heavy ivy up brick wall. That house was ghost story and block of ice, girls in dark wool slacks coming home from ice skating. That house was radio and opera. That house was Canada and Finland and 1940. That house was war and the knowledge of color. That house was a clock on the wall. How can a child survive such subtle losses? That house was number.

12

I can't remember a time when I couldn't read. The first day in school, the nun took me around from classroom to classroom, making me read from some book in front of other students. I didn't understand what was happening. I did what I was told. I read aloud. I was uncomfortable being dragged around but I did what I was told. I almost always have. Later my mother told me it was remarkable that I could read; other children couldn't, and had to go to school to learn. Why did I have to go?

13

Buildings. The green copper dome of St. Peter's church against the high skyline of Jersey City. The green copper of Queen of Angels in Brooklyn, and the Masonic Temple right beside it. The vast prow of Freemason's Hall in London, standing out of the night palpably full of useful mysteries. The low skyline of Hudson from the hospital window where I came with Mary Goodlett several times each week for her chemotherapy, for radiation, windows in the room where Mary died. *Skylines of Small Cities*—I thought that was going to be a book's title for me, the human scale of it. The exact and unreplaceable detail of the apparent. The Parthenon we could build again from formula, but the skyline of Hartford in 1968 is lost forever, a message we never read, a shapeliness that eludes us still.

Buildings. When I first began to listen to Bruckner's symphonies, I understood that "structure" in music was not about construction but about housing, interiority, carving out a space in the rock of the world we could live in, or defining by some masterstroke the templum, *space defined as ours*—a place we can live in. Hearing is a house.

14

What do I think of myself as a writer?

I think I am a great playwright, one who has scarcely ever written a play, and never a good one. I think I am writing a great play all my life and every poem a speech in it. Only to find the right mouth, the right shadow. Come, speak me. Come be my mouthed verities and bellowed tendernesses. Come be me. Every poem is a cry that matches exactly its lewd or sacred juncture in the play. Every story a precis or stage direction.

I proposed in my first book an armed descent—Valéry's mot, "He who would descend into the self must go armed to the teeth." And that is what I have tried to do, if do is the word for it, if tried is true. To go down into the self, armed with everything I have of flesh or dream or information. Armed, but not armored. To go down into the self, not especially my self but the sense of, steady beating pulsing beautiful soon lost forever physiology of the, self.

If beginnings were only as easy as they say, those French writers of our day who propose a universe not essentially different from the spin they can give to their words, who balance paradoxes on the tips of their fingers, an arm's length at least from the heart.

Linguistics is the most ironic science, and while we hear little about it these days, it casts its spell still on the devious enterprises of the educated classes, the stuff that passes for learning and teaching, the voice of not knowing you know nothing. " . . . the unbreachable demarcations of law are themselves and precisely the destinies of every transgression, which by endorsing the law it trespasses, by and in that fact proposes, beyond and unboundedly, a later and thus nonpresent limit which is both result of the transgression and source of the next." These phrases from a text of Maurice Blanchot are what happens to me when I fall into a fever of doubt to avoid responding from my heart to Georges Bataille's remark: "Coitus is the parody of crime." When you hear a sentence like Bataille's, you either hear it in silence, or fill up your mouth with words.

And right now I'm filling up my mouth with words, to avoid hearing the *tolle lege* of the Gale Research Company, or rather its *tolle scribe*. Rather than tell the story of my life, I'll say anything that comes into my head.

15

The events of my life as I remember them do not seem in any way different from actions I remember in a book. My standing outside our apartment on West Twelfth Street excitedly telling Joan that I'd just made ΦBK—though I feel the complex intertwined vulgarities of my excitement in the street, this memory doesn't seem to belong to me—except I guess by default: *there's no one else to remember it.* When there's no one else to remember it, it must be mine.

These *hapax dromena*, then, these once-only happenings, are the special burdens of memory we are bitterly privileged to bear.

Because there is no story except the story told. And what is left when I'm finished writing will be the story of my life. I tried at first to sketch it in terms of the twelve houses of the genethliacal figure, my horoscope (though that word truly means only the ascendant or degree rising over the horizon at the moment of my birth—in my case 24° Sagittarius); had I persuaded myself of the cleanliness of that procedure, I would have wound up with (been wounded by) the twelve mundane houses and their affairs: Body and Personality, Stuff and Property, Brothers and Sisters and Friends, Mother and Home, Sex and Self-Proclamation, the Body as Theater of Chemistry, Marriage and Partnership, Dream, Fantasy and Other Inheritances, Theory and Observation (thus travel and religion), Profession, Sway and Conviction in Society, and Karmic Obscuration and Constraints.

And then I thought to order the record of my days by using as rubrics the main relationships of my life—each one an era. But such a procedure, like the Winter Count of the Plains tribes pictographed on buffalo hides, would have made me seem even simpler than I am. And I am simple.

16

I am simple. There, that is a beginning, like the great first line from an early novel: "I, Clement, have been from my earliest youth a lover of chastity."

No one but the hardworking and prolific writer, dauntless practitioner of every experiment and any trick that comes to hand, no one but he can really know just how simple he is. How simple I am. And telling you about it no more convinces you of its truth, my truth, than the phrase *Pleasant downpour every afternoon at Waikiki* soaks the clothes you're wearing now.

Simple, a lover of chastity, a lover of flags and emblems and words, of contours, of answers. Science was my first love, because it told as quickly as it could what little it knew. It knows more than I ever will, and still tells quick, but it too has latterly grown sluggish in its way of telling. It argues more and more about beginnings, and shows less and less the inner life of geodes and the dreams of zooplankton. (Just as linguistics turned to issues of grammaticality and covert structure and left off cataloguing and describing the languages that are actually spoken, at least still being spoken when linguists turned away, by living human beings.) Discourse (a word Charles Olson disdained) has taken over even what used to be called the Exact Sciences; with discourse has come that flaccidity of intellect from which it is not likely we will, as a culture, recover.

Early on, very early, even from the first book I read from the library (was it called *The Stars for Sam?*) I could tell by feel, not reason but feeling itself, just when the author was saying what he knew (or what he thought he knew)—as opposed to filling in the gaps more or less plausibly. It is allergy to that specious gap-filling that has kept me from science and most scholarship.

Simple enough to know I can't find any structure for my telling, except itself, structuring its way along as writing always has, always *can*, if you let it. *No structure but structure*, then, I will claim, and obey.

17

It is not always what we want, the ability to remember. A mango left in a paper bag on a body-polished wooden bench on the Eighth Avenue subway platform. Millie Gendell gasping her lungs out with plaster dust in the coldest winter in years, scraping down to brick in her apartment on Minetta Lane. Millie Minetta millinery, Mr Buonfiglio and the sports jacket two-toned he made me, cashmere soft and paneled in buff, like buckskin, Elderts Lane with Simonetti's pizza garden, a bus on the Avenue Paul Valéry, what is it all about?

Here is the story I have tried to tell:

Armed descent, into her body which is my talisman, my weapon against time. Against time these round dances, the movement around the

"With my sister, Patricia, and father,"
about 1947

core of myself that is my enstasy—the opposite of the ecstasy people are always raving about or hoping for. I wanted enstasy, to stand inside, to be incarnate as myself, in all the full intensity of feeling *in full consciousness* from this place outward. Above me, the stages of the moon declare their lunes, which are their measures in us too, the tuneful amazements of the soul's calendar. Words are forever in service of this going that is my knowing.

That was the first chapter. Somewhere inside all that while, not published as or in a book for twenty years, was "The Exchanges" (1959–1961), the secret alchemical, Mahayana heart of what I was trying to declare.

I can admit it now—my work *has* a meaning to declare. One that I have learned along with you, clement reader.

18

Readers, raiders, you by being close and by being few have charmed me into my own intimate acts of self-awareness, undistracted by criticism in bulk. Slowly I have come to know what my work proposed, first for me to do, then for you to understand. And I am with you, reader, really, for writing and reading are the same act, only different phases of, and I am (truth to say) only this minor character among the personae of my drama, the one called towards the bottom of the column of fine rolling names: First Reader. The writer is just the first reader and seldom the best.

And waits for the Final Reader, in whose lap lies—perhaps at this moment, rising from the paper halfway to the eye, to the ear, to the heart—the real meaning of each thing I have written, and of all those things together. For surely they have their true meaning only in the great text of the whole work, the thing called context but that is really the text itself, the actual weaving.

19

As a child I wanted to be English, be in England, be there. The heavenly country, I called it later in one of the few pieces of mine where I ever tried to face that strange infant anglophile—I can't remember when I didn't want to be there. "Over there," my sad old uncles sang, and meant a different place from the one to which I ventured at their sounds. Song was a signal of that place, a flag

seen at earliest light, dim over the hill. And I knew it was an English war they fought in and sang about now. But music is embarrassing, isn't it, especially when people make it, when people make it drunken and cigarry and with the scatter of pinochle cards all over the big walnut table and the smoke going up into the nostrils of that bald old shiny-pated god in gold-wire rimless spectacles, the god of old men. Over there was somewhere else . . . was moorland and soft springy turf and lichenous stonework yellowy and green. It was old cars moving slow in crowded streets. It was rain. I knew it already, though I had never been, wasn't to set foot in the place for forty years. But I knew. I was almost content. I studied weather and language. I loved the rain and waited.

20

If I write about myself, I must circle around certain absences. If there is any excuse for writing (rather than praying) about one's life, it is this one: that it is necessary to praise certain men and women, and more than man-and-woman, who have blessed me with their kindness or their rage. *Denn rühmen ist's*—praise is the order where the mind best says itself in the world, just as a glad silly reverence is the best habit of mind to carry through the blaze of deeds and omissions.

The only unity to my life is the responsibility I might take for all the deeds and omissions of what is perceived by others as my life. For me, I see only a song that has mine as some of its words.

But there will be absences, and that worries me. Until I know, if I know, how to deal with them, I will devote myself to a history of the text. Not of the life of the weaver. A weaver's life is Bottom's dream and needs no deep expounding.

21

The life of Napoleon that vanished overnight from my cellar study, vanished with the rest of the twenty- or thirty-volume set of duodecimo classic biographies—I don't know, I didn't have them long enough to tell—that my dear uncle Owen Parry had just given me, the life whose absence made me for forty years or more refuse to read a word about Napoleon until Tolstoy made me think of that strange tormenting personage again—that life that vanished overnight because my parents deemed the print too small for my eyes, the eyes meant to be kept virginal for all the textbooks I would read in medical school, but these books in a brown paper bag, dark dusky reddish books, faded burgundy, dusty, very small type to be sure, those books I have never ceased lamenting, and never recovered from the sudden spiteful (as it seemed) destruction—never acknowledged, silently denied—of these things, books, I valued more highly than any other thing I knew then, when I was eight, and books were my savior and my hope, my silver key to the hard door out of the screaming madhouse of my unquiet mind. How wild a child's mind is, prey of every wind of desire and aversion.

What might have been if that book had stayed with me? Would the determined madness of the emperor have won my noncommittal heart, would I have joined the army, determined to rule, and kill where I could not reign?

What might have been—there was no sexier reflection as I grew up than that, what might be, and what might have been.

I used to sit on the subway and boldly watch the doors slide open at my own station, stare and stare and dare myself to let them slide closed again. And the train would take me to the next stop or beyond, beyond anything I knew. What would happen then? I would grow breathless with the excitement of the guess, burgeoning wildness of all that might come to pass. If only we broke the ordinary, the orderly, the same. How we could be touched!

Would that have tormented me, those days after days of the long summer of 1815, after Waterloo, before the ill-starred flight to England, when he, he, l'empereur, could have gone anywhere, Russia, America, the Orient? But stayed there too long in Malmaison, too long in Rochefort. The breathless hard excitement of his waiting, the scholars and biographers didn't know that, but I knew it, how he waited *because* it was the wrong thing to do, because only by breaking the pattern of all your oughts (your reason, your stop on the train), only by breaking all of that can you ever hope to meet your destiny, to meet and contradict the Daemon whose shadow lies on the pattern of your life.

It's just as well, isn't it, that I didn't know all that then? The lust to break the pattern would have overwhelmed me, left me in the world of crime or war.

And then hell would have been my portion in the next life and the next.

22

I didn't like poetry when I was a child. The artifice of it, the rhymes especially, made me feel bad. The artifices, the "marked features" so obvious a child could see or count them, "lisp in numbers," struck me as, not exactly *insincere,* but something like that, perhaps something worse. There was something bad about the poetry I saw, something that made me feel unclean or cloyed by some sentimental (which children dislike) or over-enthusiastic smarmy teary compulsion to feel. Drunken uncles at funerals, coming upstairs from where the funeral director was prudently dispensing shots of rye to the sports among the mourners—those illucid, self-involved, self-deceiving uncle eyes, breathing a sincerity on which they could not quite focus—*that* was the feel of poetry. So poetry seemed untrue. It was not till years later (as it seemed) when I finally reached fourteen that poetry appeared in my life (thanks to Arthur Pinkerton and Hugh Smith) that seemed to be about revelation, not decoration.

If as a child someone had shown me Whitman or W. C. Williams, I might have come earlier to poetry. But by the time I did find them, I had grown enraptured with artifice, and found them, both of them, huffy and secular and busy with opinion. By the time (late college) I read WCW, I wanted to read of glory and see the sunset slant in through lines of poetry as I could find it doing in Dylan Thomas.

But when I was younger, very young, turning with a literal physical sensation of nausea from rhyme and "poetic" language, then Whitman would have won me. I would have liked him well, the ardor and self-conviction, his arrant sincerity unmodulated, stark, like a penguin alone on an ice floe. But no one showed me Whitman.

23

These are the books I remember in my house: seven of the eight volumes of the *American Educator Encyclopedia;* a Catholic CCD edition of the New Testament; *Lost Horizons,* by James Hilton. (I never read it, strange to say, since I heard ordinary people talking about it. All the stranger since my life has become deeply involved with some real-time version of a Tibetan tradition I gather that novel fancied or celebrated.) Then there was a twenty-volume set of books called *World's Greatest Literature,* in false gilt cloth bindings, faux-Grolier, which my parents had gotten for subscribing to the *New York Post,* a paper which my father, by the time I could buy my own paper, judged bolshevik and vile. These are the ones I remember from the twenty: *Moby Dick, The Last Days of Pompeii, The Scarlet Letter, Vanity Fair* (never read it, still can't; Becky still scares me), *The Vicar of Wakefield, Plutarch's Lives* (a selection), *The Last of the Mohicans, The Autobiography of Benvenuto Cellini, Poe's Best* (or *Best Loved*) *Tales, Best Loved Poems, Ben Hur, Tale of the Christ, Oliver Twist, Washington Irving's Sketch Book, The Way of All Flesh, Treasure Island, Shakespeare's Plays* (a selection—I remember best the line drawings, men's calves limned as sturdy ovals, something German in the drawing, a woman cracking a lute over someone's head), *The Count of Monte Cristo, Emerson's Essays.*

Number one sustained me. And one day in number ten I found Coleridge's "Kubla Khan"— and that was it. That is the first poem I remember reading where I found something—everything—I had found nowhere else. I had found poetry.

(In August 1992, after a summer spent in the French countryside, I stood with Charlotte in the noisy MSS display room of the British Museum, and, half-bent forward over the case containing the original manuscript, found myself chanting out loud, full normal voice among the hum of Japanese visitors, the original poem of my life, "In Xanadù did Cubla Khan," I read from the manuscript and recited to the end, hoping to pay back, in the capital city of our language, my debt to its greatest poem.)

24

I should talk now of the poets in my life, starting with Samuel—Samuel Coleridge, matching Samuel Kelly, my father, named for his grandfather Samuel Marles, from Somerset or so, next county over from Coleridge's Devon, who was of an age to have been Coleridge's son. It was Samuel Marles, my great-grandfather, who presided over the fantasy-of-the-past for me as I grew up, so much so that when I first was publishing in college days, I used his name as my pseudonym. Marles must have been born around 1825, probably in Somerset. Family legend called him a painter and poet, who supported himself by japanwork on cabinetry and worked in Bristol. Some pages of his journals survive—including many poems, well-written, intelligent, with an early Victorian sincerity. The spelling is flawless, and nothing hints at

the autodidact or the insecure. He must have been educated. He got married in Manchester to Jane Brass, daughter of a clergyman—presumably John Brass (b.1790) of Bedfordshire. They moved to New York—why?—in the late 1840s, and in 1861 Samuel enlisted in the Union Army to defend his adopted country in the time of her need. My grandmother Florence was eighteen months old at the time. Samuel was wounded at the Battle of Gettysburg, and somehow never came home. He left the country, went to Australia (I was told by some) and to India (by others) to seek his fortune. Certainly I have letters from him, mailed in Karachi (now Pakistan, then the Sind) in 1865. He spoke of his hopes to have wife and daughter join him. Nothing more. Rumors of his death from cholera, of gold found, of some gold sent home expropriated by a wicked uncle. In any case, Samuel Marles has been a vital figure for me, establishing at once whatever authenticity it is to have connections with history (Gettysburg) and Over There (Somerset, Bristol), and at the same time pointing me to Asia.

25

It doesn't seem to me there is some other way of talking about my life than by talking about the people who made me me.

Who are they, though, if not the father and the mother? And everyone has been that at one time or other, even if they haven't been of the magnitude of Margaret Rose Kane (nic Aen) and Samuel Jason Kelly (O Ceallaigh) who made this body me.

Whose names should I mention, leave out, hide, disguise?

Charlotte Mandell, my wife, who moves in the room behind me, her voice soft on the telephone talking to someone a few miles from the sea?

The sea itself—Sheepshead Bay, Coney Island, Rockaway, and the vastness of the sea seen?

Nora Welcome of New Hampshire, whose gracile limbs were white but not as white as the sand scorched into 8-mm color movies from 1939, fresh from being bought at the World's Fair?

The first women and the last.

And I am all the men, or none of them.

No, there is no way to begin this, there is no meaning in a life, in a packet of names, a card catalog, a bed, a crowd in the street at a festa in Settembre, hips jostling, the saint being carried by in his golden carrozza.

A wasp in the window, wondering.
Daylight is all, just daylight.
My autobiography is any day.

The Tibetans when they write of a life story call it for short *nam thar,* abbreviating a phrase that means something like the Story of How He Achieved Complete Liberation. Only such stories are worth telling, I guess. Whereas for us, we dote on detailed annotations of failure, grief, misprision, and despair.

Shall I pretend to an Enlightenment I have yet to uncover, affect a despair I do not feel?

So hard to begin . . . to begin is to end. Well begun half done, they say.

Who say?

The English. Start with that. I think I'm English. The Brasses of Bedfordshire and the Marleses of Manchester, Somerset, Wales. But I'm born on the terminal moraine of the last glacier, a ridge which ran through Brooklyn, of an Irish (raised English by his Protestant mother Florence Marles) father and an Irish (raised American by her Catholic father Thomas Kane) mother. What does it matter where they came from? Doyle made me, and Williams and Dante and Pound and Marlowe and . . .

26

A problem suddenly encountered in writing my autobiography:

I think I'm turning into a crow.

Noisy mysterious obvious and dark
arcane mysterious overt on a tree
conspicuous in snow folkloric
dark portentous scary easy-scared
polemic but not murderous
carnivorous but killing nothing
wide-winged tasteless in people's way
eating grain I never planted
making too much noise being here
sitting apart on the highest
thing I can find apart from everybody
never far from human neighborhoods.

27

Nothing happened to me but people. The people who met me made me. That's the behind and before of it, the way it simply is. (And if we look cannily at most people, we will find it I think

the same—they were who they had beheld, they spoke what they had heard.)

Who said an autobiography is honest? It isn't—it is instead a telling of how one supposes one came to be oneself, here and now, the one who bears my name and speaks it as his own. I am telling you how I came to be me—yet I know nothing of it, nothing but guesswork and hope and fondly cherished memories of erotic blessings, sentiments exchanged, vistas seen—and even more tightly cherished memories of pain and injustices.

So Western autobiography, since it tries to tell what the author doesn't know, is a desperate genre, full of the accidental genius of trying hard—which is why autobiographies are always so full of brio and youthful charm and lies, no matter how old the perpetrator. Robert Graves writing his at thirty-five is no more juvenile than the Oldest Member grousing at his foolscap.

Nothing happened to me but other people. All I did was sometimes have the bravery to recognize and embrace them, all too often the cowardice to avoid them or turn away, mostly the ignorance not to see them really until they were gone. Chances, missed chances, chances married to the deepest and richest bottom of themselves. Known. But there are always more chances. The beauty of the world: there are always more people.

So if I can't tell their names, then I have nothing left to tell (in the old title style, *Life and Opinions of So-and-So*) except my opinions. And my opinions are precisely what I value least about me, lord, this old green shirt has more value than my views on intellectual history or the latest *lutte poétique.*

So I am left to tell you the books I wrote, by which I in turn was written into the world, such as it is, of those who read books and come to know, vaguely, at the corner of their minds, my name. The way it is.

But you understand, don't you, that all this while I'll be thinking about the people.

(One thing I could do is write their names: a real autobiography would look like an index in a scholarly text, and be, finally, as comprehensive and unreadable as an index, a book of names, a personal Deuteronomy.)

In fact, every life is the index to a lost text.

28

When I think through my life, I realize that I am sustained by an immense (that means not measurable) network of gratitudes and permissions.

Maybe the thing I mean when I say *my life* could be the same as all those who have surrounded and instructed me, plus the act of saying so, where "I" is no more than the one that says so.

Someday, someone may have the decency, courage, and effrontery to write an accurate autobiography. It would be made up of nothing other than the names of every man and woman he has ever known; at the end he would draw a line and beneath it sign his own name. Because that is who he sayably is.

I don't have the time, memory, and honesty to do that now. There are so many, and I have lost them, so many of them, into the days and the renewals.

But of the network that sustains me, some nodes are so obvious that even I can't forget them. Let me say some of them here, for the beauty of the names of them, these little murmurs of thanks that should be a mountain roar of *Gratias ago*, lords and ladies!

Friends of childhood who welcomed me into the road of excess and the palace of self-criticism, Arthur Pinkerton, the first person I could talk to who knew more than I did about what I needed to

know, and Hugh Smith who made me understand that a poet was someone it was possible to be.

Joan Elizabeth Lasker (1931–1989), my first wife, Joby—she it was who took my arrogance and mute skills and said, These will do, and treated me like a poet until I sort of was one. And who did not selfishly confine herself, or let me confine her, to Musing just me, but whose kindness and perception strengthened I think many poets, young and not so young. Long after Joby and I had separated, my parents kept sending her every Christmas as nice a check as they could from their Social Security—a little before their deaths, my mother said: She made you a poet.

Wasn't that extraordinary for a mother to say, to yield to that other woman what she, more than any, could have claimed as her own? For she had not just given me a strong body and sturdy bones, but a profound sense of that Irish quality I should call "despairing optimism," the knowledge that we are going to get what's coming to us, and that everything turns out for the best. What better paradox could an artist be armed with?

My father, for all his verbal wit and bel canto, had no such convictions, and had a typically English come-off-it attitude about most exaltations—except for country silences and rare glimpses of deer at twilight (he would have said "in the gloaming"). From him I learned that the words we choose to call them make the emotional meaning of everything we see and do. And from him too the strange (since he despised exercise and athletics, though he danced like Astaire and shamed me at any physical deed) transmission into the sacred dance of baseball: playing, observing, judging, adoring.

His name was Samuel Jason Kelly, and he was born 8 July 1900—on John D. Rockefeller's birthday, he would wryly remember. His own father, a New York detective and City Hall presence of some sort, died when my father was seven and the whole huge family had to vacate the mansion they'd lived in. They kept a few steps ahead of the bailiff, as my father described it, all through his growing up. My father had a wonderful tenor voice, precisely focused and without a trace of vibrato, even as an old man, when the voice was lower and darker. He sang, when he sang, formally and deliberately, never just humming or absent-mindedly; when he sang, he sang full voiced and with his mind on it. He loved Irish songs in the manner of McCormack, and operatic arias he'd make up imaginary French or Italian sounds for, as needed. The music was all, the

*Robert and Joby in the new apartment
in Annandale, 1963*

words nothing. *Prima la musica, dopo le parole* might have been his motto. And in a sense it's mine, since my voice is bass, heavy, unnimble to sing—so I've had to find my arias in the words. But still the music comes first.

My father retired early, at sixty, and he spent the next thirty years in a curious quietness. He would sit at the window for hours, with a strange light in his eyes, seeing I suppose nothing, or that Other Country to which meditators perhaps also hasten inward and by night. He smoked heavily— cigarettes till his seventies, then cigars—but never inhaled, drank a lot in later years, but never seemed drunk, just louder, then quieter, then asleep. He died three weeks after my mother's death, only a few weeks after we all had, for the first time in years, had the chance to spend a summer together up here in the country.

29

In the late 1950s, there was circle of kindness and decency and visionary exploration into which I, rough-hewn and suspicious and greedy, was welcomed—by Jerry and Diane Rothenberg and their friends, Armand Schwerner, Paul and Sara Blackburn, Seymour Faust, my friends Rochelle Owens and George Economou and Amy Goldin, and David Antin, who was the first of all of them I knew, and who brought me along to the Rothenberg door finally, as he had brought me through German literature and communicated even to me some glimmerings of the brittle, the fiercely detailed, the passion for the abstract, the glimmering meager of silverpoint, the passionate enough.

With the Rothenbergs and their friends, I entered for the first time a world in which the individual striving for vision, clarity, or just decency and sense, fitted into the social order—where the solitary poet ran the glad risk of becoming a man of letters. The risk is necessary—without the community, and specifically in some sense the community of letters, vision turns back ingrown. It is the community that gives language, and through language, what we see is restored to those who gave us our means. It was this specific world that the Rothenbergs, with their anthropological interests and training, would soon investigate so deeply and usefully through their work with finding a current English/American voice for Native American and other tribal poetics.

And I was caught at the pivot point, right there, and never sure, never to this day sure, which

way I speak. Because I am private and dread the tribe whose language speaks me. Crazy as Merlin or Taliesin (flattering self-images abound), I took stock of my world and found silence what I could trust most—to talk from silence. To talk from the feel of water on my skin, my feet on the rock, my eye on the contours of experience—uninstructed by the social.

Except of course the ever-present, ever-hidden "social" of poetry, all the poems I had ever read that, resonating in me and charming and changing and dying and begetting, taught me in fine not what to say but, somehow, how saying is, and that I could.

Pivot point. This is the late 1950s, 1960. We had founded The Blue Yak, a bookstore exclusively devoted to small-press books of poetry. A cooperative of us poets ran it: Rothenbergs, Diane Wakoski, George Economou, Armand Schwerner, Howard Ant, Susan Sherman, Bill May. It did enough business to support one person, and that was remarkable itself, after the low rent was paid on the Tenth Street storefront on that block of avant-garde galleries and winos. But there were eight of us, and most of us had too much on our minds to keep it open. The wonderful blue furry horned animal painted on the brick wall still stays in my mind.

30

About this time Caryl Chessman was scheduled to be executed after years of appeal. Joan and I had marched from Columbus Circle in a great crowd of protesters begging for last minute clemency from the California gauleiter. We reached Washington Square to be greeted with news of the man's execution. The grief and impotence of the social moment matched identical emotions in me about my own life and work. I felt neglected, ignored, unknown. Cheaply and silently, I resolved to die. By force of habit we kept walking down to the old Figaro, a sleazy and comfortable cafe on Bleecker, and as I came in, footsore and in despair, an older man wearing a cocoa-colored suit with an orange necktie said, "Hello, you must be the Kellys. I'm Robert Duncan."

This man had recognized me! This man, whom I regarded as the greatest poet living in my language, had spoken my name, known me. Always a knower, Duncan had here deftly, simply, saved my life, literally. The strictly angelic nature of his intervention was shocking and shamed me by

"A party at the Rothenberg's: (from left) Amy Goldin, Armand Schwerner, Jerome Rothenberg, Sara Blackburn, Joby Kelly, Diane Rothenberg," New York, 1960

its simplicity. How little I needed! And how much I got! And the basic sustaining power, the wing he gave me, lasted in all he taught: the power of attention to the dance of words that—so attended to—always would make sense of the body and all its pivots with the world. Social as Auden, fierce as Barker, incantatory as Thomas, learned as Lansing, honest as Olson, adventurous as Mac Low, musical as Zukofsky, Duncan struck me as the complete poet and one whose grace let him play and comfort and be gone. And part of his grace was his strict, sometimes even humorless, fidelity to dream and vision—which made him my key in my own struggles on the side of the surreal against the neo-classic—which is how my generation misunderstood the energy and scruples of Charles Olson:

Olson, who overpowered me and my kind with the fervor with which he, sometimes breathless and in doubt, sustained what seemed—too easily—the mind's argument against the heart. Amazing man, that such flesh and tune and ballsiness should doubt Lord Plato.

And who but Olson could read to me deep in the marches of the night, on Fort Square, within breath of the sea, that overwhelming paragraph from *Moby Dick* that warns all Platonists (and he was warning me) of the honeyhead, the sea in which they'd fall from the crow's nest of their dreamy apart—as if he, great Olson Ter-Maximus, would not have splashed that sea dry and displaced it by his own Animal Ardor he wittingly mistook for mind! For he was intelligent indeed, and knew the cunning of the knees, the care of the eye, the art of what the Icelanders, we are told, call *menskr*—all that is human.

Yet neo-classic seemed an honest word to say of all that, that early and middle thrust of Olson towards the human, the truistically over-determined Human Universe—presume not God to scan.

But in the later, more powerful days, Olson did break that too-sensible rule, and turned from the sub-Emersonian enthusiasms of "history" in America (where Pound had been all our teachers) to scan the deity, the central issue, the Angel. And in the third volume of Maximus, still underperceived by or stifled by his scholars, we find a far more telling appointment with the soul than many of his students wanted or want—they wanted to keep him to the Democratic Party, Aristotle, and coaching at third base. And in the heart of his striving we find the curious name of Amoghasiddhi, the Buddha of the possible.

31

Dear reader,

(Dear reader! How dear you are to me, really really, not just a *façon de parler,* you are the heart of me, the best of me, the part that hears.

You judge the truth of me by what I say.

Actions speak louder than words, my father used to say and say, until I feared to say a word.

Dear reader, for you this language is, for you it made me and made us as we are, prone—prompt—to answer and sullen, we are sullen, you hold me in your sullen lap and dare to doubt me, you do right to doubt me, to test what I say. Test in your body moving and at rest the cloth and fiber and fit. Test the steel on your wood. Test the insistent questions on your continual answers.)

Dear reader, I don't feel much interest in the years gone by, my imagined past. The trough of time I got through as well as I could. I don't feel close to them now, especially the 1960s and 1970s, years of putting one word after another and hoping the world would still be there. Now that the fashions of those times are with us again, if cleaner now and more whimsical and safe, no need to give much glory to those dark hopes and self-induced projected terrors, scares we used as a politics to block our always dim-enough awareness of the real terror of the situation: this mind of ours we do not know. It was a bleak enough time for all its noise and patchouli, and I am glad to be past it.

But the beloved friends of those days, let me say their names at least here, and many of them I get to call upon still, Diane Wakoski and Chuck Stein and Armand Schwerner and Helen Kelly and Jackson Mac Low and Tandy Sturgeon and Gerrit Lansing and Ken Irby and Stan Brakhage and George and Susan Quasha and Elie and Nona Yarden and Jed Rasula and Clayton Eshleman and Lisa Katzman and Michele Martin and Dennis and Barbara Tedlock, and brave John Martin whose fierce idealistic mind and sensual disposition ush-

ered to the dear readers of America half a thousand books of new poetry.

Dear reader, by the time you read this, I will probably be sixty years old. What I care about is what is happening now, the life I live now with Charlotte Mandell, my wife, who translates French and studies Tibetan with me and in her accuracy and beauty and clarity keeps me pointed towards sunrise and makes me happy.

32

Charlotte was different from people I've known. She grew up gently, fastidiously, accurately. I came to know her first in the late 1980s, when she was a student of Edouard Roditi—in the last few years of his life he taught memorably at Bard. Charlotte was of great personal beauty; her father Marvin was a novelist and teacher and an editor of *New Politics,* her mother Betty Reid a sociologist whose career was devoted to the disadvantaged, the homeless, the beneficiaries of welfare-in-name-only, and who single-handedly edited a newspaper for and about the poorest, *Survival News.* Husband and wife had moved in the same New York leftist circles I knew a few years later. So Charlotte was raised in ethical and aesthetic literacy—and that summoned me to her, to a friend raised to value articulate candor and justice.

Charlotte spent her summers in France, or on a small island near Martha's Vineyard—and from that island, Cuttyhunk, she from time to time would send me letters that I marveled at for their spontaneous serenity, a kind of razor-sharp gentle alertness. When she moved to Seattle in 1990, we corresponded. Always her letters were, as she is, precise, generous, willing to see the best of things, even of me. Late that year, after all the deaths and separations I'd been through, I found myself on a west coast trip, and we met in Seattle, then travelled by ferry to British Columbia for a week of keeping warm in the rain. We seemed to move in the House of the Raven, in the primordial powers. The following year she went to France, and when she came back in October, we began to live together—and have ever since. I had never before known the curious integration of erotic intensity with intelligent calm—truth in quiet teaches constancy.

33

What I care about is now, and the work I'm doing—long poems that go on, *Bliss, Espousals,* prose texts, theories of translation, the klondike of electronic publishing with the Himalayas of hypertext just behind, and above all else the dance I meet every morning in silence, the song, *le chant du jour* and what else is new? What else is now?

I want to write sentences they will take delight in
("feel measure!") in three hundred years
(after the baroque revival, the second Lake school,
the new Novalis and ultra-Kierkegaard,
when Marx is fresh again
and a great, bluff bully from the Touraine
weeps at the human comedy again
and Miss Baudelaire wakes up at evening's dusk
and Second Ezra wakes up what's left of London

or whatever is, whatever ever is)
                     sentences,
sentences unhinged from rule and hardware,
long lines of luminous messages, semaphores,
outrage on emulsions, screens, the sky, the eye
taught its manners by machines,
however and wherever they do it, do it,

and still my crazy grammar will make hard sense,
crazier the better, glue on every corner,
crumbs of green cheese between the fingers,
something for you! for you!

inexhaustible, indestructible, leaving
echoes and clatter and strange garlicky reeks,
a flurry of frangipani, gets stronger
when you open the windows, where's it coming
    from,
from your hands, the words infect your flesh,
keep reading, smell the weather of these words
coming over the horizon like a Viking ship
or just a sunrise, a coven of gypsies,
a crowd of giggling kids tossing your heart from
    hand to hand

34

In all the gratitudes I want to mention last the chiefest gratitude:

In December of 1981, beginning to be tired of what had begun to look like persistent patterns of greed and aggression in what I thought was my innocent behavior, I took refuge in the Buddha, Dharma, and Sangha. I recited the ancient traditional formula that makes one a Buddhist. One very cold night a month or two later a friend was showing me pictures of various Tibetan lamas. (A lama is the one who shows you your mind—something we can see unaided no more than the eye, for all its acuity, can see itself. We need a mirror, and the eye finds perhaps its best mirror in the eye of another person.)

One picture in particular struck me; looking at the face, I felt what I could now call the intense presence of near and far—at once most intimate and most exalted, the way I suppose one's own soul feels. At the moment, what I felt was yearning to meet and listen to this teacher, who was called Kalu Rinpoche.

Several months later I had the chance to make a connection with Kalu Rinpoche when he offered the Kalachakra Initiation in New York. A little later, I had the nerve to ask him to be my teacher; he agreed, but in his kindness told me that I should work mostly and directly with Lama Norlha, who lives most of the year in the United States.

Meeting these two great teachers, my root lamas, strikes me as the most important opportunity I have been given, and the greatest good fortune, even among so many kindnesses my life has known. For the past dozen years or so, I have tried to let their wisdom and compassion shape the direction of my activities. Though Kyabje Dorje Chang Kalu Rinpoche passed away in India in 1989, his presence and kindness continue to pervade my life, focused through the brilliant and compassionate instruction of Lama Norlha. It is strange in these times to meet such a being; usually, the better you know someone, the more you see his faults. With Lama Norlha, the reverse seems true; the longer I have been with him, the more I have seen of his qualities. Of all the remarkable persons I have ever had the blessing of talking with out loud, in ordinary words, as well as learning from by signs, behavior, quietness, Lama Norlha is the truest. Without any time wasted on what we quaintly call a "private" life, he dedicates all of his time, all of his life, to helping others. His teaching is penetrating and direct, and intensely personal to the one taught. The simplest thing to say about him is this: He knows.

He knows me. He has helped me to integrate all the energies and interests of my life and perceive them as continuous. The Buddhist Vajrayana is usually called tantric—and *tantra* means continuity. At root, the word means something like loom, and the seamless continuity of what is woven. The Tibetan word is clearer: *rgyud,* the thread, the line, the lineage, the continuity.

Lama Norlha teaches the Buddhadharma, yes, but I have learned from him much of what I know

Kalu Rinpoche, about 1979. "This is the picture I saw that so caught my mind."

about narrative, timing, language, and what we mean when we speak, and what we are keeping unsaid. His own teachings, and the power of his chanting, are continual reminders of what it means to speak and be heard.

Once not long ago I was talking to him and told him about this thing I'm writing (this thing you're reading now), this autobiography. My life, what can I say about my life? What is the value of writing a story of someone who has not achieved the goal, has not broken out of the system of habits and constraints?

I said to Lama Norlha, what can I possibly write in my autobiography?

He laughed and said, You like to write. Write about your future lives instead. (The past is the son of a barren mother, it is said: there is no past, only the onward hurtling energy of our own past deeds, shaping what we perceive as the world, moment by moment appearing to take form.) Write your future lives. It is the ones to come and not the ones that have gone that are important. Tell those.

Are you joking?

(In telling there is learning. Telling is investigation.)

Maybe in my very next life I will be born in Mongolia, a nomad. Looking down the corridor of Necessary Words (the world of prophecy), I see myself on a cold wide plain. Between my hands the head of a deer, his eyes turn wild at me, his breath snorting out, gushing warm on my dirty wrists. I am holding this animal by the horns, he twists his head to one side and I pull him straight, twists to the other and I right him again. We look at one another. He has the fatal, useless, beautiful wisdom of animals. I have the kind of cunning, deep esemplastic cunning, that I can hardly imagine in this present life. But when I am a Mongolian it will be different. My hands will do some of my thinking for me, twisting the deer this way and that, until we have finished saying to each other whatever has to be said. Perhaps I'm trying to tell him about this life of mine. Or all life, so short, so mysteriously projected into outrageous destinations.

I look at Lama Norlha. His hands are twisting the head of the animal back, gently, so that this unseen beast sees me.

He says, Oh, in your next life after that you will be a Chinese fisherman. (This will be hard for me, for I have never hunted, fished or killed.) And then in your next life you will be a Japanese businessman.

(And here is the hardness of money, that I never understood in this life—Saturn in Pisces in the second house—didn't understand, did love the warm feel of it in my pocket. But Japanese businessmen have no pockets, only fountain pens and documents, no sleep, Johnny Walker Red Label [I never liked scotch]. I used to go without sleep—once I managed five days without sleep and without food, lived on coffee and cigarettes and rode the subways. Was I in training for Nagoya or Osaka? Once I was a sort of businessman and wore a homburg hat to business, had the key to the office in my pocket, and knew the books. I took a course in Japanese language and culture from Professor Edwin O. Reischauer [later to become Ambassador to Japan] at City College. It was called Unattached Eight, and brought Madame Harich-Schneider [I think was her name] to play that round mountain of tubular ascensions, an ancient mouth-organ of the Japanese; she brought with her a small electrical brazier to keep the instrument warm. And someone else brought in and played the *shakuhachi*. Nineteen fifty-four, and already getting ready for that life beyond the Pan-Pacific Rim.)

Lama is still smiling at me. Maybe then you are born again as an American. You become president, you preside over America becoming at last a very spiritual country. You think that is good?

(And here I can tell the history of my *historein,* searching, researching, my quest among the so-called religions. What I saw early in the morning as Father Brady lifted up the silver cup. And how that light led me faithfully to the work of the Grail. How can a country have a religion? Can't we go to the land of the Grail, as the King of Oddiyana achieved realization, and brought the whole population of his country with him into the Pure Land? Travelers when they came to Oddiyana found a pleasant, perfectly empty country, no people, no birds, no beasts, no fish. Just trees and flowers, precious jewels lying all over the ground, smoke still drifting up from kitchen fires.)

But, Lama, is it just one life after another?

Then you get a lifetime of rest—in Tibet, watching yaks.

Maybe then enlightenment time?

Maybe.

Maybe a long time watching the yaks.

TIMELINE

1935—September 24, born in Brooklyn, New York—on Brown Street, in Marine Park, near Gerritsen Beach, the coal docks, and conduits.

1943—Birth of my sister, Patricia. (I knew her only as a baby, since after fifteen or so I hardly ever was home. I have gotten to know her in recent years, with her husband James Kimbis and my two nephews Thomas and Peter.)

1943—Simple myopia began. Misdiagnosed, untreated. For the rest of the 1940s, I would be progressively less and less able to see. Only the threat of having me put in classes for the blind

Lama Norlha at Tsopema, India, 1993

Robert in the Adirondacks, 1988

finally reconciled my parents to the "crutch" of treatment: eyeglasses. (A great moment came one December—maybe 1949?—when the doctor settled the spectacles on my nose and wheeled me around, and I saw snow sifting down over Eighth Avenue, omni-colored in neon, and for the first time I saw each flake a word apart, distinct, chiseled-clear.)

1944—"Loss" of our house—we had to move to a shabby part of town (one I later learned to roam and love). For months I would make my way, by busses and trains and walking, to the original neighborhood, not so much for the friends I had there, but for the house, the place—and the garden, which still, in its modesty, defines what flowers mean: the pansies in the windowbox on the garage, the pussy willow by the picket fence, the aisle of deep red roses, the huge blue blossoms of the hydrangea that always seemed wet with dew no matter how hot the day. How I hated heat!

1944–50—Living on Crescent Street in the Old Mill district, east of Brownsville and New Lots, south of Cypress Hills, west of Ozone Park. Walking distance from the great marshlands that bounded Long Island's south shore, which still throng with birdlife in the Hammels. In those marshes I walked a lot, losing and finding myself. Black mud, wild birds, luminous byways of water, sea creeks, endless acres of timothy and marsh grass. There were miles of old wooden catwalks and foot bridges over winding channels of the sea. These old grey wooden weathered walkways went out towards a village of houses built on stilts, called Kinderhoek, where fishing people lived. No roads—only by boat did they come to the firm mainland. And this was the place for me, these marshes, gulls, and sky. My place.

1949–51—Brooklyn Prep, a Jesuit school. I wanted to go there because it taught Greek. From the earliest sight of the place, long before school age, I knew they taught Greek and knew I needed it. How did I know? I did learn Greek and Latin there, and began German.

Worked on the newspaper. Smoked, and stored illicit books in my locker.

1950–52—*Wanderjahre*, fell through the cracks, absenteeism gradually turning into dropoutism, wandered the city, got no further than Philadelphia (Rodin Museum! Gates of Hell!), mostly Manhattan: the Village and the subways and hanging around Columbia. Era of nosleepism, no eatism, weird mentalisms, seehowfarIcangoism. My close friends in these days were Arthur Pinkerton, who disapproved, and Hugh Smith, always ahead of me in creative profligacy.

1951—Forced to choose between legal trouble (for truancy) and going to school. I had to enroll in something, so I went to college. I entered CCNY at fifteen and went sedately enough through four years of mostly immemorable required classes and met wonderful people—David Antin, Robert Levine, James Moran, Jack Hirschman. Insolent and unruly as I was, I secretly let these folk be somehow my teachers, and am grateful yet.

1954—Met Joan Lasker and began my first close relationship, in poverty and difficulty and silliness and splendor, the way it is. In the summer, I spent several weeks in Paris, studying nothing but the city, the fall of light, the wield of her streets. Supposed to go to Austria and Germany to study language, but I never did. I never do.

1955—Graduation from college. Married Joan in August. We lived in Brooklyn (again!), in Crown Heights, on a street neatly divided between Hassids and West Indians. Began working for a living: as a translator (German and Spanish mostly, medical and pharmaceutical materials—I knew all about the tranquilizers as they were being developed, thanks to the clinical papers I was assigned) for an agency run by Ralph Gladstone (poet and brilliant translator of Jarry and the 'Pataphysicals, editor of the remarkable *Wunderhorn Musette*, a single issue that glistened in Bohemia) and his brother William.

1955–58—Enrolled in the graduate program at Columbia, working first in seventeenth-century studies with Marjorie Nicholson and Pierre Garay, then in mediaeval studies, just at the end of Roger Loomis's career—his spell lingered, and I worked on the exfoliations of the Grail legend, concerning myself with Malory in particular, answering an intuition that Malory had somehow—in his sullen art, his

strange isolation, his feral apartness—enlarged nonetheless the notion of the Grail company, the sacred committee of holy knowing. I did all the course and exam work, but never wrote even a master's essay, let alone a dissertation. But I thought about it quite a while. Then rejected it.

1957—The closest friend I met in Columbia was George Economou, and with him I got started on a project of a new magazine. We invited two friends to work with us—Ursule Molinaro and Venable Herndon. We had been introduced by Joe Kling in his wonderful bookshop on Greenwich Avenue—he who linked back to Hart Crane and the Paris-American vanguard of the 1920s. Venable and Ursule were both much savvier than George and I, they were writers who had been around. I wonder sometimes how they put up with my callowness. Maybe it was my push. I have always had push. Soon we had together the first issue of the *Chelsea Review*, which we had printed in Gibraltar. Three issues more followed it before there was a change of editorial direction.

1958—On an October evening, blue sky and cool, I walked down Lexington Avenue going home from work, tired and absurd, three years in graduate school, three years translating rat tests and liver jaundice. It seemed that the sky opened quietly and an Understanding spoke in me, saying that if I dedicated myself to writing, if I gave myself to that truth I knew as somehow the sky and the voice that speaks inside and the good of the world, if I gave myself over to writing for the good of the world, it would be well, and it would be well with me. When I got home I explained all this to Joan, who encouraged me to quit my job and school and devote myself to writing. I did so, immediately. And from the end of 1958 to the summer of 1960, Joan supported us. She was working at a job she liked well, that paid poorly indeed, and we were almost humiliatingly poor in those days. She worked in the library at the Brooklyn Museum, with friends like Dorothy Billings and Lois Katz, who spent some lovely Saturdays trying to teach me Chinese.

1958–61—Amy Goldin, sister of my Columbia classmate Ruth Huston, moved to New York. Amy and I had the most intense exchange of letters I had ever known, and I revelled in the detail and emotional accuracy of her brilliant mind, her sensuous reach for art. Her coming to New York gave me someone to study with, study, be prodded by, yet also (being me) advise and console. A painter whose work never found its full reception, she later became more and more an essayist and critic in the 1960s. We were very close, and she was I think the first of my real live teachers. I still feel the excitement of her mind and her engagement with the means of all the arts; I mourn her loss, first through the natural estrangements of relationships, and then her terrible death.

Joan and I met Celia and Louis Zukofsky, and learned much from visits to them in their spotless place in Brooklyn Heights, a marvel of housekeeping, an apartment as precisely ordered as the dictionary. Their kindness to gauche and messy youngsters was impeccable. Louis Zukofsky's amazing acuity of mind's ear is of course what's most for me to be grateful for. But he also did all he could to link poets together and spread the news. He let George Economou and us print a little book of his as a Trobar Book—*I's (pronounced eyes)*.

1959—About this time I began a correspondence with Gerrit Lansing, which still continues. It brought me to Gloucester in 1962 to meet him and Charles Olson—the years 1962 to 1969 are full of Gloucester visits and adventures—it seemed to be a university of rock and sea, bitter and salty and smart, Olson and Lansing and the wind at Hammond Castle, Harry Martin. I learned to hold my own, but maybe held too hard.

1960—Through the kindness of George Economou, I got my first teaching job at Wagner College on Staten Island. Classes from eight in the morning till noon. I had to get up at five, take a subway, change to the East Side IRT, take the Ferry, then two buses to get up to the college. I was often late but seldom absent. My annual salary was $2400. At the end of the term, I resolved never to teach again. It had its advantages: the immense vista of New York harbor from Grimes Hill—a sight of my Brooklyn, not much inflected from its essential nineteenth-century self; and palling around with the old poet and filmmaker Willard Maas, who taught English with people who saw him as an eccentric, whereas I celebrate him still as the maker of that extraordinary film *The Geography of the Body* that years before had overwhelmed me, ca 1951, when I saw it at a showing of avant-garde films

Robert in the mid-1960s

at Cinema 16—a subscription to which had been my mother's surprising gift to me one Christmas.

1960—George Economou and I left the editorial board of the *Chelsea Review*. We wanted to deal with poems, not prose; American, not fashionable translations. We began *Trobar*, dedicated to what we called (by a perhaps fortunate synchrony) the new American poetry. The first issue had a strong cover by Amy Goldin and was printed on menu paper by Balys Jacikevicius in Brooklyn; he charged sixty dollars and felt cheated. But I can still spell his name and still taste his wife's sweet milky Baltic coffee.

1961—Through the kindness of Paris Leary (with whom I'd corresponded since early in Chelsea days), a poet and Anglican priest with a passion for Charles Williams, and who thought of himself as "an apostle to the rich," I was offered a job teaching German at Bard College. (I had studied German literature in college, tried to major in it, translated it for

"Charles Olson between kitchen and workroom," Gloucester, 1963

several years, but had never spoken it, never been in Germany.) Twice I refused the job, hating the idea of leaving the city, of teaching what I didn't know, of living on the edge in every sense. When they made the third offer, they asked me to come and look at the campus. The president of the college, the late Rev. Reamer Kline, picked me up at the bus station in his little VW bug—the simplicity of it impressed me. Annandale's beauty swayed me, and the gorgeous apartment Bard offered us—free—won me, after years in Rat Hall in Bed-Stuy.

Sometime in the fierce hot dry summer of 1961, we managed to move our several thousand books (managing alas to lose our collection of Joe Kling) upstate, and left our steel shelves from Brooklyn to Jackson Mac Low. All these years later I do not regret it for a moment, this rustication.

1961–62—Taught German at Bard: beginning, intermediate, and a seminar on Goethe's *Faust*. What was I doing? Exhausting, draining, almost nightmarish—yet I wrote more than I had ever written in my life—an instruction that activity is itself stimulating to the prophetic faculty, not the reverse. Lazy people have nothing to say.

And for the first time in my life, we had money, not much, but at $5500 a year and no rent, I could learn to drive. I bought a dark green 1949 Chevrolet. I was taught to drive by the poet Jonathan Greene, who had been the real instrument in getting me to Bard, and who now had to deal with the monster he had summoned. (I had met Jonathan in New York with his friend Chuck Stein, with whom I am still close after thirty-five years, both of them students of Armand Schwerner, who brought them to meet the Big Poets one night around 1958—Paul Blackburn, greatest of our troubadours, and Armand Schwerner [never in my life have I ever heard him say a boring thing, always on, always acute] himself, and Economou and me. Chuck, whose mother had just died, read some poems that struck me powerfully indeed, even though he was supposed to be along only for the ride, and for his saxophone, which he played as we sauntered "like cut-rate Montezumas," in Dahlberg's great phrase, down to the Village and the Festa di San Gennaro that thronged the streets.)

In spring of this year, Jerry and Diane Rothenberg's Hawk's Well Press published my first book, *Armed Descent*. Fifty or so books later, I'm still glad that was the first. And as hard as it was to wait (till twenty-five!) for that first book to be published, I am profoundly glad it took so long; had the book been gathered together six months before, I could not now stand by it.

1962—Shifted to teaching English at Bard; I started my first freshman English course with *Naked Lunch* and Sherlock Holmes, with pleasure to teach the things that formed me. Later I was asked by Heinrich Bluecher to teach a section of his "Common Course"—which is how I happened to begin teaching Buddhism, one of the "units" of his history-of-consciousness-oriented Jaspersian enterprise. So I found myself one day—I can still feel the feel of me, inside the chest of me, the mind of me, as I, pompous as Charlemagne, recited the triple refuge in Sanskrit: *Buddham saranam gacchami, dharmam saranam gacchami, sangham saranam gacchami.* Twenty years would pass before I had the least sense of what I was really saying. But now I can stand by the words. The words meant. The words counted. As they always do.

1962—This year I met Charles Olson.

Cid Corman, in the course of hundreds of dynamic, horrendous, instructive, benevolent, critical letters, published "The Exchanges" and other poems of mine in a featuring-RK issue of the second series of *Origin,* whose first series had clearly been the most important magazine of the 1950s for American poetry.

1963—First meetings with Stan Brakhage and Ken Irby. Margaret Randall, who opened so much of the Americas to the work being done throughout all its tongues and islands, published my second book, *Her Body Against Time / Su Cuerpo Contra El Tiempo,* in Mexico City, in a bilingual edition.

1964—Charles Olson invited me to join Dorn, Creeley, and Baraka in teaching at Buffalo for the summer. *Lunes* (embodying a three-line, thirteen syllable form I had developed) was published in an edition with Rothenberg's *Sightings,* fierce arrowheads of his work, with cover by Amy Goldin. *Round Dances* published, with drawings by Josie Rosenfeld.

1965—Meeting with Helen Belinky, who came to live in Annandale. I began *Weeks,* first of my long serial poems. *A Controversy of Poets* published by Doubleday as an Anchor paperback—Paris Leary and I had edited it over several years, and the controversy was between us, I representing the experimental/Black Mountain/avant-garde, he the "academic" poets (the ones the world already knew about). Doubleday had planned to call it the Doubleday Book of Contemporary Poetry, then got cold feet and gave it a silly donnish joke of a title which yet embodied something of the polemic going forward. Robert Duncan refused to be included because the anthology was not polemic enough. In the piebald despairs and follies of anthologists, I almost abandoned the thing, then kept myself going with the thought that Zukofsky's *A–11* could be read by thousands. The book eventually sold something like sixty thousand copies and must have done some of what it was supposed to do.

1966–67—Living in Cambridge, teaching as Visiting Professor of Modern Poetry (a title that warmed me) at Tufts. Close to Steve Jonas, Linda Parker, Carol Weston, and Robert Lee Tipps, through whom I met all these, Jim and Joanne Randall, Gordon Cairnie.

1967—Doubleday published *The Scorpions.* I began corresponding with John Martin of the new Black Sparrow Press whom I first met in Connecticut. This has been a continuous relationship with the publisher and press who made my work available to the commonwealth—my work and the work of hundreds of other new poets and narrators, in the greatest triumph of small press in our time. *A Joining: A Sequence for H.D.* is the first small book of mine from Black Sparrow. And there were samizdat books of mine this year, printed on our fancy mimeograph: *Devotions, Twenty Poems, Axon Dendron Tree, Crooked Bridge Love Society.* Residency as Fellow of Calhoun College, Yale.

1968—Moved early January into Lindenwood House, on the Triangle in Annandale, where I still live. The temperature reached twenty-six below zero a few days later, then I left for California, my first visit to the West. Stayed with Harvey Bialy and Timotha Doane, who opened San Francisco to me. *Alpha* published. *Finding the Measure* published, my first full-sized collection from Black Sparrow.

1969—Reading tour through New England. *Songs I-XXX* published. *A California Journal. The Common Shore,* first five books of a long poem about America in time. After a peaceful divorce from Joan, Helen and I married in Mexico, April 1969.

After eight years of digging in my heels, sustaining myself by the sight of the dark treetops of the century-old white pines against the blue sky on the road to Blithewood, and after much political struggle (much of which went on unconsciously or actually without my taking part), I was given tenure at Bard. Bard. What a name, and what auspices! Originally I planned to stay a year, then fell in love with the place—the telluric aspect of it first, the part the woodchuck and the crow know best. Then little by little the school part of it pleased me, gave me space, let me do my work. And to Bard came year after year brilliant students of poetry, and I had the privilege of working with them, trying to stimulate without shaping, informing without forming. Those students, who still keep coming, are what has kept me here all these years. Occasional forays to other schools would show me what is more usual in American colleges: one or two brightlings amidst the dim. But so many of them came here, men and women who wanted to write, and who would go ahead to make their lives into a long fulfillment of that double contract with the earth and with language that it is to be a poet. It was a delight, sometimes a daunting delight, to work with them, and a joy to think of them still working in the renewal of the world: Thomas Meyer, Pierre Joris, Elizabeth Robinson, Ann-Sargent Wooster, John Yau, Bruce McClelland, William Prescott, Amanda Dowd, Harvey Bialy, Josepha Gutelius, Norman Weinstein, David Gansz, Kimberly Lyons, Barbara Grossman, Juliana Spahr, Lydia Shectman, Brian Stefans, Drew Gardner, Manus Pinkwater, April Hubinger, Mary Sternbach, Mary Caponegro, Lynn Behrendt, Laura McClure, Noreen Norton, Marilyn Donahue, Susan Mernit, Peter Boffey, Phyllis Chesler, Dennis Barone, Paul Pines, Bill Wilson, Cathleen Shattuck, Jane Heidgerd, Thea Cooper, Mark Karlins, Barbara Roether, Tandy Sturgeon, Jessica Bayer, Martine Bellen, Richard Grazide, David Abel, Lisa Harris, Leonard Schwartz, Drake Stutesman, Alison Watkins, Norman Weinstein, so many, how can I number them? I am grateful to them all, for coming, for hearing, for making me speak. They made sense of my work.

Bard. I know the earth is special here. Whether it's because it's on the ancient Cape Ann—Cahokia—Grand Canyon—Temple of Moroni in West Los Angeles ley-line (as we would have said in the 1970s), or because of the grace of the earth lords, or its having been an ancient treaty region, Delos-like among warring tribes, or thanks to the blessings of some ecological conjuncture we have not yet the science to perceive, this Annandale is a place in which considerable energy is available for those who propose to work. And over the last two decades, the college itself has grown much more in harmony with that kind of renovative energy that so abounds here. When Leon Botstein came in as president to wake the faculty and bring the arts alive, he (historian, musician, a man of Olsonian reach and risk and skill) wielded the curious double power of the academy at its best: the power of finance, to provide for the livelihood of those intellectuals and artists who maintain the continuity of human culture, and the power of intellect, to declare all things open to question, including especially the comfortable assumptions of curriculum and "discipline." He has brought living people here and trusted them to do their work. And that is one of the things for which I am most grateful, the colleagues who have been brought here over recent years, colleagues who are writers and who teach as part of the strength of what they do— Norman Manea, John Ashbery, Mona Simpson, Ann Lauterbach, Ed Sanders, William Gaddis, Edouard Roditi, Lydia Davis, and further back Robert Coover and I. B. Singer and Peter Sourian and even, a decade ago, Robert Duncan, who taught a remarkable course in Poetics at Bard 1982–83, and presented a sequence of readings of all his late work. Bard is an extraordinary place, all three: ground and institute and the custom of the young.

1970—*Kali Yuga* published by Cape Goliard in London. Through these years I was associated with Clayton Eshleman as a contributing editor to *Caterpillar,* and with Dennis and Barbara Tedlock of *Alcheringa.*

1971—Death of Paul Blackburn. In the spring of the year, Paul asked me to read at Cortland, where he had finally taken a teaching job. On St Patrick's Day I read there for his class—on that same day, Paul got the diagnosis—"It's nothing," he said at the end of the reading when I asked about his trip to the doctor, "just a little cancer." That night I couldn't sleep, tormented by grief for him—and for all of us, for myself, since one death is the death of all. I grieved because of his young wife and baby son, grieved for the greatness of his work and his immense (really never saw anything like it before or since) kindness to other writers. When I was just beginning, he guided me to readings, wrote big praise about my work, tried to make things happen. And not just for me. He was always ready to put himself last. I remember sitting in his West Side apartment in the late 1950s, hearing him read, studying how he studied his own work, his careful readings, revisions, attentions, watching how everything he did—eating, drinking, smoking, talking—was done with precise focus. His care and hard work and his sinewy feeling for song made the direct link with Ezra Pound, whose

Proença left Paul such scope for our new *trobar*. And now I was watching those oriental eyes of his wrinkle with the smile of "only a little cancer." By the summer, he was weak indeed. I saw him last at the curious two-week poetry festival on the sun-battered shadeless primary shield of central Michigan, where he lugged his two-ton reel-to-reel tape recorder around to everybody's reading, just as he always did in New York, keeping track of us all. His own reading was feeble, strong only in that this dying man could read so clearly, gently, without the least glimmer of self-pity or even excuse. The young writers who came to learn to strut got little sense of the grandeur of the man. Just after I got to Los Angeles and started teaching at CalTech, Paul died back east, mid-September, just before the beginning of Monastic Lent. He was forty-four.

Cities (a novella written in the heat of energy still unspent at the end of writing *The Scorpions*) and *In Time* (a collection of essays and manifestoes) were published by Harvey Brown's Frontier Press. *Flesh Dream Book* (the title means to identify the three sources of the poem) published by Black Sparrow.

1971-72—Chosen as first Poet in Residence at CalTech, through the kindness of David and Annette Smith. Year in Los Angeles: lived up in the foothills of the San Gabriels, in Altadena; from the front steps you could see sunlight cresting on the waves coming in to the distant shore across the Basin. Behind the house was Mount Wilson, where it snowed one day. Friendship with Caryl and Clayton Eshleman, Jim and Christine Tenney, Max Delbrück, Ted Ronyon. In the fall of 1971 I turned thirty-six, thus in some literal sense outliving the predictions I had lived with since my childhood, that I would die at thirty-five. In the overwhelming gush of survival energy, I began *The Loom* and finished it, for the most part, in two months, sometimes composing (at the secondhand Olympia we had just bought) for twenty hours at a stretch.

1972—*Ralegh* and *The Pastorals* published.

1973—Back in Annandale. *The Mill of Particulars* published.

1974—*A Line of Sight* published.

1975—Publication of *The Loom*.

1976—Residency at Dickinson College in Pennsylvania. *Sixteen Odes* published.

Paul Blackburn in Annandale, 1963

1977—First teaching stint at Naropa Institute; over the years, I would read and teach often at this remarkable school that sheltered the last sparks of American protest, and the first glimmer of Dharma light. Separation and divorce from Helen. Publication of *The Lady Of.*

1978—I began to live alone, for the first time since 1954. This meant relearning the wonderful work of time. From now into the 1980s and beyond, I would enjoy friendships with Mary Caponegro, Chuck Stein, Patricia Snyder, George and Susan Quasha, Mary Sternbach, Franz Kamin, Bruce McClelland, Barbara Leon, all of whom were living within a few miles of each other—a kind of Annandale-Barrytown-Rhinebeck renaissance. *The Convections* published. *Wheres* published. Bruce McPherson's Treacle Press published *The Book of Persephone*, beginning a relationship that would shape my sense of my writing and eventually send my fictions—written at liberty—out into the world, unexpectedly, as far as I was concerned.

1979—This was a year of a major change in my life: through careful diet and through grace, I lost so much of the gross obesity I had always carried that, by 1980, I could walk down a street and not be noticed—and that is an extraordinary sense of liberty, the curious freedom of being "normal." Publication of *The Cruise of the Pnyx,* an experiment in telling, using verse and prose and something in between them, all three, in one text. Publication by Black Sparrow of *Kill the Messenger Who Brings Bad News—The World Is Only Description.*

1980—*Kill the Messenger* (under its shorter title) won the *Los Angeles Times* prize for the best book of poetry of the year. After a year or two of planning and committeeing, the new graduate program in the arts began at Bard. I taught in this every year for the next dozen years. Courseless and entirely directed to the individual encounter with work and criticism, based on endless one-to-one exchanges, the program usefully dealt with each art in the context of all the others, which was my chief concern, and avoids still the factory air of workshops and conservatories. *Sentence* published by Station Hill. The Poetry Collection of the Lockwood Memorial Library in Buffalo began to acquire my manuscripts, correspondence, and notebooks, as part of an RK archive.

1981—*Spiritual Exercises* published. North Atlantic Press published Jed Rasula's gathering together of poems of mine published in magazines but never collected, *The Alchemist to Mercury.* He described it as an "alternate Opus" and presented it as a sort of left-handed Selected Poems. I had the chance to include some pieces overlooked, and learned a great deal about my work from Rasula's admirable editing. As I did later from his long essay on my work that prefaced his bibliography (complete up through 1980) of my work, published later as an issue of *Credences* (spring 1984, edited by Robert Bertholf). On 27 December in New York City I took refuge in Buddha, Dharma, and Sangha.

1982—In the springtime, I first met Kalu Rinpoche and Lama Norlha. *Mulberry Women,* the first livre d'artiste collaboration with Matt Phillips.

1983—Travelled in India with Lama Norlha and stayed in Kalu Rinpoche's monastery near Darjeeling. While there, compiled an Indian journal never published. On return, trying to find the way of words again, worked at the composition of *The Flowers of Unceasing Coincidence.*

1984—*Thor's Thrush,* an old collection, republished by Coincidence Press, with a title in runes.

1985—Travel in England and Scotland. Beginning of a deep friendship with Mary Moore Goodlett; we worked and lived together till her death four years later. Her skills in linguistics and communication, her humane fervor and toughness, were joyously wielded for her friends. As a fourteenth-generation American from Kentucky, she made me, somehow, more American than I knew I could be. Bruce McPherson this year published *A Transparent Tree,* the first collection of my fictions. It includes the "Russian Tales—an Experiment in Telling," which is the clearest demonstration or exposition of how narrative arises from language itself: "Language is the only fable."

1986—In May, I received an award of the American Academy and Institute of Arts and Letters at their annual meeting.

1987—Visited Hawaii in January. In the summer, Jerry Rothenberg and I represented the U.S. at the First International Poetry Festival in Luxemburg. Visited France, Austria, Switzerland. *Not This Island Music* published.

1988—*Doctor of Silence* (second collection of fictions) published. *Oahu* (notations from my Hawaiian visit) published by Bruce McClelland's new St Lazaire Press.

1989—Visit to California. Last meeting with Kalu Rinpoche in January. Passing away of Kalu Rinpoche in India, 10 May. Death of Joan Lasker a week later. Through this year, Mary Goodlett's condition deteriorated, the cancer metastasizing determinedly.

1990—A full year of death: death of Mary Goodlett, January 25, aged thirty-nine. Death of my mother in August, aged eighty-eight. Death of my father in September, aged ninety. *Cat Scratch Fever* (third collection of fictions) published.

1991—*Ariadne* published. To California and Pacific Northwest. Travel with Charlotte Mandell to Victoria. In October, Charlotte returned from France, and we started to live together.

"With my wife Charlotte,"
Mohonk Mountain, 1993

Over the late 1980s and on into the '90s I have been sustained by close working friendships with Pat and Marla Smith of *Notus*, Brad Morrow of *Conjunctions* (which we were able to bring to Annandale as Bard's literary journal), David Gansz, Dennis and Barbara Tedlock, Nicholas Maw, Matt Phillips, Barbara Leon, Ken Irby, Pierre Joris, and Nicole Peyrafitte-Joris, Sarah Rothenberg, Ilse Schreiber, and Bruce McPherson.

1992—Teaching at Naropa, and travel with Charlotte in the Rockies; spent the summer in the foothills of the Haute-Savoie with Charlotte and her family. Publication of *A Strange Market*. Resignation from the graduate program, getting the summers back.

1993—Charlotte and I married on 3 June. Editing and preparation of my *Selected Poems 1960–1992*.

BIBLIOGRAPHY

Poetry:

Armed Descent, Hawk's Well Press, 1961.

Her Body Against Time, Ediciones El Corno Emplumado, 1963.

Enstasy, Matter, 1964.

(With Jerome Rothenberg) *Lunes / Sightings,* Hawk's Well Press, 1964.

Matter / Fact / Sheet / 1, Matter, 1964.

Matter / Fact / Sheet / 2, Matter, 1964.

Round Dances, Trobar Press, 1964.

Tabula, Dialogue Press, 1964.

Lectiones, Duende, 1965.

Song XXIV, Pym-Randall Press, 1966.

Weeks, Ediciones El Corno Emplumado, 1966.

Words in Service, Robert Lamberton, 1966.

Alpha, The Pot Hanger Press, 1967.

Axon Dendron Tree, Salitter, 1967.

Crooked Bridge Love Society, Salitter, 1967.

Devotions, Salitter, 1967.

A Joining: A Sequence for H.D., Black Sparrow Press, 1967.

Twenty Poems, Matter Books, 1967.

Finding the Measure, Black Sparrow Press, 1968.

From the Common Shore, Book V, Minkoff, 1968.

Songs I-XXX, Pym-Randall Press, 1968.

Sonnets, Black Sparrow Press, 1968.

Statement, Black Sparrow Press, 1968.

A California Journal, Big Venus Books, 1969.

The Common Shore, Books I-V: A Long Poem About America, Black Sparrow Press, 1969.

We Are the Arbiters of Beast Desire, MBVL, 1969.

Kali Yuga, Jonathan Cape, 1970.

Flesh Dream Book, Black Sparrow Press, 1971.

The Pastorals, Black Sparrow Press, 1972.

Ralegh, Black Sparrow Press, 1972.

Reading Her Notes, Salisbury Press, 1972.

The Mill of Particulars, Black Sparrow Press, 1973.

The Tears of Edmund Burke, privately printed, 1973.

Whaler Frigate Clippership, Tansy, 1973.

The Belt, University of Connecticut Library, 1974.

The Loom, Black Sparrow Press, 1975.

Sixteen Odes, Black Sparrow Press, 1976.

The Convections, Black Sparrow Press, 1977.

The Lady Of, Black Sparrow Press, 1977.

The Book of Persephone, Treacle Press, 1978.

Kill the Messenger Who Brings Bad News, Black Sparrow Press, 1979.

Sentence, Station Hill Press, 1980.

The Alchemist to Mercury: An Alternate Opus (uncollected poems 1960–1980), edited by Jed Rasula, North Atlantic Books, 1981.

Spiritual Exercises, Black Sparrow Press, 1981.

Mulberry Women, with drypoints by Matt Phillips, Hiersoux, Powers, Thomas, 1982.

Under Words, Black Sparrow Press, 1983.

Thor's Thrush, The Coincidence Press, 1984.

Not This Island Music, Black Sparrow Press, 1987.

The Flowers of Unceasing Coincidence, edited by George Quasha, Station Hill Press, 1988.

Oahu, St. Lazaire Press, 1988.

Ariadne, St. Lazaire Press, 1991.

Manifesto for the Next New York School, Leave Press, 1991.

A Strange Market (poems 1985–1988), Black Sparrow Press, 1992.

Selected Poems 1960–1992, forthcoming.

Fiction:

The Scorpions, Doubleday, 1967.

Cities, Frontier Press, 1972.

A Line of Sight, Black Sparrow Press, 1974.

Wheres, Black Sparrow Press, 1978.

The Cruise of the Pnyx, Station Hill Press, 1979.

A Transparent Tree: Ten Fictions, McPherson & Co., 1985.

Doctor of Silence, McPherson & Co., 1988.

Cat Scratch Fever, McPherson & Co., 1990.

Queen of Terrors, forthcoming.

Plays:

The Well Wherein a Deer's Head Bleeds (New York), 1964, published in *A Play and Two Poems,* Black Sparrow Press, 1968.

Eros and Psyche, with music by Elie Yarden, (New Paltz, New York), 1971, privately printed, 1971.

Editor:

(With Paris Leary, also contributor) *A Controversy of Poets: An Anthology of Contemporary American Poetry,* Doubleday Anchor, 1965.

Paul Blackburn, *The Journals,* Black Sparrow Press, 1975.

Other:

In Time (essays and manifestoes), Frontier Press, 1972.

Sulphur, privately printed, 1972.

(Contributor) *Likely Stories,* edited by Bruce McPherson, Treacle Press, 1981.

A recording of *Finding the Measure* was produced by Black Sparrow Press in 1968.

Walter Laqueur

1921-

Walter Laqueur

"A meeting place for writers and readers—a place where writers can present themselves, on their own terms to their audience," says the preface to this series. This statement frightened me a little; I have met not a few writers in my time. Some were grave disappointments; only in a few cases did I find them particularly interesting or contact with them of help to understand their work. Perhaps I was a little naive and my expectations excessive. Perhaps the part of the writer that is not in the work should not become more widely known. Classic mythology is full of reference to the mysteries of Eleusis, of Isis and Osiris, and to veils not to be lifted by ordinary mortals, and I have sympathy with these practices.

Some political leaders, such as General de Gaulle, knew only too well that there should be a certain sphere not in the public domain; not accessible at all times to all people. In brief, the private sphere of life should be respected. This is very much against the American grain with the "right to know" as a basic ethical principle. Unlike American presidents, De Gaulle did not give daily press conferences but just once a year, and he always appeared with four prepared answers, quite irrespective of the questions that would be asked. My sympathies were, and are, with the general, hence my hesitation. But I foresee other difficulties: most of my work has been nonfiction, some of my books are used as texts. Thus, I have a captive audience and I am not at all certain whether many of my readers really want to know more about me. The personal element in these books is, by necessity, minimal. Ranke, the great German historian, once said that all aspiring historians should obliterate, efface themselves, eliminate the "I" as far as possible, and while this injunction can be pursued to excess, there is something to be said in favor of it.

But I have by no means always lived up to my credo, being the author of two novels and, worse yet, an autobiography spanning the first thirty years of my life. Why did I write it in the first place? Obviously because I felt the urge to do so, because I believed that I had lived through an unusual period of history quite unfamiliar to those younger than myself, even though a great many books have been written on this bygone age. I mean the worlds that no longer exist—Weimar and Nazi Germany, Palestine during the pioneering years prior to the establishment of the State of Israel.

The reception of the autobiography showed more interest on the part of my contemporaries than among the young for whom it had been written. This was perhaps to be expected. There is always the comforting thought (or illusion) that one day perhaps they will rediscover it. The critics were friendly, they usually are in such cases; some

207

complained that there was not enough about myself in the book, and why did I stop at the age of thirty? Simply because I felt inhibited, nor was my postwar experience so unusual. I am a student of autobiographies, and I once read an intriguing statement by Karl Immermann, a German writer well-known in the forties of the last century. He said, "My life does not seem to me of sufficient interest to bring it on the market in all its details. I shall deal only with my encounters with history." This was, more or less, my own intention. Had I been born in a less violent age, had I not lost so many relations and friends, had there been more continuity in my life, my attitude would probably have been different. I am not a particularly modest man, but I felt that in my case, a book with the emphasis on the self, on introspection, on the analysis of changing moods and relationships with fellow human beings, would have been not just irrelevant but in bad taste. In the world I grew up, calm seas and still waters have been rare, hence my negative attitude in this respect. Introspection and self-analysis are fine, but if committed in public are of interest to me only in rare cases. Notwithstanding my family name, I do not hail from the Faubourg St. Germain and my talents are not those of a Marcel Proust. In brief, I apologize to readers for certain inhibitions which I do not wish to shed.

I was born on May 26, 1921, in Breslau, at the time East Germany's biggest city. I left it after graduation from school in 1938. Seven years after my departure, it became a Polish city and is now called Wroclaw. My parents were middle class and, at forty-two and thirty-eight, elderly by the standards of those days. I was their only child. Relations were harmonious but not very close. The open show of affection was tabu in this milieu, except with regard to small children. In later years my parents were almost wholly preoccupied with their own affairs, the financial losses which were the result of the Great Depression and Hitler's rise to power. As a child I was very much living in a world of my own in which fantasies of travels to foreign, exotic parts played a central role. I was an avid newspaper reader from an abnormally early age, but my interest was devoted almost entirely to the sports pages—soccer, track and field, and swimming. I was fascinated by films, first silent, later the talkies, and while I never wanted to be an actor, I dreamed about being a leading producer.

There were quite a few uncles and aunts and also cousins, all older than myself. I had no interest in the history of my own family. This came only much later when my own children were growing up and were asking questions. In recent years I have spent considerable time in research and trips to various countries trying to find out more about my antecedents. They lived in Silesia. I can trace them back in full detail to the early eighteenth century. But I don't know whether they came from the West (Alsace) or from the East, following the ravages of the Swedish-Russian War waged by Charles XII and Peter the Great. The family was Jewish, but there was a great deal of intermarriage during four generations: whole branches converted to Protestantism and the Russian Orthodox Church. Uncle Moritz, renamed Boris, a medical doctor, went to Russia about 1810; he was ennobled for services to the state (he had signed the death certificate of Czar Alexander I) and his three sons married into the Russian aristocracy. One of them wrote the first serious study of America in Russian in 1859 (published in English by Chicago University Press in the 1970s). Recently I met some of his offspring.

Those in Germany frequently studied medicine—one wrote a widely used textbook on ophthalmology, another was the first to produce synthetic testosterone, the male hormone. My mother's maiden name was Berliner, my maternal grandmother was a née Cassirer. They belonged to clans well-known to the student of German-Jewish history.

My parents did not read much, but they were passionate lovers of music; some of my earliest memories are listening to them playing the piano, four hands. I went to a private primary school in my hometown, and later to a "humanist gymnasium," that is to say a Latin school with Greek taught from the age of twelve. I was not taught English at school; it was my sixth language. I began to read and write English only well into my twenties, and my formal education as far as English grammar, orthography, literature, and composition is concerned is nonexistent. I was and have remained a self-made man.

My recollections of school are mixed. I did not get on well with most of my fellow pupils, which may have had to do in part with the fact that I was usually the youngest. Being a little precocious, I had been asked to skip a year; owing to the introduction of obligatory military service under the Nazis, I saved later on yet another year. As a result I graduated at sixteen, which in all probability saved my life because I was confronted with the necessity to make decisions, just in time, which otherwise might have been postponed. Thus I left Germany nine months before the outbreak of the war—when the curtain came down and emigration was no longer possible. In retrospect, I do not tend to take my social difficulties between five and twelve too seriously. I do not recall contemplating suicide—or killing someone else. With puberty my performance in school became more uneven. I was still good in the subjects close to my heart—literature, history, geography, sports—very bad in science. Relations with my contemporaries gradually improved, though I never became the soul of the party.

Among the formative influences of those years I have still not mentioned the "youth movement." These were youth groups (the literal translation makes no sense in English) somewhat similar in character to the Boy Scouts, but far more ambitious in their educational aspirations. It was not mere entertainment but an attempt at life reform, to create a new type of human being. It was a typical romantic, Central European phenomenon;

it came into existence before 1900 and petered out under Hitler. It is a fascinating subject, not so much politically for its ideas were often infantile, highly idealistic, and equally vague. But as a footnote to modern cultural history it was of significance, and eventually I became its historian. Some of the friendships of these years have lasted, and it has been one of the benefits of writing books and occasionally appearing in the media that I get unexpected letters and calls from men and women all over the world who, like myself, had the good fortune to survive.

To grow up as a young Jew in Nazi Germany should have been a horrible experience, but in retrospect it was in my case much less of a trauma than outsiders assume. I did not live in a ghetto but went to a German school (flags with the swastika, Nazi curriculum, and all that) up to 1938 and after that worked for a while in a textile plant. Life was far from comfortable but I can recall only a few incidents of persecution or discrimination. Was I

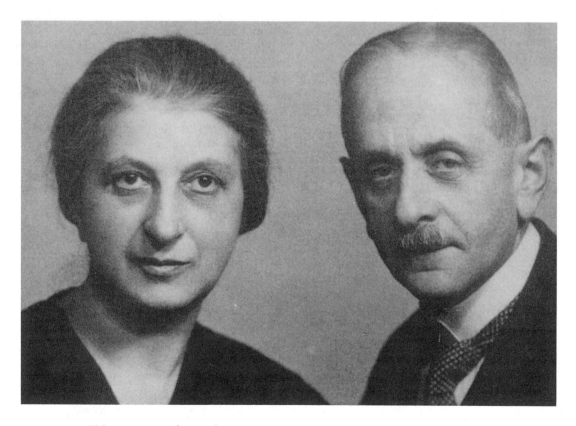

*"My parents, Else and Fritz Laqueur, on my father's sixtieth birthday,
shortly before the outbreak of war"*

Walter on his sixth birthday

obtuse, unaware of what went on around me? Perhaps to a certain extent, but it is also true that I did not have to fend for myself. I had a home and enough to eat. There was even enough money for buying books occasionally and for foreign travel, albeit on the most primitive level. Had I been ten or fifteen years older, I would have no longer been able to work in my profession but lost my livelihood and, generally speaking, have been exposed to the icy winds blowing from all directions. I was, however, not an adult but deeply immersed in the private world of an adolescent, friendships and first love, discovering nature and the world of literature and arts. True, more and more of my friends and acquaintances left, and I knew that sooner rather than later my turn would come. But a sense of great urgency was missing. Nazi policy towards the Jews (and to a certain degree Nazi politics in general) became only gradually more radical. It became unbearable only from the *Kristallnacht* persecutions in November 1938. This, in retrospect, is a tragedy, for if the true face

of the Nazi Reich had emerged earlier, more would have emigrated and escaped their fate.

To be uprooted from one's native country is usually a major shock. But looking back this is not how I reacted. In any case, those of us who went to Palestine never considered ourselves emigrants but *Olim*, which, freely translated, means repatriates. I was no fanatical Zionist, I had absorbed German culture; nor was I a rootless cosmopolitan, my background was far too provincial to aspire to anything so fancy. In fact, up to the age of thirty I had never been to a truly big city (except to Berlin for a few days), or a major museum, or seen a house of parliament, or travelled on an underground railway, or listened to a world-famous orchestra, or driven a car, or eaten in a fancy restaurant.

It is not entirely clear to me why being uprooted from the country was relatively painless, in contrast to leaving behind many people dear to me. Perhaps I instinctively felt that the world I was leaving was bound to disappear anyway and that virtually everyone in that city would vanish within a few years, that even the buildings would no longer be standing, that the streets would have different names, that people living there would speak a different language. But it could also be that I attribute to myself prescience which I did not have at the time. I did not lose interest in Germany. I have written about its history, politics, and culture. But it did not become my main field of specialization. I was preoccupied even more with other countries and cultures.

Growing up in the Third Reich was in some ways an invaluable experience for the future student of politics. Even though politics then did not figure high on my scale of priorities, it was impossible to live through that period of history without becoming politicized, to develop a sense of danger. I watched street battles on the way to school and the long lines of unemployed, hungry people with no hope. In later years there were the giant parades, the Hitler speeches, the frenetic ovations—and the resistance on the part of a few, isolated brave people. It was fascinating to watch the reaction of people, a mixture of rejoicing at the Nazi successes at home and abroad, and the fear that things may turn out badly. Among my fellow students I sensed genuine support for the regime and real enthusiasm, but also dissimulation and a certain amount of subacute fear.

I think I developed in later years, as a result of this experience, a better sensorium for what life in a modern dictatorship is like, for truth and falsehood, for the appeal of nationalism—than many of my contemporaries who had the good fortune to grow up in the United States or Western Europe. Not because of superior intelligence or more learning, but simply because of the years in Nazi Germany. For those who never lived in any other society, it is difficult to appreciate the vital importance of free institutions. Gibbon wrote somewhere that the captain of the Hampshire grenadiers was of help to the historian of the Roman empire, and this was true, *mutatis mutandis,* with regard to my own experience.

Our house in the center of town where we lived from 1930 to 1938 was adjacent to the excellent municipal library, and this became my first "university," to use Gorky's term. I read voraciously in many fields, sometimes four or five books a day. I had no one to guide my steps and read many unnecessary books. At the same time my athletic activities continued. I participated in competitions outside my hometown, and the report on the occasion of my graduation said that I was well qualified to become a sports teacher; such a career, given the circumstances, was, of course, ruled out.

I graduated from school in February 1938, and it was obvious that I should leave the country as soon as feasible. My parents' economic situation had rapidly deteriorated and there was no way to train for any profession inside Germany, let alone to attend university. But emigration had become exceedingly difficult; according to prevailing currency regulations, those leaving Germany could take with them only two or three dollars and no country was willing to accept destitute arrivals. A few exotic places were willing to receive highly skilled experts—the Dominican Republic or Manchukuo (a short-lived Japanese puppet state). America took a few thousand relations of American citizens, Britain a few thousand children. But I had no relations in America willing to vouch for me, and I was too old for the children's transports. This left a very few escape routes—travel to Shanghai which under Japanese rule was legally a no-man's-land. Illegal emigration to Palestine was then in its infancy; legal migration had been cut to a trickle by the British mandatory authorities fearful of an Arab uprising.

Nineteen thirty-eight was for me a year of waiting, of expectations and failed hopes. I wrote many letters and got but a few replies. I worked for a little while in a textile plant but was eventually thrown out because the Nazi union learned about my non-Aryan origins. Then I went

to train as a carpentry apprentice in the city of Frankfurt with a group of youngsters preparing for kibbutz life in Palestine, even though no one knew whether we would ever be able to reach that country.

Two days sufficed to persuade me that I had not the slightest aptitude for carpentry. On the third day the shop was closed because of the outbreak of an epidemic. I used the free time to read more books, to swim in various rivers and climb several mountains, alone or with friends. Above all, I cycled through the Rhine valley, visited Heidelberg, and enjoyed the mild and pretty landscape of southern West Germany, very different from the harsh and stark scenery of my native East Germany.

There was a great deal of excitement in the air. Nazi Germany's expansion gathered speed; in April of 1938 Austria was incorporated, in October it was the turn of Czechoslovakia. At the time of the Czech crisis I was in hospital for a tonsillectomy, normally a minor operation. But there were some complications, I lost too much blood and had

At age fifteen, the athletic period

to stay a week longer. During that week it seemed that war would break out and that the trap in which I was would be sprung. It was a nightmare that followed me for many years. But the danger passed, at least for a little while, and by an extraordinary stroke of good luck I got a permit to emigrate to Palestine as a student. There was then a small number of places (the student body at the Hebrew University counted five hundred) and one needed furthermore a few hundred pounds sterling, a giant sum which my parents did not have. But an uncle decided to help me—from inside a state penitentiary. He was a bachelor doctor who had been given a five-year sentence for, according to the Nuremberg laws, "defiling the German race," that is to say, sleeping with a German woman. But since he was a highly decorated World War I officer, he was given the privilege to dispose of his property, with me as one of the beneficiaries.

And so on November 7, 1938, accompanied by my parents and a few friends, I went to the Breslau central railway station to take the train to Trieste, from where a ship called the *Gerusalemme* would take me to Palestine. I was not to see my parents and those who had accompanied me again. They were killed like so many others in the death camps in Poland. Twenty-five years later I arrived again at the station.

A portrait of myself at seventeen would have probably run on the following lines: ambitious, shows qualities of leadership but in many respects quite immature. Tends to act in a foolhardy way, probably to prove something to himself and others, and at the same time suffers from hypochondria. Good when facing challenges and doing a job he likes, but lazy in most other respects, unreliable, lacking self-discipline. Widely read but confused. Shows no interest in choosing a career, lacks other middle-class virtues, could become a drifter. It is uncertain whether without guidance he will be able to stand on his own feet.

This then was the end of the German chapter of my life. There followed fifteen years in Palestine. When I left it, it was a different country not only in name. It was a very small country but colorful, incredibly complicated and difficult to understand. I have not read a satisfactory description of life in Palestine during the 1930s and 1940s, certainly not in English. There was not one Palestine but many Palestinian societies, including the Palestine of the British officials running the country. The Arabs and the Jews met in the streets and sometimes at their working places. Further-

more, there were many subdivisions mainly on ethnic and religious lines. The Orthodox Jews lived in their own quarters and had little contact with the Sephardim, those of Spanish-Oriental origin, and even less with the new, mainly Zionist, non-Orthodox community which had arrived since the turn of the century. Everything was different from the European world I had known, the bright lights, the street noises and smells, the language, the attire of the people. In retrospect I am surprised how quickly I got accustomed to the new land, at least on a working, superficial level.

I should have enrolled as a student at the Hebrew University on Mount Scopus, which was the only university then in existence. I had originally wanted to study medicine, but there was no medical school at the time, and the kind of history taught (with a heavy emphasis on the Middle Ages) did not appeal to me. Above all, it seemed virtually certain that a world war would break out soon, in which case the whole endeavor seemed pointless. At any rate, I lacked motivation and was not yet ready for the order and self-discipline of higher education.

For the next eight years I worked in a dozen different jobs as agricultural laborer, tractor driver, on building sites and in factories, as a truck driver's mate, as an auxiliary policeman, as a longshoreman in Haifa harbor, in a stone quarry, and eventually as a bookseller. I cannot honestly say that I enjoyed the work, even though physically I could cope with it without great difficulty. I did like the cowboy life in the fields of the kibbutz to which I belonged. For two summers I spent most of my time among Bedouins, was a guest in their black tents, and had to cope with the occasional rogue shepherd who drove his cows into our fields. There were the horse races, the quarrels and the camaraderie of the guards in the fields, Jews and Arabs. We had, of course, guns, but ammunition was expensive and there was little target practice. I tend to become sentimental when I think of the nights around the campfire, when I was taught songs from many lands. I had grown up in a city and even though it was not my first contact with nature (my mother had been a country girl and had taught me a great deal), I learned to watch plants and animals and to deal with them. The bourgeois world in which I had grown up no longer existed. My daily contact was with peasants and workers (and nomads and thieves) who had never read a Latin text and yet could be my teachers as far as the school of life was concerned. There was very little to eat—no meat, no fish, a lot

At eighteen (left) as a watchman at Kibbutz Sha'ar Hagolan in the Jordan Valley

of oranges and grapefruit but no sugar, little fat. It was no doubt a very healthy diet, but I was always a little hungry. My trousers had been repaired countless times, the shoes were in an advanced state of decomposition. Yet, physically, I felt better than any time before or after; it was the kind of life a young man of nineteen could dream about. And all the while Europe was going up in flames.

I should write, even if briefly, about the kibbutz—life in a collective, agricultural settlement, a new social experiment, unprecedented in the history of mankind, utopia in the sunshine, one great family, a community of like-minded young people. This, at any rate, was the theory. Reality, inevitably, was not quite up to our dreams.

In this community I met Naomi. We were not twenty yet. We lived together for a year and then got married in Haifa during an air raid. There were no rings, no guests, just a document we had to produce on a few occasions in later life. Workers from a nearby building site were enlisted to act as witnesses. The first two years of our married life we lived in a tent—a much more flimsy, less

luxurious affair than tents in these days. Whenever a high wind came, or a strong rain, the tent collapsed and the beds sank in the mud. But we were young and not very spoiled: the deprivation of daily life did not weigh heavily. If gradually I became restless, it was mainly because I did not want to be an agricultural worker or a longshoreman or work in a factory all my life. I should perhaps add here that this was just before mechanization took place in agriculture and containers became the fashion in transporting goods. Work in the fields has changed during the last fifty years more than in the preceding five thousand.

My inclination and interests were in other directions. I was acutely aware that I still had a great deal to learn. The kibbutz had an excellent library, and while the other members studied agrochemistry and animal husbandry, I immersed myself in history, sociology, and literature. I knew German and French; in Palestine I taught myself Hebrew and some Arabic as well as rudimentary English. When I broke my leg while shaving (probably a unique case in the annals of medicine)

"My wife-to-be, Naomi, at the children's village, Ben Shemen, two years before we were married," 1937

and was immobilized for a while, I studied Russian. Mrs. Pickmann, a lady from Nikolayev in southern Russia, was the mother of a fellow member, had been a teacher in her younger years, loved the Russian language and literature, and was glad to have an eager student. I read and talked Russian for ten hours a day, and when the leg had mended, the fundament existed for what was to become a lifetime interest.

If I think back on these eight years between leaving school and entering a profession of sorts, the years of manual labor, of moving and living in a milieu for which I had been utterly unprepared, my immediate reaction is that expressed in one of Edith Piaf's most famous songs: *"Je ne regrette rien . . ."* This despite inevitable disappointments and frustrations, despite the fact that my formal education was forever to remain unfinished. When many years later I entered the academic world bereft of any degree, I was usually the only one to be in such a predicament. Even later, when asked

for my professional qualifications, my academic nakedness pursued me. Whatever I would say in explanation would be wrong. To stress that I was not Dr. Laqueur, that I did not even have a B.A., would be considered a case of inverse snobbery. But if I mentioned that I had a few honorary degrees, but not a genuine, hard-earned one, this would be even worse.

If these years were wasted from the point of view of formal education, they were immensely rich and helpful as an initiation into the school of life. Perhaps Mao was right when, during the cultural revolution, he insisted on sending students to work in the fields of China for a few years. (It was probably wrong in the case of young physicists and mathematicians.) It has been one of the traditional weaknesses of intellectuals, especially young intellectuals, to develop abstract ideas concerning living people while in a kind of vacuum. I would marvel in later years when I listened to some of them talking with utter assurance about "the working class" or "violence," about suffering or reforming society, without having the faintest idea of what they were talking about. They would publish learned treatises about "decision making," but the most important decision in their own lives had been what lecture course or seminar to attend. I do not claim that it is impossible to acquire a sense of real life even on campus, but a great deal of empathy is needed which few have, and common sense is by no means as common as commonly believed.

These years outside "bourgeois" society and far from the groves of academe were a good antidote against various kinds of utopianism and theorizing, divorced from reality. If growing up in Germany had helped me to understand what it is to live under a harsh dictatorship, the years in Palestine sharpened my critical sense without having read the authors of the Frankfurt school. They inoculated me against some of the grosser forms of idiocy widespread in intellectual circles in the postwar years. They helped me to understand, to give but a few examples, the Soviet Union and Communism, the roots of political violence, conflicts between nations, and I was also largely immunized against various intellectual fads and fashions.

We left the kibbutz in 1944. I was vaguely aware that I wanted to be an author; I had written some articles on political and historical subjects, some had been published, more were rejected. But these were no more than limbering-up exercises. I had come across an advertisement for work in a bookshop at a ridiculously low salary; for years Naomi, an expert baby nurse, would earn more than I did. But I chose a bookshop because I loved books and I somehow imagined that I would, by osmosis, be able to absorb their contents (which happened to be correct up to a point—there are slack hours in this as in other trades). I also could spend a few hours each morning at the library of the Hebrew University on Mount Scopus, which excelled in the very fields that interested me most. The librarians took a paternal interest in the young self-made man, even though I made them work hard—reading back volumes of Russian periodicals which no one had touched for years.

Work in a bookshop had its advantages. One met all kinds of interesting people, and I had to know, at least on a very superficial level, what were the basic books in a great many fields, what to recommend to customers who knew even less than I did.

We lived at the time in a single room in an Arab village, unable to afford Jerusalem rents. The panorama was breathtaking when we opened the window in the morning. There were the Judaean hills to our feet and, when the weather was good, the Dead Sea appeared in the distance and beyond it the mountains of Transjordan, as it was then called. The room was small, there was no electricity, no telephone, and water had to be drawn from a well as in Biblical times.

We had no children and such primitive life was bearable; while the war lasted, there was no feeling of acute deprivation. Many people were worse off, and we had been lucky to survive in the first place. But as the war ended, the old impatience resurfaced. I did not see enough of Naomi; she worked long hours and frequently had to stay away from home nights. Above all, there was again the feeling that I had reached a dead end. True, I had taught myself a few things; I had even taken a correspondence course in journalism, which did not teach me much I had not known before.

So I began to write again without notable success, until quite suddenly, early in 1946, I got a letter from the editor of a Hebrew daily newspaper named *Hamishmar* offering me the position of Jerusalem correspondent. This was the greatest breakthrough I had had in my life, and to this day I do not know to whom I owed it. A great deal of self-confidence was needed to accept it—Hebrew is a very difficult language, and my written Hebrew was neither faultless nor elegant. Nor did I have some other essential qualities needed by a

successful newspaperman; I was no extrovert, found it difficult to make friends easily, got frequently bored, which is to say it was difficult to sit through the daily press conferences. But re-reading now some of the stories I wrote at the time, it is also true that I had a sense for news, had creative ideas, and even developed a certain style. My main weakness was that I focussed more on speculation about the future than on events that had already taken place, which is, after all, the true calling of a newspaperman.

The newspaper was small but prestigious. Some leading young writers who later made a name for themselves were attached to my office. Among my assistants, aged eighteen or nineteen at the time, were Shabtai Tevet, Amos Eilon, Naqdimon Rogel; my Tel Aviv editor became Minister of Labor, our accountant in the Jerusalem office— Minister of Health. Jerusalem was the place where the action was at the time—the seat of the mandatory government, the seat of the supreme Jewish and Arab political institutions. The major political trials took place in Jerusalem and the government Public Information Office would transport us on a few minutes' notice to Haifa, where another illegal immigrants ship had arrived, or to other places where some terrorist outrages had taken place.

Together with UNSCOP, the UN Committee which later recommended the division of Palestine into two separate, independent states, I toured every corner of the country and listened to political leaders and other experts representing the various sides to the conflict. There had been many enquiry committees before, but there was a feeling that this could be the last. There was no dull day. In addition to politics I had to report on municipal affairs, archaeology (these were the days when the first Dead Sea scrolls were found), obituaries, visiting celebrities, religious affairs (Jewish, Christian, and Muslim), social trends (including strikes and lockouts), crime, funerals, and weddings. Since I began to contribute to other newspapers and magazines, first as stringer, later as correspondent, I would produce a few thousand words every day under constant pressure, which was good preparation for later life. I never had much patience with students who claimed they needed weeks to prepare a measly term paper of a few pages.

Life as a correspondent, later as war correspondent, was not without danger. There were major explosions and later on sniping and shelling; on most nights a total curfew was in force and I still remember the eerie feeling of walking home in the darkness from my office loudly whistling or singing—to be challenged every few hundred yards by soldiers, sometimes trigger happy. My office (in the *Palestine Post* building) was destroyed in a bombing one evening in February 1948—I had left an hour earlier. Three or four of my colleagues were killed, more were wounded during those months. But there was an exhilarating tension in the air which made one forget fear, or later on hunger and thirst during the siege of Jerusalem which lasted some seven months. There must be some psychological, probably even physiological explanation. Once the shooting was over, I fell victim to a psychosomatic disorder which for a long time partly disabled me.

We had moved from our Arab village to the German colony, a mixed Jerusalem suburb in 1946. On September 1, 1947, we took possession of the first apartment we could call our own (it was rented, to be sure). It was in a new building which had been built by an Arab police sergeant. On November 1, Sylvia, our first child, was born, but later in December we had to leave the apartment because fighting had broken out and reached our small street. Thus, our happiness was very short. Like thousands of others we became refugees in a besieged city. Eventually, we found a room (later an apartment) in a building called Kadimah House, which the British government had built for its officials. When work on it was finished, Britain had decided to relinquish the mandate. This apartment was to remain ours. Our younger daughter was born there in 1950, and some thirty-five years later Tamar, our youngest granddaughter. I mention all this because it was the first case of continuity in a life otherwise characterized by constant change and enforced moving.

Elsewhere I have described my work as a newspaperman in the exciting postwar period. I should have mentioned, at least in passing, assignments to Cyprus, Lebanon, and Egypt—under King Farouk at the time. Journalism was a good school. I mingled with all sorts of people, leading politicians of various nations (including some whose names have entered the history books), terrorists, religious believers of a dozen confessions, secret policemen, union organizers, Communists and neo-Fascists, madmen and a few geniuses. On a given morning I got stuck in a terrorist hold-up at a bank; in the afternoon, being an official of the journalist union, I introduced the vice president of the U.S. at a press conference; in the evening there was a concert given by a blind pianist from Egypt. I was twenty-six at the time but

the pace did not seem extraordinary to me, for everyone was very young. I do not remember ever being tired. On the contrary, I had difficulty falling asleep at night.

Then the riots broke out in December 1947, and, a few weeks later, real war. My greatest frustration was to be stuck in besieged Jerusalem throughout 1948. As we were totally cut off, I could not get my eye witness accounts through to the editorial office in Tel Aviv. My paper had installed a powerful transmitter (war surplus) on the roof of our building, but there were high mountains between Jerusalem and Tel Aviv, and voice contact was never established. I still went on writing every day on what I had seen and heard and passed the dispatches on to all kinds of people I vaguely knew who claimed to be in touch with someone who would pass the lines at night on foot or horse or in a jeep, who owned carrier pigeons, or were privy to some even more outlandish scheme. I was convinced that none of these schemes worked. Only forty years later, working on my autobiography, did I discover that most accounts had in fact gotten through the lines and had been published, albeit with a delay of a week or two. Read with the benefit of hindsight, they are of certain documentary value, as long as I wrote on what I actually had seen. As for major military operations, the fog of war was such that I often got it wrong, including skirmishes which I had actually covered.

Then the fighting stopped with the second armistice in July 1948, though sporadic sniping went on for a long time even after. There was an anti-climatic feeling. Jerusalem was now a divided city and a backwater. The action had moved to Tel Aviv. Thousands of residents left Jerusalem; it seemed a doomed city. I had progressed to writing editorials and daily columns for various newspapers, and regularly contributed to newspapers and magazines in various lands.

But I did not feel well in my skin. There was the old unrest, the feeling of getting nowhere. The magic of immediate gratification provided by journalism no longer worked. So I went on writing every day on a great variety of topics, transferring my attention from municipal affairs to world politics and cultural developments, following from afar the great political confrontations, new cultural fashions in Paris and London, in Central and Eastern Europe. America increasingly figured on the political map. Culturally it seemed of less interest than Left Bank Paris from which at the time most impulses seemed to emanate. But how to comment from afar about countries, cultures, and people I had never known? By the early 1950s I had published, under a pen name, a number of essays on world affairs in several small but prestigious journals, above all the British *Twentieth Century* but also the *Partisan Review*, the first issue of *Encounter, Commentary, World Today*, and *Foreign Affairs*. My name was not exactly a household word, but invitations arrived to write and to attend conferences. I had become acquainted with George Lichtheim who made his home in London at the time; despite periodic quarrels we remained friends up to his suicide twenty-five years later. He provided useful introductions. George was an enormously gifted free-floating intellectual, a man of great erudition, a fiercely individualistic thinker, a master of English prose, best remembered now as a historian of socialism but with interests in many other fields. Through him I came to know Richard Lowenthal and Franz Borkenau, some of the leading spirits of the age, and also Gershom Scholem, who lived a few blocks from me in Rehavia. These and Raymond Aron, from a greater distance, were my gurus at the time.

Conversations with them made me aware of the lacunae in my own education. It was too late to be a student again, but there were other ways, slightly less risky, to improve oneself. I did take the plunge even though I was then in my thirties, father of two children. It meant above all travelling, widening my horizon, a *grand tour* of Europe, such as young men and women had undertaken in the eighteenth and nineteenth century. Naomi and I visited France, Britain, and Germany several times in the early 1950s, and in 1955 we went to London with our children, initially for six months. Such travel was much more complicated at the time than now, be it only because a visa was needed for each entry to a foreign country. I had persuaded Michael Josselson, Secretary General of the Congress of Cultural Freedom in Paris, that he needed a periodical dealing with Soviet cultural affairs; politics in the Communist bloc were widely covered, but not much attention was paid to other trends in the Soviet bloc. With considerable reluctance Mike agreed to have an internal newssheet of sixteen pages for a limited period of time. This became in later years *Survey*, a journal of ideas which I edited with the help of George Lichtheim, Jane Degras, and Leopold Labedz, to whom I handed it over in 1964. Despite its relatively small circulation, *Survey* was one of the leading intellectual-political magazines of the day (1955–1990);

Arriving in Moscow, about 1957

while still focussing on Soviet and Communist affairs, it eventually came to cover a great many other topics as well.

A history of the Congress of Cultural Freedom has been written. It is now remembered among other things because of the fact that it was subsidized up to the 1960s in part by the CIA. Its main aim was to give a platform to liberal anti-Communism through journals, conferences, and research projects. In countries such as Britain or France such activities would have been subsidized through the British Council, or the Alliance Française, but America was a newcomer to the field of public (and cultural) policy, and the only instrument available was the CIA (which also paid for the Munich-based radio stations). This was, of course, a grave mistake, and when the facts were revealed it caused much harm.

In retrospect this was not, however, the decisive issue. The crucial question was whether the Congress was needed or unnecessary, whether its basic ideas were right or wrong. Today, following the collapse of Communism, the answer seems clear: it was right at a time when so many well-meaning Western intellectuals from Sartre to Moravia were hopelessly wrong trying to justify in their political pronouncements the Stalinist dictatorship. No one ever dictated to me as editor of

Survey what to publish and what to delete; whatever my other weaknesses, I would not have stood such interference for a single day. Had I known about the sources of support of Congress, I would not have been deterred. The decisive issue for me was freedom of action. The fact that, like most of my colleagues, I was not told about the financial arrangements caused annoyance for having been duped. As it happened, I had left Congress well before the revelations were made, and thus the question of resignation never did arise. Do I feel remorse in retrospect? On the contrary, I feel some pride for having been associated with a noble (if mismanaged) endeavor, at a time when being critical of Communist dictatorship was anything but popular. Anti-Fascism had been politically correct, anti-Communism was not. We made, I think, a modest contribution to the defeat of Communism on the intellectual level. Leo Labedz became something like a national hero in his native Poland; I was widely published in Russia under Gorbachev and Yeltsin. Today Communism does not seem much of an intellectual challenge, but in the 1950s its influence in Europe was considerable.

Europe in the 1950s was not remotely as affluent as later on, following the economic miracle. But intellectually it was a far more stimulating continent, especially for a young man from the provinces for whom about everything he saw was new. We had a small apartment in North London; my salary was not princely and there was, of course, no tenure. We visited Scandinavia, eastern and southern. We were almost constantly on the move: once a month I had to be in Paris; twice a year, or more often, in Germany.

Naomi's parents had left Germany for Russia in 1937. Her father was a professor of medicine who had settled in the Northern Caucasus. Beginning in the fifties we went on annual pilgrimages to visit them. In the beginning only Moscow was open to foreigners, the second year we met at Sotchi, the Black Sea resort, then, at last, we were permitted to see their home in Pyatigorsk, the center of the North Caucasian spas, which we came to know as well as any foreigners did at the time. In fact, we were among the first, if not the very first, to visit some of the places in which now fighting rages, from Sukhumi to the Chechen-Ingush autonomous region. I came to like the Caucasus very much. We used to call it Switzerland minus the tourists (and the amenities). For me, these were not holidays, strictly speaking, for I also visited other parts of the Soviet Union and Eastern Europe on the same occasions. This resulted in a series of travelogues,

mainly for the *Neue Zürcher Zeitung,* the leading Swiss German-language newspaper. Some of these articles also appeared in languages other than English and German; a selection later came out in hardcover.

Restrictions on foreign travel in the Soviet Union and meeting with the locals remained stringent prior to *glasnost.* Owing to our family contacts we knew about as much on the Soviet Union and the Soviet way of life as any foreigner could know. This refers not to high level politics, but the way ordinary people were living, their hopes and fears. My Caucasian journeys made me realize early on that tensions between nationalities in the Soviet Union had not disappeared as the party leadership claimed and as many foreigners, not only the well wishers among them, believed. It also became clear to me that the discrepancy between the claims of the regime and its performance was even greater than I had previously thought; this in the 1960s when the crisis was by no means as acute as in later years.

I concluded my autobiography, for a number of reasons, with the grand tour of Europe in the early 1950s. As far as Weimar and Nazi Germany were concerned, as well as Palestine in the pioneering days and the kibbutz and the War of Independence (1947–48), I was writing about worlds which no longer existed, whereas my work, meetings, and peregrinations in later years were less extraordinary. Others have written on Western Europe and Russia in the postwar period with equal or greater competence. Secondly, I felt I did not have the necessary distance to my European (and American) years. I sometimes felt that I would not be able to tell the whole truth and I was not interested in an account which was less than full and outspoken. In a shorter report such as the present one, self-conscious over-the-shoulder-looking is less of an hindrance.

In the postwar period I tended to change every seven or ten years either my profession or my residence, or both. As I turned forty, I had been editor and journalist for a dozen years. The experience was definitely worthwhile, just as I am glad for the years as agricultural and factory worker. I understood early on that my future would not be in Middle Eastern studies. This demanded a much better knowledge of Arabic than I had, and preferably also of Turkish and Persian, and travelling widely in the region. But the effort seemed hardly worthwhile. I had no particular interest in Arab, Turkish, or Persian history, and the reading of the daily press was not intellectually stimulating. I did write in later years a *History of Zionism,* and a book on the War of 1967, which was hailed as the best at the time it was written. Needless to say, it was still "instant history" and thus overtaken as more sources became available.

During the 1950s I read an enormous amount of contemporary literature in Russian newspapers, periodicals, and books, until in the early 1960s I realized that I had to force myself to do so. It was repetitive and boring; with some notable exceptions, the Soviet Union was a cultural desert. Had I been an area specialist, with my interest focussed on, say, agriculture, it would have been different, but as it was my enthusiasm rapidly waned. Then, one day on an excursion with my "Russian" brother-in-law in the Caucasian mountains, I suddenly realized that nothing much was likely to happen in the Soviet Union for years to come. It was a short time after Khrushchev had been overthrown and the period has now become known in Russia as the age of *zastoi* ("stagnation"). My intuition proved to be right. I began to read general and cultural history, and this led to the study of the German youth movement (which I have mentioned earlier on) as well as a book on German-Russian relations, mainly before 1920, with the emphasis on cultural attitudes rather than diplomacy. This in turn led to a preoccupation with a fascinating phenomenon called the "Black Hundred," a precursor of modern fascism and the origins of the *Protocols of the Elders of Zion,* one of the key documents in the history of modern anti-Semitism. This study appeared in Russian with a delay of twenty-five years, and it again intrigued me in the early nineties when a new "Black Hundred" surfaced in Russia.

I wanted to leave current affairs and the opportunity arose when I was offered the directorship of the Wiener Library in London. I had known this institute as a user, had liked the atmosphere, but had never aspired to become closer involved.

But in 1964 the offer coincided with the inclinations which I have just described. The Wiener Library had been founded in Amsterdam in 1933 and transferred to London just before the outbreak of the war in Europe. It had become one of the leading study centers on Nazism, Fascism, the Second World War, totalitarianism, anti-Semitism. During the war it had been part of the British and Allied war effort but in 1945 it was "denationalized." It had no endowment and while it had the fervent support of many well-known people, most of these were academics and in no position to help. British charitable foundations were more likely to give to hospitals for sick animals or for the restoration of derelict parish churches as I was soon to find out. In brief, the institution existed on a shoestring, was partly dependent on a wealthy benefactor (who died in 1962), partly on the work of volunteers, partly on contributions from Germany. Thus the continuing existence of the place was an annually recurrent miracle.

This, very briefly, was the situation when I came in. I had ambitious plans—to turn it into a European center of contemporary history. But within a year I realized that this was quite unrealistic. I would be lucky if I managed to help the place to survive for a few more years. A few new books were published under our sponsorship, and a journal came into being (*The Journal of Contemporary History*) which I co-edited with George Mosse, a distinguished professor of history at the University of Wisconsin, Madison. It exists to this day and is one of the leaders in its field.

Once I realized that my plans were not feasible, I had to take stock. As a fund-raiser I was no good at all, yet at the same time I felt it would be dishonorable to abandon a sinking ship. Anglo Jewry is not known for its eagerness to give for cultural purposes—unlike German Jewry had been

In London, 1960

or American or Russian Jews (before 1917). When I went to their leaders they told me that since we were specializing in fascism and racialism this was not really any concern of theirs, when I went to government officials or committees I was advised to try my luck with the rich Jews. . . . It was an unedifying situation, and as a result I was looking more and more for an arrangement outside Britain. When this became known a storm of indignation broke in the pages of the London *Times* and other newspapers—how did I dare to deprive England of one of its national treasures? There was a wave of angry protest, but still no willingness to contribute to our finances. A widely publicized appeal by many leading British intellectuals resulted in donations totalling some twenty-five pounds sterling.

The history of the Wiener Library remains to be written (it is now written, in fact); all that need be said in the present context is that I succeeded in enlisting some support, enough to continue to function on a very low level. All the while I hoped that there would be a miracle, and in the end such a miracle did occur: in the early 1980s two wealthy and well-meaning businessmen walked in and offered their assistance. Together with their friends they launched an appeal which resulted by

1990 in amassing a sum guaranteeing the continued existence of the institution, even if on a very modest scale. In 1992 I retired as a director; the existence of the institute was secure for the foreseeable future—for the first time in its existence.

The fund-raising frustrations made me an absentee landlord. I continued to figure as director but was spending most of the year outside England. The library could not really afford to pay a director and I had to look for income elsewhere. I also knew that since I was no professional librarian by training, it would be a waste of my time to sit around in London where I was not really needed, since the management of the library was in capable hands.

I had come to America first in the 1950s. I had been invited by the Rand Corporation in Santa Monica, later by Johns Hopkins; I was visiting professor in Chicago and a visiting member of the Harvard Russian Research Center. Later I returned to Harvard as visiting professor. These annual visits continued until the late 1960s when Brandeis offered me a chair in the history of ideas, succeeding Herbert Marcuse, who, upon reaching retirement age, had moved on to California.

I very much wanted to be in America, but I did not want to teach full-time or become involved in university politics. The 1960s were a distracting period on campus, and my interest was in world affairs, not in university politics. And I still had the moral commitment to be in London part of the year. But Brandeis, to my surprise, accepted my conditions, and thus I became a tenured, part-time professor. To gain admission to the United States was not easy in the McCarthy and post-McCarthy era. I had been, after all, a member of a kibbutz, and a kibbutz was a "Communist organization" in the book of the Department of Justice. It took the intervention of the then junior senator from Massachusetts, John F. Kennedy, and a few others to overcome this hurdle, but the stigma continued to haunt me even when I acquired U.S. citizenship. Since I had never been a member of the Communist party, I could not leave it and acquire "defector's status."

Sylvia and Shlomit, our daughters, were in university at the time. Sylvia studied medicine; Shlomit, geography. Our frequent travel had tried them sorely when they were children; I felt uneasy (and their mother even more so) but I think that now, having children of their own, they have forgiven us. Sylvia chose England as her residence,

"Our daughters, Sylvia and Shlomit, with their Caucasian uncle Friedrich," 1963

Shlomit went back to Israel where she had been born but which she hardly remembered.

During the 1960s we went regularly to Israel, mainly to see old friends. On one such trip, lining up for the toilet in an El Al plane, I began to talk to the man next to me whose face seemed vaguely familiar. We had met years before in Jerusalem. He was a historian, specializing in ancient Greece and Rome, and he asked me whether I would be interested in a professorship at Tel Aviv University. Of course, I replied, provided I could come and go more or less when I wanted in view of other commitments. He waived this aside as a matter of no consequence. I thought he was joking, but a couple of months later I received a letter appointing me professor of history at Tel Aviv. The miracle man who had initiated it was Zvi Yavetz, well-known in his field, but also an organizer of genius, who had more or less single-handedly set up Tel Aviv University some ten years earlier (and also helped to establish Addis Ababa University). He and his wife Dvora became good friends.

I had always wanted to have a room or a small apartment near the sea, to spend a few hours every day swimming, walking on the beach, and beach-combing. And now at long last this dream was realized—we had a place about a hundred yards from the sea where I would be a part of the day, playing, thinking, reading, talking, idling. My teaching duties, a lecture course and a seminar, were not onerous, and I would come for only three months a year to Herzlia. Sunshine and warmth were more or less guaranteed. It was a very primitive but happy life. I would dress formally (that is to say shirt and long trousers) only for my lectures and the occasional dinner with friends.

I was not an outstanding teacher, better in a small group, and I preferred mature to very young students, simply because the former were usually more highly motivated and had experience in various fields. But I became friendly with some of the younger students too, and by and large did my duty by the university. This arrangement went on for about ten years. It was in many respects eminently satisfactory, but in the long run the complications asserted themselves. We had apartments on three continents and to keep them in reasonable order was a nightmare. In the place near the sea the rust was all-pervasive whereas the house in London was broken into more than once in our absence—the trips were time-consuming and expensive, the all too frequent changes of locality affected my research and writing. Above all, my employers became restive: whenever I was needed I could not be found. They wanted to have more of my time. And so, with great regret, I was forced to give up Tel Aviv, and would spend less and less time in England.

My connection with the Center of Strategic and International Studies in Washington dates from the later 1960s. The Center had been founded a few years earlier and it was at the time part of Georgetown University. My interest in the field of defense in the narrow, military sense was limited; my expertise was in international affairs and I regularly commented on world politics even after I had ceased to be a full-time journalist. For those dealing with world politics, Washington was the obvious place, neither London, nor Greater Boston, and thus Naomi and I moved to the capital. I became a member of the CSIS International Research Council, then its chairman after the death of Phil Mosely, of Columbia University. Under David Abshire in the 1980s, CSIS became one of the largest and most influential think tanks in America; I initiated some of its publications, such as the *Washington Papers* and the *Washington Quarterly.*

Washington was an excellent observation point as far as decision-making was concerned. There were frequent meetings with policy makers from many countries, press conferences, appearances in front of congressional committees, membership in committees of various kinds. In fact, there was a surfeit of politics (sometimes interpreted very narrowly)—the topic dominated not only one's working hours but also conversation during breakfast, lunch, and dinner. There was the danger of becoming blasé as one watched successive administrations repeat the same old mistakes in their learning process.

I continued to teach at Georgetown and commuted between Washington and London, and this helped to break the political monotony. A price had to be paid for this peripatetic lifestyle: we did not see family and friends as often as we liked, and there were other drawbacks. I want to mention just one: up to the age of fifty I had never employed a research assistant. In Washington I had two scores of interns over the years. Almost all were intelligent and industrious and without their help I would not have achieved remotely as much as I did. They helped to get me the source material I needed from libraries and archives, and this was an enormous saving of time and effort. But much of my satisfaction had been the result of personal exposure to archives and libraries: one never knew what unexpected material one would discover in the course of a search. I missed these expeditions into unknown territory.

In recent years I have had to face yet another problem in this context: since interns are not paid and since academics cannot afford to pay much to their research assistants, it is customary to give their contribution due recognition in the preface of books. I have been doing this conscientiously and sometimes perhaps their role has been slightly exaggerated. What was the result? One critic has compared me with a superior staff officer, overseeing an army of research assistants "who see with their own eyes not his," another has suggested that my books were, in fact, written by them. This had to be retracted with fulsome apologies. It greatly amused me but also annoyed me a little. I suppose it is one of the risks one runs if one writes more than a book or two in one's lifetime.

I cannot complain about my experience with reviewers. They have treated me fairly by and large, sometimes perhaps with excessive praise. As far as my first books were concerned, I paid great attention to reviews, was easily elated or offended.

In New York, 1980

I suppose most authors react in a similar way. Later on I faced comments with decreasing interest. One still looks for approval from one's peers, but reviews are too often written these days by authors with no special competence. I prefer an opponent familiar with the subject at hand to someone who does not feel comfortable with the subject, who cannot really judge whether the book is good or bad. True, I do not particularly relish to be reviewed by ambitious beginners who feel the urge to show that they know more than I do (for some reason they seem to be more numerous in Germany than in other countries) and who have learned the basic lesson that a negative review is easier to write and more widely read than a positive one. In some countries such as Italy and Japan, negative reviews seem to be the exception rather than the rule, and senior military officers and diplomats are ideal reviewers—they seldom give offence and usually look for the redeeming features in a book.

I have written hundreds of reviews. Have I always lived up to the high moral standards which I expect of others? I have tried to, but I certainly have not attained perfection. If I review a book by an established figure in a certain field, chances are that I had dealings with him at one stage or another and that I either like or dislike his work. Perhaps one should disqualify oneself in these cases (and they are frequent). But the alternative is to call in for review someone from outside the field, and this is no ideal solution either.

I continued to write—too much in the view of some of my critics. I have to concede that there are several books I now wish I had not written— quickies, attempts to write instant history. The temptation is always great but should be resisted, except perhaps in rare incidents. In some other cases I finished a book too quickly, the arguments were not sufficiently thought through. Lastly, as for the changes in my field of interest, this was quite customary in the nineteenth century but frowned upon in the twentieth. I was a generalist in an age of specialists. In the nineteenth century, it was quite customary to combine a political career with writing on history and politics, and an academic would change his field of interest from time to time and perhaps even try his hand at fiction. (Great fiction writers would write books on history, and no one blamed them for unbecoming, unprofessional conduct.)

I have mentioned my early works on the Middle East and also the reasons why I gave up this field. In fact, I had written two books in Hebrew even earlier on, but I would not include them in my "collected works," in the unlikely case that there ever should be such an edition. One was a small book on the oil industry, which was little more than a scissors-and-paste job and was furthermore heavily rewritten by a hyperactive editor. The other, on Communism in the Middle East, was written too hastily, but I was able to use some of the chapters in my first book in English.

My interest in Russia was deeper and more abiding. I wrote a history of Russian studies which first appeared in 1967 (the fiftieth anniversary of the October revolution); a second, updated edition came out twenty years later. I have mentioned my interest in German history and current affairs (the youth movement, the Weimar Republic, especially its cultural aspects, and German postwar developments). Two other topics which preoccupied me were modern Jewish history, *A History of Zionism,* and *The Terrible Secret*—a book on what was known, and when, about the mass murder of the Jews, and why so many refused to believe it. Out of this work came a case study written with Richard Breitman: *Breaking the Silence.* This was the story of Eduard Schulte, a German industrialist, who was the first to get the news to Switzerland about Hitler's decision to exterminate European Jewry. Since Schulte had always kept his action secret, we had to engage in a lot of detective work. It was time-consuming but rewarding, and in any case a deserved memorial to one who had done good in a time of great danger, when only a handful had the courage to act as their brothers' keeper.

During the 1970s my interest shifted to political violence. I had been asked to write the entry "revolution" for the *Encyclopedia of Social Sciences* and reading the existing literature about the subject left me dissatisfied. As so often, realities were much more complex than the theoretical concepts used to explain them. My own essay also left me dissatisfied, but then nothing is more frustrating than writing an entry for an encyclopedia, which entails an enormous amount of work. During the sixties and seventies, guerrilla warfare and terrorism were very much in appearance and the attempts to account for them struck me as unhelpful and even misleading. Some advocated political and moral relativism ("One person's terrorist is another person's freedom fighter"), others claimed that terrorists were invincible and that the state was powerless. Yet others used the term "terrorist" and "guerrilla" indiscriminately, which added to the confusion that prevailed

"With Leo Cherne, former head of Freedom House," Washington, D.C., 1993

anyway. My own approach was historical. It showed that guerrilla and terrorism were by no means new and unprecedented phenomena, and that, generally speaking, there was a tendency to overrate terrorism; more often than not it had failed. Terrorism, broadly speaking, made a great deal of noise but seldom had any lasting effect.

These arguments ran against established wisdom at the time. Some claimed that I was underrating terrorism, others missed a "grand theory" of terrorism. I had not said that terrorism would *always* remain relatively harmless; there is the danger that one day terrorists will have access to weapons of mass destruction. As for the "grand theory," I felt certain that there never would be one, simply because the differences in motivation, the traditional historical context, and the political aims were so substantial that it was hopeless to find a common denominator. With all the resistance against my approach, which was considered too unconventional and "unscientific," these books became standard texts in several countries and they were complemented by a *Guerrilla Reader* and a *Terrorism Reader*.

It would be tedious to enumerate all my writings. Over the decades I paid close attention to European affairs and some of my essays on this subject were later published in three volumes *(The Political Psychology of Appeasement, Europe and the Soviet Union*, and *Soviet Realities)*. I also wrote a history of postwar Europe which first appeared in 1969, was frequently reprinted, and reissued in an updated form in 1992. I drew most satisfaction from two novels I wrote and my autobiography. My earliest inclination had been towards fiction and the cinema. My feeling as an adolescent was that I had a great many ideas and also perhaps the ability to express them. I felt less sure about certain talents needed for meticulous scholarship—the painstaking footnoting, the inner urge to check every fact, however insignificant. To this day critics rightly blame me for using an idiosyncratic and inconsistent system for transliterating Russian terms into English. (There is no ideal system, but mine is probably worse than others.) I do not want to deride the essence and the paraphernalia of meticulous scholarship. I simply want to point to a weakness which I could not always overcome—lack of patience. But I knew from an early age that there was no future for me as a writer of fiction be it only because I had to switch languages more than once. No one in Hollywood was waiting for me and the market for documentaries did not yet exist at the time.

There is, of course, as much drama in history and politics (as Balzac and others have noted) as in "pure" fiction. But the main trend in historiography in my time was largely away from narrative history, considered unscholarly, towards disciplines considered more scientific such as social history, Cliometrics and, generally speaking, the search for "theory." This has changed to a certain extent in recent years. Fashions in history, as in other disciplines, come and go. It was the same in political science: Shlomit studied this field at the time at a leading American university and was greatly surprised that politics as taught there had more to do with calculus than with people. Since she had no bent for this branch of mathematics, she dropped the subject. The kind of history which Michelet and Trevelyan had written became unthinkable in the second half of the twentieth century. Or, to be precise, it was still written and even produced best-sellers, which were however frowned upon as amateurish. In brief, the "profes-

sionalization" of history impoverished the discipline.

I had lived through a stormy period of history, and I was reasonably familiar with what had been written about it by the professionals. The books were important and useful, but I felt that a whole dimension was missing. What did people feel at the time? What was life like in Central Europe in the age of the dictators? It was important that cabinets changed and that war was declared, that more women worked in offices and factories, that steel production rose and central heating became more widespread. But it told us little about the quality of life, about the behavior and the mood of people. This induced me to write two novels: *The Missing Years* and its sequel *Farewell to Europe*. They describe the story of a family from the turn of the century to the 1970s, and I have often been asked to what extent it was a *roman à clef* with strong autobiographical elements. The short answer is that it is a composite picture. All, or almost all, did indeed happen but not necessarily to me in person or to any other single individual. My main problem was handling dialogue. Having written nonfiction all my life, I found this very difficult indeed, and from a stylistic point of view the novels were certainly imperfect. But I felt that the story I wanted to tell had so many elements of tension and drama that interest would be sustained even if told artlessly. These novels appeared in translation and there were paperback editions; they were not runaway best-sellers, but then I had never hoped to reach a very big audience, and the letters I received from readers, some quite long and detailed, were rewarding. I had learned in Latin school that it was the assignment of the writer either to delight or to help, and if I had achieved one of these goals, however imperfectly, it was all I had hoped for.

I have been to some extent a controversial writer, largely perhaps because I did not shy away from controversy. I find, in retrospect, that I frequently saw new historical trends early on, but underestimated the period of time it would take in real life for these new developments to unfold; there were always retarding factors. When I received the *Inter Nationes* literary prize in Bonn, the speaker on the occasion, a shrewd German publisher, said: "What a pity Laqueur's books always come too early. . . ." I have learned from experience that to be prematurely correct in one's political appraisals does not add to one's popularity and fame; those eager to be popular are well advised to swim with the mainstream, even if the

"Most of the family: (from left) Benjamin, Johanna, Walter, Shlomit, Tamar, Naomi, and Sylvia," Regents Park, London, 1993

direction happens to be wrong. When it eventually appears that they were mistaken, they were in good company and it will not be held against them.

I do not relish to be called prolific. If one has nothing to say, even one book is too much. I always liked and believed in what I was doing; I never wrote a book unless I was deeply interested in the subject. The one exception (at first) was the *History of Zionism;* originally I should have written the (official) life of Dr. Chaim Weizmann, but in his absentmindedness the sponsor had forgotten that he had commissioned someone else. Since I had done a considerable amount of spade work, I decided to change focus, and as I pursued my work, enthusiasm replaced a feeling of obligation. The two authors who had been elected—Richard Crossman, the British Labor minister and Yakov Talmon the well-known historian—died before they could even start work. Eventually, the biography, an excellent work in three volumes was written by my friend Jehuda Reinharz.

I was able to work so much because conditions were almost ideal: Naomi was dealing with the practical problems of daily life, which in most other families are the preserve and the duty of the husband. Furthermore, I had the good fortune to hold positions which did not involve me in unend-

ing committee meetings but left most of the time for my own work.

Have my books stood the test of time? Almost everyone can write a book, but will it still be read ten or twenty years after? Some of my books have rightly been forgotten, but most are still (or again) in print after fifteen or twenty-five years, which is not frequent in an age when publishers let books get out of print far too early. The quality of my work will have to be judged by others. Were some of my books influential? This I find impossible to answer. Very few books have a deep and lasting impact. I found out years later that some of my work on the Soviet Union had been published in a small Russian edition for members of the Central Committee of the Communist party. But I have no reason to assume that this made the slightest difference in the end. As I write these lines, I am beyond the age of retirement, but my work in Washington continues. I have slowed down but not very much. Travelling has become more of a strain, but I hope to continue until further notice. I am at present between two books. I feel there is still some work undone.

In one of his novels Joseph Conrad has his hero say that he does not like work: "No man does—but I like what is in work, the chance to find yourself." My good fortune has been for many years to be able to do exactly the kind of work I wanted to do, and to find myself in the process. One cannot reasonably ask for more.

BIBLIOGRAPHY

Fiction:

The Missing Years, Little, Brown, 1980.

Farewell to Europe (sequel to above), Little, Brown, 1981.

Nonfiction:

Communism and Nationalism in the Middle East, Routledge & Kegan Paul, 1956.

The Soviet Union and the Middle East, Routledge & Kegan Paul, 1959.

Young Germany, Routledge & Kegan Paul, and Basic Books, 1962, published as *Young Germany: History of the German Youth Movement,* Transaction Books, 1984.

Russia and Germany: A Century of Conflict, Little, Brown, 1965.

The Fate of the Revolution: Interpretations of Soviet History, Macmillan, 1967, revised edition, 1987.

The Road to Jerusalem: The Origins of Arab-Israeli Conflict, 1967, Macmillan, 1968, published in England as *The Road to War,* Weidenfeld & Nicolson, 1968.

The Struggle for the Middle East: The Soviet Union in the Mediterranean 1958-1968, Macmillan, 1969, published in England as *The Struggle for the Middle East: The Soviet Union and the Middle East, 1958-1968,* Routledge & Kegan Paul, 1969, revised edition published as *The Struggle for the Middle East: The Soviet Union and the Middle East 1958-1970,* Penguin Press, 1972.

Europe since Hitler, Weidenfeld & Nicolson, 1970.

The Rebirth of Europe: A History of the Years since the Fall of Hitler, Holt, 1970, revised edition published as *Europe since Hitler: The Rebirth of Europe,* Penguin Books, 1982.

Out of the Ruins of Europe, Library Press, 1971.

A History of Zionism, Holt, 1972.

Neo-Isolationism and the World of the Seventies, Library Press, 1972.

(With Bernard Krikler) *A Reader's Guide to Contemporary History,* Quadrangle, 1972.

Confrontation: The Middle East and World Politics, New York Times Book Company, 1974.

Weimar: A Cultural History, 1918-1933, Putnam, 1974.

Guerrilla: A Historical and Critical Study, Little, Brown, 1976.

Terrorism, Little, Brown, 1977, revised edition, published as *The Age of Terrorism,* 1987.

A Continent Astray: Europe, 1970-1978, Oxford University Press, 1979.

The Political Psychology of Appeasement: Finlandization and Other Unpopular Essays, Transaction Books, 1980.

The Terrible Secret: An Investigation into the Suppression of Information about Hitler's "Final Solution," Little, Brown, 1980.

America, Europe, and the Soviet Union, Transaction Books, 1983.

Germany Today: A Personal Report, Little, Brown, 1985.

A World of Secrets: The Uses and Limits of Intelligence, Basic Books, 1985, revised edition, 1993.

(With Richard Breitman) *Breaking the Silence,* Simon & Schuster, 1986, published in England as *Breaking the Silence: The Secret Mission of Eduard Schulte, who brought the world news of the Final Solution,* Bodley Head, 1986.

The Long Road to Freedom: Russia and Glasnost, Unwin Hyman, 1989.

(With Leon Sloss) *European Security in the 1990s: Deterrence and Defense after the INF Treaty,* Plenum Press, 1990.

Soviet Realities: Culture and Politics from Stalin to Gorbachev, Transaction Publishers, 1990.

(With John Erickson and others) *Soviet Union 2000: Reform or Revolution?,* Tauris, 1990.

Stalin: The Glasnost Revelations, Scribner's, 1990.

Europe in Our Time: A History, 1945-1992, Viking, 1992.

Festschrift, Sage, 1992.

Thursday's Child Has Far to Go: A Memoir of the Journeying Years (autobiography), Scribner's, 1992.

Black Hundred: The Rise of the Extreme Right in Russia, Edward Burlingame Books, 1993.

Editor:

The Middle East in Transition: Studies in Contemporary History, Routledge & Kegan Paul, 1958.

(With Leopold Labedz) *Polycentrism, the New Factor in International Communism* (first published in England as a special issue of *Survey,* 1962), Praeger, 1962.

(With Leopold Labedz) *The State of Soviet Studies* (essays first published in *Survey,* January and April, 1964), MIT Press, 1965.

(With George L. Mosse) *International Fascism, 1920–1945,* Harper, 1966.

(With George L. Mosse) *The Left-Wing Intellectuals between the Wars, 1919–1939,* Harper, 1966.

(With George L. Mosse) *Socialism and War,* Weidenfeld & Nicolson, 1966.

Education and Social Structure in the Twentieth Century, Harper, 1967.

Literature and Politics in the Twentieth Century, Harper, 1967.

(With George L. Mosse) *Literature and Society,* Weidenfeld & Nicolson, 1967.

(With George L. Mosse) *The New History,* Harper, 1967.

Reappraisals: A New Look at History, Weidenfeld & Nicolson, 1968.

(With Barry M. Rubin) *The Israeli-Arab Reader: A Documentary History of the Middle East Conflict,* Citadel, 1969.

(With Evelyn Anderson and others) *A Dictionary of Politics,* Free Press, 1971, revised edition, 1974.

(With Mosse) *Historians in Politics,* Sage Publications, 1974.

Fascism: A Reader's Guide—Analyses, Interpretations, Bibliography, University of California Press, 1976.

The Guerrilla Reader: A Historical Anthology, New American Library, 1977.

The Terrorism Reader: A Historical Anthology, New American Library, 1978.

(With Barry Rubin) *The Human Rights Reader,* Temple University Press, 1979.

The Second World War, Sage Publications, 1982.

The Pattern of Soviet Conduct in the Third World, Praeger, 1983.

Looking Forward, Looking Back, Praeger, 1983.

(With Robert Hunter) *European Peace Movements and the Future of the Western Alliance,* Transaction Books, 1985.

Other:

(Compiler with George L. Mosse) *1914: The Coming of the First World War* (essays originally published in *Journal of Contemporary History,* Volume 1, numbers 3 and 4, 1966), Harper, 1966.

Walter Laqueur, Inter Nationes (Bonn), 1985, and *Walter Laqueur: A Bibliography of His Work,* Center for Strategic and International Studies, 1986. Also *Festschrift,* special issue of the *Journal of Contemporary History,* which appeared on his seventieth birthday, 1991.

Founder and co-editor, *Journal of Contemporary History,* 1966—; founder and editor, *Washington Papers,* 1972—; founder and co-editor, *Washington Quarterly of Strategic and International Studies,* 1977. Contributor to periodicals, including *Commentary* and *New York Times Magazine.*

Denise Levertov

1923-

Denise Levertov, 1985

A few years ago I wrote a biographical sketch for inclusion in a poetry anthology, but found that I could not get further than my childhood in the space allotted.[1] Since virtually all the elements which determined my life as a poet were there in the character and circumstances of my childhood, this was not inappropriate; but I shall try this time to avoid lingering there, and to move on to other phases of my life, focussing on what seems relevant to my work.

My father, the Reverend Paul Levertoff, D.D., born 1878, was a scholarly Russian Jew who had read the New Testament while a student at Konigsberg and had become a Christian as a result. He met my mother, Beatrice Adelaide Spooner-Jones, in Constantinople in 1909 or '10, where she was teaching in a girls' secondary school run by the Scottish Church. They were married in England, lived in Warsaw and Leipzig (where my sister Olga, 1914–1962, was born), and settled in England soon after World War I. My father was ordained as a priest of the Church of England a year or two before my birth.

I was born October 24, 1923, at 24 Lenox Gardens, Ilford, Essex, just across from Highlands Elementary School. My mother remembers hearing the shrill clamor of children's voices from the playground, gathered before the first class-bell rang them into the building, so I am able to tell astrologers the time of my birth, 9:15 a.m. The midwife, subsequently known as Old Nurse, was illiterate but excellent at her craft, it seems. During my childhood she used to come every Saturday for a hot dinner, and sit by the kitchen fire holding a Bible upside down, pretending to read. I was the last baby she delivered, so she took a special pride in me, and later gave me a beautiful sewing-box of inlaid wood which some grateful mother must once have presented to her. I still treasure it—though I use it for mementoes, not sewing materials. I mention it as representative of certain objects in my life which have contributed to a sense of connection to past times that is an undercurrent in my creative experience.

Lenox Gardens was a stone's throw from beautiful and historical Wanstead Park, which (together with the less romantic but also beautiful and quite extensive Valentine's Park) became very important to my life and sensibility as soon as I was old enough to look about me. My mother and sister took me there frequently during my first year, and perhaps something of its atmosphere entered me by osmosis from the very beginning. When I was eight months old, however, my father took the big step of buying a house—5 Mansfield

---

[1]Jeni Couzyn, editor, *The Bloodaxe Book of Contemporary Women Poets*, Bloodaxe Books (Newcastle-upon-Tyne), 1984.

Valentine's Park, one of the parks which figured prominently in Levertov's childhood

Road, a substantial five-bedroom double-fronted brick "semi-detached" built in the late 1890s, virtually identical with many other London houses. This was where I grew up, and where my parents lived until my father died in 1954, and my mother, a year or so later, came to join me and my husband and child in the U.S. The house was only three blocks from Valentine's Park.

My childhood was unusual in that I did not go to school but did lessons at home. I had a great deal of time to read and play, and a freedom to wander the neighborhood which in these dangerous days no cared-for child can be allowed to enjoy. I knew every inch of Valentine's so well that I can still walk there in my mind, and each part had some mythic or other characteristic significance. Wanstead Park was further from our street and was the one place out-of-bounds for me to go alone, because of a solitary incident of violence which had occurred there when I was still a baby or even before I was born, but which was so unusual in those days that people remembered it; but I would go there with my mother, and it was

always a special delight. As an adolescent I often went alone as well—and researched all I could of its history in the local public library. These parks were formative influences, providing ample experience of natural beauty with their ancient trees, their lakes and "ornamental waters," as well as a wide terrain in which to enact imaginary dramas of chivalry, Robin Hood, or of contemporary fictive children about whom I told myself serial stories. Moreover, they reinforced—as did the row of Huguenot weavers' cottages tucked behind Gibson's big furniture store on Ilford's busy commercial High Road, the stone gateposts of already demolished mansions here and there, and the rural names of certain places, such as "The Wash," where until not long before my birth the Cranbrook Road had forded a water-splash, now channeled underneath the roadway—that sense of the past I have mentioned, which my mother's love of history, and the time she spent reading Sir Walter Scott's and other historical fiction to me, stimulated and made thrilling. One of my strongest interests as a child was in finding out what kind of clothes people wore at different periods and what sorts of things they had around them: atmosphere, rather than dates of battles.

Formative, too, was the quantity of books in our house and the fact that everyone read constantly and wrote as well. Listening to my mother read aloud was the way most of our evenings (my father's, my sister's, and mine) were delightfully spent. Thus, beyond the fairy tales and other stories I heard in early childhood, I soon enjoyed much of the grown-ups' fare from Dickens to Tolstoy. Not satisfied with the family library though it was always growing, I also used my Children's Library tickets (one fiction, one nonfiction) and often purloined the adult tickets to take out extra books. Dear Miss Farmery, the children's librarian, would save the nicest new acquisitions under the counter for my next visit. We had tickets in the name of the maid (who did not use them) and—dare I admit it?—of our dog, as well as the legitimate ones. (My father was the only one of the four of us who did not use the library, for though he loved to hear what my mother read, his own interests were scholarly, and if he needed a book he did not own he would have borrowed it from a theological library. He also made frequent use of the British Museum Reading Room.)

Although I do remember my mother reading to me "The Hound of Heaven" and also, another time, "The Ancient Mariner," she restricted herself in general to prose. However, to Olga's and my amused delight, she was apt to declaim Thomas Gray—"Ruin seize thee, ruthless King, confusion on thy banners wait," etc.—with Welsh fervor as she went about the house energetically cleaning and dusting. Sometimes my sister would read one of her own poems aloud, but essentially poetry was something I discovered for myself, though Olga and I would at certain times talk about it, and she introduced me eventually to the work of contemporary poets. I started my reading of poetry with *A Child's Garden of Verses*. (There were also the fairy poems of Rose Fyleman, which I enjoyed for their content, but I seem to have been aware of a qualitative difference: Stevenson's had an emotive resonance, Fyleman's seemed made up—not because they were about fairies but because of their words; though of course I could not have analyzed this.) Then came Palgrave's "Golden Treasury," Tennyson, Walter de la Mare; and soon, Keats, Wordsworth, Coleridge, the many poets of the so-called "Georgian" years, Norman Ault's anthology of Elizabethan lyrics, some of Herbert ("I got me flowers to straw thy way, / I got me boughs off

many a tree, / But thou wast up by break of day / And brought'st thy sweets along with thee"), and de la Mare's wonderful anthology *Come Hither*. There was also Van Doren's anthology of world poetry, belonging to my sister, which I pored over, finding many wonders in its thin-paper pages. Of course the rhythms and language of the King James Bible and the Book of Common Prayer were a presence in our lives, absorbed without thinking about it. And thanks to my sister, by the time I was twelve I was reading some Auden, MacNeice, Day Lewis—the young, innovative poets of that moment—and T. S. Eliot. It is impossible for me to recall accurately the chronological order of most of my discoveries in poetry—partly because I did not give up one poet or period for another, but with an inherent catholicity of taste went on enjoying the mannered eighteenth century in Thompson or Cowper, or the lush romance of the Pre-Raphaelites, or poets of the recent past like Robert Bridges or Edward Thomas, concurrently with what was then avant-garde. In much the same way I can read John Berger or Peter Handke at the breakfast table and Trollope in the evening, and they don't cancel one another out.

As for writing poems, I know I began to do so at four or five, for until I was in my late twenties, I retained a poem of mine composed (improvised) before I was capable of writing it down, and dictated to Olga. It was a rambling account of a visit to fairyland, with detailed description of the fairies' wings and clothes. Fairyland was entered by way of a hollow tree. Later on I wrote poems somewhat imitative of Tennyson's short lyrics. I had nothing as yet to say, but was captivated by luscious-sounding, romantic and unusual words. Words such as eglantine, damask, ambrosial—Pre-Raphaelite taste. So far as these compositions expressed anything at all, it was a love of the music of language and also a kind of yearning—the same qualities which years later, when my first book, *The Double Image*, came out, caused Kenneth Rexroth to speak—embarrassingly but truly!—of "Schwärmerei." But by the time I was twelve some degree of talent must have been manifest, otherwise T. S. Eliot, even though he had some acquaintance with my father due to a committee both served on, would not have written to me so kindly, and at some length, in his letter of advice. I had sent him some poems on a moment's impulse, without telling anyone. Politeness to my father could have been exercised with a far more formal reply. My parents were amused at my temerity in having approached him, for in general I was rather shy. I

*Father, the Reverend Paul Levertoff, D.D.,
about 1950*

had become aware of being an "artist-person" in general and a poet in particular by ten or eleven years old, without ever speaking of it to anyone; possibly even earlier. I did not show my poems to anyone as a rule. Possibly my mother had come across them, for I tended to stuff my writings and drawings under the sofa-cushions; but she had the blessed tact not to mention them. I had a strong sense of the need for privacy, an instinct for shielding myself from well-intentioned definition by others and from inappropriate praise.

Looking at art and hearing good music were other formative influences. My mother sang, my sister played the piano—Bach, Beethoven, Scarlatti; Granados, Albeniz. And once we got a radio, the BBC provided lots of wonderful musical programs. Each year my father would take us to the Special Exhibitions at the Royal Academy: I remember the Persian Exhibition (those blue tiles!) and the Seventeenth Century Exhibition, which put me in a ferment—even the unillustrated catalogue can still thrill me when I come across it,

though that century did not remain my favorite in visual art later on. There were some—not many— art books at home, including a beautiful edition of Turner's *Liber Studiorum* (I wish I had it now!); and copies of a History of Art in monthly parts which had been ordered for my sister when I was a baby and which gave me great joy, although the printing was sloppy so that colors overran their borders. When I was ten or so, Olga began to take me to the National Gallery and later to some other art exhibits. After I was twelve and began to go "up to town" in the train every day by myself for my ballet classes, I began to haunt the Victoria and Albert Museum and visit other art museums; once I got courage to overcome my shyness and enter, I frequented the West End private galleries as well. Looking at art—particularly paintings—has remained one of my greatest joys and interests and has surely had an effect on my writing equal to the love of classical music, of nature, and of omnivorous reading. The basic, primary love of looking comes to me from my mother, both as an inheritance and because she pointed things out to me from the very beginning of my life: flowers, birds, clouds. . . . From my father I think I got a meditative and intellectual bent; my mother was more concerned with concrete detail. My sister conveyed to me a sense of exciting contemporary ideas and experiments much sooner than I would have had it if I had been an only child (though because of the nine-year difference in our ages, and the fact that she had begun to leave home in stages and episodes quite early in my life, I often seemed more like an only child). From all three I got a sense of commitment to righteous causes—to issues of peace and justice. And though I turned away from it in adolescence and did not fully return to it until much later in life, I took in from all three a strong religious impulse together with a powerful impression of the inviolable sincerity of their convictions—and thus of the serious nature of religious faith and practice, which I always hated to see mocked or sneered at even in my most doubting periods. I have again lingered too long on my early years, but these are indeed the elements I believe underlie my life as a poet.

The several years I spent studying classical ballet were not very influential except in friendships made at ballet school and in the exposure to the music, color, and charm of the ballets I saw (mainly the Ballets Russes de Monte Carlo—also called the de Basil Company—which had a London season each year for several years until the war made it impossible). My friendship with Betty Mitchell, a friendship which lasted till her death in 1989 (her brother David remains one of my dearest friends), was decisive, however. It was with her that I discovered Chekhov, and mainly with her that I saw some wonderful plays: Shakespeare, Ibsen, Shaw, Wilde, and Chekhov performed by Gielgud, Olivier, Edith Evans, Peggy Ashcroft, Marius Goring, Lucy Manheim, and many other marvelous actors. I not only attended these productions, but through Bet's power of critical analysis was led to understand what I'd seen in ways I could not have attained by myself.

Another lifelong friendship formed at ballet school was with two sisters, daughters of an American expatriate mother and a Dutch father, Giselle and Jehanne-Marie Deutschbein. Giselle later took her stepfather's last name—Waldman. Jehanne married an Italian and became Marchesi. Their (American) stepfather was the historian and publisher Milton Waldman, and in that first year of the war, when the school was evacuated to Buckinghamshire, he and Peggy had rented a lovely Cotswold stone house near Oxford, and I was invited for a weekend. Milton was a stiff, gloomy man of whom I was shy, but he very kindly took fourteen-year-old "Gici" and sixteen-year-old me on a tour of the Oxford colleges. I remember less of the history he imparted there than of the terraced garden full of sweetpeas and honeybees, and the delights of their house. I sat up all night reading Lamartine and eating the chocolate biscuits which used to grace the bedside tables of well-appointed English guest-rooms in the days when no one seemed to be aware of plaque and the necessity of flossing your teeth. Next day I was embarrassed in case my greed were discovered and reported.

It was only the second time I'd been anywhere for a weekend. The first had been to Shoreham, Kent, where my other ballet-school friend, Audrey, daughter of Slade School professor Franklin White, lived in a low-ceilinged ancient house of many small rooms full of her father's drawings and of work by Augustus John. Her mother and sister looked exactly like Augustus Johns themselves. During my three visits there Audrey took me to see Knole, which I'd read of in *Orlando,* and the cottage where Samuel Palmer had lived. This friendship was abruptly broken years later, after all of us had married, when Betty and Audrey quarreled and I sided with Bet.

I spent the first year of World War II in Buckinghamshire, where the ballet school had

Mother, Beatrice Adelaide Spooner-Jones Levertoff, about 1950

migrated in the general move to evacuate schools from the cities. But when the bombing actually began in the fall of 1940 I returned home to be with my parents, and in 1941 I gave up my ballet training and ambitions with a mixture of pain and relief. (The whole idea had been my sister's, not mine, but once embarked on that career I'd been hooked by it, while all the while knowing secretly that it was not for me.)

At eighteen, with a violent change of focus, I joined the Women's Land Army, in the romantic expectation of living a style of rural life nurtured by the many books on English farming and craft traditions I had read. I did not take to the experience (which differed from that ideal) despite my enthusiasm and, as I was still underage for the female conscription we had in wartime England, was allowed to resign. At nineteen, facing an alternative of military service or defense-factory work, I joined the Civil Nursing Reserve, which gave basic intensive training and then sent one out to replace nurses at civilian hospitals who were now with the troops. After a year I transferred to a regular nursing school (at an isolation hospital, then quaintly called a Fever Hospital) where I spent another year and took and passed my first big exam; but then dropped out, to continue

At age twenty-one months

working as an Assistant Nurse at several hospitals in the London area.

These events threw me into a wholly unfamiliar social world. My fellow nurses were mainly from much less affluent and less well-educated backgrounds than the girls I knew at the Legat School of Ballet or than the very few other young people with whom I'd mixed before; they were much tougher and, in a way, worldly wise. The lively ones, to whom I was drawn, went to dances with the soldiers from whatever training camp or anti-aircraft squad, etc., happened to be nearby, and I soon learned to go too, and to drink beer and whiskey and go to pubs. I'd met no boys at all before that. All this was an extraordinary contrast to anything I had ever known (or to what my life would have been like if there hadn't been a war on). I was too immature to make any sort of bridge between it and my home life or my inner life (though the two close friends I made in these years, Marya and Joyce, were very intelligent and with them I could discuss anything and everything—separately, for they did not know one another). My parents would have been shattered if they had known a quarter of what my social life was like; but when I went home for my days off I concealed almost everything from them, and when I was home for a longer leave I relapsed with relief

into an earlier mode of behavior—only to experience a reluctance amounting almost to dread when it was time to go back. Yet once back at work the strong collective atmosphere whirled me right back into itself after a few hours. It was very much like what I have read of people's feeling about going back to boarding schools, where even if they were unhappy the peer-group exercised such compelling centripetal force on their return. But I was not unhappy, on the whole, and indeed experienced a lot of laughter and excitement much of the time; as for the work itself, it had quite a strong appeal to me in some respects, though it was shadowed by chronic fear of one's superiors, for the system in British hospitals was virtually military in its authoritarianism. It was humiliating to hate that and at the same time cringe before it, and I rebelled in every way I could think of; but the ways were not many, and seem as I recollect to have consisted mainly in scrambling in through windows hours after the nurses' residence doors were locked at night, or refusing to go to (mandatory) breakfast in order to have an extra half hour in bed. Yet at the same time that I was leading this alien life I was also continuing to write; and the weakness of the poems in *The Double Image,* which were written between ages of nineteen and twenty-two, is that they reflect nothing of that world, except in so far as they convey some sense of not being at one with what surrounded me. But there was some unconscious hypocrisy in that, for if much of that world was coarse and brutal, I was seduced by it without a struggle—attracted partly by a kind of fierce gaiety that pervaded it and which I suppose was a facet of the stoicism which made most people in England endure air raids and shortages with such matter-of-factness, where Americans, I can't help but feel, would have been hysterical.

By coincidence, my first nursing job led to my first literary friendship. I had been assigned to a hospital in Billericay, Essex, after my brief basic training in the CNR, and it was there that Charles Wrey Gardiner, editor of *Poetry Quarterly,* was then living. I soon got to know him. He began to publish my work in the *Quarterly* and through him I met a number of other poets: Nicholas Moore, Sean Jennet, Alex Comfort (who decades later, in the palmy days of the Sexual Revolution, became famous for *The Joy of Sex,* but was originally known as a poet and novelist), and Tambimmuttu, the Sri Lankan founder of *Poetry London,* which quickly became better known than *Poetry Quarterly.* I didn't get to know any of these people well at all, but the occasional lunch or pub evening Charles would bring me to gave me some sense of that world. As often happened later, I did not really notice that I was the only female poet at such gatherings—indeed, the only *female,* so far as I recall, poet or not. It was the literary world, in some measure the artistic, bohemian world I had known I would someday belong to; that it was so much a male world did not occur to me, since I was somehow privileged to be in it nevertheless. It was not until the late sixties that the women's movement caused me to realize how often I had been complacent in this position, which "token woman" does not really describe since there was no sense of obligation on the men's part to provide at least a token. Perhaps I was unthinkingly accepted just because I did not expect *not* to be—for to me the camaraderie of art was innocently taken for granted, and though uncertain of myself in every other respect I knew I was a poet.

Other poets I came to know included Dannie Abse, who was exactly my age and wrote me a poem in which he identified me with his twin sister dead in infancy. A scarlet dress I wore at that time got into this somehow. He was a medical student when I was a nurse, and he was a Welsh Jew—tenuous parallels added to our both being poets. But decades later he made fun of my father, claiming that he talked of Christian doctrines in a Yiddish accent, which was Dannie's fantasy since my father did not grow up speaking Yiddish at all; Russian was his mother tongue (in which he dreamed, incidentally), and if he had any accent it was a very faint Russian one.

Through Dannie I met Emanuel Litvinoff and the Austrian poet Fred Marnau (then a refugee from Nazi Austria). I recognized that Fred and his wife, though not much older than I, were years beyond me in their cosmopolitan sophistication. They were gracious and kindly, as well; and moreover I responded strongly to Fred's poetry (translated by Ernst Sigler), which was mystical, allusive, and seemed to grow from the same soil as the Rilke poems and letters I had begun to read.

I have jumped ahead a little, for the war was at last ending or had ended by this time, and soon I

Denise Levertov, about age seven, in front of the Ilford home at 5 Mansfield Road

was no longer nursing but worked for a time at Betty's father's antique shop in Hampstead and then at a bookstore in the City. At this job my phenomenal math block caused me endless problems. But I enjoyed meeting another young poet, Keith Sawbridge, who worked nearby, during our lunch hour. Once, we went up The Monument—and I never see that column, when I'm in London, without wondering what became of Keith. At first I lived at home, then in Hampstead. The days of soldier's dances, and going on double dates with nursing friends and young men one had never seen before and would never see again, ended even before the war, when I fell seriously in love with someone who had been in the Friends' Ambulance Service, had been captured, and had spent quite a long stretch in a prisoner-of-war camp. He was a documentary film-maker and has remained a life-long friend. After we "broke up," as I learned to say later on in America—I don't recall what phrase was used in England at the time—I again fell in love, this time with a designer (who later married a dear friend of mine and also remained an ongoing figure in my life, though it is now a long time since we have had any direct communication). He was an anarchist, and through him I met George Woodcock. I had known Herbert Read since ballet school days (when he lived down the road in Buckinghamshire), and through his writings was superficially familiar with the kind of philosophical anarchism prevalent in those circles. It was in the Read's house at Seer Green that I first saw the bright bindings (with spines printed the other way up from English ones) of American books. And at George's flat to which my boyfriend took me I noticed such books again, and among them *The Signature of All Things* by Kenneth Rexroth, much to my interest—for Kenneth (then only a name to me) had just written to ask me for poems for his anthology *New British Poets,* which he was compiling for New Directions. This would have been in 1946.

It was in that year that my first book, *The Double Image,* was published by Cresset Press. I have described in the introduction to *Collected Earlier Poems* (1979) how that came about, so I will not repeat the story here.

Early in 1947 I left for Holland as an *au pair* girl, intending to return in three months and possibly marry my boyfriend. In the event, I stayed away much longer and we each married other people. The family I stayed with were friends of George Woodcock's, and my job was to speak English with the three teenagers and read English with the lady of the house. Jerry and Dini Lavies were extremely kind to me and had an extensive collection of English books—fortunately, for often I was alone all day. I had also brought a few with me, including the edition of Rilke's *Selected Letters* which has been, through the decades, an essential text in my life. But the cold of those months was ferocious—one of the coldest winters anyone could recall—and my clothes (from years of war-time rationing) were inadequate to it. Instead of the warm coat I know I did possess, I had brought (for sentimental reasons) only a gray raincoat that, before I knew him, had been left at my boyfriend's after a party. (It had belonged to someone I did not know, Lucien Freud, Sigmund Freud's grandson—later to become the internationally esteemed painter.) To my lifelong regret, I did not learn to skate in that lake- and canal-surrounded Dutch village: it was too cold for me to stay outdoors long enough to practice. However, the coming of spring that year, minimal though initial signs of it were, was momentous and poignant as never before or since. A few blades of grass, icebound boats jostling in the melt, skylarks singing . . . This was at the very end of my stay, when I particularly recall a walk with the late composer Rudolf Escher, who was staying nearby at the house of his in-laws, who kept there for his use a powder-blue grand piano on which he played for me when we returned from listening to the exhilarating skylark songs.

With £10.00 paid me by my au-pair family and £10.00 sent by my father, I set off for Paris in April 1947, armed with a few literary addresses, mostly sent by Kenneth Rexroth, a few by John Hayward, my editor at Cresset Press. (I met virtually none of these people, as often happens with travelers' introductions.) My mother as a girl had longed to go to Paris but her guardian thought it too dangerous—he let her go to Constantinople, though, because her position there was with a church school! And I too had dreamed of it—the Paris of students and artists, of *La Boheme* and *The Light That Failed* and *Trilby,* but also of Rilke's sojourns and countless paintings and memoirs. There spring was in full leaf, and I wandered the streets blissfully for weeks, too happy to pin myself down to one of the nursemaid jobs I found. Since I had no idea how much my money was worth, I was afraid to go into a restaurant, but lived on black ersatz coffee, tomatoes, and the hard-boiled eggs sold at coffee bars. I slept at a French YWCA inhabited by students and young working girls—

With Mitchell Goodman in Paris, about 1947

and later was lent for a week or two a very posh high-rise apartment near the Eiffel Tower, which however I had to enter by a scary metal outside staircase, the servants' entrance. Eventually my money ran out and I had to take a nursemaid job which turned out to be virtual slavery, describable only by a Céline. It must suffice to tell that I was given only a bare mattress—no bedclothes—to sleep on, that my hours were such that it was not possible to seek other employment options; and that when at last I escaped, I was unable to extract from my employers the payment they owed me for several weeks of servitude. My rescuer, who had previously lent me that luxurious apartment while he was away, was a Mr. McEwen from the British Council (the cultural organization, similar to the USIS), who was a cousin of Sir Herbert Read. He arranged with the Matron of the British Hospital to take me on without waiting for my nursing references and uniform to arrive from England, and he picked me up and drove me there himself.

In the months I spent at the hospital in Levallois-Perret, a working-class district, I was able to dig further into the sense of being at home in Paris—one of the few cities which, if one is not a tourist but has some kind of work or function, lets one feel accepted as part of itself, illusory though that may be. Though my job was demanding, as nursing always is, I managed to go on night duty, which meant that one's "time off" was clustered, giving longer free stretches; besides which, at twenty-three I rejoiced in being able to do with very little sleep, so I often spent the days, when I should have been in bed, wandering around the Left Bank or Montmartre. With another nurse, Margaret Carey, I once or twice went rowing in the Bois de Boulogne in the fresh early morning. I met a few people. One was a wonderful old Russian anarchist; he and his wife lived in a suburb and raised goats. I horrified (and amused) a friend of Rexroth's, Janine Lambert, who invited me to a sort of salon, by saying that Kenneth had described her as a Stalinist. I was too ignorant to understand the implications. I boldly interviewed some painter whose work I'd seen exhibited, telling him I was writing for a London magazine (it was wholly speculative and came to nothing). I missed the chance of visiting Versailles with the bluestocking daughter of a delightful lady, widow of an Englishman, who had been a patient at the hospital—I was too shy to believe she had really meant to take me, so I didn't show up. Looking back, I see I was very young for my age—impetuously daring at one moment and so uncertain of myself the next that I would "cut" people on the street, unsure if I really knew them, or if they would remember me. (This was partly due to myopia.)

After some months an event occurred which caused me to leave Paris. Sir Ashley Duff Cooper, the British Ambassador, was coming to unveil a memorial plaque of some kind and the entire nursing staff was supposed to form a guard of honor on the front steps. I refused, because the idea seemed so militaristic to me and because the demand infringed on off-duty time. (I had nothing against Duff Cooper personally—he had been helpful to my mother when she was intervening on behalf of various interned refugees during the war years.) Consequently I was fired for insubordination.

That suited me just fine, though I would otherwise have honorably stayed for the whole of the year stipulated when I was given the job. It opened up the opportunity to see more of France; and with Betty Mitchell, who came over from London to join me, I took off for what turned out to be (as the months in Paris also had done) an adventure so rich in itself that its really rather brief duration does not correspond with its importance in memory. We hitchhiked southward (first encountering the Mediterranean at Sète) then eastward into the Tarn, westward again to Toulon, and finally north through Haute Savoie to Geneva. To begin with we stayed in Youth Hostels, but soon began to go to farms instead and ask if we could sleep in a hayloft. We were never refused, and often were given a bowl of café au lait in the morning after we had washed our faces at the farmyard pump. In the warm south we would simply lie down in a field at night, with our clothes strategically applied—e.g., legs thrust into arms of sweaters, a second sweater tied around our hips. We had no camping equipment, wore skirts, not jeans; we spoke not of hitchhiking but of "getting rides" or "faire le stop," and when a vehicle hove in sight we did not stick out our thumbs but our whole arms, stepping out dramatically into the middle of the road. There were no Americans and very few non-French hitchhikers in the summer of '47; the French ones were mostly young workers

on vacation. Gasoline was still in very short supply and almost all our rides were in trucks. One *camion* had a wood-burning engine and every few miles we and the driver had to get out and go in search of brushwood. The atmosphere in that brief idyllic time between the war's end and the beginning of the Cold War was hopeful, generous, unsuspicious. We were unafraid and were never threatened in any way—just one driver (of a private car) got a bit fresh: we dismounted at the first opportunity and decided he had undoubtedly been a collaborator during the Occupation (which may well have been true). That summer remained for both Betty and me the most lyrical of our lives.

Once again, I had started out with £10.00 as had Betty, and once again it was giving out when we reached Geneva. Betty was interested in possibly enrolling in the Institut J. J. Rousseau and we knew we might get work in prosperous Switzerland. While staying at the Youth Hostel in Geneva we met two Americans, Harvard graduate students on their way from Italy to Paris. At the same time, my former boyfriend the film-maker showed up from Czechoslovakia where he'd been working for the International Student Service. As a result of this meeting, one of the Americans, Stan Karnow (later the famous journalist), married a girl to whom the film-maker had given him an introduction—Claude Sarraute, daughter of Nathalie Sarraute, the novelist; Betty fell in love with Stephen, the film-maker (who remained an important person in her life, as in mine); and I married the other American, Mitchell Goodman. This was in the fall of 1947. During the winter of 1947–48 all of us were living in Paris—Mitch and I (and, I suppose, Stan) in cheap Latin Quarter hotels, Betty (teaching English to a little boy and some other pupils) in one of those tiny servants' attics up in the mansards of so many French city dwellings, Stephen in a similar one elsewhere. He had various irons in the fire, and on one occasion took me to the studios of the BBC's Paris service to read a poem for a program directed by the son (and namesake) of the Irish poet Sturge Moore.

In those months I experienced my third sense of Paris. My first had been that of an unemployed pedestrian wanderer, speaking to no one for days on end but happy just to be "a pair of eyes on legs." My second was while I felt myself a working girl, learning the metro system and a bit of (long forgotten) *argot*. Now, meeting mainly American students (Mitch enrolled at the Sorbonne under the GI Bill), living in hotels, and eating in cheap restaurants, my relationship to the city changed again, though I don't know how to characterize it. Perhaps it became less intense, less intimate. I had become a visitor, if not a tourist.

In early spring, while it was still cold and damp in the city, we moved to Florence, where I discovered the USIS library and began to read American poetry. (I had "discovered" Stevens and Williams in Paris.) But Florence was as cold and damp as Paris, or more so, and we took the train down to Sicily. No tourists—neither English nor German—had yet returned to Taormina, and when we arrived there with our rucksacks and stringbags, both of us barely twenty-four years old, the touts from the somehow-surviving hotels almost tore us limb from limb in their eagerness to capture two customers. After one night in a palazzo where we dined one each end of a long marble table, we found a room in a peasant's house more suited to our estate. On the way from Messina we had ridden in an open train carriage, sitting on the floor with our feet dangling out, eating little sweet blood-oranges; the conductor leapt out to gather me a bouquet of wildflowers, and easily hopped back in. The empty streets of Taormina were lined with little palazzos and Saracen castellations. Everywhere were almond trees in full blossom. Far below, the sea was a sparkling dark blue; and on the horizon was Etna, white and dreamy. Not until I came to know Mount Rainier in the last few years have I encountered so powerful a mountain presence.

We went also to an inland town, Pallazuolo Acreide, chosen at random from the map. It took all day to go maybe fifty miles on a narrow gauge railroad. Trains of mules and muleteers could be glimpsed among the wild sun-scorched hills. We alighted after dark, and would have been totally at a loss but for a self-appointed (and, as it turned out, perfectly disinterested) guide, a real guardian angel. He found us a room in what had once been a fine palazzo. There were four or five beds in the room, but no fleas; traces of an eighteenth-century painting of gods and goddesses decorated the ceiling and a corner balcony overlooked the main piazza, dominated by a vast baroque church. Grass grew between the stones of the piazza. Our angel came next day to show us the Greek theater (grass-grown too) and the Millionaire. The Millionaire was a large man in a Borsalino fedora, smoking a cigar, who sat in a little store (not as shopkeeper but as patron) receiving admirers. He had been foreman in a Connecticut shoe-factory and had retired to his hometown, set his relations up in business or working some land he had purchased,

and was enjoying leisure, power, and universal admiration.

Back in Florence I began to learn something of Renaissance art; but at that time so much was still not on view after the war, or was so badly lit, that on visits to Italy in later years I realized how much I had missed in 1948.

We spent the late summer and fall of 1948 in England with my parents, with some excursions to see relatives in Wales, and to spend a rainy night in a tent close to Stonehenge, where we saw the sun rise over the altar stone when no-one else at all was there. I was incensed at there being barbed wire (which we scrambled through) around the stone circle, and a little sentry-box where in the daytime someone took entrance fees, but there was none of the large-scale vulgarization I'm told has now despoiled it.

Late in 1948 came the momentous voyage to the U.S. I was statistically a GI bride, though Mitch had been discharged from the army without being sent overseas. The ship was a troopship and the majority of passengers were genuine war-brides, many already married and with young children, others going out to rejoin fiancés and meet their in-laws. A great many had destinations in what Mitch told me were rural areas in the plains or "badlands," and I've often wondered how many of these young women, especially those from urban backgrounds, stuck it out. Most of them—like myself!—had very little idea of what America would be like. My own impressions when we at last arrived were, first, a vision of downtown Manhattan's towers evanescent in early morning mist and touched with pale rose, while, close by, dark marker posts accentuated the Venetian, Turneresque mirage: a sense of the city never recaptured even from the Staten Island ferry later on. Then, the shock of the Bowery with its dirt, litter, and drunken figures stumbling along or prone on the sidewalks—a sense of filth, poverty, and decay worse than anything I'd seen anywhere at that time (including Naples) and wholly inconsistent with my assumption that New York was new, modern, and prosperous and would therefore be very clean and shiny—more like Geneva. My third initial impression was that the big electric sign I saw as we crossed the bridge to Brooklyn, which flicked on and off saying "Kinsey," "Kinsey," indicated that best-selling books were advertised in lights over here—for I took it to refer to *The Kinsey Report,* which had just been published. Mitch and his brother, in the front seat, were deep in talk and I did not find out until the next day, when I alluded to this, that Kinsey was a brand of whiskey.

After a year of living in European hotel rooms and eating in bistros, we commenced a more settled life, supposedly more "real," in a tiny Greenwich Village "walk-up" which had been passed to us while we were in Paris by a Radcliffe student Mitch knew. We repainted it and played house. The toilet was out in the hall, and the shower was rigged up over a washtub in the kitchen so that one had to climb on a chair to clamber into it; the circular plastic curtain wrapped horridly around one. But it was all exciting and fun to begin with, and the Village was still a rather quiet, calm area with a lot of charm, a bit like (London's) Chelsea. After our son Nikolai was born in June of 1949, however, things became difficult—indeed, even before that there had been the frightening necessity of daily stepping over the drunken, snoring body of a certain neighbor who used to pass out on the stairs (we lived on the top floor). I was so afraid he would wake and grab at me–especially as I got bigger and bigger in my pregnancy. And after Nikolai was born several neighbors, in our building and the adjoining one, harassed us in a variety of disgusting (and anti-Semitic) ways every time the baby cried. In various ways I was unconsciously suffering culture-shock as well, but the term had not yet come into use.

Busy trying to be a proper grown-up wife and mother, I was not a very prolific writer during those first two years—but three important new friends became part of my life: the painter Al Kresch; Barbara Bank, my first American woman friend who, a few years later, married the painter Howard Fussiner, who also became a close friend; and Robert Creeley, through whom I came to know many people and ideas. I was already reading Williams intensively, but it was Creeley who turned me on to Ezra Pound, whose *ABC of Reading* and some of the *Literary Essays* (more than the *Cantos*) were very influential on the development of my intellectual or reflective understanding of writing, which up till that time had been almost entirely intuitive and emotional. I had an impulse to comprehend and analyze what I was doing and why I liked or did not like what others did, and Pound's criticism helped to give me some acceptable guidelines, although I did not accept all of his prescriptive canon.

I did not confront and judge his racism until a later date—the prose I read was free of it, and though I knew *about* it I dismissed it as an aberration afflicting only inessential sections of his

work. That it permeated and infected more than that was something I reluctantly perceived in time; but I continued to feel that one cannot therefore forego all that his work offers, as some maintain. (The same applies, for me, to a number of other major writers—Wallace Stevens, Céline, etc. Why should I not cut the worm out of the apple and eat the rest, if it is a fine juicy apple otherwise?)

When Nikolai was fifteen months old we returned to Europe (Mitch had some more GI Bill coming to him), and lived at first in a village near Aix-en-Provence. It was an idyllic time in many ways. As I drew water from the well of our cottage I could gaze, as if from within the canvas, at what appeared to be a Cezanne painting, dominated by the austere planes of the Mont Ste. Victoire. Once a week we went to Aix to the public baths (very civilized, quite Etruscan in atmosphere as husband and wife reclined and conversed in two big bathtubs and little Nik slithered delightedly on the tiles from one to the other). Bob Creeley and his then wife Ann and their children came to live in an adjoining village. We exchanged baby-sitting, and sometimes two or three of us would bicycle to a concert. Or when Bob came over we would sit in the field and talk about poetry. Nikolai took long deep afternoon naps (no wonder he was insomniac at night!) and Mitch and I sometimes left him in care of our landlady, who lived next door, and took long walks in a countryside wholly unspoiled at that time. In spring the fields were full of wild narcissus. The shepherd leaned for hours on his crook, coat flung over his shoulders like a cape, or walked his flock to new fields. There was wild thyme on the slopes of the low hills just north of us, and many little irrigation canals in which to bathe hot feet in the summer. I learned to cook on a wood stove or, in hot weather, on charcoal. And in the garden of a nearby small chateau to which the owners came only rarely, there were lichened eighteenth-century statues, periwinkles around a fountain, and many nightingales. But we were plagued by the multitude of half-feral, sick-looking cats our landlords kept but did not take care of, and which would snatch food from the baby's hands; and by a disgusting outhouse which I will not describe. So after a while we moved on and went to live in Sori, a little town on the Ligurian coast between Genoa and Rapallo where Jehanne and Gisela's parents had a house. Gisela helped us find an apartment in a building right on the beach. The lower floors had no windows facing the sea because, though tideless, the Mediterranean beat fiercely on the thick stone walls in time of storm.

Our flat was on the top floor and when wind and waves were high the spray would fling itself through the open casement. The first day, I thought we could never bear the loud sound of jostling pebbles, but a week later I had to make an effort to hear it, as with a ticking clock. Some of Nik's growing vocabulary had been French, but in Sori he went most days to the Asilo (a day-care center run by the nuns for the working mothers of the little town) so that he would have playmates, and soon he was chattering away in dialect much of the time. Towards the end of our stay my parents came to visit. My father was a fine linguist but knew no Italian; however, he managed to converse with the village priest in Latin. The dear old nuns were impressed. That visit was the last time I saw my father.

A year or so after we returned to America, we moved to a larger apartment on West 15th Street just over the line into Chelsea. This was the building my close friend Barbara lived in. As Nik began preschool and then kindergarten I began writing a lot more. Mitch, all this while, was also writing (fiction and travel journalism). I worked as a nurse for a few months, at James Ewing and St. Vincent's, but was not properly accredited by U.S. standards and did not like the working atmosphere

*The poet with her son, Nikolai Goodman,
in New York City, mid-1970s*

anyway. I also had a number of minimum-wage jobs—proofing department store credit cards, selling greeting cards, copy-holding at a linotype shop, and as a proofreader at a large office typing pool. I applied for a job at the New York Public Library, but though it was only for pushing the book returns cart around the shelves they could not hire me because I had no school certificate; I told the lady my book was in their catalogue and she laughed and sympathized, but a rule was a rule. Soon, though, Mitch found he could make enough by writing travel articles to support us, and I did not go out to work again until I started teaching some years later.

The period after our return from Europe was marked by other momentous friendships: I went to pay homage to William Carlos Williams, and thereafter visited him at Rutherford every few months, with the exception of the two years I spent in Mexico, and also corresponded with him. His letters to me (few of which have been published[2]) are now at Stanford's Green Library. I felt his approval and affection as a powerful blessing upon my vocation.

After the publication of *Dr. Zhivago* I longed to know Boris Pasternak, and wrote to him, sending him *With Eyes at the Back of Our Heads*, which had just come out. He wrote back saying, "I feel that we shall be friends." Alas, that was not to be, for he died soon after I received his letter; but the relationship that might have been remained as another benediction. And it was in the 1950s, also, that my long close friendship with Robert Duncan commenced, first by mail and soon with a meeting as he and his partner, Jess, passed through New York on their way to a year's sojourn in Majorca, where Creeley was living at that time. This was a rich and influential association on many levels and I have written at some length about it elsewhere.[3]

My father having died in 1954, my mother came over to live with us in New York, and in 1957 we all went to spend two years in Mexico. The impact of Mexico—of place, flora and fauna, sights and sounds—was almost immediately apparent in the many poems I wrote during our stay, whereas my great love of the English countryside and of London and all the scenes and places I'd

---

[2]*Stony Brook*, a short-lived literary magazine, published a selection in 1968.

[3]"Some Duncan Letters—A Memoir and a Critical Tribute," in *New and Selected Essays*, New Directions Press, 1992.

Bach Mai Hospital in late October 1972. "The doctor standing next to Muriel Rukeyser and pointing to a crater is the Director. I am at far right."

witnessed in Holland, France, and Italy, though felt intensely, had made little or no overt appearance in my poems. The difference may have been partly due to the absolute ignorance of Mexican culture I brought to Mexico, so that what I encountered was exotic to me as nothing in Europe could be. But I believe it was more the result of my having imperceptibly developed sufficient technical strength and flexibility to extend into a new articulation of response. Some of my early New York City poems had begun to reflect this ability, but Mexico brought it out strongly, and from then on the impact of the various places I have lived or stayed for a while has been an evident, though not constant, factor in my work.

Our return to the U.S. after two years was via San Francisco, as Robert Duncan had arranged for me to read at the Poetry Center—my first public reading anywhere. Duncan had gathered a large audience, mostly young and very enthusiastic (my first U.S. book, *Here and Now*, having recently appeared from City Lights) who

did not seem to mind my conscientiously over-long performance. (Duncan, on my enquiring how long it should be, blithely told me "at least an hour and a half" and I had timed it accordingly. These were, of course, the days of the San Francisco Renaissance and audiences were more than averagely tolerant. . . .)

Back in New York City, hard times, both economically and emotionally, were alleviated by some positive events. Mitch's novel, *The End of It*, completed in Mexico, found a publisher after a long painful search for one, and was a critical success though not a financial one. James Laughlin (thanks to Rexroth's having brought me to his attention) invited me to become a New Directions author, which I have happily remained to this day; he became a lasting friend. And I was asked to teach a weekly workshop at the Poetry Center in New York.

The summer after that first ten-week experience of teaching, we visited Barbara and Howard Fussiner in Deer Isle, Maine; and on a hot day I was sitting on a rock just offshore, in a little cove, when a summer neighbor of theirs, Professor John Bicknell, swam out and perched himself beside me to ask if I'd like to teach a poetry workshop at Drew University in New Jersey that fall. Thus began my college teaching career. As I've described in "The Untaught Teacher,"[4] I had to make everything up as I went along since I'd never seen a classroom before I entered one as the teacher. And as the years passed, whatever I learned about teaching was acquired by trial and error, since I have almost never had the opportunity to see my academic colleagues in action. Exceptions have been Paul Lacey at Earlham College, where I have visited a number of times, and John Felstiner at Stanford, who has occasionally invited me to classes of his. Both are magnificent teachers; but it was probably too late for me to learn much from them about pedagogy.

I have not found teaching fundamentally incompatible with my primary creative work except in the time and energy it consumes. When critical, or "left brain," activity becomes too dominant, poetic creativity is inhibited; but that can occur during any analytic or expository writing or during heavy involvement in other types of tasks, such as political or community organizing or various domestic events. It is not specific to teaching, and in fact contact with imaginative, gifted students can be beneficial—in moderation. Close scrutiny of their poems, and the demands on their care and craft I found myself making, made me demand more care and attention of myself, which was beneficial. But it's a matter of balance, and writers whose work as teachers involves larger, non-elective classes, heavy course loads, and lots of committee work might be better off in a nine-to-five job, except for the long vacations academia provides. Myself, having come into the academic world not through the career door, I have been extremely fortunate in having small classes of hand-picked students, and teaching only writing workshops, modern poetry, and self-designed courses such as "Poets on Poetry" and "The Prose of Poets."

In 1961 Mitch was commissioned to write a travel piece about Greece; as Nikolai was at a summer camp that he liked, I was able to go with him. On that journey I also saw Venice for the first time. Only a single poem (about Delphi) reflects that memorable journey; but our purchase that year of an old farm in Maine—a house of seven

rooms, in fair shape, and fifty acres of overgrown pasture and woodland, all for a flat $3,500 (which for the first time in our lives we were able to come up with)—led to a great many of my poems in the succeeding decade, when I spent all my summers there except for two- or three-week visits to my mother (who had remained in Oaxaca, Mexico). My books from that period, even after our anti-war activity accelerated and intensified, are full of poems that sprang very directly from the fields, woods, streams, and weather of Temple, Maine. It was a rich experience of communion with nature (and our earlier years there were an important part of Nik's later childhood—he was ten when we started to spend the summers there). It was in the sixties, too, that friendships with Adrienne Rich, Hayden Carruth, and Galway Kinnell developed. (But for every friendship I mention, many others go unnamed. My life is very rich in friends—the greatest blessing there is.)

Although I was already involved, as was my husband, in protesting the Vietnam War (and even before that, in the "Ban the Bomb" anti-testing demonstrations), my association with students in the 1960s and '70s had a strong influence on what I did in the sphere of political activity and how and with whom I did it, both during the war, and on into that phase of the peace movement which, bringing together veterans of the sixties' war resistance with a new generation of post-Earth Day environmentalists, focused on the dangers of nuclear power. Our efforts were often mocked, but Three-Mile Island and then, incalculably more so, the Chernobyl catastrophe proved us right, though even so the lesson has not yet been learned.

Among writer friends first met in other circumstances who became political comrades as well were Grace Paley and Muriel Rukeyser. In 1972 I travelled to Hanoi with Muriel, along with Michigan Senator Philip Hart's wife Jane, at the invitation of the Vietnamese Writer's Union and the Women's Union. That brief but highly charged journey was not only a memorable experience but necessitated many months of subsequent work for each of us, speaking and showing slides, etc., to tell people (mostly on college campuses) what we had seen, both about the positive and amazingly generous spirit of the Vietnamese we met and about deliberate U.S. bombing of hospitals and residential areas and use of anti-personnel weapons on civilians. Even apart from this trip to Hanoi, I spent a lot of time in the 1970s speaking at rallies and demonstrations and doing various kinds of organizing. This extended beyond the war

---

[4]*The Poet in the World*, New Directions Press, 1973.

issue into working with political exiles from Greece, Iran, and Chile. In time, it was to a considerable extent my involvement in peace and justice causes which led me to define and develop my latent religious faith, which in turn resulted in the themes of many of my poems in recent years.

During the seventies I began to return almost every year to England and sometimes to France and Italy for long visits and the renewal of old friendships. International poetry festivals and the like also enabled me to travel to many other places in the seventies and eighties, including Russia, Japan, Bulgaria, and Australia. I spent a term as a Writer in Residence in Sydney, and some weeks of fruitful solitude in the South Pacific, mainly in Tonga. In 1973 Mitch and I had parted company, and our son was, of course, grown up by then.

While we lived in New York City we had moved from West 15th Street to an apartment in an industrial building on Greenwich Street between Warren and Murray, across from what was then still the fruit and vegetable wholesale market, picturesquely active all night under arc lights and half-deserted by day. A close friend, jazz pianist Race Newton, and his then wife lived in the loft below us, and when Race left for England after his marriage had ended we sublet it for him, first to Galway Kinnell and then to Wendell Berry, who was spending a year at New York University. Race eventually married an Englishwoman and never returned; the round oak table he had had to buy when he originally leased the flat, and around which so many interesting musicians and poets had gathered while it was still downstairs, became ours when Race gave up his tenancy, and is at this moment in my Seattle kitchen, which is also my dining room.

After Mitch's 1968 trial as a co-defendant with Dr. Spock, William Sloane Coffin, Marcus Raskin, and Michael Ferber ("The Boston 5" charged with "conspiring to aid and abet young men to avoid the Draft"), we spent half a year at Berkeley, and on our return to the East Coast moved from New York City to the Boston area, living first in East Boston, then in Brookline. A year before we decided to part we bought a small house in West Somerville, on the edge of North Cambridge. When we divorced this house became mine and the house in Maine his—an arrangement which undoubtedly helped to minimize the bitterness normally involved in a marital breakup. Quite by chance I was offered a job at Tufts when we were moving into Glover Circle; Tufts was in walking distance, and I not only accepted but soon

was given tenure. I taught there for six years. I resigned over a department issue and, after living exclusively on my reading engagements for a year or so, began to teach in the fall term at Brandeis, where I remained for three years, and in the winter quarter at Stanford, where I have gone each January ever since until the present. This annual three-month sojourn in California led to many new friendships, with colleagues and others, not least with some of the gifted poets who have been Stegner Fellows during my years there.

I had grown quite fond of the house in Somerville and expected to live there for the rest of my life (so far as I ever have any such expectation), but in 1988, returning from Europe, the surroundings struck me as unduly unappealing and I realized that I had been feeling increasingly cut off from nature. I resolved to move.

I chose Seattle because of its milder, more English climate and because I believed I could find a house there from which I could walk directly into somewhere beautiful. (I don't drive, so cannot—in the U.S., at least—live anywhere really rural.) I

Levertov with former students at a war protest, San Francisco, 1990

*Seward Park, near Levertov's home in
Seattle, 1993*

was lucky, and quickly found a suitable house close to Lake Washington and to a beautiful park with woodland trails in it. I can see a shoulder of Mount Rainier from an upstairs window. The cross-country *déménagement* was a delightful adventure. Two friends—a professor of English and the twenty-three-year-old son of my friends the Fussiners—drove me and all my belongings across the country in a huge Ryder pantechnicon. I had made the trip often by air and twice by rail but never before by road.

These new surroundings have not resulted in a less busy, more reclusive life, though that had been one of my hopes in making the move; but once again the experience of place has had an effect on my poems. In the four years I have spent here so far, the mountain in particular has seemed an inexhaustible source of inspiration. Moreover, having beautiful places nearby in which to walk has proved to be indeed the resource I longed for, and many pieces of work begin, or problems are solved, peripatetically; I try never to be without pen or pencil and some scrap of paper in my pocket. A

poem may not be directly connected with my immediate surroundings, but strolling by the lakeshore or through quiet woods helps me discover the words nevertheless. So I find, late in my sixties, that I am again living close to a large park, within city limits, yet offering an intimate and nurturing relationship with nature, as did the parks of my childhood; although the sense of connection to history I received in Valentine's and Wanstead is missing here and, as some of my poems tell, the magnetic pull of the Old World remains strong for me despite the impulse that has brought me to dwell on the northwest edge of the New World. A poem called "The Two Magnets," written in Italy just after I had moved to Seattle, probably says as much about who I am as any single poem can say about its author.

The Two Magnets

Where broken gods, faded saints, (powerful in
    antique presence
as old dancers with straight backs, loftily
    confident,
or old men in threadbare wellcut coats) preside
    casually
over the venerable conversations of cypress and
    olive,
there intrudes, like a child interrupting, tugging at
    my mind,
incongruous, persistent,
the image of young salmon in round ponds at the
    hatchery
across an ocean and a continent, circling
with muscular swiftness—tints of green, pink,
    blue,
glowing mysteriously through slate gray, under
    trees
unknown here, whose names I forget because
they were unknown to me too when I was young.

And there on the western edge of America—
    home to me now,
and calling me with this image of something I love,
yet still unknown—I dream of cathedrals,
of the worn stone of human centuries.
Guarded by lions with blunted muzzles
or griffins verdant with moss, gateposts open in me
to effaced avenues.
Part of me lives under nettle-grown foundations.
Part of me wanders west and west, and has
    reached
the edge of the mist where salmon wait the day
when something shall lift them and give them to
    deeper waters.

BIBLIOGRAPHY

Poetry:

The Double Image, Cresset, 1946.

Here and Now, City Lights, 1957.

Overland to the Islands, Jargon, 1958.

Five Poems, White Rabbit, 1958.

With Eyes at the Back of Our Heads, New Directions, 1959.

The Jacob's Ladder, New Directions, 1961.

O Taste and See: New Poems, New Directions, 1964.

City Psalm, Oyez, 1964.

Psalm Concerning the Castle, Perishable Press, 1966.

The Sorrow Dance, New Directions, 1967.

(With Kenneth Rexroth and William Carlos Williams) *Penguin Modern Poets 9,* Penguin, 1967.

(Editor) *Out of the War Shadow: An Anthology of Current Poetry,* War Resisters League, 1967.

A Tree Telling of Orpheus, Black Sparrow Press, 1968.

A Marigold from North Vietnam, Albondocani Press-Ampersand, 1968.

Three Poems, Perishable Press, 1968.

The Cold Spring and Other Poems, New Directions, 1969.

Embroideries, Black Sparrow Press, 1969.

Relearning the Alphabet, New Directions, 1970.

Summer Poems 1969, Oyez, 1970.

A New Year's Garland for My Students, MIT 1969–70, Perishable Press, 1970.

To Stay Alive, New Directions, 1971.

Footprints, New Directions, 1972.

The Freeing of the Dust, New Directions, 1975.

Chekhov on the West Heath, Woolmer/Brotherston, 1977.

Modulations for Solo Voice, Five Trees Press, 1977.

Life in the Forest, New Directions, 1978.

Collected Earlier Poems, 1940–1960, New Directions, 1979.

Pig Dreams: Scenes from the Life of Sylvia, Countryman Press, 1981.

Wanderer's Daysong, Copper Canyon Press, 1981.

Candles in Babylon, New Directions, 1982.

Two Poems, William B. Ewert, 1983.

Poems, 1960–1967, New Directions, 1983.

Oblique Prayers: New Poems with Fourteen Translations from Jean Joubert, New Directions, 1984.

El Salvador: Requiem and Invocation, William B. Ewert, 1984.

The Menaced World, William B. Ewert, 1984.

Selected Poems, Bloodaxe Press, 1986.

Breathing the Water, New Directions, 1987.

Poems, 1968–1972, New Directions, 1987.

(Editor) *The Collected Poems of Beatrice Hawley,* Zoland Books, 1989.

A Door in the Hive, New Directions, 1989.

Evening Train, New Directions, 1992.

Essays:

The Poet in the World, New Directions, 1973.

Light Up the Cave, New Directions, 1981.

New and Selected Essays, New Directions, 1992.

Translations:

(With Edward C. Dimcock, Jr.) *In Praise of the Krishna: Songs from the Bengali,* Doubleday, 1967.

Jules Supervielle, *Selected Writings,* New Directions, 1968.

Eugene Guillevic, *Selected Poems,* New Directions, 1969.

William Meredith, editor, *Poets of Bulgaria,* Unicorn Press, 1985.

Jean Joubert, *Black Iris: Selected Poems,* Copper Canyon Press, 1988.

(With Samuel Beckett and Edouard Roditi) Alain Bosquet, *No Matter No Fact,* New Directions, 1988.

Jean Joubert, *White Owl and Blue Mouse,* Zoland Books, 1990.

Other:

In the Night: A Story (fiction), Albondocani Press, 1968.

Conversation in Moscow, Hovey Street Press, 1973.

Denise Levertov: An Interview, New London Press, 1980.

(Contributor) *The Bloodaxe Book of Contemporary Women Poets,* Bloodaxe Books (Newcastle-upon-Tyne), 1984.

(With Peter Brown) *Seasons of Light,* Rice University Press, 1988.

Guy Murchie
1907-

THE SOUL SCHOOL:
CONFESSIONS OF A PASSENGER ON PLANET EARTH

Foreword

I am a citizen of the twentieth century, perhaps the most turbulent century in human history. I was born in the first, almost Victorian, decade, and I have lived into its last. I have seen the horse-and-buggy age when airplanes were not around, when space and polar regions were still unexplored, when world wars could scarcely be imagined.

Something happened early in this century that had never happened before. Our planet Earth germinated. Like a budding blossom, it opened up with startling speed. Before the century was half over, newly discovered flying became the cheapest and easiest means of long distance travel. Automobiles, leaving the horse behind, took us everywhere easily, indispensably. The invisible atom turned out to contain unbelievable energy that gave us weapons we had not expected nor were mature enough to cope with. We fought two world wars and got into space so fast that in less than ten years our rockets put man on the moon. At the same time scientists discovered that genes are spiral-shaped and began learning how to make them and how to steer evolution. We began to see the necessity of controlling our burgeoning population. Computers were conceived, able to accelerate human thought a billionfold.

I grew up in all this, struggling to comprehend and make the most of it. I managed to make my way through Harvard despite the ubiquitous tin lizzies and beautiful girls. I worked my way around the world alone—drifted a thousand miles down the Yukon, was clapped in irons when stowing away out of Alaska, got arrested as a spy by Japanese police in Nagasaki and by the secret GPU in Siberia. Writing a diary of my adventures, I strove to decide what to do with my life as the Great Depression arrived in the 1930s. It seemed I was destined to become a feature writer for the

*Charcoal portrait of Guy Murchie
by Polly Starr*

Chicago Tribune, directed somewhat by a medium and letters from my mother who had died when I was four. Under the auspices of the *Tribune* in the thirties I learned to fly in an airplane smaller and simpler than the Wright brothers' first craft. I was the *Tribune*'s first war correspondent in World War II and later navigated the great oceans for airlines while writing books like *Song of the Sky, Music of the Spheres* (about stars and atoms), and *The Seven Mysteries of Life* (about life and mind and the meaning of existence on a planet unlike any other yet known.)

On a *Tribune* assignment I discovered Baha'i, a new Persian religion that seemed more reasonable and broad-minded than any other I'd heard of. I married my college roommate's mother, who replaced my own mother. I got some real education while writing for my paper, flying, farming and running an interracial children's camp, then living ten years in Europe, followed by expeditions to Persia and Africa. At thirty-four I married an Irish midwife and refugee from wartime England, followed by a superb illustrator of children's books, later a Prussian refugee from Hitler's Germany, and eventually I wedded a lovely Dutch girl my own age who became my final partner.

I sought and continue to seek an answer to the mysteries of life and death. I am of the ancient race that dwelt in Karnak and Jericho and Cnossus—in Olduvai Gorge and the Dragon's Mountain. My body was shaped in the rivers where vertebrates developed and the lung was born. My apprenticeship was in the trees where I grew my hand. I was once Proconsul, the pre-man. After the uplifting of the continents produced the grassy fields, I learned to stand up and look far and to outthink the lion.

If my honored ancestors once arose from sea to land and into the air, is it not my turn now to move onward beyond air into space? For I am also the creature that learned to weigh stars. I know that any world may die and be born and that my own world shows signs of being the cell of a greater life. I accept as man's normal business: to reach for the sun, to build things reachable out of things unreachable. Yet, before reaching out with my hand, I reach out with my mind—a human mind which can pass through the hottest fire and the blackest space, a mind which has never been taught to shun the moon nor to fear the stars, and which has, for a reason still unknown, been endowed with a swiftness greater than light.

Background of Glamour

I heard a lubb-dup-lubb-dup-lubb-dup sound and felt comfortably warm as if I belonged wherever I was. There was no one to tell me when an odd disquietude began that I was in a womb which was due soon to thrust me outward into a strange, new world I had never known nor imagined. If I had been a twin, sharing the womb with a brother or sister, and had been capable of thinking, I might have noticed a sudden flash of light followed by

the disappearance of my twin. If I'd been capable of speech, I might even have murmured "goodbye" as he seemed to depart into the equivalent of death, somewhere beyond my simple world and into something utterly unknowable. I might have missed the comfort of his nine-month presence. He was gone. He was "dead." But death then was just nothing—something unknowable and undreamable. I took everything for granted and made no choices. I had no alternatives. I knew nothing about worlds that transcend into other worlds and that might give me a hint of life beyond life. I did not really wonder or think at all. I only felt and let happen whatever would happen.

There was a gradual sensation of constriction and pressure which eventually reached a climax when I burst forth into what would turn out to be a bedroom at night. I was born, whatever that was. My little warm, liquid world had exploded into an undreamed dimension. I did not care why or where I was, nor who were those beings hovering and fussing over me. Or the lights. For it all seemed so natural, indeed inevitable, as I gasped and drew my first breath from the invisible atmosphere of a planet I had never heard of but which in time I would learn to cherish.

Long afterward I was told by my aunt May that I was lucky to be born in America with a silver spoon in my mouth, whatever that meant. Mother was the dark-haired lady who seemed to own me. And it was surely good to be owned. For she let me suck at her warm, soft breast. That was about the only thing I knew as I snuggled in my swaddling clothes and breathed and caught a glint of snow out the window.

From an outside perspective I was indeed privileged. Our four-story house was made of red brick like all the other houses around it and like the snow-swept red brick sidewalk before it. It stood in a then-fashionable part of Boston on Mount Vernon Street (No. 62) near the crest of Beacon Hill, just above Louisburg Square, in the heart of what came to be known as Brahmin territory. Occasionally I heard a jingling sound, far off—sleighs, as I was to learn—and the twittering of sparrows. It was Friday, the 25th of January, 1907, the dead of winter in the time before they plowed snow. The elms and roofs outside were blanketed in white, as was my infant world.

But I could not yet know about the burgeoning world beyond where, that very morning, at a remote strand known as Ormond Beach in a faraway balmy region called Florida, a man named Frank Marriott drove his Stanley Steamer one hundred and fifty miles an hour to set a new world speed record. The old record, made in a locomotive, had been pushed upward by thirty miles per hour in one blow and would not be raised again for a whole decade. And then only by a flying machine, a fabulous and improbable man-made contrivance designed to fight in the skies of a world war no one thought could ever happen. It was all part of a great germination process the planet Earth, my world, was going through, affecting not only the speed of transportation, but of communication, exploration, liberation, the spread of knowledge, and other things I would someday learn and ponder and write books about. But my part in the germination would have to wait and wait. It would take time, seemingly endless time, and then more time—a quantity still unknown to me on the first day of my life.

My mother had a nursemaid helper, a woman called "Googoo" (for Gertrude). And I soon discovered I had a big brother, usually referred to as "No no," who was rarely allowed to touch me. Later it turned out that his real name was Donald and he was not as dangerous as he seemed at one year old. I was to learn in the distant future that Donald was my mother's maiden name, for she had been born Agnes Donald, the only daughter of the late rector of Trinity Church, Dr. E. (for Elijah) Winchester Donald, who had been called to that exalted station on the death of his illustrious predecessor, Phillips Brooks, in 1893. Brooks had been a bishop, a renowned preacher and author of the charming Christmas carol "O Little Town of Bethlehem."

Everyone said that Mother was an unusually warm and sympathetic soul. And she had lovely dark skin with glowing cheeks. She was also full of energy and high spirits, and loved to ride horses, climb mountains, and walk twenty miles while pushing a baby buggy.

One of her early beaux, twenty-five years after it happened, told my younger sister that one day, during a hike in the country, he and Agnes came to a river which they wanted to cross. There was no bridge but fortunately no people around as well, so they quickly took off their clothes and, holding them aloft in one hand, swam across, then redressed and walked on.

My father was almost as energetic as Mother, and hardly less ambitious. His name was Guy and he got to know Agnes best on mountain trails. He had been born in the little town of Calais, Maine, on the Canadian border, where his father, William Andrew Murchie, ran a lumber business.

Father was a glamour boy, if one is to believe a Boston debutante who described him half a century later. His eyes were blue, his hair a sandy gold, and he sat tall on a horse. Unlike his younger brother and two sisters, he was considered promising enough to induce his father to send him to a large private prep school: Exeter in New Hampshire. From there he went to Harvard where he was chosen captain of the freshman football team, a success that soon got him talked about and into exclusive Boston and Cambridge society.

He caught the eye of a thirty-year-old Spanish poet and philosopher named George Santayana, who liked to go on long country walks with attractive Harvard boys. Early in the summer of 1894, when Father had just completed his junior year, he went on a month-long jaunt through England with Santayana and John Francis Russell, Bertrand's older brother, known as Frank. The following summer Santayana and Father took a "short walking trip" (about one hundred and fifty miles) through eastern France and developed such a warm relationship that the poet began sending him sonnets, including one penned specially for him as a graduation gift. It began: "To Guy Murchie. No flower I bring you but the scentless weed / That in my youth's deserted garden grew / Wherein no zephyr of soft passion blew / Nor gust of anger bent the barren reed . . ."

By 1896 my father, now graduated, was courting a tall Boston debutante named Katharine Dexter. But Santayana wrote him a long, fatherly, and cautioning letter on March 12, saying " . . . I think marriage for you extremely risky. You have not the gift of being easily happy or of making others so. You are inconsequential, and the more one loves you the more one must suffer from such vacillations of your sympathy. . . . It is hard for a young man like you to distinguish the charm of a particular woman from that of women in general, to distinguish affinity from proximity."

Urging him to await "a man's love, which is a better and safer thing than a boy's," Santayana went on to say that that kind of love is "what I feel for you, dear Guy, who are a great deal more to me than any of my friends could be when I was a young fellow, and could not really know either myself or other men. There is resolution in this sort of love . . ."

Luckily for me, Father heeded Santayana's advice and did not marry Katharine Dexter. Instead she married Stanley McCormick of the McCormick reaper family in Chicago who, to her dismay, soon went insane. However, now controlling his great fortune, she engaged a chamber ensemble to play his favorite music to him as long as he lived and became an important philanthropist in her own right. Besides music and education, her principal beneficiaries were her friend Margaret Sanger, and the emerging birth control movement, in particular (many decades later) the inventors of "the pill."

Somewhere Father also met Theodore Roosevelt, fifteen years his senior, and when the Spanish-American War broke out in 1898, he corralled a contingent of his more exuberant Harvard friends and they enlisted in the Rough Riders. On short notice, they embarked to fight Spaniards in Cuba. Roosevelt admired him and wrote in his book, *The Rough Riders* (1899), that "Murchie of Maine . . . saw all the fighting and did his duty with the utmost gallantry."

When Father began practicing law, one of his first clients was the renowned American novelist Winston Churchill. Father had just introduced the Churchills to Roosevelt, now vice president of the United States, and was visiting them in Cornish, New Hampshire, when President McKinley was shot by an assassin in Buffalo on September 6, 1901. The very next day Roosevelt wrote a letter to Father, without even mentioning McKinley who had been taken to a hospital in critical condition. In it he said:

> Dear Guy,
>
> I have just received your letter of August 27th, and it really touched me. Of course you can do me good, and exactly along the lines indicated. My judgment, however, would be that we had better wait a little while before beginning active operations. I will talk it all over with you when, in accordance with your promise, you pass that night at my home.
>
> What trumps the Churchills are. I was so glad to meet them.
>
> Ever yours,
> Theodore Roosevelt

I have no idea what "active operations" T.R. referred to, but he is reported to have gone moose hunting in the Adirondacks the next day and, when McKinley finally died on September 14, he was nowhere in sight. Some say they practically had to beat the bushes, calling "Hey, Teddy, come out o'there. You're president of the United States."

In any case, some five years later during Roosevelt's second term, by when I had put in my own appearance and after Father had been pleading with him for about a year to honor the whole family by becoming his son's godfather, the president finally agreed to do it. It was 1907. He was coming to Boston for one day during the third week in February and would be on a tight schedule. He would be leaving the Riverside Press in Cambridge at ten thirty. "From there," he wrote, "we could go instantly to your house for the christening. Could we get away from it at a quarter to eleven?" It was a good two miles from the Riverside Press, across the pepperpot Longfellow Bridge and up the steep hill to our house. If his cab horse could keep to a lively trot for ten minutes, including the climb, hopefully there would be five minutes for the ceremony.

The victor of San Juan Hill was game. With Colonel Leonard Wood he had routed the Spaniards from Cuba in a few hours. This, by comparison, should be a cinch.

As the clatter of hoofs stopped at No. 62, everything was ready. Donald and I were suitably ensconced and waiting in the second floor parlor with Father and Mother. Bishop Lawrence of Massachusetts presided. As T.R. charged up the stairs, followed by Captain Frank McCoy, his White House aide, the fifty invited guests cheered and hands were shaken all around. The bishop wasted no time as the president of the United States became my brother's godfather and Captain McCoy (substituting for Leonard Wood, then governor general of the Philippine Islands) mine. And whom did I get for a godmother but Katharine Dexter McCormick (and her mother for Donald)? A congruous arrangement.

Altogether it was an almost mystical welcoming ceremony into the world to have the head of state of a great nation get down on his knees before a three-week-old baby and brother to "renounce the Devil and all his works" as part of the Episcopal service. Yet it really happened and in ten minutes the president was gone.

It wasn't long after this that Father hosted a party at the exclusive Tavern Club (of which he was a member) in downtown Boston for his friend Winston Churchill on the occasion of an early visit to America of W.C.'s younger namesake from England, then still unknown in America, who wanted to meet his American cousin. And I've been told that it was on this occasion that the English Winston agreed to use his middle name of Spencer in future so he would not in any way dilute or endanger the growing reputation of his eminent cousin. Which is why the great future prime minister of England, who was to stand firm against the menace of Hitler in World War II, always signed himself Winston S. Churchill. He thus proved a man of his word. And, incidentally, his faithful adoption of the initials W.S.C. helped him disassociate himself from the unavoidably ubiquitous facilities that by then were proclaiming themselves in every hotel and public place in Europe as simply the W.C.

Growing Up

It was June 1907 when Father moved his growing family from Boston to Ipswich, an attractive coastal town some twenty-five miles to the north, near Cape Ann. From there he could easily commute by train to his office while Mother kept house in the farm home he had bought beside the salt marshes, with big trees and a long driveway, a congenial and restful spot. She was not greatly burdened with work here because Gran, her mother, lived in a very old house close by and there were plenty of servants. Almost every family had servants in those days. At wages of three to five dollars a week and keep, why not? So Mother had leisure to go riding or hiking when she wanted to, and I can remember her appearing in her riding habit at teatime. In summer she often wore straw hats and mannish clothes with neckties, and she even smoked cigarettes and drank cocktails. Some described her as rather wild.

The farm included cows, pigs, and chickens, besides a horse or two needed for going to town. When they took us boys in the carriage, I recall they put each of us into a sack drawn tight at the neck with our hands inside so we couldn't get into much mischief. One brown horse responded to the name of Worgz. I think he was a veteran of the Rough Riders. But Donald and I ran loose at home and got into a peck of trouble. We wore rompers and so, quite naturally, romped. I remember eating soggy toast out of the garbage pile, and when I was two and a half, following Donald, I tried to jump across a sewage ditch leading to a marsh but fell in and caught typhoid fever. I recall lying in bed in the attic bedroom for weeks, playing with a toy steamroller. We had a baby sister by then, whom we called "Titi." Her real name was Agnes.

I guess I was happy most of the time despite more than normal unpleasantness in what might be called toilet training. At times Googoo seemed outright cruel, switching me for wetting my bed or

pants in a way that made me fear going to the bathroom, which of course led to more "accidents" and worse switchings. I don't know whether Mother ever knew about it, but it became a bitter ordeal for me until I was old enough to understand what the bathroom was really for.

By then the beginning of a conscience seemed to be budding in me, something I first became aware of after I made the exciting discovery of the sugar bowl full of delicious white lumps of sugar standing on the tea table within easy reach. I would creep into the dining room when no one was around and swipe a lump, then take it outdoors to suck in secret joy. The sugar lasted me for what seemed hours. At the least, each lump lasted so long that it never occurred to me to take more than one at a time. But one day, running around the house with a fresh sugar lump in hand, whom should I meet at a corner but old Gran? She started to speak to me, not suspecting anything, but I turned in a panic and ran in the opposite direction, out of sight around the back of the house. I was sure I'd be in for a whipping or worse if she found me out, and my conscience was throbbing like a dagger in my heart. Where could I hide the evidence? I instantly dug a hole and buried the lump, vaguely intending, like a dog, to return someday and recover it. And Gran, though puzzled by my unexplained retreat, never found out.

Dr. Tucker, the Ipswich physician who attended the delivery of my sister Agnes in May 1908, did not manage to get to our house in February 1910 when a new baby was coming at the same moment as a raging snowstorm. I guess he didn't consider it that much of an emergency. So Father himself, with Googoo for midwife, helped my second sister, Janet, into the world.

That also was the year when the famous Halley's Comet appeared, and I can just remember the starry summer night when we were all brought outdoors to see it, a "star" with a funny tail. But exactly what it was doing up there in the sky, nobody seemed to know. Which reminds me that on the comet's earlier appearance in 1835, Mark Twain was born. And when he saw it in 1910 he reportedly said, "That's *my* comet. This is where I came in." And he died the next night.

By the same reasoning, Halley's Comet this time around was *my* comet (almost) and when it came back again in 1986, it provided more than a hint that I'd about used up my term.

Father and Mother of course had plenty of guests in those days even out in far Ipswich, but

Guy in Boston, about 1920

the guests were more often artists than philosophers; some of them asked to paint Mother's portrait, and did. Santayana never came, evidently because he got disillusioned with Father after Father took up with swashbuckling types like Teddy Roosevelt and tooted off to war. So far as I know, he did not communicate with Father at all after that. Other philosophers around Harvard, moreover, like old William James, knew Father but evidently never exactly warmed up to him. Speaking of war, however, these spirited personages were not quite above battling each other when an opportunity arose. Rumor has it that there was a memorable spat between Santayana and James that actually blossomed into a snowball fight just before the turn of the century. According to the *New Yorker,* which wrote it up eighty years later, after Santayana "made an ill-natured crack about James' 'Swedenborgian connection,' James responded by suggesting that Santayana had fallen in love with another dead hypothesis." Then one snowy night, James spotted Santayana in the street and "on impulse, scooped up a handful of wet snow,

compacted it, and sent a looper that splattered on the back of Santayana's neck. The ensuing battle lasted thirty minutes, with no clear victor."

By the summer of 1911 things appeared to be going auspiciously for the Murchie family of six. And Mother, having had four children in a little over four years, was expecting a fifth. But, without warning, disaster struck. I don't know whether she overdid on some athletic venture or what, but in the middle of August Mother came down with a fever and, feeling very weak, took to her bed. Dr. Tucker said it was pneumonia, a truly deadly ailment in those days before sulphur drugs or penicillin. When the crisis came, Father sat up all night nursing her, feeding her hot lemonade and whatever medicine the doctor ordered, but her lungs had filled and, at dawn, she stopped breathing. He was stunned and found it almost impossible to believe that such a vital life had so suddenly been snuffed out at the age of twenty-eight. No one had the heart to tell us children about it. All Googoo would say was that "Mother has gone away, far away on a long journey."

But things soon happened that had never happened to us before. Father inexplicably decided to move back to Boston. Donald was five and I four, "old enough for school," he said. He employed a highly recommended nurse or governess to mother us and the girls. Her name was Abbie May Burt, and she came from Vermont, of Irish extraction. I don't know why but we called her "Ahyou" and, though she was strict, we knew she loved us and we soon learned to love her in return.

Our new home was at 46 Mount Vernon Street, just a few doors uphill from old No. 62 where someone else now lived. There were four stories and a basement with kitchen and laundry in traditional upstairs-downstairs fashion, with dumbwaiter to the pantry, coal bin below, and attic under the mansard roof made of slate. At sundown the lamplighter walked up the street carrying his short ladder which he used for climbing each lamppost and lighting the gas street lamps, one by one. Pigeons and English sparrows inhabited near by trees and gutters, and squirrels were frequent visitors. Occasionally we saw or heard an owl.

Every weekday morning at eight o'clock, Donald and I walked a quarter mile to school on Beacon Street. We were both in the first grade. At recess we played on Boston Common. It was really a girls' school but they stretched the rules enough to accept little boys in the first few grades. The lady teachers were competent and had no difficulty in teaching us to read and write. I clearly remem-

ber my first sentence: "Run to the tree with me."
It was a fairly painless process.

At home Ahyou got us into a daily routine: up
at seven, breakfast at seven thirty, then off to
school at eight. We got home again about noon;
then, after lunch and an hour's nap which seemed
interminable, we went out with Ahyou for the
afternoon, usually to some place like the Common,
the Public Gardens, or the Esplanade, where we
could roller-skate along the Charles. Donald and I
often made believe we were animals, usually of
some species he had heard or dreamed of. My
usual question after naptime was "What'll we be
today?" One day he chose "water hens" and, as
usual, he was the male bird and had most of the
excitement of crowing, wing flapping, and flying
about while I was relegated to the "nest" to lay
eggs and sit for long hours "hatching" them. I
think that's how I learned patience.

After supper, we often had homework to do,
then bedtime was drawing near. Of course there
was no radio or television in those days, but Ahyou
often read us a story, typically about animals or
Indians. Then Father would show up and usually
would play with us, crawling on all fours as we
rode his back across the nursery floor. He called it
an elephant ride. Then it was prayers, perhaps a
psalm read by Father and ending with "Our
Father Who art in Heaven . . ." as we knelt with
palms together. So to bed.

We always got dressed and undressed in the
same room with the girls when we were little, and I
noticed they were made rather differently from us
boys. But I was too shy to ask why. It was just one
of the mysteries of life, like why was God always
invisible? Or why did Mother go away and never
come back? Only gradually did we get to understand that she had died and must now be in some
hard-to-visualize place called Heaven. It seemed
unfair, and I wondered why God let it happen?
Would we too have to die someday? Although
Ahyou said "yes" to that one, we were not very
happy about it and many of our questions had no
answers at all. Does the sky and space end somewhere? And, if it does, what is beyond that end? I
got the feeling that such questions are not really
meant to be asked, at least not by humans in the
world we are in now. Even Father did not offer any
real solutions, and he said we had best just do
whatever we are supposed to each day and not
worry about the sky or space or next year.

Something terrible happened in the spring of
1912 way out in the ocean. A brand new and
wonderful ship named *Titanic* hit an iceberg and

sank—and more than a thousand people drowned.
It was hard to imagine it, but our Auntie Hunter,
an old friend of Mother's who lived alone at
Squam Lake, New Hampshire, told us she was
once on a ship that sank at sea and she was sucked
down with the ship—way down deep, she said—
but she was a strong swimmer and swam and swam
upward until finally she came to the surface and
was saved. Auntie Hunter never got married and
always seemed unusually tough. People said that
when she was about fifteen, her parents offered
her a choice between dancing lessons and boxing
lessons and she chose boxing lessons. Maybe that's
what scared off the boys.

In June 1912 Father took us on the train
down to West Barnstable on Cape Cod, where we
got into an open flivver called a jitney and drove to
Cotuit on the south side of the Cape. I think it was
almost the first automobile I had ever seen, and
quite a thrill for us all. There were seven or eight
of us: Father, Ahyou, and Nellie, the cook, besides
us four kids, and maybe Zeta, Nellie's younger
sister. I think the jitney cost only a nickel apiece,
but Father probably gave the driver a tip for the
extra miles.

The cottage he had rented was just right for
us. There were kerosene lamps to read by at night,
a woodstove in the kitchen, and a windmill to
pump the water up to a tank on a tower. Electricity
had not come to that area yet. Neither had the
telephone, but we got one the following summer,
the kind with a crank to make the bell ring. Father
would call a number and say, "Hello, Fanny. Is
that you?" We kids thought that was hilarious. He
was talking with Fanny Howe, wife of Mark
deWolfe Howe, the well-known man of letters who
lived on Brimmer Street in Boston and owned a
summer place in Cotuit.

Every morning Ahyou took us to the beach,
which was close by, down a long flight of wooden
steps. There we saw a new world of amazing
creatures, from dainty fiddler crabs and jellyfish to
big bluefish and occasionally a small shark. We also
learned to swim, at first with the aid of inflatable
rubber collars around our necks to keep our heads
from going under. But in a week or two Donald
and I could swim confidently and no longer
needed our rubber collars. And we were given a
ten-foot catboat and learned to sail it. Before the
summer was over, we even won a sailing race
around Dead Neck Island in the harbor, managing
to drag our little craft across a mud flat to shorten
the course. The prize was a pirate flag displaying a

skull over crossed bones, which we proudly attached to the top of our twelve-foot mast.

We continued going to Cotuit every summer for the next four years and Father saw to it that we were given special training in everything from carpentry to making blueprints of flowers and painting them in their true colors. We also were provided with bicycles and learned to ride them. And Father tried to inspire us to take a cold bath every morning on arising, as he did (inspired, in turn, by Teddy Roosevelt), but when he was not around, the inspiration soon eroded. At the same time, I still had not completely licked my bed-wetting problem and Ahyou was trying hard to bring me under control, threatening me with everything from a "good horsewhipping" to dressing me like a girl. Naturally the threats did little good because the occasional wetting was not voluntary, at least no more so than other dream actions are. I did not much mind wearing a dress either, though my short hair and narrow hips made me into a very dubious-looking "girl." (Why should Ahyou think it shameful to be female anyway? I suppose she just assumed I'd be ashamed. Women's "lib" was unheard of then. Women did not even win their right to vote until 1920. But they were important in our lives and not least in keeping us in touch with history; I remember one "old" lady who vividly described to me her remembrance as a child of sitting in Abraham Lincoln's lap in the White House.)

All sorts of surprises popped into our lives, some really devastating, like the time a doctor and assistant suddenly appeared at 46 Mount Vernon to extract our tonsils and adenoids, whatever those were. The worst of it was the ether, administered right in our own nursery by having a rubber cup clapped over one's nose and mouth while the doctor's impersonal voice intoned "now breathe deeply." It was like being smothered to death.

Christmas, on the other hand, was a pure delight even after we began to suspect that the true story about fat old Santa Claus coming down the chimney was kid stuff. The one thing that Donald and I wanted most for Christmas was a gun but Father knew better and neither of us ever got one. Instead we usually were given more constructive things like an Erector set, a paint box, or a book. In return we were induced to make presents to give to the aunts and uncles who habitually gave to us things like a set of twelve place cards with a different bird or animal painted on each.

Birthdays were also special days and on them, after supper, Father would produce the "grab bag" into which each of us was allowed to reach deep and grope for one of the mysterious wrapped presents he always kept for such occasions. And the Fourth of July was even more exciting, with lots of firecrackers and occasionally a wanton deed like throwing a lighted firecracker into some strange house through an open window. And nice questions arose such as whether a boy were admirably brave or just stupidly dumb if he held a firecracker between his teeth, lit the fuse, and waited without flinching for it to explode. At Halloween we had different temptations for devilment like cutting clotheslines and starting fires in rubbish barrels in dark alleys but, to tell the truth, such pranks were much more talked about than done.

In 1915 another huge ocean liner, named *Lusitania,* was sunk at sea, drowning more than a thousand men, women, and children. This time, to make matters worse, the deed was reportedly done on purpose by a submarine in which "bad" people called Germans fired something called a torpedo. It was all part of a terrible world war being fought in faraway Europe which affected us mainly in that we learned to knit and made scarves and mufflers to help the shivering Belgian refugees.

Another year (I think it was 1916) Father took Donald and me "out West" to see his "gold mine" in southern Colorado, in which he and Uncle Walter had bought stock. We went in style on the famous "Twentieth Century Limited," the super train that, at full speed, scooped up water for its steam supply from a long trough between the rails. In Chicago we stayed overnight at the Blackstone Hotel, then it was across the great prairies to the Rocky Mountains and south into sagebrush country where rattlesnakes and prairie dogs lived and where a narrow-gauge local train took us to the mine and a nearby ranch. Learning to ride and throw a lasso were new to us, but we reveled in it for nearly a week.

In the summer of 1917, instead of returning to Cotuit, Father sent all four of us to a children's camp in Eliot, Maine, called Camp Lanier. It had been founded by the son of Sidney Lanier, the poet, on his property on the north shore of the Piscataqua River, which separates New Hampshire from Maine. Ahyou got a job there too, in maintenance, as part of the deal. The girls' camp was located only about a hundred yards from the boys' camp, and we all ate together in one dining hall. I was in a group of boys known as the Buckskins and, after a few weeks, I began to hear some of the boys in my cabin mentioning the name of a particular girl or other as "my girl." Not "having" a girl myself, I felt I was missing out on something—I wasn't sure just what—and determined I had better do something about it.

So the next day, while on the way to the dining hall for lunch, as I happened to overtake a nice-looking girl (nice-looking from behind at least), I got up enough nerve to ask her, "Will you be my girl?" I didn't know her name or anything about her, and I hardly expected her to be receptive. But, to my delight, she said, "Yes." And she was "my girl" from then on for many years.

Her name was Maria and we both took violin lessons that summer and I wrote to her and got letters back. They were the first letters I ever wrote to anyone (with the possible exception of my immediate family) and took much mental effort. I could barely manage one or two a year and they came out very stilted: "Dear Maria, I am at the Country Day School and am having quite a good time. We played football this afternoon. Do you still take violin lessons? . . ."

Donald did much better in school than I did. Not only did he get better marks but he had a strong sense of drama and wrote exciting stories for the school magazine and even a play, which we acted out at home for an invited audience. He also painted pictures and played the piano. He was popular, too, and I was impressed. I tried to write and paint and was given a few lessons in charcoal drawing at the Museum of Fine Arts but couldn't seem to catch up with Donald in anything or really compete with him except that, by the time I was eleven, I was an inch taller than he. I looked for other ways to express my individuality. People said I was "stubborn" and none too bright. I was made to repeat a year in school. My front upper teeth stuck out even when my mouth was shut, so I had to wear braces to correct it. And I was given elocution tutoring so I might overcome a stammer and speak more distinctly. Sometimes I heard a ringing in my ears, felt faint, and thought I was going to die.

I was getting to be what psychologists might have called an introvert. But, in reality, we never knew of any psychologists, for the new "science" of psychology had just been introduced to the world by the likes of William James and Sigmund Freud and struck Father's conservative mind as rather too weird for any normal people to bother about. It was 1919 then. The Great War in Europe had fortunately ended and Father began to look around for a boarding school to send us boys to— someplace where we would get "proper discipline"

and where even my stubbornness would hopefully diminish.

Boarding School
1919–1925

Upon enrollment in September 1919 in a small boys' school in Brookfield Center, Connecticut, the elderly headmaster, Mr. Curtis, gave each boy a number (I became "number three"). He also assigned each of us a bowl-shaped boulder and a hammer for pounding stones into gravel on a small hill in back of the main building. It was the Curtis method for dealing with any infraction of the rules, such as slamming one's desk lid, whispering in study hall, or dropping a book. This plus corporal punishment.

Once, during a pillow fight, I hid behind a door and bonked someone entering who, to my horror, turned out to be the headmaster's son and assistant, "Mr. Gerald" as we called him. Surprisingly I received no strapping but instead was condemned to sleep all night curled up on a chopping block in the cellar—which gave me plenty of time to meditate on my crime.

This may sound like a penitentiary, but it really wasn't all that bad—more like a quaint carryover from Dickensian times. I was there two years and only got a strapping twice. Mr. Curtis was usually warm and approachable. I remember when one boy asked him what was the most beautiful thing in the world, and he surprised everyone by replying, "A nude woman." Nudes weren't around much in 1920 and I had no idea what the old man was talking about. His positive response to feminine nudity, however, enhanced my sense of the mystery and wonder of the adult world.

At the age of thirteen puberty had not quite arrived and, like the others, I was hazy as to the famous "facts of life." Sure, we all had observed that babies grew inside their mothers—nothing very exciting about that—but few of us had got around to wondering how the babies got there or got out, and even fewer had thought to speculate upon what fathers had to do with it. Once a year, Mr. Curtis would give a talk to the older boys about relations between men and women but it was all up-in-the-clouds stuff about the sacredness of marriage and the need for chivalry.

It was not until a rather rough farm boy named Griff, who spoke out of the corner of his mouth, explained things one afternoon while we were busy pounding rocks on the pounding hill that my eyes were opened. "You've got something that sticks out," he said, pointing to my groin. "And girls have something that goes in. I mean a hole. So the man just puts his thing down her hole, and that makes the baby." Very simple. I assumed he did it only when he wanted her to have a baby. None of us imagined he might have another reason.

One of the boys, however, had heard that married men and their wives spent a lot of time in bed together, and he thought it must take many hours or days to make the proper connection to produce a baby. "I guess it's sort of an operation," he surmised. "Someone has to bring them their meals during that time so they won't starve . . ." It sounded complicated and appropriately mysterious. Presumably that was what "breakfast in bed" was all about—another of the wonders of the coming adult world.

Remember that the Victorian Age had only recently ended and the "facts of life" were rarely talked about. My first wife, who grew up in that age, later told me that she was six months pregnant before she learned what part of her body her baby would come out of.

Something else of a not-unrelated character happened suddenly one spring day in 1920. A nice lady arrived in her Rolls-Royce and said she wanted to meet Donald and me, because she was going to marry Father. We were surprised but accepted her announcement at face value and were delighted when she invited us to take a ride in her elegant car. She said we could call her "Aunt Jane" and we sat with her in the backseat as James, her chauffeur, drove along country roads. We had never ridden in a car like this before and when Donald asked how fast it could go, Aunt Jane replied, "Very fast" and instructed James to "step on it and show the boys what speed is like." Without hesitation James put his foot down and the big car leapt forward, swooping down the dales and over the hills. The road was not paved or well graded so sixty miles an hour was hair-raising. Donald and I tried to stay in our seats, and chickens and ducks barely fluttered out of our way as we whooshed by, leaving clouds of dust.

Aunt Jane also gave Donald and me impressive presents of model airplanes we could assemble and fly. She was obviously determined to make a hit with us, and she succeeded. We didn't notice it at the time but, as we grew older, we began to realize that showing an interest in his children had been a sure way to please the "old man" (as we had

come to call him). He married Jane a couple of months later and presumably thereby got substantial help in paying school bills, for her maiden name was Eaton and she was rich. But she avoided mothering us by retreating during our school vacations to a house she owned in Cohasset, even though Father had bought an old house in Dedham which he said would be the future home for our whole family.

Father said our new home had been built in 1660 and its beams were plainly put together with wooden pegs. He named it "Highland Mary" and surmised that at one time it had been a tavern on the post road from Boston to Providence. Its large central chimney made of red bricks included three fireplaces, each in a different room, and the one in our living room (originally the kitchen) had a crane and Dutch oven. Most interesting to Donald and me was the fact that the fireplaces did not fit together, so there had to be an odd-shaped space between or behind them, which was not visible from any room. We explored the many cupboards and closets, including those upstairs, and finally, by some judicious deduction and prying out of boards in the back of an upper closet, discovered an empty place we called "the secret passage." To our delight, we learned to worm our way through it and down to the hidden hollow chamber between the fireplaces. We imagined that in the Indian days when the house was built this passage must have been a place of last resort where the white settlers could hide from the "savages" and perhaps hold onto their last precious chance to avoid being scalped.

In any case, it was an exciting thought and added immeasurably to our appreciation of our part-time home. We even shared the secret with our closest friend and neighbor, Nancy Hale, an only child about Agnes's age, who lived across the road. Her father, Philip Hale, was the son of Edward Everett Hale, the famous clergyman and author whose statue stands in the Boston Public Garden. Philip Hale taught art in Boston, including among his students Polly Starr who, half a century later, sketched my portrait, which opens this essay. As for Nancy Hale, it was she who became a well-known writer, starting her career as the first "girl reporter" on the *New York Times* and later writing satirical accounts of her childhood for the *New Yorker,* followed by several novels. Having no brothers or sisters of her own, she naturally became a virtual member of our family and in 1972 published a small novel titled *Secrets* about us, and especially our secret passage. The jacket of this book featured a charcoal drawing of Highland Mary during a snowfall as viewed by Nancy's artist mother from her living-room window, a hauntingly sensitive work with snowy elms.

In 1921 Father entered me in a Connecticut prep school called Kent for the fall term. I was impressed with Kent School, which appeared very imposing after Curtis School with lots of big sophisticated-looking boys around. I tried not to admit to myself that it was scary. The headmaster was the renowned Father Sill, who wore white robes with a black wooden cross around his neck. I must have been in a state of nervous tension because when he put his arm around me in a fatherly gesture, I burst into tears. It surprised me as much as it did him, but he accepted me in the school. He said he knew I would grow up to be a big man because my hands were big.

At first I felt rather out of place at Kent, and not just because my bed was so far back under the sloping eaves that I had no room to stand up near it. I made a few friends, but felt awkward with most of the boys, some of whom took to calling me "urch Murch" in a less than sympathetic tone. I

The caption to this newspaper photo reads: "A Tribune correspondent makes a rescue—Guy Murchie, himself injured, carrying a hotel receptionist from the wreckage of the bombed building in Dover," England, 1940

got to be almost six feet tall but weighed scarcely a hundred pounds, and so was almost pathetically skinny and lacking in confidence. I don't know why I got homesick because my motherless home didn't offer a very loving atmosphere. (Ahyou was no longer there.) But I felt terribly lonely at Kent that autumn, profoundly rejected, and I had no idea whether I could ever pull out of it.

Attending chapel was compulsory and I discovered I got some comfort from the singing of hymns. But one or two tough-minded boys rebelled on the ground that God was a hoax and the Episcopalian service nothing but a "superstitious farce." A sixth former named Jim Cozzens even convinced himself with "infallible logic" that Christ had no leg left to stand on and went to Father Sill to have it out with him, which he was vain enough to presume would redound to his credit. All that is known of the meeting is that the headmaster was heard to bellow, "Get out of my study, you dirty, stinking little coward," while Cozzens backed down the stairs protesting, "But sir, this is most unfair. . . . But sir . . ."

Father Sill was inclined to blow up like that at times and had no compunction about using strong language. Almost every month, or whenever he suspected something amiss, he would without warning work himself up and go "on the rampage" as we called it. It was a frightening performance, especially for those who chanced to cross his path or in any way became victims of his wrath. Only occasionally did his temper backfire on him. The time I remember best was one evening when he got the notion that the school was becoming seriously depraved and started barging into the boys' rooms, looking for sexy pin-up pictures that he regarded as proof positive the owner was going down the drain. Like a bull seeing red, he yanked picture after picture off the walls but after he had thrown on the floor one particular photograph of a beautiful girl with a revealing neckline, stamping it in his righteous rage, he noticed that the boy in whose room it had hung was in tears and inconsolable. Only several minutes later did the truth come out when the boy sobbed, "That was my mother."

I don't mean to give the impression that Father Sill really ever made a fool of himself as a fanatic, for he was widely respected, wore his robes with religious dignity, and fearlessly dealt with all his problems from financing and building a run-down farm into a first-class modern school to coaching a champion eight-oared crew on a flooded windswept river. He had both warmth and humor for nearly every occasion. He was one of a kind.

Come spring I decided to build myself a hideaway. My impulse was mostly subconscious or close to the animal level. I had vague fears and no reliable friends. Clearly I could not count on Father Sill to rescue me from bullies—he was capable of being a bully himself—and I was being picked on by many of the older boys in the thoughtless and heartless ways typical of teenagers. Although I could not articulate it even to myself, it got so bad that the urgency of finding a place of refuge dominated my thoughts. I craved the kind of ultimate retreat in which—if things got worse (as I expected they would)—I could hole up until the crisis blew over. The kind of solitary retreat to a log in the woods as done by the arrogant Jim Cozzens was not for me. (He enjoyed hating Father Sill and used his escapes to write. One of his essays was even published by the *Atlantic Monthly* while he was still in school. Thus began the memorable career of James Gould Cozzens, who in time became a legend, a brilliant novelist, and winner of the prestigious Pulitzer Prize.)

As for me, I was actually digging a cave—all by myself. Other boys were making huts in the woods, usually two or three friends together, and I had a momentary leaning in that direction. But a hut is conspicuous. I needed seclusion, and I was not social. Going underground like a fox or a woodchuck was the obvious answer. Finding a shovel and other materials was easy, and I came upon an ideal spot in a field half a mile downstream from school where the river bends eastward. There was an old rubbish heap there, and nobody around. Nothing to attract attention. There I dug out my cave under the rubbish, which I moved aside temporarily to roof it over with boards, covering the boards with dirt, then dumping the rubbish on top again, spread out to look "natural."

It took me only a couple of afternoons to dig out the main room of the cave: about ten-by-six feet and six feet deep. Next I dug a tunnel as an entrance way, about forty feet long with three right-angled turns in it, but only two feet wide and three deep. For a door I dragged over the crumpled side of a junked car from the dump and placed it in such a way that I could open up its rusty door and step down a three-rung wooden ladder into the passage, then crawl to the main room of the cave. I also built myself a fireplace inside the cave, using bricks and mortar from the new infirmary then being built at school (I waited

until the workmen had quit for the day and found it surprisingly easy to load and take off with a wheelbarrow full of bricks). Then I found an old window sash with six panes and used it to make a skylight so my cave was illumined (at least by day). I carefully concealed both the skylight and my chimney with judiciously piled junk and, when I had my fire burning, I found it cozy and warm down there while I relied on the top appearing no more suspicious than any other old smoldering rubbish heap.

I kept supplies of food and fuel in my cave, two candles, matches, a few books, and even an old mattress and blankets. I must admit it got pretty swampy there after substantial rain, but I wasn't one to worry over petty details like mildew or the drainage problem. More important, it was there that I started my writing career by writing a story in a notebook about a voyage to Mars. I was inspired by Percival Lowell's descriptions of what he perceived as the canals of Mars. I illustrated it and included such exotic details as a sophisticated language for the Martians: "Urga vodar kitshkeen, batoolshvo hlevchinkof voodetreentrish, horromchetavuilt mnosgraznov zenzovneestvui kakaburroj mugozmi schloognit . . ." The Martian language went on and on like this and became an unearthly creation that, I prided myself, was in no danger of ever being understood by anyone on Earth but me.

Remarkably enough, the cave remained my sole secret for more than a year until one day in 1923 I heard two boys from the school walking nearby in the field while I crouched apprehensively inside. I could plainly hear them talking and expressing their curiosity about some fresh footprints they noticed going toward my entrance. Then, to my horror, one of them opened the old car door and saw my ladder and the passage. Of course they were instantly excited with this discovery of what they speculated might be a "bootlegger's den" or worse. Soon one of them got up enough nerve to climb down the ladder and start crawling toward the inner cave. By then I had put out my candle and was waiting in the semidarkness, my mind going at top speed trying to decide what to do. But I held my peace until whoever-it-was had rounded two corners and was getting what seemed awfully close. Then I let out a bloodcurdling yell. I tried to sound as inhuman as I could—certainly as wild as my idea of a panther. And it worked. For whoever-it-was backed out of there in a hurry and I soon heard the two of them running away, evidently in full panic, toward school. At the same moment I realized that, unless I acted very quickly, they would surely tell others about their adventure and in no time the whole school would know about my cave. So I hastily scrambled out the passage and ran after the boys until I caught up with one. It was Harry Helliwell, about my age. He seemed relieved to know it was only me, and I took him back and showed him the cave and pledged him to secrecy. And he in turn fortunately managed to stop the other boy before he spilled the beans. So my secret still held. And by the following year I had grown another inch or two and gained thirty pounds, and no longer felt picked on or in need of a refuge.

By that time my mind had developed noticeably and I began to enjoy the risqué jokes told by the older boys such as the classic one about the little dog who fell asleep beside a railroad track, carelessly leaving his tail over a rail, so that when a train came along and ran over his tail, he turned his head around to see what had happened, letting the train run over his head too. The obvious moral: don't lose your head over a piece of tail. "Piece of tail" was a new expression to me at the time, but I felt more than sophisticated enough to guess its meaning.

Mathematics was my best subject in school and its ramifications endlessly fascinating. I even got interested in playing chess. My next best school subject was English composition. Certainly I found it congenial and felt little difficulty in writing a weekly theme. But it struck me as strange that the same theme could get such different grades from different teachers. One story I wrote about a panther in the Maine woods, titled "The Last Sock," was given a mark of forty in 1922 by Ted Evans, who taught the third form. But when I submitted the same theme again in 1923, teacher Cuthbert Wright, an admirer of Jim Cozzens, graded it sixty. I was sufficiently encouraged by this to try it for a third time in my fifth form year on Mr. Hilliard, and he rewarded me with an eighty.

My last two years at Kent School were a lot more enjoyable than the first two, mainly because I grew to be the biggest boy there and began to do well in sports, particularly rowing. Father Sill had introduced rowing at Kent as soon as he could afford it, I think in the spring of 1922 after he had begged some of the richer parents to donate a couple of racing shells, oars, and a motor launch. But the Housatonic River in those days had a lot of stumps sticking out of the water along its sides, so we sometimes had to pull in our oars to get around the bends. I remember Father Sill in the launch, wearing his cap and turtleneck sweater and yelling to us through a megaphone: "Pull ahead starboard, back up port," then, as we got safely out to midstream, "Let 'er run."

I rowed in the number seven position in Kent's "first crew" in the 1924 and 1925 seasons, and we managed to win most of our races, in fact all except the ones against our main rival, Choate, a much bigger school than Kent.

If Kent had had a track team in those days, I would have tried out for it. Instead, I contented myself in off-season afternoons with such unsocial activities as ropewalking and throwing the boomerang.

For the summer of 1924 Father decided that, at seventeen, I had outgrown camp, and he tried to give me a special treat and challenge by signing me on as an O.S. (ordinary seaman) on the crew of a square-rigged ship called the *Nereus*, due to sail out of Boston harbor in June. I would be a working member of the crew. On my first climb up the shrouds, I felt numb and dizzy looking down at the deck more than a hundred feet below. I didn't know that my reaction was entirely normal or that it would pass after a few hours of experience. It took all my nerve, when the shrouds converged to the crosstrees some eighty feet up, to keep going still higher, which required my reaching backward, partly upside down (hanging by my hands) out and around the crosstrees, then unavoidably up to the upper crosstrees (at one hundred fifty feet), and finally up the third flight.

I had never imagined that what was expected of me and a few other teenagers who had signed on as "ordinary seamen" would be so gruelling. It was an experience most of us anticipated with barely concealed dread. But to our dismay the *Nereus* never left Boston because it had not met the safety regulations of the Port Authority and we had to abandon our inflated hopes. Instead, I spent August at Camp Devens, a Citizen's Military Training Camp where Father had a hunch the army discipline might do me good. According to my own hunch, it probably did.

Back in school, I roomed with my friend Jonah Sherman and his friend Phil Rhinelander, both sons of clergymen and top scholars. Somehow I could not interest myself in my studies seriously enough to emulate them even in literature.

I remember that on a hot afternoon in June just before the end of school four of us sixth formers went swimming at a quiet spot a mile up the river, and we got to talking lightheartedly about the mysteries of physical lovemaking which none of us had experienced. Being naked in that lonely surrounding, we were quite uninhibited in our speculations, and we even tried molding life-size female images out of mud at the river's edge to express what we imagined the ideal nude woman should be like, inevitably with wide hips, full breasts, and of course a hole in what we considered the right place. When we wildly conjectured as to how it would feel actually to push into that hole, one boy argued that it would have to be wet and warm in there and another surmised it surely must have a heavenly juiciness so delicious it would be unimaginable until experienced. The third boy almost exploded with delight, exclaiming "and once you're in there, boy, you've really got 'er. That's for sure. She couldn't get away if she wanted to." I didn't think to ask him how he knew.

Somehow I managed to pass my college board exams in the spring of 1925 and, though Father had difficulty believing it, I was accepted as a freshman at Harvard for the academic year beginning in September. By then Donald had completed his freshman year at Harvard, rowed bow on the freshman crew, and was considered bright and promising in every way. He got a summer job tutoring the children of Thomas J. Watson, founder of IBM, through whom, after graduating from Harvard in his junior year, he was given a good position in the IBM organization and, everyone agreed, measured up to all of Father's expectations.

Labrador 1925

For the summer of 1925 Father arranged for me to go to Labrador and work in one of Dr. Grenfell's mission hospitals. It was a sort of missionary job without pay, but at least I could earn my keep and see a goodly part of the north country where I had never been before. After taking the train to Quebec I caught a little steamer called the *North Star,* and we steamed northward down the St. Lawrence River, thence eastward across its gulf toward the Strait of Belle Isle, which separates Newfoundland from Labrador.

There we dropped anchor at Harrington Harbour, our destination. The coast was rocky, without a tree or a bush in sight, and the town just a few dozen blocklike houses scattered among the ledges, with racks of drying codfish everywhere and packs of wolfish sledge dogs lolling around. A

lighter took a few of us ashore, including a scientist studying magnetic variations (we called him "the magnetic man"), the elderly Archdeacon of Quebec named Frederick Scott who wrote poetry and had been senior chaplain of the Canadian Forces in World War I, and a cheerful boy my age from Vermont named Freddy Lee (bound, like me, for a summer hospital job and Harvard in the fall).

On the wharf to greet us stood the hospital staff—Dr. Wasson, his assistant Mrs. Murray, and a young French Canadian nurse, Jean Egbert—all a little excited by the arrival of the steamer. After introducing ourselves all around, it was only a short walk up to the three-story hospital, the largest building in sight, while the *North Star* soon weighed anchor and steamed off northward up the coast toward Battle Harbour, Indian Harbour, Goose Bay, and other ports, none of which were connected by roads, leaving the sea their only practicable link with the rest of the world.

Freddy and I soon got into the routine of our duties, such as unloading thirty tons of coal from an old barge and carrying it in bags to the hospital. We had to carry it on our backs because there was no such thing as a wheelbarrow here, nor any sort of wheeled vehicle. No horse either. In fact, the horse is just a legendary creature in this region. None of the one hundred fifty residents of Harrington Harbour had ever seen one.

The people of course were fishermen, not farmers, and there was no school—yet. Few could read or write so much as their own names, which were mostly biblical, and nearly every man over forty was called "Uncle." There was "Uncle Ham," "Uncle Jacob," "Uncle Matt," etc.

When Freddy or I went visiting the families on outlying islands, they usually assumed we were doctors. One mother asked me to "sound" her baby, and it turned out she wanted me to listen with a stethoscope because she feared the baby had worms.

About once a week we got a day off and a chance to go exploring in the hospital motorboat. It was exciting because, they said, this coast had not ever been thoroughly explored, so Fred and I hoped we could penetrate to country never seen before by white men and maybe even get to name places after ourselves. Wouldn't it be a neat surprise if some friend someday discovered in some future atlas such features as Lake Lee spreading out below beautiful Murchie Falls?

Sad to say, we never actually got that far all summer because there wasn't nearly enough time or fuel to go more than about twenty miles beyond

Harrington. But we were lucky enough on one occasion to become real castaways on a desert island, an adventure becoming all too rare in this twentieth century. It happened because a dense fog bank rolled in off the sea before we had time to return from an expedition northeast to Mutton Bay. There were four of us, all men, and as we were threading our way among the Bald Islands off Tête-à-la-Baleine, we found ourselves suddenly in the soup, with visibility down to about a hundred feet. Although we continued putt-putt-putting ahead, trying to find our way home, we soon realized that our fuel would run out if we kept wandering aimlessly in the fog, so we put ashore into a tiny cove on a rocky island perhaps three hundred feet long to wait for the fog to lift.

It was windy and a gentle drizzle descended on us, making us not only wet but undeniably cold and hungry with little prospect of comfort on that bleak strand. The few scraps of driftwood we found seemed too wet for kindling a fire and there was nothing edible in sight nor any obvious way to keep warm in our light summer clothing. So we tried to keep active and looked for ways to better our lot. We explored the island for nearly an hour but found nothing significant except for two fresh water pools, some seaweed on the lower rocks, and a few barnacles. One of the boys wondered whether the seaweed might make a salad, or if we could possibly break the barnacles out of their shells and eat them like clams. The seaweed, however, tasted like nothing so much as rubber dipped in salt and, after we ground up a few barnacles, we could scarcely find any meat at all among the splintered shells.

It got dark by ten o'clock when, as we had no feasible way to sleep, we just walked and jogged around all night to keep warm and told stories until we couldn't remember any more. Then at three o'clock dawn came and the rain stopped, but the fog was denser than ever. We were glad it wasn't December when dawn doesn't show until nine and the fog can last a week. Hunger gnawed at us so much that, as soon as the light allowed, Freddy and I started searching for food with intense concentration and, at a little after four, by digging into a mud flat that had been exposed by the low tide, he found some mussels and presented us with about a dozen. Then around five, peering into a crevice, I discovered a seagull's nest with two nearly grown chicks in it. They were fat and fluffy but obviously too young to fly. I picked them up and they just looked at me as if I were their mother, opening their big mouths for food. It was

a strain on what little maternal instinct I had, but hunger and a sense of duty to my companions somehow prevailed and, without giving myself time to weaken, I picked up a five-pound rock and bashed their heads against a ledge as instantaneously and painlessly as I could. It was an emergency situation, I told myself, and these delicious mouthfuls of meat had been heaven-sent to sustain us.

While Freddy and I were plucking and cleaning the gulls, one of the boys whittled shavings from some driftwood and, using a few drops of gasoline from the boat, finally got a small fire going. We found an old can near the engine and, after scouring it out with sand and salt water, tried boiling the mussels and seagulls in it. Unfortunately, the mussels remained very tough and the baby gulls, though almost as tender as chicken, took on a definite tinge of gasoline and fish. So, after a few bites, we roasted what was left of the birds directly on the fire and they tasted a full magnitude better. This was largely due to the circumstances no doubt but, although we never could completely put out of mind the fading Standard Oil flavor, I don't remember enjoying any roast fowl of any breed quite that much before or since.

By noon the sun had burned through the fog and we chugged home without incident except for meeting another motorboat sent out by the worried Harrington hospital staff who, not knowing what had become of us, thought we might need rescuing. Thus ended my one and only adventure of being marooned on a desert island which, though no ship was wrecked and the setting was neither tropical, balmy, nor romantic as one's dreams would have it, and, lamentably, lacking even a hint of beautiful girls, was something I could not possibly, nor would I wish to, forget.

Speaking of romances, obviously I had only the vaguest idea of what the word meant in that summer of 1925. But I would soon be going to college where I would be free to make my own way, pick my own friends, including girls. It was an exciting thought, as I had never really had a chance to get to know a girl. True, I had been corresponding with Maria for eight years at the rate of about one or two letters a year, and I wrote her again in August.

It wouldn't be quite accurate to call them love letters though I usually signed them "lovingly, Guy." But I did write something approaching a love letter from Labrador to another girl I had met only in June 1925 at a house party (my first) in Hancock, New Hampshire, just four days before taking the train to Quebec. She was Dolores de Pierrefeu, known to her friends as "Dodo," whose mother, the Countess de Pierrefeu, had been married to a French count and knew my father well. Dodo had impressed me enough during the weekend of the house party that I wrote her some thirty pages illustrated with my own drawings, a sort of diary of Labrador.

In the meantime a girl came into my life even in barren Labrador. One couldn't have called her pretty or very unusual but she was there, and there was no other. She was Jean, the little black-eyed nurse in the hospital. Fred didn't seem particularly interested, but I had long conversations with her and found her responsive and, as some would say, cute. She took quite an interest in my long letter to Dodo, which I let her read, and asked about my future plans. She liked my descriptions of the sledge dogs, their size (up to eight feet, nose to tail) and fierce way of defending their territory against other packs of dogs, and their otherwise lovable dispositions. When out in the sunshine, her black eyes looked dark brown, exactly the color of stewed prunes, so I took to calling her Prunie. Interestingly enough, she enjoyed it. We went out on walks together over the rocks and reindeer moss and held hands but never got to the point of kissing. I guess I just didn't known how, having never been exposed to boy-girl kissing. And she, brought up strictly Catholic, apparently did not feel competent to teach me. Prunie was fun, nevertheless, and used to bring me lots of goodies from the hospital commissary to assuage my ravenous teenage appetite.

We saw Archdeacon Scott only twice all summer when he stopped briefly on his Anglican mission rounds. He was invariably jovial, and entertained us by imitating farm animals and quoting his own inspired poetry. He was quite a contrast from Father Sill, who in school had preached sermons with a lofty moral tone obviously intended to inspire young men to hold to their ideals of chastity, sermons about the mysterious virtue of saving oneself for true love in the future, of sacrificing ephemeral delight today for the sake of everlasting happiness later, of controlling the body and its desires now for the benefit of the soul and its eternal well-being.

I doubt if any of the boys at Kent, whose only experience of sex was an occasional wet dream or some secret experimenting with himself, knew what that monk really meant—if, indeed, he knew himself. And as for me, I was far from convinced that these earthly sex temptations would turn out

to be all that irresistible. Or, if they did, exactly what could I count on gaining by holding out? What was the unmentioned taboo of sex all about anyway? If sex was really so powerfully beautiful as to motivate all the great romances of literature, why did it have to be taboo at all?

When September rolled around, a big schooner tied up at the main Harrington wharf to load up with salt codfish for the Halifax market. As Freddy and I were due in Cambridge by mid-September and the captain agreed to take us to Halifax for nothing, from where we could easily go to Yarmouth and catch the overnight boat to Boston, we eagerly signed up for the adventure. Normally it would take at least two weeks to sail the three hundred-odd miles across the Gulf of St. Lawrence through the gut of Canso and another hundred and fifty down the coast of Nova Scotia to Halifax. But because a big storm blew up out of the northwest with gale-force winds behind us, we made Canso in three days despite trouble such as having our mainsail rip right down the middle during our first night out. Fred and I could have sewn up the sail ourselves I guess, but were glad that, as passengers, we were not expected to. Because the sea was so rough we were both rather sick, and the skipper swore he'd never seen a worse storm in the Gulf. The waves seemed as high as the mast top when we were wallowing in a trough between them, and our whole horizon then was just one gigantic wave. The worst of it, however, was that every wave broke over the ship with an avalanche of icy water crashing down upon the deck, so we had to duck inside and slam the hatch shut for fear of being washed away. But it was hard to breathe inside the cabin because the violent motion riled up the bilge water, a mixture including rancid whale oil, blubber, and rotten codfish that whooshed acrid fumes up through the cracks in the cabin floor fit to stifle us.

Even the captain, though long used to it, looked slightly green, and I noticed he didn't finish his lunch which, like every meal, was nothing but salt cod and plum duff (sticky dough studded with stale plums). Fred and I passed up lunch too, but the captain settled his stomach with occasional swigs of port wine. All in all this 1925 voyage under sail served to redeem for me at least some of the sea voyage I had been denied in 1924.

Fred and I, anxious to get home, debarked at Canso and, after taking the train to Yarmouth, which fortunately included a dining car, we shipped out that very evening to Boston.

College
1925–1926

Harvard was like a big city after Kent School, and my class of 1929 with some 1050 members so numerous that I could see no likelihood of ever getting to know more than a tiny percentage of them. Even my friend Freddy was lost in the crowd, and I did not run across him for months.

It was exciting, moreover, to be managing my own affairs at last, deciding what courses to take, buying books and clothes. Father had agreed to give me $1500 a year out of which I must pay for my tuition ($900), board and lodging (about $500), and everything else I needed from laundry and carfare to movie tickets and incidentals. I could earn as much additional as I wished by getting jobs, especially in summer.

If this was adult life, I was glad I was an adult. My assigned room was in Persis Smith Hall, and I ate my meals in the Smith Dining Hall, attending classes like English A, European history, calculus, French, and a reputedly snap course in field artillery. Most of the classrooms were in Harvard Yard, a beautiful walled-in park full of graceful elms and old ivy-covered brick buildings, one or two of which had been the center of the college since its founding in 1636. Undergraduates were all required to participate in a sport of some kind. Despite some misgivings, I signed up for football along with about a hundred classmates. I didn't do any better than I expected, and even felt relief when I did not make the team. Certainly I entertained no thought of achieving such glory as my father had won for himself thirty-four years earlier.

I made a number of new friends while trying out for football, however, such as Allerton Cushman who happened to have a locker next to mine. Finding him high-spirited and amusing, I joined him in other college activities such as attending a varsity football game against Dartmouth in the Harvard stadium one Saturday afternoon in October. And there he introduced me to his mother, Eleanor, who, ever since she had divorced his father fifteen years earlier, had been generally known as Mrs. Parker, "Parker" being her maiden name. She was the eldest daughter of James Parker, a retired major general in the cavalry.

Now forty-five years old and wearing a red-fox fur around her shoulders and a brown tweed suit, Eleanor had a strikingly vivacious personality with flashing brown eyes and plenty to say on nearly every subject. I think we went for tea after the game to her small apartment in West Cedar Street on Beacon Hill. Not having a mother of my own, I found Mrs. Parker's warm enthusiasm and maternal hospitality very enjoyable. She told me that she had known my mother twenty years earlier and had once had dinner with my father and mother before I was born. It also came out in the conversation that she had been in an Indian war in 1880 shortly after her birth because her father, then a cavalry lieutenant, was in Arizona pursuing Geronimo, the famous Indian chief. The house where she and her mother lived had been fired on by the Indians and Indian bullets had made holes through the sash of the window of her room. It was almost the last Indian battle ever fought by the United States and the memory of it brought history very close to home.

As autumn advanced, the social season in Boston blossomed as I had never known it or even heard of it. Teenage girls of socially prominent families traditionally became debutantes at about eighteen, which meant that their parents usually felt obligated to give them a "coming out" party or ball sometime between October and April. These affairs usually took place at the Somerset Hotel in Kenmore Square, occasionally at the Copley Plaza, and about a hundred girls would be invited along with a somewhat larger number of supposedly eligible young men, many of them undergraduates at Harvard, whom the girls' parents considered properly brought up and safe. Through no fault of my own, I was one of them but, if I really was safe, it was only because I was too inexperienced and unsure of myself to be anything else.

In that winter of 1925–1926 I tried out for the freshman wrestling team. I had always preferred wrestling to boxing and, in childhood scuffles, noticed that, if another boy took to punching me, I could usually get the better of him by grabbing an arm or leg and wrestling him to the ground. I knew nothing of the science of wrestling or even if wrestling was a science.

The wrestling coach, W. E. Lewis, was glad I showed up because I was clearly the biggest and strongest of the fifteen boys who went out for wrestling at Hemenway Gymnasium. I had a lot to learn, but I was immediately picked as the "unlimited" member of the team, mostly because at six foot five and two hundred pounds, I was four inches taller and thirty pounds heavier than anyone else there.

At a match I had to be patient while the lightweights wrestled first, sitting on the bench for most of an hour, wrapped in a crimson blanket over my undershirt, red wrestling tights with leather knee patches and sneakers. I would watch the contending wrestlers on the mat before me, tumbling about, sweating and grunting, but usually I was too nervous to enjoy it, for behind them on the opposing team's bench sat my own personal opponent, always the biggest and heaviest man on the other team.

At first wrestling was hard, and I discovered I could be overpowered or outmaneuvered by experienced wrestlers smaller and lighter than I. Thus I lost my first two matches. But I learned as the season advanced and won my third and all my four bouts after that, including the one against Yale.

By the end of the winter I found myself a member of the freshman rowing crew and we became known as "the giant crew" because our average height was 6 feet 3½ inches, taller than any crew on record, including the varsity. I was given the number seven position, and the composition of the crew remained unchanged all season because we won all our races.

I had a few interests besides rowing, I hasten to tell, and one of my most significant achievements in the spring of 1926 was acquiring a girlfriend of my very own. This time the event gave every promise of being the real thing. Certainly it was the first time I had ever fallen wholeheartedly in love or had my eyes opened all the way as to what the love emotion is about.

It began quietly enough at a dance in Brookline. There I met a girl named Molly Farnham with blue eyes, blonde hair, about five foot two, with a pleasingly ample figure and eager mind who seemed very responsive to all my ideas. I was much taken with her right away and danced with her many times, finding her light on her feet and invariably easy to lead.

I offered to take her home when the dance was over at midnight, and she readily accepted. Although I didn't have a car, I managed a ride with a friend and delivered Molly to her door on Pinckney Street at the foot of Beacon Hill. Having already embraced her so much while dancing, it was easy to hug her some more in the dark vestibule. And then I found myself kissing her—my very first kiss, probably more like a puppy than a human.

When it came time to release her so she could go upstairs to her parents' home over an antique shop, I indicated I couldn't bear to let her go and

Murchie made this drawing of an English tank factory while a member of the Chicago Tribune *foreign staff, London, 1940s*

she, though hesitant, said I might come upstairs with her "just for a minute to say good-night." I was thrilled at this unexpected acceptance and eagerly followed her up the two flights to the apartment where the Farnham family lived on the two upper floors. Of course her father and mother had long since gone to bed, so Molly and I had the living room to ourselves and we hugged each other and talked much longer than we meant to.

I saw Molly pretty regularly after that. Both her father and mother were nice and unpretentious. They seemed to like me, so I felt welcome at their house and dropped in to see Molly every few evenings all spring. She was my chosen partner for the Freshman Jubilee, our class's biggest social event. We danced until after midnight despite crew training regulations which would have had me retire much earlier.

That heady spring I also learned to drive a car. My brother Donald had acquired a Model T Ford, then regarded the acme of practical personal transport. A common ditty ran: "A little spark, a little coil, a little gas and a little oil; an old tin can and a two-inch board, put 'em together and you've got a Ford." The thing had to be cranked, of course, and it had "planetary transmission," requiring the driver to keep his left foot on the clutch pedal "halfway down" if he wanted to be in neutral gear. It was tricky but, with Donald's help, in half an hour I could do it pretty well. Licenses were not required in 1926, and traffic was generally light and slow, with almost no red lights. So I was soon driving all around Boston and its environs with a wonderful feeling of potentiality and liberation. Even Attie Cushman's mother, Mrs. Parker, got herself a vehicle about this time, a Ford roadster which she referred to as "the hoptoad," and ventured into the streets with carefree abandon. Her main trouble was that, having been brought up a horsewoman, she tended to leave it to the car to get her out of jams, and I think she felt more than slightly betrayed every time the "toad" behaved indifferent to her needs.

In the summer of 1926 I got what seemed an ideal job, mostly through the good offices of a girl named Georgia who worked in the Student Employment Bureau. As Georgia presented it to me, I would be paid a hundred dollars a month for serving as companion to a seventeen-year-old boy named Jack, and I would be expected to teach him and his two younger sisters how to play tennis, swim, and sail a boat. I couldn't imagine a cushier deal, and it certainly seemed a cinch after the previous summer in Labrador. Best of all, I would be living in as part of the family, named McFarland, in their summer home on Cape Cod. And I was to have a day off once a week with use of one of the family's cars, and as it was only fifteen miles to Falmouth where Molly would be spending the summer with her family, obviously I should see a lot of her.

On my first day off I of course headed straight for Falmouth and the Farnham's cottage. There was Molly in the kitchen, bright-eyed and expectant, busily filling a basket with sandwiches, fruit, and hard-boiled eggs for the picnic we had planned. She had on a very fetching green jersey and matching green skirt, and I felt fetched. This would be the first time we could be completely on our own, unchaperoned and free. Molly's mother seemed a little nervous about letting her daughter go off like this for the whole day, but after our promise to be back before supper she was all smiles and waved us off.

What a thrill to have Molly utterly to myself for the next seven hours. It seemed like heaven on Earth. We drove east along the coast to a neck of wild land Molly knew about. It was covered with sand dunes. There were no houses within miles and no people in sight. We turned off the main road onto a narrow sandy track through scrub pines heading toward the beach and, after a mile, came to a place wide enough to turn around. There we left the car and walked eastward among the dunes, carrying our basket, a small blanket, and towel. The sun was high and bright and the gulls circled above us and over the sea, uttering their familiar high-pitched cries. We saw no footprints but our own as we climbed one dune after another, up through the marram grass on the windward side, then jumping down the steep leeward side into soft sand.

On impulse I suddenly picked Molly up, with the basket on my left arm, and carried her like a baby over the next small dune and down to a sandy hollow where beach plums grew. I knew she was thrilled to be lifted off her feet by powerful arms. My energy seemed boundless then, and I sensed the indescribable exuberance of youthful potency. With the warmth of her young body snug against my chest, I could have walked for miles. But a stronger impulse soon made me put her down on the warm blanket in the soft sand. Her head was against my shoulder. "You are so big," she whispered.

We laughed and hugged each other as if we could never let go. Presently fingers groped for buttons and buckles. Clothes were peeled off and skin slid against skin, down down . . . My eyes took in the lovely lines of Molly's shoulders, her slim torso, hips and thighs. She seemed surprised at my reaction.

"Haven't you ever seen a nude girl?" she asked.

"No," I said. "Not since my sisters when they were tots."

"Well, now you have." She snuggled close. "I am a woman in case you didn't notice. And I am your woman—if you want me."

I rolled toward her and moved my knee between hers. Our thighs met all the way to our knees. I could smell the salt air and the dry grass and beach plums near by, and I felt the sand give under the blanket. Things happened with remarkable ease and I had a feeling of power and relief and assurance.

It was a man's voice that woke us up. I was startled. It seemed far away, but it was indubitably a man's voice. And then there was another male voice.

"Somebody is coming," I said. "Two men. Maybe more."

Molly sat up. "It's probably clam diggers," she said. "They're the only people that usually come to these parts."

"We'd better get out of here," I suggested, pulling Molly to her feet. She agreed and we started off eastward, away from the voices which might be a quarter mile distant. Side by side we walked up and over dune after dune. We could hear the voices going toward the beach where they would undoubtedly go if they were clam diggers. After it became obvious that the men were not coming our way, we loved each other some more and ate our picnic lunch with our clothes on as proper as could be.

When you are in love, how can you help wanting to get as close as possible to the one you love? But after being brought up to think of modesty as a virtue and that a body in the buff is something indecent or, as some see it, disgusting, and fornication a flagrant sin, we just knew that some of the older generation probably would not understand what we did or how we felt. After all, they were Victorians who grew up in the days of Queen Victoria who somehow managed to remain every inch a lady while producing her nine royal children. What I still never could understand was why so much of the love emotion, the inspiration of so much beauty in art, music, and literature, should be tabooed as if it were ugly and evil.

The summer passed quickly. I saw Molly every week but sometimes we just sailed in her catboat, went to parties with her friends, or did something athletic like running along the beach. I got to enjoy distance running at this time and I remember once running clear across the Cape, south to north, on sandy roads. Marathon running wasn't a popular sport in those days, but it came naturally to me.

I hesitate to mention it, but I also began to indulge in what's called juvenile delinquency, mostly for fun with my suggestible young friend Jack McFarland. One day, seeing a road sign saying "CHOWDER AHEAD," somehow I couldn't resist the temptation to swipe it and I tore it off a tree so I could triumphantly hang it in my college room. Yet I guess I must have taught Jack and his sisters enough in swimming, tennis, and sailing, between secret shenanigans, because Mrs. McFarland judged me worth hiring to go out West with the family the following summer, 1927. And

that would include a tour of the Canadian Rockies, Yellowstone Park, the Grand Canyon, and a three-week pack trip with Jack through the Shoshone Mountains of Wyoming. Life was really opening up.

Sophomore Year 1926–1927

Back at Harvard I roomed with Attie Cushman in Claverly Hall. As sophomores were provided no dining hall in those days, we ate in various little cafeteria nooks like one in the basement of the Lampoon building called Arthur's Lunch, and often bought groceries and cooked on a hot plate in our own room. Canned salmon from Alaska was very cheap then and made a satisfying meal when heated for three or four minutes in a frying pan.

As fall rowing occupied me only for an hour or so on a few afternoons a week, I filled my extracurricular time with seeing Molly and expanding my social life, occasionally going out to our old house in Dedham, "Highland Mary."

Needing personal transport about this time, I bought a secondhand Buick roadster for twenty-five dollars and, although Attie didn't know how to drive, he paid half and considered himself half owner. After his first driving lesson, when he still had trouble distinguishing the brake from the accelerator, he managed to drive up the front steps of Claverly Hall one evening where the steep incline barely braked him in time to spare the door. With the aid of kindly gravity, he worked his way back down to the sidewalk and parked on Mount Auburn Street as he'd meant to all along.

The Buick had a top that would come down and a horn that blew by squeezing a rubber globe. It was suitably sporty and just right for driving Molly out into the country on weekends when we would always look for wooded places with no houses around, or at worst a farm big enough so the farmer wouldn't yell at us to get the hell off his land. I guess Molly's mother had her suspicions as to where we went and what we were up to, but she evidently considered me to have the makings of a "gentleman" and didn't say anything, just kept wistfully hoping Molly would behave enough like a "lady" to keep out of serious trouble.

In some ways it was easier to make love in Molly's house than in the country because her mother usually went upstairs around nine, leaving us to ourselves in the living room. The only hazard there was the possibility that Mom might come downstairs again unannounced, which she occasionally did at a fast trot. I can't think she was really trying to catch us. It was just her way.

The closest call of all happened when Molly and I were making the most of a rare opportunity on the dining room rug. It was on a sunny Sunday morning and Mom came trotting down the stairs at the climactic moment for a near disaster. We barely had four seconds to get on our feet before she rounded the corner from the living room. Molly's skirts were down by then but all I could do was turn my back on Mom and walk away toward the kitchen, trying to appear casual. While Molly distracted her and somehow kept her from following me, I very deliberately entered the kitchen. Luckily it was unoccupied. But not knowing whether Mom was still behind me, I dared not turn and just kept going, at the same time trying to think of something plausible to do in the opposite direction. Seeing a closed closet door at the far side of the kitchen, I walked straight to it, opened it, and stepped in. And there in front of me stood a large flour barrel, so I reached into it and pretended to be scooping up flour, wondering whether Mom could possibly believe me if I explained that I just wanted to mix up some pancake batter. Unfortunately, the wet spots on my dark pants got dusted with the white flour, making them very conspicuous, not to mention suspicious. Fortunately, however, Molly detained her mom long enough so I could mop up and look reasonably presentable—but I always wondered what shenanigan she imagined I was up to in her kitchen. She never said, and of course I never asked. I was a fairly established member of the family by then (at least I imagined I was), so I presume she just tolerated me as a necessary part of her daughter's development.

In college I was studying English literature, physics, psychology, and German. I didn't really know what I wanted to do with my life and thought vaguely of becoming an architect. I also felt I didn't know enough about the world and developed a strong urge to go around it and see for myself what people were like in China and other far places. I went to see Mrs. Parker and talked with her about all this, including the idea of leaving Harvard after two years because I didn't think college life was doing me much good. She was very sympathetic and made me feel I wasn't being foolish to think that way, and she obviously approved my yearning for some firsthand adventure instead of the secondhand book learning I was getting.

The first letter I ever received from her came just after Christmas 1926, and I kept it and luckily still have it. She wrote:

My dear Guy,
   I have here a book [*The Call of the Wild* by Jack London]—the one I spoke to you about—and I hope you will like it. I shall try to get Allerton to bring it out to you—what time I can get hold of that elusive galumpher!
   I've been thinking a lot of what you told me about your speculations as to going around the world and all—I'd like so to talk to you again about it. I love your idealism & desire for adventure—but you must be careful not to set that great young strength of yours into a wasteful or badly directed course. Every pound & every day of it should give you something that was worth what you were paying. If you can stand any more of my senile chatter, call me up when I get back from N.Y. & we will have tea together & consult with one another. Best luck for the new years.

                                        Yours,
                                        E.F.P.

In the book itself was written: "To my very dear friend Guy from his aged admirer, Eleanor F.P." She was forty-six at the time, and I was nineteen.

Among distractions like Molly and Mrs. Parker, there were also undoubtedly the clubs. The best known, and perhaps least exclusive of these at Harvard, was the Hasty Pudding Club. Being invited to join depended mostly on how well one was known and therefore how many votes one might get. Having been on the "giant freshman crew" of 1926, I had recently received more than my due in publicity, including numerous write-ups in Boston and New York papers, and having an older brother in the Class of 1928 helped. So it was no surprise to me when I was tapped for the Pudding. And having been told by Donald about the archaic initiation tradition—including the public attempts to humiliate sophomore candidates during initiation week—I was not entirely unready.

The final day of the initiation involved solemn ceremony and being blindfolded for several hours, during which time we candidates were driven to "the cemetery" and made to "kiss a corpse" (actually a hunk of rotting pork, according to Donald), then, after being commanded to drink a full quart of strong liquor, made to slide headfirst down a chute into a mysterious subterranean pool.

Forewarned of the pool by my brother, I took a deep breath on my way down the slide and remained motionless on the bottom for nearly a minute until my mentors, fearing I might have had too much booze and drowned, fished me out. It was good to see their relieved expressions as I finally "came to," a full-fledged Pudding member.

After that, most of us ate lunch regularly in the club and enjoyed its pool table, stage, and piano. It was reasonably inexpensive. But numerous other clubs, the exclusive so-called social clubs, soon made themselves known. Father had been a member of the Fly Club since 1893 and Donald belonged to the Delphic Club. "Don't you want to be one of the boys?" he once asked me. And both these and the Iroquois Club made overtures, all citing what seemed to me exorbitant initiation and seasonal dues. But I couldn't see how I could possibly benefit enough in joining them to justify all it would cost. Besides, I thought I sensed a faint but pervasive aura of snobbery about them that somehow went against my grain. So I decided I just wasn't cut out to be a club man and turned them down, one and all. Maybe I never knew what I was missing but, if so, at least I could bask in the peace and economy of my ignorance, and never since have I uncovered any convincing reason to regret it.

By Christmas I felt so sure of the wisdom of my decision to quit Harvard in June and work my way around the world that I no longer took my studies seriously and made a point of revealing my plans to Father even though he was sick abed in Highland Mary at the time, probably with the flu. I was not surprised that he took it hard, but the depth of his bitterness in calling me heartless for "kicking a horse who was down" struck me as not at all understanding. And he not only seemed to consider me disloyal to oppose his wishes but foolish in the extreme not to appreciate the rare educational opportunity that I had been blessed with. Furthermore, he indicated he would do nothing to support my harebrained scheme financially and, if I were stubborn and foolhardy enough to persist in attempting it, I would have to do it entirely on my own. I half expected him to add, "And may God have mercy on your soul." But he just slumped back in his bed with the incredulous look of one who has been stabbed in the back. I reflected, however, that he had recently turned fifty-four and at that age I didn't think he could really have become too frail to cope with my juvenile intransigence.

And it turned out that he could and did cope with it and in the one way that offered a real promise of success. He had heard of my close friendship with Mrs. Parker whom he already knew and regarded as a respectable lady with some standing in Boston society. I don't think he could have understood our relationship but at least he realized she must be listed in the social register, a mark of solid distinction to him. And he wrote her a letter appealing to her to use her influence on me before I threw away my life by abandoning Harvard and everything it promised for my future.

Of course she did not wholly agree with him but, to my surprise, Mrs. Parker did accept the possibility that I might later regret having precipitously dropped out of college in my immature state and she urged me not to be hasty but rather to try to allow for the possibility that I might eventually gain more than I could yet imagine by remaining at Harvard and, on graduating, that I might conceivably get even more from seeing the world as a voting-age alumnus of twenty-two than as a bemused dropout of twenty.

Her perspective on the question was hard for me to take but her eloquent appeal to reason eventually penetrated my mind and, with a lingering feeling of doubt, I finally resolved to study harder and stick with Harvard until I graduated. I had not abandoned my independence of mind, however, and I always enjoyed the unorthodox and the unexpected. That is mainly why I rarely won Father's approval. I remember I used to think how dull it was when people shopped for groceries and invariably asked for "a dozen of your best eggs" or "a pound of your very best butter." Why not put them on their mettle once in their lives, I decided, by doing it differently? So I would ask in a polite and matter-of-fact tone, "May I please have a dozen of your worst eggs, and a pound of your very worst butter?"

In 1927 Attie and I sold our Buick for thirty dollars after I bought a handsome red Indian Chief motorcycle for thirty-five dollars. It was a third-hand machine with two cylinders that had once been used by the Boston police. It weighed four hundred pounds, would go sixty miles on a gallon, and seemed impressively powerful, especially to Molly and other girls whom I later invited to ride on my backseat. It is wonderful how impressed girls are by powerful-sounding engines and brass buttons. I had a shirt with brass buttons and usually wore it when out cycling. It somehow gave me confidence.

I tried to make the most of this discovery but ran into unexpected trouble in April of that year when Ed Brown, the new varsity crew coach, picked me for the varsity crew and found out that I was riding a motorcycle.

"Hey, Murchie," he said in his dictatorial voice, "you can't ride that motorcycle any more. Not if you want to row. I can't risk any injuries during crew season."

Understanding something of this and not wanting to get into disfavor with Ed Brown, who had the power to make or break my own career as an oarsman, I did not argue with him but immediately agreed to quit riding my motorcycle. So I was faced with the problem of what to do with it. I could leave it in the garage at Highland Mary until after the rowing season. But, on reflection, it would be even better if I could rent it. And, by good luck, an old friend named Dan Codman offered me ten dollars to rent it for the next three months. I closed the deal without hesitation. But Dan had never ridden a motorcycle and needed to be shown how. So I gave him a short demonstration. It was on Memorial Drive along the river. He sat on the backseat while I showed him how to work the starter and, on moving off, the hand accelerator and the gears.

We had no sooner got comfortably under way, however, and were tooling along at an easy twenty-five miles an hour when who should we encounter smack in front of us but Ed Brown!

"What do you mean, riding your motorcycle?" he roared. "Didn't you promise me you would not?"

I had difficulty explaining that I had just rented it to a friend and was only taking a short spin to show him the ropes. But, although he muttered a while, Ed Brown eventually realized that Dan really had rented the thing and began to calm down after Dan rode off alone somewhat shakily into the distance, no doubt a little unsure as to whether Ed Brown might somehow contrive to confiscate his new possession before he had mastered it.

I didn't see much of Dan Codman after that but Ed Brown loomed large in my life as the crew season got into full swing. We rowed on the Charles practically every day, and Ed loved to try us out in different positions with three crews designated as A, B, and C, racing each other with different men in each boat each time. Ed Brown, of course, supervised these activities, bellowing at us through his red megaphone from the deck of his motorboat, the *White Pup,* which was driven by a

bright young man from Minnesota named Harry Blackmun. None of us knew anything about Harry at the time or had the slightest suspicion that four decades later he would become renowned as a justice of the Supreme Court.

As our first race approached, against the Naval Academy at Annapolis, Ed finally settled on who would be on our varsity crew and there were daily comments in the sports pages of Boston and New York papers. I was assured of a place in the number seven position, they all predicted, and several of the sports columnists referred to me as the "Tarzan of the crew," a "remarkable sweep oarsman," and occasionally they used even more extravagant terms.

Unfortunately, we lost to the navy, but by only twenty-five feet on a mile and three quarters course. And we did better after that, beating MIT, Penn, and Cornell—all by comfortable margins despite the fact that our captain, Jeff Platt, was laid up with a serious sinus ailment and unable to row in any races through May. There was also some very interesting news that month about an ambitious young pilot named Charlie Lindbergh who used to fly the mail out west and astonished the still complacent world by flying nonstop from New York to Paris in his single-engined plane. It seemed to me that a whole new age in aviation and world travel was trying to be born—and I itched to be part of it.

Barbara Cooney and Guy Murchie at Fort Des Moines, Iowa, 1942

Then in early June we took the train to New London, Connecticut, for three weeks of training for our four-mile race against Yale on the Thames River. The Harvard camp was called Red Top and thirty-nine of us stayed there, including three crews, waiters, coxswains, launch drivers, managers, doctor, coaches, and a French proctor to oversee our exams, whose main qualification was impartiality in that he didn't give a sou whether Harvard or Yale won. Attie Cushman was one of several waiters who not only served our food at the training table but rowed daily to keep in shape as substitutes in case any regular oarsman became incapacitated.

We were very conscious of our task in attempting to beat Yale, because Yale had lost only one race to anyone in five years, and Ed Leader, the Yale coach, was considered a real genius who demanded the ultimate in disciplined perfection of his men. More specifically, Yale had beaten Harvard on the Thames every year since 1920, six times in a row! And Yale men were pretty smug about it and many thought Leader didn't have a thing to worry about, even though our crew averaged nine pounds per man heavier than theirs. In football our extra weight indeed would have been considered a major advantage but in rowing, where every man must pull more than his weight and our hundred surplus pounds (twenty-five pounds of it due to extra bracing in our overloaded shell) made our boat sink at least an inch deeper in the water, it was debatable and many coaches would not under any circumstance allow oarsmen heavier than one hundred eighty pounds on their crews.

We rowed four-mile time trials every two or three days and so did Yale, and everyone commented on how smooth and confident the Elis (Yale boys) looked in what the papers called their "scientific perfection." Ed Brown got very excited about these time trials and tried to schedule ours at unexpected times so the Yale scouts could not spy on us, yet he always had binoculars and stop watches ready to clock Yale whenever he suspected they might pull a trial. Thus the tension mounted day by day and people expected this would be the closest Harvard-Yale race ever and that 800,000 people would come to watch it in many hundreds of boats and luxurious yachts, including a new three hundred-foot submarine at the sub base in Groton and an unknown number of airplanes.

The most palatial of the yachts was undoubtedly the *Corsair,* owned by J.P. Morgan who went to Harvard and was rooting for us. His rakish vessel arrived two weeks ahead of time and, following a tradition of many years, Mr. Morgan graciously invited all the Harvard company for a Sunday cruise on Long Island Sound.

When we filed up the gangplank, J.P. was there to welcome us, putting out his portly arm to swing each of us aboard with a hearty greeting. Then we were free to enjoy the luxury of dozens of lounge chairs, sofas, and hammocks with mountains of cushions and the most scrumptious luncheon you could imagine. Most of us had second and third helpings of the dessert of strawberries and thick cream, and few of us gained less than five pounds, with the possible exception of J.P. who was built like a walrus from gaining so much in past years that he could hardly gain any more. This J.P., by the way, was not the famous nineteenth-century financier, John Pierpont Morgan with the big nose, who died in 1913 at the age of seventy-six, but his son with the same name and financial proclivities.

The *Corsair* was over a hundred feet long with a crew exceeding a hundred and an indication of her luxury was that her normal accommodations were for only six persons or couples, each provided with a suite of several rooms with such touches as gold faucets in the bathrooms for filling the marble basins and bathtubs. The towels were as big as horse blankets and as soft as wool. Footmen were standing around everywhere, handing out boxes of candy, glasses of milk or fruit juice or wine for those allowed it. And apparently every room had a fireplace and there were palm trees in huge pots on deck and in many of the halls.

J.P. strolled the decks and obviously enjoyed seeing the boys helping themselves to his cigars, engraved cigar rings, and colorfully decorated stationery. "Take all you want, boys," he would say with a sweep of his arm, but I doubt that he realized how many of the boys would use his invitation cards (with blank spaces for pier numbers, dates, etc.) to send plausible formal invitations to the wistful mothers of their girlfriends whose dreams of glamour might in consequence never again settle back to normal.

In mid-June I wrote a letter to Mrs. Parker from Red Top. I addressed her as "My dear Worgzle." By that time I knew her well and, noting that her eyes were the color of my father's horse, Orgz, I called her Worgzle. And, ardent horsewoman that she was, she accepted it.

After telling her that I had just completed my exams, getting a *C* in English, a *B* in physics and a *C+* in psychology, I said:

We've been having a terrific number of time trials lately. [We had twice covered the four-mile course in less than twenty minutes.] We are getting used to it, I suppose, and tomorrow is our last one before the race. I don't think four miles is so bad, and I like it better than two miles because you don't get at all winded and have plenty of time to think things over. The last half mile isn't very pleasant though.

I hope we can beat Yale, and if nothing goes wrong I don't see why we shouldn't. They did a good time trial last Friday and are quite confident, but we've made some good time too. . . . The course record (in a race) is 20 min. and 2 secs. We've done it in 19 min. 42 secs. but the race record is often beaten in time trials, because in the trials (unlike a race) you can pick the best conditions.

Well, . . . I'll be very glad when it's all over 'cause it will be a big load off my mind . . .

With lots of love,
Guy

On race day, June 24, things started off well for Yale and the large crowds, which seemed to favor them, were enthusiastic. Yale won the freshmen and junior varsity races in the morning, coming from behind in both cases. Evidently they were coached to row at a relatively low stroke per minute to conserve their strength for most of each race (two miles), then to raise the beat for an all-out spurt at the end—and it worked as planned. For our part, we on the varsity just intended to jump Yale at the start and try to keep ahead for the whole four miles.

Partly because a brisk southerly wind arose during the afternoon, our race was scheduled for eight o'clock, just before sunset. We drew the east lane and would row downstream, starting near the Yale camp at Gales Ferry. At half past seven we heard the observation trains coming up from New London, one on each side of the river. They were about half a mile long, each holding five thousand spectators and, according to reports, were completely sold out, notwithstanding the work of a few hawkers who had cornered the last two hundred seats and let them go at departure time for fifty dollars apiece.

Most of the crowd, variously estimated at more than half a million, had to content themselves with standing on the banks on rooftops, with tens of thousands clinging to the New London bridges and of course uncountable other thousands on the boats and gaily decorated yachts that lined both sides of the river five or six deep. The *Boston Globe* said that "the Harvard-Yale varsity classic had brought out the biggest yacht fleet ever assembled in the river and lower harbor which contained at least a thousand yachts, including those moored off Eastern Point, stretching up above the bridge along the racing course," and the article named nearly a hundred of the better known ones from such ports as Boston, New York, and Philadelphia.

We of the crew were only dimly aware of all this as we paddled out to the stake boats at quarter to eight, our oarlocks carefully sealed against any mishaps during this biggest event in our young lives. Next thing I knew, there was the Yale shell beside us on the line, backing up to her stake boat, the men looking very efficient. I was glad, however, to see that some of them showed signs of nervousness, for I felt as if I were sitting on air myself instead of on a hard, wooden sliding seat. My grip on my oar seemed very unreliable, my numb fingers touching only emptiness. . . .

Now our shirts are off, and have been passed back to the man in the stake boat, who is holding onto our rudder to keep us in position until the start. Here comes the referee's boat, the referee with a megaphone in hand on the bow, and a dozen gaily dressed passengers. Beyond him are more launches, full of people—all eyes, eyes, eyes on us.

"Are you ready, Harvard?" from the referee.

Our captain nods, "Yes."

"Are you ready, Yale?"

"Ready all!"

We are taut as fiddle strings and with sinking stomachs as the seconds tick slowly, slowly . . .

"GO!" roars the referee.

A wild splash! Our blades churn the choppy water like mill wheels in a racing start of forty-two strokes to the minute. Dimly we are conscious of the hum of launches following us and the roar of the crowd, and the steady "chuff, chuff" of the train starting up.

I can see we are gradually pulling a little ahead of Yale as we strain in quick strokes to gather speed before settling down to our steady four-mile pace of thirty-two. We are swinging well together: forward till our shoulders are between our knees, a quick flip up with the wrists to grip the fleeing water, and back hard—eight tugging pairs of arms, eight backs, eight driving pairs of legs—till the oar handle bounces off the chest and forward to another stroke.

I am slightly out of breath, but no longer have that numbness of before the start. In a staccato bark the coxswain is yelling out our strokes and giving us encouragement.

"Now we're goin' ahead of 'em—steady—huoo—huoo! Give her ten good ones now—one, two, three, four—now we're goin'—five . . ."

It is a relief to be ahead and I breathe more easily as we settle at thirty-two, spacing out in almost even puddles as we drive forward. The water slaps our blades as we feather, and some of it slops into the boat to swish up and down as we change our momentum with each rhythmical rush of slides.

I am not supposed to look away from the man in front of me, but cannot help hasty glances at Yale between strokes. Minutes go by. We struggle on. Yale is three-quarters of a length behind.

I feel very tired for a while and take it a little easier. I wonder if I can hold out all the way at this pace. And then soon I feel more rested and can pull harder. This is the phenomenon we know as the "second wind" and I thank God for it. And it is a great relief to see those flags, red and blue, go zipping past every half mile.

Hours go by. Where are the two-mile flags? Ah, there they are at last. I think to myself: "Twelve minutes to go—only twelve minutes." Yale is a length behind. I am sweating hard. My mouth is dry.

Yale is gaining now, slowly pulling up to us. Perhaps she has been saving up for a surprise as in the morning races. It is going to be harder than we thought. We must go faster.

Our shell is equipped with a system of little electric buzzers to be operated by the coxswain as a signal for a "silent sprint." This kind of sprint which is revealed to the opposing crew only by our increase in speed instead of by the usual frantic yelling of the cox, is believed to have a much more devastating effect on their morale. Now is the time to spring it.

Bzzzz—zzzzz! Away we go! Straining to our utmost, we gradually pull ahead until we have a half length of open water on the enemy. What a joy to see them struggling along behind us. We settle down again. We pass the two and a half mile mark.

I am more tired than ever. I hear familiar grunts from Tim Clark behind me. Yale is gaining again. I see that our wake has curves in it and wonder if the coxswain has lost any distance by careless steering. Each foot, each inch, mean everything in the world to us now.

Yale is still gaining. There is no more open water. Maybe they have had a secret sprint of their own. They are pulling up with what seems alarming ease. My breath wheezes through my throat, my body trickles with sweat. My oar seems clumsy to hold and splashes more than usual. I think for a moment that I cannot hold on.

Suddenly our stroke, Jack Watts, seated in front of me, changes his rhythm. He is excited. He has seen something. I glance at Yale. Someone in their boat has "caught a crab." His oar, twirled out of his fingers by a wave, is momentarily out of control. Yale's numbers three and four seem to have stopped rowing while they struggle to retrieve the loose oar. Their shell has lost speed till they recover from their confusion and set after us once more.

Meanwhile Jack has seized the opportunity to put us into a sprint. It's exciting! I feel I could go ten miles now as Yale falls back into our wake. We pull with wild joy for there is only a mile or so more and Yale is now two full lengths behind. The taste of victory is in our blood. There, the three mile mark!

Crack! My oar! Has it broken? I look out to see, but am relieved to find it undamaged. It had evidently struck a bottle which I can see floating back in our wake. Somebody on some yacht probably threw it overboard without a thought. Whew! I wonder what I would have done had my oar really broken. Should I have jumped overboard?

Where is that three-and-a-half mile flag? I suddenly feel pretty far gone, my throat like the inside of a smokestack, dry and hot. All around my stomach region feels weak. I keep going from momentum. I feel as if, were I stopped, I couldn't start again.

Yale is slowly but steadily coming up. Much as I want to beat them, that idea has become secondary to the much more vital need of seeing the finish line.

Zip! The three-and-a-half mile flag! Three minutes more to go. Everything is swimming in a fog of weakness—but the stroke must soon go up, and keep going up to the finish.

Yale is still gaining, if slowly. There's only a little open water left. Are they about to pour on their famous final sprint? Every physical reaction is swallowed up in the effort to keep going, but I can still think, "This stroke tempo must increase a little. I must pull through a little faster . . ."

The coxswain blows his whistle. "Forty strokes to go!" he yells. Our beat goes up to thirty-four, to thirty-six. Vaguely I hear the sirens, whistles blowing, a roar from thousands of throats, the shrill screams of women. Yale is gaining.

All I can feel is that I must give every last drop. The sense of rhythm with a yank in it is all I have left.

"Thirty strokes more!" the coxswain screams above the whistles. He counts them out: "One—two—three—four . . ."

I can see the Yale bow opposite our stern. We are holding them about even.

"Eight—nine—ten . . ."

The stroke is going higher. Nearly forty to the minute now.

"Ten more to go!" yells the coxswain. "Four—five—six . . ."

Between each stroke my mind wanders. I think of friends on the observation trains. "Nine—ten . . ."

Then: "Ten more to go!" The cox must have misjudged it. I feel that I can just hold on, but I sort of pray that I can do it. Yale can't catch us now and I think we're actually running away from them. "Three—four . . ." I hear myself saying to myself: hold on. Only a few seconds more. Nothing can stop us now.

"Three strokes to go!"

Yale is a length and a quarter behind. We've got 'em licked.

"One—two . . ."

Zip! The finish flag!

"Let her run," says the coxswain.

We all slumped in our seats and it was pure joy to realize we had won and were suddenly "heroes" to the cheering crowds. But five minutes later we had recovered and were paddling leisurely back to Red Top where we collected nine Yale shirts (crews traditionally bet their shirts on races), threw cox Fred Sullivan into the river (another tradition of winning), and elected Jack Watts captain for the next year.

Parties of celebration at the Griswold lasted far into the night and morning, and we joined them. Some of us drank too much and got sick, but not me—for I have never really liked the taste of liquor and even less the feeling of losing control of my body or mind. So I stuck to ginger ale or fruit juice; this decision and custom helped me avoid a lot of woe in future years, perhaps more by luck than virtue. Not that it seemed so then, but my stubbornness in resisting offered drinks turned out to be a life-and-death issue, and I was glad that some mystic guidance helped steer me from mortal

danger. Mrs. Parker seemed glad too that I abstained for her husband had ruined their marriage through drink and her younger son seemed to have inherited the tendency.

Junior Year
1927–1928

After some relaxation in Dedham and seeing Molly and Mrs. Parker for a couple of weeks, I set out for the West by train on July 11 because that was when my summer job with the McFarland family began. I was to meet them in Cleveland the next day, and it seemed a golden opportunity to visit the most spectacular parts of North America not only without expense but with an assured salary of one hundred dollars a month plus, as it turned out, a sizeable bonus if I wasn't too scrupulous about reforming my delinquent ways.

At the end of a day in Cleveland we all boarded the train to Chicago and, after a night in the Blackstone Hotel, caught the "Mountaineer" at the Soo Line station for our three-day journey to Lake Louise in Alberta, travelling in plush Pullman sleeping cars of course. There were six of us, Mrs. McFarland and her three, plus Miss Armstrong (nursemaid to the two girls) and me. Following a natural inclination, I wrote a 150-page diary about our adventures that summer (up to Labor Day), which included forty-eight illustrations (mostly postcards).

Without doubt I was bursting with energy in those days for, at almost every stop and opportunity, I would head for the nearest mountain and, despite a lack of proper gear, climb it and look over the countryside collecting flowers and bird feathers, taking pictures and drawing maps. I usually went on these side trips alone because my charge, Jack, while game enough, was not used to such strenuous activity. At Lake Louise I rowed the length of the lake and back (three miles) with Trudie, the youngest McFarland girl. Then, finding the water only 38 degrees Fahrenheit, preferred the hotel's 100-foot outdoor pool for swimming.

On July 19 we headed West again and next day got to Vancouver where we took the steamer across the Strait of Juan de Fuca to Seattle on Puget Sound, a four-hour voyage I was to repeat two years later under strikingly different circumstances on my way around the world. Then, riding the train south to San Francisco, Jack and I intermittently amused ourselves by trying to see how much silverware we could swipe from dining cars without being noticed by either the family or the waiters. To our surprise, it was ridiculously easy.

As the big bridges had not yet been built in San Francisco, we had two interesting ferry rides, including the one from Oakland to the city itself where we stayed at the palatial Fairmont Hotel atop Nob Hill and explored Chinatown. Next we were off southward again for San Luis Obispo and then Santa Barbara, where we put up at the El Miramar Hotel, had a swim in the Pacific and, being too late for the hotel lunch, enjoyed some "purloined steak" from a society picnic we had quietly infiltrated.

Although I inwardly squirm now for the need to recapitulate and mention our unconscionable light-fingeredness, it was all part of our enjoyable delinquency at the time and, if you can believe it, it was actually widely acceptable among our adventurous contemporaries, most of whom would mature into quite respectable lives as doctors, lawyers, financiers and, in several cases, headmasters of leading schools where memory of their youthful delinquency undoubtedly gave them more than a few invaluable insights into the psychology of their errant students.

As a matter of fact, I had estimable moments of my own right there in Santa Barbara because my devoted uncle Walter and aunt Mary lived nearby and, by extraordinary coincidence, my godmother occupied a luxurious annex of El Miramar itself. I did not realize then that Aunt Katharine had just returned from hosting an important reception for something called the World Population Conference at her chateau in Prangins, Switzerland, or that she was deeply interested and involved in trying to keep the world's population from getting hopelessly out of control, which was why she enrolled as a student in biology at MIT (Massachusetts Institute of Technology). This was in 1896 at the age of twenty-one, just after breaking off her romantic relationship with Father. She never spoke to me about such things but I was aware that she had a strong character (probably strengthened further by the tragedy of her marriage), that she was a serious pianist, and as the decades passed I eventually got to know that she was deeply determined to do whatever was needed to promote birth control. That, of course, was why she befriended and financed Margaret Sanger when birth control was taboo, illegal, and dangerous to be associated with, and why she risked jail in smuggling diaphragms

from France to America through most of the twenties to aid her cause. Of course she had no idea that I would have appreciated a diaphragm in 1927 (for Molly)—she viewed birth control almost solely on a world scale, though she evidently practised it herself and remained childless—so we spoke mainly of conventional pleasantries and probably about my mother and how sad it could be to lose a dear one. Katharine was far too reserved to mention that her hopelessly demented husband, Stanley, was then upstairs listening to the private symphony orchestra she had employed for the past twenty years specifically to soothe his raging phobias and depressions, and which she would continue to engage for another twenty years until his death in 1947.

Next day Jack and I, having separated ourselves from the family for our scheduled August camping trip in Wyoming, took the train for Los Angeles. As we boarded the coach with our heavy luggage (including our purloined dining car "silver"), I heard some member of the family behind us sigh and remark, "Well—*they're* gone!" For our part, we had a momentarily giddy feeling as the apron strings slipped away and out of sight.

Today, sixty years later, I retain no important memories of Los Angeles or the Mohave Desert we subsequently crossed into Arizona, but the Grand Canyon unquestionably did impress us. I see in my diary that I wrote that the canyon "is more mysterious in its depth than the Himalayas in their height, and bestows a new conception of space, and of the size of the earth." We rode on mules with eight other tourists down the Bright Angel trail to the bottom which is vertically more than a mile below the rim. My mule had the name of Domino "which I changed to Dynamo because of his dynamic will and personality. . . . He loved to show off by tripping merrily along the very edge of the trail, on the brink of some stupendous chasm, gargling softly to himself with delight. . . . And he would frequently stop to reach, goatlike, out into space, for a choice mouthful of willow leaves or refreshing pine needles. . . ."

At the bottom the temperature was around 125 degrees in the shade and "the only water clear enough to be drinkable was a tiny, trickling brook . . . as hot as soup." The Colorado River here was a "bare 100 ft. in width," muddy and very wild. To ease Dynamo's burden, I returned on foot all the way back up to the canyon's rim, collecting on the way such flowers as columbine, mountain aster, and wild geranium which I pasted into my diary. By supper time the harsh red glare

Louise and Guy Murchie, Sr., (standing) and Janet (Bell) and Guy Murchie, Jr., (seated) at Apple Hill, Nelson, New Hampshire, about 1950

of the Grand Canyon faded "under the enchanting spell of the ever-increasing softness of the rays of the setting sun. Peaks began to shift and glow, walls darkened, crags took fire, and gray-green mesas, dimly seen, took on the gleam of opalescent lakes of mountain water."

When we got off the train in Cody, Wyoming (named for Buffalo Bill), on August 3, our lives underwent a complete change for, as prearranged by Mrs. McFarland, we took a three-week "pack trip" through the Shoshone Mountains with two cowboys as guides and nine horses to ride and carry our camping gear and grub. It was a most enjoyable adventure in almost virgin country teeming with game, and I wrote sixty pages in my diary, mostly about the animals we saw, the wild flowers and Indian relics we collected, and the unexpected events we experienced each day.

Our last week in the West was spent in Yellowstone Park where we saw lots of tame game,

begging bears, hot springs and geysers but hardly anything worth retelling now. We saved money on one or two occasions by climbing through the window of unoccupied cabins and sleeping on whatever beds we found, but we tried to leave things inside so neat in the morning that no one could tell we had been there.

We had some interesting news at the Grand Canyon Lodge where Jack found a letter from his father who had somehow discovered we would be in Yellowstone Park about now. And Mr. McFarland, it turned out, wanted to see his only son so much that he actually invited us both to visit him at his home in Pittsburgh on our way home. And, to make sure we would accept, he even enclosed a check to cover our fares from Yellowstone to Pittsburgh. We somehow got to Pittsburgh and, from there, home in good time, both well and prosperous.

That September I rented a room by myself at Harvard and took up what was, for me, the serious study of economics, government, philosophy, and social ethics. I was "on probation" because I had not applied myself hard enough the previous semester after planning to drop out of college, so now I had to work really hard to make sure I would regain eligibility for the crew season in spring. And, perhaps subconsciously, I felt some sort of an impulse to undertake the study of social ethics in order to reexamine my delinquent rationalizations. I must have told Molly something about our summer's pranks but she, still a teenager, seemed more inclined to be an accomplice than to suggest that I rethink my principles of living. It was different, of course, with Mrs. Parker, who undoubtedly wormed the significant facts out of me and, while continuing our warm relationship, began to suggest that my childish egotism had outlived its usefulness and was due for progressive replacement by a more mature and balanced outlook.

I really needed this kind of parental guidance. Father was clearly incapable of giving it to me because he was utterly out of touch with my mind and my dreams of the future. However, he had been unwontedly impressed with my success on the Harvard crew at New London and, reflecting on it, invited the whole crew to a gala party at the Tavern Club in Boston on my twenty-first birthday, January 25, 1928. This he declared to be in honor of my having achieved my majority and the legal right to vote. He was likewise pleased to hear that, by then, I was off probation and eligible to row, an issue publicized probably more than he thought warranted by the sports writers in the Boston and New York papers.

My relations with Molly, on the other hand, continued without outward change and, though we rarely talked about it, we thought of ourselves as engaged for probable marriage sometime after I finished college, went around the world, and settled down into some sort of a steady occupation. Her family remained more than a little conservative about letting her go off with me on any kind of extended date, and I remember the lengths I sometimes went to to maneuver her out of the house on weekends. I recall one Sunday in particular that demanded unusual ingenuity because, as Molly said, she didn't really dare go out with me if her parents specifically forbade it, as they were then inclined to do. To defy them in such a matter would have seriously queered our relations for the future. So my problem was how to wake her up early enough in the morning so she could get up, dressed, and away, before either parent awoke to find her gone. Once she had flown, of course, unless one or the other had acted in anticipation, they couldn't reasonably claim to have forbidden her.

An alarm clock was impractical in this situation because it would likely waken the whole household. All the bedrooms were close together with thin walls. So I told Molly to find a string about forty feet long which she could tie to her big toe before retiring, leaving the rest of it hanging out her open window and down to Charles Street three stories below. This I could pull when I arrived at about six, and it should surely waken her.

She agreed. So I arose eager and early that Sunday and drove in my aging Buick to her house, parked quietly on Charles Street, and found the string in the dawning light. Of course any passerby could have pulled the string, and some fellows probably would have if they'd noticed it and been capable of imagining what might be on the other end. But that was far too improbable to worry me. I eagerly pulled at 6:02 and in a few seconds saw Molly's head out the window with a finger to her silent lips. Then I waited a long five minutes while she hastily dressed and slipped noiselessly downstairs. And hooray, hallelujah! We were off, and free!

I don't remember just where we went that day, but I'm sure it was fulfilling. Almost invariably it was. We had the world to choose from and, though we might get frustrated momentarily by picking some quiet lane that turned out to be the back entrance to a mansion defended by Dobermans, we could try again and, if need be, again.

I got *C*s in economics and government and a *B* in philosophy that fall and winter. And I was on the crew again in spring, and we won every race before we went to New London in June. But something happened to us while we were training for the Yale race. It may have had to do with Ed Brown's paranoia about Yale's progress for I have a letter I wrote to Mrs. Parker from Red Top saying:

> Whenever [Ed Browne] discovers Yale is about to have a time trial, he gets terrifically excited and begins rushing around with his stop watch, booming out orders to get the launches ready and everything . . . Afterwards he gets out paper and pencil and starts figuring out how we compare with Yale, taking into consideration tide, temperature, wind, humidity, size of waves, room for improvement, our physical condition, how the boat was rigged, surface tension, etc. He multiplies a lot of numbers together, then adds 4 (he won't say why), then he does a lot more figuring and in about an hour arrives at a startling decision. If the decision is too startling, he says he made a mistake and does it all over again differently. That's how he spends his evenings. . . .

Perhaps, because of all this frenzy, we somehow got overtrained and went into a slump. In any case, we lost to Yale by almost nine lengths, the worst drubbing I ever had in my six years of crew racing, and my only loss to Yale in five encounters. And we didn't do much better in the Olympic trials in July, although I did not feel noticeably different.

Senior Year
1928–1929

I had been planning to take a job in western Canada during the summer, a payless charity job working on a railroad with shovel, pick, and sledge hammer each day and teaching my largely illiterate fellow laborers at night. It would have been an enlightening contrast to my last summer's activities, but our Olympic trials prevented me from keeping the appointment and someone replaced me by July first. So, after a few days visiting Worgzle (Mrs. Parker), who had rented a small apartment on the second floor of 18 Louisburg

Square in Boston, we decided I had best go up to Northeast Harbor in Maine for at least the hot weeks of July and August. Her younger son, whom we called Park (for Parker) or Bub, was there, and her aunt Frances, about seventy, owned a summer home there. Aunt Frances was her father's younger sister, had married Henry Parkman (son of the historian), and lived in cool seasons in a brownstone house on Commonwealth Avenue in Boston. Worgzle herself could not go because she had a job in Boston, needed to supplement the two hundred dollars a month allowance she got from her father. I think she was selling bonds that year.

No longer having the Buick, my obvious mode of transport was my motorcycle which by then I called "the thunderbolt" or simply "the bolt." I set out from Boston on a rainy afternoon and had hardly crossed the Charles River before I had a strange accident. In those pre-highway days any long-range wayfarer had to traverse all sorts of cobblestone byways in endless sequences of towns, and I was slowly rumbling along a cobblestone street in Charlestown when I overtook a man leading two large draft horses. I could not see well as I was wearing goggles, all smeary and wet from the steady drizzle, and as the animals seemed placid enough, I did not consider them dangerous and steered to pass about six feet to the left. But, without warning, the near horse suddenly swung his hind quarters toward me, reared, and let go with his great hind legs, kicking me off my machine. The next thing I knew, I was lying in the street beside the motorcycle with its engine still running and rear wheel turning in the air, and the man with the horses was leaning over me trying to express his concern while the horses just stood there slobbering and glowering against the dull sky. I guess I'd been knocked out for a few seconds. I shook my head, trying to get rid of the stars. In the next minute I got up and set the thunderbolt aright and told the man not to worry as I didn't feel much hurt, then I proceeded on my way north. Evidently I'd been kicked in the right hip and the steel horseshoe had cut into me but luckily broke no bone. However, I was oozing blood down my right pant leg all the fifty miles to Exeter, New Hampshire, where I stopped at an inn for a hot bath, supper, and a good night's sleep.

By morning I felt pretty normal and cycled the rest of the 250-odd miles to Northeast Harbor and moved into a rooming house with Bub. It was beautiful and cool there on Mount Desert Island and we shared a big double bed for $7.50 a week, so we weren't exactly splurging. The only trouble was that Bub, despite his rare sense of humor, was shy about meeting people, especially the young, rich, self-centered crowd of merrymakers in this summer resort where swimming, tennis, and sailing were the main occupations along with picnicking by day and dancing by night. It was naturally easier for me, being two years older, because, even though I had yet to go around the world, I had already had enough exploits and adventures to make me a "man of the world" compared to these starry-eyed kids and, once I got to know a few of them, I found myself being invited out to meals or sporting events almost every day and dances several times a week. Only rarely could we get up the nerve to call on old Aunt Frances which, we hoped she didn't notice, was always close to mealtime.

One sporting event was a swimming meet in Bar Harbor in which I competed as a member of the Northeast Harbor 200-yard relay team. We raced against both Bar Harbor and a Navy team of four sailors picked as the fastest in recent competition among the crews of several destroyers anchored in Bar Harbor. Surprisingly, we won, and each of the four of us was awarded a prize of a small cup made of German silver. The last time I got such a mug was summer before last when I was even more surprised to win a tennis tournament near Falmouth when visiting Molly. On both occasions the cup turned black in a couple of months and didn't seem worth polishing or exhibiting on a shelf. More of a problem was my twelve-foot oar which Harvard awarded me (with a bill) every time we beat Yale, not to mention the shirts of defeated crews of MIT, Cornell, Navy, Penn, and Yale. I guess we were expected to hang them up in our rooms as trophies. Oh well, it was a nice custom for the next year or two but, after that, the likelihood began to fade.

That was the year when Tunney retired from the boxing ring after twice defeating Dempsey as heavyweight champion of the world. And Worgzle got so excited thinking about it that she began to wonder why I, bigger than either of them, couldn't become a prize fighter and eventually world champion. It was characteristic of her to get "brain waves" of the sort, but it didn't take long for me, with Attie's help, to talk her out of it.

She was living near Newport, Rhode Island, that August on the turkey farm owned by her father, the retired general, then in his seventies and fading. He and her mother must have given her a rough time as their unmarried and dependent daughter whom they could boss around, for unthinkingly they treated her as a child even as she devotedly took care of them in ways they failed to appreciate.

I don't remember writing to Molly anymore during this time, but I did write frequent love letters to Worgzle and told her I wanted to go to Rhode Island to be near her whether or not her parents would invite me to their farm. She was much more than a mother to me but I could not really think of her as a girlfriend. Ours was primarily a spiritual relationship with the potentiality to grow into I didn't know what. Almost all her friends were close to my age and she often said wistfully, "If only I were thirty years younger . . ."

Meantime I tried to make the most of Northeast Harbor. One day when a bunch of kids were admiring my thunderbolt, I offered them a ride around the town, as many of them as could climb on. Seven managed it: one on the gas tank, two on the rear seat, one on the rear mudguard, one on my lap, one on the handlebars, and one on the front mudguard. That made eight of us in all, and I carried them for two miles at about 20 mph. I believe it only because I was part of it. It made such an impression on them that long after I'd forgotten it, one reminded me of it in 1953.

Unfortunately, the bolt broke down occasionally at which times I resorted to other means of travel. One night after a dance at Northeast, I emerged with my friend Bob Sewall, anchor man on our relay swimming team, and we were itching for more fun. So we decided to hitch a ride to Bar Harbor. We hopped on the rear fenders of a big limousine bound in that direction and took a bumpy ride. After twenty minutes we were glad for the chance to get off our cramped perches as the car entered a magnificent driveway and halted before a majestic stone mansion. Alighting and stretching, we saw two beautiful young ladies getting out of the limousine, obviously very surprised to see us. We introduced ourselves and told them of our devotion in escorting them for so long on the stern of their chariot. They seemed impressed and amused and invited us into their house for a repast and a warming before the fire.

By the end of August I had decided to accept a request of my father to visit him and my stepmother, Jane, at her plush home in Cohasset. I had misgivings about going there because I knew how critical Father could be and, for some reason (I can't remember what), I had run out of clean shirts to wear. I was probably short of money too and had not yet been invited to Rhode Island. So,

being still young and foolhardy in some ways, I took what seemed the lesser evil and arrived in Cohasset to find myself in instant hot water.

When I was in Boston I didn't have a clean shirt so I borrowed one from a fellow. But it was so small I couldn't keep the collar closed and it got dirty on the way because I was so dripping wet with my heavy suit on such a hot day. My stepmother wasn't especially pleased by my appearance, so I went in for a swim to get cooled off and figure out what to do. When I came out I decided it was imperative to get a clean shirt before supper if I expected to be allowed to spend the night. I went to Father's room and began looking for a shirt and while searching for a collar button, a terrible thing happened. I saw a little gold box with a lever on the side and thought it might be a jewelry box with collar buttons inside, so I pushed the little lever. To my amazement and terror a little bird about an inch long suddenly sprang up and began to sing at the top of his lungs—it was some kind of a music box. My position would surely be given away if I couldn't shut him up somehow, so in desperation I seized a blanket to muffle the piercing noise. In my haste I knocked over a vase of flowers which didn't help much, and the bird sang on, very cruelly, by himself. At last he stopped and I hoped against hope that the singing hadn't been heard. But it was too late. I heard my stepmother, despite being quite fat, charging up the stairs and demanding, "What are you doing in my room?" And I only had a ragged undershirt on above the waist.

Well, that lecture was over in about half an hour: she wasn't as slow at lecturing as Father was, but much fiercer. Then I went upstairs and tried to get a shirt on without collar buttons. Eventually I got it tied together pretty well and came down to supper. Father was there by that time and wanted to know where all my clothes were, why I hadn't let him know I was coming, why I had left Maine so soon, what I had done with the money he had given me, where were my accounts, and many other difficult questions—meanwhile rubbing in the fact that Donald and Agnes had been working all summer while I had loafed.

I didn't have a very enjoyable evening. I thought many times I wouldn't stay and finally went upstairs to sleep it off. In the morning it wasn't quite so bad but I received short lectures on the same old question of the previous night and in addition a ferocious one on my lack of education. Then Father said I must be sure to vote Republican in order to help the Hoover cause. And when I said I didn't think I could vote for Hoover, he laughed at me as if I were crazy and asked me pityingly if I knew what the issues were.

I went out for football that September because I felt pressure to do it, even from Ed Brown who seemed to feel I had let him down in the Yale race in June. At the same time Father, who once did well in football and liked it enough to coach it, wanted me to give it up, saying I was prone to get injured, hadn't enough experience to have any chance of making the team anyway and that, even if the team were so poor they'd want me on it, that I'd surely get on probation again from neglecting my studies. I never heard such a pessimist.

However, even though I did better than I thought I could in the early season, I soon had serious troubles with football, particularly recurring headaches because the biggest headguard I could obtain pinched my head whenever I got hit. After the doctor took an X ray of my head in October, he advised me to quit and, with an inward feeling of relief, I did so.

Then I tried my hand at a sport that seemed much more congenial to me: running cross-country. At first everyone was surprised and skeptical that I, who weighed 210 pounds, could even think of competing with these skinny little harriers of 130 to 140 pounds, but on my first attempt, before I had bought track shoes, I qualified for the team, finishing eighth out of thirty. As expected, I was *slow* going *up* the hills, but I found I could largely make up for it by going *fast down* the hills.

The Harvard cross-country course covered five miles up and down the Charles River, taking in several hills and, through some streets in Watertown where one had to dodge pedestrians, hurdle baby carriages, and deal with dogs yapping at heels and kids making snide remarks. Our best runner was Jimmy Reid, who weighed seventy pounds less than I did and broke all records for our course and won all his races including the ICAAAA (Inter-Collegiate American Amateur Athletic Association) meet in Van Cortland Park in New York City where he outran all the hundred best distance runners in the country. Later he became a judge in Maine. The only thing about my own running that could be considered remarkable was the fact that I ran carrying the equivalent weight of an eight-year-old boy around my shoulders and chest, something believed hopelessly detrimental in competitive long-distance running. Yet, to my coach's amazement, at the season's end I was one of five Harvard runners awarded gold medals for scoring in our victory over Yale. The cross-country team had a party to celebrate and we all ate, drank, sang

"My father, Guy Murchie, Sr., at christening of my daughter Gretel," 1944

songs, and made sentimental speeches until the wee hours. When we dispersed about 4 A.M. it was so quiet in the streets that, as I joked to Jimmy, "a caterpillar sneaking along a velvet sidewalk wearing greased rubber soles would sound like a royal coronation in the Fiji Island".

Worgzle knew about Molly, of course, and met her once or twice for tea in Boston. On one occasion when Molly missed her period and thought she was pregnant, Worgzle tried to help with advice such as having her take a mustard bath. I didn't see how she could be pregnant after all the care I had taken to protect her. I didn't know about diaphragms or how to obtain a condom, but I was using balloons from the ten-cent store and felt sure they were safe even though the colors (red, blue, green and yellow) ran when wet. Despite all this, Worgzle was concerned enough to lecture me on my duty to marry Molly if, for any reason, she should bear my child. "An honorable man would have no alternative," she said.

It turned out that Molly was not really pregnant but only a little irregular. And Worgzle, coming to understand that my affair with Molly was primarily based on physical attraction, began to point out that, although Molly and I seemed to get along well at present, my future development would likely become so different from Molly's that we might not be at all suited to each other in five or ten years. For that reason, she said, "I really fear you would be taking a reckless chance if you didn't think twice about marrying her."

In retrospect one might wonder whether Worgzle had any sort of surmise that she herself might marry me one day and therefore could subconsciously be trying to leave open the possibility. Somehow I cannot quite let myself believe that. At least once that spring of 1929 when she was criticizing my naive delinquency and contrariness, she said with some feeling that I was "the last man on earth" she would ever think of having for a husband. I'd have to admit that it was not exactly what one could call a verifiable declaration.

As for Molly, who at the time was the only woman I had ever "known" in the biblical sense, she naturally was on a pedestal as a kind of angel in my affections. I was unacquainted with any other girl with whom I could even begin to compare her. So inevitably I idealized her and, if I had married her then, I might well have lived with her all my life, blissfully unaware of what life could be with someone else, someone perhaps closer to me intellectually or spiritually.

That is how it was in the winter of 1928–1929 when Worgzle opened my eyes to a realization that I might be missing something. And, to my wonder, she actually started pointing out other females to me, ranging from a picture of the Venus de Milo to a live young ballet dancer, whom she fancied I might consider. If I was determined to go around the world, she said with a wide-eyed look, it behooved me at least to develop the perspective of a man of the world.

Perhaps I was getting to feel a little that way (though not as Worgzle meant it) by early March when I attended an illustrated lecture by a British geologist and mountaineer named Odelle who was freshly back from Mt. Everest. He had gone above 28,000 feet (only 900 feet below the top) on the most recent Everest expedition during which the dauntless pair, Mallory and Irvine, lost their lives. I wrote her excitedly as soon as I got to my room, saying:

I would really like to go on the next expedition if I get the chance, and I think the summit will surely be reached then. The only reason they failed on Everest last time is because they didn't have time to get acclimated on account of the unexpectedly early storm season. . . . But it will be hard to launch another expedition for awhile, because the Tibetans have gotten superstitious about the death toll of the mountain and won't allow any foreigners near it.

Odelle had some marvellous pictures of Mt. Everest, which is so high that its summit is subject to a terrific trade wind caused by the earth's rotation, all of which results in tremendous clouds of ice crystals being blown perpetually from the peak in a snowy streamer that extends miles to leeward. Oh! It's a magnificent mountain, Worgzle, I'd love to try it some day . . . It makes me restless just to think of it. Gosh, I'll be glad when I get loose and can start around the world.

I didn't do well in rowing that spring, mainly because Ed Brown seemed to regard me as a Jonah. So, after a few weeks in April of trying to recover my reputation, I decided to quit—and went out for track instead. As there was no long-distance running event in spring, I tried the shotput and discus but, although I showed "promise" at first and made measurable progress, one month wasn't enough time for me to prove my potential. Besides, I had some tough exams to pass and, as soon as I finished them, I wanted to be off on my way around the world. With all that looming and beckoning before me, it was not easy to concentrate on such exam questions as "How do fiscal machinery and methods of obtaining money affect the progress of a people toward civilization?" or "What are the social problems inherent in the existence of a leisure class?"

All this time Worgzle, bless her, had been struggling to improve my character, mostly in letters pointing out that I tended to dramatize too much and, by telling people of my bumming adventures and how I enjoyed them, giving the false impression that I was just a bum.

I wrote back that my saying how much I enjoyed bumming was not strictly false because I really did like to bum. If I didn't, why would I want to bum my way around the world? And, if people got a wrong impression of me, it was only because they didn't really know me, and that in turn was because I hadn't told the whole truth but just a small part of it. "It takes time," I explained, "to give the whole truth." But I believe in the truth, I told her, which is in every way better and more exciting than any made-up drama because it is real. It is fact. It is true.

When she questioned my sincerity, I responded with some heat: "My life has not really even begun and I can't prove anything until it does—but by God! I'm going to then." When she mentioned that some people thought me conceited, I said that my sincerity probably gave that impression and not without reason. I admitted to being conceited and "in that I sense I have an advantage over other people because I understand things they don't, but I don't believe it is an objectionable kind of conceit if it is understood." I said I felt sure I was happier than most people and, since everybody seeks happiness, I must be to that degree more successful. That was the basis of my conceit.

It also had something to do with being true, which I called "the most beautiful thing in the world . . . and the strongest power under heaven," something that "when you have it, you know it beyond the shadow of doubt" because "beauty and strength really are the same thing."

By way of an example, I told her that I had a picture in my hand that was the most beautiful thing I had ever seen. It was a photograph of Abraham Lincoln taken in 1860 during the campaign that made him president. "Some call it ugly," I wrote, "but to me it is absolute beauty. . . . To see that utterly honest, sincere face and then to think of what he did with his life . . . I get tears in my eyes almost every time I look at it. Those lean, strong jaws and that steady, unfearing look reveal a faith that I cannot hesitate for an instant to believe comes directly from God . . . I just know it. It doesn't need any proof for me to believe it."

Pouring out my soul to her, I declared that "I never can give my true self to anyone until I have lived my life. That will be me—as it is with everybody, if you understand it. The thing I must do is try to keep from giving a false impression in the meantime. I must keep from pretending things, especially to myself. You have taught me this, Worgzle, and I am going to show you in time how well I have learned it."

I had already made my break with Molly, telling her (as gently as I could) that I had to be free while I was still growing up and setting forth around the world, and that we should not consider ourselves engaged anymore. It was quite a wrench, for me too, but she took it pretty well—and even

seduced me on one occasion shortly afterward, with commendable subtlety and finesse, perhaps to demonstrate that anything is still possible. However, I dated a few other girls too, one whose body odor and perfume surprisingly kept me at arm's length, another a doctor's daughter, quite alluring but nervously unsure of where to draw the line. I told Worgzle enough of these ventures to alarm her, so that she warned me repeatedly against getting entangled emotionally at my callow stage of life.

Once in a while Worgzle would get mad at me and, if she seemed unjust, I would respond in kind. But it never lasted long and invariably cleared the air. Referring to it in a letter, I said "When we get mad I always learn something by it, and then when everything is OK again we love each other more than ever, so it is worth getting mad almost . . ."

In a profound sense we had a kind of dream of love, which I tried to describe in one of my letters:

> I wish the same way you do sometimes, that I were with you somewhere in a little warm hut or a cave—where we two could lie in peace in a beautiful country full of great mountains and bleak cliffs above us and great forests of unblazed timber all about—where we could go tramping through the wind over the long mountain trails, and be friends with every great thing all about us, and love each other, undisturbed forever . . .

And now I see that Worgzle sometime later wrote five words in her own hand upon this page, calling it "The old old lovely dream."

The last few weeks between my final exams, all of which I passed, and my departure were hectic with getting my passport and visas, three typhoid inoculations a week apart, going to the dentist, acquiring an AB (able-bodied seaman's) ticket, and a minimum of packing. Instead of a suitcase I decided to take an old laundry bag I had which was colored red, blue, green, and yellow in a kind of Czechoslovakian pattern. I liked its toughness and flexibility.

Father was not in favor of my going at all and referred to it rather sarcastically. He was convinced I was not very bright, not just because my marks at Harvard were mediocre but because obviously I couldn't learn by being told and therefore would have to learn the hard way: by experience. At first he tried to control me by refusing to give me any money. Then when he realized I was stubborn enough to go anyway and intended to earn my own way, he tried to bargain with me, saying he would give me a letter of credit if I would promise to return within a year. When I replied that, although I hoped to be back that soon, I did not know enough of what my circumstances would be while travelling to be able to promise anything, he eventually backed down and gave me the letter of credit anyway. But he kept on referring to my venture as a happy-go-lucky vacation and let me know that he considered me basically ungrateful and selfish not to respect his wishes or follow his advice as Donald had. Donald by this time was about to begin his third year with IBM, and he was generally considered not only promising but definitely headed for the top.

If I had known about Santayana's letter to Father, calling him "inconsequential" in 1896 when he was recently out of Harvard, I might have been tempted to remind him of it, but I knew nothing of Father's own youthful struggle to find his way and he never mentioned it, leaving me to discover it only from his widow when she handed me a packet of letters half a century later.

I had heard of an oil tanker due to sail from Boston on June 1 and thought of bidding for a place in her crew. But I had to go to New York to visit Worgzle in the last week of May and there, hearing of an army transport named the *Chateau-Thierry* (for the World War battle) docked in Brooklyn and scheduled to sail June 7 for the West Coast via the Panama Canal, we decided she was the one for me and I would go around the world westward.

When I showed my AB ticket at the shipping office on June 6, they signed me on straight away and, after an intimate farewell from Worgzle, I walked up the gangplank on the morning of the seventh with my sack over my shoulder—ready for the world.

Alaska 1929

It was something of a shock to feel the abrupt change in my circumstances as I beheld the motley crew of the *Chateau-Thierry*. One sailor with a mug like the front end of a freight locomotive spat over the rail and said, "This is a hellova time ter be on a boat. Kericed! Just the woist time o' year. Think what we could be doin' this summer if we stayed in New Yoik!"

Another, known as the Wop, snarled, "God, that's a lousy stink-hole they give us to sleep in."

Then, "Hey you, Slim," shouted the bosun, with gimlet eye upon me, "stow your stuff in the fo'c'sle, then go get up steam on winch number two."

I sprang to do his bidding. I knew the forecastle must be forward and I found it. But after leaving my bag on the only vacant bunk, I wondered where was winch number two. Able-bodied seamen are presumed to be familiar with such things but, despite my AB ticket and brief experiences on sailing vessels, I was a very green sailor. By beginner's luck I hit upon the right winch, second from the bow, and by trial and error found a valve that hissed with steam. But there was still time to kick me ashore if the bosun found out how little I actually knew—so I assumed a confident air and toyed, casually, with winch number two until, to my great relief, we cast off and I could watch the towers of New York sinking behind us.

I enjoyed my voyage through the Panama Canal despite the bedbugs in the fo'c'sle. I was impressed with the casualness with which most of the sailors invaded the red-light district in the town of Panama where booths lined both sides of the streets, each booth barely big enough to hold a double bed with large doors that could be closed when the bed was in use. Betweentimes, of course, the girl entertainer (if that's the phrase) sat outside, presumably trying to look seductive. But business was so thriving (at a dollar a shot) that the more seasoned ones no longer bothered with their looks. In fact many appeared utterly dispassionate, if not hard-boiled, and I heard one sailor complaining that, during a whole entertainment, his hostess had been preoccupied with a large bag of peanuts.

When we got to San Francisco I left the *Chateau-Thierry* and in a few minutes signed on a small freighter for Seattle. Then again in Seattle I joined the crew of the SS *Admiral Rogers*, bound for Alaska. I was eager to get a good look at that young, untamed country where a population less than a hundredth of New York City's is spread out over an expanse a fifth as big as the whole contiguous United States. I wanted to see the wilderness and its animal life in their pristine splendor before going on to the old, old civilizations of the East.

I think I more than earned my passage on the *Rogers* because she often put into small cannery villages and we of the crew did all the stevedoring, loading gold at Juneau in 200-pound sacks and in other ports mostly unloading machinery, cement, coal, and salt bags.

At Skagway on Alaska's panhandle, our most northerly destination, I was glad at last to jump ship and take the "Trail of '98" inland over the mountains. That's the route trudged by the thousands of prospectors who came this way headed for the Klondike in the wild days of the gold rush, the same year that Father was a Rough Rider fighting the Spaniards in Cuba. Only now there was a single-track railroad which easily took me the hundred miles to White Horse on the Yukon, a bleak hamlet of three hundred people, the junction between railroad and river. There, along the river's edge, hauled up on the bank beside the houses of logs and mud, lay the worn-out hulls of old scows and steamboats—leftovers from the rush days.

I lingered in White Horse only a couple of days, working in the boatyard (for four dollars a day) to finish a freighter which would add one more to the little fleet of three stern-wheelers that plied up and down the great, rushing Yukon. After painting her thirty-foot smokestack in a bosun's chair one afternoon with an old captain and an Indian boy holding my rope, I went to a dance with a fellow named Leskosek. For partners we took along the only two available girls in White Horse. Leskosek, accustomed to unfavorable arctic conditions, thought they were pretty hot; but I,

used to more favorable temperate conditions, described them in my book as "a sallow, skinny bartender's daughter with hair like dried spinach and a sickly, flat-breasted waitress with goldfish eyes and a burlap skirt." In any case, we pumphandled around with them for an hour to the 1906 tunes of a rickety phonograph while, not unexpectedly, there was "no conversation for the simple reason that no one had anything to say."

Next day I decided I would waste no more time in White Horse but go straight away northward, down the river into the heart of Alaska. I had been offered a job as fireman on the freighter when she was launched, but that seemed weeks away and I was raring to be off. So I bought a twelve-foot square-ended rowboat with oars for ten dollars through a boiler-maker friend and made ready to depart. "It's yust der t'ing," said the boiler-maker, "for goin' down der river. Yer wanna be careful in the rapids though. It's wery few that escapes if they gets dumped over in this river. Wery fast river and wery cold river—but you'll get along all right I guess. You'll have a long row gettin' 'crost der lake down dere—Lake La Barge—it's forty mile long—but after dat you get a strong current ter help . . ."

For grub I collected beans, raisins, bacon, and hardtack—and also got a fishline, cooking pot, ball of twine, matches, mosquito net, tarpaulin, and map. I had a last large meal of moose steak and lentil soup, loaded everything into my little craft, and was about to go when Leskosek, who had come down to see me off, asked me if I had a blanket. As I had none, he offered to give me an extra one of his and, although it was full of holes and rather smelly, I accepted it with a gratitude that was to increase through each cold night. He wished me luck—and I pushed out into the stream.

In two minutes the current had carried me three hundred yards down the river, around a bend, and out of sight. There was no sign of habitation within my horizon. Nothing but the vast spruce forests stretching from the top of high clay riverbanks back into the mountains. All about me the rippling, swirling river, making a soft swishing sound like a steaming kettle. The next town I should see would be Dawson, center of the gold rush, four hundred and eighty miles through the mountain ranges to the north. It was after 10:00 P.M. and the long arctic twilight was descending.

Next morning, July 15, I awoke in my drifting boat at the southern end of Lake La Barge. I was glad I had planned it this way for I needed a long day. As far as I could see, the lake extended like a

"My son, Jed Murchie," 1953

mirror of deep blue, spreading its narrow arms in among the spruce-clad mountains. Picturesque all right—but a tremendous obstacle to me, all alone in a little boat in dead water. There seemed nothing to do but row, so I headed north, starting off at a steady easy stroke, calculated to last a long time. But the outlook was a little grim.

Four miles in a shell with seven other men to help you is bad enough, but forty miles in a rowboat all alone seemed somehow unfair, maybe even unnecessary. So, as I rowed along and the shore seemed to remain in the same position hour after hour, I kept looking and wishing for . . . for I didn't know what. Then I saw it—and consciously thanked God. I noticed a slight ripple on the previously smooth surface—a following breeze! Perhaps I could sail!

I hastily made for shore, cut two strong driftwood poles for masts, and rigged up a sail with my tarpaulin. Having no hammer or nails, I managed, by the liberal use of twine, to lash my two masts erect, one on the starboard and one on the port side of the bow, with the sail stretched taut in between.

It worked perfectly, and to my great joy, the breeze strengthened, coming still from the south. I took my place in the stern, steering with an oar, and soon was skimming across the huge expanse of water at about four knots. Although by afternoon the waves got so high they slopped over the side with alarming frequency, I bailed with my cooking pot and made over toward the nearest shore—just in case. But in time the wind lessened and, as the sun finally swung below the northern horizon, I had crossed the lake and reached the river again. I felt happy to relax my steering arm, and go ashore to cook a few beans before starting once more on my downstream drift.

July 17. It was a great feeling to be totally alone, drifting, drifting through the endless wilderness, never knowing quite where I was and always wondering what would show up around the next bend, perhaps another lake, perhaps an Indian camp, perhaps a woodchopper's shack or a swift rapid to be navigated. Sometimes near some hut I would see a fish wheel or two, being slowly turned by the river's current, automatically scooping up an occasional unwary fish and dumping it into a gutter that led to a basket. Several times I saw eagles, moose and caribou, once a bear, and once, I think, a wolf. Wolves are shy, more often heard than seen, but sometimes their singing was hard to distinguish from that of sledge dogs whose

wailing customarily announced a habitation about an hour before I reached it.

When I heard rapids I would hastily cover my chattels with canvas in preparation for the spray, and stand by the oars. It was usually over in a minute: a sudden boiling sea, hard holding on the oars, and a flash of chill water, then calm again, drifting on and on. Although the rapids never really amounted to much, it was always exciting. That was because my boat didn't really amount to much either.

I got to Dawson on the nineteenth and stayed three days, working one day in the placer mines. It was hot, around 90 degrees Fahrenheit in the middle of each day, mostly because there are no real nights here this time of year to cool things off. I met several odd characters who had dwelt in Dawson ever since the rush days, including one shabby old duck who had shrewdly taken a job sweeping the dance hall floors. He told me he had noticed that, because of the shortage of cash here in 1898, most of the prospectors would pay for their drinks and their girls in gold dust, by the ounce. And, after they had had a few, inevitably they would spill some of the dust on the floor. So he just swept up the dirt and sawdust each morning and quietly took it to his room and panned it.

"Would yer believe it," he grinned. "I got ten times as much gold from the dance halls as them poor suckers got outen th' sluice."

Dawson in those days had a temporary population of several thousand. People lived in tents or shacks and a good many just squatted in the scows that had brought them downriver. But no one really had time to sleep for saloons, gambling houses, and dance halls were running and packed full all the twenty-four hours.

I asked my dilapidated friend where the girls came from and how they got here. "Oh, they came from all over the Pacific Coast," he replied, "from Seattle, Victoria, Vancouver an' all around. They came by the hundreds, on the ships with the men, workin' as waitresses an' such, an' then over the mountains an' down the river wit' the crowd. They gener'ly showed up in bunches—and they would be sayin', "When yer go down back home, don't tell Mother where I am, will yer. She thinks I'm workin' in Vancouver. Whatever yer do, don't tell her I'm here!"

It took about three days to drift from Dawson to Circle, a hamlet near the Arctic Circle. This was actually only a collection of mud huts with sod roofs growing grass so tall that the town looked as if it needed a haircut. But the important reason I left the river at Circle was that my map showed a road connecting that settlement with Fairbanks, Alaska's central town at the northern end of the Alaska Railroad. When I sold my boat, I was glad to get five dollars for it because downriver boats are cheaper than upriver boats on swift rivers like the Yukon, and it was more than obvious that the nearly a thousand miles I'd travelled since White Horse were well worth the five dollars' loss. Roughly fifty cents per one hundred miles.

As for my next destination, I planned to hike the 175 miles to Fairbanks, sleeping a few hours each warm day and walking every night so I wouldn't need to lug a blanket. But, as luck would have it, a car came along the very first day and gave me a ride, so I never found out whether I would have made it in the five days I'd allotted.

On my second day in Fairbanks I had no trouble hopping aboard a freight train bound for Seward on the coast and found it a surprisingly easy way to travel. The train crew were friendly and every evening we stopped for the night and the crew slept in a bunkhouse while I retired to a boxcar. I had discovered by then that, once you get used to it, there's hardly any bed more comfortable than a good wooden floor—that is, when you're young. And I didn't forget to say "hardly."

I was not long lonely on the train either for I had a prospector companion most of the time, who shared my bread and raisins but offered only conversation in return. "When Pa was up here prospectin'," he confided, "he was drunk the whole time. Yeh, I'd say he was drunk a good six years. An' he had four squares, Pa did. I never have more'n one m'self—but Kericed, I'm not rich like Pa was."

When I told him how I'd drifted down the Yukon, he couldn't understand why I had no squaw along in my little boat to cook and keep me company. 'Smatter of fact I had seen a few fat squaws on my way down the river but hadn't been seriously tempted. And what do you do with a squaw at voyage's end? Somehow I didn't really mind when he compared me unfavorably with his father.

We got to teeming Anchorage on the third day, having halted frequently to pick up scrap iron en route. My companion told me that a Japanese freighter was loading the scrap in Seward and it was to be used in building battleships for the Japanese navy. That seemed an eminently reasonable explanation at the time.

It was about midnight, July 31, when we finally rattled into the port of Seward in pitch blackness and fog. It was my first full-fledged night in a month. We were on a long, lighted wharf where many men were working. The Japanese freighter lay alongside and I could hear the intermittent thunder of the iron being dumped into her hold by a huge magnet that would lift it from a flatcar, then swing it over a hatch, and shut off the current to let it drop.

At ninety cents an hour, I saw my chance to make good money as a longshoreman. One day I worked sixteen hours and made more than fourteen dollars, which would be a real help when I got to the Orient.

The scrap-iron job, however, was both dirty and dangerous. Down in the hold you felt as if you were under shell fire. The nuts, bolts, flatirons, wheels, grubhoe heads, axles and other odds and ends of the mechanical age landed on the cargo surface with a deafening explosion only to bounce like shrapnel in every direction as we hid behind posts to escape the barrage.

When a ship called the SS *Yukon* docked, bound for Seattle, I tried for a job but was told that no places in the crew were available, either on deck, in the engine room, or the galley. Nor was any sort of passage to be bought, neither first-class nor steerage, nor on any of the next four boats south. All the steerage bunks, in fact, had been reserved by contract for Filipino and Chinese cannery workers, and the other passengers had all bought their return tickets before coming north in the spring.

So, if I didn't want to spend a long winter in Alaska, that meant I must stow away, and soon. I bundled my belongings into my laundry bag and looked for an opportunity. That very night it came. At low tide the ship's deck had subsided to the level of the wharf so one could step aboard anywhere without using the gangplank. I boarded the *Yukon*'s fore well deck under the cover of midnight darkness and immediately went down a companionway into the bowels of the steamer, apparently unobserved. According to my diary:

I soon found, way down in the hold, a secluded space in the overflow cargo, which is stacked near the steerage quarters. This, my lair, is up on top of the salmon cases, just under the steam pipes along the ceiling. I think I am pretty safe and I know I am very warm. I am below water level so there is no fresh air nor light—but to be aboard at all is enough to keep me contented under any

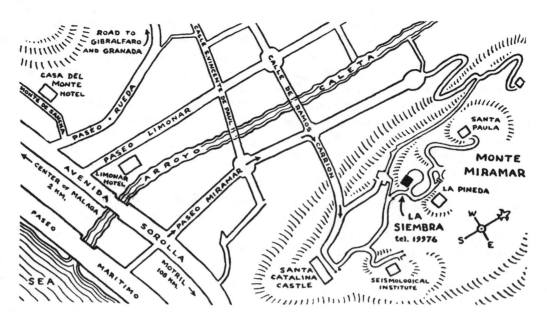

"Map of our house in Malaga, Spain, 1966"

conditions. The situation is more hazardous from the fact that I went to every officer on the ship with my story of being unable to get passage, and they all know me by sight.

I have one piece of chocolate to eat from time to time, but otherwise remain unnourished. This has been my lot for the last thirty-eight hours, ever since we sailed . . .

August 12. The night before last, I got my first real food. I was looking around in one of the forward holds when I found two bear cubs which were being shipped in crates among the rest of the cargo. There was a large supply of raw meat there for them, but they were already stuffed, and it made a regal feast for me, much to their grunted disapproval.

Returning to my lair among the steam pipes, I watched the rats scurrying about and grew to admire their extraordinary agility, even gracefulness, in negotiating the hot pipes at lightning speed.

The next time I was really hungry I grew reckless enough to approach the firemen's mess where, meeting a fireman obviously primed but hospitable, I attended a kind of "firemen's ball" and managed to stuff my pockets with three hash sandwiches besides eating several helpings of bacon and eggs, while listening to a lurid tale about a

very tough old-timer named Cast-Iron Fred who was fond of spreading canned heat as a delicacy on his bread. And one day, related the fireman, after hauling two half-drowned friends from the sea, Cast-Iron Fred ate four tins of canned heat for extra strength, then hefted his friends, one on each shoulder, some twenty miles to a hospital where, having heroically saved them, he himself died a horrible death. Wood alcohol, it seems, can be dangerous when immoderately ingested.

August 14. At last I need worry no longer. We are in the Gulf. We left Cordova late last night . . . and I decided to risk confiding in one of the stewards. He is a kindly, sympathetic fellow, fixed me up a bunk, and sold me a ticket for five dollars which he says will get me by all right. He went so far as to invite me to visit him at his home in the States. . . . Protected by my ticket, I can now go out upon the open fo'c'sle head. The wind, as we plow eastward across the Gulf, feels delicious beyond expression after the cramped murk of the hold . . .

August 15. Times have changed. My situation is very different from what it was yesterday. This morning the mate, who was naturally suspicious of me, asked for my ticket, and, upon examining it, pronounced it "no good." It was careless of me to have neglected making certain that my ticket was OK.

I was taken before the captain, a salty, grizzled old scoundrel, to be arraigned and sentenced for my crime.

"Well, what're you here for?" he bellowed, trying to look as terrible as possible.

"I'm a stowaway, sir," I answered.

"A stowaway! Hah! And where did you get this fake ticket yer tried to pass off on us?"

"A feller sold it to me," I said.

At this the blood showed red in his leathery face. He was getting mad.

"Come on!" he roared. "WHO sold it to yer?"

I hesitated. My steward friend would be in dire trouble if I weren't careful. He had tried to help me, and perhaps had made a mistake about the validity of the ticket. At any cost I must remain true to our collusion, however illegal it had been.

I tried to explain this to the glaring skipper, but it was like spraying gasoline on a forest fire. His rage grew almost unmanageable. Holding it barely under control, he settled slowly back in his chair, glanced briefly at the mate and chief purser, who were looking on, and then, turning to me, grinned from ear to ear. There was no love in that face, however. It was a cold dental smile—about as friendly as the scoop on a steam shovel.

"So yer are standin' in wit' th' rest o' th' bums, eh?" he muttered, in a voice tense with suppressed wrath, "an' yer don't give a damn about us, eh?" He paused, and his rage seemed to grow till he could control it no longer.

"Whirling toward the mate, he said viciously: "Put him in irons, and lock him up in the brig! Give him water, but I'll fire any man caught givin' him anything to eat!" And to me, "Yas, yer goddamned————! I'll find out from yer yet who gave yer the ticket. Yer————!"

Well, it's a grim outlook for a while. It seemed best to submit peaceably to the handcuffs, so here I am. This is the ship's storeroom, but serves as the brig on occasions, as I see by writing on the wall. One inscription reads, "H.S.S. kept prisoner here on bread and water—May 18th, 1928—caught two hours out of Seattle."

Apparently the captain intends to keep me here until we reach Seattle, which will be about four days. He hopes to starve us into squealing on the steward. The nights will be hard, because I am shackled to a short cable leash, the other end of which is fastened to a steel stanchion, and they don't give me a blanket or anything to keep me warm. I don't mind the iron floor, but the cold is weakening, and it is drafty. A little open hatch in the ceiling lets in a chilling wind all night. . . .

I am much comforted to hear the swish of the waves outside our hull as we continue to plow southeastward. At least I am leaving Alaska. The storeroom door is locked and it is very dull here, but I can keep occupied, as my handcuffs are far enough apart to let me write in this little notebook. . . .

August 16. Things are much more comfortable. I was rather cramped during the night, but solved the problem of keeping warm by wrapping up in a piece of sail which I found behind some nail kegs, luckily just within reach. The sailor and my friends, in spite of strict orders to the contrary, come and talk with me through the door cracks and through the little hatch. I don't like to ask them for food, and haven't, but several have brought me candy and raisins, so I am having a good time.

The mate came in just after we left Wrangell last night, and let me out for a drink before leading me back to be shackled to my post for the night. It was hard to sleep because of the tight handcuffs, which cut my wrists, but I had rope for a pillow and, with my sail blanket, did quite nicely.

In the morning, the mate appeared again.

Guy and Katie Murchie in Malaga, Spain, 1965

"How do you feel now?" he said.

"All right, sir," I answered truthfully.

He was looking more sympathetic than he did yesterday and, as he unlocked my handcuffs for my morning drink, he said: "It's too bad you have to stay this way. I don't believe in this sort of stuff, but I have to obey the old man's orders."

One of the ship's officers, a little later, crawled down through the narrow hatch into my prison—I can't say who he was, as it might lose him his job—with a napkin full of buns and sausages from the galley.

"Here," he said, in a low voice, "take this, and don't let anyone know you've had it. And if, by any chance, the old man hears of it, for God's sake don't let him know who gave it to you—or I'll lose my job."

The number of my friends seemed to increase as presents of sandwiches, candy, apples, oranges, cookies, eggs, meats and other goods kept coming through the hatch so fast I had a big supply stocked secretly under various piles of rope. Each donor thought he was my sole benefactor and faithfully contributed his little offering after each meal, entreating me not to tell a soul. I didn't, and consequently my food supply was continuously augmented and more people took pity on me every day. I didn't know where I could put all the food.

August 17. My friends are getting very bold now. Even the Chinese take pictures of me through the hatch and ask all sorts of questions. Evidently there are rumors around that I have murdered a woman back in Seward . . . [But that only fascinated them the more, and the gifts increased until late in the evening.] Finally, after a hearty feed of chicken, cold lamb, salmon croquettes, lettuce, buns and jam, with dessert of apples, oranges and chocolate cake, I rolled up in my sail for the night. I dreamed of a sandy island somewhere in the South Seas. The beach was coral, the air was balmy, the girls were broadminded.

I woke to find myself in irons in a ship's brig. We were at Ketchikan. In a few minutes the mate came in and unlocked my cuffs. I thought it was for my usual morning drink—but no.

"Follow me," said the mate.

He led me to the gangplank and told me I was to be taken ashore. At the foot of the plank, on the wharf, I saw the marshal of Ketchikan and his lieutenant, waiting to meet me. All about were the mountains, spruce forests, bleak cliffs, and the ragged town upon a blue strait.

I didn't like the idea of going to jail in this little town, but realized that it could not be for long, and went peaceably to the marshal's office, where I was put behind the bars in a small, three-cell jail . . .

Here, after a few hours' waiting, my Russian jailer gave me a breakfast of hot cakes and syrup, while the marshal, fat and goggle-eyed, investigated my baggage and read this notebook. At ten o'clock my case was taken up—all very informal. . . . They concluded that I was neither a pauper nor an habitual criminal. And when I paid my fare all the way down from Seward to put things right with the steamship company—which I had offered to do all along—they turned me loose.

The marshal conducted me about the town and introduced me to various fishermen with whom I might get passage to Seattle. Ketchikan—which name struck me as being peculiarly appropriate, both to its circumstances and to my own—is a fish and cannery town: salmon, halibut and herring. Everybody talks fish. Owners talk of the various species of salmon—kings, pinks, reds, and sock-eyes. Workers talk of salmon—sock-eyes, reds, pinks, and kings. Men who are not working sit around on the fish wharves, talk fish—pinks, sock-eyes, kings, and reds—and clean their fingernails with scaling knives.

I got a room for the night and a much-needed bath, also a date with a deputy clerk girl whom I had met at the marshal's office. But I couldn't keep it, as a little freight and passenger steamer, loaded with salt herring, was sailing at once for Seattle. In midday sunshine we chugged out of the dock, limping along on three propeller blades, the fourth having been broken off on a log on the way north. I watched the fish wharves gradually fade into the distance, with the men still sitting, still talking fish, of kings, pinks, reds, and sock-eyes—and cleaning their fingernails with scaling knives.

And Around the World
1929–1930

From Seattle I took a bus to San Francisco, the best port for shipping to the Orient, and signed on as deckhand and night watchman on the SS *Manulani* of the Matson Line, a sugar ship then offloading Hawaiian cane in Crockett, California. By mid-September we docked in Hilo on Hawaii's big island, taking on a new cargo of sugar, and it was there that I met a beachcomber named Gus who, it turned out, had once been in the same jail I'd recently been in Ketchikan. We immediately became warm friends, for it seems that a jail can be an even closer human bond than an alma mater.

Gus also informed me he had been in Hilo a long time and, having tired of his hand-to-mouth existence, was terribly anxious to get to Honolulu, where his opportunities should be enhanced. I felt sorry that we had no vacancy just then in the crew of the *Manulani* but, being night watchman, I could easily stow him away for the 200-mile overnight voyage to Honolulu. It was the least I could do for my old jail mate.

Two days later at 6:00 A.M. I found myself on the *Manulani*'s bridge, a deckhand steering our 10,000-ton freighter into Honolulu harbor. It was an unprecedented thrill—the biggest mass I've ever been privileged to move. And by ten o'clock I was walking the streets of this capital of an exotic land. Quoting my diary:

Japanese, Portuguese, Chinese, ease and disease, with modern American improvements and tropical surroundings, make up the city of Honolulu.

It is a relaxed and crowded city, set among green volcanic hills and translucent waters—a city where everyone seems sufficiently prosperous without undue effort; where electric lights break the warm seduction of tropic nights, and trolley cars clang through every shining hour. . . .

Next day I repaired to an oriental rooming flat run by a deep-voiced Hawaiian assisted by a couple of wrinkled Chinamen who talk with their hands and smile eerily in the presence of strangers. There are also several small black-eyed Hawaiian entertainers, females whose company, I understand, involves an extra expense of three dollars. On inspection, I decided to remain unentertained, but, not wishing to hurt anyone's feelings, I evaded the issue by explaining that, to my capricious taste, these girls were too little. Having disposed of this problem, I went "proprietously" to sleep.

Sometime in the middle of the night, I was awakened by a stealthy someone entering my room. I thought at first it was a thief, and was acutely aware of the disadvantages, in any possible altercation, of my being so extremely lightly clothed. It was no thief, however, but a Hawaiian entertainer, dark-skinned and very, very, very fat. My obliging host, wishing to please, had scoured the neighborhood for hours for an entertainer who was not "too little." This lady, hopefully

provided according to specifications, and who closely resembled a stout orangutan, was about five feet tall and must have weighed well over two hundred pounds. She was pertinacious in her intention to entertain but, without unduly hurting her already lacerated feelings, I finally persuaded her to retire on the ground that I was too sleepy to receive callers.

Since then I have dwelt uneventfully in this crude abode, though not without hearing much of interest through the thin partitions.

I did not long remain in the rooming house, however, for the silver spoon factor from Boston overtook me in Hawaii in the form of a letter from Mrs. Ronald Lyman, Worgzle's younger sister Bussie, introducing me to one Walter P. Dillingham, an extremely prominent businessman and notable in Honolulu society, whose father, if I remember right, owned the Oahu Railroad and Land Company and brought Walter up to be perhaps the city's most popular tycoon. At any rate he invited me to his elegant home and drove me out to his ranch where he raised polo ponies. A letter from Worgzle mentioned that he had a pretty daughter who might be something for me, but I resisted this and other attempts of hers to promote romance in my life.

It took more than a month to get out of Hawaii because ships stopping there seldom changed crew members and vacancies were as rare as peacock's eggs on the 31st of June. But finally, on October 27, I got an extraordinary break when the SS *President Monroe* docked at 6:00 A.M., for she was known as "the worst ship" in the Dollar Line fleet. There were seven vacancies: three on deck and four below.

My diary records:

I signed on in the "black gang" as a wiper, it being an unskilled engine-room job. They would care little when I quit. The two wiper vacancies were caused by the first assistant engineer, who sent the boys diving in the bilge for his pet wrench. They dived—and deserted. The oiler who quit was lovesick and wanted to get back to 'Frisco. A fireman had to be taken ashore because Bunny, the Hawaiian junior engineer, accidentally broke four of his ribs with a sledgehammer. This engine room seems full of human interest. . . .

Heat and sweat and oil. That's all we see, feel, hear, smell, and taste in the engine room. Everything, even the railing, is too hot to touch. Gloves are a necessity, and our pockets are stuffed with dozens of rags to supplement the gloves in handling hot machinery. We glisten all over from oil and sweat; we drip and trickle all day long, and drink water constantly—four of us emptying a two-quart pitcher every fifteen minutes. Even so, our mouths are so dry we can't spit. The water pours through us like a brook, and our sweat is almost as pure as the water. The heat is so terrific that we must stand one minute under the ventilator to about every three minutes of work. . . .

You wouldn't think the boiler room would be a congenial place for an Eskimo. But, believe it or not, we have a contented Eskimo fireman aboard. His name is Pooooph, and he tolerates the heat better than anyone else. Pooooph doesn't say much, and usually just grunts, but he went to high school and, when he feels confidential over a bowl of fat broth, he has been known to confide that, contrary to the common belief, Eskimos live in quite a high temperature and are used to a stuffy atmosphere. According to him, they spend almost all of their lives indoors. He thinks that the thermometer in a well-run igloo, if there were one, would seldom register below 80 degrees Fahrenheit, and more generally approach 90. A fire is constantly going and the family, usually fat and wearing caribou underclothes, fills up most of the igloo. Eskimos are also used to grease and oil, so Pooooph feels much at home among the boilers and frequently chuckles.

Chicago
1934–1936

Five years later, it was late in March when I got back to Chicago and, after subletting a small apartment, found my way to the *Chicago Tribune* Tower and reported to Bill Wisner, the Sunday editor, to begin work. The *Tribune* Tower, one of Chicago's landmarks, is on North Michigan Avenue beside the Chicago River. The lobby is elegant in creamy marble, with two illuminated letters from Abraham Lincoln written to the *Chicago Tribune* when he urgently needed publicity on running for president in 1860. The paper evidently did right by him for he surely hasn't needed publicity since.

My first assignment presumably originated with managing editor Lee, for Wisner handed me the note he had just received: "Mr. Wisner, in view of the anti-Jewish activities, let's have a double [double page article] on modern Jerusalem, pix

[pictures] of Tel-Aviv, and how this ancient bit of soil still maintains its place in the world. L."

Wisner assigned me a desk in the big high-ceilinged room where some dozen writers were at work, and introduced me around. The men were all in shirtsleeves and the women in light dresses for, though it was cold and blustery outdoors, the air conditioning inside kept the air at a semi-tropical 75 degrees Fahrenheit.

After a couple of hours of sorting, reading, and making notes, I started writing my story: "A horse struggles across the grassy hillside. He pulls a plow of shiny steel. Behind him as he walks spurts a new furrow of sandy loam . . ." And behind the plow came a man, "Menke the Jew." Of course I was thinking of Menke Katz.

The story was published on a Sunday in April of 1934, under my own byline on the front page of the magazine section, and was distributed to more than a million subscribers—an exciting experience for me. In ensuing weeks I was assigned to write other feature stories with dramatic pictures in color about famous murders, assassinations, and other sensational episodes in history.

I also got to know the city, which in some ways seemed like a collection of hundreds of villages, in each of which lived thousands of people who knew each other intimately. Evidence of this came to me one hot morning in May when I set out to call on my friend Ross Langdon, who had told me he lived on East Division Street, a short street on the near north side of town. I couldn't remember his house number and he did not yet have a telephone, but I noticed that the windows of most of the houses were wide open, so I just walked slowly down the middle of the street calling his name in a loud voice. And within five minutes he heard me and answered.

One of my early Chicago assignments was to write up the sewage system, an appropriate subject seeing as I was perceived to be starting at the bottom to work my way up. Right away I learned that Chicago was proud of having three times as much sewage as New York. To which New York replied, "Yes, but our sewage is stronger than yours in Chicago." Then I met the fellow whose job it was to watch the grating that Chicago's sewage passed through, and I learned from him that a few days ago he had spotted a ten-dollar bill drifting along on the noxious tide and had retrieved and washed it and hung it up to dry. After this extraordinary bonanza, moreover, his eyes opened a little wider as he thought "maybe someday a twenty-dollar bill will come along." But, seeing me jotting down notes, he said out loud, "Oh, don't write it up in the paper." For he had fears that the *Tribune*'s huge circulation might bring out hordes of prospectors to pan out the sewage like the Gold Rush of forty-nine, in which case his job could literally cease to be.

Another side of sewer life showed itself in the phone calls the sewer workers were getting from hundreds of people who had lost some treasured article down the drain: a wedding ring, false teeth, a gold piece, a pet alligator, a string of pearls. And the tone of such calls, more often than not, was emotional. Few people, furthermore, had the capacity to see things from what might be called a sewage-eye view, nor could they begin to plumb the true depths of sewage philosophy. Indeed, most factories and industrial plants produce some sort of by-product that is no good to them, so they throw it away, which usually means they dump it down the drain. But in the sewage business one cannot do that. One cannot get rid of anything down the drain, because in the sewer, you ARE the drain. And no matter how many hundreds of thousands of gallons of the worst stuff in the world comes along every day, you cannot throw any of it away. You have to do something else with it. That is the great challenge of sewage. You are the bottom line, the very nadir of pollution.

After three days in the depths I arose to the heights. I had since married Worgzle and now called her Pig, a term of endearment that she loved, as I told her that she resembled a newborn pig upon awakening in the morning. She arrived in May, and in less than a week she had made our little apartment into a real home. She obviously got great satisfaction from my new job and all it implied, and started entering into the social life of the bustling city. Of course she well knew what a vital part she had played in my getting the job. But as time went on my new prominence also made her feel she had served her purpose with me and perhaps subconsciously she gave up trying to be my wife. She ceased all effort to diet and deliberately let herself get fat. She even encouraged me to see other women, such as Josephine Patterson, the attractive daughter of Joe Patterson, Colonel McCormick's first cousin and founder of the *New York Daily News*. Jo, as we called her, was asserting her independence in a reporting job for the *Chicago Daily News*.

Then suddenly Pig attempted a drastic exit—out of my life! When I came home from work one Monday evening in early August, I found she had packed up and gone, taking her two little dogs with her. It was a severe blow and I wandered around the apartment in a daze for hours, trying to adjust to the gaping hole in my life. To refresh my memory after half a century, I have the twelve-page letter I wrote her before going to bed. "Darling Pig, it is now night—I've been trying to write to you for hours . . . my eyes are red and my nose stopped up. Pig, I never knew how much I loved you till now. You'll never know what a shock it is to come home and find an empty house, to look and look through the rooms, then think my darling must be out shopping and then find a note saying 'good-bye' . . ."

I told her it was the hardest thing in the world for me not to jump on the next train to New York to get her back, but I was enough of a realist to understand why she felt she had to go.

She wrote often, but the only answering letter from her that I still have said: "Guysling sweet—I wish I had enough gift in words to tell you what I feel . . . You must not doubt, ever, that I am the same brand of soul as you . . . I am—I know it . . . All I can say, my sweetest heart, is that I love you with my soul and that I feel I will love you forever—as I know you love me with your soul and . . . will love me forever . . ."

Late in September I was assigned to write the history of the Gypsies and it was like a tonic to my loneliness. The Gypsy language has no words for "duty" or "possession," for they are probably the world's most carefree and freedom-loving people. I was interested to learn that they originally came out of India as a tribe of "untouchable" Dravidians with semi-mystic aphorisms like "the music is more than the lute" and "the odor more than the rose." And they would sing unrestrainedly: "Love is the wind—let it blow! The wind is wild—purer than snow. Let your tent flaps fly, let your heart strings go! The wind is free—let it blow, blow . . . blow!"

In October I was given a two-week vacation and used it to drive my jalopy to Rhode Island to fetch Pig "home." I had a wild ride through a storm, during which one of my doors blew off, though I managed to tie it back on well enough. Once I arrived at Greenvale Farm, it wasn't too difficult to persuade Piggie to return to Chicago, and we bought an old Packard phaeton to replace the jalopy before it totally collapsed.

Among new assignments in early 1935, I was asked to interview Grace Wiley, curator of snakes at Chicago's Brookfield Zoo. As soon as I met her I could see that she was a gentle, unassuming lady, but her accomplishment in being the first person in the world ever to succeed in raising rattlesnakes in captivity was impressive.

"They are much like cats," she explained, "only not at all playful." She kept them in their natural state with fangs still in place. "But you have to move very slowly in picking them up," she said, "because they are easily frightened and if they get frightened, they will probably try to strike you."

As she said this, she slowly picked up a four-foot diamond-back rattler, taking about thirty seconds to do it, the while murmuring, "Poor little Tommy. Don't be frightened, Tommy. Nobody's going to hurt you." Aside she told me, "He'll get over it after a while. He's young. But his father and mother were nice sociable snakes. They have personalities just like people. I know that a lot of folks don't believe there's such a thing as a nice snake. That is why snakes are the most abused and misunderstood of all creatures and, ever since the Garden of Eden, have seldom had a fair deal."

Grace Wiley obviously loved her snakes and considered them her own children, giving them warm baths, rubdowns, and swabbing their sore throats. If they got indigestion she would feed them castor oil with a spoon.

Picking up a rather fat king cobra, one of the deadliest of snakes, she whispered, "Sam here has been overeating and I'm going to have to cut down on his meals. You can see that his waistline is nearly a foot around. He has a shameful figure." Sam's countenance, however, revealed not a hint of penitence, nor a wish to turn over a new leaf, and the whereabouts of his waistline was anybody's surmise.

Several months after my snake article was published in the *Tribune*'s Sunday Magazine, Grace Wiley got into trouble because she had put some of her deadliest snakes out on a flat rock for a sunbath after the "poor things" had been cooped up all winter, and two got away. The zoo director fired her. She was upset to find herself destitute with no money to pay her rent or keep up payments on her furniture, but she was plucky enough to get a job in a circus sideshow in St. Louis after travelling there with her sole remaining treasure: an imitation alligator skin suitcase containing five rattlesnakes and a green mamba.

The last I heard of her she was a curator of snakes in the San Diego zoo where, sadly, she came to a tragic end in 1948 after being bitten by a king cobra. The cobra serum she had relied on for such an emergency was unusable in an old and defective syringe and the hospital to which an ambulance rushed her possessed no cobra serum. Despite all the doctors could do, poor Grace died an hour later gasping for breath in an iron lung.

In the summer of 1935 I decided to take up flying. I had always had a yen to do it, and frequently I'd had vivid dreams of flying, usually without wings. Intuitively I knew it would come naturally to me. So when I suggested doing a series of articles on learning to fly for the *Tribune* and found that they would pay most of what it cost (some $150), it seemed a perfect opportunity.

On the advice of Wayne Thomis, the *Tribune*'s aviation editor, I went to Stinson Airport on a sunny June afternoon in 1935 for my first lesson. It was a small airport and the little aeronca I would fly stood less than five feet high with side-by-side seats for two. It could be picked up by the tail and wheeled like a wheelbarrow, and was in several ways simpler than the Wright brothers' first airplane, having only half as many cylinders (two) and half as many propellers (one). Slim Tiedt, owner of the airfield, didn't seem to mind the power lines and deep quarries around his place and advised me with a cynical grin that, if I got lost flying, I could always find an airport by following a power line until it crossed another power line. There at the intersection, especially if quarries were near, would be an airport.

I reported my progress in the *Tribune* in some detail from simple acquaintance with the stick and rudder to flying on an even keel, then to figure eights, vertical turns, landings, and takeoffs. The important thing in landing, Slim explained, is to keep up your flying speed until just before your wheels touch down because flying speed is what gives you lift and control. Once you lose that critical speed, you are mushing or stalling and in danger of an uncontrolled crash.

Slim gave me early lessons in spinning and how to recover from a spin. Wearing parachutes because of the danger, we climbed high, then deliberately raised our nose until the airplane slowed down, stalled, and dove out of control. It was confusing at first because the earth whirling beneath us gave no indication of which way was north or south. But by the second or third spin, I learned to keep track of direction and also how to regain control through speed until I could safely pull out of the spin.

During World War I when flying was new, flying instructors, I understood, did not give spinning lessons but concentrated instead on take-offs and landings. If a recruit could not qualify in four hours of instruction, he was "washed out."

But now in 1935 they were taking more time. However, after four hours of instruction which included "precision spins," Slim said I was ready to fly solo.

So I drove out to Stinson Airport one Sunday afternoon in July all ready for my first time alone in the air. But I had a rude shock for, as I approached the field, I could see our little aeronca all crunched on her nose in the grass and another small plane lying in a distorted heap near by. There had been a collision a hundred feet or so above the edge of Stinson Airport as both planes approached the same runway to land. Although two men were in each airplane, evidently not one of them noticed there was another plane near until too late as one descended on top of the other, the impact knocking both planes out of control. Only one of the four men survived.

I had to wait a month until Slim obtained a new aeronca. Then, although the accident had been decidedly unnerving so close to my scheduled first solo flight, my solo took place without incident. In fact, a first solo flight is naturally made easier when the instructor gets out and says, "She's all yours now. You're on your own," for the total load is lightened by the absence of his weight and you, the pilot, take off after a shorter run and climb with unwonted ease. It is hard, nevertheless, to find words to describe the exhilaration in one's first solo flight, when one has just cut one's umbilical cord to all terrestrial things, including the rest of humanity. In my case it was a spiritual experience bordering on exaltation.

After a few flights alone, the body of the airplane becomes so attuned to one's own body that the wings turn into simple extensions of your arms and the ailerons are your own fingers confidently gripping and guiding the passing air. Then at last you are at home in your maternal element, the sky. Not long after realizing this, one day, playing with my little aeronca in the upper meadows, I discovered something Slim had never mentioned. I could fly her without touching either the stick or the rudder pedals, just by leaning: forward to go down, backward to climb, to the right for a right turn, to left for a left turn. I even did figure eights—no hands—and felt completely at home way up there among the clouds. My life had truly expanded into a new dimension.

The next major series of articles I wrote for the *Tribune* brought me tumbling back down to earth—way down. It was on gangsters, particularly the mob warfare between Al Capone and other notorious Chicago racketeers whom Prohibition

had made powerful through the 1920s and early 1930s. It required me to spend days interviewing the city police, detective specialists, and checking reams of court records. I made a list of the thirty-three men Capone was believed to have murdered, giving the dates and motivations in each case. Even though Capone was never indicted for any of them, the list was published in the paper.

Another thing I undertook was to draw a map showing the territories of all the Chicago gangs, which was particularly difficult because the boundaries were continually changing and overlapping. The map made quite a stir when it appeared in full color in the Sunday magazine.

After I finished my gangster series I started on a new assignment: to write the "true story" of the famous mutiny on the *Bounty*, a fiction version of which had been very prominent in bookstores and movie theatres in recent months. In writing of the *Bounty*'s mutiny I was struck by how young everybody was, the sailors mostly teenagers, Captain Bligh himself only thirty-three and Fletcher Christian, leader of the mutineers, twenty-five. A vital factor in the mutiny, missed by Nordhoff and Hall who wrote the fiction trilogy, was that Bligh was lowborn with a cockney accent and therefore had difficulty getting his men to respect him. Indeed, he felt he had to resort to unusual and unpopular strictness to win obedience. Almost all British officers of the period were aristocrats who spoke with variations of the Oxford (or BBC) accent. On the other hand, Christian, though not an officer, possessed just such an accent and thereby found it easy to lead the ill-educated sailors who had never known the kind of democracy then being cultivated in America.

After the mutiny, when twelve mutineers fled to remote Pitcairn Island taking six Tahitian men servants and fifteen Tahitian women, trouble arose, mainly because there were too few women and no prospects of any replacements. When one mutineer's wife got killed, falling from a cliff while gathering eggs, and he took a servant's wife, feuding began between the white men and the Tahitians and within three years all the men but one were dead, and that one brought up the dozen mulatto children, using the only book available, the Bible from the *Bounty*, to teach them English.

How the colony brought up on Bible stories turned out to be as law abiding as their fathers were unruly was told in my book, *Mutiny of the Bounty*, published by the Spencer Press of Chicago in 1937. I thought it had become part of an obscure collection of sea stories until I chanced to see it on the bookshelf of a new neighbor when, fifty years later, I moved to California.

I got an important new assignment on March 15, the Ides of March. It was to be a dramatic presentation of how the United States Army fought in the World War (1917–18) from the viewpoint of a combat intelligence officer—a perspective that had never before been utilized. It would be an epic military story of special interest to Colonel McCormick and very difficult in many ways as evidenced by the fact that no less than four *Tribune* writers had already been assigned to it and all, for one reason or another, failed.

Col. Tom Gowenlock, McCormick's close friend who served as the G-2, intelligence officer on the staff of the First Division, was to be the prime source of information. The main problem seemed to be in learning how to handle Gowenlock so he would tell the dramatic details without going endlessly off on tangents. My first installment was about espionage, the best-known and most dramatized aspect of military intelligence. After a second

installment on the rapid war preparedness of America in the spring of 1917, I wrote about the arrival of the First Division of our army in France and particularly of the first American battle at the village of Cantigny, an engagement which included Colonel McCormick himself as a commander of artillery. When I had a conference with Kennedy, the new Sunday editor, and Lee about how to write it, Lee said, "Be sure to do Cantigny thoroughly. Cantigny is OUR battle, you know," and his eyes rolled suggestively up toward the twenty-fourth floor. Continuing, he cautioned, "And be sure to explain how the artillery is much more important than the infantry, how the artillery in fact takes the territory while the infantry merely occupies it. Never forget that the *Chicago Tribune* is in the artillery, and we gotta eat."

I did the battle of Cantigny to Colonel McCormick's obvious satisfaction, having consulted various officer veterans of World War I such as General McCoy and Colonel George Marshall whom Pig and I had met while dining with the McCoys. I think Marshall, with his modest mien

At work, 1975

and leather gloves in hand, was the most immaculately dressed and courteous man I've ever known, and extremely knowledgeable concerning every detail of the war. As he had been Pershing's G-3, or chief of operations, in 1917–18, he had planned and directed the battle and seemed to remember everything of importance about it.

I was not aware at the time that, as Pershing's chief advisor, Marshall had been the top brain guiding the American forces through World War I, and of course I could not know that in half a decade more he would become the world famous genius who would lead all the allied forces to victory in World War II.

One would have supposed that such an attractive and successful officer of World War I would have become a general long before 1936, but army promotions can be very flukey. I knew this from having married into an army family, and Pig told me a lot about the rivalry between Douglas MacArthur and Marshall, which seemed to be the real key to their fortunes of rank. Although they had entered the army at the same time, just after the turn of the century, and both had performed brilliantly in France in 1918, MacArthur as commander of the proud Rainbow Division and Marshall as Pershing's vital right hand, their personalities were utterly at odds and bound to clash.

It happened in the last week of the war that Marshall wrote an order at the behest of Pershing authorizing the first American army troops to enter and take the city of Sedan. This led to a scramble between various divisions of the army, including MacArthur's Rainbow Division, but when the flamboyant MacArthur walked forward to see what the confusion was about, a young lieutenant from the First Division took one look at the angry figure, dressed as usual in a floppy hat and muffler, without the required gas mask over his shoulder, and arrested and disarmed him on suspicion that he might be a German. Of course he protested violently but he had no proper identification and they kept him locked up until an order came through from divisional headquarters.

Although MacArthur later spoke of the incident as a big joke, he had seen Marshall's signature on the directive that led to the race for Sedan and never forgot it. And when MacArthur, with the help of family strings, was made chief of staff of the U.S. Army, which automatically made him a major general and then an acting four-star general, Marshall remained a mere lieutenant colonel in charge of the Illinois National Guard. That is what he was when I met him in 1935 and, although

neither he nor his attractive wife Katherine gave any hint of it, they felt there was scant hope of his being promoted to the rank of general during that slack time in army affairs, especially while MacArthur remained chief of staff and holding the reins of promotions.

Pig and I saw a lot of the Marshalls in 1936 and had them to dinner in our apartment as well as dining more than once at their house in Wayne, Illinois. His war stories were not only delightful, but reliable and he turned out to be my most solid source of information in writing the remaining installments of my history of the First Division in World War I, which later came out in book form as *Soldiers of Darkness*.

At the time I was still flying every few days and it so happened that the first place I landed my aeronca outside the airport was in the field beside Marshall's house. And I recall that after our potluck lunch that day, it was Colonel Marshall himself who held the tail of my little plane to keep it from flying away unattended when I spun the propeller, thereby enabling me to get safely inside, wave good-bye, and swing around into the west wind for takeoff.

Happily for Marshall, Douglas MacArthur resigned as chief of staff that summer of 1936 to become commander in chief of the defense forces of the newly created Commonwealth of the Philippines. And almost immediately Marshall was promoted to brigadier general by the new chief of staff, Malin Craig. And when Craig's term came to an end in August 1939 just as World War II was about to begin, all the army people in Washington wondered who the new chief of staff would be. Obviously, with a major war looming in Europe, it would be an extremely important position. No one imagined that George Marshall, the junior brigadier, had a chance. He was outranked by twenty-one major generals and eleven brigadier generals, so would have to leapfrog over thirty-two higher officers to be picked.

But Marshall had by then learned something about maneuvering politicians as well as armies, and when he discovered that a good half dozen major generals were desperately vying for the job—notably Hugh Drum who had been in command in Hawaii, John De Witt, president of the Army War College, Frank Powell and Walter Krueger, each scrounging all the influence he could—he decided that his own best chance, probably his only chance, would be to play it cool. So he sought no influence and just lived quietly. He had already demonstrated to President Roosevelt that he was no "yes man" by bluntly disagreeing with him about Roosevelt's pet plan for building ten thousand war planes for Britain and France in 1938. And he won FDR's instinctive respect while their relations were still cool and, though his rank was lower than any of the other staff officers, the president surprised everyone by appointing Marshall chief of staff of the United States Army in April 1939, charging him with full responsibility for building up the nation's armed forces with a degree of trust that could only have enhanced America's all-out drive to victory in the years that followed.

In that same period many of my most influential friends were military men. I didn't plan it that way. The war was on and it seemed inherent in the age, an age in which armies made history and might made right. Not only was my godfather a general but I had married a general's daughter and wrote military history for the colonel who owned the *Chicago Tribune,* and I knew important military figures from Admiral Byrd to General Marshall.

In October 1936 I made a date with Pig to fly precisely over our house in my little aeronca at an altitude of one and half miles. In spite of a powerful west wind, somehow I managed to get there at exactly eleven o'clock when I had told Pig to look straight up from our backyard if she wanted to see me flying, and to wave something big and white like a sheet so I could spot her. She did and I actually saw her do it. It seemed almost magical to be picking out one woman, my own, from a city of four million people all spread out in plain sight beneath me—and I wagged my tail to let her know I had her message of love.

The Janet Problem
1943

At about this time, Pig and I separated, got divorced, and Barbara Cooney came into my life. I saw Barbara's illustrations for children's books before I ever saw her and liked them so much that I wrote to her at her home in Maine and found that she had just enlisted in the Women's Army Corps (WAC) and would soon be on her way to Des Moines, Iowa, to become a WAC lieutenant. I arranged to meet her en route to Chicago, and we got along so well that I married her on Christmas Eve in 1942. We settled on a farm called Windy Dip in Illinois until the ATC (Air Transport Command) moved me at the end of 1943 to

New York, their navigation school in Chicago having folded by then. My base being now in New York, Barbara and I drove our beat-up Green Hornet, decorated with Barbara's paintings of Windy Dip farm scenes, to our new home at the Sanford Hotel in Flushing, Long Island. It had been provided for us by American Airlines, partly as a base for further training because in preparation for future emergencies all the navigators were now required to become radio operators and all the radio operators to become navigators, while all pilots were expected to be proficient in both these disciplines.

It was near the end of November 1943 that my father presented me with the Janet problem. It seemed that no one in the family had heard from my sister Janet and evidently, since Father had stopped sending her any allowance in the hope of inducing her to get a job and make something of her life, she didn't feel the need of writing. Now he wanted to know where in the world was she? And in what sort of shape?

At the age of seventy, he didn't feel able to cope with the problem himself, and I was aware that he was beginning to think of me as someone who might turn out to have qualities beyond his understanding. Why I might have such qualities that Donald and my sisters lacked I did not know and I had never thought much about it. Was it my unexplainable luck that I had no taste for liquor or cigarettes or was it some mysterious inheritance through my genes? I had had little experience with alcoholism, which did not seem a deadly danger in the family, but Donald was obviously becoming less promising and more alcoholic all the time, though Father seemed hardly aware of it even though he had an alcoholic younger brother and Uncle Graeme (Mother's brother) was obviously alcoholic. Father was understandably apprehensive about calling on the police or the Bureau of Missing Persons so, in some desperation, he turned to me. Who else had he to turn to?

Naturally I offered to help as best I could in the difficult circumstances of having a wartime flying job and a wife in her eighth month of pregnancy.

Janet had last been seen by Donald sitting in a bar in the skid-row district of South Boston, but he didn't know where she lived. All he could say was that she then had had a little black dog and was probably hanging out with some man who had picked her up in the bar.

The prospect of finding her was not good, but I went to Boston and started visiting bars around

Columbus Avenue, one of her haunts, inquiring in each case whether anyone there had seen a woman with a little black dog. The response was discouragingly negative for quite a while, but finally I met a fellow who suggested that I check the bars near Central Square in Cambridge.

I did, and it didn't take long to find Janet. She was living in an abandoned house as the guest of a man who had bought her a drink. It was very primitive. The water had been turned off so she had to use the backyard as a bathroom and there were no sheets or blankets on the beds. She slept in her overcoat and it was getting chilly those November nights. She was also four months pregnant. And she said the man who got her that way was Irish.

Talking with Janet, I learned that the father of her child was not at all close to her and neither he nor she wanted any lasting friendship like marriage. So I didn't see much point in trying to pressure them to hitch up. Instead I decided I would try to find some unmarried old man who, for some monetary inducement, would agree to marry her. After all, I didn't necessarily have to find her a real husband or even a man she could live with. When I reported all this to Father he was pretty upset, and his interest was primarily that she be provided with a married name, to make her an "honest woman" so his next grandchild would not disgrace him by being a bastard.

Janet was too impassive to care much about what a baby would do to her life, and she hardly could imagine having a real husband. Perhaps that was why she never had a real husband. She joked about it but was easygoing in the extreme and more than willing to let happen whatever would happen, leaving it entirely up to me to solve her marital dilemma.

As my job did not permit my remaining in Boston, I took Janet to New York so I could more conveniently work on the case. It wasn't easy to get her an apartment or even a room, the city being very full in the war years but, after looking at a dozen possibilities, I finally found her a passable pad and she gratefully moved in and accepted the renewal of her allowance from the "Old Man."

Then I went downtown to Union Square on Fourteenth Street which seemed a promising place to find her a "husband," for lots of elderly men were sitting around on benches or at tables with nothing much on their minds, apparently just passing the time of day. The weather was rather pleasant for late November, and I looked about for likely candidates. I wanted a man with an Irish name if possible, since he was to be the legal sire of a half-Irish baby. So I sat down at a table beside a mild-looking man of sixty or so and engaged him in conversation. Yes, indeed, he agreed it was a pleasant day and New York not a bad place to live. After a bit more of introductory chitchat, he allowed that his name was Reynolds and I thought of Sir Joshua and wondered how Janet would take to becoming "Mrs. Reynolds." Then I broached the subject of having a pregnant sister who needed a married name and asked if he would be interested in giving her one—for a consideration of course. At that he moved forward toward the front edge of his chair.

"Sure, I'm interested," he said. "And I'd like to meet her." He seemed more interested in her than in the fifty dollars I mentioned—and the prospect of some amorous adventure to enliven a dull life obviously had a strong appeal.

"Can you bring her around to my place tomorrow?" he inquired. "What about noon time?"

So it was arranged. But when I brought Janet to his rooming house I found he was not there and his landlady, in whom he had confided, had talked him out of my "dubious scheme" and wanted to hear no more of it.

Back in Union Square I sat down with other prospects, many of whom turned out to have unsuitable names like Wajewski, Brandhorst, Basilthwaite, Paduchak, or Langenberger. One backed away, commenting that marrying my sister was not quite in his line.

"What is your line?" I asked him.

He replied that he had a "common-law wife" at home who would surely take a dim view of my plan.

After many such turn-downs I was sitting one evening in Union Square with Barbara. It was about nine o'clock and she was tired and wanted me to take her "home" to the Sanford Hotel, but I had a feeling that I was about to succeed in my quest and I asked her to allow me one more try.

"Give me ten minutes," I said. "Then we'll go home."

"All right," she agreed. "Ten minutes."

I stood up. But not seeing any likely prospects in the almost deserted square, I wandered eastward on Fourteenth Street to Third Avenue, then turned southward toward Thirteenth Street. And right there I chanced to see a sailor coming out of a bar. I'll never forget it. He was fairly young, probably in his thirties, and he wore one of those little round caps favored by men of the merchant marine.

We conversed and, after telling him a little about Janet, he said his name was Charles Bell and that he might marry her himself. "I once almost got married," he confessed. "But the day before the wedding my best man fell in love with my bride and the two of them just upped and ran off to marry each other. It was a terrible shock. I've been off women ever since and decided marriage was not for me. But your suggestion is something else." He said he had been a nurse before the war and obviously he had developed a missionary attitude toward anyone in need. That must have been why my proposal appealed to him. And he didn't mind when I told him that Janet was alcoholic and not much of a catch. His present job, he said, was loading convoys in New York Harbor but he had ample time ashore and, after two more minutes of talk, he said he wanted to meet Janet and, no matter what, he would marry her if she would have him. He refused to accept any money for this either but said I could pay for the marriage license, the required Wasserman blood test, and the wedding itself. We shook hands heartily and arranged to meet again the next day when I would introduce him to Janet.

Barbara was impressed with my serendipitous success, which hardly took ten minutes, and we introduced Janet to Charles as planned, and made all arrangements for the marriage, which we agreed would take place in our room at the Sanford at two the following Saturday afternoon.

On Saturday morning Janet prepared for her wedding day by taking a bath in our small bathroom. She sorely needed it, but in the process she lost her wedding ring down the drain. It took me half an hour of fishing with bent wires and some luck before I could retrieve it. Then the minister appeared—but no Charles Bell.

We waited until three o'clock, then the minister went home. But there was still no groom at half past three. Could Charles Bell, the eager missionary, have decided to stand up my sister? It seemed unlikely. We were puzzled and getting discouraged—but then at ten minutes of four he finally arrived and apologized. He had been loading a ship in the harbor when a strong wind arose, so strong that the navy would not let him go ashore. Thus he got delayed two hours until the wind died down. It was clearly not his fault, and we fetched the minister back and had the ceremony—and Janet became Mrs. Charles Bell.

Unfortunately, Charles was not enough enamoured of Janet to stay with her, and they went their separate ways. But I delighted Father with the news of her marriage and we never heard from Charles again.

I don't think the strain of the nuptial accomplishment was particularly hard on Barbara who rested at home in the Sanford much of the time, but the weather turned raw in December and she came down with pneumonia by the fourteenth. So I telephoned the army air force hospital at Mitchell Field on Long Island, where she was scheduled to have her baby, and they sent an ambulance for her. And on the sixteenth she was delivered of a very pink five-pound baby girl, whom we named Gretel.

My feeling about naming a baby was that the name should have a definite gender, rather than be ambiguous like Beverly, Leslie, Marion, Lee, or Pat, and it should be simple and easy to spell yet not so common as to cause confusion with others similarly named like John, Mary, Elizabeth, Jane, James, William, David, and Robert. And, above all, the baby should not have the same name as its father, mother, or grandparent. I myself had been named after my father, which is how I got stuck with a "junior" after my name. I disliked it intensely and discarded it as quickly as I could. "Junior" is really a number, not a name, and is both awkward and ugly, not to mention unnecessary. And it is only a misguided modern idea that our ancestors did not value. How would you like to have the father of your country known by the name of George Washington Jr., or the great emancipator as Abraham Lincoln Jr.? Would that not detract from the lustre or dignity of their names?

At any rate Gretel, though only an eight-month baby, grew up well and loveable and was even warmly accepted by her maternal grandmother. I was still regularly navigating the Atlantic, usually by way of Newfoundland and Iceland to Prestwick, Scotland, sometimes through the Azores to Morocco and Senegal.

When it came time for Janet to give birth in April, she went into the maternity ward of the New York Hospital. But, as God decreed it, her baby girl was stillborn. Which was probably just as well because Janet seemed ill-suited for motherhood and continued her visits to bars at every opportunity.

Meanwhile Barbara and I lived in Bedford Village, New York, near my other sister, Agnes. I continued with my flying job, which was fairly routine most of the time though I was always looking for something of interest, especially on the face of the earth where I could never forget that a world war was in full progress. When flying out of Britain that year we occasionally saw ships far below, slowly plying the watery seas—and I wondered if some of them might be ships I had sailed on in my younger days. It seemed unlikely that I would ever know, but one dark night when flying from Scotland to Morocco off the west coast of France, when I as navigator was not at all sure of where we were, I chanced to hear a radio signal from a ship in the Mediterranean which gave its position in latitude and longitude, helping me pinpoint our own position. The ship's radio officer signified that there were more than 350 wounded soldiers aboard, which gave it the rating of a hospital ship, and it therefore could safely reveal its position in wartime. He ended the message by stating that it was the *Chateau-Thierry,* the very ship I had once sailed on as a deckhand in June 1929 when embarking from Brooklyn, New York, on my way around the world. How comforting it was to receive a helping hand from my old friend, the *Chateau-Thierry,* on which I had once been a hand!

I guess my old friend was having trouble getting through the war, however, for some time later I chanced to hear of a conversation between an elderly mess sergeant and an ordinary sailor on some army transport in 1942. "This scow," said the sergeant, "reminds me of the rusty old hulk they sent us overseas on in World War I."

"What was her name?" asked the gob.

"The *Chateau-Thierry.*"

The sailor raised both eyebrows, then said, "This *is* the *Chateau-Thierry.*"

I think it was on a later flight from Scotland to Morocco that a passenger came into our cockpit and engaged the pilot in friendly conversation. He spoke English with only a slight accent and said he was interested to see how we conducted our operation because he too was a pilot. As a result he was soon invited to fly our airplane, which he did for some twenty minutes. But during the ensuing conversation he revealed that he was a German fighter pilot who only last month had been flying regularly off the west coast of Nazi-occupied France in an attempt to locate some of our planes and shoot us down. Obviously he was a new prisoner-of-war under the charge of an armed guard who judged it safe to let him wander about our C-54 while he was being transported by a roundabout route to the U.S. for internment. As it

didn't seem exactly proper to have an enemy in control of our airplane while the war was still on, he soon yielded his place to our pilot again.

At the same time the incident made me wonder who is really fighting whom in a war these days. I was sure that none of our crew members felt any great hatred for Germans who, we realized, were simply obeying their orders in opposing us. So the real war seemed to be between persons of strongly contrasting views on each side, such as hawks and doves, or between those with racial or religious antagonisms. Perhaps it would take only a single fanatical individual like Hitler to trigger a world war involving hundreds of millions. I had no way of knowing then that for most of my life I would be married to a Prussian with whom I could share everything from thoughts to earthly goods of every kind. We would have a baby in 1952 but in thirty-eight years never a serious clash that could have led to a war.

By 1944 the American and British armies had successfully invaded western Europe and the Russians were rebounding from the east and it was plainly only a question of time before Hitler would be finished. So I resigned my position with American Airlines under the ATC and repaired to a dairy farm in central New England where an old friend offered to try me out as a potential partner in a beautiful pastoral setting where I might find it possible to write books and Barbara could pursue her career as an illustrator, while we brought up Gretel and any new members who might arrive.

Milking at Five
1944-1945

You've got to be on deck before dawn tomorrow morning," said Henry. "The milking machines are all washed and ready, and Joe will help you—but the job is really yours alone."

That is how Henry Renouf introduced me to my new job as a hand on his 100-acre farm in Belchertown, Massachusetts, where I was expected to milk eighteen cows every morning and evening at five o'clock and, between times, feed a thousand chickens, not to mention chopping wood for the stove in the bungalow he provided for Barbara and me. Henry had been born in China, the son of a German missionary, but grew up in New England and now owned this prosperous dairy farm a few miles north of Springfield where he lived with his wife Robin and two small daughters.

I had agreed to work as a farmhand for six months, after which, if all was well, we would decide how to go into some sort of partnership. In the meantime I would work about six hours a day taking care of the cows and chickens which should allow me perhaps eight hours for writing a book about flying, aerial navigation, meteorology, and other aspects of the sky.

I was given an assistant named Joe Ludchuck whom Henry had borrowed from a state institution for the feebleminded with the understanding that Joe was not to be paid but hopefully he could do enough useful work to earn his keep, and his life thus could be as normal as he was capable of. Joe could carry the big cans and drive the cows very well. He also knew them all by name. There was Rita, Nellie, Mildred, and Bessie. But most were named after flowers, like Violet, Rose, Lily, Daisy, and Buttercup.

Most of the year they would be let out of the barn right after the morning milking and would spend the day grazing in the fields, wandering to wherever the grass looked greenest. But as five o'clock approached they would head back to the barn. By then their udders were nearly full and they wanted to be milked, and each one knew her stall and would willingly walk to her own stanchion to have her neck locked in place for the night. The stanchion is a wonderful invention, by the way, that keeps a cow securely under control with her head over her manger while her neck is free to slide up or down between two vertical steel poles, permitting her to lie or stand at will and eat or drink as she chooses.

In the dark at half past four I would quietly go to the barn. There I would first feed the hens, scattering or strewing the kernels of grain over the whole surface of the floor so the birds could eat their fill. Every few days I would also give each pen of hens a bucket of manure to eat. Being scavengers, they loved it, and Henry had discovered it was an economic and efficient way to interrelate cows and chickens: every pen of 260 layers ravenously consuming a full bushel (68 pounds) of fresh cow manure per day. It was still a new and experimental concept but it already showed signs of improving the quality of the eggs.

Down on the main floor of the barn, I would put the milking machines on the cows, dumping the resulting chambers of milk into the big milk cans. Then I had to strip each cow of cream which meant milking her by hand to get out whatever fluid was too thick for the machine. It was slow work and it often got my fingers tired but it took only two or three minutes per cow. There is a restful rhythm to hand milking that makes it a pleasure to see and hear the jets of white liquid shoot into the pail with steady force. The first few streams would play a tune on the metal and, by the end, the squirting cream would sink into a bubbly mass of foaming froth. If one were cautious, one might have tied the cow's tail to her far leg so she couldn't switch it freely because it is not exactly delightful to be waked up of a sleepy morning by a wet tail across the mouth. Joe expectably got the worst jobs such as shoveling the night's fresh manure into the manure spreader each morning. He didn't seem to mind. Then it was my job to hitch the tractor to it and haul it out into the hay fields for spreading, rain or shine.

Some days my job required me to treat ailing cows, or shovel chicken manure out of the pens amid dusty clouds of it fit to make me choke. But I spent the middle hours of most days writing and, when need be, gathering and sawing wood for my stove. The best wood in those days was chestnut, still plentiful in the surrounding woods, though virtually all chestnut trees in America had died when the chestnut blight struck early this century. Chestnut wood, however, is slow to rot and lots of it was around among the fallen trees and readily available to saw up and split. Not only did it make excellent firewood but I could see why Abraham Lincoln, the classic rail splitter, specialized in chestnut which has so few knots that rails more than ten feet long can be split with an axe alone, without need for wedges or sledges.

Barbara had not been brought up to be a housewife, as her wealthy parents always had servants to cook, sew, and keep things in order, but she was a serious student of art, especially of book illustrations. So she spent time almost every day drawing, but she also read cookbooks and made herself into an excellent cook as well as housekeeper and mother. About once a month we were invited for a meal in the main house with Henry and Robin and the little girls who were apt to ask questions of us very uninhibitedly. I remember that a few days after they had witnessed the breeding of cows with Henry's bull and then saw our baby Gretel at her first birthday party, one of them evidently put two and two together and suddenly asked Barbara, "Did Mr. Murchie breed you?"

When I got into the barn at five in the morning the cows were usually awake, but sometimes Joe and I found one so sound asleep we had trouble waking her. Rita, for example, who had a black face, was so habitually asleep that Joe suggested we buy her an alarm clock. He thought that that would be easier than just shaking her as we often did and shouting in her ear, "Wake up, Rita. It's time to get up, Rita. Come on, old girl, we don't have all day."

I can remember some of these details because I kept a "Dairy Diary" all that autumn. And I see an entry I wrote for Monday, November 27, about another sleepy cow. "After I milked Daisy tonight, she lay down and went to sleep. I don't mean just an ordinary doze but real deep sprawly sleep. In fact she put her long head down sideways against the concrete rim of her manger and in less than ten seconds was dead to the world."

Whenever this happened Joe tiptoed by her, whispering "Shhh—Daisy's asleep. Don't make so much noise."

"Maybe she's tired," I put in. "I think she overdid today. I'll see if I can get her a blanket."

"I've got a blanket," said Joe. "Let's tuck her in for the night."

Another unusual cow was Debbie, who groaned unrestrainedly and sighed every few minutes. "Debbie is dying," said Joe. "Call the doctor. Call the undertaker."

"She's not dying," I said. "She's already dead."

"Then hand me the shovel," said Joe. "We'll dig her grave."

Another cow named Rebecca, with a mostly white face, would worry Joe by giving him what he called "dirty looks." When that happened, Joe would shrug his shoulders and say, "She thinks I owe her some money."

I suggested to Joe that "maybe it's because Rebecca overheard you telling her age. You know, that's something women can't stand."

"Yeah," said Joe. "Did you know that today is Rebecca's forty-fifth birthday?" Then, after some thought, he added, "And I forgot to mention that she is my wife—until death do us part. Yessir, we'lla been married thirty years come December." And he pulled a plug of Day's Work chewing tobacco from his pocket and handed it to Rebecca who, sure enough, nibbled off a piece and ate it.

"And look at that hair!" he exclaimed. "See those curls. Did you ever see anything like that on a cow?"

"Probably she's been going to the hairdresser's," I ventured.

"Yup, that's where all my money goes," he continued. "She thinks I owe her thirty dollars. Look at that dirty look!"

Though it had been an interesting intermezzo in my life to work on the farm for half a year, my back ached almost every day and I found it not a very enjoyable shift from navigating the ocean and the pay not really worth the effort. So Barbara and I decided to quit Robin Farm in April 1945 and to find ourselves a place to live elsewhere in New England, probably farther east and north. We were not sure how we would earn our living, but I wanted to write and she wanted to illustrate and we knew we could make it somehow. So exactly six months after we had arrived in Belchertown and, having concluded our promise of a half-year's trial at farming, we packed up, said "good-bye" to the Renoufs, and headed east in our Green Hornet for come what may.

Katie's Sunset
1986

I met Katie in 1948 by answering an ad she had placed in the personal column of the *Saturday Review of Literature,* as it was then called. It said "Industrious young woman" looking for something or other (I don't exactly remember), presumably a job—in which case, she got one. Anyway I liked her immediately and hired her to work in a children's summer camp called Apple Hill.

She was well geared to it, having been trained as a Froebel kindergartner in Jena University in Germany, near where she was born. And we soon developed it into an interracial camp, something virtually unknown in those days. To the campers she was "Aunt Katie" and I was "Uncle Guy." Dividing our work, I generally enrolled the campers, we both interviewed and hired the staff, and Katie did most of the detailed supervising during the eight weeks the camp was in session in July and August. We always gave scholarships to needy campers and spent more than we had intended, so we didn't make much profit—yet, by rarely hiring contractors, and doing almost everything ourselves, we made out nicely.

After the kids went home at the end of August I had time to write and, in some years, to take flying jobs. Thus I completed a book about the sky which, becoming the Book of the Month for December 1954, liberated us enough so that we sold the camp and moved to Spain. Katie, being a European, took easily to Spain, especially during our first few years there. She became fluent in Spanish in no time and was going to market and haggling for fish with the best of them. We lived

With Katie at Wind Rose Farm, New Hampshire, 1977

simply there—twenty dollars a month rent for the first four years—and in summer, when it got very dry and hot in Spain, we drove north and swapped houses with people.

Then in 1967, mostly at Katie's suggestion, we came back to live in New England where she felt more at home than anywhere else—and she lived her last nineteen years in this house, which she named Wind Rose Farm for the wind roses on ancient maps. As opportunity offered, Katie and I not only saw Europe but most of the world, accepting invitations from book readers in Africa, Asia, and Latin America. We lived in Mexico more than once, owned a house there in 1955, and several times wintered in California. She adapted to living in other people's houses very well and was welcome anywhere.

Katie was in every sense not only a lady but a complete woman of the world. Despite being brought up as an only child in very limited middle-class circumstances, she was at home with people at all social levels from ditch diggers to queens. Many of you have probably heard the story of how she literally crashed the royal household in England and was invited to tea by old Queen Mary, widow of George the Fifth. It happened because she worked for a man named Oliver who ran the royal

bank—and one day, riding in his Rolls-Royce being driven by his young French chauffeur, there was a crash in the London traffic when two Rolls-Royces collided. Katie wound up on the floor and the next thing she knew there was somebody at the window asking, "Are you hurt, my dear?" It was Queen Mary who had stepped out of the other car. Katie apologized for not curtseying but the Queen, who said she quite understood, invited her to tea in Buckingham Palace and, a few weeks later, she went. Ushered to the door by a lady-in-waiting, she made a real curtsey, German style, begging Queen Mary's pardon for not knowing the English style. And the old queen smiled and said, "It's in the family."

Katie's use of the English language, which she learned only in her twenties, was one of her greatest attractions. She would say things like "I went to a party yesterday where there were three unsuspected guests and two dead strangers." A lively party, one can readily agree. When she was watching the first moon walk on TV, she asked, "When are they going to go back into the looney nodule?" And describing a Nutcracker ballet, she said, "Barbara and Phoebe sat in a box by themselves, all dressed up to the hills." Although she seldom seemed to care what people said about her, once she complained, "I always keep hearing about people saying things behind my back and making allegations. But the trouble is it's so hard to find out who the alligators are."

I can't at the moment locate any diary or old calendar to remind me accurately of our doings in early 1984, but Katie and I realized that Wind Rose Farm with its many lawns, its garden, and acres of growing brush was becoming a chore to keep up. So we offered it for sale and a month later managed to sell it to (of all people) Austin Olney, our old friend, the editor-in-chief of Houghton Mifflin. He was a generation younger than we, due soon to retire and already looking for an attractive and practical country estate. It was a fortuitous but satisfying decision. He was glad to pay $190,000 and would not need our place until 1986, so we could rent it from him while investing the money, and take our time in considering where to move to afterward.

To help us with the impending decision, I drew a chart, listing six areas of Earth and seven factors for consideration. The areas were New England, Southeastern U.S., the West Coast, Europe, South Africa and New Zealand. The factors were Quality of Life, Climate, Accessibility, Economy, how would it do if World War III happened?, and would Katie like it as a widow? I thought the West Coast had the best climate and a good quality of life, but Katie thought Europe had the best quality of life with New England next. She said if she became a widow, she'd have a hard time choosing between Europe and New England.

About the late spring of 1984 we had a visit from Eugene Mallove of the "Voice of America" radio program in Washington, D.C., who had read books of mine and wanted an interview. He came and talked with me about life and philosophy in our living room for three hours and recorded it, then boiled it down to about twenty minutes, which included comments from Katie and was broadcast a month later to some sixty nations of the world. I received letters from as far away as China that summer, which made me think deeply of the meaning of existence, including Confucius's saying that "Man is a third partner between Heaven and Earth," although that did not fit easily into today's terrorism or our struggles to work our way out of the nuclear stalemate or the three *B*s of babies, bombs, and blight (over-population, over-armament, and too much pollution) in the germinating world.

I note that all archeological and other evidence now shows that our Earth has reached only the dawn of her eventual enlightenment—that there seems not to have ever existed on Earth any creature before man with intelligence comparable to his—no advanced fish or insect or spiritual bird or highly sophisticated mammal who built up any appreciable civilization such as Atlantis or Mu and left a clear record of it. Which means that almost certainly we humans are still in the ancient history phase of the total Earth and that our souls have scarcely begun to sprout.

If this is a fact, should we be surprised to discover that our souls can look forward to a long continuity, that the reincarnation theory is in a sense reasonable and true, that man's self is basically the mark of finiteness of the present earth life and that in the long run all souls are really one, like leaves on a tree? Under such a hypothesis you and I will live out the lives of all humans, each of us separately eating, sleeping, loving and living as our selves, yet in effect simultaneously as a kind of superorganism outside the apparent time-space continuum, all first persons singular progressively becoming absorbed into third persons plural until no lingering taint of "I" remains and all souls can be viewed dispassionately but with increasing perspective from a dimension outside themselves.

If a hypothesis may be something like an angel, not strictly real yet valuable in conveying an inspiration to the open mind, I postulate that our material universe of stars and worlds is not only basically mental in its nature but that its spiritual aspect is even more fundamental. To say, as did Sir James Jeans in the 1930s, that the universe is coming to look more like a great thought than like Newton's great machine is not giving it much purpose—but to see it as a great development of spirit is to give it both joy and hope and even a means of reconciling and clarifying such bewildering paradoxes as ugliness, pain, and evil.

Early in the summer of 1985 Katie had stomachaches which gradually got worse as time advanced. Dr. Snowman thought they might come from a hernia of some kind, but X rays and other tests were inconclusive. After Snowman retired, his successor, Dr. Kim Temple, gave Katie more exhaustive tests and in October concluded that she almost surely had cancer in her pancreas, and that it probably had spread and was inoperable.

Our lives did not immediately change after that but a surgeon in the Hitchcock Hospital in Hanover scheduled an operation for Katie early in November to open up her pancreas and find out exactly where and how big her tumor was. The surgeon telephoned me to say that Katie's tumor was next to her pancreas and appeared "the size of a tennis ball." I asked him if he had removed it and he replied he had not because it would have been of "no use." Cancer cells were growing all over her stomach and lung areas and trying to remove the tumor would likely have killed her.

She felt weak and took pain killers though she did not yet need them often. She was as cheerful as ever, seeming to accept the prospect of dying with remarkable equanimity, almost as if it would be a welcome relief. I was glad of that. We joked about her being a "terminal case" and reflected that everyone in the long run is a terminal case. It is just a question of when. The doctors offered chemotherapy or radiation treatments but Katie did not want either. She had read that they involved severe nausea, diarrhea, and the loss of hair, not to mention frequent trips to the hospital.

Told she could eat anything she enjoyed, she got her friends to bring smoked oysters, smoked salmon and pickled herrings—but she could not eat very much and steadily lost weight. We borrowed a hospital bed and set it up in the living room so that every day she could see the fields, the trees, and the birds.

November passed quickly until one evening, a few days before Thanksgiving, I was in the kitchen and trying to get a jar of marmalade off a top cabinet shelf. As it was hard to reach even at my height, I got a chair to stand on. I had often done this before and was quite casual, in fact too casual, for my left foot did not quite reach the seat of the chair as I intended but tripped on its edge, and the next thing I knew I had fallen backwards down to the floor, landing first on my left hand, then hard on my left side. I knew immediately that I had broken something. At the hospital, the X ray showed that my left hip was fractured and needed pinning together.

Of course I was uncomfortable and rather depressed, because Katie could not drive anymore and did not come to the hospital and I had only myself to blame for the carelessness that had caused my trouble. They discharged me shortly before Christmas, and the ambulance delivered me back to Wind Rose. What heavenly joy! Medicare provided me with a hospital bed for a month so Katie and I were together again at last, sleeping on two hospital beds in our living room.

Katie, of course, knew that Wind Rose Farm had been sold to the Olneys and that they expected the house to be vacated by the end of the year, but she couldn't bear the thought of moving all our things away somewhere and said she would just like to stay at home—and looked forward to seeing the red-winged blackbirds arrive in March along with the crocuses and the bluebirds in April. I told her she would not have to move—ever—and that I would stay with her to the end.

In late February Katie agreed to try chemotherapy treatments when told that otherwise she would likely lapse into a coma within ten days, for chemotherapy had recently improved and would not likely produce side effects such as nausea or hair falling out.

At about this time I received a letter from a British physicist named Rupert Sheldrake, inviting me to be a delegate to a conference on "Resonance and Vibrations" at the Esalen think tank in Big Sur, California, from June 1 to June 6. Katie urged me to go and thought it quite important for future development of ideas expressed in my *Seven Mysteries.* But of course I declined the invitation on the ground of Katie's terminal condition. I could not possibly leave her to die alone, but might still accept if conditions significantly changed. Rupert Sheldrake understood.

By late April Katie was getting close to her end. She did not suffer much now as she was taking morphine pills almost hourly and the hospice girls gave her injections when she needed the relief. She said she didn't think she would last long but she could walk and actually went out into the garden on Wednesday, April 30, to tend her flowers and hear the birds sing. Bluebirds were building a nest in one of the birdhouses I'd built for them, and she loved to see them.

By Thursday she was slipping into a coma and no longer could swallow food or get out of bed by herself. I had thought a coma was a state of unconsciousness, but although Katie's eyes were now shut and she breathed with difficulty she became very sensitive to touch. When one of the girls tried to turn her over so she wouldn't get bedsores, Katie screamed with pain and I stopped the girl, saying, "Let her be in peace. Bedsores don't matter anymore."

By Saturday morning Katie became very sensitive to sounds as well as touch, though her eyes were still shut and she was breathing in short gasps, about one every second. She quietly stopped breathing at 5:40 and I knew she had finally gone. Everything was strangely still and it was a peaceful spring evening.

Epilogue

My son-in-law, Steve Goldsmith, had been urging me for years to buy a word processor—and I had been resisting on the ground that it did not make sense, at my age, to take on such a complicated machine that would require me to learn a whole new language and system of codes. But, coming to realize that publishers and printers were introducing word processors as well as computers into their production of books, I eventually succumbed and bought one. Steve helped introduce me to this extension of my life. It has been a struggle but, if I live a few more years, probably worth it.

Summing up my present way of life, I am more than content with my current wife Marie, who is a charming girl in her eighties. In her youth she was a dancer and champion swimmer. Later she was an outstanding researcher on violence at Brandeis University. She has long been a member of peace and freedom organizations striving to unite the world. We have much in common, and I consider her a perfect partner for our old age. And really, I think the second half of life can be much more productive and exciting than the first half. Donald, Agnes, and Janet sadly missed most of what was offered them. They hardly realized that the world was changing fast, much faster than anyone knew. It was exploding. And so was my life! *Seven Mysteries* may well be too far ahead of its time for even such a perceptive editor as Clifton Fadiman who, in reviewing it for the Book of the Month Club, did not seem to notice that it was primarily a book of philosophy. And how many of its readers understood its message? Who on Earth yet realizes the abstract nature of the world or how all creatures are related? Who really yet notices our Transcendence? And how many are aware of the Germination of Earth?

One new problem I encountered was the fact that my heart seemed to be wearing out. Early in 1989 I was feeling dizzy and out of breath, and cardiologists, observing my heart with echocardiograms, etc., found that one of its valves was getting so clogged with calcium that it could hardly pump much blood. So, on the recommendation of two heart surgeons, I had open heart surgery on March 23, 1989, when a pig's heart valve was sewn into my heart with an estimated 85 percent chance of

survival. I accepted that as fair enough and, after eight days in the hospital, Marie literally "brought home the bacon" and I recovered normally for a couple of months.

But in early June I felt sick again, and doctors sent me to the emergency section of Cottage Hospital where it was found that I had pneumonia in both lungs, anemia, a collapsed lung, and blood clots. In addition, during my month there, I suffered two mild strokes from lack of oxygen, both caused by the hospital's neglect. On two occasions the staff somehow forgot my much-needed oxygen tank. Marie was alarmed as my speech was temporarily affected. Fortunately the strokes were not paralyzing for more than a week, but during that time I could not breathe while sitting up. Marie came to the hospital faithfully for almost twelve hours every day, bringing me flowers and special food. She also massaged and loved me, which did wonders for my morale while, according to one doctor, I was "a very sick puppy." To raise me from puppy to dog, he gave me big doses of antibiotics, a lung pump, breathing exercises, and

Marie with her two sisters, Lucille (left) and Margaret (right), 1982

physiotherapy. My weight dropped more than fifty pounds (to two hundred) during my month in the hospital and some doctors thought I might have to go to a nursing home for treatment indefinitely. But gradually my breathing improved, walking became easier and I went home on July 5. I still had little appetite except for soft-boiled eggs at breakfast.

Then one night I dreamed of Indians, one of whom handed me a jar of peanut butter, saying, "Try this. You'll like it." On awaking I asked Marie to get me some peanut butter and it truly tasted good. My appetite picked up. I also yearned for canned grapefruit sections, which had always refreshed me—and I began to regain my weight. By October I felt fully recovered at 220 pounds and Marie and I took to walking for twenty minutes around the park every day, which did both of us good.

By this time I was getting used to my new word processor and found that I could work at it for many hours a day, stopping to lie down and rest only when I occasionally got sleepy. Sleepiness had been a chronic problem with me ever since I was a teenager. Marie had long had a similar problem, but in my case sleepiness had seriously slowed my production in creative writing for more than half a century. Contemplating this got me to wondering what is the real purpose of sleep anyway? And what of dreams, like my dream of Indians? The Indians helped me, yes, but were they Indians only in my mind? Or in my subconscious memory? Or were they in some mystical way giving me a message from another world?

We on this planet, both animals and humans, spend about a third of our lives asleep. And evidence is accumulating that all of us dream, probably all the time, though we are rarely aware of our daytime "dreams" and forget most of our night ones by the time we are fully awake.

But why do we sleep? Is consciousness so new in evolution on Earth that we cannot yet have it continuously but must pay for it by sleeping about a third of our time? Why do so many "defenceless" prey animals risk their lives by closing their eyes and damping down their senses for hours every night or day? Do the body's nerves really need to be turned off that long and that often? Would not breathing, drinking, eating, and resting be sufficient to replenish our energy and keep us going? Why should we sleep ever? And if, as it seems, we MUST sleep, do we necessarily have to dream?

Psychologist Christopher Evans, in his *Landscapes of the Night,* gave me new insight into the function of dreams as the relaxed way the human mind has of solving problems that in waking hours are surrounded by distractions and anxieties. Evans compared the brain to a very sophisticated computer, defining the dream as an interception by the conscious mind of programs that the brain (temporarily "off-line") was sifting for future use.

I often have dreams that seem to deal with research in another world, such as David Bohm's hologram universe in which the form and structure of the whole is enfolded within each part. It is like the now-known fact that every gene in the body is capable of directing any bodily growth. It is a universe in which consciousness creates all, and every remembered dream can be viewed as a mystic preview of the greater world beyond space, time, and self.

Returning to the mortal world in which I am writing, I reflect that, at intervals while not writing, I have planted thousands of trees, some already forty feet high, I've built almost five hundred feet of stone walls, steps, benches, posts, etc., not to mention a lot of woodcutting, carpentry, masonry, some plumbing, grading, and digging, which kinds of work I find much easier than writing. In fact, it relaxes my mind and in many ways my body and, along with reading, illustrating, watching birds and animals, and playing the piano, is an enjoyable change that refreshes me for the next bout with conjuring up ideas and fitting them into sentences that I hope will be worth reading.

With all this I live in a mad world where my buttons keep coming off, shoelaces keep breaking, and my clothes are either splitting at the seams or constantly needing readjustment. The man at the furniture store just shrugs: "It's all coming through that way. Maybe the trees are more warped than they used to be."

There is also a quiet searching for knowledge that goes on continuously. . . . I am only a passing thought in this world, a ship in the night of time, a material illusion that will soon be gone again over the horizon of death. In this piece—in everything—the universe is whispering to itself.

I am intrigued with the impending possibility of colonizing space and I often let my mind run loose there. Home building thousands of miles up in the sky may ultimately turn out to be easier and safer than living on planets where weather, volcanoes, earthquakes, and other natural phenomena must continue to be periodically uncontrollable. And the three *B*s of pollution will almost certainly become more manageable in space where bombs can be rigidly outlawed, birth control diligently

"My sketch of our view," Santa Barbara, California

applied, and someday perhaps, should we make contact with other life, we may gain indispensable assistance from the outer majority.

Speaking of other life, astronomers are seeking it all over the sky at an accelerating rate with more and more powerful radio-telescopes aided by more and better computers every year. So far nothing even hints at intelligence. But the potential rewards of success are so exciting that no one wants to stop listening.

Astronomers, astrophysicists, and philosophers like me are increasingly wondering why ETI (extraterrestrial intelligence) is so elusive. They ask "Where is everybody?" As our technology is so new, we are likely the most naive civilization around while other presumed life could be millions of years older and more mature spiritually, possibly more than familiar with the mysteries of death and the purpose of our existence in the mindboggling nursery of the Milky Way. If so, they may be wisely letting us cope with all such philosophical bewilderment alone.

I cannot resist setting before you some of the more fantastic possibilities. Imaginative speculators think that life in other worlds may not be based on water, oxygen, or carbon molecules as it is on Earth. It may have evolved in ammonia, or perhaps is based on molecules that can stand the heat of molten iron and depends on organs sensitive to radiations, colors, or sounds far beyond our worldly range of sensitivity. Or small organisms may have evolved over millions of years into superorganisms big enough to occupy whole planets as

single beings. And they may even have evolved ways to modify biological creatures through chemicals and artificial organs resembling computers to extend their functions in fantastic ways. This is called the Cyborg concept. Perhaps some advanced civilizations have tired of adapting and improving themselves by old-fashioned thinking and resorted to mechanical automata that can store vast quantities of information and make rapid and important decisions through artificial intelligence, enabling their populations to advance, intelligence building on intelligence, at unbelievable speed.

My friend Harlow Shapley of the Harvard Observatory thought that in addition to the 100,000 life-bearing planets he surmised existed in the Milky Way there might be another class of little-known celestial bodies capable of sustaining life there. These would be neither stars nor planets but between them in size. They would be warm from the radioactivity in their massive interiors but at the same time not hot enough to blaze like stars. They would get along without a sun, illumined only by starlight. He thought life might evolve into intelligent forms in such worlds which, being dark, could not be seen with the biggest telescopes though they might well be more numerous than visible stars.

Eventually it is believed that man will have to rearrange the solar system to fulfill humanity's future. . . . Meantime, perhaps by late next century, we may presume that our planet will have started building Saturnian rings as people accommodate to the freedom of space and assemble their giant habitats, beginning at 22,300 miles above the equator (where fixed satellites are already in place) and working from there up and down like an orb spider web until the structure is rigid enough to include space elevators for cheap transport between heaven and earth—something Arthur Clarke has been actively promoting for years. All this of course will take centuries and more, by when all people should have been long convinced that our planet is essentially one country with its federal government firmly in control of pollution, with our depopulated continents definitely becoming more natural and pastoral as the frontier of action moves upward and outward toward the universe as a whole.

I spoke of some of this at the symposium during my fiftieth reunion at Harvard in 1979, and also in my *Seven Mysteries of Life.* The evolution I describe, however, is not just a material evolution but more profoundly a mental and spiritual one, which will in time inevitably embrace all consciousness and the greater worlds beyond space, time, and death. Significantly, this ties in with the aforementioned revolutionary theory of physicist David Bohm that the universe is constructed like a hologram, every part containing all the information for the whole.

This idea is coming to be called by physicists the anthropic principle, for it advances the concept that it may be only man's intangible consciousness that creates the total environment he finds around him, from the heart of the atom to the farthest star.

One of my personal minor challenges is to try to determine whether the mysterious coincidences in life, of which I think I've had more than my share, are really random or could have been created by some mystic influence beyond my comprehension? This makes me muse that consciousness is in essence nothing but a growing memory associated (during earth life) with a certain organism, but is there any reason why (when the organism disintegrates in death) the memory may not go on growing? Could it be that the texture of abstract memory (something nonphysical) is all there is to consciousness, and that the association of a physical body is minor and unessential to it? Does that throw light on the body-mind mystery?

Marie and I sometimes delve into the world's mysteries together, and she skillfully edits my manuscripts. I do a few odd jobs around the house, sometimes solving little intricacies that baffle her. She also lovingly massages my curly gray head—

Guy and Marie Murchie at home,
Santa Barbara, 1987

we call it scratching my brains—when I tuck her in at bedtime.

I sum up the "Two and Twenty Codes for Living" I have collected during my more than four-score years on the planet, of which Marie approves on the whole and observes in daily practice:

- Do not promise more than you will do, nor do less than you promised.
- Know what you live for. And so live that anything less than immortality would be unjust.
- Know no strangers. Imagine no enemies.
- Bear no arms. Rather dispel fear with the "weapon" of love.
- Be on friendly terms with the Universe and welcome its laws for your own.
- Love everyone, including yourself, as a bosom relative in the world's family.
- Be joyful at work, as at play, and you won't need to know the difference.
- Act immediately on your worthy impulse lest memory or opportunity fade.
- Stand back that you may see the world in big perspective.
- Be humble for you are made of rain. Be noble for you are made of stars.
- What you are, seem. What you seem, be.

- Order begins with calling things by their right names.
- Be prepared at any moment for death. And welcome it as a glorious unfoldment of life evolved for you by the wisdom of the Universe.
- Be generous in giving your labor, time, information and worldly goods when they are needed.
- A man is not wholly a man except he be part of mankind.
- As a galaxy may contain a quintillion minds so may a mind contain a quintillion galaxies.
- Like the flying kite, your loftiest freedom is won by welcoming the string that ties you to a will greater than your own.
- As every world contains a potential seed, so every seed contains a potential world.
- Plumb the depths of yourself and you will taste the Universe.
- If your spirit be weak, try to think and behave AS IF you loved or believed, and in time you will.
- Look upon the world with your own eyes. Look upon God with His own.
- Thank God for your problems, for they will feed your soul.

These precepts have sprouted from observations of life across the world, some expressed in comparable vein by sages from Confucius to Baha'u'llah, all more or less hoed, chewed, digested, and here humanly raised to the warm light of today. One knows not whence they came since all writers, poets or seers, wittingly or no, snuff up the passing air and gather grist from the towns, hills, and seas around them to grind in the mill of mind and soul to serve anew to their fellow wayfarers on Earth. Let's just say they are nuggets from the riverbed of human transcendence, tenderly picked and sorted for your final look into one man's soul.

If to MIND we pay no mind
And MATTER matters not,
There's nothing left before, behind,
But SOUL. It'S OUL we got.

"A wonderful way to end it," says Marie, "for the time being! . . ."

BIBLIOGRAPHY

Fiction:

(And illustrator) *Men on the Horizon,* Houghton, 1932.

(Editor and contributor) *Mutiny of the Bounty and Other Sea Stories,* Consolidated, 1937.

(With Thomas Russell Gowenlock) *Soldiers of Darkness,* Doubleday, 1937.

(And illustrator) *Song of the Sky: An Exploration of the Ocean of Air,* Houghton, 1954, revised edition, Ziff-Davis Publishing, 1979, abridged edition published as *The World Aloft,* Houghton, 1960.

(And illustrator) *Music of the Spheres: The Material Universe from Atom to Quasar, Simply Explained,* Houghton, 1961, revised edition for young adults published in two volumes, Dover, 1967.

(And illustrator) *The Seven Mysteries of Life: An Exploration in Science and Philosophy,* Houghton, 1978.

Veil of Glory, forthcoming.

Author of full-length memoir "The Soul School: Confessions of a Passenger on Planet Earth," from which this essay is excerpted.

Contributor to anthologies; also contributor to annuals, including *The Old Farmer's Almanac,* and to newspapers and periodicals, including *Atlantic, Holiday, Reader's Digest,* and *Science Digest.*

Norman Spinrad

1940-

Although it presents certain technical difficulties, maybe you shouldn't write an autobiography until you are dead.

The story of a life, even if your own, published for the benefit of readers, becomes, well, a *story*. And true or not a good story requires, if not necessarily a traditional beginning, middle, and end, then at least certainly *some* sort of structure leading to a sense of satisfying resolution at the end of the reading experience.

But since I'm fifty-three years old as I write this, not exactly on the brink of retirement, I can hardly be expected to bring *this* story to a successful thematic closure in any of the usual manners.

Then too, while "write what you know about" may be the hoariest of literary maxims and autobiography seemingly the ideal exemplar thereof, upon a moment's uncomfortable reflection, maybe not.

Sure, you know the sequence of events better than you know anything else, but it's no easy task to negotiate the treacherous literary waters between the Scylla of the extended brag and the Charybdis of a deadly dull recitation of the complete bibliography and nothing more.

So what I've opted for here is a rather experimental form, itself perhaps a bit of autobiographical characterization, since fairly early on in my career I came to the realization that form should be chosen by the requirements of content. And *this* particular content certainly seems to call for something rather schizoid—a montage of split points of view, *persons* that is, in more than the usual technical sense.

So this autobiography is divided into three clearly labeled tracks.

"Continuity" is, as Sergeant Friday would have it, just the facts, Ma'am, written in third person as if "Norman Spinrad" were someone other than the author thereof.

"Flashbacks" are little novelistic bits and pieces designed to illumine some of the events of "Continuity" with some more intimate visions of what the character in question was thinking and feeling at the time.

Norman Spinrad on the French Mediterranean, 1990

"Frame" is what you are reading now—the author and the subject, the novelist and the literary critic, speaking to you and maybe myself as directly as I can manage under the circumstances, and trying to extract some overall meaning from it all.

CONTINUITY

Norman Spinrad was born in New York City, on September 15, 1940, the son of Morris and Ray Spinrad. Except for a brief period in Kingston, New York, he spent his entire childhood and adolescence residing with his parents and his sister

311

Helene in various locations in the Bronx, where he attended Public School 87, Junior High Schools 113 and 22, and the Bronx High School of Science.

In 1957, he entered the College of the City of New York, from which he graduated in 1961 with a bachelor of science degree as a pre-law major.

FLASHBACK

I was a subway commuter as a college student, living in the family apartment in the Bronx, hanging out in Greenwich Village on the weekends.

My father, eldest son of a family of five, had never finished high school, having left to earn family bread, and only after serving as a medical corpsman in the navy during World War II did he realize that medicine would have been his calling, and by then it was much too late. Like many such children of the Great Depression, he wanted nothing more or less for _his_ son than a secure professional career, ideally the one he wished _he_ had been able to have.

So I was always under pressure, not just to perform academically, but to follow a path towards the bankable sciences. I passed the stiff entrance test for the Bronx High School of Science, graduated in 1957 at the age of sixteen, and, at the behest of my father, seeing as how medicine obviously actively turned me off, entered City College as an engineering major.

This lasted about a term and a half, terminated by my confrontation with the horrors of pre-electronic-calculator calculus. Okay, said my dad, what about chemistry? You don't need so much math for that. So I became a chemistry major long enough to convince me that I had no genius for the subject and less interest in it as a life's work.

Okay, said my dad, with less enthusiasm, what about, uh, psychology? He seemed to view the vector from medicine to hard engineering through stinky liquids into the murk of the social sciences as a kind of intellectual slippery slope.

What did _I_ want to do with my life at this point?

Hey, come on, I was about nineteen years old!

Although it's common enough for one's parents and guidance counselors to demand that one get serious and make a commitment, it's both cruel and naive to suppose that a nineteen-year-old kid is intellectually or emotionally equipped to decide

what he's going to do with the rest of his life. What did _I_ want at this point?

I didn't really want to be in college at all. I didn't want to be living _en famille_ in the Bronx until I graduated. What I wanted was _la vie bohème_ in the Village.

F R A M E

What is included here and what is left out:

Unless you've lived an extraordinarily dull and uneventful life under a bell jar with your typewriter, and I haven't, you will have broken hearts, had your own broken, and engaged in any number of acts sexual and otherwise that were politically incorrect at the time or, in hindsight, illegal, or even the sort of thing your older and wiser self may now find immoral.

Then too, my life has intersected, in various degrees of intimacy, the lives of many people of more than passing literary interests—Philip K. Dick, Timothy Leary, Theodore Sturgeon, Harlan Ellison, J. G. Ballard, William Burroughs, Frank Herbert, Michael Moorcock, to name a random sample of a long, long list.

Some of these luminaries were or are real friends, others acquaintances of one degree or another. I've written about many of them extensively in various places already, and so you must take my word for it that it's length limitations rather than ego that limits mention of them in this compass to the effect they may have had on _my_ life or career.

I have been commissioned to write a short literary autobiography, and as I interpret that commission, this is supposed to be the story of Norman Spinrad the writer, not a juicy exposé of my private life, nor of the private lives of people who may have been involved with it.

However . . .

However, there are times when such matters _do_ impinge on what gets written, and I _am_ trying to tell the true story to the best of my ability, so when they do, I guess I'm going to have to try to bite the bullet. . . .

FLASHBACK

The Village, circa 1959, pre-Beatles, the Beat Era. Coffee houses. Craft shops. Folk music. I remember seeing a fat-faced kid from Minnesota performing for free at a Monday amateur night at

Gerde's Folk City. Name of Bob Dylan. A hot act was the Holy Modal Rounders, a bluegrass group which later metamorphosed into the Fugs. One of its members was Peter Stampfel, who is now a science fiction editor at Daw Books. Another was Ed Sanders, who was to cover the Manson family trial in Los Angeles for the *Free Press* while I was writing for the same paper.

But in 1959 I never knew Sanders, and Stampfel, whom I did party with upon occasion, would not remember the me of that era. They were culture heroes, and I was just another day-tripping college kid.

Another culture hero of sorts in this space-time was Bruce Britton, proprietor of the Britton Leather Shop. Bruce was a famous sandalmaker. Bruce Britton was a charismatic party animal, and the Britton Leather Shop was a major party scene. When work was done (and sometimes when it wasn't), it became an open house, and also a place where you found out where the *other* parties were.

The Britton Leather Shop became my central weekend hangout, and Bruce became my friend, an older role model of sorts, and later one of the earliest patrons of my writing career.

But I didn't aspire to a writing career at that point. Truth be told, and my father not, I didn't aspire to a career at all. From his point of view, what I aspired to was quite appalling, namely, to spend all my time the way I spent my weekends—as, well, a beatnik in Greenwich Village.

Norman, about two years old

FRAME

Beatniks, even teenage wannabee beatniks living with their parents in the Bronx, did drugs. Mostly pot, which was readily available, but I was introduced to consciousness-altering chemicals with rather stronger stuff, namely peyote, which I experienced before I so much as puffed on a joint.

Ah yes, we've all committed our youthful indiscretions. Why, even President Clinton has copped to tasting the Devil's Weed, though since he didn't inhale, he didn't enjoy it. I, however, did inhale, and therefore did get off. Often. And to my creative advantage. Nor do I regret it.

If there's one gaping void in the story of American literary history in the second half of the twentieth century as currently promulgated, it's the influence of grass and psychedelic drugs, not only on the lives of writers, but on the content of what's been written, and on the form and style too. It's hard to be critically or biographically coura-

geous when so much creative work was done under the influences of jailable offenses.

In the Beat Era, however, the literary culture heroes of bohemia—William Burroughs, Jack Kerouac, Allen Ginsberg, and company—were not only entirely up front about it, but openly advocated the chemical enhancement of consciousness as a literary, spiritual, and cultural *virtue.* And wrote much stylistically mighty work under the influence to prove it.

Even a mainstream literary lion like Norman Mailer wrote a famous essay called "The White Negro" extolling the "Hip" world of sex, dope, and transcendence over the "Square" workaday world of the Lonely Crowd, though elsewhere he was to correctly opine that writing *final draft* stoned was maybe not such a terrific idea.

I raise this issue now because I would be lying shamelessly if I denied that I was a devotee of this tradition or renounced herein my belief that on the whole a bit of grass and a more significant trip now and again is beneficial to the creative juices. Nor could the story of the sort of writer I became make much sense in the absence of its consideration.

Most writers of science fiction, at least prior to the New Wave of the 1960s, emerged as writers from a formative adolescence immersed in the hermetic subculture of "science fiction fandom," reading science fiction obsessively, attending science fiction conventions, as well as writing letters and articles in science fiction fanzines. SF fans even have an acronym for it, FIAWOL—Fandom Is A Way Of Life.

Not my teenage planet, Monkey Boy. I didn't even know that this subculture existed until after I had published about a dozen stories and a novel. Yes, I read a lot of sf—Sturgeon, Bester, Dick, Bradbury being early obsessions—but I was just as deeply into Mailer, Kerouac, William Burroughs, and their precursor, Henry Miller.

And *theirs* was the subculture I wanted to grow up to live in before I even had any serious thoughts about a writing career; the hip world of free love, pot, psychedelics, literary and personal transcendence—all that which, with the addition and via the medium of rock and roll, was to call into being the Counterculture half a decade later.

FLASHBACK

This was something I could hardly admit to my parents, the guidance counselor, or even quite

*About four years of age
during World War II*

to myself at the time. And at least being a psych major was something I found far more congenial than my previous provisional career choices.

However, two unpleasant academic satoris were to convince me that this was not to be my planet either.

I was fortunate enough to be assigned to a section in motivational psychology taught by Dr. Kenneth B. Clark, who, among other things, had written part of the brief in Brown versus Board of Education. There were no tests. You discussed texts that had been assigned for consideration in class and you wrote three papers, and Clark marked you on that.

At the beginning of the term you were handed a list of the books and papers that would be discussed. In addition to the expected scientific treatises, there was a five-foot shelf of novels, plays, and assorted literary works. How could anyone be expected to read through all that in a term? They couldn't. Clark believed that any college upper classman who hadn't already read most of this stuff didn't belong in a class on this level in the first place.

I loved this class. It was worth the price of admission. Clark was brilliant and witty and brought out the best in his students. The class was educational, but it was also a kind of high intellectual entertainment.

All during the term Clark complained of the conventionality of the papers students were turning in. Can't you give me something *original?*

I admired Clark greatly and for my final paper I determined to write something that would pay him back intellectually and knock him out of his socks in the bargain.

I had read my way through all Kerouac, Ginsberg and on into Herman Hesse, Alan Watts, and D. T. Suzuki, a common intellectual vector in my Village extracurricular circles, and so I knew quite a bit about Buddhism.

So I wrote a paper comparing Buddhism and Freudian theory as systems of psychology.

This is brilliant, fascinating, Dr. Clark told me after he had read it. I glowed.

"But I can only give you an A-."

"Huh? Why?"

He shrugged. "Because I don't know enough about Buddhism to judge whether you really know what you're talking about," he admitted.

And had not been willing to make the intellectual effort to acquire the necessary background.

Another required course that I had to do a term paper for was abnormal psychology. I suggested to the professor that I do it on the mental states induced by consumption of peyote. He seemed quite interested.

"But as far as I know, there's not much source material in the literature," he added dubiously.

"Don't need it," I assured him. "Not only do I have plenty of primary experimental subjects to interview, I have firsthand experience myself."

Did he gape at me as if I was some kind of crazed dope fiend?

Nope.

That wasn't what made him refuse to consider the subject appropriate for a term paper in his course. If I could have rehashed secondary sources and studded the paper with appropriate footnotes, no problem. But original research in the form of direct reportage of the mental states in question was not academically acceptable.

CONTINUITY

In his senior year at CCNY, he took two courses in short story writing and made his first submissions to magazines. Having secured entry to Fordham University law school, he spent the summer of 1961 traveling in Mexico with friends.

FLASHBACK

By my senior year, all I really wanted was out—out of college, out of my parents' apartment, out from under their pressures and influences, out of the square world and into the hip.

But I still had it in my head that I had to get a degree to please my parents. By this time, I had changed my major so many times that the only way to graduate was to lump together what I had already taken with a few more random courses, call it a "pre-law major," and bullshit it past the guidance counselors by being admitted to law school.

One course I took in short story writing was formative. It was taught by a writer named Irwin Stark who had sold fiction to magazines and had not lost the habit of submitting. Stark, like Clark, bitched about the conventionality of what the students were writing, and I took another shot at taking a teacher at his word.

I wrote a story called "Not With A Bang," in which a couple finds true love screwing in a bathtub full of chocolate syrup during a nuclear apocalypse, good enough to eventually sell to a low-grade men's magazine about a decade later.

The look that Stark gave me when he handed back that week's assignment was choice.

"I can't have you read a thing like that in class," he told me in his office later.

Uh-oh.

"Why don't you submit it to *Playboy?*"

"*Playboy* . . . ?"

"Yeah, it's a long shot, but they're the top market, and if you start at the top and work down, you can take the first offer you get for a story and know it's the best you can do."

And he told me how to submit stories to magazines: stick them in an envelope with a cover letter and a self-addressed, stamped return envelope, and drop 'em in a mailbox. If you get a check, cash it before it bounces. If you get a rejection, submit it to the next best market.

I submitted "Not With A Bang" to *Playboy.* They didn't buy it, so I sent it elsewhere. And elsewhere. And wrote some more stories. And started submitting *them.*

And that's how I became a writer. Not yet a published writer, that was about three years in the future, but by the time I graduated from CCNY, I knew what I wanted to do with my life, and how one went about doing it. You write 'em, you drop 'em in the mail, you wait.

Best advice I ever had. Best advice any would-be writer can ever get. It's ultimately all you need to know. The Big Secret is that there is no Big Secret. It drives me crazy how many wannabee writers just won't believe it.

CONTINUITY

Upon returning to New York, he decided not to attend law school but pursue a writing career instead. He rented a cheap apartment in the East Village, secured part-time employment in a friend's leather shop, wrote a first novel which has never been published and about a dozen short stories, finally making his first sale to *Analog* in 1962. The story, "The Last of the Romany," was published in 1963.

FLASHBACK

Actually, the thought of entering law school in the fall of 1961 was filling me with nauseous dread before I even graduated. By this time I knew I wanted to be a writer, but what I lacked was any notion of how to support myself while doing it, plus the courage to make such a beatnik move sure to outrage my parents. The road trip to Mexico in a rotten old car (*never* buy a car from a relative!) with two college friends, Marty Mach and Bob Denberg, was part temporary escape from this dilemma, part personal vision quest, part hopeful emulation of Huck Finn and Kerouac.

When we finally managed to coax the wretched clunker back to New York after an exhaustive education in automotive Spanish, the Greenwich Village outdoor Arts and Craft Show was in full swing. One weekend afternoon, I took over the Britton Leather Shop's table as relief for an hour and moved two hundred dollars worth of goods, about what they had done all week.

Bingo! I had a part-time job. Bruce Britton, and later his partner and successor at the leather shop, Ken Martin, supported my writing ambition and more or less let me make my own hours. And my own wage, since what they were paying me was a commission on sales.

I found a foul little apartment in the East Village that I could rent for $36 a month, meaning, what with food and utilities, I could survive on about $120 a month, and in a good week I could make $40 at the leathershop working twenty hours.

I could survive, more or less, as a would-be writer.

F R A M E

My naivete was total. I knew no other writers, I hadn't published a thing, and my brilliant notion was that I would support myself writing short stories while working on my first novel. I wrote an unpublishable novel, which, years later, I was to some extent to cannibalize in the writing of *Bug Jack Barron.* I wrote stories and sent them off to magazines, mostly science fiction magazines.

When I finished the novel, I knew nothing better to do with it than pay my thirty-five dollars to have it "evaluated for the market" by the Scott Meredith Literary Agency, who advertised this service in various magazines. They rejected it, as they did 99 percent of such fee submissions, as I was soon to learn in another incarnation, but the "agent" who wrote the rejection letter over Scott Meredith's signature met me in secret, praised my talent, and wised me up to the SMLA fee-reading

scam, strongly suggesting that I not waste my money on it again.

Nor had I sold anything. And the final turn of the screw was that *Analog* had been sitting on "The Last of the Romany" for an unconscionable six months.

What I didn't know was that the reason for the delay was that John W. Campbell, Jr., the legendary editor thereof, had discovered the lion's share of the major science fiction writers of the last quarter century or so by the tedious and time-consuming process of reading his entire slush pile himself.

Needless to say, when his acceptance letter arrived in the mail, all was forgiven.

CONTINUITY

He sold several more short stories during the next year or so, on the strength of which he secured a professional agent, the Scott Meredith Literary Agency.

F R A M E

I had been dead broke before I sold a novelette to Campbell for the princely sum of $450, so broke that I had taken a job as a welfare investigator in Bedford-Stuyvesant for a month to keep me going.

When I made my third magazine sale, I wrote a letter to Scott Meredith, the only agent I knew, and was accepted as a client on a professional basis.

Meanwhile, an ulcer I had developed under the pressure of adolescent angst, and no doubt exacerbated by eating all that cheap hot stuff in Mexico, landed me in a hospital for an operation. The operation was successful, but the patient should have died. They screwed up bad and infected me with something called toxic hepatitis, supposedly universally fatal. I ran a fever of about 106 degrees for days. I lost about twenty-five pounds. I survived. Still running a fever and looking like death warmed over but not by much, I took a cab directly to the draft board and got myself reclassified 4-F so it wouldn't be a total loss.

FLASHBACK

A prolonged ultra-high fever, aside from usually being fatal, makes a 1000-mile acid trip seem like a warm glass of 3.2 beer. I was not only hallucinating, I had . . . Powers.

Laboring under the hallucinatory delusion that I was being tortured for secret rocket fuel information by spies, I had the hysterical strength to snap the bandages tying me to my deathbed, yank out the IVs, and hold off a squad of interns while I used another Power on the bedside telephone.

It was the wee hours of the morning. The hospital staff must've thought I was raving into a dead phone; understandable, considering what they were hearing on my end.

Somehow I had fixated on the name of what turned out to be a real air force general. I got an outside line. I got a long distance operator. I made a collect long distance call to said general at the Pentagon. He had long since gone home to bed. I did . . . a thing. I ordered the Pentagon switchboard to patch me through to his home phone, validating it with a blather of letters and numbers that was my top secret command override code. They did it. A bleary general's voice came on the line.

I started babbling about spies, rocket fuels, send a rescue squad to—

"Huh—? What the—?"

At which point, the interns jumped me from behind and hung up the phone on the sucker.

By the next morning, my fever had broken.

And the hospital had some tall explaining to do when the Pentagon traced the call back.

F R A M E

Qué pasa? I've contemplated that question ever since, my best take being the story "Carcinoma Angeles," a literary breakthrough for me that I wrote about three years later, and which, long after that, seems to have been picked up by a doctor in Texas as a treatment for cancer.

As on an acid trip, only more so, I think the fever warped me into a metaphorical reality in which the disease ravaging my body was transmogrified into a paranoid image system overlaid on actual real-world events. By giving *that* story the ending I wanted, by actually waking up the general, I somehow was able to triumph over the infection for which the whole thing was metaphor.

Unless you've got a better explanation.

The facts are that I survived a fatal disease, that this experience, whatever it was, later was the impetus for the story that was the real take-off point for the writer that I was to become, and I don't think I was the same person afterward.

CONTINUITY

SMLA made no sales for him during the six months, and he was economically constrained to seek full-time employment.

He answered an ad in the *New York Times* offering an entry-level position as an editor. When he took the test for the job at the employment agency, he realized that the prospective employer was his own literary agent, Scott Meredith. Armed with this knowledge, he did very well on the test and was tentatively offered the position by the employment agency.

FLASHBACK

As a client, I had never even met Scott Meredith. When I showed up in the office as a job applicant, he was nonplussed. Many writers who later became clients had worked for him, but Scott had never hired one of his own writers through the employment agency cattle call and didn't want to do it.

"What do you mean, you won't hire me?" I demanded. "The only reason I need this damn job in the first place is because you haven't sold a thing for me in six months!"

Having never confronted this argument either, Scott relented. Voila, the twenty-four-year-old kid whose own stuff wasn't selling had a job anonymously representing a list of something like a hundred established writers, some of them, like Philip K. Dick, Philip Jose, Frank Herbert, John Brunner, and Jack Vance, among others, literary idols of mine at the time, and people who were later to become my friends.

F R A M E

The pro desk at SMLA was an excruciating experience. Scott Meredith was a genius at squeezing work out of his peons by force of paranoid pressure, and after a full day's work writing letters under his name to authors, sometimes typing them over and over again until he was satisfied, you had to read manuscripts on your own time at home. It was like being back in *school*. It was nearly impossible to get anything of my own written. And there I was, agenting stories and novels anonymously for the very writers whose illustrious company I longed to join myself!

On the other hand, it was a crash course in the realities of publishing from the inside out, and the bottom up. By the time I was twenty-five, I had more publishing street smarts than venerable greats twice my age, and before I was thirty found myself playing the strange role of career advisor, father-figure even, to my own literary idols, like Theodore Sturgeon and Philip K. Dick.

CONTINUITY

While working at SMLA in various capacities from 1964 to 1966, he continued to write stories, some of which sold, and completed *The Solarians,* his first published novel, which appeared in 1966.

F R A M E

I have always been a lousy typist, and, in the end, I simply couldn't keep up with the workload on an SMLA pro desk. Scott fired me. He then rehired me for a part-time job supervising the fee-reading operation, where piece-work editors wrote

The author signing autographs in the Ambiance Bookstore in Paris, about 1989

letters of criticism on submissions from amateurs for a fee.

Somewhat morally ambiguous maybe, but I had time and energy to write my own stuff again. Stories sold, including one to *Playboy:* "Death-watch." I wrote a space opera, *The Solarians,* which SMLA sold to Paperback Library for $1250.

After I left the Meredith agency for good, I never held another job and, for better or worse, sometimes much worse, have survived on my writing ever since.

And though I seriously suspect that years later Scott Meredith was responsible for the non-publication of *The Children of Hamelin,* I doubt whether I would be saying that now, if it wasn't for the education I got in his rough school of hard publishing knocks.

CONTINUITY

In 1966, he decided to move to San Francisco. He gave up his East Village apartment and his by then part-time work at the Meredith agency, bought a $300 Rambler, loaded his worldly goods in it, and set out for California.

F R A M E

Bruce Britton and his wife, Marilyn, had moved to San Francisco in the train of their psychotherapy guru (a story that was to be an inspiration for a part of *The Children of Hamelin),* somehow bringing a curtain down on part of my life. But it also meant I now had friends in California.

And California, San Francisco in particular, for me like so many others, was the mythical Golden West towards which Young Men were supposed to go, the land with no winter, North Beach, the Sunset end of the Road, the object of a thousand and one vision quests, the Future itself, somehow, the glorious leap into the Great Unknown.

Appropriately enough, Frank Herbert and about three hundred milligrams of mescaline sent me on my way.

FLASHBACK

Walking west through the Village night on Fourth Street, peaking on mescaline after reading the final installment of the magazine serialization of "Dune"—a powerful meditation on space-time, precognition, and destiny soon to launch a hundred thousand trips—I had a flash-forward of my own.

I would be a famous science fiction writer; I would publish many stories and novels, and many of the people who were my literary idols, inspirations, and role models, and former clients, people I had never met, would come to accept me as their equal, as their ally, as their friend.

And my life's mission would be to take this commercial science fiction genre and turn it into something else somehow, write works that transcended its commercial parameters, works that could aspire to the literary company of Burroughs and Mailer and Kerouac, that would help to open a new Way. . . .

This is what you're here for. This is why you passed through the fever's fire and didn't die in that hospital bed. This is what you must do. You must go West to meet your future.

The mescaline talking? An overdose of twenty-five-year-old ego? A stoned-out ego-tripping wish-fulfillment fantasy?

Call it what you will.

Everything I saw in that timeless Einsteinian moment would come to pass.

CONTINUITY

On the way to San Francisco, he attended the Milford Science Fiction Writers' Conference in Milford, Pennsylvania, to which he had been invited by the organizer, Damon Knight.

FLASHBACK

Damon Knight had invited me on the basis of "The Equalizer," a story I published in *Analog*. The only other science fiction writers I had met before had been Terry Carr and Barry Malzberg, fellow SMLA wage-slaves, and suddenly there I was in Damon's huge crumbling Victorian manse for ten days of workshopping and socializing with a couple dozen of them, a few whom *I had actually agented anonymously,* though considering what had habitually come down, I wasn't about to mention *that.*

Damon's motto was "No Chiefs, no Indians." This was a professional workshop and everyone invited was by definition a professional, hence an equal, whether they were Damon, Gordon Dick-son, James Blish, Judith Merril, or one of the selected new guys like me.

What's more, I was indeed accepted as an equal colleague on a certain level, and the sense of awed isolation I felt when I first stepped into the house's big kitchen and met all these people who were names on book jackets lasted maybe an hour and a half.

You can say a lot of critical things about the community of science fiction writers, and down through the years I certainly have, but it really *is* a community that not only tends to protect and nurture its own but actually *welcomes* newcomers into the fold. Like all gatherings of writers, the sf community engages in bragging, backbiting, vicious gossip, and cruel games, but nowhere else in my experience are established writers so genuinely openhearted to the new kids on the block.

CONTINUITY

He became fast friends with Harlan Ellison, who was at Milford, and was strongly attracted to Dona Sadock, with whom he was to live many years later, who was there with Ellison.

FLASHBACK

Harlan arrived in Milford in a flash of Hollywood street punk ectoplasm with the tiny elfin Dona in tow. It was just one of those weird chemical things. He hadn't been in Damon's kitchen for twenty minutes before we were talking as if we were already old buddies picking up a conversation that had been going on for years.

Harlan at that time was about thirty, dressing and bullshitting like the Hollywood star writer. Dona was this tiny little twenty-year-old groupie, or so it seemed until she opened her mouth and out came this preternaturally powerful voice redolent of fifty-year-old sophistication and speaking for someone who seemed about a thousand years older than that.

Instant fascination. Unrequited love that would go on for years.

The beginning of the two longest friendships of my life.

CONTINUITY

Instead of driving directly to San Francisco after Milford, he passed through Los Angeles and looked up Ellison, who put him up at his house for a week or so, persuaded him to try Los Angeles instead, and found him an affordable studio apartment.

F R A M E

I hadn't intended to stay more than a few days in Los Angeles. I took a random exit on the Hollywood Freeway and called Harlan, the only person I knew in LA. He invited me to crash in his little house up in Beverly Glen. Before I quite knew what was happening, he was persuading me to give LA a try and finding me an apartment. All in a week.

It couldn't have been a week after that when he asked to borrow two thousand dollars, about half my net worth, this from a guy who was knocking down a thousand a week on contract to Paramount. Just for ten days, he assured me. How could I say no to a guy who had been so generous to me?

Thus began a weird pecuniary relationship that went on for years. Harlan would borrow large sums from me for a week or two, pay them back, then borrow the bread again a week later. The same few grand got recycled over and over. No matter how much money he made, Harlan had the creative need to ride the edge of insolvency. No matter how much he borrowed, he always paid it back.

CONTINUITY

He stayed in Los Angeles for about six months, where he wrote, among other stories, the now-much-reprinted "Carcinoma Angels," the very first story purchased for Harlan Ellison's landmark anthology *Dangerous Visions.* A previous attempt at a story for *Dangerous Visions* turned into an outline for the novel *The Men in the Jungle.* Doubleday gave him a contract and a modest advance, and he moved to San Francisco to write it.

F R A M E

Why did I leave Los Angeles after six months? Why did I stay that long?

The Summer of Love, the Counterculture, might be two years in the future on a mass level, but the tension between the hip and the square

from which it was to emerge was a very real identity crisis for a young writer from Bohemia.

I had made one lifelong friend in Los Angeles, I had made the stylistic breakthrough of "Carcinoma Angels" there, and the attempt to write *The Men in the Jungle,* my take on Vietnam and professional revolutionaries, as a novelette for *Dangerous Visions* had led to my first hardcover contract, so I can't say the atmosphere wasn't creative, but there didn't seem to be any *there* there. No street life. No scene like the Village.

San Francisco, on the other hand, the chosen object of my odyssey in the first place, was still mythical country, Kerouac's North Beach, the Village West, the California capital of hip. Harlan's and Los Angeles' distant disdain for the misty metropolis to the contrary, I had to at least check it out myself, now didn't I?

FLASHBACK

When I hit San Francisco, the first place I went to was Bruce Britton's apartment, since I knew no one else in town. Bruce being Bruce, and as luck would have it, he and his wife were going to what would be one of the historic parties of the decade that very night.

Yes, I spent my first night in San Francisco at Ken Kesey's very first Acid Test blowout in Seaman's Hall, an event often considered the birth of the Counterculture. Thousands of stoned people, loud music, acid in the punch, general frenzy, the whole tie-dyed ball of wax.

What a homecoming to the hipster community!

And yet . . .

F R A M E

Fabulous North Beach proved to be an expensive bummer. The Beat scene having turned it into a primo tourist attraction, the authorities in their infinite wisdom figured all they had to do to make it *perfect* was to get rid of the dirty beatniks who had made it famous in the first place.

The result was a depressing mixture of high-rent apartments, plastic coffeehouses and topless bars, and a hip scene that had followed the low rents elsewhere.

Namely to the Haight.

CONTINUITY

In San Francisco, Spinrad lived on a street close by Buena Vista park, bordering on the Haight-Ashbury. There he wrote both *The Men in the Jungle* and *Agent of Chaos* in the space of less than a year.

F R A M E

The bohemian communities of Greenwich Village and North Beach had had economic bases in the arts, the crafts, the tourist industry, but Haight-Ashbury in 1966, the year before the Summer of Love, had no such legitimate economic base at all. People like me, actually making a living in an artistic endeavor, were rare; people with straight nine-to-fivers even rarer.

The unfortunate result being that the economy of the hippie community there (so named by *Time* in 1967) could only be based on the drug trade. At street level, indigent connections collected money for nickel bags of grass or crystal meth or individual tabs of LSD from high school kids or day-trippers, and scored ounces or lids from the lowest true dealers, their cut amounting to ten dollars or so or a nickel for their own stash. The low-level dealers bought from wholesalers in maybe kilo quantities, and so on up the food chain, which in those days did not extend to drug lords, narco terrorists, or the Maf.

Not my planet either, not what *On the Road* had advertised as the hip scene in San Francisco at all, though there seemed to be no other. In the process of cleaning up North Beach, the powers that be had created Dope City in the Haight.

Call it street smarts, or call it luck, I found myself a nice little garden apartment on a hill just above this scene, where I could write *The Men in the Jungle* and later *Agent of Chaos* during the day, and boogie in the Haight at night and weekends.

No doubt some of the nastiness in *The Men in the Jungle* owed as much to the environment of the Haight as to the Vietnam War, which was beginning at the time. For sure, the *three*-sided conflict between Establishment, Revolution, and Forces of Chaos in *Agent of Chaos* owed even more to my identity crisis at the time.

I was a hipster, right? A Beat, a bohemian; these were my people, weren't they? *Weren't they?* The square world sucked, didn't it? Official reality was boring and oppressive, for sure, and, hey, it was the Establishment itself that created the Haight by driving the Beats out of North Beach. Surely I didn't want to be part of *that*.

But I saw things in the Haight . . .

I saw people smoking coffee grounds because they had nothing better. I saw people smoking *match heads* to get off on the sulfur fumes. I saw needle freaks shooting up with *hot water* just for "the Surge." A guy said to me, "I'd eat *shit* if I thought it'd get me high," and he wasn't joking.

And there were people who regarded me as a square because I wouldn't get involved in dealing.

I spent a long time looking for a third way. So did the country. And maybe we're all searching for it still.

CONTINUITY

A certain deterioration in the cultural milieu in the Haight persuaded Spinrad to return to Los Angeles.

FLASHBACK

One day two Texan girls I knew pleaded with me to come over to their apartment and rescue them from a couple of dealers for whom their kid brother was a connection, and who were refusing to leave.

I put on my White Knight suit and drove over.

Given the level of paranoia in the Haight, ejecting them was easier than it might seem. All I had to do was glower at them enigmatically until they started giving *me* paranoid looks.

"Whatsa matter, you guys think I'm a *narc* or something?" I snarled defensively.

"Oh, no, man, nothing like—"

"Yeah, I think you *do!* Whatsa matter, I look like a cop to you?"

"Oh, no, man—"

"You think I'm a fuckin' *narc*, don't you?"

Sinister these schmucks were, but they *were* schmucks, and after about a half an hour of this, they slithered out the door. But not before telling a story that they found highly amusing.

They were big-time acid dealers, or so they claimed. Peace, Love, Higher Consciousness in hundred tab lots.

"An' two out of every hundred hits are cyanide, some people are in for a really heavy trip, haw! haw! haw!"

I left the Haight for LA the next week.

F R A M E

I spent about a month living in Harlan Ellison's large new house with Harlan and one of my main literary heroes, Theodore Sturgeon. Both Sturgeon and I were chasing unsuccessfully after Dona Sadock, who had arrived in LA, and it got kind of weird.

I was still trying to digest the results of what I had seen in the Haight. The Counterculture hadn't even been born yet, but I was already thinking twenty years ahead to what would emerge out the other side. Ted and Harlan were both working on TV scripts, and I was thinking about what immortality would mean as an item of commerce too. *Bug Jack Barron* was somehow coming together in my mind. . . .

CONTINUITY

Spinrad drove to New York, where he secured a contract from Doubleday to write *Bug Jack Barron,* and then to Cleveland, where he attended his first science fiction convention.

F R A M E

The elusive Dona had fled from Sturgeon and myself back to New York, and I did another transcontinental run, in pursuit of her and a book contract from Doubleday. Didn't catch her, but I did cadge the contract for *Bug Jack Barron,* at a rather wet lunch with Larry Ashmead, who had been my editor on *The Men in the Jungle,* then about to be published.

Ashmead grandly assured me that there were no taboos, that I was free to follow my literary star in writing this novel of immortality, television, and American Presidential politics.

FLASHBACK

Harlan was also in New York, on his way to be Guest of Honor at the World Science Fiction Convention in Cleveland. "You gotta go to the Worldcon," he told me.

"Worldcon? What's that?"

"Two thousand fans of writers like us, half of them women. Need I say more?"

I had failed to connect up with Dona once more, so enough said, he didn't.

I pictured a thousand literary groupies of the sort one might in one's dreams encounter in a Village coffeehouse, avid for intellectual discourse and fornication with science fiction writers.

Instead, I had my first encounter with the subculture of science fiction fandom—dominantly male, adolescent, overweight, and literarily jejune to say the least. An unsettling experience for writers who come to science fiction from elsewhere for strictly literary reasons. J. G. Ballard didn't write for a year after his first and last convention. When I encountered Keith Laumer after his first convention, he was in a state of gibbering shock.

Not my planet either, but being the venue of much publishing wheeling and dealing—as well as places to meet your friends and colleagues—sf conventions, I was to find, are rather seductive to science fiction writers; bad for the head, but hard to avoid.

CONTINUITY

Upon returning to Los Angeles, Spinrad rented an apartment in Laurel Canyon, where, in 1967–68, he wrote *Bug Jack Barron,* as well as short stories, journalism, and two scripts for *Star Trek,* one of which was produced as "The Doomsday Machine."

F R A M E

Los Angeles seemed a lot more like home the second time around, or rather Laurel Canyon did—wild overgrown hills five minutes off the Sunset Strip, inhabited by wild overgrown people—and I've never lived anywhere else in LA ever since.

Harlan introduced me to Jared Rutter, editor of *Knight* magazine, and I wrote a piece about science fiction fandom for him which led to a monthly column chronicling the times as we passed through them, collected in 1970 in *Fragments of America.*

This was to be published by something called Now Library Press, another line of a large porn publisher, who at *this* time was doing the Essex House line of literary porn novels under the aegis of Brian Kirby. The writers who wrote the novels—and there were some formidable ones like Theodore Sturgeon, Philip Jose Farmer, David Meltzer, Michael Perkins—got $1500. I got $300

With Yeremy Parnov of the Soviet Writers' Union and his wife Elena Parnov of Novosti Press Service, at the Peking Hotel, Moscow, 1989

to read them and write six pages afterwards justifying their redeeming social significance.

Thanks to another Harlan Ellison connection, I wrote a piece for *Cinema* magazine, and thanks to a favorable mention of his pilot for the show therein, I was invited to write a script for *Star Trek* by Gene Roddenberry, and then a second.

Thanks to all of the above, I managed to survive economically for the eight months or so it took me to write *Bug Jack Barron* on the first half of a $1500 advance from Doubleday.

This was, in retrospect, the apogee of the countercultural revolution, when everything seemed possible, when the world was being made anew, when even *Time* could do a naively positive cover story on the Summer of Love.

I was writing commentary on it all every month. I had been invited to write for *Star Trek*. My first hardcover had come out. I was riding as high as the times.

So I took Ashmead at his word, sat down with my copy of *Understanding Media*, a lid or two of

grass, and the blithe assumption that science fiction could also be made anew, that is, that all the commercial, political, stylistic, and linguistic strictures no longer applied, and I let the muse, the evolutionary imperative of the time, take me where it would.

Where it took me was into a highly political tale of love, sex, immortality, suicide, drugs, idealism lost and ultimately regained, informed by a sexual explicitness the science fiction genre had never seen before, though, in 1990s retrospect, relentlessly heterosexual, and almost naively free of anything that would today be called "perverse."

The style that seemed to move through me in a great Kerouacian gush was curiously similar in spirit to that of Norman Mailer's *Why Are We in Vietnam?*, Brian Aldiss's *Barefoot in the Head*, and even Robert A. Heinlein's *The Moon Is a Harsh Mistress*, all of which had to have been written at roughly the same time, and none of which could have influenced any of the others. None of the four of us had written anything like that sort of thing before, and none of us really ever did again.

It may sound arch in 1993 to suggest that the spirit of the times must have been speaking through us. But not in Psychedelic Sixty-Seven.

CONTINUITY

Doubleday rejected the finished manuscript of *Bug Jack Barron.* Spinrad spent the next year or so trying to sell it to major hardcover houses without success.

FLASHBACK

On the other hand, the years 1968–1969 were, as I called them in the title of one of my *Knight* pieces, "Year of Lightning, Year of Dread."

Martin Luther King, Jr., and Bobby Kennedy were assassinated, Russian tanks crushed the Prague Spring, Richard Nixon emerged as president after Lyndon Johnson was driven from office, and Doubleday bounced *Bug Jack Barron.*

Not to suggest that these were events of similar magnitude, but the nature of the clashing forces were the same in the microcosm as in the macrocosm.

"Take out all the sex, drugs, and politics, and we'll publish the book," Doubleday told me.

"All that would be left would be a novelette," I pointed out.

Multiply this by ten million such incidents, small and large, and you have the transformation of the cultural awakening of 1967 into the cultural war of 1968–72. Hip versus square. Counterculture versus Power Structure. Revolution versus Establishment. Sex, Drugs, and Rock and Roll versus the Judeo-Christian Tradition. Me versus You. Us versus Them.

Bug Jack Barron bounced around New York from publisher to publisher, rejection to rejection. The mainstream publishers rejected it because it was too much like science fiction. And I resisted the easy out of publishing it as a genre book.

As in the macrocosm, so in the microcosm.

CONTINUITY

During this period, he took the manuscript with him to Milford, where he met Michael Moorcock, British fiction writer, literary theoreti-

cian, and editor of the experimental magazine *New Worlds.*

F R A M E

In the microcosm of science fiction, the countercultural literary trend was called the "New Wave."

So dubbed by critic Judith Merril to describe a recondite *stylistic* revolution within the genre taking place primarily in Britain under the theoretical aegis of Mike Moorcock. But by 1968, the term had come to include *anything* that its proponents considered taboo-breaking or that conservatives believed polluted the vital bodily fluids of the science fiction genre, as exemplified by the stories in Harlan Ellison's landmark *Dangerous Visions* anthology.

And of course by *Bug Jack Barron,* "New Wave" by all three definitions and a novel that had become notorious before it even found a publisher.

It was already notorious in part because I had already gone public on the subject in articles in science fiction fanzines, in appearances at science fiction conventions, even on the radio. I definitely did not want *Bug Jack Barron* published as just another genre sf paperback, but things being what they were, I used my voice wherever I could make it heard.

And took the manuscript with me to the Milford Conference.

CONTINUITY

Moorcock was very enthusiastic about *Bug Jack Barron,* and serialized it in *New Worlds* in six monthly installments. The magazine had a grant from the British Arts Council, and when the W. H. Smith bookstore chain refused to stock it because of their objections to *Bug Jack Barron* and the Arts Council successfully pressured them to rescind the ban, questions were raised in Parliament, where Spinrad was called a "degenerate."

Meanwhile, Spinrad was finally persuaded to sell the American book rights to *Bug Jack Barron* to Avon Books as a science fiction paperback original.

F R A M E

Mike Moorcock was not the only one at Milford who was enthusiastic about the notorious

Bug Jack Barron when they got to read a piece of it. The encouraging reception it got from writers on both sides of the so-called New Wave controversy pulled me out of a personal pit and dropped me in the middle of a paradox with which I have wrestled ever since.

Ever since *Bug Jack Barron,* it has always seemed to me that what I was writing, like much else that got published as "sf," did not belong in the sf marketing category, genre sf being commercially targeted at an audience of literarily and politically unsophisticated male adolescents, while what I wrote, judging from reader response, was appealing to a demographic slice that was older, more female, more interested in literary and political matters than in the "action adventure" formula dominant in the sf genre.

A more general audience, conditioned by decades of sf genre packaging *not* to seek out such fiction within such covers, where in fact, paradoxically, much of the best of it is in fact to be found, precisely because the writers thereof have been ghettoized therein by the mainstream publishing apparatus, itself conditioned by the very prejudices its own sf lines have done so much to promulgate.

Like other science fiction writers of my generation and our older soul mates of similar literary ambition—Ellison, Moorcock, Thomas M. Disch, Barry Malzberg, Robert Silverberg, Samuel R. Delaney, Philip K. Dick, Brian Aldiss, Fritz Leiber, Alfred Bester, Theodore Sturgeon, to name a few—I have fought to break my work out of this literary ghetto.

The paradox being that there has always been more comprehension for this desire to break the bounds of the genre, more emotional and intellectual support for literarily adventurous speculative fiction, *within* the walls of the very ghetto from which it seeks to escape than from without.

This being the short form of the long analyses in my teaching anthology *Modern Science Fiction* and my critical overview of the literature and its place in society, *Science Fiction in the Real World,* both published quite later.

FLASHBACK

A year or so of trying to sell *Bug Jack Barron* as a major mainstream novel finally convinced me that I was banging my brains out against a stone wall. And indeed, as soon as I gave up and unhappily agreed to let Scott Meredith try the sf publishers, the book was involved in a kind of half-

assed auction. And after I reluctantly sold the novel to Avon as a paperback original, I managed to secure a simultaneous hardcover edition from Walker Books.

Still, I wanted out. Or rather, in. To larger literary realms. And the only way to do it seemed to be to write a novel that was not science fiction, and to do it without a contract.

This, after having had a *contracted* novel rejected and bounce around for a year without selling, was *scary.* Though, upon reflection, maybe not. After all, the three thousand dollars I had finally gotten for *Bug Jack Barron* via competitive bidding was still less than what I had made in two weeks writing a *Star Trek* script. And my *Knight* column covered the rent.

And I had a story to tell, or rather several of them that fit together thematically. I would write *The Children of Hamelin,* relating the karmic connections between the roots of the Counterculture in the old Village bohemia, drug dealing, psychotherapy cults, and the fee-reading operation at a literary agency not entirely unlike Scott Meredith's.

CONTINUITY

About this time, he met Terry Champagne, with whom he was to live for the next year or so.

After he finished *The Children of Hamelin* and persuaded Meredith to agent it, he and Terry Champagne moved to London in 1969.

FLASHBACK

Yes, Theresa Louisa Champagne was her real name, and in retrospect it was a relationship that was not so much doomed as destined to be a limited run for a certain season.

Terry was still married to a friend of mine while she was chasing after me, and I was too square to let her catch me until she had resolved her situation. Terry was not into monogamy except perhaps of the short-term serial variety. Terry was not looking for a permanent relationship, and I was.

Or was I?

For by the time she moved into my Laurel Canyon apartment, I was committed to moving out. All the way to London.

The American publication of *Bug Jack Barron* was set, and I was in the process of finishing *The*

Children of Hamelin. I had become something of a minor countercultural hero in "swinging" London in absentia. Who could resist? Why should I?

Hooking up with Terry didn't change my plans. Terry was an archetypal child of the sixties, a stone willing to roll wherever. An artist, a topless dancer, a jeweler, a dealer, and when, through me, she got to take a shot at writing stories and doing journalism, she succeeded at that too, albeit, on her usual terms. "It's all the same shit," she used to say to me, to my consternation.

If I had ever thought of *myself* as a hippie, living with Terry Champagne disabused me of any such notion.

Still, for a time, it worked. I finished *The Children of Hamelin,* somehow managed to bullshit the Scott Meredith Literary Agency into marketing it despite, uh, certain aspects, and off we went, in March of 1969, via a flood in LA, a blizzard in New York, and a five-day, barfing seasick crossing on the SS *United States* to London, to a Europe that neither of us had ever seen.

F R A M E

Neither Terry nor I had been outside of North America before, and now here we were in London. At first it was all an adventure: the scene around *New Worlds,* the fringes of the Countercultural underground, Midsummer's Eve at Stonehenge. It was all new, even the *smell* of everything was subtly different.

But after we had sublet an apartment in Bayswater and started actually *living* in London, it all settled into a sort of normal routine, something like living in New York for me, but more alien for a California girl like Terry.

Which is to say that London in the end was more interesting to me than to her. She was writing about as much as I was, and good stuff too, but she was never as *serious* about the literary scene as I was, or for that matter, about much of anything else.

Nor was I getting much writing done, waiting for *Bug Jack Barron* to be published, waiting for *The Children of Hamelin* to sell as it bounced from publisher to publisher, talking literary theory with Mike Moorcock and colleagues, playing the minor underground literary celebrity. . . .

FLASHBACK

After J. G. Ballard and Mike Moorcock backed out, Christopher Priest and I were invited as the token science fiction writers to the Harrogate Festival of Literature and Science by the noted publisher and literary figure John Calder. Off we went by train, Chris and his wife, Terry and I; Chris nervous about mingling with all the awesome literary luminaries.

Calder, quite frantic, met the train with his humongous Jaguar saloon, the four of us and two Indian professors stuffed ourselves into it, and Calder started to drive out of the parking lot . . .

"Oh no, man!" I shouted. "You're gonna—"

Too late. Calder had already driven the Jag halfway down a flight of stone steps, where it hung quivering on its belly-pan.

Calder, freaking, had no idea what to do next.

Somehow, this grand entrance into the literary high life ended any trepidation I might have felt about being a twenty-eight-year-old sf punk amidst my intellectual betters.

"You stay behind the wheel and gun the engine when I tell you to," I told him, "and the rest of us get out and lift the rear end."

And that's how we did it, bouncing the car down the steps in stages. It managed to get us to the hotel before all the oil leaked out, but the repair bill was enormous.

So it goes, as Kurt Vonnegut would say. So it went.

The theme of the conference was the interface between science and technology and literature, but they had one microphone to be passed among twenty panelists, like an exaggeration of a typical science fiction convention. My experience therewith served me well, and I sort of began to ooze front and center.

Then, Erich Fried, a German Marxist writer, and his attendant groupies decided to organize a revolution. This was 1969, I was the author of the notorious *Bug Jack Barron,* and thought my heart was surely in the right revolutionary place, so I attended his evening strategy session in the auditorium as invited.

Fried's thesis was that the relationship between the speakers up on the platform and the audience down here in rows of seats facing them was hierarchical, therefore fascist. He would demand that the seats be rearranged in a circle with the audience surrounding the speakers on the same equal level. Much more democratic.

Okay . . .

But when I looked down, I observed that the chair I was sitting on, like every other seat in the auditorium, was quite thoroughly nailed to the floor. It would take a team of carpenters days to move them all.

When I pointed this out to Fried, he scowled at me with bemused contempt. "Hardly the point!" he sniffed.

Uh-huh.

The next day, Fried stood up in the audience and made his demand, backed up by many shouts of "Right On!" from his supporters. There then ensued half an hour of tedious argument about seating arrangements to the discomfort of the paying customers and the total befuddlement of the chairman, science writer Nigel Calder (no relation to John), who had completely lost control.

After a half hour of listening to this totally pointless argument, I had finally had enough. I snatched the one free microphone and gave Fried what he wanted.

I observed none too gently that, the seats being nailed to the floor, the argument was moot, the audience was bored with it, and it was time to get on with the program.

"You, sir," Fried shouted righteously on cue, "are a fascist swine and a bastard!" And stormed out of the audience at the head of his troops, as he had obviously planned to do all along.

It was the major media event of the conference. It made all the papers. That's how I got called a fascist swine and a bastard in every major newspaper in Britain.

Well, not precisely. Because John Calder had spelled my name wrong in the press kit, the fascist bastard was "Norman Spinard."

F R A M E

Bug Jack Barron had been published, *The Children of Hamelin* hadn't sold, I was still writing my monthly column for *Knight* but had no other significant source of income, Terry was getting homesick for California, the sublet on the London apartment was up, so, somewhat reluctantly on my part, perhaps, after a month staggering about the continent after the car we had borrowed from Mike Moorcock expired in Germany, we returned to Richard Nixon's America in the fall of 1969 and rented a house in Laurel Canyon.

FLASHBACK

Coda to Harrogate:

We took the train back to London in the company of, among others, William Burroughs. We had to change at York. Burroughs went to a newsstand after reading matter for the trip and returned with a handful of sleazy British tabloids.

"Look at this stuff!" he chortled. "Juicy!"

They were all full of this lurid Hollywood murder story. Pregnant actress Sharon Tate, wife of Roman Polanski, famous hair stylist to the stars Jay Sebring and several others had been gorily murdered by a tribe of drug-crazed hippies in thrall to some weirdo named Charles Manson.

I never paid attention to crap like that and marveled at how someone like Burroughs could.

Little did I know how close I was to get to the Manson Family.

Too close for comfort. And soon.

CONTINUITY

There Spinrad, in 1970–71, wrote *The Iron Dream,* his satire of science fiction, Nazism, and Adolf Hitler, which had emerged as a concept from a conversation in London with Moorcock, during the writing of which his relationship with Terry Champagne ended.

During this period, he was also writing political journalism, film criticism, and the occasional book review for the *Los Angeles Free Press,* America's best-selling weekly underground newspaper.

F R A M E

A crazy time.

My relationship with Terry was breaking up. I was writing a novel that amounted to channeling the consciousness of Hitler in order to exorcise the demon of Nazism. And I had become a main man of the Underground Press on the side.

Arthur Kunkin, founder of the *Free Press,* had hired Brian Kirby as managing editor, and I was one of the writers he brought in. The money was next to nothing, but as a film critic I was on all the freebie review lists, as a political columnist I developed a certain following, and I loved the instant feedback of weekly journalism, a welcome relief from getting inside the head of Hitler while my relationship was falling apart.

But what I, and everyone else at the paper, could have done without was the Mansonoids.

Kirby had brought in Ed Sanders, poet and former Fug, from New York to cover the murder trial of Charlie Manson. As soon as he hit the tarmac at LAX, Ed was writing stuff about how the Establishment was railroading this innocent hippie tribe in order to crush the Counterculture.

Charlie and his Family *loved* the coverage. They *loved* the paper. They *loved* Ed. There were more of them on the loose than anybody not at the *Freep* realized. And as the trial progressed, every stoned-out nut in California seemed to want to join the Manson Family too. . . .

The Mansonoids *trusted* Ed. They trusted him so much that they told him about *all these other neat snuffs* they had done that only their good buddies at the *Free Press* now knew about, hee, hee, hee. . . .

So early on we all knew that Manson and company were indeed the crazed killers the wicked Establishment claimed they were, but Kirby had to keep on their good side, such as it was; the *Freep* had to hew to the Mansonoid line, print Charlie's poems and manifestos, or the murderous creeps hanging around the paper *might not like us any more.* . . .

Years later, I met Ed Sanders in New York.

He told me that even there, even then, he still slept with the lights on.

One good thing did come of it, though: one of the best front page headlines ever.

Remember when Richard Nixon butted into the trial? "MANSON GUILTY, NIXON DECLARES," screamed the headlines in the Establishment papers.

The next issue of the *Free Press* carried a piece by Charlie himself about the then-unfolding Watergate scandal.

"NIXON GUILTY, MANSON DECLARES," said Brian Kirby's headline.

How right they both were!

CONTINUITY

The Children of Hamelin still hadn't found a book publisher, and Brian Kirby, editor of the *Free Press,* began an unprecedented weekly serialization of the novel in the paper.

FLASHBACK

Speaking of Watergate and the Underground Press, if George McGovern hadn't won the Wisconsin Democratic primary in 1972, I would probably have made him president.

A couple of weeks before the primary, I got a call from a guy who was an admirer of the political analysis I'd been publishing in the *Free Press* and who'd been offered the job of press secretary for the McGovern campaign in California.

He wanted my advice. Should he take the job? McGovern seemed like such a loser, but what other instrument of change *was* there? We kicked it around a bit.

"Look," he said, "McGovern's probably gonna lose in Wisconsin, and then he's gonna be receptive to some changes in his campaign. Would you be willing to fly there with me to talk to him?"

"Well, sure." How could I resist?

"Well, what would you tell him? What would be *the* winning campaign issue?"

"Watergate," said I.

"Watergate?"

This was before the real story broke, before the hearings, before the tapes, back when the whole thing seemed to be just a bunch of isolated dirty tricks and a bungled amateur burglary and was being covered as such in the Establishment papers. McGovern had hardly mentioned it.

The paranoiacs of the Underground Press, though, were convinced that Nixon had planned a coup against the Constitution. Concentration camps set up for dissidents. Enemies lists and use of the IRS against those on them. Illegal bugging. Financing of Nixon's campaign by the Mafia through the Teamster Pension Fund and Bebe Rebozo's bank.

Crazy, right? Only drug-crazed hippies would believe such stuff. Only those Underground rags would print it.

Art Kunkin, however, had his mitts on something hot enough to blow the whole lid off if someone like McGovern chose to push it. . . .

An airliner had crashed killing all aboard, including the wife of one of the then-key Watergate figures, upon whose person was found a large bag of cash. That much had been covered in the Establishment papers.

The FAA report had found cyanide in the lungs of the victims.

The White House had suppressed it.

Kunkin had somehow gotten hold of a copy and printed it in the *Freep.* But the *Free Press* was only an Underground paper. . . .

"Watergate is a complex conspiracy by the Nixon administration against the Constitution, is what I would tell George McGovern," I declared. "Half the dirty tricks are the Nixonoids' efforts to keep the lid on till after the election. But if you make it the centerpiece of your campaign, George, I'd say, hit it hard, hit it often; you can make the story break early enough to count. Yeah, this sounds like science fiction, but I kid you not; there's enough dirt under this rug not only to defeat Tricky Dick in an election, but, who knows, even get him *impeached.* . . ."

George McGovern, alas, *won* the Wisconsin primary.

The rest, alas, was not history.

CONTINUITY

About two-thirds of the way through its serialization of *The Children of Hamelin,* the *Free Press* was taken over by a pornographer to whom Arthur Kunkin had become indebted, and the staff and writers of the paper left en masse to found the *Staff,* which published the rest of what was to be twenty-eight installments.

FLASHBACK

A crazy time.

How crazy?

I had been in the same room with Philip K. Dick only once, and I had been too much in awe of this literary idol of mine to actually *talk* to him.

Then, late one night in 1972, I got a phone call from Vancouver. It was Phil Dick, and the conversation started like this: "My girlfriend just left me, and I think I'm going to kill myself, but I read your story "Carcinoma Angels" in *Dangerous Visions,* and I thought I should talk to you first."

And that was how my friendship with Phil began, in midstream, as if it were a pre-existing condition. All at once it seemed natural to be deep in a long intimate conversation with this old friend who had been a total stranger before my phone rang.

"On the other hand," Phil finally said, "I've got this offer from Willis McNelly at Cal State Fullerton to come down there to Orange County to live. What's your honest opinion? Now don't

bullshit me. Would I be better off moving to Orange County, or killing myself?"

"Well, Phil, personally, I can't *stand* Orange County," I found myself saying, "but you might as well give it a try. If you don't like it, you can always kill yourself later."

"Yeah, that makes sense," Phil said reasonably, and moved to southern California.

CONTINUITY

Even though *The Children of Hamelin* appeared every week for six months in papers with a circulation of about 100,000, the Scott Meredith Literary Agency still didn't find a book publisher for it, and in 1973, Spinrad finally fired them and secured the services of Lurton Blassingame.

F R A M E

Was the Meredith Agency actually trying to keep *The Children of Hamelin* from being published in the guise of ineptly agenting it? Were they submitting it to publishers out of one side of their mouths while making it known that its publication would vex Scott out of the other?

Quien sabe?

What I *did* find out for sure was that it was no longer being submitted. Months previously, they had talked me out of my carbon copy on some pretext, and on a trip to New York, I discovered that the top copy had been either lost or destroyed, and they were paying peon wages to a professional book editor to (badly) retype a new one from my carbon *very* slowly.

Without ever telling me what was happening.

CONTINUITY

In 1973, Spinrad secured a contract from Putnam Berkley to write *Passing through the Flame,* a long novel about, among other things, filmmaking in Hollywood, the rock music industry, the death of the Counterculture, and the takeover of an underground paper by the porn mafia.

FLASHBACK

Stone-broke, the IRS having cleaned out my bank account, I flew to New York on a credit card to try to sell a novel version of what was later to become my oft-printed novella, *Riding the Torch*, maybe my own choice as my best piece of short fiction.

George Ernsberger, who had been my editor at Avon on *Bug Jack Barron* and *The Iron Dream*, was now editor in chief at Berkley Books, a position of much more power.

Blassingame and I had lunch with him at a Moroccan restaurant to pitch the science fiction novel proposal.

"Naw," said George, "I think you should write me some kind of big mainstream novel instead. . . ."

"Well, George, I dunno. . . ."

"Give me an eight-page outline I like, and I'll give you an advance of ten thousand dollars."

I think I played it cool. I think I managed to avoid choking on my couscous.

Ten thousand dollars seemed a princely sum at the time, more than twice what I'd gotten for anything before.

"Well . . . I'll think it over, George. . . ."

I went straight back to the friend's apartment where I was staying and banged out the outline in five days on my portable typewriter.

F R A M E

Around this same time, one person I met and one I failed to meet were to have serious career consequences. The person I met before I got the contract to write *Passing through the Flame*, was Larry Schiller, later to collaborate successfully with Norman Mailer on *The Executioner's Song*, but then as broke as I was and my unsuccessful collaborator in any number of Scams of the Week.

The person I failed to meet was L. Ron Hubbard, once and future science fiction writer and founder of the Church of Scientology. Hubbard had never granted a major interview. I knew A. E. Van Vogt, who had been quite close to him in the old days, and through Van I got in touch with the upper levels of the Scientology hierarchy in Los Angeles.

This was one Scam of the Week that went on for months, as I pursued the journalistic coup of the Hubbard interview while they strung me along, playing with my head, suggesting that if I played my cards right, I might get to write the authorized biography, and so forth. I found out much more about Scientology than I wanted to, maybe more than it was entirely healthy to know.

Of course, I never got the interview with Hubbard.

But several years later the experience was to be the inspiration for the novel I was to write after *Passing through the Flame: The Mind Game*.

FLASHBACK

When I finished writing *Passing through the Flame*, I flew back to New York to deliver it and to do some final work on *Modern Science Fiction*, the teaching anthology I was doing for Anchor Books.

There I chanced to meet Dona Sadock, whom I had pursued futilely for so long way back when, at the tag end of a bad marriage. Now, somehow, the time was right for us. She came back with me to Laurel Canyon, the beginning of a series of transcoastal staggers which were finally to end with us moving back to New York about the time of the first publication of *Passing through the Flame*.

Before that, though, we were visited in Los Angeles by Richard Pinhas and his significant other, Agnetta Nielsen.

Richard had been described to me as a French rock musician so deep into *The Iron Dream* that he had named his group after the mythical country in the book, Heldon, and we nervously awaited the arrival of Nazi skinheads in jackboots.

Instead, Richard proved to be the most intellectual of musicians, a pioneer synthesist who was also to write a thesis in philosophy, and Agnetta a Swedish model rather than Eva Braun in black leather. Both of them were about as right wing as the Paris student movement of 1968, of which they were veterans. We hit it off right away, and today they are two of my oldest friends.

More to the point here, their visit was the beginning of my relationship with France, and *Little Heroes* is dedicated to Richard, who was to be instrumental in its conception years later.

CONTINUITY

After *Passing through the Flame* was accepted by George Ernsberger, Walter Minton, owner of Putnam at the time, arbitrarily decided to publish it as a paperback original, despite Ernsberger's previous assurances to the contrary.

Spinrad got on a plane to New York to object strenuously, and after much argument, Minton agreed to do the book in hardcover.

FLASHBACK

I had George's assurance that *Passing through the Flame* would be a hardcover, but nothing in the contract. I was quite cross when he told me Minton's plans. I called my agent, Lurton Blassingame. Minton, it turned out, had discussed the matter with him, and it was Lurton's considered opinion that, Walter Minton being one of the most powerful executives in publishing, it would not be wise for either of us to take him on.

We'd see about that.

I called George back and told him to tell Minton that I would be in his office next Monday, and that if things were not settled to my satisfaction, I would "pull him across the desk and beat the living shit out of him, or worse. Maybe *much* worse."

I then called Larry Schiller, who just happened to be in New York at the time, trying to sell some scam with Mario Puzo to none other than Minton himself. I asked him to impress Mr. Minton with the idea that I was a dangerous hothead with unsavory connections who just might be pissed off enough to have him offed.

Minton was ever so polite when I arrived in his office. Not a harsh word was spoken between us. *Passing through the Flame* was done as a hardcover.

With, however, no support.

CONTINUITY

Ernsberger was later fired by Minton, and when the paperback of *Passing through the Flame* was published, the dedication to Ernsberger, which had appeared in the hardcover, was removed. During this period, MCA bought Putnam and eased out Walter Minton, and Spinrad changed agents again, signing on with the Jane Rotrosen Agency.

FLASHBACK

By the time the paperback came out, Dona and I had moved back to New York, and I saw the first copy in the Putnam office. In the absence of Minton, I raved on about how I was going to talk to certain people in Hollywood who would see to it that he would be gone ere the year was out.

It was admittedly a cheap thrill. Putnam had already been bought by MCA, and from the experience of my friends Betty and Ian Ballantine,

I knew all too well what happened to owners who sold their companies to such conglomerates believing they could cash the fat check and still retain effective control.

Then too, Minton was not exactly a hero to his troops. He once fired a couple dozen people at the office Christmas party, to give you an idea.

I was at a big publishing party when it came down. A whole bunch of people from the Putnam office arrived, drunk as skunks, and lugging champagne, which they proceeded to pour for me.

MCA just axed Walter Minton, they told me. How did you do it?

I just smiled enigmatically over the rim of my glass and toasted his demise.

CONTINUITY

In another attempt to secure major mainstream hardcover publication, Spinrad wrote *The Mind Game* without a contract. Though the completed book seemed on the verge of being accepted by major hardcover houses several times, something always seemed to happen between the editorial and legal ends.

FLASHBACK

Was Scientology or the fear thereof responsible? They had certainly complained when their street-solicitor minions appeared in my comic short story in *Playboy*, "Holy War on 34th Street," and had tried unsuccessfully to get Anchor Books to edit my comments on Hubbard out of *Modern Science Fiction*.

And while *The Mind Game* was bouncing around, we did have this rather peculiar burglary. The apartment was ransacked, but nothing was taken. Not the stereo, not the TV, not Dona's mink coat which was hanging in plain view, not even cash.

A search for a manuscript?

A not-so-friendly warning?

The cops said it was probably crazed dopers.

I could hardly tell them that the burglars hadn't taken my grass either.

FRAME

Whatever the cause, *The Mind Game* wasn't selling, so I decided it was time to write another science fiction novel, and wrote an outline for *A*

World Between, my meditation on sex roles, feminism, media, and electronic democracy.

My friend David Hartwell wanted to buy it, and I had been instrumental in securing him his position, but unfortunately that position was sf editor at Putnam Berkley. I had recommended him to Ernsberger, but at this time George was already gone and Walter Minton was still in power.

So Jane Rotrosen auctioned the outline, and the winner was Jove Books, the hot new paperback line just started by Harcourt Brace Jovanovich. And they made a deal to do new editions of *The Iron Dream* and *Bug Jack Barron.* And bought *The Mind Game* too.

For the first time in my career, I had some significant capital.

CONTINUITY

Jove published *The Iron Dream,* but before any of Spinrad's other books there could be published, corporate upheavals at Harcourt Brace Jovanovich intervened. The Jove science fiction program expired, and Jove itself was sold to Putnam Berkley, under which corporate aegis it finally published *The Mind Game* in 1980.

Spinrad, meanwhile, had moved *A World Between* to Simon and Schuster/Pocketbooks, where David Hartwell had started a new line of books, Timescape. Hartwell published *A World Between* as a paperback original, but published Spinrad's next two novels, *Songs from the Stars* and *The Void Captain's Tale,* in hardcover.

F R A M E

Songs from the Stars was a post-apocalypse alien-contact story, among other things, and I wanted the "narration" of the alien data-packets to be, well, songs . . . poetry, that is. Could I pull this off? Fortunately, David Hartwell was an experienced poetry editor whom I could count on to tell me if I was making a fool of myself.

David thought the verse worked, with some tinkering, but felt that the forty pages or so of description around it should be in metric prose.

"Metric prose? What's that?"

David proceeded to teach me, as we went over forty pages of manuscript, syllable by syllable, phoneme by phoneme.

Somehow, this learning experience, combined with a scene that had been kicking around in my

With English novelist Doris Lessing outside conference center in Valbonne, France

head for years without leading anywhere, synergized into *The Void Captain's Tale,* a (non-)love story of the far future written in a kind of "world-speak" called Lingo, my first piece of book-length fiction in experimental prose since *Bug Jack Barron,* although in a style light-years apart.

I had written three novels since the publication of *Passing through the Flame* in 1975, but owing to all these publishing upheavals, none of them were published until 1979–1980, when all three of them were published in a space of eighteen months. First it looked as if I had had a four-year writing block, then as if I had written three major novels in less than two years!

CONTINUITY

In 1976, soon after the writing of *A World Between,* Spinrad's relationship with Dona Sadock ended, though the two remained good friends. Between 1980 and 1982, Spinrad was twice elected president of the Science Fiction Writers of America. During this period he also began a quarterly column of criticism for *Isaac Asimov's Science Fiction Magazine,* which, at this writing, still continues. In 1982, Universal Pictures, which had previously had the book *Bug Jack Barron* under option, bought the film rights for $75,000, the film to be written by Harlan Ellison and directed by Costa-Gavras.

FLASHBACK

Universal was trying to get me to sell them another cheap option. I knew that I could force them to pay me the pick-up money, only because Costa-Gavras wanted Harlan to write it. It was a high-stakes game of chicken.

Finally, I got my long awaited $75,000 phone call. I had about two hours to enjoy it. Then I got another phone call telling me that Phil Dick had had a massive stroke and had lapsed into a terminal coma.

Universal still owns the film rights to *Bug Jack Barron*. To this date, they have pissed away maybe $2 million on the project, and the film has not been made.

CONTINUITY

During this period, he began visiting France, the first time as guest of honor at the Metz Science Fiction Festival. On this trip, in Paris, he recorded two tracks on Richard Pinhas's album *East-West* as a cyborged vocalist.

FLASHBACK

"*Me* sing on a record album, Richard? Are you nuts? I can't even carry a tune with a forklift!"

"Not to worry," he told me, "just write some words to this music, chant them into the microphone, and I, the vocoder, and the computer will do the rest."

So we went into the studio, and I put on the earphones, and started just chanting these simple lyrics. We did some takes like this, and then . . .

And then Richard tried something. He let me hear my own voice being processed through the vocoder circuitry in real time and something happened. . . .

I was supplying analog input to the electronic augmentation circuitry, in a positive feedback loop with the vocoder, collaborating with it, with whatever Richard was doing, manipulating it as it was augmenting me; and out the other end *something* was singing . . . me, maybe, but not quite not-me either, and then . . .

And then, unbeknownst to me, Richard cut the vocoder out of the circuit like Daddy surreptitiously removing the training wheels from a kid's bicycle.

And played the result back to me.

"That's you," he told me, "au naturel." And so it was. And so it is. For better or worse, you can hear it on the album, re-released on CD in 1992.

I wrote a piece on the experience for a magazine. And started playing with the first little electronic keyboards. And got to thinking . . .

Electronic circuitry can replace human drummers, even do whole rhythm tracks untouched by human hands. . . .

And if electronic circuitry can make a singer out of *me*, it can make a rock star out of *anyone*. . . .

And if out of anyone, why not out of *no one*, why not *virtual* rock stars who aren't there to not show up for concerts, or get busted for drugs, or command all that money . . . ?

If the music industry *could* do this, they sure would, now wouldn't they?

And that was to be the genesis of *Little Heroes*.

FRAME

But *Little Heroes* was one book in the future. I had never done a sequel to anything before, or since, but I wanted to do a sequel to *The Void Captain's Tale*. Sort of.

The Void Captain's Tale, narrated in his own "sprach of Lingo," that is, his private melange of human languages, by the Captain in question, takes place entirely on a single spaceship, and is written in a rather hermetic Germanic sprach.

I didn't want to keep the characters, or the setting, or even the style. I wanted to write a wider-screen, more up-beat, joyous bildungsroman from a female point of view, and in a more Latinate, baroque, wise-cracking sprach of Lingo. . . .

CONTINUITY

After the hardcover publication of *The Void Captain's Tale* by Timescape in 1983, David Hartwell made a deal for a new thematically and stylistically related novel, *Child of Fortune*, and Spinrad once more returned to Los Angeles and rented yet another house in Laurel Canyon in which to write it.

FLASHBACK

The breakup with Dona left me emotionally devastated. New York was filled with memories, bad karma, high rents; I was getting homesick for California, and *Child of Fortune,* with its long sequence in an alien forest of flowers, seemed like a California book. . . .

But I had friends in New York, I had plenty of money from various books and the movie deal. So I decided to give New York one more try. I'd make a fresh start, I'd move into a nice new apartment. After all, I could now afford *twice* the rent I was presently paying for my crappy little three-room railroad flat on Perry Street.

I looked, and looked, and was finally about to give up when I saw an ad for an apartment that seemed perfect. Double my current rent, but I was prepared to pay it.

"Large beautiful four room apt. on tree-lined Village street, eat-in kitchen, sunny garden view. . . ."

Only wasn't there something familiar about the phone number . . . ?

Indeed there was, as it turned out when I called it.

It was the number of my current landlord.

The wonderful apartment I could move into for twice the rent I was paying was a clone of my own in the same building two floors down.

CONTINUITY

Before contracts for *Child of Fortune* could be drawn up, the Timescape line got caught up in a power struggle between Richard Snyder, head of Simon and Schuster, and Ron Busch, head of its Pocket Books subsidiary. Snyder canceled the Timescape line and caused Busch to fire Hartwell, simultaneously making a deal with Scott Meredith for his literary agency to package a new line of science fiction for the company.

FLASHBACK

David Hartwell used to throw Friday afternoon parties in his office. Dick Snyder's office had a private dining room and attached kitchen. One Friday, after Snyder had left, Dave snuck up to his office to cop some ice from the machine in his private kitchen.

He returned with a bucket of ice cubes and a dazed expression.

Snyder's ice machine had embossed the cubes with his monogram.

F R A M E

Which will give you some idea of the egos involved. But it was corporate hardball too. Busch, not Snyder, had hired Hartwell to start the Timescape line, and now Timescape was doing *Pocket Books hardcovers,* which Snyder chose to see as infringement by Busch on his turf. So canceling Busch's sf line, and making a deal with his good buddy and my ex-agent Scott Meredith to package a replacement, was a ploy in a larger power struggle.

Making *Busch* take the public heat for a move that was directed against *himself* was pure Dick Snyder.

CONTINUITY

The Science Fiction Writers of America, under President Marta Randall, strenuously objected to this obvious conflict of interest. Randall had been Spinrad's vice president and his choice to succeed him, a task she had accepted only on condition that Spinrad make himself available if called upon by her in an emergency. During the period when this crisis broke, Marta Randall found herself teaching a writers' workshop on an isolated island with only a pay phone as her contact to the outside world.

FLASHBACK

So I found myself representing the SFWA in a loud, national, four-cornered media battle against my former agent and employer, and two competing powers within the publisher of my own last three novels!

They never had a chance.

For an agency to package a line of books featuring work by its own writers was a blatant conflict of interest that stank like a codfish in the media moonlight. And to make my job even easier, when Busch canceled Timescape and fired Hartwell, he had told the press that he had done it because the *literary quality of Hartwell's product was too high.* Meredith would do a *much* better job of providing cynical schlock.

Guess whose side *Publishers Weekly* was on? Guess how it looked in the *New York Times* and the *Washington Post?* Guess how happy Gulf and Western, who owned Simon and Schuster, was with Snyder and Busch as they devoured their own feet in public print?

For about ten days, I found myself dribbling Busch, Snyder, and Meredith in the press like a basketball, not that you had to be a media Magic Johnson to do it.

When they finally capitulated, Busch actually complained to the *New York Times* that the SFWA had thrown its weight around unfairly, that we had *bullied* poor Pocket Books, Simon and Schuster, and Gulf and Western, that I was guilty of practicing "gunboat diplomacy."

CONTINUITY

The winners, paradoxically enough, were the SFWA and Dick Snyder. For the first time in American publishing history, a writers' organization used the public press to overturn a high-level corporate decision at a major publisher. On the other hand, while Snyder was unable to consummate his deal with Scott Meredith, he won the power struggle with Busch, eventually forcing him out of the company.

Timescape, however, was still canceled, Hartwell was still fired, and Spinrad was understandably less than confident in his future at Simon and Schuster/Pocketbooks.

He moved *Child of Fortune* to Bantam, who published it in 1985.

From 1984 to 1986, while writing *Little Heroes,* under contract to Bantam, Spinrad taught the novel at the Clarion West Science Fiction Writer's Workshop in Seattle, where, in 1985, he met Nancy Lee Wood, who writes under the name N. Lee Wood and was there as a student. In 1986, she moved into his house in Laurel Canyon.

FRAME

Science fiction writing workshops had proliferated, and I had often expressed my dubious opinion thereof, much preferring Damon Knight's old "No Chiefs, No Indians" formula to the hierarchical structure of teachers and students, established writers and wannabees.

"Don't knock it till you try it," I was told, particularly by Harlan Ellison. So finally, when I was invited to teach a week at the six-week Clarion West Conference, I accepted on condition that I teach the novel, which no one else had tried to do,

the idea being to teach novelistic *structure* by having the students turn an idea into an outline.

Somewhat to my own surprise, it worked well enough to persuade me to teach it three years in a row, which had never been my intention.

Lee, a resident of Portland at the time, was one of my students in the middle year and showed up in Los Angeles a few months later.

We met at various events and venues in between Portland and Los Angeles. During the next year, I went to visit her in Portland, and she finally moved into my house in Los Angeles.

Terry Champagne had written and published while living with me, but this was the first time I had lived with someone who had been a writer *before* I had met her, and who was as serious about it as I was.

And we've actually been able to work consistently while living together. I've written two long major novels, 100,000 or so words of short fiction, and much else as of 1993. And Lee has written two complete novels and parts of three others and quite a bit of short fiction during the same period.

If you don't think this is rare, you don't know that many writing couples. Which is exactly the point—a writer has a hard enough time living with *anyone* and working at the same time. For *two* of them to do it sharing the same space-time ain't smooth and easy!

CONTINUITY

In 1987, Spinrad and Wood traveled together to Europe for the first time, to England, and then to Paris. The conjunction of their mutual love for the city and the political changes occurring in Europe caused Spinrad to conceive *Russian Spring* in New York on the way back to Los Angeles, and secure a contract to write it from Bantam.

FLASHBACK

By this time, I had been to Paris by myself several times; most of my books had been published there, I was popular in France, I had a circle of friends in Paris. I had always fantasized living there at some time, but had never gotten up the nerve to do it alone.

What I *had* done, years earlier, while still living in New York, was write the beginning of something I called "La Vie Continue" in which my future self was living as a political refugee in Paris,

*The wedding of Norman Spinrad and N. Lee Wood, Fort Myers Beach, Florida,
April 28, 1990, with Morris Spinrad, Norman's father, and Christine Goddard,
Lee's grandmother, looking on*

in which the Soviet Union had undergone a "Russian Spring" analogous to the "Prague Spring" of 1968. . . . About twelve pages into it, I realized I had the beginning of a *much* longer work than I had bargained for, and set it aside.

Now, years later, in Los Angeles, I owed Bantam a long novella for *Other Americas,* a collection they were going to publish, which seemed just the right length for "La Vie Continue," so I sat down and wrote the first draft in LA.

That's right, I wrote "La Vie Continue" *before* I moved to Paris. Call it prescience. Call it a flashforward. Call it a self-fulfilling prophecy.

FRAME

One anglophone writer living alone in a francophone culture had always been a scary creative prospect to me, but Lee fell in love with Paris on this first visit, and together I felt we could live in France successfully for a protracted period, even though she spoke no French at the time and my French was what I had learned on my previous visits.

Then too, I was between drafts on "La Vie Continue," scouting locations for the rewrite, going around Paris contemplating the life of this American exile who was myself, living in the very same city, while at the same time, thanks to Gorbachev, the future I had envisioned for Europe years earlier in New York was beginning to unfold here in real time. . . .

The setting of *Russian Spring,* the characters, the context, all began to come together, and so too the adventure of writing it. This would be a novel dealing with the future of Europe, the Soviet Union, and the United States, and would be primarily set in Paris, so we had an excellent excuse to live there for a year or so while I wrote it.

CONTINUITY

In the summer of 1988, Spinrad and Wood moved to Paris, and soon thereafter Spinrad was elected president of World SF at a meeting in Budapest, an international organization of which N. Lee Wood was later to be elected general secretary.

Shortly thereafter, Spinrad began writing *Russian Spring*, and after finishing the first draft, he and N. Lee Wood traveled to Moscow in the winter of 1989 as guests of the Soviet Writer's Union to do further research for the book, which was not finally finished until about three months before the August 1991 coup attempt, and which

Spinrad holding the very first copy of the Russian edition of Russian Spring *to come off the presses, in the office of* Literature Gazette *in Moscow, 1992. Lenin still on the wall. From left to right: the editor of the magazine; Volodya, Marketing Director of TexT; Spinrad; Vitaly Babenko, President of TexT; another editor of the magazine.*

was published in the United States the month afterwards.

FLASHBACK

At the World SF meeting in Budapest in 1988, we had met Vitaly Babenko, then a depressed Russian writer having a hard time getting anything published. When we visited Moscow in 1989, he felt he had to sneak into the Peking Hotel where we were staying courtesy of the Writer's Union, and I felt I had to be circumspect about seeing him.

By 1992, he was the president of TexT, the second biggest private publisher in Russia, and he had brought us there for the publication of the Russian edition of *Russian Spring*. Mad, mad Moscow!

He paid me my advance in the form of a huge bag of rubles. "Spend it all before it disappears!" we were told by one and all.

It wasn't easy, but we did. Like everyone else in Moscow, we became obsessive shoppers. It was a crash course in the psychology of inflation, believe me!

And how right they were. When I was handed the money, the ruble was 135 to the dollar. Less than a year later it was to be about 1000 to the dollar.

Moscow is a tough, crazy town, but one of the most exciting places I've ever been at this mad moment in history, and as we stood atop the Lenin Hills with some Russian friends the day of our departure, one of them gave me a strange look.

"You *like* it here, don't you?" she said in some bemusement. "You could *live* here. . . ."

Maybe she was right. Maybe I could.

CONTINUITY

Spinrad and Wood decided not to return to the United States as residents, though they returned for visits, and were married on one of them in Florida in 1990.

Norman Spinrad's latest novel, *Pictures at 11*, though set in Los Angeles, was written in Paris where he still resides, and deals partially with the strains of German reunification. Completed in the middle of 1993 under contract to Bantam, it will be published in the fall of 1994.

Farewell to Moscow, atop the (former) Lenin Hills: (from left) Babenko,
Vanya (our grand prix driver and puppetmaker for the Moscow Puppet Theater),
Luda (friend and translator), and Spinrad.

F R A M E

CONTINUITY

FLASHBACK

FLASH-FORWARD

This close to the real time of me sitting in my Paris apartment writing this attempt at the closure of a story that is not yet finished, they all finally merge.

The story of how two American writers came to Paris for a year or so and ended up staying is certainly material for a whole novel, several of which have probably already been written.

The historical context in which it took place is a novel *I* have already written, namely *Russian Spring*, conceived on a one-month visit to Paris, developed in New York, treatment written in Los Angeles, first draft written in Paris before Wall came down, before our first trip to Moscow at the time of the death of Sakharov, and finally published in Russia itself in 1992, in a society not that much unlike what is described in the book, but which didn't exist before it was written.

So why is Norman Spinrad still living in Paris?

The answer is *not* to be found in "La Vie Continue." The Norman Spinrad in that novella is ten years older than the present writer, and the present writer does not consider himself an American exile, political or otherwise.

I'm not living in Paris because I can't bear to live in the United States.

I'm living in Paris because I want to live in Europe.

We've been here five years now. We've braved the Russian winter. We've walked *through* the Berlin Wall in the very process of its demolition. We've both been officers in an international writer's organization. We've made friends in France, Russia, the (former) two Germanies, (former) Yugoslavia, (former) Czechoslovakia, Italy, Holland, points between. We've been part of our friends' lives and they've been part of ours, at a time of rapid-fire evolution that is transforming this supposedly tired old continent into the cutting edge of the twenty-first century.

And I'm doing another cut on one of Richard's albums via the very instrumentalities I predicted in *Little Heroes*.

Why would an American writer of speculative fiction choose to live in Europe?

Why not?

Or, as I usually say when asked this question, hey, to an American science fiction writer, Europe isn't merely another planet, it's a whole other *solar system!*

Planet France, Planet Germany, Planet Russia, Planet Italy, and other major bodies, plus untold scores of ethnic asteroids! And each of them a world entire!

I'm fifty-three now, improbable as it seems to me. I've lived by my words for thirty years. I've witnessed three decades of history in many places, and been part of some of it. I've been rich and poor. I've been flush and broke. I've fought the good fights, and I've won and lost. I've achieved a certain amount of literary recognition, but not, of course, what I consider my just share. I've had my ups and downs. I have my good moments and my bad.

And when I'm really feeling down, I remember a twenty-five-year-old kid stoned on mescaline, walking across Fourth Street to the Village, high on "Dune," and dreaming those crazy prescient dreams. . . .

He was going to be a famous science fiction writer, he would publish many stories and novels, and many of the people who were his literary idols, inspirations, and role models would accept him as their equal, would become his allies, his friends.

And his life's mission would be to take this commercial science fiction genre and turn it into something else somehow, write works that transcended its commercial parameters, works that could aspire to the literary company of Burroughs and Mailer and Kerouac, that would open a new Way. . . .

This is what you're here for.

And so I was. And so I am.

When I look into the mirror and am appalled to see this middle-aged guy looking back, when my latest novel fails to make the best-seller lists, when the bills start coming in faster than the checks, and I bemoan all that I haven't done, all the just

desserts that haven't been piled up on my plate, all I long to be and haven't achieved . . .

Then that twenty-five-year-old kid grins back at me and gives my fifty-three-year-old self a swift kick in the psychic ass. At my age now, maybe I know much too much to feel the same, but *he's* certainly got cause to feel entirely satisfied with the story so far.

Everything he saw in that timeless Einsteinian moment has come to pass.

Everything he wanted to be, I have become.

I look out my window onto my Paris garden. And when I finish this, I will walk out into the summer streets of Paris, a minor princeling of the City of Light.

Beyond the wild dreams of that twenty-five-year-old kid!

I've become what he wanted to grow up to be and so much more.

I should be satisfied, right?

Sure.

I've spent my whole life looking forward, not back. Sure, this fifty-three-year-old has got what that twenty-five-year-old wanted.

But I'm not him, and it's not enough, and I'm old and wise enough now to know that it never will be.

If I live to be a hundred with a Nobel on the mantelpiece, I'll probably say the same thing.

I'll probably even believe it.

This story doesn't end here.

It begins tomorrow.

BIBLIOGRAPHY

Novels:

The Solarians, Paperback Library, 1966.

Agent of Chaos, Belmont Books, 1967.

The Men in the Jungle, Doubleday, 1967.

Bug Jack Barron, Walker Books, 1969.

The Iron Dream, Avon, 1972.

Passing through the Flame, Putnam, 1975.

Riding the Torch (bound with *Destiny Times Three*, by Fritz Leiber), Dell, 1978, published separately, Bluejay Books, 1984.

A World Between, Simon & Schuster/Pocket Books, 1979.

The Mind Game, Jove, 1980.

Songs from the Stars, Simon & Schuster, 1980.

The Void Captain's Tale, Simon & Schuster/Timescape Books, 1983.

Child of Fortune, Bantam, 1985.

Little Heroes, Bantam, 1987.

The Children of Hamelin, Tafford, 1991.

Russian Spring, Bantam, 1991.

Deus X, Bantam, 1993.

Journals of the Plague Years, Bantam, forthcoming.

Pictures at 11, Bantam, forthcoming.

Short-story collections:

The Last Hurrah of the Golden Horde, Nelson Doubleday, 1970.

No Direction Home, Pocket Books, 1975, Millington Books (London), 1976.

Le Livre d'Or de Norman Spinrad, edited by Patrice Duvic, Presses Pocket (Paris), 1978.

Au Coeur de L'Orage, Presses Pocket, 1979.

The Star Spangled Future, Ace, 1979.

Other Americas (four novellas), Bantam, 1988.

Les Années Fléaux, Deoel (Paris), 1990.

Television scripts:

"The Doomsday Machine" (episode of "Star Trek" series), NBC-TV/Paramount, 1967.

"Tag Team" (episode of "Land of the Lost"), NBC-TV, 1974.

"Gray Wolf" (episode of "Werewolf"), Fox, 1987.

Other:

(Contributor) *Dangerous Visions,* edited by Harlan Ellison, (includes "Carcinoma Angels"), Doubleday, 1967.

Fragments of America, Now Library Press, 1970.

(Editor) *The New Tomorrows,* Belmont Books, 1971.

(Contributor) *SF: The Other Side of Realism,* edited by Thomas D. Clareson, Bowling Green University Popular Press, 1971.

(Editor) *Modern Science Fiction,* Anchor Press, 1974, hardcover edition, Gregg Press, 1976.

(Contributor) *Threads of Time: Three Original Novellas of Science Fiction,* edited by Robert Silverberg, Thomas Nelson, 1974.

(Contributor) *The Craft of Science Fiction,* edited by Reginald Bretnor, Harper, 1976.

(Contributor) *Experiment Perilous: Three Essays on Science Fiction,* edited by Andrew Porter, Algol Press, 1976.

Staying Alive: A Writer's Guide, Donning, 1983.

Science Fiction in the Real World (essays), Southern Illinois University Press, 1990.

Author of weekly column on politics for Los Angeles *Free Press,* 1970–71; monthly column on writing and publishing for *Locus,* 1979–85; quarterly column of criticism for *Isaac Asimov's Science Fiction Magazine,* 1980—. Contributor of political and social essays to *Knight* magazine, film criticism to *Cinema,* Los Angeles *Free Press,* and *Staff,* and fiction to *Analog Science Fiction/Science Fact, New Worlds, Playboy,* and other periodicals.

Audrey G. Thomas

1935-

Audrey G. Thomas, about 1992

Several years ago my mother wrote me a letter and enclosed a clipping. The former secretary of one of the First Ladies, Lady Bird Johnson perhaps, had just written a book which was auctioned to a New York publisher for some incredible amount of money: thousands and thousands of dollars. Wasn't it about time, wrote my mother, that I admitted I was not a success as a writer, gave up this foolish dream, and went back to what I studied in college, was it medieval history? Perhaps I could get a job teaching. What I studied in college was Anglo-Saxon and Middle English, but my mother is old, very old, so it didn't bother me that she had got it mixed up. What did bother me was my own reaction, after all these

years, to her not-so-subtle ways of putting me down. I laughed but I also felt again the self-doubt that has plagued me all my life about my writing: that I had somehow, as usual, ended up chained to a large hungry dog (my writing) and would give anything if someone would come along and release me, unchain me, shoot the damn dog, or at least find the dog another home. Maybe the old lady was right—give it up.

Easier said than done, of course, so I put the letter away and kept on with the only thing I know how to do. It would appear that I have no choice, although it wasn't my first choice or even my second. But therein lies a tale.

I come from a small city in western New York State, at the junction of the Chenango and Susquehanna Rivers. My mother's family had been in that general area since 1790, first in northern Pennsylvania (they named the town of New Milford) and then across the line in Conklin, New York. They had been in Massachusetts for over a hundred years before they "went west" so they were a very old family indeed. They made their money in lumber, and one branch of the family was in the acid factory business up and down the east branch of the Delaware until the 1930s. My grandfather came in on the very end of this—my mother talks about going to live near Shinhopple where they were not allowed to play with the company children. She remembers seeing men with huge arms, stripped to the waist and covered in sweat, feeding the furnaces which were the first step in the "destructive distillation" process which led, eventually, to acetate of lime. Some of those villages still remain: Acidalia, Burntwood, Methol, Corbett, New York, and I have been to see them. However, by the time I was born my grandfather lived in Binghamton and was head of the mechanical engineering department at IBM. THINK, said a brass plaque on his enormous desk. He was my hero when I was a child. I remember my grandmother, his wife, only vaguely. She wasn't a well woman and she died a day or two after a heart attack at my kindergarten Christmas party. My

Father, Donald Earle Callahan

grandfather lived another thirty years after her death; the last time I saw him he called me by her name—"Is that you, Grace?" (Still in his own house then and not senile, he quickly corrected himself and made a nice attempt to admire his great-granddaughter Sarah. We were on our way from England to British Columbia, where we were to settle, but I had taken the baby on a side trip to show her off to my mother and father, my sister, my grandfather. It seemed terribly important to do this even though it meant I would travel by train from Boston to Vancouver by myself, with the baby, as my husband went on ahead once our ship docked at Montreal.)

My father's family had also been in the area for a long time and also came there from Massachusetts. He was a member of the Sons of the American Revolution, somebody having fought in the Revolution but I can't remember who, some connection with General Joseph Warren and the Battle of Bunker Hill. His father died before I was born but had run a very successful hardware and sporting goods store, Callahan and Douglas, for

years before he sold it to his partner. He was a keen fisherman and so was my father. One of my favorite breakfasts as a child was brook trout freshly caught, rolled in cornmeal, and fried in a cast-iron frying pan. I love living out here by the ocean, feasting on salmon and cod, oysters, clams and crab, but there are days when I yearn for the clear lakes and brooks of my childhood and the silvery treasures, laid so carefully on ferns, in my father's creel. My father talked a lot about that sporting-goods store—I think he missed it and would have liked that sort of a life for himself, discussing lures and rods and guns. He loved to "jaw," as my mother called it. Instead, he taught general science and history at a high school across the river. And although he had two degrees I never saw him read a serious book the whole time I lived at home. He read *Life* and *U.S. News and World Report* and the *National Geographic,* a lifetime wedding gift from my grandfather Corbett. (My mother read the *Ladies' Home Journal,* the *Woman's Home Companion, McCall's.*)

I think my father, a short, rather nervous man, was ill-suited to be a high school teacher, and one of the ways he showed this seemed very peculiar when I was young. My grandfather Corbett had a summer camp in the Adirondack Mountains, and we went there every summer until I was seventeen years old and he was forced to sell it. We left home the day after school was out (returning at least twice to make sure the gas stove had been turned off and the notes had been left out for the milkman and the mailman) and we didn't come back until Labor Day. Our first stop was the Esso station to fill up with gas. "Yep," my father would say to the owner, whom he knew, "me and the missus and the kids are headin' up to camp for the summer." And as we progressed—a stop at Utica for lunch, a stop at the General Store in Pisco, if it was still open by the time we got there, a stop at Red's Baits to get worms and other crawly things that lived in soil-filled trays in an old shed—his diction and accent became more and more "country boy." It drove my mother nuts, but then just about everything my father did or didn't do drove her nuts. (It was years before I realized that husbands and wives actually shared one bedroom.)

Both my mother and father thought of "success" in terms of money, nice cars, nice *things.* They argued about money all the time, terrible arguments and nearly every night. Neither could manage money and although a teacher's pay was very low in those days compared with the salaries in any other profession (teachers were like nurses and ministers; they were expected to have a vocation) I don't think we needed to be as hard-up as we were. My father was always asking his unmarried sister, Ethel (who was a maths professor at an upstate college), to bail us out; my mother would ask her father. Sometimes my parents hid when bill collectors came to the door. Sometimes the telephone was cut off. After my grandmother Callahan, who had been crippled for years, was moved up to Syracuse with my uncle and his family (they all lived next door but my mother didn't speak to them), we moved into the family home, a dreary house with faded brown wallpaper and a general air of decay. Except for a few months near the end of his life, when they wanted to be closer to my sister and her family in Massachusetts, they lived there until my father died. (They rented, they didn't own; my aunt owned the house, another thorn in my mother's side.) There were attempts to fix the place up from time to time, but I remember it as shabby and depressing. It had a nice backyard, however, with an apple tree, a cherry tree (pie cherries), and a small vegetable and flower garden. My father tended all this and was very proud of his tomatoes and his roses. His other great interest, besides fishing, was the Masons, and at one point he was master of his lodge. He used to pace up and down in his room upstairs at the back of the house practicing his degrees: "Hail, Brother from the South!" etc. All of this was very secret stuff, of course, but we couldn't help overhearing from time to time. He loved the Masons (successful men belonged to the Masons) and always took us to the annual father-daughter banquet and talent night where we knew he wished we could twirl batons or play the piano. (I wrote poetry but it never occurred to me that poetry might come under the classification of entertainment. My poems were not humorous.) He also liked parades and took us to the Shriners parade every year. I think there was a streak of showman in him. He told me that when he was a child he had wanted to join the circus and that later he had wanted to be a minister. There was something wistful about him although I had nothing but contempt for the way he measured success and the way he engaged in these dreadful quarrels with my mother. I see now that he tried to escape, in his own way, tried to make some kind of a life for himself outside the home, and I wish I had known him better. The last time I saw him was the winter of 1963, when he and my mother had rented a

Mother, Frances Waldron (Corbett)
Callahan

small house in Holbrook, Massachusetts. My sister had phoned me to say that he was terribly ill and that, although he didn't know it, he was dying. "When are you going to come and see him?" she said. "At the funeral?" I left my husband and the youngest child and flew with our eldest, then four-and-a-half, to the U.S. Kennedy had been shot just a few weeks before and the country was still in a state of stunned disbelief. There was a lot of snow and Sarah had fun playing with her cousins although she ended up with tonsillitis and the trip back to British Columbia was a nightmare.

The night before we left I sat up with my father and watched *Goodbye, Mr. Chips,* of all things. The rest of the family insisted he didn't know that he was dying, but I was sure he did. I wanted to talk to him about it and about his life, but I didn't know how to begin. I was a graduate student at the time, taking a leisurely M.A. because the children were so young, and earning baby-sitting money by teaching freshman English. He was very proud of all this and talked a bit about his days at Cornell. I asked him if he remembered when he was getting his M.A. and we all went up to Ithaca with him, how he used to bring home stuff from the experimental farm: three-legged turkeys and blue eggs, things like that. I wanted to *cheer him up*. I should have taken his hand, but we had been trained by our mother to be such a non-touching family I was afraid to do so. We sat side by side while the tears rolled down my cheeks. "I always cry in sentimental films," I told him.

He died in June and had a Masonic funeral. My mother sold the house (*her* father had died in July) and moved to Massachusetts. She gave away a lot of my childhood toys and books, threw away my box of school certificates and awards, and cleared out a lifetime of old magazines from the spare room. I couldn't help her because we'd gone to Africa to work for two years. When we stopped in to see her on our way, she told me I had killed my father because he was so afraid for us "going out there." She'd worked herself into such a fury about that and other things by the time we left that she began running after the taxi that was taking us to the station, running down the street in her nightdress, barefoot, yelling. My husband held my hand tight: "Don't look back," he said, "just don't look back. It will all be all right."

When you have parents who behave like children, parents who refuse to take charge of their own lives, then how can you ever be a child yourself? *They* are having the tantrums, the crying spells, the fights. You learn very early on to keep your mouth shut if you know what's good for you. But you can't help seeing and hearing; you hear because even with the pillow over your head the voices come up the hot air registers; you see the broken dishes, the smashed picture frames, and the endless letters, written on secretarial pads, shoved under your bedroom door during the night. You feel trapped and helpless and at the same time furious—that they won't behave, that they can't be relied upon to act like other parents, that they have staked everything on you and your sister: "We stayed together for your sake; we sacrificed everything for you."

If you can't open your mouth to question any of this and if you don't keep a journal because there is nowhere safe to hid it, you memorize, you can't help but memorize. You can't get rid of all this and so it remains inside you, imprinted. My ex-husband still says "you have an incredible memory!" and I do, I do. He says it, now, with admiration, but I see myself like Marley's ghost, clanking along through life, weighed down by all this memory.

In *A Prayer for Owen Meaney*, John Irving says "Your memory is a monster; you forget, it doesn't; you think you have a memory; it has you." Only I don't forget; so am I a monster, too?

My first choice for "what I want to do with my life" was "visual artist." Why, I don't know as I have no talent in this direction at all. My mother had gone to Pratt Art Institute for a while (she said recently that she had wanted to be an interior decorator) and her old drawing board was used in the kitchen as a pastry board. She also sharpened pencils with a paring knife; nobody else's mother did this. I never saw her draw anything and still don't know whether she herself had any talent for design. A few years ago I bought her a drawing pad and some crayons and suggested that she might like to do some sketching. Last year she gave them back to me, unused. "You might as well give these to the grandchildren." Her father could draw. I have hanging in my guest cottage a large pencil drawing he did when he was at Stevens Institute. It's a very carefully rendered drawing of a column, a geometrical figure, and a round bean pot. It looks very "modern" and yet he drew it in 1887. It has a photographic quality as well; this was a young man who understood angles and volumes and lines. Did *he* suggest that I should take up drawing? I know only that he bought me a complete set of oil colours, in a wooden box, when I was in junior high school, and I did some *copies* of paintings that weren't bad and some charcoal drawings of log cabins in the snow. And once I answered one of those Famous Artists ads which appeared regularly in the magazines my mother read: CAN YOU DRAW THIS PICTURE? Since I was good at copying I sat down and drew the picture (I think it was the head of a girl) and not long afterwards a salesman came to the door. I didn't sign up for the course he was offering; perhaps it cost too much money or perhaps I knew in my heart that I wasn't any good at this. I did, later on, take visual art for a year when I was at college, but I think it was more because I loved being around an art room than because I had any illusions about myself as an artist. I do remember one painting, however (done in poster paints I think), that would have been a psychiatrist's delight. The painting showed a group of girls in yellow slickers and yellow rain hats on one side of a street; on the other stands a solitary girl in a red velvet party dress. My professor saw it; I'm surprised, now, that he didn't ask me about it. I gave the girl black hair but she was obviously me.

I still like being around visual artists. I married one, lived with another, and my eldest daughter is both an artist and an art therapist at a veterans' hospital. All three of my daughters, in fact, have a strong sense of colour and design and were encouraged, when young, to explore paint and clay and printmaking. I think they were very lucky to have a father who would "play" with them in this way. Of course there were books around, lots of books, but they had the added pleasure of "making a mess" and nobody minded. A friend said to me one day that she didn't know anybody else who wrote about landscape the way I do. I think that's an exaggeration, but I do think that I have "the painter's eye" if not the rest of the equipment. When I write I actually see the place I'm writing about, see where the sun is (if there is a sun), see where the shadows fall. However, working with black marks on white paper isn't nearly so satisfying as squeezing out a colour, mixing it with another, laying it on. My vegetable garden is my canvas now, I suppose; I can get very excited seeing my purple burgundy beans climbing the fence with the orange and gold nasturtiums, the ruffled purple lettuce next to the dusty green broccoli.

There was a war on when I was young, but it was all happening "over there." The quarrels of my parents were much more frightening to me than the possibility of an enemy attack. I remember the posters, which seemed to be everywhere. "Shhh. The Enemy May Be Listening" or "Loose Lips SINK SHIPS"—and I remember air-raid drills at school where we went down into the basement and put our heads between our knees. My father tried to enlist but he was over forty and had flat feet so they turned him down. He was welfare commissioner for part of the war, however, and he enjoyed that very much. How he got the job and what qualifications he had, God knows; it probably had something to do with the Masons and the fact he was a Democrat. (My mother was a Republican; she liked to think she cancelled out his vote.) Now he had a big desk and even a secretary, Betty, who took dictation. We had a cocker spaniel named Skippy and my father would stand at the door saying, "Where are we going, Skippy? City Hall? City Hall? City Hall?" until the dog was nearly frantic. My father loved being a big shot, even if he was only a minor big shot (and out on his ear as soon as the Republicans came back in.) Later, he worked briefly as an inspector for the

OPA and travelled the state checking up on businesses and staying in hotels; he loved that, too (and of course it got him away from home).

I remember my mother kneading a bag of margarine (called "oleo" then) with a small colour capsule inside. Margarine didn't come coloured then, you had to do it yourself. (I don't think it came coloured in Canada until fairly recently.) She was working this and working this but it never lost its streaky appearance and my father hated it— "none of that ersatz stuff for me!"

I was good at singing and loved all the war songs: "Don't Sit Under the Apple Tree," "Comin' in on a Wing and a Prayer," "From the Halls of Montezuma (to the shores of Tripoli)." We listened to Kate Smith every Sunday and prayed for our boys in church. At my grandfather's summer place, things went on much as usual. He had a housekeeper who knew how to get extra treats from butchers and grocers so we ate very well. On the outhouse he tacked up a sign you usually saw at the gas station: IS THIS TRIP NECESSARY?, and bought toilet paper printed with the faces of Hitler, Mussolini, and Hirohito. "Wipe out the Axis" it said. But not a single member of our family was "over there." Some cousins were in the ROTC but I don't think they ever went overseas. The war wasn't real to me; it was something happening somewhere else. I don't think I had any idea, then, what was happening to the Jews; it certainly wasn't talked about at school. Children today are so much more aware of what's going on in the world—they are bombarded with images of suffering, starvation, and death. I suppose they still believe, here in North America, that wars always happen someplace else, but teachers talk about things that never came up in my youth: prejudice, racism, the possibility of war itself being wrong. I do not think we should take away the innocence of children or make them feel guilty if they are white and middle class. But to make them aware of a wider world than their own safe neighborhood is not a bad thing.

We were at my grandfather's the day the war ended in the Pacific; this was the only time I ever saw him take a drink. My father, who had been a bugler boy in the First World War, although he got influenza and never went overseas, took down the bugle which hung on the front porch and played TAPS.

And that was that. The only other thing I remember is seeing the front page of a newspaper with a picture of the mushroom cloud and a reference to President Truman. Because I was fascinated by words from a very early age, I could never take his name seriously. It was like having a president named Mr. Goodfellow. But what he'd done was real all right and now he was a hero.

(A few years ago in Ottawa I saw a travelling exhibition of paintings done by survivors of the atom bomb; I believe most of them had been children at the time. I stood in the corridor and wept.)

From the time I was nine until I was about thirteen I wrote poetry. Some of it won prizes in the annual contests sponsored by *Scholastic* magazine. I wish I still had some of these poems so that I could include an example here. All I remember is the opening lines of one: Beyond the gates of sunset lies / the shining realm of Paradise, where little boys with golden curls / stoop down to sing with little girls. I wish I could forget THAT! The others were of the same ilk: princes and princesses, knights and lepers—dreadful stuff. I'm surprised I didn't become a writer of greeting card verse. I think I wrote this stuff to *please*, and to try and elevate my soul from the drab reality of the house at 13 Chestnut Street. It was like covering a cake of shit with sickly, sugary icing and hoping no one would notice what was really inside. I never admitted to anyone what my life at home was like, and my sister and I never talked about it; we still don't. People must have known, though, at least about my parents' improvidence. The milkman knew, the electricity company, the telephone company, the insurance agent, the department stores where expensive dresses for my sister and me were put on lay-a-way every year, the dancing-school teacher, the dentist (who would wait until I was in the chair, with the drill turned on, before he said, "Would you ask your mother to call me about her bill?"), the bank managers. And all of these people had families; some of them had children at our school. I wrote those poems because it seemed to me that these were the sort of poems teachers (and judges of contests) expected from nice little girls. Perhaps, if I wrote enough of them, they would think I *was* a nice little girl, just like all the others. It took me a long long time to get over the feeling that I had to please people with my writing, that I shouldn't write about anything dark if I wanted to be liked and/or accepted. And I have never got over the fear of being in debt; I pretty well have to know, down to the last dollar, what I have in the bank. I'm amazed at people who don't balance their chequebooks—how can they stand it? I still see the awkward bill collectors turning their hats in

their hands, looking sideways at my mother and father: "Well, perhaps if you put a little something on the account?"

When I sold my first published story (to the *Atlantic Monthly*), we were living out in West Africa. They wrote and asked for a brief biography and where to send the cheque. (Five hundred U.S. dollars! A fortune!) I wrote them a (very) brief history of my life and at the end I put, "to speak of something as sordid as money, please don't send the cheque here, but deposit it in my bank account in Canada." Shortly after that I received a letter from Edward Weeks. He said I should get one thing straight right at the beginning of my career; there was nothing sordid about money except the lack of it.

My children used to say, "You must have really liked school, you're so smart." But I didn't. I hated it most of the time and wished I didn't have to go. I was shy and awkward and always on the outside of things. And I wasn't really all that bright; learning did not come easy to me, only reading. I spent half my time looking out the window and the other half trying not to be called upon. Junior high was even worse, except that I took journalism instead of English (this was an option if your English grades were high) and finally had a group I belonged to. (I think we all had the same homeroom.) I learned about column inches and layout and design, went round to local businesses and shops drumming up advertisers, wrote feature articles, book reviews, sports columns. I think that was in grades seven and eight but it might have been for three years, I can't remember. The editor of the *West Junior Leader* was the daughter of the editor of the Binghamton *Sun.* Naturally I thought *I* was a far better writer, and the two of us were rivals. As my mother would say, I felt she got the job through "pull."

I also played in the junior high school orchestra and sang in the glee club, for music was my second choice after art. One winter—I think I was in the third grade—I came down with a cold that turned into severe bronchitis and I was forced to stay home from school for weeks and weeks. I didn't really mind because the old radio, a small, wooden table-top model with its wonderful glowing tubes in the back, was brought up to my room. I slept, I listened to soap operas ("The Romance of Helen Trent," "Ma Perkins," "Young Dr. Malone," "Our Gal Sunday"), I cut out pictures from ladies' magazines and stuck them on white paper, designing "rooms." I must have been quite sick because once I saw a sign on the front door: Please

Don't Ring Bell—Sick Child. Even today, if I get a cold it easily slides into bronchitis and I have a permanent cough, rather like a smoker's cough. I suppose that all started that winter.

One day my grandfather came to see how I was and he brought me a small violin in a case lined with purple plush. I thought that violin was absolutely beautiful. I would take it out and run my fingers up and down the rich, honey-coloured wood, smell the block of resin used to lubricate the bow, pluck notes on the strings. I still don't know why he decided to buy me this present but I wanted to get better fast so that I could take lessons. We did have my grandmother Callahan's piano downstairs in the living room, and my sister had begun piano lessons but there wasn't much interest in music in the family except for listening to the Lucky Strike Hit Parade once a week. My sister and I both sang in the junior choir at the First Presbyterian Church, and I continued to sing in choirs and glee clubs right up to the time I graduated from university. (I still slip into a church from time to time on a Sunday morning, in order to sing a few of those lovely old hymns.) My father knew some Gay Nineties songs and taught me "A Bicycle Built for Two," "Bill Bailey," and "The Band Played On" (Casey would waltz with the strawberry blonde), a song I particularly liked because my hair, when I was very small, was red-gold. And up in the attic there was a gramophone with two horns, one for everyday, functional, adult brassy colour, and one for special occasions—a morning-glory horn. This had been left behind when my uncle and his family moved up to Syracuse. There were wax records too, stored in padded cardboard cylinders. Every so often my father would get out this gramophone and play a few songs or recitations. Strangely enough the only one I can remember was about Jealousy, the Green-Eyed Monster. The voices were scratchy and faint, like the voices of the Munchkins in *The Wizard of Oz*, but I was fascinated. Who knows where that gramophone ended up; how I should love to have it today!

My mother had an old beau named Harvey Fairbanks; his wife was a peripatetic music teacher and often visited our school. Harvey Fairbanks gave violin lessons at the big music store near our church and it was arranged that I would take a half-hour lesson once a week at some bargain price (I seem to remember it was fifty cents) "for old times' sake." Later on I would visit that store many times, as a teenager, to select a record and go into one of the soundproof booths to listen. We didn't

have a record player although my sister finally got one as a present the year *South Pacific* appeared. Mostly I listened to music on the radio or in one of those booths at Weeks and Dickinsons.

The music studios, very cramped and tiny, were on the second floor. Harvey Fairbanks taught me some simple tunes and told me I had to practise, practise, practise in order to strengthen my fingers. But it was hard to practise at home in the living room with my father trying to read the evening paper, my mother working on the evening quarrel, and our dog howling whenever I hit a high note. And I was lazy about it as well; playing the violin was hard work! However, by the time I reached junior high I knew enough to win a place in the second violin section of the school orchestra. We didn't do much except supply a kind of underpadding for the first violins. There were two boys in this section who could *really* play, had real talent, but of course they were looked down upon by the other boys—and a lot of the girls. It just wasn't "manly" to play the violin. I remember one song, "Dark Eyes," where all the second violins did was go *uh-uh uh-uh uh-uh* throughout the entire piece. *La la la:la la* went the melody and paused: *uh-uh*, we replied, *la la la:la la (uh-uh* and so on). At some point, perhaps when I entered junior high, my grandfather gave me *his* violin, which was very old and came with a battered wooden case. I had never heard my grandfather play the violin but he must have, perhaps in his youth. I hated that case, so shabby and beat-up; I was beginning to fall for my mother's belief in appearance and "nice things." I must have made quite a fuss because eventually I was given, for Christmas, a new violin case from Weeks and Dickinsons, but I was already losing interest in pursuing the violin in any serious fashion. By the time I was in senior high I had ceased playing altogether, and the violin went up to the attic. I still think music is the highest art form and envy those of my friends who stuck to their music lessons and derive great pleasure from playing. (This is usually the piano or the recorder.) I recently went to a drumming workshop here on the island where I live, twenty-four of us and a wonderful assortment of African drums. By the end of the afternoon our hands were buzzing, but we were actually producing music. It was wonderful, and now all those yearnings have begun again.

My grandfather had a record player up at his camp; it was the latest thing, with a device which allowed several records to be stacked, one on top of the other, a new one dropping in place when the old one had finished. One record was Fritz Kreisler (violin music!), one was North American Bird Songs (a set), one was Bob Hope, Bing Crosby, and Jerry Colonna. My grandfather was very fond of Bob Hope and Bing Crosby and during the winters he took us to the latest "Road" movie, although my mother thought they were too risqué (her word). Afterwards we went to the Ritz Tearoom where the hostess, a tall blonde in a black dress, took us to our seats. My grandfather was a flirt, even in his seventies, and if we called him "Grandpa" when the blonde with the peek-a-boo bob was around, he'd say, "Now that did I tell you girls?" We were supposed to call him "Uncle Larry."

He was very sarcastic towards both my mother and father, particularly my father, who smoked and who therefore represented a fire hazard when we were up in the woods. He usually walked up from his house on Walnut Street to eat Christmas dinner with us but would make cutting remarks about all the fancy gifts under the tree. I was always a little frightened of him but he was, in fact, a good grandfather. (I know now what a stern, cold father he was and how his children suffered because of this.) I think it was those summers at his camp that kept me sane. My parents didn't dare to quarrel so much—at least not inside or where he could hear them—and my sister and I were allowed a lot of freedom. The cottage, a big log house with a screened porch in front and a workshop and garage underneath, was on a rise above the lake. The nights were very cool—we wore drop-seat pajamas with feet in them called "Dr. Dentons"—but by midday it was high summer and we were down on the sand in our bathing suits, running in and out of the water or taking out the rowboat which was ours exclusively, "The Pin-Up Girl."

It took a long time for the lake to drop off so we were quite safe, even when small, and once we learned to row a boat we were trusted on the water by ourselves. My grandfather had a series of housekeepers with unusual names (Mrs. Thing, Bertha Pullum, Johnnie Coffee) and that also allowed my mother some freedom as she didn't have to cook or plan meals. She often went fishing with my father over at T-Lake mountain, and I liked to think they were actually happy together at those times. They could be like the children they were, with no real responsibilities (as my grandfather was paying for everything). My mother sometimes complained about the fact that we lived off

"My grandfather's summer camp in the Adirondack Mountains"

my grandfather every summer because my father wasn't a "good provider" and she often resented the housekeepers, particularly the very attractive Mrs. Coffee, but in her heart I felt she liked having someone else in charge of all the domestic and financial arrangements.

There was a huge stone fireplace in the main room, with a buffalo rug on the floor in front of it. My grandfather got up about 5 A.M. and lit the fire (and the fire in the woodstove in the kitchen; even after we got electricity and an electric stove, breakfast was usually cooked on the woodstove), and after a while we raced in with our clothes and dressed in the warmth from the fireplace. Now I cook on a woodstove in the winters and enjoy coming downstairs in my nightgown and lighting the fire. Even as I write this, the wood is snapping and crackling and giving off a kind of purr. There is no other sound like it.

We ate very well. Fresh-squeezed oranges (a job for my sister and myself, using a metal contraption that looked something like an earth-mover's shovel), pancakes, bacon, and maple syrup for breakfast; fried chicken and corn on the cob for dinner, or fish and coleslaw and baked potatoes; sandwiches and soup for supper. And there were always blueberry pies or a dish of boiling blueberries and sugar, with dumplings plopped in called "blueberry grunt." Wild blueberries grew in profusion all along the sandy road which led out to the main road. It didn't take long to pick a bucket or two as well as a posy of black-eyed Susans, Queen Anne's lace, and clover.

The waters of the lake were so clear you could see to the bottom even when you were quite a ways off shore. Clear and cool. We ran across the burning sand in mid-afternoon, our feet about to burst into flame, or that's the way it felt, and ran out into that lovely cool water. Out here in British Columbia the ocean is cold; it turns your bones to glass and you hesitate, will I, won't I, on all but the hottest day. Not the same thing at all.

My grandfather sold the place in 1953. The camp burned down shortly afterwards and, as he had sold it "lock, stock and barrel" as my mother said, a great chunk of my childhood went up with the house: the big old radio next to my grandfather's chair, the slippery black sofa stuffed with horsehair, the cotton Navajo blankets and lumberjack shirts that hung on pegs by the back door, the stereopticon with its views of foreign castles and cathedrals, the jars of arrowheads, the old books for rainy days, the Ouija board on which we tried to foretell our futures, the beds we slept in, everything.

I've been back once. The people who bought from my grandfather are there still. He has a

"With my sister (I'm on the left). The handtinted picture was taken for my grandfather who kept it on his desk in a frame that said 'The pin-up girls of L. B. Corbett,'" about 1942.

business in Amsterdam, New York, and there's a float plane moored at the entrance to the creek. They said my grandfather had installed a sawdust-burning furnace shortly before he sold the place and something went awry. They've built a nice house on the property and they were certainly welcoming but I couldn't wait to leave. Everything had shrunk from the mythic to the ordinary; I doubt I'll ever visit there again.

When I entered senior high school I became very depressed. My teachers did not inspire me, not even my Latin teacher, and I felt very alone and awkward. Both my parents had gone to this high school and my sister seemed to be doing fine. She was very active in the drama society and had joined a "second-string" sorority after neither of us had been pledged to either of the "top" sororities, Delta Kappa or Tau Epsilon. Sororities were a big thing in those days and your whole social life revolved around them. There were meetings every Friday night and after the meetings the boys (who had their own fraternities) came over, milled about, and joined up with the girls for Saturday movie dates. I was very ashamed that we hadn't been asked to join, especially as my mother was so upset about it, as was my father. My mother wept and my father muttered and of course they fought about who was to blame. There was also the implication that it was our fault as well and that we had let them down. I think now it probably *was* our fault, if fault is the right word. Neither of us knew much about socializing and we had become very self-centered. One could argue that our upbringing had caused this, but I don't think we should be let off that easily. We were older now; we could see through a lot of the pettiness and envy of our mother, the weak-willed behaviour of our father, and yet we continued to view life through their eyes—as victims as "acted upon." It took me a long time to get over this, and the feeling still creeps in occasionally through various cracks and crevices. And I long ago forgave my parents; it seems to be harder to forgive myself!

One day, in study hall, I talked to a girl I knew slightly. She said she hated high school too and was going away to boarding school in just a few weeks. Her father worked in one of the big banks; I'd seen him when we were dragged in by our parents as ocular proof that they needed yet another loan, so I imagine he made a fairly good salary. I went home and told my mother I hated school and wanted to go to boarding school. She asked me if I was crazy—where would they get the money for something like that when our father couldn't keep us out of debt as it was. I said the girl had mentioned scholarships; maybe I could get a scholarship or something.

I don't know why my mother agreed to write. Did she sense how desperate I was or was she so used to asking for money, for favours, that she saw nothing out of the ordinary about writing such a letter? I still don't know what she said, but a few weeks later they drove me to New Hampshire and deposited me at St. Mary's-in-the-Mountains; I was the recipient of a Bishop's scholarship, me, a Presbyterian! There had been an early snowfall but the leaves were still on the sugar maples. I felt as though I were in Paradise, truly, as they drove away and left me there surrounded by all that beauty. This turned out to be one of the happiest years of my life.

I am not going to give a blow by blow description of the rest of my life up to now but St. Mary's was such a turning point for me that I must try and set down why this was so. This was a small school, maybe not more than seventy girls, Anglican, and with great emphasis on strong minds in strong bodies. Classes were small, teachers were dedicated, and the girls themselves were a mix— tall, short, pretty, plain, shy, outgoing. We wore a uniform, grey skirt and navy blazer for class, navy ski pants and pale blue parka when we skiied on nearby Cannon Mountain. Of course there were party dresses for various social functions and some of these girls came from very wealthy families, but most of the time we could simply forget about what we wore. That was a great plus for me, right from the start. Secondly, classes were small and we were given not only the set texts but as much extra work as we wanted. It was *okay,* in fact it was great, to want to learn more. My English teacher, seeing that I had finished all the books for the year by Christmas, gave me Tolstoy, Dostoevsky, Chekov, Thomas Mann, Ibsen, even, I seem to recall, Gertrude Stein. He told me I wrote very well and had I ever tried my hand at writing stories? The history teacher gave a special class in Far Eastern history; until then I had known little or nothing about China or Japan. I began to realize how truly ignorant I was, but this didn't depress me at St. Mary's. I suppose what I discovered was the joy of learning and that joy led to other joys. Soon I was quite a cheerful person, dreaded going home for Christmas, couldn't wait to get back.

I was in the choir and we sang not only at school but on Sundays, in red robes and white surplices, in the choir of the Anglican church in Littleton. We sang our responses in Latin; we sang a sevenfold A-men. The music teacher had just come from England (she was quite young and I don't think she was English although she affected an English accent) and was full of the works of Ralph Vaughan Williams. On Sunday afternoons there was Music Appreciation and I heard whole operas for the first time, heard Strindberg, Dvorak, Erik Satie.

And then there were the sports. I had never been terribly good at sports (my eyesight has been bad since I was seven) but I'd played grass hockey and volleyball back home as well as softball. I was also a good runner. Now I learned lacrosse and how to ski. I was never good at either of these things but I was out there trying and nobody made fun, quite the opposite. I loved coming in from outdoors on a winter afternoon, my whole body glowing and alive.

When the school decided to put on *Macbeth,* I tried out for one of the witches. I closed my eyes and tried to imagine the blasted heath, the thin scratchy voices of the witches, who weren't evil themselves but knew evil when they saw it. After I spoke there was a sudden burst of applause. I had discovered another aspect of my personality: I could "do" voices. (This has proved very useful when I do public readings of my own work.)

There were just two flies in the ointment, as my mother would say: the minister who taught us religious studies and was also the priest at the local church and the headmistress herself. I did not get along with either of them. Rightly or wrongly I felt that the headmistress picked on me, that she didn't like scholarship girls and was the only member of staff who looked down on me. The minister didn't like me because, like the Queen of Sheba, I asked him "hard questions." I was becoming known among the other girls for my rather sarcastic "wit" and I expect I gave the minister a hard time just to show off. Anyway, whatever the cause, I didn't get my scholarship renewed. Mother wrote to another place, in Massachusetts, and I went there for my final year of school. It was all right but it wasn't the same as that lovely little school tucked up in the mountains of New Hampshire. After that year I knew, somehow, that I would survive, that I was never trapped unless I chose to be trapped, that my "background" was simply that and I should start getting on with my life and let my parents cope with theirs as best they could. Not a bad lesson to learn when you are sixteen.

There is a family story that my mother trots out from time to time. She says that when I was about three and my grandmother Corbett was still alive but frail, lying on the big sofa up at the woods and requesting that "somebody take that child down to the beach," I shouted back up at the house, "Well I don't care! Someday I'm going to Europe!" It's probably apocryphal although I did know at a very early age—because of the stereopticon and some old photograph albums—that there was such a place and that it was far away. Nobody in the Callahan family had been to Europe since they came over from Ireland before the Revolution but my aunt, my mother's sister, had been to Europe in her youth and my grandfather's parents, accompanied by their youngest daughter Mabel, had done the grand tour. That was when Mabel danced with the Prince of Wales. ("Before he met Mrs. Simpson, of course," says my mother.) And when I was in grade school there was a series of rather sugary books about children from other lands ("Little Anne of England," "Little Jan of Holland," "Little Marie of France"; I'm making these up because I can't really remember the titles, but you get the idea.) There was also the ubiquitous *National Geographic* with the pictures of sturdy, happy people from other parts of the world. Every so often the magazine would come with a map which my father unfolded carefully and I borrowed from him later.

I didn't know any people in Binghamton who had been to Europe, although certain fathers and sons had been overseas during the war, not only in Europe but also in the Pacific, the Far East. Girls at St. Mary's and the school I went to later had been to Europe, usually with their families, but I imagined going on my own, perhaps living in Paris or London for a while, writing books which would be instantly acclaimed. The more I read, the more I wanted to travel.

I won a scholarship to Smith College, which had (probably still has) a junior year abroad, but I knew I could never afford that and it still wasn't exactly what I had in mind. Then, near the middle of my second year, I became friends with a girl who intended to head off to St. Andrew's in Scotland for her junior year. A friend of her older sister had done this and loved it. Why didn't I come along? She had a copy of the catalogue, which was nothing like the glossy catalogues put out by American colleges: just a thick book listing rules and regulations and all the courses offered. Scotland was cheap and if we went as nonmatriculating students we need pay only twenty-five

pounds (about seventy-five U.S. dollars) in tuition. I went home at spring break and told my parents I wanted to go to Europe for my junior year. How would I get the money? I'd go back to The Hill, I said.

In 1884 or shortly before, the first inebriate asylum was opened on a hill to the east of our city centre: two hundred and fifty-two acres of land high above the Susquehanna and Chinango Rivers. The cornerstone was laid by the Grand Master of the Free and Accepted Masons, and part of his speech is recorded in *A History of Broome County* (with illustrations), 1885:

> As I looked last night at the flaming comet in our sky, and saw it inclined and plumed like a pen [there had been a comet in the sky the night before] fit and ready for the Almighty's own hand, I could not but feel that if He should seize it and inscribe with its diamond point upon the sky the chief event of this *annus mirabilis* it would be the foundation of a policy and a usage that we now celebrate—of an institution, the first of its kind in the world, which proclaims that mercy is better than justice; nay, that mercy is an exacter justice.

Whether there weren't enough inebriates who were willing to come forward or what, I don't know, but the experiment failed. Within a few years, the place had become the Binghamton Asylum for the Chronic Insane, called by the locals "The Hill." I had heard of The Hill, not just in the ordinary way—that everybody in town had heard of it and knew where it was—but because my mother's sister had spent some time there after her second suicide attempt. However, it wasn't the sort of place you went for a field trip with Brownies or Scouts and I had never even been near it until I started to look for a summer job that would pay real money, at the end of my freshman year. I had seen an ad for someone to demonstrate hair brushes at a local department store and, as I had an abundance of nice-coloured hair, I went downtown for an interview. But I had got up late and the job was taken by the time I arrived. What to do? I went over to the New York State Employment Commission and told the woman behind the desk I had to have a job. Could I type? No. Could I instruct children in riding? No. Could I drive a car? No. She said she didn't see how she could help me since I had no skills. "Isn't there *anything?*" I said. "I really need the money."

She hesitated, then handed me an index card. "There's an opening for two orderlies at The Hill. You could start tomorrow."

"You mean—work at the insane asylum?" She nodded. "It just says someone in good health and prepared to work hard."

I could see by her face she knew I wasn't going to take it. College girl, too good for that sort of thing.

"I'll take it," I said.

My sister, who was away somewhere that summer, had a friend whose father was a doctor. My parents said I had to call him up to make sure it was safe to work there. My father, who hated mention of illness of any kind, kept muttering and shaking his head, but I knew it was my mother who would decide. And the doctor said it would be perfectly all right to work there—they'd never put me on the Violent Ward. In fact, his daughter was looking for a job as well; he'd mention to her that The Hill had two openings for female orderlies. When she came home she called and said she was coming too.

The next day we borrowed her brother's convertible and drove up for our interview. Naturally we were hired on the spot—they were very short-staffed—and half an hour later we had caps and a series of keys which were fastened to a lanyard tied around our waists. She was to go to one ward, I to another. We looked at one another: "We thought we'd be together," I said. The director shook his head. No, we were to act as "reliefs"; we'd be moved around from ward to ward wherever we were needed. He took Joan up to her ward while I waited in his office, then he came down and got me. I was on the fourth floor of the main building, Ward 88. He knocked on the heavy metal door and after a few minutes a nurse unlocked the door and we stepped in. Even today I don't know why I didn't turn and run. The noise! The smell!

"Welcome to the Shit Ward," she said, taking my arm and leading me down the long corridor. "Come and I'll introduce you to our ladies."

Joan quit the next day; I stayed all that summer and went back the next. If anything made me a writer (if writers are made, not born) I think it was The Hill. For although my family life was pretty terrible emotionally I had, in fact, led a sheltered existence. I wasn't even allowed to go to funerals when I was young. Ward 88 was crammed full of mad old ladies, incontinent, abusive, hideous to look at (most of them), terrifying. I had not known there were people like this in the world, *women* like this. Skin and bones, most of them, with huge bedsores painted with gentian violet. This was still the era of straitjackets and "baths" (with

"The wonderful ship that took me to Europe for the first time"

canvas covers and a hole for the patient's head so she stuck up like a pie bird in a pie).

I worked on other wards besides Ward 88—the shock ward (insulin shock, which is terribly dangerous and makes you fat, as well as electroconvulsive therapy, where I often had the job of holding down a patient's legs), an ambulatory ward, the operating room. In fact, during my second summer I worked almost exclusively in the O.R., witnessed lobotomies and amputations as well as the birth of two babies, born to women who had no idea what was happening. I worked 7:00 to 3:30; I worked 3:30 to 11:00; I worked midnight to 8:00. I made friends with the nurses and some of the other orderlies. The world of The Hill became much more real than the world outside, down in the town. When I wasn't working there, I was asleep. And at the end of the second summer, with a little help from the Daughters of the American Revolution (another of my mother's letters) and all my savings, I flew to Boston to join my friend and we set sail for England. Boston-Halifax-St. John's-Liverpool. It took us twelve days to cross the Atlantic and by the time we stepped ashore, I felt ready for anything that life could offer; I felt free. (It wasn't until several years later that I began to have nightmares about The Hill.)

About fifteen years ago I made a sentimental pilgrimage to St. Andrew's and to No. 10 Hope Street which in my student days was a co-ed boarding house. Now it was a bed-and-breakfast run by a dour Scots woman who was very reluctant to let me in the door when I said I had lived there as a student. She obviously didn't like students very much even though she lived in a town which depended on the university for a lot of its revenue. (It is also the home of the Royal and Ancient Golf Course; no doubt many of her clients were well-behaved golfers, not rowdy undergraduates.)

I went up to the top floor where we had a room directly opposite the stairs. The room was unoccupied so she let me have a look in although she stayed right behind me, looking from time to time at her watch. I had had no brothers and so had never shared a house with boys before; it took me a while to get used to a boy coming out of the (bitterly cold) bathroom in his dressing gown, to the way people popped in and out of rooms, sometimes without knocking. We all had various interests outside the house but we were also the Hope Street Gang and would go en bloc to the movies, where we sat in the shilling seats and smoked and made rude comments if we didn't like

the film, or went to the Cross Keys for beer and crisps and noisy discussions about Life. On Tuesdays we gathered in one room and listened to the Goon Show. We made fun of the food we got, the inevitability of it—Mondays, bangers and mash and turnips; Tuesdays, floating mince and mash and tinned peas; Wednesdays, rissoles; Thursdays, stewing steak with gravy; Fridays, plaice and chips. I can't remember Saturdays and Sundays, probably a "joint" of some kind on Sunday. Porridge (always) for breakfast. Pot after pot of tea.

The academic work was hard and nobody stood over you to read that book by Wednesday or get that essay in. At that time only about 5 percent of young people went on to university so it was still a privilege, not a right. Most of the students were on grants and had very little spare cash. But they knew how to have fun (there were lots of parties and dances and walks along the sea) as well as how to make best use of their study time. After the first quarter, when I nearly failed Moral Philosophy because I hadn't read the books the professor had "suggested" we read, I smartened up and learned how to study myself. I think that basic grounding in self-discipline, setting aside a certain portion of the day for intellectual work, has been of great benefit to me as a self-employed writer. When I am working on a story or a novel, particularly when I am working on the first few drafts and have no deadlines, no editors, no *anyone* breathing down my neck, I have to set myself a schedule and try to stick to it. Now I find it hard to work for anyone else!

At the end of the academic year my roommate and I went walking in the Highlands and on Skye, staying in youth hostels, hitchhiking occasionally when we got tired. I have always been drawn to hills and mountains and the sometimes bleak beauty of the Highlands really spoke to me. The weather held and we came back feeling very fit after our year of books and bangers and beer. During the long Easter break, we had gone to Spain and now we decided to go to Scandinavia (her grandfather was Danish), Holland, Italy. It was safe to hitchhike in those days; we never had any trouble even though she was very blonde and I was a redhead. We were followed a lot in Italy (*che belizza! che belizza!*) but no one really accosted us. Times have changed; a woman would be a fool to hitchhike in most parts of Europe any more. (And perhaps our innocence protected us; I don't know.)

One of the many songs we learned at parties was "Come Landlord Fill the Flowing Bowl" (before it doth run over). The refrain is:

"Two of the children from 'Gem Street,' Bishop Ryder's Church of England Infant and Junior School, where I taught. Ian drew pictures of most of the children while I was teaching there."

For tonight we'll merry, merry be
For tonight we'll merry, merry be
For tonight we'll merry, merry be
Tomorrow we'll be sober

The first novel I attempted to write, about that year at St. Andrew's, was called *Tomorrow We'll Be Sober*. I think I wanted it to be a cross between *Zuleika Dobson* and *Our Hearts Were Young and Gay*. I abandoned it fairly early on and God knows where it is now; I'd love to have it. I was so in love with the whole student world of St. Andrew's that I even toyed with the idea of staying on. I would have to learn Greek in order to matriculate and I would have to find some more money; the last didn't worry me so much even though I was on a student visa and forbidden to work. There were always odd jobs about and after The Hill I knew I

could do anything, however unpleasant, if I needed to. But I was a scholarship student at Smith and I felt a certain duty to return and finish my degree. Maybe obligation is a better word. So, in late August I sailed for home (via the port of Montreal) on the *Franconia*. There were quite a lot of college kids on that ship; they seemed terribly *immature* to me, especially the giggly girls. After all, I hadn't just spent the summer cruising around Europe with my pals; I'd been a student. I'd had an affair. I'd actually lived there. I wasn't a *tourist*. What a snob I must have seemed to the others! What a phoney.

But one thing was real—I knew I was going back just as soon as possible. I'd been bitten. The New World would never again hold the attraction of the Old. Or so I thought—leaning on the rail as we sailed up the St. Lawrence on that warm afternoon in August 1956.

By November 1957, having graduated from Smith and worked in a bookstore and then the advertising department of a department store ("Crisp as an autumn breeze these pleated skirts are just the thing for the smart schoolgirl"), I had saved enough money for a passage back across the water. In the late summer I had also become engaged (wasn't that what all our mothers wanted?) to a man I had known at St. Andrew's. I already knew, by the time I sailed, that this wasn't going to work out but I decided I wanted to go anyway. I shared a room in a house in Ladbroke Grove near the Holland Park Tube Station with a friend from our house at Smith, and I answered ad after ad trying to find work in London. The Aliens Act had come in and I had to prove that I was better qualified to do the job than a British person. I couldn't type or do shorthand and I had no real "qualifications" other than a B.A. so I soon became very discouraged. I tried the BBC, the film studios (I almost got a job with Columbia Pictures, doing publicity, but there was no particular reason why they should hire an American so the home office said no). I think my lowest day came when I answered an ad for a temporary nanny, went all the way to Highgate, only to discover that my future employer would be an American woman who only wanted a girl with "a good English accent." (She apologized for not having made that clear in the ad.) December was cold and bleak and foggy. Sometimes, when you crossed the street, you could only see the orange globes at the sides of the zebra crossings. It was like living in a bag of damp, dirty white wool, and the ambulances went all night, taking the elderly to hospital with pneumonia. For the first time I understood what a pea-soup fog really was. Just before Christmas, when all I had left was a few pounds and my return passage, a young man I'd met on the ship suggested I try Birmingham, where his father was a teacher. Apparently they were always short of teachers in Birmingham. I said I didn't have a teaching certificate. He said that didn't matter; I could teach with a degree.

I really didn't want to leave London. Why would a would-be writer go to *Birmingham?* Who, of note, had ever come from Birmingham? I liked London; I liked the parks and the museums and galleries. I even got to see some good plays (parts of them) by hanging around theatres waiting for doctors to be called out on emergencies! I was never afraid in London, even in those Dickensonian fogs. I went to free lectures and struck up conversations in coffeehouses (expresso bars were just becoming the rage) and pubs. This sometimes led to free coffee or lager or even a meal. But I knew I couldn't stay if I had no work at all, and my visitor's visa would run out in a few months.

Just before Christmas I took the train to Birmingham, talked to my friend's father who set up an interview with the Education Authority, and I was hired on the spot, to begin the first week of January. They sent me back to London with a letter for the home office saying it wasn't a question of someone else doing the job better, there was no one to do the job. (They were 500 teachers short in Birmingham at that time.) The night before I was (reluctantly) to leave London, the man I loved called me up. We hadn't seen each other for a while because all we did was fight. He wanted to know how I was doing and would I like to meet again and talk. I remember holding the black receiver in my hand (the telephone was in the downstairs hall) and thinking, "I can't go to Birmingham; I love this man; surely we can work something out.") "I've got a job in Birmingham," I said, "teaching primary school. I leave tomorrow." "Best of luck," he said, and I never saw him again.

Someday soon I intend to write an entire book about my time in Birmingham at Bishop Ryder's Church of England Infant and Junior School, a fancy name for what was really a very old school in the slums. I had Class 3, ages six and seven, and I think there were about forty-eight of them, all but a few (the boy whose father was a fireman, the little girl whose father made coffins) very noisy, cheeky and dirty. I had a high, slant-top desk at the

top of the room and took attendance in a huge register, dipping a pen in an inkwell. "John Fulford?" "Here, Miss." "June Binnell?" "Yes, Miss." At break I sold biscuits from three separate tins at three separate prices. Janine Dodgers were the most expensive, a penny ha'penny. There were also Lincoln biscuits and something else I can't remember. The children all crowded round shouting out their orders and I was always short at the end of the week. Every schoolchild in England got a free pint of milk at break but a lot of my children didn't like it—they preferred tea—until I suggested to the headmistress that perhaps they could have chocolate milk. Trucks were lorries, elevators were lifts, cookies were biscuits, your "front passage" was what you peed out of, not the entrance way in your house. When it was my turn to supervise school dinners, I and another teacher walked the school down a few blocks to the Salvation Army Hall where good, nourishing food

"My oldest child, Sarah, at her christening with Ian's mother at back, his grandmother holding Sarah, and me in my very '50s 'bandeau plus veil.' We were about to sail for Canada," Sussex, England, 1959.

was ladled out by two deaf mutes. (Eventually the hall was burnt down by some of the older boys at the school.)

The other teachers were mostly much older than I was, very good at their jobs, and knew how to keep order as well as teach; they overlooked the bedlam coming from my classroom and gave me lots of good advice. I'm not sure what those children learned (except a lot of songs; they loved to sing), but I learned a lot.

I lived with two other young teachers miles away in a house owned by the Education Authority and used to teach home economics to secondary school students. My housemates were *real* teachers, had been to teacher training college, and both had steady boyfriends whom I suppose they eventually married. There was a good fish-and-chips shop at the end of the road where I got off the bus, so I would often bring home big newspaper-wrapped bundles of fish-and-chips or roe-and-chips, and we'd sit around the kitchen table eating all this lovely, greasy food and drinking endless cups of tea. We paid almost no rent, but we had to make sure the place was spotless on Monday mornings.

I discovered Birmingham was full of culture: the Birmingham Rep, the City of Birmingham Orchestra, the wonderful art gallery, the Cathedral, the excellent library. And I hadn't been there long when I met a young man in his final year at the Birmingham College of Arts and Crafts on Margaret Street, the first college to be built outside London during the arts and crafts movement. He had a book in his pocket. It turned out he always had a book in his pocket. I think, in many ways, he was better read than I was. He introduced me to the happy-go-lucky world of the Art College (just to go in the door of that place made me feel good) and soon he was doing the art lesson, on Friday afternoons, for my little monsters.

We "courted" in pubs and coffee bars and curry houses. We spent Saturdays wandering around the Bull Ring listening to the hawkers, watching the Strong Man get loose from his heavy chains (he was married to a girl at the Art College), eating cockles off the end of a pin. He invited me to come out to Solihull where he lived, to meet his parents. He said he wanted to emigrate, to see the world; I said I had wanted to settle in England but I too wanted to see the world. I don't know whether we "fell" in love so much as realized, gradually, how very much we had in common, that we loved one another, yes, but would also be good companions in the adventure of our lives. We decided to get married. (His parents had quite liked me up to then but they didn't like Americans much and they never expected their son to marry one. They never got over it.)

In 1959, with our infant daughter, Sarah, we sailed to Montreal on the old *Empress of France*, in the cheapest cabin on D-deck, right next to the engine room (the baby seemed to find the thud-thud soothing) and then came to British Columbia where we have lived—more or less—ever since. I had never seen the Pacific Ocean until then and I am now a complete convert to the Pacific Northwest. Although Ian and I are no longer together, we live very similar lives on separate islands in the same archipelago between the mainland and Vancouver Island. We have vegetable gardens and he has geese and ducks and chickens (I had chickens until recently) and we live in wood houses on land that we own and love. We have three daughters all very much "West Coasters" and all just a ferry-ride away. It seems impossible that thirty-four years have gone by since I held the baby up to the train window as we sped across Canada ("these are the lakes these are the hills these are the prairies these are the prairies these are the prairies—this is your country now, Baby"). I wrote to someone the other day, "If Time flies, he goes by Concorde." There are two little grandsons in Victoria. Is that possible?

I have not said much about our time in West Africa, where Ian was offered a job at the (then) Kwame Nkrumah University of Science and Technology in Kumasi, Ghana. We sent a telegram "yes" and then said to one another, "Where's Ghana?" It had been the Gold Coast when we were in school. My family said, "You're taking your children to *Africa?*" *His* mother said, "Lucky you, fancy having servants." (We were there when Nkrumah was overthrown and overnight, almost, his name was painted out from everything; it was like something out of *Alice in Wonderland*.) I was pregnant with our third child when we arrived and lost the baby when I was nearly seven months along and I nearly bled to death, a horrible experience in every way. I was ill for a long time, both in body and spirit, and lived on the edge of a breakdown for several years. But about six months after I got out of hospital I wrote a story, a very stylized story, trying to come to terms with what had happened. (Nobody wanted to talk about it. After all, it wasn't as though I had *known* her, was it? I must "buck up" and not mope.) I would have had more sympathy with a broken leg.

"I'm pregnant with Claire. Vickie on left, Sarah on right,"
Stanley Park, Vancouver, 1967.

I sent the story off to the *Atlantic Monthly*—I had several encouraging letters from them in the past few years—and two months later they wrote and said they'd taken it as an Atlantic "First." I sat staring at the letter with the tears rolling down my face. I would give anything to have had the baby rather than the letter! However, it was from that moment on that I decided to write about reality, about what it was like to be a woman in the second half of the twentieth century, decided that I had to be *true*, not "nice," if I was to be an artist (and was to save my soul).

Edward Weeks saw the story and wrote me a letter from Atlantic Monthly Press. Robert Amussen at Bobbs-Merrill saw the story and wrote me a letter from Bobbs-Merrill in New York. Both wanted to know if I was working on a novel. I wrote back, to both, that I could only imagine writing short stories as I had two young children and my life was very fragmented. Atlantic Monthly Press said they'd be delighted to see a book of stories when I finished. They heaped praise on me,

comparisons to "the early James Joyce" and Katherine Mansfield. Bob Amussen said, "We'll sign for a book of stories right now if you will do a novel later on." I was in such despair and confusion at that time I couldn't imagine a "later on" but Ian, who I think now must have been terribly worried about my sanity, said "sign it, sign it." I think maybe he held my hand as I signed it, I don't remember.

The *Atlantic* story came out in June 1965, almost thirty years ago. I have been writing stories, novels, and radio plays (radio is a great passion of mine; I don't own a TV) ever since. Looking back on this time I would say that writing has never brought me happiness, that it has got in the way of my human relationships, that if I knew how to do something else I would. "It's so *isolating!*" I said to one of my daughters last year. "I want colleagues; I want office parties." She just laughed. Most people envy me because I am my own boss and can take a day off, without asking permission, if I want to. But I have no dental plan, no company pension to look forward to, and I pay all my medical plan myself. (How fortunate I am to live in Canada with its national health care plan!) I teach from time to time at universities but I don't really like university life; I think, on the whole, it's death to artists. I'm glad, most of the time, that I didn't opt for *that* life, but I get a little wistful when I discover somebody is getting $91,000 a year teaching Canadian literature and I'm on the reading list! But money (or the lack of it) isn't my real problem. I've never had much and I can't imagine I ever will. Money doesn't bring automatic happiness, although it's useful when the old fridge packs in or the dentist hands you a bill you'll have trouble paying. I *did* think writing well, as best as I knew how, and trying to be a good mother and good wife would bring happiness—and for a while, a long while, it did. But writing by itself? Forget it. And I am more and more cynical about the publishing world. Publishers are looking for profits—can we blame them? And people like me, who have a small but loyal following, are barely tolerated any more. I never get an advance over $10,000 (Canadian), and for my last book, which took seven *years*, that was paid out in three installments, the last $3,333 on the week of publication. How is one to keep on writing with "encouragement" like that? I can't get an agent because I've written too many books, have too big a backlist of critically acclaimed but financially unsuccessful titles. Agents want to discover people or snap up people who've become "hot." I'm not even lukewarm. Believe me, I've tried and been turned down again and again. Without an agent to negotiate for me (I used to have an agent but she retired, then I had another but he moved to Dublin), I haven't a chance of pulling together enough money to give me some peace of mind. There are days—more and more frequent—when I hate the writing, when the appetite of the large dog seems insatiable, when I have the feeling he will eventually eat me up. I still feel I should be doing something useful. The world is in a "terrible state of chassis" and there must be something I could do to help, something more useful than chronicling what it's like to be a woman in the second half of the twentieth century. I don't think that what I have to say about it is very important. Eliot again—"The great poet, in writing himself, writes his time." What about the not-so-great, the really-rather-ordinary-but-she-has-a-way-with-words? Some days I want to say to young writers—don't do it, run from it as fast as you can. It's not worth it, none of it. Find something else to do, less isolating, more

fun, with colleagues and office parties. Artists can't really share—or only with people who would pass them by on the street. Give the large dog back while it's still a puppy or you'll end up discovering you don't own it, it owns you.

© 1993 Audrey G. Thomas

BIBLIOGRAPHY

Novels:

Mrs. Blood (also see below), Bobbs-Merrill, 1970.

Munchmeyer and Prospero on the Island, Bobbs-Merrill, 1972.

Songs My Mother Taught Me, Bobbs-Merrill, 1973.

Blown Figures, Talonbooks (Vancouver), 1974, Knopf, 1975.

Latakia, Talonbooks, 1979.

Intertidal Life, Stoddart (Toronto), 1984, and Beaufort Books, 1984.

Short-story collections:

Ten Green Battles, Bobbs-Merrill, 1967.

Ladies & Escorts, Oberon (Ottawa), 1977.

(With others) *Personal Fictions*, edited by Michael Ondaatje, Oxford University Press (Toronto), 1977.

Real Mothers, Talonbooks, 1981.

Two in the Bush and Other Stories, McClelland & Stewart (Toronto), 1981.

Goodbye Harold, Good Luck, Viking/Penguin, 1986.

The Wild Blue Yonder, Penguin, 1990.

Radio Plays:

(With Linda Sorenson and Keith Pepper) *Once Your Submarine Cable Is Gone, What Have You Got?*, first broadcast on Canadian Broadcasting Corp. (CBC-Radio), October 27, 1973.

Mrs. Blood, first broadcast on CBC-Radio, August 16, 1975.

Untouchables, first broadcast on CBC-Radio, December 5, 1981.

The Milky Way, first broadcast on CBC-Radio, November 26, 1983.

The Axe of God, first broadcast as part of *Disasters! Act of God or Acts of Man?*, CBC-Radio, February 24, 1985.

The Woman in Black Velvet, first broadcast on CBC-Radio, May 17, 1985.

In the Groove, first broadcast on CBC-Radio, November 4, 1985.

On the Immediate Level of Events Occurring in Meadows, first broadcast as part of *Sextet,* CBC-Radio, January 26, 1986.

Contributor of short stories to periodicals, including *Atlantic Monthly, Canadian Literature, Capilano Review, Fiddlehead, Interface Maclean's, Saturday Night,* and *Toronto Life.* Also author of five other radio plays.

George Zebrowski

1945-

So much of the writing life is spent undoing the damage, delay, and wasted time caused by being, economically, "a parlour guest of the rich," as one writer recently put it, that I often think of those more lasting wellsprings which, if they do not run dry, give a writer the will and courage to stay the course. Staying the course is everything, because only by staying do you have a chance of learning what success you may have, however modest. To give up partway toward success or failure is to condemn one's self to nagging doubt about what might have been.

Of course, success and failure are most easily judged in their extremes, and perhaps not even then are they clear; so the only path for talent is to do its best and let both today and tomorrow judge as they will, since they will do their usual myopic job whether they declare one a success or not. If I have learned anything as a writer, it is that no matter how good or bad or middling a work turns out to be, there will be those who love it and those who hate it; and there will be readers who like your work for reasons you may despise, or hate it for reasons with which you may even sympathize.

Between such goings on, and those of economics, a writer might be discouraged early on if he knew about them in advance. Fortunately, many writers wear the protective blinders of denial, longing, and ambition, and by the time these fall off it is too late; their best work has been accomplished through sheer momentum.

Talent doesn't much care what happens to its holder, as long as it is fulfilled. People in sports and ballet pay a heavy physical price, so why shouldn't it be the same among writers? Getting published shouldn't be too easy (occasionally it is), but not so hard that it destroys its own principal product (this is too often the case and getting worse). It should not face talented people with a choice they cannot make: to write the works or not; since they must write, they accept, too often, *any* circumstances that are available, because not to do so would mean strangling their works in the cradle.

It is perhaps most difficult for the long-term writer, who will continue to develop well into his

George Zebrowski

fifties and sixties, who already knows all the obstacles, who knows what price will have to be paid, and must now reach back more deliberately into the wellsprings and make sometimes painfully conscious the resources that first moved him to write—and to give himself some kind of explanation of what he is doing, if anything, and what he still hopes to do; and perhaps to give up, if need be—because the tendency of talent is to blame itself exclusively for its own failures.

So let us see if it is possible to see.

My earliest memories are clear, dramatic images of a stormy night in a small English town in the late 1940s. The community of Polish war

"My beautiful, sharp-eyed parents, Anna and Antoni, whose youth and intelligence were wasted by World War II. I'm wearing the expression I seemed to have been born with."
England, 1947

refugees from Europe had been given temporary housing in a camp near the town, and one night a storm threatened to knock down power lines in the nearby road, sending all those in danger to stand outside until the storm was past.

Later images seem, by comparison, like a resurrection: sunny days, green fields filled with wildflowers. I remember escaping into warm, glorious afternoons, from which only my mother's melodious voice was able to call me back. That voice seemed to be able to reach me anywhere I went, because the park area which I explored was not very large, but it was a vast world to my child's eyes. I had made this bargain with my mother, that I would call back and come home as soon as I heard her voice. It was a bargain that gave me the freedom to explore.

One green hillside, rolling gently down into a small valley, still lives within me, a permanent dream of bliss. I would go down into this valley and up toward the trees beyond, as if trying to find

a way to "get behind" the scenery, to find out what the vision was "really" made of, but, of course, I only found more of the same.

It seems to me that I was wise beyond my words as a child. Insights flashed within me but remained inexpressible. Today, I can say how I felt, but I hold dear the fact that I will always suspect more than I can say; no matter how skilled and observing the writer becomes, the inexpressible will continue to escape his nets, because while the "edge" of the inexpressible nearest to you may yield to expression, the outer edge will continue to grow. To know this, to feel it deeply, is to know an inexhaustible reservoir.

As a child I would sometimes recite the events of the day to myself before I fell asleep—to turn them into a scheme of words that would make sense after the experience, which could not be understood while it was happening but would all fall into place later. I remember being startled by this activity of mine only when I heard my mother describe it to another adult; before then it had seemed a perfectly natural way of grasping the world.

Earlier, I had spent many months in an Oxford hospital after a hip operation that went wrong because I tried to get up in my sleep. Here I learned to speak English from the nurses and doctors. I already spoke Polish, but today I only vaguely remember ever knowing one language before the other. I now consider this second language to have been a great gift given to me by my illness, since learning it then prepared me for English grade school and for our move to the United States in 1951; but the Oxford accent got me several bloody noses in American grade school, until I took on the protection of a Manhattan manner of speech and dress.

The summers of '52, '53, '54, and '55 were a special time, so much so that these are the only times I still dream about while forgetting that I am dreaming, although as the memory has grown older I occasionally remind myself in my sleep that I am dreaming, while marveling at how realistic the dream seems to be! Without a doubt this is the expression of my desire to regain the earlier dream state, in which I accept the dream as reality.

In these summers I was sent away from our apartment in New York, on Ninth Street between First and Second Avenue, to a camp in Southampton, Long Island. It was a camp for boys and girls between the ages of seven and twelve. One feature of the daily schedule was that we spent the time from breakfast until noon in a single-room schoolhouse which had been joined to a structure of older buildings and dorms. This building had a large glass cabinet against one wall, and here I found a complete set of the Oz books by L. Frank Baum.

One day, after we had been let out to play on the huge grounds of the camp, I wandered back into the schoolhouse, took out *Tik-Tok of Oz* from the cabinet, settled down on my stomach on the shelf of one of two large bay windows, and read until I had finished the story. This and *The Wizard of Oz* were probably the first books I read, and they were miraculous. Whole worlds of vivid imaginings, feeling, action and drama, characters and their thoughts and feelings would appear in my mind whenever I wished to open a book and set my eyes on the pages.

Between my interest in lepidopterology (butterfly collecting and specimen classification) and reading, I led a rich inner life during those Southampton summers. The countryside and the beautiful beaches, and the company of other children (I had my first puppy loves with a young blonde girl and later with a pair of twins), together with caring counselors (I developed affectionate friendships with both male and female counselors) brought my life into a vivid, orderly balance to which I looked forward all during the school year in Manhattan. The counselors took us into town to see films like *Moby Dick* and *The Great Locomotive Chase*. Southampton became a joyous retreat for me, making my mother wonder why I never seemed eager to come home. Once, the camp had an open house, which my parents did not attend. Waiting to see if they would arrive was a bit irritating, but I was not very upset when the time for their arrival passed. I had trouble understanding those kids who would cry out of homesickness.

After my parents separated in 1955, my mother, brother, and I lived on Webster Avenue in the Bronx for three years. Although this time was filled with interesting events, it did not become the kind of wellspring that I wish to concentrate on in this memoir. In 1958 we moved to Miami, and the next year became the decisive time of my life.

My mother took my brother and me to the Miami Public Library and got us each a card. We did not have a television set during our year in Miami, and I quickly rediscovered that reading was an overwhelming experience. I began to read science fiction, science, and biographies with a hunger that has never returned to me. This was the year in which I began to suspect that I wanted to write, and I sought to learn something about the craft. Writing seemed to me to be only the flip side of reading.

The various works of science fiction that I read in this time were an extremely personal form of exploration for me. Arthur C. Clarke's *Against the Fall of Night,* for example, was, from the first page of its beautiful Gnome Press edition (now an expensive collector's item), a book that seemed to have been written for me alone. Its story of the distant future is linked with my time of growing up, when I lived in the shadow of rockets lifting off from Cape Canaveral, and the night sky existed as a glittering, starry, blue-black field for my telescope. Here I first viewed the Moon through a telescope, and the plurality of worlds, which I had known only intellectually, flooded into my mind with all the reality given to young sight—clear and sharp, almost three dimensional. The simple power of being able to adjust the focus of the telescope to the attainable clarity was a miracle of optics that I understood as if I had suddenly adjusted my mind to the same sharp clarity.

The marbled library from which I borrowed Clarke's novel remains associated in my mind with Diaspar, the city of Clarke's far future. Every Friday after school I went to the library with a bulging leather briefcase to exchange my weekly hoard of science fiction for a new load. I read one or two books a day in that year—at breakfast before school, at the bus stop, on the bus ride, in the schoolyard before the bell rang, at lunchtime, on the bus going home, before doing my homework, at the beach, and before going to sleep. Sometimes I even read at night, finishing Robert A. Heinlein's *Starman Jones* by the pale light of the street lamp shining in my window.

One day on the bus ride to school, a man of middle years, whom I was to know only as Jim Loomis, saw me reading Edward E. Smith's *Chil-*

"My grandparents, on my mother's side: (left to right) Grandfather Piotr, Grandmother Jadwiga, and her brother, Andrzej," Poland, late 1930s

dren of the Lens. The next day on the bus he loaned me the same author's *The Skylark of Space.* In later weeks he loaned me, in complete confidence that I would return the book on the bus, without knowing my address, *Slan* by A. E. Van Vogt. I read the novels with delight and returned them promptly. To this day I don't know whether Loomis ever learned what became of me, and I never learned a thing about him except that he worked for a Miami movie chain and had the same last name as Noel Loomis, a science-fiction writer whose work I discovered years later.

It seems to me now all but impossible to convey the magic that novels by Arthur C. Clarke, Robert A. Heinlein, Andre Norton, and many others worked on me from the summer of 1958 to the summer of 1959. They were everything I had imagined science fiction would be—far-ranging, poetic, peering into distant times and places, and with an attitude that prized intellect and knowledge. They gave me a sense of the universe's real size, that the Earth wasn't everything, that there was so much more to reality than anyone could imagine. Reading science fiction taught me that humanity was my culture, that the Earth was my country, and that the ideals of science—knowledge joined to critical doubt—were my best hope as a thinking being. I was thus spared from falling into the cultural, national, religious, and racist niches that wait for every generation. To belong to any of these backwaters without taking on their chauvinism seemed unlikely to me then, and I still think so today.

In the summer of 1959—just after my mother, brother, and I returned from Miami, my mother remarried, and we moved into a large apartment near Bedford Park on the Grand Concourse in the Bronx—I entered the Hospital for Special Surgery in Manhattan to again correct my hip problems. I stayed from August to Thanksgiving, during which time major surgery was done on both hips and I was imprisoned in a body cast that forced me to sleep either on my stomach or back, with no ability to turn over without help. Nevertheless, I have long viewed this time as a positive experience, however alloyed a benefit it turned out to be.

Surgery was scheduled for the day after I entered the hospital. I remember standing looking out the window at the river on Seventieth Street, feeling foolishly grown up at thirteen years of age as I tried to understand what was going to happen to me. I understood and had some faith in the technical aspect of the surgery that was going to be done; emotionally, I had been awaiting this time for as far back as I could remember. The early teen years, my doctors had advised, would be the best time to do the corrective surgery, since I would be growing quickly. I was quite strong after the year in Florida. Remembering my resolve and brave, rational outlook today makes me shudder, as I realize that it was more than anyone should ask a thirteen-year-old to face.

As I went under anaesthesia the next day, the thought crossed my mind that I might die, and a strange curiosity came over me—at the fact that I accepted what might happen and that I didn't care; I knew that I should care, but I didn't. Later I realized that this was the lowest point I would ever know. Nothing like this uncaring has ever come into me since then.

The surgery was brutal—first one hip, followed by ten days of incredible pain; then, just as it was easing, the second hip, with ten more days of pain. The painkillers were a welcome lie, but I knew that behind their shield, the pain was alive and waiting to grip me. My own willfulness to get through was best illustrated by what happened when my mother visited me in the recovery room. I saw her dimly and told her to stay, thinking that I would shake off the anaesthetic in a few minutes, as if I were simply going to wake up. Of course I didn't, but I was convinced that I could.

Within a month much of my pain was gone, but it now dawned on me that I faced at least twelve weeks of a turtle-like existence in bed and on a mobile stretcher, which I learned to operate. I began to count the weeks, reading Clarke's *Childhood's End*, Orwell's *Nineteen Eighty-Four*, Bradbury's *The Martian Chronicles*, Robert Heinlein's *Waldo, and Magic, Inc.* and *Starship Troopers*. A few weeks in I lost my composure, threw a dinner tray at the wall, wept, and shouted to be freed from my prison.

A positive experience? This is how it became one: I had to get myself together and decide what I was going to do. I had to get well, to look forward to it, to know that I would. This took a kind of self-programming, a disciplined remaking of one's self that leaves a permanent mark on how one goes about doing things for all the years after.

I was released on crutches, but had to return two to three times a week for physical therapy. In the following weeks it became clear to me that this would only improve my condition up to a point. The surgery had improved the amount of support I would have in my hips and straightened my back,

"Manhattan, early 1950s. America's influence on two nice European boys. I'm on the pony. Standing, my brother, Zbigniew."

but it left me with stiffness in both hips, restricted motion, and the prospect of arthritis in later years, despite the improvements. My walk is still noticeably different to observant souls, especially to children, who have no shyness about looking. What this forced me to face was simple: would I develop the outlook of a handicapped person or not? I decided not, that I would not be stopped; and I succeeded, although looking back on the year that followed my release from the hospital makes me marvel at the person who could do what he did and wonder how much he was in fact slowed down. I sometimes feel that I have all the wounds from a war without having fought it.

From November of 1959 to August of 1960 I stayed at home. A tutor got me through eighth grade and prepared me for high school, but for most of each week I lived a life of solitude that I still dream about quite often. Solitude freed me from distractions and peer group pressures, helping me to think for myself by forcing me to go through all the choices that might be open to me in regard to a problem or an issue until I glimpsed a path I could follow. I read a lot, exercised, and went to a movie matinee several times a week, usually to the Loew's Paradise on Fordham Road, where I sat in a nearly deserted theater which was for all practical purposes my own private screening room. I clearly remember every film I saw there, and even today I cannot watch one of these without being vividly thrown back to that time.

Gradually, my skill with crutches enabled me to go out and buy each monthly issue of the science-fiction magazines, which I read avidly. Soon, I was able to ride a bicycle, even though I needed my crutches to get to the bike. The bike freed me to go bookhounding, and I soon found every bookstore, new and used, that the Bronx had to offer. My science-fiction collection began to grow. When I parked my bike by a store, I had to hobble inside, but this provided me with a transition from my crutches. Soon I could do with one crutch, and the time came when I could simulate a nearly normal walk and even stare down people who looked at me with pity. I discovered that I could learn a lot about people from how they reacted to my disability. When September of 1960 came, I was determined to go to my first day of high school without crutches, and I did, even though I still needed them. I even came home on a bus, carrying all my books under one arm. I simply had to let go, and I did.

The first two years of high school were exciting. I breezed through courses with an *A* average, was chosen for the college-preparatory Scholarship Class, and was generally happy about how I had met everything head-on. Writing was already beckoning. I had rejection slips from John W. Campbell of *Analog* and Cele Goldsmith of *Amazing,* with encouraging words.

In early October of 1961 I attended the American Rocket Society's gathering at the New York Coliseum. This was an open exhibition of the history and current state of space technology and exploration. I wandered around the main floor, clutching my copy of *Booster,* the society's daily newsletter, marveling at the numerous exhibits. At one booth I saw a short Soviet film about the launching of the first two Sputniks, and I still remember the chills of excitement that this film sent through me as I understood its historical meaning: humanity (I didn't much care whether it was American or Soviet) was beginning to look beyond the world of its origins!

Then I drifted over to a photo display of spaceship designs.

"That's a Clarke Moonship," someone said next to me, and my ears turned like radio dishes toward the familiar sound of the name. "And that's Clarke himself," the voice added softly. I can't remember the person who pointed Clarke out to me.

"Where?" I asked with astonishment.

"Right there, next to you."

I turned with disbelief and saw a sandy-haired gentleman bending down to get a better look at a picture of a lunar spacecraft. He looked exactly like the photograph on the book jacket of *The City and the Stars,* the expanded and revised version of *Against the Fall of Night.*

Dazed, I said hello and introduced myself, then managed a few clumsy words about reading his novels. He signed my copy of *Booster* (which I have next to me right now as I write this) and suggested that I attend an open reception later that evening. When I arrived, Clarke noticed me at once and introduced me to Willy Ley (whose science books I knew) and to Wernher von Braun, who at that time was regarded as a necessary evil by some, since he had designed the V-2 rocket for Hitler and was now working for NASA, and as a great engineer and remarkable human being by others. He was a tall, imposing figure, even more legendary at that time than Clarke.

"What are you going to be, young man?" he asked me as we shook hands.

"A writer," I replied.

"Good, good," he said, smiling at me, and I forgot to have him sign my copy of *Booster.*

This was all too much for a high school student. I had not expected to meet any of these people. I had already stretched my stay to attend the evening reception, and then lost all track of time. My stepfather gave me a tongue-lashing for getting home late, but I didn't much care. I had met Arthur C. Clarke! As I tried to explain who he was, a strange, jealous look came over my stepfather's face, and he accused me of caring more for this Clarke whoever-he-was than I did for my family. I almost agreed out loud, but held back. Years later, when *2001: A Space Odyssey* came out, I reminded my stepfather that the writer was the same man I had met.

In trying to recapture my feelings about these encounters at the Coliseum, I recall an immense sense of growth, of development, of seeing

"Washington, D.C., 1963. World Science Fiction Convention attendees. The callow, shy youth in the top right hand corner is myself at seventeen. The white-jacketed man in the foreground is Fritz Leiber, who would be my teacher at Clarion in 1968. Far left, author L. Sprague de Camp."

through the exhibits and the people I met that future-oriented concerns, expressed as science fiction, science, and technology, were real things with which living people were involved; and I wanted also to become involved—after a suitable period of education and preparation, of course. Astronomy beckoned as a career, and I had already tried my hand at two or three short stories. It seemed impossible, as I went home that evening, that I might be able to have what I wanted; but I was determined to try.

So when I got home in this hopeful state of mind, I was not prepared for my stepfather's hostility. He had already ridiculed my reading of science fiction and had made it difficult for me to watch "The Twilight Zone" on television, yet still I half expected that he would be happy for me, that he would be encouraging; and when he was not, I only wound myself tighter inside, resolved that I would show him one day. It may well be that teenagers need some skepticism from their parents

against which to push; but I shudder to think how many talented people have parents whose skepticism and ridicule are too effective.

Some of the other happy times of my high school years (1960–64) were spent bookhounding. I would take a subway from 200th Street in the Bronx to Fourteenth Street and spend the afternoon going from one used bookstore to the next. My money was limited (usually saved up from lunch money), so I sometimes bought a book in one store that I could trade for more money in another. A few of my "captured prizes" included *H. G. Wells: Journalism and Prophecy 1893–1946*, edited by W. Warren Wagar; *The City of Man*, by W. Warren Wagar (who would become my friend in the 1970s); *Persons and Places*, by George Santayana; and *Skull-Face and Others*, by Robert E. Howard.

I also visited the only science-fiction specialty store, Stephen's Book Service, whose owner always saved items for me, the most important of which were the British magazines *New Worlds, Science Fantasy,* and *Science Fiction Adventures,* which gave me great pleasure when they were edited by John Carnell and influenced me greatly when Michael Moorcock took over and started the "New Wave" of the 1960s. It was at Stephen's that I met Donald A. Wollheim, the writer-editor who would later accept my first novel at Ace Books.

In 1963 I attended the twenty-first World Science Fiction Convention in Washington, D.C., where I met Isaac Asimov, James Blish, E. E. Smith, Robert Silverberg, and other writers known to me from my reading. John W. Campbell signed his *Invaders from the Infinite* for me, in the Fantasy Press edition, and from Lloyd Arthur Eshbach, the publisher, I bought a dozen other titles—now all expensive collector's items—and was careful not to let my parents see that I had spent most of my money (which I had earned working at the Fordham branch of the public library) on books. The whole convention weekend cost about a hundred dollars! While in Washington, I also bought William Hope Hodgson's Arkham House edition of *The House on the Borderland* for the great sum of four dollars!

The effect of the convention on me was to spur my own writing. My teachers encouraged me, and I won an essay contest. A short story of mine was published in an amateur science-fiction publication, and Cele Goldsmith rejected, but with kind, encouraging words, a first attempt at a portion of what would become my 1979 novel, *Macrolife.*

My college years at the State University of New York, Harpur College (now Binghamton University) were a constant struggle between increasingly dull course work and my writing. I had one outstanding teacher, Robert Neidorf, who taught me philosophy of science and showed me what a student could do out of real interest. There was a way to avoid the make-work aspects of education! I still draw on what this man taught me about science, the philosophy of science, and about myself, in such stories as "Gödel's Doom," which was later reprinted in the Bertrand Russell Society's publication (Russell, along with H. G. Wells, had a great effect on me), and in the science essays I recently have been writing for *Omni* magazine.

But the most important and exciting event of my late college years was my attendance at the very first Clarion Writer's Workshop in Science Fiction and Fantasy at Clarion, Pennsylvania, in the summer of 1968. The year before, I had left school,

worked as a copyeditor at a local Binghamton newspaper, then gone back to college with grave misgivings about ever being able to write, even though I had published a translation of a Russian science-fiction story and, in a state of near desperation, begun my first novel, *The Omega Point.* I heard about Clarion through a science-fiction magazine ad, and knew at once that this was something different, because working writers whose work I knew would be the teachers. I had even met one of them, Harlan Ellison, at the Twenty-fifth World Science Fiction Convention in 1967. My college roommate heard me talking about Clarion, but concluded that all I would do is talk and never attend. To this day I am grateful for his ridicule.

Pamela Sargent, whom I had met in 1964 and grown close to, knew that something was happening to me. I was actually building up to something in regard to my writing. She confessed that she felt somewhat threatened by my stiffening resolve—I was going to do something, and it might even work out!

Jack Dann, whom I had also met recently, sensed that something was brewing. I knew that he also wanted to be a writer, and that he had been startled by my meager publications. He liked to sit around and propose one story idea after another,

"Spring 1965. The State University of New York at Binghamton (now Binghamton University), Harpur College. The earliest surviving photo of Pam and myself. I'm trying to look like Steve McQueen, and Pam is wearing my flannel shirt."

endlessly. I think I felt a bit shamed by his enthusiasm, since it contrasted with my doomed mood about the possibility of writing, publishing, and maybe even making my living at it. Jack, who became one of my best friends, didn't know it yet, but we were already unstoppable.

So I went to Clarion, after my mother twisted my stepfather's arm and loaned me the money to go. The bus came within eighteen miles of the town, and I hitchhiked the rest of the way, carrying a suitcase and the typewriter I had bought, along with a pair of glasses, with high school academic award money some years earlier. As I came in the door to the dorm, I was met by James Sutherland, Neil Shapiro, Evelyn Lief, Ed Bryant, and Judith Merril, the writer and anthologist whose work I knew. Someone immediately asked me if I had "published anything." I said yes and received a friendly hiss.

My teachers at Clarion were Harlan Ellison and Fritz Leiber. Ellison's energy and example of productivity—he wrote a story during the workshop, in one day—took me aback, but I persisted in being unimpressed by him: P. T. Barnum was not my idea of a writer. Ellison had his quieter, serious moments, which only served to confuse me at first, but eventually I discarded my impression of him as a promoter. Happily, Harlan praised my stories in the workshop, and they were eventually published.

Fritz Leiber was my idea of a writer—tall, gray-haired, with the voice of a Shakespearian actor. He held private sessions with each writer, in which they discussed their plans with him. When my turn came, I waxed enthusiastic about *Macrolife*, and he, like Wollheim before him, urged me to write it; and he praised the three pieces that I showed in the workshop. I asked him why he was so encouraging to the students, and he replied that, for one thing, they had all been through a selection process to be here, and whatever their talents, they would face enough discouragement anyway when they tried to publish—some would quit, of course, or find they didn't want to keep trying—so there was nothing to lose by encouraging them.

Still, I felt a bit down at Clarion, and did not attend all the sessions, and did not complete new stories while I was there; but I did send back completed short stories after I went back to Binghamton. One of these, "The Water Sculptor," which became my first published story, drew the attention of an editor at Charles Scribner's Sons, who had been shown a collection of new fiction

from the workshop, and in 1972 he gave me a contract for *Macrolife*, the novel I had been dreaming about throughout high school and most of the sixties.

Clarion was for me a practical, not an artistic spur, although my admiration for Fritz Leiber led me to learn from his work. Generally, I do not believe in workshops, because too many voices in your ear can prevent you from hearing your own, and you write a kind of consensus fiction, or at the least you follow currently fashionable models for what is fiction. Deviation from this model is often interpreted as a failure or lack of ability. I have more regard for the apprenticeship model of becoming a writer, in which a hopeful would become an established writer's assistant, typing his manuscripts, sweeping the floor, taking phone calls, and talking about his own fiction, until the reality of being a writer takes hold.

In 1970, after a six-year, sometimes catastrophic close-approach and wide-swinging cometary orbit of each other that might be described as a mutual reraising and reeducation rather than a courtship (although we did get engaged), Pamela Sargent and I moved into an apartment at 141 Oak Street in Binghamton and set about in earnest to become writer-editors. A writer-editor is the kind of complete professional who, in the traditions of science-fiction and fantasy writing, not only contributes with his or her own work but also looks out for the welfare of the field by editing.

Writer-editors established the SF field, and there is scarcely an important editor who was not a writer. From the 1930s onward, SF has been shaped by writer-editors, among them John W. Campbell, Donald A. Wollheim, Frederik Pohl, H. L. Gold, Damon Knight, Anthony Boucher, Lester Del Rey, Michael Moorcock, and Judith Merril. There were notable exceptions like Cele Goldsmith, Edward L. Ferman, Groff Conklin, and Britain's John Carnell, but none of them shaped the field as decisively as did the writer-editors. Much that has gone wrong with SF publishing in the last decade can be attributed to the passing of the great writer-editors and the inability, for various reasons, of the younger writer-editors to exert the proper influence on how SF is published. Not that it was ever easy to get publishers to do the right thing for any particular book; the design and art departments, the advertising and sales people all seem to think they know better; and the result is that books are published from outside their center of strength by people who, in effect, try to fix horse races rather than try to learn something about the horse.

My first five years as a full-time writer were quite naturally filled with "firsts." My first short story, a revision of a Clarion effort, was published, as was my first collaboration with Jack Dann, at nearly the same time. My fourth published short story was nominated for a Nebula Award and appeared in the Nebula Awards annual anthology as a runner-up. Donald A. Wollheim accepted my first novel at Ace Books, but it was Frederik Pohl, who took over Don's job, who saw the book through publication in 1972. I edited my first anthology, *Tomorrow Today.* The first foreign editions of *The Omega Point* were published in German, Dutch, Portuguese, French, and British editions. I acquired and then parted company with my first agent, and went from Scribner's to Harper and Row with *Macrolife* when Scribner's cancelled their SF program. I began to make public appearances, with speeches, panel discussions, television and radio, and think-tank roundtables. All of these firsts will never come again, but there are a few I have not yet had.

One source of strength for me in the seventies was the completion of *Macrolife,* about which I had

"My beautiful Pam," mid-1970s, Johnson City, New York

dreamed since the early sixties. This background of mobile, interstellar, self-reproducing space habitat societies is one against which I planned from the first to write a mosaic of novels, novellas, novelettes, and short stories. Some of these already exist in draft, or are about to be published. "These are your Foundation Stories," the late Isaac Asimov said to me. "Don't neglect them, even if your publishers do." Praise from Arthur C. Clarke for *Macrolife* was a welcome tonic against uncomprehending, nonplussed, and hostile reviewers. If H. G. Wells had risen from the grave to encourage me, I could not have been happier. Praise from fellow writers Michael Bishop, Gregory Benford, and Howard Waldrop, among many others, kept me going.

The other, continuing source of strength is my companion, Pamela Sargent, who brought to our life together another writer's understanding of what happens day to day. She knows what happens to me because it also happens to her as a writer. What might have been intolerable to a nonwriter, however understanding she might be, is quite normal to another writer who is "inside" the daily efforts. "When will you be finished?" is a rarely asked question between us, a technical question rather than a show of impatience. We both know that watching another writer work is often much like watching grass grow or paint dry. I once had a relative staying with me for a few months, during which I wrote a useless draft of a novel because I was constantly trying to be done by a certain hour each day in order to be "available." The presence of an outsider in your house can fatally distract a writer's subconscious.

Happily, Pam "goes under" in her own office, and I am at peace, knowing that all writers must stand alone. No one can write the novel for you; no one can see, feel, or think as you do; this individuality is all that an artist can hope to offer. Dilute it with too many other voices and that uniqueness is modified or destroyed. Even the best editors fail to learn this lesson and blur the line between editorial suggestions and collaboration with the author. Maybe there *is* too much Maxwell Perkins in the works of Thomas Wolfe. Maybe there shouldn't have been *any* Perkins there, and it should have been all Wolfe, flaws and all; but they would have been Wolfe's flaws, not Wolfe-Perkins compromises.

I think Pam goes under more deeply than most writers. Electric currents of feeling and thought flow through her work, sometimes overwhelming readers who expect something more

"The writer, early 1970s, 141 Oak Street, Binghamton, New York, with a black Woodstock typewriter from the 1940s. Philosophy books (left), science fiction (right). The science fiction is in alphabetical order; the philosophical tomes are unsorted."

amiable. Pam opens up the hearts of men and women as few writers of SF have ever done, with a spare, flinty, sometimes nervous prose that does not reward the lazy reader. She has the full array of thought, feeling, and technical skill to do justice to genuine science-fictional subjects, to what is often called hard SF. The ability to think through subtle ideas does not often go hand in hand with skills of characterization and writerly prose; too often readers are satisfied with the sheer dazzle of ideas and miss the equally interesting human impact of such toys. The lack of writers like Sargent is what stops SF from achieving its full potential more often.

With her counter-melodramatic, Greek-tragedian's methods, Sargent confronts readers with the human consequences of science, technology, and future changes. She is neither technophobe nor technophiliac, or ideologue. There is wonder in her work, but no easy fantasy or wish fulfillment. I've read her as a reader, as an editor, and as a

fellow writer, and what I've seen happen over the years is the growth of a vehement talent finding its own way while I've had to find mine. An awesome talent has come to life within the person I love, within the same human being in whom I have also known frailties and faults. When I read her, I forget that I am a writer and that she is the person in the next room. When she interrupts me, I ask the intruder to leave, so I can read the writer I admire. Watching her succeed over the last two decades has been both heartening and pleasurable, and instructive. We continue to trade editorial services such as line editing, which is a lost art among today's so-called editors, who are really no more than office caretakers. Pam belongs to the great tradition of SF's writer-editors, and I can't imagine being without her.

As a writer I am committed to SF. The tributaries that feed it are science, history, and the writing crafts of prose and storytelling. My love of

SF continues to be a happy wellspring, because at its best SF looks toward a creative humankind that may learn and grow, and perhaps become something finer, if it does not perish or destroy itself. I have always sought to contribute to SF, in the way that is unique to SF, with a disciplined, imaginative foresight that tries to understand human possibilities. I do not do this for money. I do work for money in order to continue doing what I love. In one way or another, an accountant could easily say about me that, balancing costs against profits, I have given my work away. I don't mind this being true.

But aside from SF, there is an unhappier wellspring that has always waited inside me. This is my family history, about which I often question myself, asking what does it mean to me? What can it mean to me? This history has always cast an uneasy shadow over my life. My parents, especially my mother, want me to keep it in mind, without letting it overwhelm me. Should I simply ignore it, or regard it as a history whose connection with me is too distant to mean much? After all, I have had enough physical suffering of my own. What can it mean to me that I never knew *any* grandparents, aunts, or uncles? Is it important that Hitler and the Germans killed a lot of Poles? Should I live my life differently because I grew up with this knowledge? Remember, I tell myself, that you missed the real horrors, so why should you care? I'd like to believe, and it may even be true, that I have understood what happened to my parents and how it happened that I was born. With my novelist's imagination, which many claim is often stronger than experience, I glimpse their war years and wonder how they recovered to any degree.

This past has certainly crept into some of my work. In my afterword to the 1983 edition of *The Omega Point Trilogy,* I wrote:

> The story seems to me to be a strangely transformed echo of a war-torn Europe where I was born and lived for the first six years of my life. That world lives in me more through the force of my parents' memory than my own (I remember only England); but the rest is there, no doubt about it.
>
> Gorgias, my main character (named after the great Greek Sophist of the ancient world, about whom I learned during a love affair with Platonic philosophy) is a ghost from the Hitlerian War. Alone, deprived of the civilization that might have flourished around him, he turns to terrorism and revenge. It was no accident that, as I planned the story, I saw how

well such motives are suited to the wish-fulfillment power fantasies of much SF. Revenge and pursuit often make for a good story, and a beginning writer needs all the intensity he can get.

> *The Omega Point* is an example of what happens when the son of Polish war survivors (my parents were kidnapped and made slaves by the Germans for the duration of the war— imagine that as the centerpiece of your parents' teen years!) writes a genre night's entertainment. He can't quite escape serious issues, and he is at an age when he still can't look critically at the kind of science fiction and fantasy he grew up reading.

And the book finally suggests that there is no solution to the past except the creation of more past that will never truly be past. Human memory must turn to creative foresight in order to shape genuine progress. In *Macrolife* I tried to look forward and to escape commercial demands for "entertainment" in favor of being provocative and thoughtful.

Yet my background has left me with a legacy. I see people as allies or collaborators with the enemy, often unconscious of themselves in a civil order that tends to disguise who we are. Under the kind of enemy occupation that Europe experienced, people either banded together to resist, collaborated with the enemy, or turned a blind eye. In every civil order today, human nature remains unchanged; there are people who will sell you out for their own benefit, and those who will stand up with you for what is right. Those who would throw you overboard have very plausible reasons—they have to keep their jobs; they have children to raise (yours don't count); "it's not personal, only business" (a vicious piece of sophistry, that). Much of Europe is still struggling to face the unpleasant truths that people learned about their neighbors and associates. Apparently everyone was in the resistance!

What my parents experienced has given me a way of seeing through people, of seeing in their small, peacetime actions what would be writ large in more extreme circumstances. But make no mistake about it, the failure is the same, only better concealed.

For example, nothing has ever changed in how publishers and editors treat authors day to day. Editors wish to believe that "they do no harm," and want to be assured of this by their authors; mistakes are covered up; inexplicable things happen to the best and brightest; editors

Hotel McAlpin, New York City, Spring 1973. Nebula Awards weekend: (back, left to right) Pam Sargent, George Zebrowski, Audrey Genn Bilker, Jack Dann, Evelyn Lief, Susan Casper, Gardner Dozois; (foreground, right to left) Arthur Saha, Isidore Haiblum, Harvey Bilker, and Poul Anderson.

and publishers actually prevent good works from being written. There is no accountability except in court, where a publisher can wait out the author's charges, then informally blacklist him despite the outcome. As Isaac Asimov told me toward the end of his life, "Money is the curse of America." And when a certain administrator's name came up, I was startled to hear my friend say, "What do you expect of a thug?" I was startled because Isaac had always tried to get along with publishers and concentrate on his work, but now he told me he was too old and too sick to care what anybody thought, and came to my defense.

One of the most personally rewarding aspects of writing science fiction was that I came to share the fellowship of writers I grew up reading. Isaac Asimov, Arthur C. Clarke, Chad Oliver, Charles L. Harness, Harlan Ellison, James Gunn, and others became my friends and demanding colleagues, proving to me that SF is not only a literary movement, but also a kind of extended family, many of whose members care greatly about each other, who get upset at the unworthy among them; who do not, ultimately, care for money, but prize a certain kind of accomplishment on which publishers place their bets without any real knowledge that the product may be much more than a commercial genre of fiction.

It is precisely because SF is so pervasive, existing at every level of accomplishment from the cookie-pattern amusement to the serious philosophical novel, in every form from the poem, opera, play, teleplay, motion picture, short story, novelette, novella, novel, comic book, and comic book novel, that it must be seen as the literature of a technological-scientific culture, expressing deeply held hopes and fears about change.

The ultimate, often vaguely held, fear is that the growth of science and technology will give humanity the chance to abolish its past and transform itself into something horrendous; the hope is that change will be creative. In either case there is the fear of an impending loss. We are approaching an event horizon of discontinuity, and from that far side, human history as we have known it may lose all meaning.

As a purveyor of these hopes and fears, SF appears to challenge the traditional fiction of the last two centuries, and is often viewed with hostility by literary editors and relegated to minor hands in most houses. It is for this reason that the importance of writer-editors of SF cannot be overestimated; they are the proper custodians of SF, which deserves so much more than the repetitive form of publication that it gets from publishers.

SF at its best shows the possibility of assimilating the meaning of science and technology in human cultures, of widening the meaning of cultural artifacts such as literature, and of suggesting bridges into possible futures.

Meanwhile, writers of every kind belong to what has been described as the class of the "privileged poor" and are used by business to produce a kind of drug—something that hooks readers. Even when some writers become wealthy, they remain marked by their poor period and are reluctant to rock the boat.

How are a writer's wellsprings poisoned? The reality of writing and having one's work published reveals itself slowly to the writer, who naturally is distracted by having to pay close attention to his guiding impulses; the reality sometimes does not reveal itself at all to the part-time writer, the commercially successful writer, or one with private means. But for the artistically ambitious professional who knows what he most desires to write in a given number of years, the publishing world has made it harder to keep the wellsprings flowing when faced with a publishing industry that seems hostile not only to the excellence of the product it sells but even to its very production. Writers are discouraged by a variety of bureaucratic and commercial circumstances from ever writing their works. It is a myth that no good book goes unpublished; but much more destructive is the fact that publishing has no answer for the writer it can't sell. He or she may have greatness, but this counts for nothing with the young Pharaohs who couldn't spot Joseph with a searchlight. Their only answer is "too bad," and in practice this means no publication, or at least catastrophically delayed publication.

The constructive answer to such difficulties would be to reexamine how a writer might be published to good effect. The fact that R. A. Lafferty, Philip K. Dick, Avram Davidson, Fritz Leiber, Chad Oliver, Ward Moore, William Tenn, Wilson Tucker, and other greats have not received the publishing support that they deserve, and were denied the acceptance that might have made them more secure, is an indictment of publishing creativity. The myth is that these writers "just didn't sell." The truth is that the people in charge failed, that they didn't know what to do. What to do is not a secret, but like an open-book test it cannot help if you don't already know the subject matter. Publishers buy too much, then don't have the money and creative resources to present their inventory to the public. Instead, they try to bet on as many horses as possible; better still, they do market research and don't run any horses at all, but simply fix the winners. Publishing is profoundly unbusinesslike, too often failing to reach its audience with the right packaging, distribution, and promotion. "Outsiders" try to market-analyze what "insiders" already know.

Writers in the meantime are slowed down or silenced, and wonder whatever made them want to write in the first place. I certainly didn't want to write SF for the money, but I expected it to be there when I paid the electric bill for my computer and lights, so I could continue to write. And then I heard from an underpaid editor, who earns less than I do and is twenty years younger than I am, that she must "follow orders or lose her job"; and from another source I heard that a higher-up was upset that my paperback novel *Stranger Suns* had made the *New York Times* Notable Books of the Year list. Even though this book also sold much better than expected, it was denied reprinting or any mention of the *Times* honor.

One of the most revealing aspects of publishing since I started is the ballooning of the standard book contract from the single, double-sided legal page to a document of some twenty pages or more filled with ominous, self-serving language whose bottom line might just as well be "We're not responsible for anything, even if it's our fault." Another telling point is that publishers rarely pay an author what it costs to write a book. There are always more writers waiting, willing to do it for next to nothing to get into print.

Where is the sunlit English field where I first sensed infinities? Where is the little red schoolhouse in Southampton where I first read L. Frank Baum, or the white-marbled Miami Public Library where I discovered the works of Arthur C. Clarke? They are within me still, these images that somehow still bring nourishment and strength—but how long can they continue to do so?

What am I doing? What is this act of writing or telling a story? It is a way of knowing, and probably the oldest form of explanation that we have, connecting people and events together in the way they were—and in SF in the way they might be—through the distorting and illuminating lens of an individual writer who has taken the trouble to be articulate, suggestive, critical, and often accepting. "Stories must be told," Simon Wiesenthal has said, lest we forget. Memory is all as we sum up each day. A piece of fiction, if it is about something important, however small, is a treasure of understanding, a way of shining a light into the hidden regions of ourselves. I was a writer when I recited the happenings of my day in my child's bed, grasping its meanings again, and I still do so, on screen or paper, but now I probe and uncover so much more, and look forward into futurities.

A good writer is always recovering stored documents for which there are no file names. Working on a screen since 1986 has made me reflect about the nature of information versus raw experience. Everything we can hold onto exists in our understanding, but only after it happens, since we can never freeze any moment; it flees, and we remember it as a mini-story, which becomes fixed long after the experience.

In my "history machine" stories I envision a time when all of human existence will be obsessed with information processing. All that was recorded, from scholarly works to entertainment, exists in a computer called the cliometricon, and is accessed by a population of historians and citizens

"Harlan."

"Yes, George?"

"We have achieved . . . hair!" A spirited 1991 reunion with the author's Clarion '68 teacher, author Harlan Ellison, at SUNY Stony Brook, Long Island, during ICON, a yearly SF convention.

which has no other life. Human consciousness has become a sluggish cursor floating across an infinity of information—the ultimate meaning of the phrase "all we can ever own are our memories."

Today, writers continuously turn human experience into words. "Daddy, are we live or on tape?" a child asks, as if it were the most natural question in the world. We are unable to understand anything except by reflection. As a writer I have come to see that I try to grasp the world through the explanatory potential of narrative, through the way of the historian who connects pieces of time. Even in abstract areas like logic and mathematics, we are given connected descriptions that reveal a storylike process of beginning-middle-end.

In recent years "narrative dysfunction" has been put forward as a character disturbance. People who cannot construct a story from their lives lack the ability to explore themselves and justify their way of life. A story is a way of knowing, of seeing a larger picture, a context in perspective. If our civilization continues to turn away from the witness of remembrance that exists in literature, then we will lose ourselves as surely as the loss of the natural environment will mean the end of our lives. We must be constantly trying on story structures that explain our history and personal lives, discarding and revising our civilization as we go along, aided by the existing and constantly birthing literatures that reflect and interpret what is happening to us.

Now let us enter even deeper waters. People prattle about responsibility, adulthood, and reality—and they may achieve a kind of illusory security that will reveal itself as illusory only when time runs out, at the price of what may be termed, with no religious intent, their souls. The wellsprings that renew them are gone, because practicality stole all the time one might have given to friends, lovers, music, books, theater, and healing personal accomplishment. They defer everything until it can't be had at all, or do them much good even if they can get it. Health and mental acuity, the basis of all appreciation, is gone. The child's capacity to be surprised and delighted is gone.

Those who weep for their lost youth never learned how to keep it with them. They sold it off, piece by piece, to the merchants of practicality, and they know they are poorer for it, yet convince themselves that they must accept the loss. True, the wisdom of the young is erratic and unconscious, but I have noticed that children up to the age of ten can spot phoniness in adults. They can't say much about it, but they feel it. Most teenagers already accept it as the way things are, and are well on their way to joining the club of adult *patzers*, that vast majority of people who freeze their level of performance in every field at the level that will be accepted by other *patzers*.

Learning to think for yourself, to revise your thinking, to resist peer pressure, to make one's own mistakes, especially, is the finest road one can travel. It's also hard work, to start every examination of a problem or an issue from scratch, to be able to distinguish between what is known (some people debate over dead horses all their lives), what is unknown, and what may never be penetrated.

The most important feature of being able to think for yourself is letting the cards fall where they may—to adjust one's emotional will to follow where the facts and good arguments lead, not where one might wish to go. It's a matter of setting one's loyalty in a certain way—to the best view of facts and the best arguments one can make, and to the acceptance that error will be a guide, ignorance a map. And that there is an ethical component to following this way: it will set you at odds with people who have vested interests in holding unexamined ideas. When you begin to think for yourself, the first feeling is a fearful stab of nostalgia for the loss of received opinions.

Throughout my writing life, I have kept an erratic journal in which I try to do some thinking. At first I called it "Herding Words." A large sampling from this handwritten, chaotic manuscript of yellow, ruled pages with a date at the top of each can be found in the British magazine *Foundation*, number 23, October 1981, and number 28, July 1983. I now call this continuing journal "The Secret Shift," since it consists of unpaid work done in between and after my normal working hours. I have come to see these scattered pages as another wellspring, since I have taken to pillaging their contents for stories, essays, and interviews. Some entries are merely clever, others I have come to disagree with; but many startle me in the same way that old photographs do—is that me, did I say that? Even as I add to this journal, I have started to gather the older pages in one place, knowing that I will draw on them in the future. Here is a new selection:

29 June 91

Every generation is a collection of survivors from the disaster of life, inheriting less than was lived and trying to pass on more than the next generation can carry. Life is a fire from which children are always escaping—into the next fire.

When I was a child adults told me that I should not be so eager to know so much, because I'd have nothing left to discover when I grew up. This took me aback, because it meant that grownups already knew everything but didn't want to let me in on it—for my own good.

30 January 83

Nothing can penetrate human reality as well as fiction, or distort it more. The same is true of theater and film. It is this waiting failure, often made possible by the demands of entertainment and profit, that so distressed Plato in his view of art as a poor third-hand copy of truth.

15 March 83

Reason was so outraged by human history that it conjured up ideologies—fantasies which hold that if only we could know what was wrong with us, then we would set it right. Idealists should be people without illusions about human nature. Only they who know the darkness can best light strategic candles. A full understanding of human nature might be very shattering; we might have to reject

ourselves. We often sense that something like this is true, but in our self-serving way we push it away.

10 August 92

Why did the ancient cave artists put their works in dark, nearly inaccessible places? I think they did it not only to save their works for posterity, but to insure that only genuine appreciators would view them. They put their paintings in dark caves to save them from defacers and . . . from critics!

Today, critics and reviewers may be seen as censors and defacers. Their repressive hand functions more in the manner of customs officials, who let in the acceptable and keep out the dangerous. Above all they forbid any questioning of their own legitimacy.

Given future technologies, might not writers be able to do again what the cave dwellers did—by encrypting their works in such a way that they will reveal themselves only to those who know the values and traditions? A reader might have to earn the right to unlock a work, by showing what kind of person he is. And even during the reading of an "opened" work he might be cut off, and have to reclaim his right several times before finishing the work.

12 January 83

Good science fiction should include what was, what is, what might be; and at its most sublime, what should be.

12 August 82

What I resent most about being a human being is the endless sense of ignorant newness. Yet we are ancient, culturally and biologically, and our knowledge must always be recovered at tenth-hand or more. Why are we so hidden from ourselves? So there can be an unfolding of knowledge, a filling of the books at the glowing end, when all will be present and inescapable?

11 April 84

Self-awareness is a visitor living in an old structure. Self-awareness is ignorant of what the edifice contains, but it assumes that it knows all the rooms. But the reality is that self-awareness is fed information in obscure and unconscious ways.

13 August 90

The trouble with fictional characters is that they turn out to be themselves, not what they should have been. This happens if the writer has done his job correctly.

New York City, 1973: (left to right) Jack Dann, Pamela Sargent, the author

31 August 90

Great art is a microscope, exaggerating subtleties, so everyone may see and understand.

25 August 90

There is a kind of bloodless, lifeless person I sometimes meet, who can be said to lack a "database." They often show impatience with hearing about anything, and ask that you "fill them in" later. It's like listening to an open grave.

20 August 90

Everyday words are cruel, clumsy comedies that cannot catch what goes on inside human beings. Fictional story-structures attempt to speak from inside the merry-go-rounds of perception, feeling, and thought. Everyday words are walls, before which the artist stands, hoping to find the brief crack through which he might pull out an insight.

29 December 90

Young people know that the adult world is corrupt, often stupid, perhaps fatally flawed. They express this knowledge vaguely, with an emotional opposition that senses the inevitable: that they will be forced to become adults and make a dishonorable place for themselves.

29 May 91

A man in his forties, if he's observant enough to notice, sees that this is the decade of shell shock, when he begins to see that life is short and strange.

28 February 88

Is a question an incomplete answer?

4 March 88

The most telling characteristic of the past is its lack of preoccupation with the future.

17 January 89

Adults don't want to tell you the truth about the world, especially if they are parents. You'll find out soon enough, they say, what they're ashamed to tell you.

23 March 89

The day-to-day of writing is a series of defeats that you hope will be reversed on the following day.

13 April 89

Computerese often gives new voice to older insights. A "computer virus" is a distillation of an old fear—the dangerous idea. A computer virus that protects itself we also know as a "reinforced dogma," a stated conclusion that includes within itself an injunction against questioning it. All dogmas are viruses for the human mind. Example: Archie Bunker's definition of faith: "It's believing something that no one in his right mind would believe."

16 April 89

No man is an island. Too bad.

5 April 84

A writer needs a platform from which to survey and shape his material. This platform consists of a good night's sleep, good nutrition, exercise, and a plan of the day's goals in dramatic-story terms. All of this gives the writer the composure from which to reach out and will the order of words that will shape the reader's response to the work.

13 October 85

The words are all in the dictionary. All the writer has to do is trot them out, train them, and make them march in the right order.

12 May 88

Writing is like listening to someone you can't hear clearly. Characters are talking to you, telling you how they will behave, and you're trying to hear. Eventually you may hear. If you don't, then you've failed.

3 July 83

Reason cannot win against will; so reason created the distancing effect of humor, which can sometimes convince, even disarm will. Most of the time, will, which is all assertive style, cannot stand mind's asceticism.

27 July 88

Intellectuals deal with the merits of matters; artists confront the powerlessness of merit.

30 July 88

The last crime of the oppressors is revolution.

22 December 85

The writer, whether he likes it or not, is the judge of every age he lives in. He may not have this opinion of himself, but this is what he is, however exalted it may seem to the casual mind.

The casual mind measures by rule of thumb. All precision, depth, or long-chain thinking appears to it as pretension. The casual mind is tone deaf before incisive reasoning. Unable to see or judge itself, it does incalculable damage to its betters, who often lack courage to do battle with the only weapon feared by the casual mind: ridicule.

With Pam at Windsor, New York, 1984

4 August 92

The bureaucracy of a story or drama demands delaying the outcome.

10 November 83

Civilization is an attempt to fix the vast game of nature.

2 September 84

The great mystery of love between a man and a woman is a matter of immortality, the binding of one time to another through children, defeating death with an unbroken line of personal vanity. In the love of two people this vanity is shared through the glowing communication of sexual delight that conceals the impersonal nature of the union; but deeply they know and feel it as a mournful sadness after lovemaking, as an insufficiency of life that can never be abolished, even when immense personal creativity is set against it by exceptional individuals. Follow the program I have set for you, nature whispers. Feel the pleasure with which I reward you, dream a little, and then die.

5 November 84

Youth struggles to pull the sword from the stone, but age, always confounded by the act, fails to send youth on a worthy mission.

7 November 84

I sometimes wish that I could write myself out of life, into another state, one in which all the endless repetitions of human existence are left behind . . .

23 February 92

Many of the practical, realistic people of the world, who can afford to imagine and accomplish what is creatively possible, are the most evil. They are all around us, but we notice them only when their faults are magnified in positions of authority and power. At the ordinary level they might be petty crooks, grocers and plumbers, grade school teachers and university professors. They can be unmasked only in extreme conditions, as when a country is invaded—and we see these pragmatists as the collaborators with the enemy that they have always been, giving in to the "realities," doing what is "possible." They all share one characteristic—an inability to understand that the right action, the moral position, the humane and compassionate way, might cost them something, perhaps even their lives. They're willing to stand up for ideals, even be moral, when the cost is trivial. When it will cost them, then it's time to be practical.

14 March 92

A great book is an act of atonement, a vindication, a reversal of wrongs through a public explanation. It is an inquiry into a wrong, a failure of character, a lack of understanding. It may also be a form of honorable revenge against the past. The best fiction is an *inquiry,* into a character, a community, a nation, a world—and in SF into the possibilities open to intelligent life.

October 92

Does America ask its writers for their best? No—mostly it asks to be entertained. Yet there are days when I want to go out and find a news stand, anywhere, and find again the SF magazines of my boyhood and teen years. I want to play and be pleased. Thus I am divided within myself.

14 June 93

"Judge not, lest ye be judged" has never made any sense to me. "Judge, and be prepared to be judged worthy" is what it should say.

26 June 93

The *experience* of reading a particular author, the *sensation,* the feeling, the side thoughts . . . the way one is touched beyond explicit understanding and critical judgment, may exist in the reader's imagination as much as in the author's intentions, and may withstand nearly all critical assessments of a book. Reading critical discussions, a reader who is aware of such qualities may feel that the critic has missed the vital experience of a novel.

"The Secret Shift" is now a habit of mine. I worry when a month brings fewer than the usual number of pages. But there are other kinds of notes that I also delight in making, and they too refresh and move me forward. I have no special name for these, so they often get into "The Secret Shift" file. They should be called "Orphans," because they are passages of fiction, or at least bits of prose that sometimes fit into a larger piece of fiction. This happens often enough that I regularly go seeking among the "Orphans" to find something appropriate; and lo and behold, they do yield

a title or a thought that is exactly what I need for the story or novel on which I am working.

Here are some "Orphans" that have not yet been assimilated—but beware, you may meet them again:

Ideas come with the blood. They build rafts and small boats, even small, intricate ships, with which to make the journey to the brain. As they near that organ and then enter it, they cry out to be heard before they are swept back into the body and have to make the vast, circuitous journey again . . .

*

The world teetered on the edge between striptease and revelation. Truth sat shamefaced in the shadows while illusions dazzled the credulous. Lies lay in bed with half-truths, and even with quarter-truths, while rumors and innuendos whispered through the trees . . .

*

The peeling red sign on The Philosophy Store announced: "Learn Everything Here." And on the glass store front, in green letters: "The Secrets of the Universe. Money Paid For Good Questions."

*

She shook my hand and looked at me carefully, as if trying to find me in my face, the person she expected to fit the idea of me that she had brought to our first meeting.

*

These excerpts show the writer constantly sifting the world's grains of information and experience, through himself, looking for the telling detail, the flash of observation or insight. That his work is fictional is only a technicality; he is always looking to tell the truth about his characters and their world. A bad writer gets his fictional world and characters wrong—by pushing his people into uncharacteristic actions and by forcing dramatic resolutions until they ring hollow. That is why good fiction can sometimes be more "true" than the reality. A legend may actually capture more of what was worthwhile than a literal account, by offering a perspective that is true but not obvious.

If it seems to the reader that I have wandered away from purely autobiographical concerns onto tangents, I can only reply that I have tried to

The author and his friend Isaac Asimov, Nebula Awards ceremonies, Roosevelt Hotel, New York City, 1991

convey something of my inner life, as well as make an assessment of the more important outer events that have shaped me. I know that I have given the impression of someone who spends his life at a desk, but this is not entirely true. I live in a working-class neighborhood that seems unchanged to a large degree since the forties and fifties, and I have over the years labored at carpentry, plumbing, and electrical work, and even run swimming pools for the city of New York. I have also managed an apartment building and have dealt with a variety of human beings. These toils have taught me to value the craftsman, who makes it easy for you to turn on your lights or walk through and close a door behind you, and to appreciate the hard work it takes to make possible the simplest things we take for granted. Some of these experiences may be found, vastly transformed by the imagined life of the next century, in my novel *Sunspacer.*

I am certain that everything is autobiography and history—even a mathematical paper, despite the efforts to remove the human being from it and give it the semblance of objectivity. I have never been comfortable with anything until I have written about it, explored and discovered its deeper textures, whether it be an idea or an experience. I like writing best when it is *an exploration,* so I don't know what opinion or conclusion I will hold at the end. People who hold instant views about anything—making it up on the spot—would never dream of deciding their bank balance in advance of their calculations; yet this is what too many do in their thinking about much more important issues. Writing, then, has been for me a way of life and thought, as well as an aesthetic pleasure.

BIBLIOGRAPHY

Novels:

The Omega Point (second book in trilogy; also see below), Ace Books, 1972.

The Star Web, Laser Books, 1975.

The Monadic Universe and Other Stories, introduction by Thomas N. Scortia, Ace Books, 1977, 2nd edition, revised, additional introduction by Howard Waldrop, 1985.

Ashes and Stars (first book in trilogy; also see below), Ace Books, 1977.

Macrolife, Harper, 1979, reissued with an introduction by Ian Watson, Easton Press, 1990.

The Omega Point Trilogy (contains *Ashes and Stars* and *The Omega Point,* both revised, and *Mirror of Minds*), Ace Books, 1983.

Sunspacer (young adult) Harper, 1984.

The Stars Will Speak (young adult), Harper, 1985.

Stranger Suns, Easton Press and Bantam, 1991.

Nonfiction:

Beneath a Red Star: Studies on International Science Fiction, edited by Daryl F. Mallett, Borgo Press, forthcoming.

(With Jeffrey M. Elliot) *Perfecting Visions, Slaying Cynics: The Life and Works of George Zebrowski,* Borgo Press, forthcoming.

Editor:

Tomorrow Today (anthology), Unity Press, 1975.

(With Thomas N. Scortia) *Human Machines: An Anthology of Stories about Cyborgs,* Random House, 1975.

(With Jack Dann) *Faster Than Light: An Anthology of Stories about Interstellar Travel,* Harper, 1976.

The Best of Thomas N. Scortia, Doubleday, 1981.

(With Isaac Asimov and Martin H. Greenberg) *Creations: The Quest for Origins in Story and Science* (anthology), Crown, 1983.

Nebula Awards 20: SFWA's Choices for the Best Science Fiction and Fantasy 1984, Harcourt, 1986, *21* (covering 1985), 1987, *22* (covering 1986), 1988.

Synergy: New Science Fiction, Number 1, Harcourt, 1987, *Number 2,* 1988, *Number 3,* 1988, *Number 4,* 1989.

Editor of ten-volume "Classics of Modern Science Fiction" series. Editor, *Bulletin of the Science Fiction Writers of America,* 1970–75 and 1983–91.

Has published numerous short stories for adults and children, and contributed letters, articles, essays, and reviews to publications, including *Collier's Encyclopedia, Magazine of Fantasy & Science Fiction, Science Fiction Review, Omni,* and *Washington Post Book World.* Works have been translated into French, Dutch, Portuguese, Japanese, Italian, Spanish, Swedish, and German.

Manuscripts, drafts, first editions of published works, and letters are collected in the David Charles Paskow Science Fiction Collection, Rare Books and Manuscript Division, Temple University Libraries, Philadelphia.

Cumulative Index

CUMULATIVE INDEX

The names of essayists who appear in the series are in boldface type. Subject references are followed by volume and page number(s). When a subject reference appears in more than one essay, names of the essayists are also provided.

INDEX

INDEX

INDEX

INDEX